Praise for *Paris: The Secret History*

"This 486-pager is an easy read filled with insight and trivia that's amazing and—the subject being Paris—salacious. It's a pop history that covers a lot of ground, from its pre-Roman inception on a reedy riverbank to its rise to be what is arguably the capital of the Western world. Paris itself is always front and center; along the way you meet iffy saints, literary lions and an array of wily or witless monarchs, movers and mobs who've helped shape the place. Best of all, Hussey tells you where to go to find a good bit of the inspiring and oddball past that has somehow survived centuries and redevelopment."   **—Raleigh News & Observer**

"Noteworthy."   **—Publishers Weekly**

"A compelling history . . . An immensely readable, richly detailed and sometimes disturbing chronicle that explores much of the darkness in the City of Light."   **—Kirkus Reviews**

"Impressive, fascinating, and highly readable . . . a timely book."
                                        —Library Journal

"Forget *The Da Vinci Code*; here's the dark side of the City of Light. A mixture of enjoyably sinister trivia and deep scholarship, taking in the Knights Templar, ancient cemeteries, Joan of Arc, whores, flâneurs, poets and criminals."   **—Independent (UK)**

"More than four hundred acute, riveting pages full of thousands of colorful characters, references, details and colors . . . At every turn, on every corner, the idle traveler through the book finds something new."
                                        —Observer (UK)

"Fascinating . . . greatly readable."   **—Daily Express (UK)**

"Masterly. Fragments of sinister trivia and captivating alternative histories bob up on every page . . . passionately entertaining."
                                        —Independent on Sunday (UK)

"Vivid, informed, delectably readable . . . an enlightened introduction to the city's best-kept secrets. No visitor to France should go without it."
                                        —Sunday Times (UK)

Paris

Paris

The Secret History

ANDREW HUSSEY

BLOOMSBURY

Published by Bloomsbury USA, New York

All papers used by Bloomsbury USA are natural, recyclable products made from
wood grown in well-managed forests. The manufacturing processes conform
to the environmental regulations of the country of origin.

LIBRARY OF CONGRESS CONTROL NUMBER FOR THE HARDBACK EDITION: 2006043038

ISBN-10: 1-59691-323-1 (hardcover)
ISBN-13: 978-1-59691-323-3 (hardcover)

First published in the United Kingdom by Viking in 2006
First published in the United States by Bloomsbury USA in 2007
This paperback edition published in 2008

Paperback ISBN-10: 1-59691-425-4
ISBN-13: 978-1-59691-425-4

1 3 5 7 9 10 8 6 4 2

Typeset by Rowland Phototypesetting Ltd., Bury St. Edmonds, Suffolk, England
Printed in the United States of America by Quebecor World Fairfield

To my mother, Doreen
And to my father, John Hussey – *flâneur extraordinaire*

I have run so far to make this portrait of Paris that I can honestly say that I made it with my legs. I have also learned to walk on the stones of the capital in a nimble fashion, quick and lively. This is the secret that one must acquire in order to see everything.

Louis-Sébastien Mercier, *Le Tableau de Paris*, 1782–8

To explore Paris . . .

Ivan Chtcheglov, *Internationale situationniste*, 1957

Contents

Contents

List of Illustrations

Page 2: Lutetia during the Roman occupation (*c.*50 BC to AD 400).

Page 30: Paris during the Merovingian period (*c.*490–640).

Page 44: View of Paris in the eleventh century by Adolphe Rouargue (1810–70). (Mary Evans Picture Library)

Page 106: A plan of Paris, *La Ville de Paris, par tout tant renommée, & principalle ville du royaulme de France, en 1548*, by Sébastien Munster, 1568. (Bibliothèque Nationale de France)

Page 154: View of Paris, coloured engraving by an unknown artist, seventeenth century. (Musée Carnavalet, Paris; © Photo RMN/Bulloz)

Page 208: View of Paris from a balloon above the Île Saint-Louis by Louis-Jules Arnout, 1846. (Cliché Bibliothèque Nationale de France, Paris)

Page 256: Road development in Paris between 1850 and 1914.

Page 308: Plan of the Paris metro in 1900. (© Collection Roger-Viollet)

Page 352: German street signs in Paris, 1942. (Keystone/Getty Images)

Page 382: 'La Beauté est dans la rue', graffito, May 1968, Paris.

Plate Sections

1. The Gaulish leaders in league against Julius Caesar (100–44 BC), led by Vercingetorix (d. 46 BC), from a protective sleeve for school books, late-nineteenth-century colour lithograph. (Private collection; Archives Charmet/Bridgeman Art Library)

2. Lutetia or the second plan of Paris in the fourth and fifth centuries AD, French School, 1722. (Bibliothèque des Arts Décoratifs, Paris; Archives Charmet/Bridgeman Art Library)

3. *Sainte Geneviève gardant ses moutons*, oil on canvas, French School, sixteenth century. (Musée de la Ville de Paris, Musée Carnavalet, Paris; Archives Charmet/Bridgeman Art Library)

4. The Cathedral of Notre-Dame, Paris. From an old picture postcard, undated.

5. Epitaph of François Villon (1431–?) from *Le Grant Testament Villon et*

Acknowledgements

It is an obvious fact that exploring Paris is a lifetime's work, but this is a list of some of the colleagues, friends and others who have helped me along the way so far.

They include Abdellatif Akbib, Lisa Allardice, Khalid Amine, Françoise Bailly, 'Béatrice', David Bellos, Gavin Bowd, Constant, Jason Cowley, Martin Crowley, Anne Cunningham (who went with me there first), Shigenobu Gonsalvez, Juan Goytisolo, Michel Guet, Cécile Guilbert, Chantal Guillaume, Sophie Herszkowiscz, Allen Hibbard, Les Hodge, Michel Houellebecq, Isidore Isou, Aimé Jacquet, Mark Kermode (for backing vocals), Ramez Malouf, Patrick McGuinness, John McHale, Anna McIver, Jeffrey Miller, Sophie Morel, Ovidie, Laura Owen, Paul Quinn, Tariq Ramadan, Ralph Rumney (deceased 2002), Roland Sabatier, Jeremy Stubbs, Yves Trentret, Zinédine Zidane.

I should also like to thank my sharp-eyed and wise editor, Kate Barker, at Penguin and my agent Peter Robinson.

And always, with love, Carmel Regan of Roscommon, for being herself.

Introduction
An Autopsy on an Old Whore

Paris arouses strong emotions. 'How different was my first sight of Paris from what I had expected,' wrote Jean-Jacques Rousseau, one of the first explorers of the modern city. 'I had imagined a town as beautiful as it was large. I saw only dirty, stinking alleys, ugly black houses, a stench of filth and poverty. My distaste still lingers.'[1] Years ago, I arrived in Paris for the first time, stepping down into the street from the metro station at Barbès and, like Rousseau and countless others arriving in the city for the first time, I did not see what I had expected to find. The streetscape was confusing, impossible to understand at first, a riot of alien colour and noise. Years later, Barbès remains one of my favourite places in Paris precisely because it is chaotic, occasionally sordid and always uncontrollable. It thrilled me then, and fascinates me now, because it belongs to several centuries all at once.

It took me a long time in Paris, and endless journeys around the city, to grasp the complexity of this fact. In its long and vast literary history, Paris has been variously represented as a prison, a paradise and a vision of hell. It has also been characterized as a beautiful woman, a sorceress and a demon. In this case, literature is not a refraction but an accurate reflection of daily life: Paris really is made up of radically different spaces and multiple personalities, always at odds with each other and often in noisy collision. It has been like this for nearly two thousand years.

In a shorter space of time, Paris has been reproduced in posters, postcards and prints that are sent around the world as empty metonyms for art, sex, food and culture. The Eiffel Tower, the Sacré-Coeur, Notre-Dame are all part of a global visual culture, a Disneyfied baby language that distorts and destroys real meaning. This process is greedy and all-consuming: not only monuments and churches but also the paintings of Degas and Manet, the photographs of Robert Doisneau or Willy Ronis, the films of Marcel Carné or François Truffaut have all been separated from their true context, reduced to cliché and commodity. Little wonder that in recent years it is the vibrant and unpredictable territories of Sydney, New York or London that have captured the world's imagination. And little wonder either that in the gloomiest of recent times, as its city centre has been once again violated by

state and capital, one former lover of Paris, the English artist Ralph Rumney, has likened the city to 'the corpse of an old whore'.[2]

But, alive or dead, the old whore still casts a powerful spell.

This book makes no claim to be a definitive history of Paris. The millions
of words devoted to the city over the centuries suggest anyway that there
is no such thing. Instead *Paris: The Secret History* aims to tell the story of
Paris from the point of view of 'the dangerous classes', a term used by
French historians to describe marginal and subversive elements in the city
– insurrectionists, vagabonds, immigrants, sexual outsiders, criminals – the
account of whose experiences contradict and oppose official history.

One of the inspirations behind this book is Peter Ackroyd's *London: The
Biography* and, in particular, Ackroyd's notion that history is not a fixed
narrative but an unfinished dialogue.[3] In this spirit, the narrative of *Paris*
tries to trace the ever-changing geography of Paris, examining its history
in space, in time and on the street. Neither travelogue nor guidebook, *Paris*
is above all written to be *used*. It is a history book that can be taken to the
bar, on to the metro, into the heart of the labyrinth itself – and there to be
engaged as interpreter, guide and interlocutor.

Edmund White's slim and elegant volume *The Flâneur* also seeks to
'read' the city.[4] More precisely, White's investigations borrow from the
nineteenth-century Parisian practice of *flânerie* – aimless wanderings through
Paris during which a gentleman might, in a spirit of detached irony, uncover
the detailed contradictions of urban pleasure, from an encounter with an
individual prostitute to an evening at a cabaret or an opium den. Unlike
the *flâneur*, the subterranean adventurer here is not simply looking for
pleasure – although I do not avoid it! – but also the associative significance
of sites in the city. The explorer seeks intoxication, deliberately disorientates
himself and sets out to get lost in the city in order to find his own way out.
As the familiar becomes unfamiliar, the new and old meanings of buildings,
roads, streets signs, squares and open spaces are revealed.

As he sketched out his own mental maps of Paris in the 1930s, the
German critic Walter Benjamin insisted that it is in the shifting movement of
everyday Paris that we can glimpse what it is that makes history. Benjamin's
contention was that everyday experience – aimlessly strolling the streets,
drinking coffee or alcohol, picking up someone of the opposite or same
sex – always contains a larger, more complex meaning. Seen in this way,
the life of the city is revealed as an endless series of moments, always
ephemeral and sometimes baffling, that are also its real history.

Paris is above all, as Benjamin would have it, a city of secret adventures. Parisian mysteries appear on the surface of everyday life – the smile of a stranger on the metro, a bar you've never been to before, a visit to a forgotten part of the urban hinterland. The pleasures of the city can also be occluded, impenetrable and sometimes dangerous. Paris has always been a carnival of light and terror.[5]

One of the cornerstones of the mythology of Paris is the notion that the city's architecture makes an ideal décor for a love story. The metaphors used to describe Paris in the nineteenth century – such as 'queen of the world' – emphasized the opulent and sensual nature of the city, feminizing it and making it the passive object of pleasure. The death of Diana – the final car journey from the chintzy elegance of the Place Vendôme to the mangled wreckage in the tunnel under the Pont d'Alma, where tourists still lay wreaths – could only have happened here.

But Parisians are not sentimental. They believe that the world is ruled by an ironic theory rather than by God. The stock character of the Parisian *parigot* is a native urban dweller whose dry black humour constantly and consistently works against government and state. Yes, love is central to both myth and reality in Paris, but so are food, drink, religion, money, war and sex. With this in mind, *Paris* is history told in the form of a journey – or rather several journeys – from bar, brothel and backroom, to the deprived estates on the city's outskirts and to the elegant *salons* and the citadels of power, everywhere interrogating, dissecting or simply being seduced by the spellbinding myths of Paris.

And Paris seduces without mercy. Diana is only the latest and most famous example of those who have been fatally seduced here. It is of course the cruellest paradox, as Diana discovered too suddenly, and then too late, that the old whore's spell is also a deadly curse.

The Invention of the Parisian

The history of Paris is not simply a tale of princesses and kings: in some ways, it is quite the opposite. Paris is, after all, the city where, after centuries of bloody conflict, the people's revolution was invented. Paris may be a world capital of politics, religion and culture, but it is also one of the defining truths of the city that its history has largely been forged in hardship by its inhabitants – the so-called *petites gens* (the ordinary people). This is why it is so important to be able to distinguish myth, legend and folklore from the way that real Parisians behave and see themselves.

As countless historians of Paris have already pointed out, it is no accident that the word 'Parisian' has long been synonymous with the word 'agitator'. This is a tendency that can indeed be traced in the Parisian and provincial imagination as far back as the Middle Ages, when Parisians were commonly described as *trublions* ('disturbers of the peace') or *maillotins* ('war-hammers').[6] These terms always had a meaning that was both specific and political. The word *maillotin* was, for example, taken from the heavy lead mallets, or *maillets*, which angry rebels used in the fourteenth century to smash statues and heads (usually of money-lenders and tax officials, who were generally Jews and Lombards). Other agitators, *trublions*, led the disorderly and often spontaneous insurrections, or *jacqueries*, against government and king in the name of hunger and injustice. The most famous and successful of such *jacqueries* was led in 1357 by Étienne Marcel, who launched a workmen's strike and killed a prince, spattering himself with blood. Marcel's statue still presides over the Seine from the front edge of the Hôtel de Ville.[7]

Outside Paris, the rebellious Parisians were laughed at as well as feared. In the mid-sixteenth century, Rabelais described the 'Parisian' uncharitably as a 'gros maroufle',[8] an unscrupulous, vulgar and dishonest alley-cat. He confidently expected his description to raise a laugh of recognition throughout France as well as in Paris. Over time, the word 'Parisian' has also been used in French to describe fashionable cigarettes, numerous sexual positions (generally variants on sodomy, depending on which part of France you are in), trousers of blue material, biscuits, a useless sailor, a type of cooking, typographical plates. For provincials, *à la parisienne* meant a job not finished, or badly done. Provincial contempt for Parisians is caught in the children's rhyme 'Parisien, tête de chien, parigot, tête de veau' ('Parisian with a dog's head, Parisian with a calf's head').

Within the city itself, however, Parisian identities have long been divided on a strictly hierarchical class basis. In the eighteenth century, Louis-Sébastien Mercier counted over a dozen different classes, but admitted he may have been skimming the surface. In 1841, Balzac used the word *parisiénisme* (a term first used in 1578) to refer to a complex series of codes and social patterns unique enough to make Paris and Parisian self-worship a target for satire: 'L'atticisme moderne, ce parisiénisme . . . qui consiste à tout affleurer, à être profond sans en avoir l'air' ('The modern Atticism, this Parisianism . . . which consists in making everything superficial, being profound without seeming to be so').[9] Parisians of a high social standing deliberately construed *parisiénisme* to mean fashionable, sophisticated, delightfully and charmingly light, elegant and witty. These were the sort of Parisians who deliberately cultivated the *accent pointu* – all words were 'hissed', with a sharp emphasis on a clipped pronunciation of short vowels at the end of a word – which for many provincials is the characteristic of the haughty and snobbish upper-class Parisian. This accent is still heard and continues to irritate contemporary non-Parisians as much as it irritated Balzac.

There was (and indeed there still is) a native Parisian accent common to the streets. This was originally a confluence of sounds from Picardy, Flanders, Normandy and Brittany. It was most probably first heard in the early 1100s as the low Latin of the rue de Fouarre – the ecclesiastical quarter of the fledgling city – disintegrated into French. It was modified in the sixteenth and seventeenth centuries by an influx of workers, mainly boatmen and traders, from the Berry, but otherwise has remained relatively untouched by outside influence.[10] The common feature was (and is) a tendency to roll the 'r'. The sound *er* or *el* is often elongated or opened into the sound *ar* or *arl*. It is a tendency that can be traced back to the fifteenth century and the poet François Villon, who constantly mashes rhymes such as 'merle' ('blackbird') into 'marle'. A comic play at the time of Louis XIV has a character named Piarot (rather than 'Pierrot') after this same slurring tendency, and in the nineteenth century this sound was noted as the characteristic feature of the accent of Belleville and Ménilmontant, where a concierge was a 'conciarge'.

This was when the term *parigot* first became widely used to describe native working-class Parisian males. At first, it was used to deride and mock the lower orders. In literature, the *parigots* were laughed at, sexually exploited or dismissed as a caricature. In real life they were apparently just wicked: 'The Parigots are born bad,' wrote a hack journalist. 'They admire crime, take part in it when they can, avoid work, and also seek an advantage for themselves whenever they can.'[11] Only slightly less aggressive and derogatory than the word *parigot* was the term *titi*, a childish word used in the nineteenth century to describe a young worker, usually dressed in cap, scarf and smoking a pipe, with a cheeky manner. The style was so common as to be easily imitated by well-heeled and rebellious young men seeking to shock their peers: this masquerade of course carried with it the real danger of being discovered and beaten up as an insulting phoney by the real working classes.

Working-class Parisian women were, similarly, mysterious and threaten-

ing in equal measure. The working-class Parisian woman was above all not
to be trusted – although she was worth cultivating for her sexual availability.
By the nineteenth century, the working-class *Parisienne* was also termed
parigote – and usually described as a harridan who did not hesitate to hurl
insults or invective at any respectable *bourgeois* who crossed her path. These
women were also, at least in the male imagination, amazingly good at sex.
This image can traced back to the late Middle Ages, to François Villon,
who holds a particular affection for a whorish lover, La Grosse Margot:

> Puis paix se fait et me fait ung gros pet
> Plus enflee qu'ung vlimeux escharbot.
> Riant, m'assiet son poing sur mon sommet.
> Gogo me dit et me fiert le jambot.
> Tous deux yvres comme ung sabot
> Et au resveil quant le ventre luy bruit
> Monte sur moi que ne gaste son fruit.

> [We make the peace then in bed. She takes my fill,
> Gorged like a dung beetle, blows me a bad
> And mighty poisonous fart. I fit her bill,
> She says, and laughing bangs my nob quite glad.
> She thwacks my thigh and, after what we've had,
> Dead drunk we sleep like logs – and let in the fleas.
> Though when we stir her quim begins to tease.][12]

The image of the tender-hearted whore has persisted long into the
twentieth century. Most notably, La Grosse Margot is evidently the ancestor
of the most famous *parigotes* – the actress Arletty and the singers Fréhel and
Édith Piaf. For obvious reasons, however, none of these women was ever
entirely at ease with this caricature of their gender and social class.

Arletty, for example, lived and died in a plush apartment on the western
side of the city, in every sense diametrically opposed to the areas of Belleville
or Ménilmontant where her screen persona was born. Accused of collaborating with the Nazis (it was rumoured that the Parisian resistance planned
to slice off her breasts as punishment) and cut off from the city culture that
had inspired her, she died a melancholy, lonely figure.

Fréhel was in fact a native of Brittany who took her stage name from the
Cap Fréhel of her native territory. She came to Paris as a child and worked
as a street singer, making her name in the music halls of the period with a

mixture of wit and melodrama. Her most famous moment came, however, when she was already past her peak. This is the role of Tania, a down-at-heel former star, in the 1937 film *Pépé le Moko*. She comforts Pépé, a stylish Parisian gangster (played by Jean Gabin) who is on the run in the casbah of Algiers, by singing him 'Où est-il donc?' ('Where is it now?'). This is a haunting and nostalgic lament for the Old Paris of the Place Blanche, an imaginary Paris that Fréhel can never return to. She ended her career in poverty and destroyed by drink. Serge Gainsbourg, no stranger himself to alcoholic disaster, took her as an inspiration and recalled with affection buying her a drink – an exotic old lady, shaking with thirst, in a bar in rue du Faubourg du Temple in 1951.

Most iconic and damaged of all the *parigotes* was Édith Piaf, who was born in Belleville, the very heart of the working-class city. Her most famous songs exalted the myth that a *parigote* urchin from this part of the city could find love and happiness in 'le Grand Paris'. She sang brilliantly of cobbled streets, accordion players, whores, tough but vulnerable soldier-lovers, giving Paris a whole new mythology. When she became truly famous after the Second World War, she was never forgiven by those who knew her well and who said that her act was a lie at the service of those forces who kept the *petites gens* in their place. Friends and admirers from her early days, such as the pianist Georges van Parys, despised the post-war Piaf as a 'phoney' and described her as a traitor to her origins. Little wonder that Piaf – intelligent, shrewd, highly sexed and crushed by a celebrity that destroyed every inch of her true identity – took refuge in destructive love affairs and alcohol. Intriguingly enough, it was Piaf's 'authenticity' that ruined her. This was the very quality that she herself cherished more than any other. When it was gone, and she realized how distant she had become from her roots, she finally wrecked herself in drink.[13] The Parisians who had once loved her accepted her squalid death with a characteristic lack of sentimentality.

Parisians are indeed a famously hard-headed race. The *parigots*, *titis* or *gamins de Paris* never or rarely describe themselves as such: they see themselves as shopkeepers, barmen and waiters, labourers, artisans, musicians, pickpockets, rag pickers, drinkers, socialists and anarchists. Above all, Parisians see themselves as a class or series of classes as varied and rich as the city itself. The image of the Parisian people created in literature, art and cinema is dismissed by them at best as folklore, and at worst a deliberate attempt on the part of the ruling élites – whoever they are – to subdue and subjugate the naturally rebellious moods of the people.

One of the few clichés that working-class Parisians do identify with is the habitual use of *gouaille* ('cheek' or 'guile'), usually in league with *l'esprit frondeur* (an aggressive use of wit – literally a 'slingshot wit' – named after the *fronde*, a catapult used in street rebellions in the seventeenth century). But even this has recently come under threat. Most notably, in late 2001, there was a drive to clear out prostitutes from the rue Saint-Denis. The local press were immediately up in arms at this attack on one of the last vestiges of Parisian heritage. More specifically, it emerged on closer reading of the most strident articles in *Le Parisien*, the older prostitutes – called the *traditionnelles* – were particularly prized by clients not simply for their sexual allure but also their *gouaille*. Driving these women from the city streets, it was argued for several weeks on television, radio and in the press, indicated that the shiny new 21st-century city had no room for old-style Parisian street culture. This was as serious, for example, as the problems facing traditional cafés and bistrots, which were similarly being driven out of the city by high rents and the fast-food culture. The forced migration of these native Parisian whores was indeed, it was further argued, a powerful metaphor for the larger identity crisis that the city had been facing since the end of the twentieth century.

The question was asked yet again: can anything of the real Paris still exist in the twenty-first century of image, illusion and spectacle? More to the point, what good was the city of Paris without Parisians?

Paris, Under the Ground

In the high summer of 2001 – when I started writing this book – one of the few cafés that stayed open during the summer break, when Parisians traditionally flee to the mountains or the coast, was La Palette on the rue de Seine.

A few years ago, this bar had been seen throughout the world as the setting for a Kronenbourg ad in which a henpecked and lugubrious *patron* dodges his wife's insults behind the bar, taking solace in a cold glass of the famous French lager. For millions who didn't know its name, La Palette, with its immaculate wooden bar, tiled mirrors and funny little tables, represented an ideal of French alcoholic relaxation. In real life, the bar is the haunt of art dealers, agents, publishers, gallery owners and, very occasion-ally, artists who come here because it is the best place on the rue de Seine to have a drink and broker a deal. It is, in the classic Left Bank tradition, extremely posh and scruffy at the same time. It is exclusive and can be intimidating. The waiters share private jokes with regulars; to the rest of us they serve sarcasm and contempt with evident relish but no extra charge.

But in the summer of 2001 even La Palette had a relaxed air. The fat waiter, who wore a leather jerkin and specialized in humiliating anybody he didn't know, was joshing with obviously foreign customers, one of whom couldn't even speak French. The dealers, movers and shakers had gone, or were in disguise as ordinary people drinking, laughing and evidently having fun. For some reason, everywhere in Paris during the summer months of 2001 felt carnivalesque, uncanny and festive at the same time. Everybody commented on this new and puzzling phenomenon. Even the Brazilian transvestites in the Bois de Boulogne reported a boom season, and this at a period, as one of them chirpily pointed out in the pages of *Le Figaro*, when they traditionally felt the pinch.

As I watched the city scene around me, I reflected on Louis Chevalier's book *L'Assassinat de Paris* ('The Killing of Paris'), which I had been reading that summer.[14] I enjoyed the detail of Chevalier's book, the insight into those obscure corners of Paris and Parisian life that even lifelong students of the city would not know about. I had followed his maps and instructions and visited the sites he said were losing their magical or totemic importance.

But I did not believe his thesis – his argument that Old Paris was dead and buried for ever – for a moment. Even from a café table on the rue de Seine you could see it was not true. What is more, Chevalier contradicted himself when he talked about the history of Paris being lost under our feet. Surely underground Paris, like the metro, was an invisible living presence that could be encountered by excavating layers of the city, in oral histories, literature and music, digging ever deeper, beyond the sewers and the catacombs, into its essence? The novelist Louis-Ferdinand Céline, perhaps the greatest chronicler of the secret history of the city in the twentieth century, had described the life of the city as a 'métro émotif', a ceaseless subterranean movement between light and dark, one place and another, different spaces and different times.[15] The metaphor now made sense. I put down my copy of Chevalier's book on the café table of La Palette and knocked back what was left of my beer. I decided that the aim of my own book would be to show that Chevalier was wrong: Paris was changing in a way that no one could predict. It made no difference if Paris, the old whore, was dying or even dead; her seductive and fatal spell still lingered in the evening air.

In the footsteps of Villon, Mercier, Restif de la Bretonne, André Breton, Walter Benjamin, Georges Perec and all the rest, I set off and started to make my own maps of the city.

PART ONE

The Old Ocean

Prehistory to AD 987

Old Ocean, your waters are bitter.
I salute you, Old Ocean!

Comte de Lautréamont,
Les Chants de Maldoror, 1868

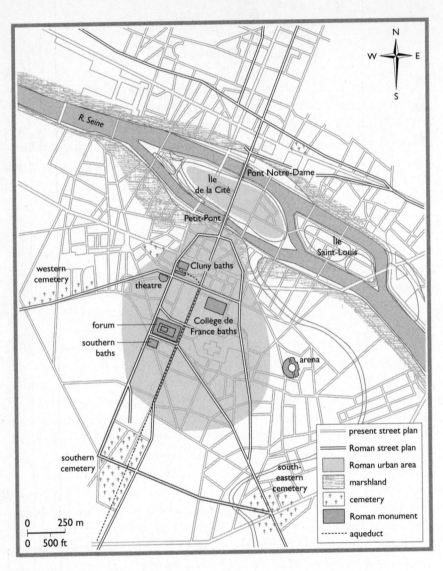

Lutetia during the Roman occupation (c. 50 BC to AD 400).

1. Dirty Water

The Old City is still there. The Roman town was built on Île de la Cité, the geographical centre of the city, eventually spilling over into the heart of the Left Bank on to the steep incline of what is now Montagne Sainte-Geneviève. Even now you can still find your way, tracing a diagonal line, guided by the old stones of Roman civilization: an arena, a temple to Jupiter, a vomitorium, the remains of a forum, a bathing house and a city wall.

These walls, bricks, frescoes and open spaces are not the most ancient traces of life here, although they are the most easily decipherable. Hand axes of design belonging to communities from Algeria and Morocco are regularly found in the washes of the Seine and its tributaries. Their relative sophistication indicates that the wandering tribes of North Africa crossed the straits of Gibraltar sometime after the invention of writing in Mesopotamia – the era that French historians commonly call the proto-historical period – but still long before the first Europeans could put written word and sound together. Arrowheads made to an asymmetrical design unknown in other parts of Europe have also been found here. There was never a period, archaeologists and historians agree, when this fertile and productive land was not occupied. The territory was made into a fixed settlement by the pre-Celtic and then the Celtic peoples, among them a tribe called the Parisii, who arrived here a millennium after the North Africans.

Above all, the Parisii revered the water (a branch of the tribe settled on the Humber near Hull for this same reason). They built boats, long canoes and vessels for fishing or carrying freight, whose remains are still being dug out at Bercy and Seine–Oise–Marne. They were sharp traders and conducted business with the other Seine valley tribes – the Senones, Sequani and the Meldi – whose coins have also been found in the heart of Paris. By the time of Tiberius in AD 14, the Celtic shipbuilders of the Seine had formed a powerful corporation, controlling a lucrative river trade that had been too often foolishly neglected by the Romans. There was, for example, a flourishing trade in pottery, mainly wine-cups, with southern Italian towns that long pre-dated the Roman conquest of the settlement in 54 BC, when the Celtic territory was given the name Lutetia.

The Parisii had always allied commercial nous with an ever-present sense of the world beyond. Their everyday art rarely depicts farmers or merchants, but is rich in gods, demons, princesses and heroes. At the heart of it all, then as now, lay the river, grey-green, sinuous and fast-moving, winding through the city like a snake. The Parisii believed the river had magical properties – this was why they had come here – and they prayed to it for luck in farming and hunting. By 250 BC, their settlement was a centre for trade and shipping.[1] But the fledgling city was far from being enchanted, at least in any benign sense. It was a place of water-borne diseases and unpredictable climate. Its only real advantage for a long time was that it was easy to defend, mainly because it stood on water, but also because it offered no real military value to the predatory tribes that stood at its northern and southern axes.[2]

The Parisii made the first real maps of the city, marking the dangers of the river, its flood tides and sandbanks. The river also carried corpses and disease, spreading panic through the population. The last time this happened was all too recently, in 1961, when the bodies of hundreds of Algerians were washed up at various points. They had been dumped there by the police who, in the aftermath of a political demonstration turned massacre, had been stupid enough to think that the river told no tales (see Chapter 42).

From Parisii to Parisians

The Parisian Celts were eminently practical in most matters. They minted their own money and were the economic superpower in the region long before the Romans arrived. But they also believed that the practical advantages of the islands were as nothing compared to their magical properties. The corpses of those sacrificed to Dispater, the three-headed deity worshipped by the Parisii, were usually hung from trees, but sometimes they were thrown into the dirty-green water of the river. When, like the murdered Algerians in 1961, the corpses returned to the surface, it was assumed that the river gods hated the city and its people. The population fell quiet and wondered how to save themselves.

The Seine was then twice as wide as it is now. At the centre of the swirling green tides was an archipelago of ten or so islands covering some 8 hectares (the area of Île de la Cité is now around 17 hectares). Over the coming centuries, these islands, by natural and artificial means, would coalesce into what is now Île de la Cité and Île Saint-Louis. They stretched from the present-day Bibliothèque de l'Arsenal on the eastern Right Bank to the Île aux Treilles (the Isle of Climbing Vines) at what is now Les Invalides and the Île aux Cygnes (Isle of Swans), previously called the Île au Gros-Caillou (the Isle of the Great Stone), a treacherous sandbank, sacred to the Celts, just beyond the site of the Eiffel Tower.

During the time of the Parisii, the only way to get on or around the shifting spaces of the islands, known collectively after the Roman conquest as Lutetia, was by navigating the river, which was also the main commercial artery of the settlement. One of the first actions of the occupying Romans was therefore to build wooden bridges at what is now Pont au Change and the Petit-Pont, linking the islands to the northern and southern banks of the Seine,[3] and ultimately to the larger world of the ports in the north and the road south towards Orléans and Rome. Until the Roman occupation, the Parisii lived as they had always done, in homely clusters of huts with stockades for animals. Society was based around tribe, clan and immediate family. Faithful to their nomadic origins, the Parisii remained resolutely non-urban – they built no temples or streets – and took to urbanization slowly and grudgingly.

The Roman conquest of the so-called 'nation of the Parisii' (how Roman commentators described the territory) in 54 BC was brutal but definitive, marking a decisive shift in the fortunes of the Roman Republic. By that date, Julius Caesar had already conquered and subjugated a good part of Gaul, whose borders lay to the south in the Po Valley in northern Italy (Cisalpine Gaul) and to the north in Belgium. The original motivation for Roman incursions into Gaulish territory had begun in 121 BC as defensive manoeuvres against bands of marauding Celts. Caesar had turned this self-defence into an active programme of conquest, controlling the territory with a series of brilliantly executed battles. This was a significant prelude to the development of what would become in later centuries the heartland of an empire. Most importantly, Caesar was establishing Gaul as his power-base before turning his attention, in 49 BC to the war against Rome that would lead to his establishment as dictator with absolute control. In 53 BC, the principal Gaulish nations, that is to say the territories belonging to the tribes of the Treviri, the Carnutes, the Senones, still lay outside his control and, what was worse, openly defied his authority by refusing to attend a general assembly he had organized. Caesar was informed by spies that the nation of the Parisii was militarily weak and that for this reason they had not taken part in the general resistance against him. He consequently called a new assembly in Lutetia, with the sole intention of launching an attack against rebellious tribes from this base. Success did not come as quickly as Caesar had anticipated, however, and twelve months on from his original assault most of the Gaulish nations were still ranged against him.

The previous year, Caesar had decided to fix on the Gaulish settlement as his base in the north. He dispatched one of his best and most experienced generals, Labienus, to seize and control the place, which several neighbouring tribes had also made their capital and a centre for fomenting insurrection. Labienus, favoured by a violent storm that wrecked the Gaulish lookout positions, outmanoeuvred the Gauls by sailing down-river with some fifty boats and several hundred heavily armed men. The Gauls responded with a scorched-earth attack led by Camulogenus, setting alight the ground at what is now Quai de Grenelle. For this reason, both historians and radicals have often claimed Camulogenus as the first truly Parisian revolutionary. His efforts were in vain, however. Labienus was now master of Lutetia, and by extension the nation of the Parisii.

Caesar had no specific quarrel with the Parisii, and even expressed admiration for them. This was in fact an unusual attitude among Roman military men of the period. Most Romans traditionally saw the Gauls as the antithesis of Roman civilization, providing the one overriding reason why they had to be subjugated. Most crucially, they were entirely lacking in the austere values of *industria*, *gravitas*, *constantia* and *severitas*. Roman commentators on Gaulish life, including sharp-eyed near-contemporaries of Caesar such as Diodorus Siculus, described the natives as given to 'simplicity and high-spiritedness . . . boastful and scared out of their wits when worsted'.[4] These first Gallic stereotypes introduce us to a people who show off in flamboyant clothing, brag at every opportunity and are given to high-minded wittering, as well as being fanatical sensualists greedy for sex and food, and always keen to drink themselves regularly into a stupor.

Caesar himself noted that, like all the Celts, the Gauls worshipped a variety of gods. With a well-practised colonial insouciance, he immediately assimilated these into their Roman counterparts, noting only that Mercury, god of commercial prowess, came to enjoy a special privilege in these parts. Caesar also referred to simulacra, symbolic statues, which were placed enigmatically around the settlement. These were not in imitation of the Roman forms of worship, but magical emblems, intended to draw down supernatural forces and bind them to the material world.

The Parisii indeed feared little in the physical world. They wielded swords and axes – weapons normally used for fighting human enemies – against the natural and supernatural forces that conjured up storms and other disasters. But they did share a powerful collective anxiety about the end of the world, that the sky would literally fall on their heads (this is the villagers' greatest fear in the stories of Astérix the Gaul). Similarly, like all Celtic tribes, the Parisii traced their own history according to an interchangeable variety of legends.

The Romans brought their own myths with them and added to the store of tales about the settlement. One of the most popular Christianized Roman myths was that Lutetia had been founded by Lucus, the seventeenth descendant of Noah, who came here to make a city on the water. Another was that Hercules led a tribe called the Parhassians here from Asia Minor to make an earthly paradise. There were half-whispers in the Middle Ages of a connection with fugitives from Troy, indicating a nostalgia for the most antique and pagan past possible; as well as a possible desire to elide the history of Rome with that of Gaul.

Other myths contained political messages: one of the most long-standing of these, persisting well into the nineteenth century and beyond, was that the Parisii of Lutetia, although still essentially rustic in character, were 'free allies' or 'friends of Rome'. Lutetia was not therefore a colony but a municipal partner of the imperial capital.[5] This presaged the great rivalry Paris would share with Rome throughout the centuries and was indeed proof that Paris had never been properly subservient to Rome. But the truth was that Parisii were not especially blessed, nor did they have a special relationship with Rome. They were simply shrewd enough to know that avoiding war led to prosperity. The battle for Lutetia was short-lived and easily won by the Romans for this reason.[6] It is possible, however, to trace the disastrous Parisian fascination with imitating Rome in style, language and manner, stretching through to the careless faith placed in the word 'empire' in the nineteenth century, all the way back to this point, two thousand years ago, when Gaulish reality was made into Roman myth.

Isle of Rats, Isle of Crows

The Roman name for the settlement in fact derives from its original Celtic one. The Celts had the habit of naming their settlements after their physical qualities. The islands, whose stinking and greasy banks made the site an unlikely halting-post, were for this reason originally named Louk-tier or Louk Teih – the place of the mud, marshes and swamp. Another half-accepted etymology is Loutouchezi, said to be a Gaulish Celtic term meaning 'among the waters'. This word has persisted through to late-twentieth-century Paris.[7] Most notably, the author and occult investigator Guy Breton, in his book *Les Nuits secrètes de Paris* ('Secret Nights of Paris'), an endlessly intriguing tour of secret societies in modern Paris, describes an encounter with a group of self-styled 'Druids' who worship in the woods of Meudon and chant incantatory verses in praise of 'the men of Loutouch-ezi' and their 'virile and cosmic sexualities' (male Parisians of all eras have always prided themselves on at least the first of these qualities; *Parisiennes* often take another view).[8]

Such etymology was unknown to the Romans, who, with true imperial arrogance, never bothered to translate the language of the Celtic peoples they conquered. The name Louk Teih, the most widely accepted approximation of the Celtic, was simply absorbed by them into Latin as 'Lutetia', and it was left to future writers and historians to guess at what the name might have meant in the beginning.

Strabo, the Greek historian and philosopher, called the settlement Lucotocia and Ptolemy, with a minor vowel shift, called it Lucotecia, but these are mainly Hellenized versions of the same name. Other translations of Louk Teih have it as a pre-Celtic word, meaning variously 'the isle of crows', 'the isle of rats', 'shelter from the water' (the Welsh word *llygod* and the Irish term *luch*, 'mouse' or 'rat', are held to play a role in this etymology).[9]

Or it could have been 'isle of white'. This translation has its origin in the Greek *leukos*, referring to the gypsum deposits near the settlement that were made into plaster. Rabelais makes fun of this suggestion, proposing that the Greeks were referring to the pure white thighs of Lutetia's women. Earlier, Romans had commonly assumed that the name Lutetia stems from *lux*, or 'light': the reality – a name derived, as we have seen, from the site's hazardous physical characteristics – seems to indicate a truer and less fanciful account.[10]

The name Lutetia lasted only a few hundred years into the life of the Gallo-Roman town. The Emperor Julian was sent to Lutetia in AD 360 and he found it civilized enough to make him forget the Middle East where he had been headed. 'I spent the winter close to my cherished Lutetia,' he wrote the same year:

This [Lutetia] is what the Celts call the little town founded by the Parisii – which is really no more than an island surrounded by water on all sides with wooden bridges from either bank. The river floods very rarely: it is the same in winter or summer . . . The temperature in winter is mild because, according to the people of the region, the island is warmed by the ocean . . . the soil is good for vines and the Parisii even grow figs, wrapping them in straw to protect them.[11]

The name Lutetia – usually softened in French to Lutèce – still lingers all over the city. It appears as the name of a luxury hotel (the Hotel Lutetia was also a nest of collaborators during the Second World War), of countless bars, either elegant or scruffy, and even as the name of a malty beer which, although it claims to be in the oldest traditions of the city, is actually brewed in Brussels.

The city became 'Paris' under Julian, who named it Civitas Parisiorum 'the city of the Parisii'. The reason for this was, on the face of it, entirely political. Until this point, the Gaulish name of the city, which indicated the relatively independent and therefore unguarded nature of the settlement, was an open invitation to predatory neighbouring tribes, who took advantage of the thinly manned Roman military outpost. After a series of catastrophic raids, Julian had come to the city to bolster its defences. He named it after its principal inhabitants, as was the tradition in the empire, sending out a signal that the city was under his protection. By using this phraseology, Julian also indicated that the settlement had completed the movement from *pagi* to *civitates*, the Roman terms used to describe the development of a tribal village into a town. More than this, Julian signalled that the small and muddy village of the Gauls now belonged to the larger and more complex world of the Roman Empire, and held an important and prestigious position within that nexus. He further honoured the city by having himself crowned emperor there.

Julian was not just a Roman commander but also a philosopher. Most crucially, he had been initiated into the Eleusian Mysteries, a mystical corollary of neo-Platonism most powerfully at odds with nascent Christianity. With an edict of religious toleration, Julian sought to restore pagan practices as the foremost religion of the city. Similarly by naming the place 'the city of the Parisii' he was paying homage to the pre-Christian origins of the settlement. His intention was to re-invest the city with an earlier sense of the sacred. He was only partially successful in this but, unlike the Celtic language, the pagan tradition persisted long into the Middle Ages and beyond.

In one founding myth – a conflation of Roman, Hellenic, Egyptian and Celtic stories – Isis, female prophetess and supreme magician, is supposed to have visited the city and enchanted the spirits of the air and water. This tale was first quoted in literature in lines by Abbon, Bishop of Fleury-sur-Loire, at the end of the first millennium.[12] The quotation was entirely misleading, however: Abbon was a literary trickster who perversely described the muddy plain as 'the most beautiful port on earth' and was fond of making puns. In his reference to Isis, he was simply playing with the Gaulish name of Iccius (a land-owner who gave his name to what is now the suburb of Issy-les-Moulineaux). Still, the myth in this confused form was persistent. Until the sixteenth century, women would pray to a small statue in female form called Isis, brought to Paris from Issy, at the entrance to the church of Saint-Germain-des-Prés.[13] The pun echoed down the years to the mid twentieth century, with the near-blind Joyce evoking it again in the dream dialogue in *Finnegan's Wake*: 'Parysis, tu sais, crucycrooks,' says Shem to Shaun, 'belongs to him who parises himself.'[14]

In the late-medieval period, the poet François Villon called the city 'Parouart'. This was a term taken from the slang of thieves and deserters – a codeword for the underworld of taverns and brothels. The poet Arthur Rimbaud came to Paris some four hundred years later to drink, write and discover the arts of sodomy in his rooms in the dark twisting lane that was then rue Monsieur-le-Prince. Rimbaud was less than impressed by Paris and growled in his letters home that he had found the city to be no glittering capital but rather 'Parmerde', a disease-ridden place that smelt of shit both day and night.[15]

By the late nineteenth century, some sixteen hundred years after Julian had first named the city, it was common for Parisians to call Paris 'Paname'. This term was in part inspired by the notoriety of the Panama Canal and its associated financial scandals that paralysed the French government in the 1890s. Hence the name 'Paname' was loaded with a sense of double-dealing and disaster. But it also referred to the waters that cut through the dead centre of the city like the great trans-continental canal itself. These waters included new canals and waterways as well as the dying river Bièvre, a thin, smoky channel that criss-crossed the eastern edge of the Left Bank.

'Paname' is still used these days, in the media and advertising, to evoke a folkloric Paris that has only recently passed away. It also remains a staple of everyday language – mostly used by rappers, Islamist preachers, drug dealers and the dispossessed of the northern edges of the city in the suburbs of Seine-Saint-Denis. These people identify only with their own community and for them Paris, or 'Paname', is usually a term of contempt, indicating a murky and corrupt place on dark, polluted waters.

This usage still carries the imprint – even if it is now faintly traced – of the city's most ancient names.[16]

The Secrets of Lutetia

The history of antique Paris was long neglected, at least until the late Renaissance. If Lutetia was known at all to the average Parisian before this time, it was usually as the backdrop to one of the gory legends of the religious martyrs of the city. In more practical terms, the inhabitants of Île de la Cité and other parts of Paris that lay over the Roman town had been long accustomed to pillaging masonry for new houses from the long-buried streets of Lutetia. From the sixteenth century onwards, there were nevertheless efforts to make sense of the past, even if the work was all too often conducted by amateurs, like the antiquarian Gilles Corrozet, fantasists such as the cleric Père de Breul or, during the latter part of the seventeenth century, the lawyer, politician, historian and philologist Henri Sauval.

The real hero of the rediscovery of Lutetia in the nineteenth century was a distinctly unpoetic small man who cherished a passionate and irrational lifelong dream to bring the Roman city to the surface. Théodore Vacquer was, in the words of his friends, 'discreet but stubborn, absolutely inflexible'.[17] He first came to prominence in 1844, when still in his twenties, having been made Director of the Historical Research of Paris, an office under the aegis of the city government. Vacquer was ordered to inspect building works around Paris, recording items or discoveries of archaeological importance. His approach to history was distinctly practical: 'We value the facts before anything else,' he wrote. 'We use few texts. Until now the history of Paris has been written by the fireside.'[18]

Vacquer's men accordingly eschewed the literary imagination and scavenged for hard evidence on the ground. It was a superb accident of timing that his work gained its greatest momentum and urgency during the 1850s, the period when Baron Haussmann was systematically ripping apart the old alleys and labyrinthine quarters of the medieval city. Haussmann's project, as we shall see in Chapter 31, was to make way for a glittering new city of wide boulevards and open avenues, a city of spectacular pleasure which would at once define modernity and be the envy of the world (in his self-justifying and deliberately skewed memoirs, Haussmann evokes the original meaning of Lutetia as a 'filthy marsh' to vindicate his plans).[19]

With the fierce passion of the lonely fanatic, Vacquer found a kind of comfort in the presence of the secret city underground. Perhaps his greatest achievement was the excavation of the Arena at the heart of the Left Bank, near the rue Monge. Parisians had known about this site from the thirteenth century, but Vacquer was the first to set about the complex task of mapping and digging out more or less intact Roman remains. He did this from 1869 onwards with a severe indifference to the great events unfolding around him – the Franco-Prussian war, the Commune – and the individual suffering they brought in their wake.

Vacquer's real quest was for the centre of gravity of the ancient city. The question he asked himself was when and how the Celtic settlement had ceased to be more than just a muddy village and become a truly urban space. He guessed that the city had been founded on Île de la Cité and then spread mainly southwards to what is now the Panthéon and the Jardins du Luxembourg. Intuition had already proved him right about the dimensions of Lutetia, stretching from the rue de Rivoli to Gobelins. The problem he never solved was how to trace and understand the movements of population during Lutetia's long history.

This was also one of the great questions taken up in the twentieth century by Michel Fleury. Like Vacquer, Fleury was a fanatic. He was a historian by training and solitary by nature: his students and acolytes described him as 'Le Grand Fleury', a loner who worked long hours and would read all of Hugo in one sitting to prove a point. Fleury was a pedant and an eccentric (he was, for example, the kind of committed Anglophobe who would spell 'weekend' as 'ouikènde'). There was more than a hint of mysticism in the way in which his closest disciples argued that he was on 'intimate terms with the invisible'.[20]

Most of Fleury's discoveries were also based on inspired guesswork. He stalked the oldest quarters of twentieth-century Paris – the rues Rataud, des Feuillantines, de l'Arbalète and Llomond, all in the Latin Quarter – in pursuit of broken pieces of pagan art, to prove his thesis that the Gallo-Roman town was truly a city of two cultures. Validating this argument was his sole agenda. His most controversial thesis was that Paris had been more or less unaffected by changes of its governing authorities in the centuries between the collapse of the Roman Empire and the establishment of the Capetian kings in 987, and that its true heritage was therefore Celtic. He traced the fluctuations and shifting movements of the population during this period, wondering why the pagan cemeteries at Val-de-Grâce had suddenly been abandoned, marking the growth of the Left Bank settlements and the destruction of the outer villages.

As a Gaulish settlement, he argued, the site depended on its river trade and life first centred around where goods were landed. Originally this was situated at Place de la Grève (where the Hôtel de Ville now stands), a marshy swamp on the Right Bank, which was the original Parisian business district. On the Left Bank, where Caesar formerly made his camp, there came the monasteries, churches and then later the University of Paris.

Hence the separation of the city into the Right Bank, the profane domain of work and commerce, and the Left Bank, the spiritual and intellectual centre of the city, dates from the city's most ancient origins. Fleury concluded that everything began and ended – as the original inhabitants always had known – with the river, which with its subterranean moods, its tides and dangers has the unpredictable quality of the sea.

Fleury's discovery gives an historical basis to a long tradition of writing about Paris that describes the city as a seascape. 'Paris is an ocean,' wrote Balzac. 'You may cast the sounding-line, but you will never fathom its depth.'[21] For Baudelaire too, Paris was a 'black ocean' of deep and limitless waters.[22] The most grotesque and chilling example of the use of this image is by Isidore Ducasse (a near-contemporary of the fastidious Vacquer but his opposite in every way). Ducasse came to Paris in the 1860s from Montevideo, called himself the comte de Lautréamont and died in the city, probably of drink. In his long poem *Les Chants de Maldoror* ('The Songs of Maldoror') of 1868, the eponymous hero – murderous, impotent and Luciferian – rages against the poisoned 'Old Ocean'.

It is never made clear whether the 'Old Ocean' is a metaphor for the unknowable depths of Paris, death, eternity, or the endless sea of alcohol that drives Maldoror mad. Either way, it is a vivid and haunting evocation of the lethal effect of polluted water.

2. Severed Heads

The villages and small encampments of Louk Teih were first made at a bend in the Seine at the central point of hills stretching north and south. It was a natural shelter that offered protection from the worst storms, blowing wildly and savagely in from the east and the north. The hills also functioned as a wall against predatory invasions from neighbouring tribes. The first settlers were farmers who came from Central Europe and the south, bringing with them an advanced form of agriculture, and a pattern of settlement, in tightly clustered villages of fifty to two hundred inhabitants (their remains are in Meudon, Cormeilles-en-Parisis and Choisy-le-Roi). This was the model assimilated by the later Parisii, who stayed because the soil, the river, the landscape and the climate offered sustenance and comfort.

What lay there in the beginning was a limestone plateau covered in fine, chalky soil, through which rainwater was naturally filtered and which in times of drought allowed water to be drawn up to the surface. The ploughing and digging was easy in these fertile fields, and nowhere more so, as the first farmers discovered, than in the plateaux of the Beauce, the Brie and the Soissonnais, each covered with a soft silt. The view from Montmartre during the Gallo-Roman period would have revealed intensely cultivated fields and orchards producing apricots, figs, asparagus and vines. The vineyards are evoked in the street names on the slopes of Montmartre – the rues du Clos, Clos-Breton, Clos-Bruneau and so on (a *clos* is a vineyard). Peasant vocabulary and superstitions are still heard across the city in street names such as rue de l'Abreuvoir ('street of the watering trough'), rue des Terres au Curé ('street of the priest's lands'), rue du Puits de l'Ermite ('street of the hermit's well'). There was an altar to Bacchus, god of wine, on what is now the Montagne Sainte-Geneviève. Julian had noted that the Parisii 'freely and generously used his gifts'.[1] This much had also been noted by the first Romans to settle in Lutetia, who reported back to their sceptical countrymen that they had found a gastronomic paradise and that the Gauls were men of high alcoholic culture. The pagan god lingered long in the memory of the Christian city, when he was nicknamed Saint Bacch and his good health celebrated on 7 October, the pagan festival of the wine harvest.[2]

Although Louk Teih evolved into Lutetia only slowly, the Gallo-Roman town was prosperous and politically stable for over three hundred years. Hostility to the Romans had largely melted away by AD 100 (a putative insurrection launched by two Gaulish nobles near the end of the first century of Roman rule was, for example, defused by the Parisii themselves on the grounds that it was harmful to their economic interests). By the second century, the town was expanding with impressive confidence. A forum was established near Montagne Sainte-Geneviève, an amphitheatre at what is now rue Racine, as well as the Arena with a capacity for 18,000 spectators. A wall was built around this new urban area, which now stretched towards what are still the northern and southern edges of 21st-century Paris. The beating heart, and economic centre, of the town was a road, uncovered by Vacquer, that ran across two bridges from north to south, through the present faubourgs Saint-Martin and Saint-Denis, and which was the first road ever to be constructed away from Île de la Cité.

By this time, even those born in Rome or who felt themselves to be ethnically Roman had come to admire the Parisian Gauls. Writing in AD 125, in the *Epitome bellorum omnium annorum DCC* ('Epitome of Roman History'), the poet and historian Florus, disgusted with the decadence of Italy, praised the Gauls for their economic energy and vigour and as the most likely saviours of the empire. The Gaulish aristocracy of Lutetia now occupied the highest positions of command, as magistrates, administrators and soldiers, modifying only slightly the tax demands made from Rome. This was, from all points of view, a settled and successful province, a fully integrated and economic nexus of the empire. There was a long-established tradition that the local Roman commander-in-chief, who was sometimes a Gaulish-speaking native of the lightly garrisoned city, had little to do but rule with minimum force and a light touch. This complacency would prove to be the undoing of Lutetia, however.

The Mount of Martyrs

Until the priests began handing out his story to panic-stricken congregations, Denis was only one of a long line of murdered Christians, most of whom had been killed for public amusement in the Arena and who, like Saint Lucian or any other Christian martyrs of the era, have been long consigned to oblivion. The legend of Saint Denis grew in precise relation to the Christian fear of Barbarian invaders from the east, and then of Islam as, towards the end of the eighth and ninth centuries, the Muslim hordes had penetrated as far north as Poitiers and Tours. There was no specific response to the Barbarian or Muslim threat to be found in the saint's story, but it did offer a chastening account of Christian fortitude in the face of the most severe danger.

This danger was not immediate or obvious to the inhabitants of Lutetia in the second and third centuries. They were none the less sufficiently disturbed by raids across the border made by the Franks and Alemanni to seek comfort in the newly arrived religion of Christianity. At this stage, it had only a precarious foothold in Gaul, and was mainly confined to the small Greek-speaking communities in Lyons or Marseilles. When Saint Denis, the first patron saint of Paris, made his appearance in the third century, probably around AD 250, Christianity was still a marginal and unpopular cult in Paris.[3] It was about this time that Gaul felt itself to be properly under threat from its barbarian neighbours, as well as the menace of mass banditry and peasant insurrections led by a disaffected Gaulish rural population. For the first time, in AD 260, a Gaulish officer, Postumus, was made Emperor of Gaul. He succeeded in pushing back the raiding tribes for another eight years. By then, there was hardly any part of Gaul which had not heard the terrible stories of massacres at the hands of the invaders.

In the first versions of the story, Denis had been sent to Lutetia from Athens to convert the Gallo-Roman Parisians, who were notorious for their pagan ways. He did this mainly by smashing pagan statues. Unsurprisingly, Denis soon exhausted the patience of his hosts and was arrested in the quarry of Faubourg Saint-Jacques, near what is now the axial meeting point of Denfert-Rochereau, where deposits of gypsum were used to make plaster simulacra or icons for pagan worship.

In the company of his fellow evangelists, Eleuthère and Rusticus, Denis was taken to the prison of Glaucus, the site of the present flower market on Île de la Cité. On the orders of the prefect Sisiianus Fesceninus, they were tortured over several days before being led up to Montmartre – which, historical linguists disagree, could have been a corruption of *Mons martyrum*, the Martyrs' Hill, or *Mons Mercurii*, after a temple to Mercury, or could have been *Mons Martis*, honouring a temple to Mars. Far from the city centre, this was where they were to be decapitated. The soldiers who accompanied the evangelists through the marshes of the Right Bank, too tired to take them all the way up the steep slope, chopped their heads off before the Temple of Mercury at the foot of the hill, in what is now rue Yvonne-le-Tac. This is where Denis apparently picked up his head, walked over to the fountain, at the corner of what is now rue Girardon and rue de l'Abreuvoir, and marched across Montmartre intoning prayers until he fell. The body of the ecstatic martyr was buried by Catulla, a pious Christian widow, in a place called Catolucus.

The headless saint has proved an unlikely hero over the years. He is supposed to have appeared before Dagobert, briefly a king of Paris in the seventh century, to protect him from demons. Dagobert asked to be buried in Saint Denis's tomb, but his real contribution to posterity was as the target of an anti-monarchist song of the Revolution of 1789. Having famously conducted kingly business with his breeches the wrong way round, he became a clear example to the Revolutionary songwriters of royal stupidity, clumsiness and sheer buffoonery. (Dagobert may have been a fool, but he was also a mass murderer: in 631 he ordered the night-time slaughter of nine thousand or so Bulgars, dispossessed of their lands and who had come to him for protection.)

Denis has proved a remarkably ineffectual saint in other ways. He was often wrongly associated with Dionysos, the Greek god of drunkenness, or the early Christian philosopher Denys the Areopagite, but has an everyday presence now, enjoying a lowly but homely status as a saint whose main powers are curing dog-bites and, somewhat inevitably, headaches. For the Germans, he is associated with syphilis, which, in the wake of their occupation of the city in 1870, they called *le mal français*. Few theologians take him seriously. Indeed, the well-known and sneering complaint of those who work in religious orders is that Paris is 'not a Christian city'. Perhaps it never truly was. Where Denis took his final steps is now the heart of the city's sex industry, and the street dedicated to him, the rue Saint-Denis, winds down through the city to the river, where pagan pleasures, at 40 euros a throw, are on offer at every few paces.

Speaking in Tongues

Nearly all the citizens of Lutetia were to some extent bilingual, in Gaulish and Latin, long before the arrival of Christianity and Saint Denis. Many of the sharper commercial operators often had a smattering of other tongues important for business, such as Greek, dialects of Old Brythonic (although Breton itself did not arrive in France until the sixth century, as an import from Britain) or the Germanic languages. Before the arrival of the Romans, the Gauls used the Greek alphabet, and long after the conquest business contracts were often drawn up in Greek, demonstrating that the language did not belong to an aristocratic élite and partly supporting the thesis of the nationalist historian Camille Julian that if Caesar's wars had failed, most of Gaul, including Lutetia, might well have ended up like Marseilles, as an integrated part of Hellenic Mediterranean civilization.[4]

The Romans might have at first imposed their own language and religion, but assimilation came easily to the Parisii. By the end of the first hundred years of its existence, Lutetia was a bilingual and multicultural city: trade, religion and politics were conducted in Latin; everyday matters, such as sex, food and farming, were expressed in the old language. The same distinctions characterized life at street level. Lutetia was in essence a market town, a busy and hard-headed place. Although the Parisii had minted their own money until the Roman occupation, most business and trade was a matter of reciprocity and barter. Now coins minted in Rome were the common currency. Long into the Gallo-Roman era, most men still dressed in the Gaulish manner, sporting a moustache and long hair and wearing a *cucculus*, a long blanket thrown over the shoulder. Women too were unimpressed by Roman fashions and generally preferred the braided hair, brooches, amulets and tunics of Celtic design.[5]

Despite the tenacity of Celtic ways, the Gaulish language eventually collapsed from within and was all but lost or forgotten by the fourth century. It is difficult to pin down with any precision the moment when Gaulish disappeared. As late as 363, a dialogue in Latin records a Roman commanding a Gaul to 'speak Celtic if you prefer'.[6] The language lingered in the countryside until the fifth century, where Sidonius Apollinaris, an astute and generally meticulous historian of Gaul, noted that the peasants of the Auvergne had only just rid themselves of 'the ignorant filth that is the Gaulish tongue'.[7] The administrative business of the empire was of course entirely conducted in Latin, and it did not help that the Druidic tradition dear to the Celts was an oral one.[8]

Centrifugal forces were also at work on the Roman language: although by the seventh and eighth centuries the written Latin of the city still corresponded to classical standards, the spoken Latinate language of the city, packed with neologisms, appropriations from Gaulish and other tongues, was, by the sixth century, no longer recognizably Roman. By the end of the first millennium, a distinct new language, the remote and distant ancestor of Modern Standard French, had emerged.

Some of the oldest words in French can, however, be traced back to the time when Gaulish Celtic was the first language of the city. For example, the word *seine*, *senne* or *saine* in Old French means 'fishing net'. Its first written usage can be traced back to Étienne Boileau, who used the word in 1269 in his *Livre des métiers* ('Book of Occupations'), an inventory of the working life of Paris. The Gallo-Roman version of the word is *sagena* – possibly derived from the Gaulish word for 'fishing basket' or 'net' – *sin-ane* or *sôghane*, meaning 'slow river'.[9] The word *seine* is used with its old meaning as a fishing net by Balzac, and indeed crops up with a degree of frequency in nineteenth-century literature; it has, however, referred to the river for as long as anyone can ascertain. The other Gaulish words that made it through to Vernacular Latin and eventually to Modern French (it is estimated that there are some four hundred of these) apply to clothing, food, tools, animals, birds, vehicles and weapons: testimony to the practical nature of the tongue. The earliest form of Parisian contempt for non-Parisians can be traced back to the ancient word *plouc*. It is still in common use, meaning now as it did for the Parisii, a gormless or oafish outsider to the city.[10]

The Sharp Edge of the World

The first Parisians, whether of Celtic or Roman origin, were deeply super-stitious, especially in times of political uncertainty. They feared the river, of course, but also the woods and forests. These were particularly dense in the west and the south-west, between Le Gâtinais and La Laye; most impenetrable were the great forests of Bière, Brie and Senlis.

The islands and southern bank of the river were now a thoroughly urbanized environment and resembled any number of Romanized centres across the Gaulish territory. The Gallo-Romans of Lutetia lived mainly in villas or *insulae*, crowded city dwellings. The wild places outside the city were fraught with danger, from hungry wolves to murderous bandits; they also presented a psychological threat as unknown spaces which challenged the instinct for protection and which had led the early Celts and then the Parisii to huddle together in their first villages. Later, as the Gallo-Roman city grew beyond its first boundaries, beyond the *ager* or *laboratorium*, the cultivated land at its edges, the forests became, in the stories of Lutetia, not only places of real danger but also emblems of an untamed and untameable libidinal world beyond the control of the strictly organized and hierarchical city. The woods and forests were, in the most literal terms, the 'outside' where evil spirits and barbarians raped young virgins, Mass was said to the

Devil and the open sky was blackened into night even at midday. Anybody who rode through a forest at night would be driven mad, it was said, or was already a criminal.

Despite these anxieties, the forests around Lutetia also had a long-standing economic role. They provided grazing grounds for flocks. During the occasional emergencies when hay was in short supply, leaves (mainly elm and oak) could be gathered to provide winter fodder for sheep and cattle. The leaves were also used to fill mattresses or as compost. In addition, the forests provided the fuel for cooking, heating and myriad industries, including breweries, ironworks, glass-works and refineries; their wood provided coopers with a living and the basis for building (houses, city walls) and transport (boats, carts). Hence the price of wood was a key factor in the economic well-being of the city.[11] More than this, it was a political weapon, especially at times of crisis, famine or constitutional instability.

Fear of what lay beyond the city's edges found its justification in history. Until around AD 330, the received wisdom was that the main threat to Lutetia's stability, indeed to that of any of the Gaulish provinces, was either from mutinous Gauls, seditious Christians or slaves in revolt. Then, in the fourth century, as the Roman Empire began to crumble at the edges, something potentially far more dangerous became apparent. Lutetia was suddenly revealed as lying on a geographical and political fault-line: only a few days' march from the Germanic borderlands, it lay almost on the border between the Roman world and the rest of Europe.

The Roman Empire had been displaying all the signs of decay for around a hundred years or so before this period. The rottenness was most clearly visible at the centre, that is to say Rome itself, which was dominated by political instability and where in the ninety years from AD 180 there had been more than eighty emperors, each one of whom had signally failed to control the growing chaos. Barbarian hordes regularly flooded over the edges of the empire, growing increasingly daring and devastating with each new success. The sacking of Athens in 268 sent shock-waves through the Roman world. In Gaul itself, a short-lived 'Empire of the Gauls' was founded by the Romanized Gaul Postumus in 258, briefly flourishing then adding to the mounting disorder. The breakdown in political order was often accompanied by disease or famine; harvests failed, goods were not moved or were stolen; the towns were badly maintained; taxes were not collected and the universal Roman coinage fell in value. One of the problems for the imperial administrators was that this was a highly bureaucratic and centralized empire (all documents on soldiers above the rank of centurion were, for example, held in Rome no matter where the legion was stationed). As a response to this, the Emperor Diocletian broke the empire into two halves in the late third century. The administration and military efficiency briefly improved, but the economy continued to fail. The empire was reunited under Constantine the Great, a native of Serbia who moved the capital to Byzantium, which was then renamed Constantinople. The founding of the great holy city on the Bosphorus in AD 330, and its establishment as the official capital of the Roman Empire and the seat of Christian power in AD 331, arguably restored order to a territory that for centuries had been slowly drifting towards chaos.

However, with this one single and swiftly executed decision, Lutetia had been placed further from the imperial capital and its protection than it had ever been. At the same time, to the north and the south, the Germanic and Slavonic tribes had already begun moving westwards. The Goths had marched from the Vistula to the Dnieper. The Franks were now camped on both banks of the Rhine. The forces were gathering that would smash the imperial province of Gaul into ruins.

3. Sea Gods

By the end of the fourth century, Gaul had fallen into a steep and irreversible decline. Governmental authority in the urban centres was weak and divided, while in the countryside higher taxes, famines and the threat of a total collapse throughout the last decades of the century provoked a wave of revolts that took on an unstoppable momentum. These rebels were called *Bagudae* ('fighters', a word taken from the Celtic *baga*, 'to fight' – a term which persists in the French word *bagarre*, a fight or a scuffle) and owed allegiance to no one. Even more dangerous to the Gallo-Roman authorities was the way in which these outlaws invited barbarians – Saxons, Burgundians, Visigoths and Franks – on to Gaulish territory, haggling with them over land, cattle and money, and acting entirely beyond the reach of the law. The so-called 'great invasion' of 406, led by the Visigoth Radagaisus, when tribes from the east swarmed over the border with no intention of going back, was partly encouraged by this behaviour. There was no decisive moment when it could be said that Roman rule in Gaul had completely ended, however. For the Gaulish Parisians the break with Rome occurred at the end of the fifth century when the Franks took over Paris.

The Frankish assassin and bandit Clovis marched into the city in 486. His name, pronounced with a hiss, is a contraction of 'Chlodovech', later to become 'Louis', the name of future kings. He was only twenty years old and had just beaten the Roman governor Syagrius in battle, humiliating his forces (prisoners were laughingly sodomized by the Frankish soldiers as a matter of routine). When his father had died in 481, Clovis had assumed command of the Salian Franks. He was then only sixteen, but already long blooded in battle. Now he controlled a city.

Clovis ran riot through the surrounding towns and villages, pillaging churches, stealing women. His wife, Clotilda, was a Christian, but he sneered at her faith, trusting the magical arts of the pagan gods over the Divine Power. The death of two sons in early infancy only hardened his scepticism about this religion of the meek. The most enduring legend about Clovis was actually invented in the seventeenth century by the historian Henri, comte de Boulainvilliers, and then taught to generations of French schoolchildren as an anti-monarchist parable.[1] The gory culminating point of the tale is that Clovis smashed open with an axe the head of a soldier on parade on the Champ de Mars, accusing him of clumsiness. This murder was also an act of revenge upon the same soldier, who had rebuked Clovis after an earlier battle for taking a vase (known as the vase of Soissons) as his own booty, arguing that treasure won in battle belonged to all who had fought. Clovis conceded the point there and then, but later took his revenge.

Although an invention, this was a highly symbolic anecdote, intended to illustrate the undisputed savagery and arrogance of the Franks. It also, as other commentators have pointed out, demonstrates a tendency in Parisian governments to match civil authority with military force, pointing to the absolutist regimes to come.[2] Still, this was hardly yet a civilization but rather a new and rather fragile society, caught, in Flaubert's phrase, between 'the death of the old Gods and the coming of Christ'.[3]

For Clovis himself, the turning point in his career came in battle with the hated Alamanni, a Germanic tribe who, despite overwhelming strength in numbers, collapsed in the face of the Frankish onslaught. Clovis had made a vow to Saint Rémi of Rheims that he would convert to Christianity if he managed to overcome such impossible odds. Under the influence of Geneviève (as we shall see, the most important political and religious figure of the time), he turned somewhat reluctantly towards God, if not to Christian charity, and became the first Christian king of Paris.

His first significant action as sovereign, and with the most long-lasting consequences, was to declare all Franks free men and all free men Franks. It is from this point on that the term 'frank' is associated not only with the territory of 'Francia', which would slowly but eventually become France, but also with the notion of being 'free'. (This is the meaning contained in the name of the rue des Francs-Bourgeois – translated by the drunken Jack Kerouac in the 1950s as 'the street of the outspoken middle-classes'[4] – which runs parallel to the Seine through the present-day Marais. The street was given this name in the sixteenth century because it housed an almoner's lodge where forty-eight townspeople of diminished means could live free of tax – although given its current gentrified status, Kerouac's translation may indeed be nearer the mark.)

Clovis also established the 'Salic Law', which debarred women from inheriting land, and thereby the throne of France. Under the Franks, Paris was still not a huge town, yet it was the capital of a country. From this point on, it would occupy a defining and central place in the history of Francia.

The First Ruins of Paris

The Franks were originally a loose confederation of barbarians, with their roots in western Germany. Roman historians first referred to them in AD 241, naming their main headquarters as the town of Dispargum, now the neat town of Tongres in Belgium. They were violent and flamboyant warriors who wore their long hair flowing over their shoulders and claimed a sea god as their ancestor.

The Frankish kings were also known as Merovingians, taking their name from Mérovée, the grandfather of Clovis. The dynasty founded by Clovis lasted until the death of Dagobert in 638, when control of Paris and all the Frankish territories passed over to successive *maires du palais* ('mayors of the palace'), heads of the royal household who effectively ruled the country. The Merovingian line continued up until the reign of Pépin le Bref, father of Charlemagne, but as the kings had no real power they have commonly come to be known as *rois fainéants*, the 'do-nothing kings'.

The Franks excelled at terror. The killing of Brunhild, wife of King Sigebert, in Austrasia (France was then composed of kingdoms with similarly strange-sounding names) in 613 demonstrated the brutality of Frankish law. Brunhild's crime had been that for three decades she had sought to play kingmaker in areas controlled by Paris. She was eventually betrayed by those she tried to control and was found guilty in Paris on the charge of the murder of ten kings. Her punishment was to be tied to a camel for three days, and to be beaten and raped by anybody passing by. This all took place at the meeting point of what is now rue Saint-Honoré and rue de l'Arbre-Sec, now a busy intersection fringed with cafés, banks and department stores.[5]

The violent Frankish city was still very much a place with a pagan culture. It was a busy commercial centre and visited regularly by Syrians, Jews and North Africans. Gregory, Bishop of Rome, wrote angrily to the Queen of the Franks in 586 to complain that, according to travellers' reports, the native Parisians had yet to submit to the 'discipline of the Church and they must stop worshipping trees, hanging in public the heads of animals which have been sacrificed in an impious manner. We are even informed,' gasped the bishop, 'that some Christians – O abominable thing! – worship demons there.'[6]

The Franks themselves were reluctant Christians and not above adding their own barbarous beliefs to the stew of Gaulish and Roman superstitions swilling around in the city. They were great believers in sympathetic magic, carrying talismans, casting spells and divining auguries in the entrails of murdered enemies. Gregory of Tours was too cowardly to rebuke Clovis when he came to him looking for a magical way of reading the future, but out of his presence condemned his barbarous practices. Other priests, even less bold, stopped preaching Christian morality under the Franks, reducing the word of Christ to the observance of certain ceremonies and rituals which were more or less interchangeable with pagan rites. The Frankish kings also earned a reputation for laziness and stupidity. One scholar, self-evidently oblivious to delicate nuances of the French post-colonial heritage, memorably described Frankish chiefs as 'clinging obstinately to the tatters of Roman pomp, like a Negro king wearing European uniform'.[7]

Lutetia had now begun to crumble away for ever. The great Roman buildings were ruins, their bricks and marble taken away for Frankish churches and houses, which spread out in all directions towards the old villages around the city. The old gods were gradually being abolished or killed off by Christianity; Frankish law was made and carried out from the old Roman basilica – now long buried beneath the parvis of Notre-Dame – and palace of justice opposite what is now the Hôtel-Dieu. As the city grew, and the old Roman walls turned to dust, it also became more vulnerable than ever.

The Nurse of Paris

Although this was a violent and unstable period in the history of Paris, it was also when the first literary texts in what can be identified as the French language emerged. These were usually tales of Christian martyrs, such as Saint Denis, who undergo torture and death rather than relinquish their faith. These legends were originally conceived by churchmen as political propaganda. As the city slowly emerged from the wreckage of an earlier civilization, their widespread popularity, which spread quickly from the pulpit into the street, demonstrated that this was a place that, lacking in conventional forms of self-defence, was desperately in need of a mythology to underpin it.

Geneviève, who was to become twin patron saint of Paris with Denis, did not undergo torture and was not killed for her piety. Rather she was a skilful manipulator of people and situations, well versed in the black arts of diplomatic negotiation, who ruthlessly intimidated lesser male political opponents while still shrouding herself in the mystique of being a holy woman. The later myth of Sainte Geneviève, for historians and religious thinkers, was built on these two facets of her character.

Before the arrival of the Franks, the greatest threat to the city came from Attila's Mongol horsemen, who by 441 had slaughtered their way to Rheims, within a day or so of the Parisian city walls. The saviour of Paris at this moment of deadly threat was not a commander or warrior in the field, but Geneviève, a slight and pious young woman who had received a vision from God in which she was told that the city would be spared. The terrified inhabitants of Paris desperately needed to hear this, and Geneviève did all she could to stop panic turning into mass flight from the city. There was a political as well as a spiritual dimension at work here: Geneviève effectively prevented surrender at a point in Parisian history when that would have almost certainly meant the destruction of the city.

One of the most famous depictions of Geneviève is *Sainte Geneviève gardant ses moutons*, an anonymous painting of the sixteenth century that now hangs in the Musée Carnavalet. Here, Geneviève is depicted with a mild, motherly face and an ample form, an image somewhat at odds with the historical account of her as a self-starved, highly strung young girl. In the background there is a row of standing stones (another invention of the painter) and the city of Paris, waiting to be saved, in the middle distance. Most importantly, Geneviève is shown as a country girl, connected to the not-so-distant Celtic past and outside the corrupting influence of pagan, decaying Rome.

In reality, Geneviève was born into an aristocratic Gallo-Roman family in 420, in Nanterre, just outside Paris.[8] The popular legends of Geneviève show her as a peasant girl who shivered herself into fevers and convulsions. In fact she was born into a prosperous and well-established family who had high political connections. Although Gallo-Roman Paris was disintegrating before her eyes, Geneviève was shrewd and hard-headed enough not to lose faith in the power of political office. Women were at this time excluded from all power-structures except religion (Geneviève had taken the veil under the Bishop of Paris at the age of fifteen) and it was Geneviève's reputation for mysticism that propelled her at a young age, following in her father's footsteps, into the key role of adviser to the ruling authorities of the city.

She was at first distrusted and disliked by the Parisians. Not everybody was impressed by the mystical claims made by the intense, skinny girl with staring eyes. Mostly she inspired fear, dread or awe. But her anxiety captured perfectly the collective mood of the time. Roman Europe was fragile and under attack. As Attila's armies moved ever forward and nearer, Paris welcomed wave after wave of refugees from the east, seeking asylum en route to the calm and prosperous south. They told stories of terrible massacres, whole towns and villages razed, virgins raped, thousands of men slaughtered. Parisians quivered with fearful anticipation. This was the wrath of God, the refugees told the terrified Parisians, the end of history and the end of the world.

Geneviève heard all of this and witnessed the starving and brutalized refugees praying to God. She starved herself (barley and beans only twice a week) and worried. Her anorexia gave her a luminous countenance and when it seemed that Attila was about to enter Paris, still a young virgin girl, she walked calmly around the streets of Île de la Cité, the marshy field around the river, and to the empty palaces (Aétius, the Roman prefect, had long since fled for Spain on the pretext of seeking help), saying that God had told her that Paris would be preserved.

Most Parisians, particularly the women, dismissed her as a hypocrite and an impostor, or a madwoman. But then Attila, suddenly and miraculously, turned his attention further south to the richer and more prestigious prizes that could be more easily won (cynics of the period slyly suggested that Attila's change of course was because he had been told the women of Paris were not worth raping). Yet more astounding miracles were reported in other places (a bishop in Orléans hurled his own boiling spit at the invaders, who, startled and panic-stricken in the face of such a 'supernatural' military response, immediately withdrew). But none were as powerful or as touching as that of the young girl – apparently no longer regarded as a self-seeking religious maniac – who saved a city.

In the foremost churches of Paris, Genevieve (alongside Saint Denis) was hailed as saviour by nervous priests with one eye on preserving their own position and safety in a place which, like its neighbours to the north and east, might easily have been ravaged and destroyed. One of the few surviving buildings of the period is the church of Saint-Julien-le-Pauvre, now at the heart of the Left Bank tourist industry, but in the time of Gregory of Tours a refuge for travellers and Parisians who feared for their lives during the raids made on the city. Its survival was testimony, the Christian Parisians whispered among themselves, to the endurance of the city.

But this was also a time of omens and signs whose meaning could never fully be made clear. Gregory of Tours himself, first chief propagandist of the Parisian Church, speaks with horror of the discovery of two golden statues of a serpent and a lion in a disused Roman sewer. A devastating fire in the southern part of the city followed shortly afterwards, to no one's great surprise. The larger message was clear: the immediate past and its pagan mysteries were still to be feared. Geneviève's most important religious role was to make the transition from the pagan world to Christian civilization a journey from which there was no going back. For this reason alone, she was commonly described by the later generations as the 'nurse and mistress of Paris'.

Capital Visions

Geneviève's most remarkable achievements were entirely political, however. She lived to an exceptionally old age for the period (dying at the age of eighty) and by the time that Clovis arrived, she was, at the age of forty-six, an experienced and wily power-broker, well used to the murderous caprices of the Franks and other ambitious, self-serving criminals. She was not only responsible for the baptism of Clovis, but also persuaded him to make his capital in Paris. The boorish and bloodthirsty Frank was even persuaded by her to found on what is now the Montagne Sainte-Geneviève a place of learning and study for poor students, which would eventually become part of the University of Paris.

The stories of Denis and Geneviève are the founding myths of the 'great civilization' of which the Christian city of Paris would soon be the capital.[9] Most crucially, however, like the political founder of Paris, Clovis, both saints combined the gift of violent vision with theocratic propaganda at a precise moment of political crisis. Their true role was to mark the establishment of a myth of the city that transcended the religious, social and political constructions of the old Gallo-Roman town.

The Franks ruled France for nearly two centuries. Although they unified the territory, albeit through brute force, the accepted wisdom is that their only true legacy was to bequeath a rigid hierarchical system of social rank. In this system, the lower ranks were occupied by what remained of the rustic Gaulish world (peasants, labourers, artisans), while the ruling aristocracy constituted an endless parade of feckless, dim-witted warriors. This account is obviously attractive to anti-monarchist historians of France.

The historical reality was rather more complex: from the time of Clovis onwards, Gauls, Gallo-Romans and Franks quickly mingled and even intermarried to an extent that made racial or ethnic distinction impossible. What was true, however, was that the royal office was more often than not occupied by destructive fools. The Franks' qualities, or rather their lack of them, were immortalized in a Greek proverb, translated back into the vernacular by

Éginhard, a Frankish scholar of the eighth century at the monastery of Fulda and the author of a Latin life of Charlemagne, as: 'You can take a Frank for a friend, but never a neighbour.'[10] In 574, the Frank Sigebiert, in a perfect demonstration of the truth of this saying, wrecked what remained fully intact of the old city – the villas, the baths, the arcades – setting fire to several areas of Paris all at once in a war against his brother Chilpéric.

Even so, the rule of the Frankish kings was not all catastrophe. Despite the blood-feuds of princes and heirlings, relative stability held good for most of the period, largely because the German border was quieter than it had been for centuries. Goods, people and property moved freely around the *regnum francorum*; markets and fairs flourished; near Paris the fair of Saint-Denis attracted traders and pilgrims from all over Europe and the Levant. But even though during this period the towns of Gaul had come back to life and the economy was steadily growing, political and cultural developments were slow and unspectacular. This stasis was reflected in Paris itself, which, although now an important political and military capital, was scarcely larger when the Franks left it than when they had first arrived.

There were also larger historical forces at work, however. During the Roman conquest of Gaul, the river had formed a frontier between Latin civilization and the unknown and terrifying barbarian north. After Clovis it was intimately associated with the destiny of France as a whole, an incarnation of its cultural, political and historical destiny.

The Frankish nation that was born with Clovis and which had Paris as its capital was, argues Michel Foucault, not just an administrative instrument but a visionary project, an hallucination of supreme sovereignty.[11] This took its most concrete form with the nation as an active engine of war, dedicated to the subjugation of the Gaulish people as they emerged from the chaotic aftermath of the Roman Empire. The French state thereafter, even in its most exalted Napoleonic form, Foucault concludes, was nothing more than the sublimation of this master–slave relationship.

It is, more appositely, a poetic coincidence – and one which says a great deal about the dual nature of the power, both spiritual and political, later invested in Paris – that the Montagne Sainte-Geneviève, the small hill on the Left Bank dedicated to the persuasive anorexic virgin, ends abruptly at the rue Clovis. Parisians still ask favours of the saint in the church of Saint-Étienne-du-Mont, where her remains lie. Across the street the future power-brokers of the city are educated in the austere surroundings of the Lycée Henri IV, once part of an abbey dedicated to Geneviève and where Clovis and his wife were buried.

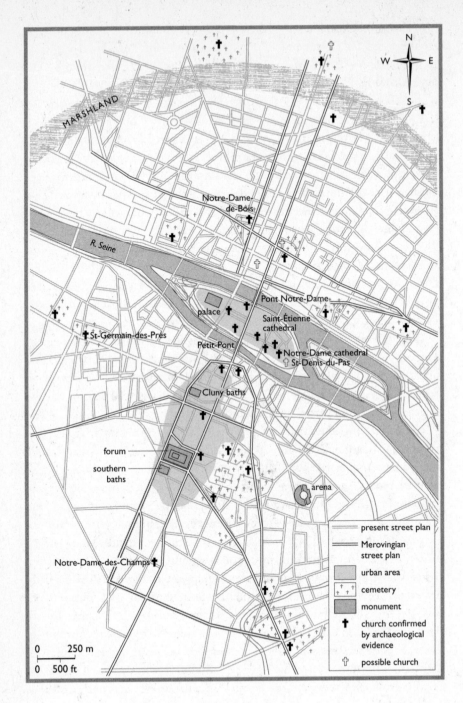

Paris during the Merovingian period (c. 490–640).

4. Infidels

The kingdom of the Franks was always a fragile entity. By the eighth century, it had settled into a loosely fixed order, into a territory known as 'Neustria', soon to be renamed 'West Francia'. But this was a fraction of the size of contemporary France. To the south of the boundary made by the Loire were the Romani, as Frankish and Gallo-Roman Parisians now called them, who inhabited a very separate world in terms of both language and culture. To the east lay the Rhine and a border with armies and tribes who shared a common violent culture with the Franks. The political and economic instability of this region and its hinterland made it an area to be feared. To the west, invading armies from Cornwall had conquered Armorica (what is now roughly Brittany), bringing with them a new language and a distinctly Celtic social organization centring around clans and chieftains.[1]

All of these borders had to be constantly and carefully watched. The eighth and ninth centuries were consequently difficult times for Paris and the Parisians. During this period, great upheavals and migrations were taking place all across Europe. The frontier between the ancient and the medieval worlds is often fixed in AD 331, when Constantinople was established as the capital of the Holy Roman Empire. The Emperor Constantine had aimed with this move to bring Christianity and empire together as one. The results were, however, far-reaching and unpredictable as, over the next four centuries, the complex and plural communities tolerated under the authority of empire were slowly being destroyed or displaced by the rise of Christendom.

Against this background, the Franks Christianized the Gallo-Roman city of Paris at a steady and determined pace. The impact on the city was dramatic, as churches – Saint-Germain l'Auxerrois, Sainte-Colombe and Saint-Paul – were built on the Right Bank between what is now the Louvre and the Bastille. These developments were neither as sophisticated nor as intricate as the vestiges of Gallo-Roman Lutetia on the Left Bank, but they did mark a further encroachment of the city towards the rural areas of Charonne, Montmartre and La-Chapelle-Saint-Denis. The general movement was towards the east; the western end of Paris was still then mainly marshland. A new settlement was founded at Saint-Marcel on the road towards Lyons and Italy. Throughout this period, Île de la Cité was still surrounded by a fortified wall and could only be entered via two huge gates at the northern and southern edges. On the island itself, life was harsh and the muddy streets crowded with clerics, students, nobles, peasants, dockers, whores and itinerant merchants.[2]

One of the best places in contemporary Paris to get a flavour of the city during this era is the church of Saint-Julien-le-Pauvre on the street of the same name. The present structure dates from the twelfth century but there are traces of the original chapel for pilgrims that, from the sixth century onwards, flanked the vestiges of the main Roman and then Frankish thoroughfare across the city. Just over the river to the north, the Frankish kings proclaimed Christ in the cathedral of Saint-Étienne (remains of this church were found at the eastern end of the parvis of Notre-Dame) and disparaged Rome as a weak and dying force.

Yet despite the doom-laden accounts of witnesses such as the Roman Boethius or Gregory of Tours, who were endlessly sceptical of the Franks, the end of the old Roman order did not seem to ordinary people to be inevitable or wrong. Although Christianity was associated with high politics, it was also, at least according to its own propaganda, the religion of the powerless and the weak. Moreover, in a place like Paris, where Franks and Gallo-Romans worked, worshipped and slept together, the sustaining myth of a division between the 'civilized' world of the Romans and the alleged savagery of 'barbarians' was clearly both artificial and redundant.

After two centuries of Frankish rule in Paris, there was in fact no longer any important distinction between the Gallo-Romans and the Franks. In the time of Clovis, it had been fairly simple to distinguish between Franks and Gallo-Romans on the grounds of social class, name, dress and probably language. By the eighth century, long years of intermarriage and breeding now meant that Frankish and Latin tombs lay side by side. The corpses of the two races lie beneath the modern-day traffic of the crossroads of Gobelins, where a vast necropolis swallowed the dead of the city. This was a place of miracles, visions; monsters and dragons were regularly seen here in the fifth century, and Parisians later often prayed here to Saint Marcel, the ninth Bishop of Paris, in times of extreme terror.

The truth was that there were two greater historical processes at work, spanning centuries. These could not have been halted by any amount of military might or administrative efficiency. But they were driving the end of empire more effectively than any local ethnic conflict. The first of these was that the cultural and political distance between the eastern and western halves of the empire had widened over the centuries, weakening what remained of the old order.

A second process, which was partly a result of this incoherent administration, was the steady influx of so-called barbarians from eastern Europe and Asia into what were formerly 'Roman' territories, either as marauders or as immigrants. The sacking of Rome in AD 410 by an army of Goths sent shock-waves throughout the empire. It was a moment that, like the 11 September attacks on New York in 2001, terrified every member of a civilization now revealed as newly vulnerable.

Islam at the Gates

A third element running parallel to these historical shifts in early medieval Europe was the astonishing and apparently unstoppable rise of a radical new cult in the desert sands of the Middle East, in which God was known as 'Allah' and the cult as 'Islam'. To the outsiders who first encountered it, the Christians and Jewish traders of the region, it resembled a ruthlessly efficient war-machine rather than a religion.

The Prophet Mohammed had died in AD 632. Since then, Arab armies had rolled across Arabia and North Africa, conquering all that stood before them in the name of the religion he had helped give birth to in his visions. By the autumn of 732, these same Arab armies had conquered huge swathes of the Iberian peninsula. Soon they were deep in Frankish territory, threatening the city of Poitiers and heading towards Paris. Their only enemies were the bitter cold of the October winds and an army of long-haired Frankish soldiers.

This was no mere border raid for plunder in 'Dar-al Harb', 'the House of War' (the term used in Arabic to describe non-Arab lands), where theft and pillage were usually the most legitimate, if limited, battle aims. This was part of a wider war which claimed territory in the name of Allah. As such, the Arab march on Poitiers was a deliberate assault on the integrity of the kingdom of the Franks. The ultimate aim was to sack Tours and Paris, the holiest centres of the region as well as the most prosperous trading centres.[3]

In 732, Charles, *maire du palais* in Paris, led the Franks to a site now known as Moussais-la-Bataille, where he confronted the Arab troops. He organized his men into a large infantry square that, in the words of a contemporary chronicle, resembled an 'immovable wall' and a 'glacier'.[4]

The swordsmanship, heavy cavalry and resolve of the Franks overcame the Muslims, who abandoned their tents after a day and night of savage fighting during which their leader, Abd-ar Rahman, was killed. Arab chronicles were silent on the outcome of the battle. The term 'Frank', however, now entered Arab legend some two centuries before the Crusades. The word persists in Modern Standard Arabic where 'Europe' is most commonly translated as 'Bilad al Firanj' – 'the domain of the Franks'. Charles himself returned to Paris with the nickname 'Martel', the hammer.

The battle of Poitiers had a massive historical significance. It would be of course another seven hundred years before the Arabs would finally be expelled from Europe with the Christian 'reconquest' of the Iberian peninsula in 1492. The victory at Tours–Poitiers was, however, not merely a successful defence of the road to Paris but also a decisive turning point in the history of Western civilization.

In 21st-century Paris, where politics and religion still sit uneasily together, and where radical Islam is the dominant cultural force in the surrounding suburbs, there are many who would argue that the conflict is not yet over. One of these is Tariq Ramadan, self-styled leader of Muslim youth in France and a controversial figure on both sides of the Atlantic for his alleged murky links to Islamist terrorism. Ramadan himself is no crude ideologue but an urbane and sophisticated thinker; this is why, in the eyes of the French authorities, he is such a dangerous figure (he was indeed barred from entering the United States in 2004 on account of his sulphurous reputation).

Ramadan's views are straightforward enough, however: there will be no peace in the West until the message of Islam is an integral part of 'European' culture. 'It is not a question of a clash of civilizations,' he said to me in the Islamic bookshop in Saint-Denis where he has his base, 'but rather Muslims standing firm in the face of distrust and prejudice.' There is an obvious irony in the fact that Ramadan preaches this message from an office a few streets away from the Basilique Saint-Denis where the first Christian kings of France have been laid to rest for over a thousand years.[5]

Siege and Slaughter

Charles 'Martel' not only saved Paris from Arab invasion but also gave his name to the Carolingian dynasty. He did not himself aspire to become king but his prestige, acquired in the hardest of battles, allowed him to place his own son, Pépin, on the throne in 754. This dynasty, or 'second race', ruled Paris and France until 987. The Carolingians were less pagan and less brutal to their subjects than the 'first race' of Franks had been, but like their predecessors, they lacked any of the Roman virtues of civic duty and dedication to administration. Paris was their power-base for military and not cultural reasons.

The overwhelming military strength of the Carolingians was partly due to the way they regularly deployed heavy cavalry on the battlefield. This was a tactic unknown to the Romans but its devastating effect in close combat made the cavalry of Carolingian armies the eighth-century equivalent of armoured vehicles and gun-ships. These horses were best stabled in the oat-growing regions of the north, with Paris as the most easily defended and loyal base.[6]

The many threats to the Frankish kingdom and Paris itself became briefly and temporarily less overt when the city fell under the control of Charlemagne in 771. He is often celebrated in the mythology of the city as one of its greatest heroes. Like most of the legends surrounding the king, however, the greyish-green statue of Charlemagne that stands today outside Notre-Dame is entirely misleading. It was put there in 1880 on the site of the old Hôtel-Dieu and portrays the noble, all-conquering king at the centre of his empire, uniting all Christendom. Charlemagne, emperor of the Western world, greatest of Carolingian kings, was in fact squat and bald. He only ever came to Paris twice, and then only for festive occasions. His real capital was made in 800 at Aix-la-Chapelle (Aachen) and it was under his control that Paris began to drift away from the centre of political life, even as its influence as a commercial and trading centre grew. Charlemagne and the Carolingians who followed him encouraged this process to continue. Jules Michelet describes the barbarians who came to destroy Paris as 'trembling' in the face of the great civilization that it represented during even its darkest periods.[7] This was not really true: the city was under almost constant threat of siege during the ninth century from new invaders from the north and east. Having shrunk back to its island origins, it was at times no vaster or greater than it had been when it was the pre-Roman capital of the Parisii.

The first attacks from the north came around 808, after a period of relative stability and peace largely determined by Charlemagne's firm rule. He died in 814 but for a while longer at least Paris and the other territories that made up the western empire, stretching from the Atlantic to the Danube, enjoyed economic growth and a certain political unity. In the borderlands on all fronts, however, the predatory armies of the Magyars, Avars, Saracens and Norsemen were standing ready to open up any breach in the dividing line.

The Norsemen, who had been making raids all through the lands to the north of Paris for nearly two hundred years, exploited a sense of growing disorder in the region. In 820, they began making their first incursions in the lands around the Seine. These were mainly unchallenged and encouraged the invaders to slaughter their way down the river. On Easter Sunday 845, led by the brigand Ragenaire, a potentially lethal force of 125 black dragon ships, from England and Rouen, arrived in the heart of Paris.

The Parisians were terrified but looked in vain for political and military support from their commercial allies in neighbouring towns. There was not even a token pretence at defending the city and many people left as quickly as they could. Leading the way were monks and priests, loaded with treasures and relics, making for shelter in nearby abbeys before heading south to safety. An undignified deal was brokered by Charles the Bald – one of the so-called 'Robertine' family of nobles – in which he paid off the raiders, who themselves then proceeded to move on to Burgundy with devastating effect. The Burgundians never forgave Paris for this act of treachery, and paid them back by collaborating with the English during the occupation of the city during the Hundred Years War. The Parisians themselves thanked all the saints they could think of. It was no shame on them either, their leaders reasoned, that the Norsemen had been bought off with 700 livres – an enormous sum for the period – of silver and the promise of the rich pickings of Burgundy.[8]

The reprieve did not last long. In December 856, the Norsemen were back and this time were in no mood to be bribed or cajoled into sparing Paris. The city was still without an adequate defence system and Louis, Abbot of Saint-Denis, and his brother Goslin were easily taken prisoner and held for an exorbitant ransom. Meanwhile, the invaders joyfully stabbed, speared and sliced their way across the islands. 'The Danish pirates invaded the Lutetia of the Parisians,' wrote Saint Bertin in his *Annales*, 'and there they devastated with the sword everything which they had not destroyed in fire.'[9] They came again in January 861 and burned down the newly built churches of Saint-Vincent and Saint-Germain-des-Prés and the surrounding areas, smashing up the Great Bridge at the northern edge of Île de la Cité. They then pushed on to cause havoc deeper inland, to the Marne, Meaux and Melun, pausing to wreck Paris again on the return journey to the coast.

Charles the Bald took refuge at Senlis for the duration of these raids. He was determined, however, not to let Paris be sacked a third time, and with the help and advice of Goslin he undertook a series of building projects to strengthen the city's defences and prevent the Norsemen from ever entering the city again. Most importantly, he rebuilt and fortified the Great Bridge, which the raiders had destroyed so easily on each previous incursion. By 870, lined with sentry towers and high walls for archers, it stood guard over the river and the city. For twenty-five years, Paris enjoyed peace. The defence systems ensured stability and a growing confidence, and within the city limits new churches were established, loaded with relics and treasures. The economy finally began to flourish again and the population grew, consisting mainly of immigrants attracted by the promise of a stable economic and social environment.

The raiders came again in 885. They travelled down the Seine in black dragon ships and, as they had done so many times before, demanded the destruction of the Great Bridge and free passage to the lands beyond the Seine. They promised no harm would come to the city or its citizens. Once again the Parisians were terrified, but this time Goslin and the Count of Paris, Odo (another Robertine), held firm and refused to let the Norsemen into the city. The men of Paris rallied to the cause and flanked the city walls displaying their arms, aiming weapons at the foreigners from the surrounding towers of the city.

Paris was encircled by 30,000 Norsemen under the command of Siegfried, a notoriously ruthless and bloodthirsty pirate, who declared a siege of the city. This was in November, as the first hard frosts of winter were beginning to bite, and Siegfried expected an easy victory. He began with an assault on a wooden tower that overlooked the bridge and which, being still under construction, was clearly the most obvious weak spot in the city's defences. The Norsemen were surprised to find that their opponents were tough, committed and resilient fighters and even more stunned to find themselves pushed back into their own defensive line. Eight further attacks on the city followed in the next twelve months as the siege tightened. Goslin was killed during one of these attacks. Still the Parisians resisted hard, defending the tower over the Seine through the winter. A flood in February 886 swept away one of the smaller bridges crossing the river, further exposing the city. The inhabitants were finally overwhelmed by the invaders in the spring of 886. The marauders slit the throats of all those they found inside.

It seemed that salvation was finally on the way when Charles the Fat arrived in Paris in November with an army which camped at the foot of the hill of Montmartre. Like his ancestor Charles the Bald, this Charles not only lacked physical charm but was a coward too. He refused to move his army any nearer the city and concluded a disgraceful treaty with the Norsemen that involved the payment of 1,400 pieces of silver to Siegfried and his men by March 887. This was a ruinous sum and a massively unpopular manoeuvre with the Parisians who had fought so fiercely to defend not only their city but their honour. It was hardly surprising that in the wake of the siege, the discredited and treacherous Charles found himself unseated by his kinsman Odo, one of the heroic defenders of the city. The Norsemen came again in 890 and 925, but this time were happy to ravage surrounding districts and the towns of Beauvais and Amiens. There were skirmishes and even battles around the city up until 978, but no foreign force would enter the city again for several hundred years.[10]

Rebuilding the City

Despite having been in a state of almost constant siege in the ninth century, the city in the tenth century faced the future with a degree of relief and confidence. The renewal of Paris can indeed be traced back as far as the aftermath of the siege of 885, when Odo, Count of Paris, had led the resistance and, in the face of terrifying adversity, given the city a sense of its true strength and importance.

These factors were crucial in the dying years of the millennium as Hugues Capet (named after the *cappa* he wore as a mark of religious faith) presided over the coming together of Neustria, renamed Western Francia, and the city of Paris. Hugues's coronation in 987 indeed marked a definitive moment in Parisian history. It was the moment when France and Paris became indissolubly associated. Unlike the city of the Frankish kings, Paris was now a capital not only in name but in function. It was this aspect of the Capetian dynasty, which would rule France until 1328, that did indeed change the country for ever. Although this family produced a line of mediocre and often guileless kings, they would also lead a court of cunning politicians, brave and skilled soldiers, shrewd administrators, and a clutch of internationally famous scholars and saints who ensured that the reputation of France by the fourteenth century would be higher than that of any other kingdom in western Europe.

At the time, however, these events were not merely lacking in drama, but seemed irrelevant to the more pressing demands arising from the military threats to the fledgling kingdom from the east and the south. Parisians themselves were more concerned with the social changes which were taking place all around them at an unprecedented pace. The most striking aspect of Paris under the first Capetian kings was the rise to power of the vassals of the nobility. Within a short time, many of the important territories in and around the city that were not in royal hands were controlled by vassals at the Capetian court, who put in place a complex set of regulations and taxes governing fishing, the use of mills and the right to unload goods on both banks of the river. The lives of the servile classes (the serfs or *servos*, as they were still called, from the Latin) were, in contrast, barely noted or recorded in literature. But their presence in the city, as well as that of soldiers, freemen workers, prostitutes and vagabonds, was a source of potential disruption and anxiety to the ruling classes: by remaining literally beyond the law or military control of the king these outsiders were able to weave a fine thread of anarchy into the social fabric.[11]

Paris was not yet the first city of Europe – as one king would claim in the near future. Indeed for most of its history up until then Paris had been, at best, not much more than a provincial town where commerce flourished, and a military base for two dynasties of kings who were indifferent to its status. At worst, as the Roman Empire had disintegrated, pushed ever further from the centres of power and civilization, the city had come close to destruction at the hands of invaders.

None the less, it emerged in the early years leading up to the new millennium as a burgeoning economic and religious centre. A century or so on from the destruction wreaked by the Norseman, Paris once again began to extend the limits marked by the ancient villages to the north and south. At its heart, the bridges had been rebuilt and churches constructed on both sides of the river. Vineyards flourished on the Left Bank, from what is now rue Galande to rue Saint-André-des-Arts.[12] Priests, evoking Geneviève and Denis of course, attributed the survival of the city to the bravery and faith of its citizens when confronted by infidels on all fronts.

'Listen to the Parisians sing!'

This, in part, also explains why the first mark of Parisian identity has traditionally been fear of the world beyond the city walls. The *Annales* of Saint Bertin in 891 reported the regions outside Paris as rife with bandits and prey to 'horrible anarchy'. For their part, provincials laughed at Parisian pretensions (the city was a long way from being the most important in what had been Gaul) and habitually accused Parisians of all manner of crimes, from incest to cannibalism. Fom the earliest days of Lutetia, however, the city was the mongrel creation of Celts, Romans and Franks. Then later came Burgundians, Bretons, Auvergnats, Normans, Picards, Belgians, Jews, Alemanni, Greeks and even Englishmen, who settled here for reasons of love, trade or religion. In the early Middle Ages, waves of mass immigration provoked and sustained by famine and war meant that Parisians defined themselves by comparing their language and manners to those of their rural cousins. Parisian identity was, and is, a matter of style and behaviour and never a question of territory.

Accordingly, the secret languages of present-day Paris are now being made and passed outside the city, in the *banlieue* where Arabs, black Africans, Eastern Europeans and Asians are stamping their own hybrid identity on to the French language. Words from Polish, Arabic, Romanian, Turkish and Serbo-Croat are now, in the eyes of racists and purists, contaminating the official language in the same way that, through the centuries, words from Picardy, Flanders and Constantinople, from Yiddish, Roma, Syriac and Aramaic 'infected' the language and became part of the everyday linguistic armoury of the street-level Parisian. The principal language in the rue de Belleville these days is Mandarin Chinese and most of the traditional bars in this part of Paris are now run by South-east Asians. Most prostitutes in the streets of Saint-Denis are Albanian or Kosovan or from sub-Saharan Africa.

But there is still, in 21st-century Paris, a tribe called the Parisii – the original name of the Celts who founded Paris. Throughout the winter and most of the spring, they gather together on Stand Boulogne R2 in the Parc des Princes, the stadium at the western edge of the city. They come here to support the Paris Saint-Germain (PSG) football team. The Arab-looking kids, fellow supporters of PSG but with an entirely separate cultural agenda, hang together at the opposite end of the stadium, marking themselves out from the *fils de Clovis* ('the sons of Clovis' – North African slang for white Parisians) with their green and red *Algérie* team-shirts or sharp Italian clothes. The Parisii, and a smaller, more vicious-looking cluster of their mostly suedehead mates, called Lutèce Falco 91, scorn such pan-Mediterranean or pan-European sentiment. Their patriotism is uniquely and specifically Parisian.

Their favoured targets are not Arabs but the inhabitants of Marseilles. 'Allons enfants du Grand Paris ... Qu'un sang marseillais abreuve nos sillons (Let's go, children of Great Paris . . . Let the blood of a Marseillais flow through our terraces),' they sing to the tune of the *Marseillaise*. This anthem is taken up by thousands of supporters, even when the Olympique Marseille team are not playing in Paris and may indeed be hundreds or thousands of miles away.

The songs of the modern Parisii also carry clear historical echoes. 'Nous n'irons pas à Saint-Denis, /C'est au Parc que l'histoire s'écrit. /Nous sommes rouge et bleu pour la vie, /Notre amour s'appelle Paris! Écoutez chanter les Parisiens! (We won't go to Saint-Denis, /It's in the Park that history is being written. /We're red and blue for life, /Our love is called Paris! Listen to the Parisians sing!).' The reference to Saint-Denis is to the new stadium in the outlying town, where the French team won the World Cup in 1998, and where PSG never play. The song is, in football terms, a conventional show of support for club over country.

But no Parisian reference to Saint-Denis – the burial place of French kings – can ever be innocent. It reveals an opposition between French and Parisian history that dates back to the moment that Clovis made Paris the seat of all power and authority in the territory of France. The role of the Capetian kings was to reinforce this position and therefore to widen cultural divisions in the kingdom. At the same time, the city became a magnet for the greedy, the disaffected and the ambitious: all those who needed to come to Paris, to a great capital, to make their mark. There has never been any racial basis for the antagonism between Parisians and non-Parisians. Indeed, one of the insults that provincials habitually use against Parisians is that there has never been any such thing as a true Parisian race. For Parisians this crude jibe indicates only a rustic attachment to *terroir* (native land) and territory that they have long since overcome.

They are indeed singularly proud of the fact that – whatever provincials, novelists, artists or historians claim – there has never been, from the earliest days of Lutetia, any such thing as a typical Parisian.

PART TWO

City of Joy

988–1460

Paris is a good place to live but a bad place to die.
It is where the beggars warm their arses making fires
From the bones of the dead.

Rabelais, *Pantagruel*, 1532

Paris is the city of joy where the naïve are taken by the neck and blackened on the scaffold, and where villains hold all sway. Get out of the thick city walls as quickly as you can! Purse-cutters and knifemen lurk in the dark. Beware of the rope!

François Villon, *Ballades en jargon*, 1460?

*View of Paris in the eleventh century from an engraving
by Adolphe Rouargue (1810–70).*

5. A Cruel and Brilliant Place

At the end of its first thousand years of history, Paris was not yet a great or beautiful city. Anna of Kiev, who came to it in 1051 to be the queen of the widowed and childless Henri I (who had taken up the throne in 1031), was shocked by the filth and squalor. Paris was a squalid and disorganized settlement no better, and in some ways worse, than the old Ukrainian city she had left behind. Her thoughts were noted in the chronicles of her home town, where she moaned loudly and long, in Greek, about her exile in 'a barbarous country where the houses were gloomy, the churches ugly, and the customs revolting'.[1]

Anna's astonishment at the state of this city was no doubt justified. The capital of Clovis was by now a tatty wreck. The main churches pillaged by the Norsemen in the ninth century – Saint-Julien-le-Pauvre, Saint-Séverin, Saint-Baque, Saint-Étienne-des-Grés – had not been restored and in some cases been left to rot. Similarly, although the houses, shops, streets and passages on Île de la Cité were more or less intact, it had not been a priority of the Frankish kings, who prized war and sloth as their chief pastimes, to make this settlement either beautiful or even especially habitable. The crumbling ruins of the Gallo-Roman city were still visible in the brickwork of the new buildings and the stonework of the squares, but there was none of the sense of urban order which had characterized life there five hundred years earlier. The streets away from the centre of the city, especially on the Left Bank, were a stinking labyrinth: a filthy swamp of livestock, dung and semi-rural stockades.[2]

The first years of the new millennium were harsh. In the countryside, famine, caused by the failure of successive harvests, had driven starving peasants to dig up corpses for meat. In Paris, law and order had all but collapsed under a succession of weak kings. The cruel laws brought in under Charlemagne were still in place and in the streets it was possible to see criminals naked but for chains, women accused of loose morals stripped to the waist and whipped, and the bloodied bodies of convicted thieves, their throats slit like sheep. This was all to little effect as the population continued to suffer from political instability and petty but punishing wars.[3]

The historian Fernand Braudel describes this century as the era which marks the beginning of 'the rise of Europe' as a cultural and political force. What Braudel means by this statement is that this was when Christendom became not merely a religious idea but a living political entity, uniting and unifying the cultural bases of the vast territory which stretched from northern Europe to the eastern Mediterranean. The process had begun centuries earlier, culminating in the alliance between Charlemagne's Frankish kingdom and the Roman papacy.[4] It was impossible, however, to be aware of such developments at street level. Most Parisians of the period were delighted to find themselves still alive, relieved that the end of the world, scheduled for the turn of the millennium, had not actually happened. None the less, the raised levels of anxiety were not entirely dissipated in the new age, no matter how many sacred buildings were erected across Paris.

These fears were cancelled out in the dark city streets by a fierce passion for pleasure, music, wine and poetry, with both men and women, true to their Gaulish origins, favouring bright colours and sporting, whenever it could be afforded, gold and silver jewellery. More than this, by the end of the long slide down the first millennium, despite the complaints of Anna of Kiev or visiting priests from Rome, Paris had begun to assume the form if not the substance of a great city.

One of the key forces for change was the vision and skill of l'Abbé Suger, the Abbot of Saint-Denis and chief adviser to Louis VI. Under Suger's control, Paris became a truly centralized administration, setting up professional guilds and adroit financial checks on the busy traffic of the Seine. In addition, Louis was no fool: he was indeed a skilful tactician in political and military terms who never capitulated to the Norman English or the feudal lords of France. He was also wise enough to allow Suger to more or less rule Paris, which he did for thirty years, establishing himself in this way as the first in a long line of ministers who really understood domestic politics and who truly held the reins of power. Suger, a small man with a pale countenance, was shrewd and able to adapt quickly to changing circumstances. Louis VI died of dysentery in 1137 without an heir (his son Philippe had been killed in an accident with one of the wild pigs which roamed the streets of Paris). Suger had already made sure that the king's successor, Louis le Gros ('Louis the Fat'), had made a good marriage to Eleanor of Aquitaine, ensuring political dominance for Paris in the south-west of France. As a consequence of these political manoeuvres, by the time that Philippe-Auguste was born in 1165, the city, although hardly more than a settlement, half built and half destroyed, stood poised to become a great European capital.

The King Given by God

Philippe-Auguste had been nicknamed at birth Le Dieu-donné ('the gift of God'). According to one account, he was given this name because he was born in the twenty-eighth year of his father's reign, when all hope of an heir had apparently been abandoned. According to another, the forces of destiny were already at work: on the evening of Philippe's birth, two old women approached an English student in the streets around Montagne Sainte-Geneviève and told him, cackling, that 'God has given us this night a royal heir, by whose hand your king shall suffer shame and mishap'.[5] Philippe-Auguste had been born, they prophesied, to deliver Paris from servitude.

On Sunday 27 July 1214, the old women's prophecy was fulfilled when Philippe's men, against all odds, battered the Plantagenet forces of King John of England. Until then the English had swaggered through France more or less at will, adding Guyenne and Gascony to their territorial claims of Flanders and Normandy. The battle at Bouvines in Flanders would determine the future of France in an opposite direction some seven hundred years later. In reality, there should have been little or no surprise at John's defeat. This was indeed the culmination of a long series of skirmishes and military stratagems that Philippe had mounted against him for several years.[6]

The victory removed at a stroke the Plantagenet threat from all-important French territories – particularly Normandy, which was dangerously close to Paris. It also established France as a nation with Paris as its capital. There were celebrations throughout the country – peasants and townspeople danced in squares, bells were rung and special Masses said. Country people who had never left the villages of their birth rushed to Paris from every point of the realm to hail the king and gawp at his prisoners. The story of the victory became an emblem of nationhood that lasted for the next seven centuries.

Yet even before Philippe-Auguste's famous victory, Paris had long since begun to look like a powerful and important city. Philippe's great defensive wall, first planned twenty years earlier, was completed shortly before the battle. Despite his preoccupation with external political and military affairs, Philippe was immensely proud of the wall and took a close interest in its planning, even supervising some of the building work himself when he was in Paris. The wall stretched from the Right Bank, near the Pont des Arts, through the lower reaches of the Marais, in a semi-circle towards the Left

Bank at Quai de la Tournelle and back towards what is now the Institut de France via the boulevard Saint-Germain. One of the best places to see what is left of the wall in present-day Paris is at the Jardins de Saint-Paul in the Marais. The rampart, which was excavated in 1945, stretches 120 metres or so across a school playground. It still looks strong, thick and firm and casts a deep shadow in the late evening. This wall encircled the whole of Paris and when it was built ensured the city would not come under serious attack for another hundred years.

No less important to Philippe-Auguste was the construction of the Louvre and the covered market at Les Halles. The first of these was planned apparently because Philippe had felt constrained and limited in the old palace on Île de la Cité. This was not simply a monument to prestige, however. It was an immensely practical construction designed to defend Paris if it was ever attacked again from the river. A heavy chain was stretched across the Seine at its eastern and western approaches. This was raised and lowered to permit the flow of river traffic as well as deter marauders.[7]

Just outside the city walls at the western edge, an imposing tower, some 30 metres high, was built to survey and defend the surrounding territory. This was nicknamed the *louver*, an old French term for 'stronghold'. It became the first point of defence for the city. Within the walls, two towers, Grand- and Petit-Châtelet, stood facing each other across the river, providing a second line of surveillance and defence. These were also used as administrative buildings and, most notoriously, as prisons. The old walls of the *louver* are still there beneath the contemporary museum. They are cold, solid and appear to be absolutely impenetrable.

The construction of the market of Les Halles was the result of a decision to take at least some trade away from the Grève, the area just behind Grand-Châtelet. After long years of varied use as a landing stage, tannery, slaughterhouse, knackers' yard and open-air brothel, this area had become an overcrowded, chaotic and disease-ridden space.

The destruction of these old quarters meant more traffic passing in and out of the island and its periphery. The river traffic, too, was increasing fast and overcrowding could be dangerous as well as slowing down commerce. Wine merchants, in particular, complained that it took a long time to transport their merchandise to the city and to its market. The docks at what became, on the Right Bank, Place de la Grève (and these days the area called Place de l'Hôtel de Ville) were extended, but the bridges over the river, crowded with wooden houses and shops, presented the greatest obstacle to traffic as well as a potential danger. Instead of building new bridges, however, the city authorities decided to shift the city's activity to the north. Butchers and fishmongers clustered around the docks, stretching markets towards rue Saint-Denis, while the riverside itself and the bridges were packed with dubious foreign traders, money-changers and hustlers.

Philippe-Auguste was a ruthless king and his admirers at street level inevitably imitated much of his brutal energy. This busy and mercantile Paris was a hard city with no room for the old, weak or the sick. Peasants feared the place – it was packed with dangerous criminals as well as unholy whores – and once they had done their business at market they could not get back to their lands fast enough. Still, Philippe had brought to Paris a political and military brilliance which meant that the city soon outshone its most powerful and distinguished competitors in even the most distant lands. A hundred years after Philippe's death, much of his city was still intact, and this provided the starting point for the rapid expansion of the early Renaissance.

Vermin

The first great change to occur in this swarming city at the end of the first millennium was a slight but discernible loosening of the bonds of what was until then a strictly hierarchical society. Although both the Church and lay society had a fixed idea of a social world based on immutable links between what the chronicler Raoul Glaber termed the *maximi*, *mediocres* and *minimi* – the king, knights, nobles and their vassals – the reality was often confused and arbitrary, the result of fragmented political authority and a matrix of geographical ambiguities.[8]

The city was always less open socially than it seemed, however. There were, of course, by now also Jews in the city. They had in fact been there since the fifth century (Gregory of Tours records their presence) and had, through the last centuries of the millennium, traded and lived at the edges of the city, establishing links with the southern cities and the Levant. In 1119, a synagogue and a bath house were founded on rue de la Juiverie which, with rue de la Lanterne, linked the Petit-Pont and the Grand-Pont. There were other settlements on rue de la Pelleterie and rue de la Vieille Draperie and important cemeteries on the cheaper land of the Left Bank, between what is now rue de la Harpe and rue Pierre Sarrazin.

The presence of Jews was testament to the wealth and international renown of Paris, but the first waves of anti-Semitism were not slow in

coming. In the wake of the First Crusade, the Parisian knights setting off
for Palestine had already cultivated a deep mistrust of the Jews' predominant
role in the city's economy (they handed out loans, with often punitive
interest, to all manner of small businesses, from cobblers to wine-growers,
who supported the 'holy war' with their own money). This mistrust hardened into active violence, as the whole of France was shaken by a fierce
wave of hatred for the Jews in the 1180s. By the end of the century, many
Jews had left Paris for ever, settling instead in the south, or in Champagne,
Burgundy or Alsace.[9]

Those who did eventually come back occupied their old haunts or
made for the newer enclaves around Place de la Grève or the markets at
Champeaux. It was during this period, at the turn of the thirteenth century,
that Paris also became a centre for Jewish learning. Scholars arrived from
all over the Jewish world to hear the great master Juda ben Isaac, otherwise
known as Rabbi Sire Léon, the intellectual leader of the Jewish School of
Paris. Notwithstanding, as the Crusades and then the Inquisition took their
hold on the European Christian imagination, the anti-Jewish feeling grew
and was matched by actions of increasing spite and severity. Judaism was
also confused with the Cathar heresy, then sweeping through south-western
France, and in 1242, on the orders of Pope Gregory IX, twenty-four
cartloads of Talmudic writings were set alight in Place de la Grève. There
were individual murders too: a Jew named Jonathas was burned alive in
1290, accused of blasphemy and usury. This became a popular charge against
Jews and such burnings were soon commonplace.

The Jews were expelled, massacred, insulted, humiliated over the next
few hundred years, but they still came back. Paris needed them, especially
their financial expertise and acumen. As a compromise manoeuvre, the
city powers, with kingly authority, decided to place restrictions on the
movements of Jews, confining them first to the city and then to certain
streets: rues Saint-Merry, du Renard, de Moussy, Saint-Bon and de la
Tacherie. They eventually spread east to rue des Rosiers. This street was
formerly the interior rampart of Philippe-Auguste's wall, and is now the
heart of Parisian Jewry, a thriving, busy slice of downtown Tel Aviv in
modern Paris.[10]

This area is generally friendly but it can burn with a slow tension. There
are plaques in memory of Holocaust victims at regular intervals. In among
the cuttings of restaurant reviews in the window of Jo Goldenberg's Deli
on the corner of rue des Rosiers are yellowing newspaper articles from all
over the world written in 1982 when Arab gunmen shot seven diners dead

in this same restaurant. This one may be the most recent but no one here needs reminding that massacres like this have been a constant feature of Jewish life from the most distant era of Parisian history.

6. Sacred Geometry

Despite the cultural advances made in the early twelfth century, Paris lacked a great cathedral and, although it was regularly crowded with pilgrims and relics, it had not yet really become a great religious centre. The claims, often made by clerics and ordinary Parisians alike, that this was a holy city forged in the fire of faith rang hollow without a testimony in stone to this religious passion. No less important to Parisians was the plain fact that without a cathedral the city could never fully rival the great cities of Christendom in any meaningful sense. In 1163, however, two years before the birth of Philippe-Auguste, the first stones of Notre Dame were laid under the watchful gaze of Maurice de Sully, the son of a peasant from the Loire who had risen to become Bishop of Paris.

Sully had brooded for a long time on the absence of a cathedral. It had also been the dream of l'Abbé Suger, the wily power behind the throne, who in 1150, a year before his death, had donated a stained-glass window to the cathedral he would never see (no one else can see it now either: the window, celebrating the Virgin, was cruelly smashed in an accident in 1731). There were also political considerations that directly influenced the decision to build a cathedral. Paris still saw itself as the rival of Rome and Parisians did not like feeling inferior to the intellectual and aesthetic monuments of the Italian city. If Paris was to be taken seriously as a religious capital, and become more than what it evidently was – a successful trading post – it needed to commemorate its status architecturally.

Sully not only took charge of the construction of the cathedral, often making daily visits to the site, but also funded much of the work himself with the revenues of his lands around Paris. The first major task was to destroy what was left of the old Merovingian church of Saint-Étienne and the remnants of an adjoining market, both of which were now no more than ruins. Work began in earnest in 1180, as the nave finally took shape.

The plan was to build a cathedral that 'sat on the waters like a great and majestic ship'.[1] The careful observer could see a distinctly Parisian style emerging: this was a decorative art that prized intricate detail over grand gestures (Parisian craftsmen were proud of their light touch with stone), and which was distinct even from that of the cathedrals of near-neighbours at Saint-Denis and Senlis.

Stones were brought over from Vaugirard and Montrouge. New streets were carved through the labyrinth of Île de la Cité, to make way for these and other construction materials to be hauled up from the Seine. The cathedral was not finished for another two centuries – Sully was not to see anything but the completed altar for ten years – but from its inception a fervid and busy urban life flourished in and around the building site and the main square, the parvis of Notre-Dame, which is still designated as the geographical centre of France.

This part of the city was bawdy and rough, far rougher than the embroidered portrait of late-medieval life that Victor Hugo paints in his epic novel *Notre-Dame de Paris* of 1831. The area swarmed with whores, beggars and thieves, and in the frequent times of epidemic (water-borne cholera was a habitual visitor to the city) the stench of the dead carried tens of miles upriver. Still, Sully was inordinately, and rightly, proud of his achievement, which he crowned in 1180 with the baptism of Philippe Dieudonné Auguste.

On a more elemental level, as Victor Hugo himself noted much later, Notre-Dame changed the cityscape in its most fundamental aspects. Most notably, it stood higher than any other building had ever stood in the history of the city. It could be seen from miles around and its fame quickly spread across Europe as the emblem of a new civilization. Closer to home, Parisians were able to climb its spires and gaze down upon their city, seeing for the first time its immensity and infinite detail.

'A monument to the end of time'

The central motif in *Notre-Dame de Paris* is the apparently hidden significance of the cathedral. Like many progressive thinkers in the nineteenth century, Hugo was able to combine a rigorous belief in science and progress with an equally passionate interest in occultism. In the 1830s, the architect Viollet-le-Duc was commissioned to restore the cathedral. The project was finished in 1846, under the watchful eye of a committee that occasionally included Victor Hugo himself. Over the years, the work has been criticized as a pastiche of the medieval Gothic style. This much was, however, entirely appropriate to the medieval fantasies provoked by the old stones.[2]

What seized Hugo's imagination most vividly is the old legend that the church is no more nor less than a form of sacred geometry. More precisely, it is claimed that windows, doors and portals, indeed its very architecture, are made up of allegorical symbols that reveal the mysteries of the ancient 'science' sometimes referred to as 'Hermetic philosophy' or 'spiritual alchemy'.

Hugo's incarnation of evil in *Notre-Dame de Paris* is the priest Claude Frollo, who spends hours meditating upon the enigmatic central portal of the cathedral. It is here that Frollo 'risked his soul, and seated himself at that mystic table of the Alchemists, the Astrologers, the Hermetics, Guillaume de Paris, and Nicolas Flamel which occupies one end in the Middle Ages, and which reaches back in the East, under the rays of the seven-branched candlestick to Solomon, Pythagoras and Zoroaster'.[3] Frollo's fascination with occult philosophy is ultimately tragic and serves mainly to illustrate Hugo's notion that individuals are helpless in the face of the unstoppable and all-powerful dynamic movement of the universe.

This mode of thinking can be traced back through the Christian and pre-Christian eras to Greek mythology and a divinity dear to the old alchemists called Hermes Trismegistus, a god of magic and writing alleged to have authored many of the texts that medieval and Renaissance magicians referred to when conducting experiments and spells. The supreme symbol of the 'great art' of the alchemist is the Philosopher's Stone, sometimes called the Green Lion in the deliberately obfuscated language of alchemy. The precise angle of the glance of a crow on the left side of the portal, looking into the cathedral, is said to indicate the exact location of the Philosopher's Stone hidden there by Guillaume de Paris, one of the first bishops of Notre-Dame.

The living flame of 'alchemical philosophy' was carried into the twentieth century by the Surrealists, led by the poet André Breton. This group (covered in more detail in Chapter 37) was founded in Paris in 1924 with the express aim of launching a 'revolution of the mind', a shift in the consciousness of the human race which would lead the way to a new era.[4] The Surrealists were religious – they believed in a universe where all contradictions were subsumed in the One, or the *prima materia* of alchemical thinking; it was just that they hated Christianity. If not moved to awe by Notre-Dame, the Surrealists understood that the church had a meaning separate from Christian symbolism.

The Surrealists learned the language of alchemy from a variety of sources – most notably from André Breton's early readings of Hegel alongside

Giordano Bruno and Arthur Rimbaud. But nothing was more enticingly enigmatic than the writings of their contemporary 'Fulcanelli'. No one was actually sure whether Fulcanelli really existed, although his calling card was frequently left at Le Chat Noir in Montparnasse and other fashionable haunts of the period. His most famous book, *Le Mystère des cathédrales* ('The Mystery of the Cathedrals'), published in Paris in 1926, claimed to unravel the secrets of Notre-Dame.

Fulcanelli may have been a myth or a charlatan, but his book is both brilliantly written and, with its punning wit and obscure references, entirely puzzling. It made him a legend in the schism-ridden world of the Parisian occult underground, as well as the avant-garde circles of Surrealism and experimental psychiatry (it was even rumoured that Breton had conducted secret meetings with the mysterious adept, who claimed not least to have conquered time-travel). Fulcanelli's book describes the stones of the great cathedral of Notre-Dame as the alpha and omega of the city of Paris or, as he puts it, 'a monument to the end of time'.[5]

In contemporary Paris there is a small but conspicuous number of Parisians who are as fascinated by the magical arts as the inhabitants of pagan Lutetia and early Christian Paris. Occultist bookshops thrive on both sides of the river. The most busy and successful – like La Table d'Émeraude at 21 rue de la Huchette – are on the Left Bank and literally in the shadow of Notre-Dame. In the mind of those who claim to understand and practise magic, this is clearly no accident. Where Notre-Dame stands has always been a sacred site, a place of Druidic sacrifices and pagan worship. Even as the great church was being constructed, elements of earlier religions, which lingered in the Parisian sensibility – either as day-to-day superstitions or the actual practices of secret societies – were assimilated and incorporated into its body. The 'Fête des Fous', an orgiastic four-day saturnalia that took place in the cathedral, often ending in murder and group sex, was tolerated long into the sixteenth century as an echo of antique religious rites.[6]

In 1992, the poet Alain Jouffroy wrote a short text about the magical significance of Notre-Dame, partly in homage to Fulcanelli. Jouffroy had been André Breton's secretary and had known all the other leading Parisian Surrealists. It had been a habit of Breton, Jouffroy and their friends to visit churches in order to laugh out loud, deliberately debasing religion and insulting priests. Jouffroy recalls in his book on Notre-Dame visiting an old church in Finistère in Brittany in the company of an aged Breton, who mockingly compared it to an aquarium.

A few years after he had written the book, I ran into the now elderly

Jouffroy and asked him what he had learned about Notre-Dame from the Surrealists. He said it was that in the city everything that looks permanent is in fact changing all the time. There was indeed no better example of this notion, he said, than Notre-Dame: that the building was or is, depending on your vantage point in history, a symbol of hope, an emblem of transcendence, the home of the torturers of the Inquisition, a base for pilgrims, a temple of Reason, a shelter for magicians or the church of emperors.

Or simply a tourist trap. It was all just a point of view.[7]

7. Lovers and Scholars

By the time that Philippe-Auguste died in 1223, Paris was the undisputed cultural capital of western Europe. This reputation was the result of its intellectual activities rather than the quality of its daily life: the city was strengthened and developed under the king, but it was still a dark place, rife with disease and dangerous hatreds.

None the less, the city attracted scholars, traders, politicians and poets who came for its renown as a centre for learning and artistic achievement. The high prestige of those who studied law or the classical disciplines in Paris was entirely matched by the illuminated manuscripts, the stained glass, the sculptures and the architecture of its great religious buildings which now covered Île de la Cité south to Montagne Sainte-Geneviève and westwards to Saint-Germain-des-Prés. The streets were still filthy but the architecture was starting to become magnificent. The ruins of the church of Saint-Paul-des-Champs, built in 1107 and a popular place of worship in the twelfth century, can still be seen in the form of a wrecked, open wall at 32 rue Saint-Paul in the Marais. On the Place du Louvre, you can see the detailed carvings in the ruins of the church of Saint-Germain-l'Auxerrois under the layers of five centuries of church architecture dating from the sixth century. The nearby streets of rue des Prêtres-Saint-Germain-l'Auxerrois and rue de l'Arbre-Sec are not the only ones in the present-day city which date from the thirteenth century, but they are more or less intact. Most importantly, they mark the edges of what was the burgeoning religious centre of the medieval city.

Paris had yet to become a great political capital. This was largely because it still faced strong external threats, mainly from the English whose energy and greed propelled them all too often towards the gates of the city through-out the thirteenth century. The internal political machinery of Paris was further damaged by being too closely bound up with royal power, which diminished steadily through the course of the century as Philippe-Auguste was succeeded by a series of weak kings from the Capetian line who were obsessed with religion, money or their own status. Little attention was paid by these kings to either the changing shape of the city, its lack of finance or its growing population.

Philippe-Auguste had made great efforts to improve everyday life in the city, which ranged from installing a rudimentary police force to building a sewage system. Philippe himself was so sickened and revolted by the stench he met when leaning out of a window in the newly built Louvre (now become the king's palace rather than simply a defensive tower) that, according to his physician, he resolved to clean up Paris there and then. This was an almost impossible job in a city where livestock roamed the streets, there was no drainage and most people's notion of sewage disposal was to throw their waste and excrement into the street.[1]

But this was also a holy city. It now possessed more than twenty churches, a cathedral and the most important university in Europe. Philippe-Auguste was succeeded by Louis VIII, who died three years later in 1226, either of dysentery or poisoning, during a campaign in the south-west. Louis IX was only twelve years old when he came to the throne. His piety and incessant prayers already distinguished him and he had the reputation of being the holiest of the Capetian line he came from. He fasted constantly and acquired a slightly terrifying look of ascetic righteousness. Louis's reign took France backwards in many ways and among his most dubious achievements was to encourage the Inquisition to operate in France. He fancied himself as a mystic and was often incompetent in worldly matters of state. He was criticized, for instance, for signing away great chunks of France to England in the 1259 Treaty of Paris. Louis was, however, surrounded by efficient and dedicated advisers under whose watchful eye Paris, and indeed France, grew prosperous none the less.

Under Louis, Paris was also in the process of becoming beautiful. The Sainte-Chapelle, for example, built by the king to meet his fevered impulse to pray day and night, held some of the most important Christian relics in Europe, including a crown of thorns and a piece of the true Cross. It enjoyed a reputation across Europe as a particularly exquisite work of sacred art and architecture. The art of poetry, often influenced by southern models, also flourished here. Most importantly, there was a renewed interest in classical literature, particularly the works of Ovid.[2] These cultural undercurrents came together in the legend of Abélard and Héloïse. The story belongs properly in the twelfth century, at least in terms of strict chronology. However, the tale only really took on its full significance in the mid thirteenth century, by which time it was known across Europe and considered to be an emblematic warning against the dangers of confusing philosophy with lust.

It was also satisfyingly gruesome and, from a later, psychoanalytical point of view, rich in masochistic detail. The legend was to become a favoured fable of the Renaissance, mainly on the grounds that Abélard himself was the very model of a thinker torn between a passion for the truth and the truth of his passion. For this reason it was included, for example, in *Le Roman de la rose* ('The Romance of the Rose'), the long poem started by Guillaume de Lorris in the first part of the thirteenth century and finished by Jean de Meung between 1275 and 1280. This poem was read in several countries as both a guide to the 'art of love' (following Ovid's example) and as a philosophical primer on the more practical aspects of sex and marriage. Chaucer translated the first and most of the second part of this poem into English, while in Italy it was rumoured that Petrarch had an original manuscript of the letters exchanged between the lovers.

The events of the story of Abélard and Héloïse took place in Paris in the 1100s and in an atmosphere – relatively speaking – of intellectual tolerance. Its currency as a legend had the highest prestige, however, at the point in the 1250s when the University of Paris was properly establishing itself in the city and beginning to spread its sharp and cruel influence, particularly in matters of heresy and faith, across Europe. The appeal of Abélard and Héloïse for intellectual Parisians of this period lay in the way in which the story brings together high philosophical and theological speculation with the most venal forms of violence. It still stands as an accurate representation of the intellectual mood of the city under the holy rigour of Louis IX. Indeed it barely deserves to be called a love story at all.

'A story sweeter than honeyed wine'

The provincial Pierre, or 'Petrus', Abélard, came to Paris in 1106 to study logic and philosophy. Paris was then reaching new heights with its reputation as an intellectual capital. Students from all over Europe flocked to the Cathedral School at Notre-Dame to study logic, philosophy and theology under the Archbishop of Paris, Pierre Lombard, the moralist Pierre le Chantre and the theologian Pierre le Mangeur, and lesser lights held tutorials in the shadow of Montagne Sainte-Geneviève.[3]

Abélard had been a pupil of Roscelin at Locmenach (now Locminé near Brest). He was at first a follower of Roscelin's Nominalist doctrine, which held that all earthly phenomena were only dim echoes of God's perfect mind. When Abélard arrived in Paris, it was first to study under William of Champeaux at the Cathedral School. It was not long before Abélard, who was already possessed of a magisterial arrogance, rejected Roscelin and began openly to challenge William's intellect and authority. Most significantly, William had declared that all universal phenomena demonstrated the universal essence of existence; it followed from this that individuality was the product of accidental circumstance. Abélard rejected this and it was not long before he set himself up as an independent rival teacher, earning along the way a high income from the students he seduced away from the angry and vengeful William.

It was at this point that Abélard fell in love. He had been employed by the canon of Notre-Dame, Fulbert, to tutor his niece Héloïse in theology and philosophy. Abélard had already been lodging in Fulbert's house (a substantial building that can still be found on rue de la Chanoinesse on Île de la Cité) and the task proved initially to be no great hardship, merely the return of a favour. He was brimming with self-confidence and self-importance, endlessly admiring himself for his brilliant career and mind and, as far as women were concerned, 'dreaded rejection of none'.[4] He was handsome and skilled at singing the *versi d'amore*. Héloïse was, at eighteen years old, not only nearly twenty years younger than Abélard but also witty, clever and, most crucially for the celibate scholar, endowed with 'other qualities wont to lovers'.[5] In other words, she was luscious and obviously available.

The days passed in love-making and 'lovers' chatter'. Meanwhile Abélard's scholarly work went into a dramatic and public decline ('kisses far outnumbered reasoned words', as he put it).[6] Students complained that he was ill prepared for lectures and grumbled that he offered no new propositions, only reworkings of old questions or readings of love poems. In confusion, Abélard temporarily abandoned his responsibilities in the city and took Héloïse back with him to Brittany, where they married in secret and she gave birth to a son called Astrolabe. However, Abélard, through vanity and a sense of shirked intellectual duty, was not ready to give himself over entirely to a domestic life. Instead, he wheedled an agreement from Fulbert that he would keep the marriage under wraps and take up his teaching duties again (although not against the law, it was unheard of for a scholar to be a married man at that time).

It was on his return to Paris that Abélard made his most fatal error, sending Héloïse away to take the veil at the convent at Argenteuil. Fulbert took this, understandably, as an attempt by Abélard to get rid of Héloïse altogether and, with Abélard once again lodging in his house, he began to plot a dreadful revenge. 'They plotted against me with fierce indignation,' wrote Abélard, 'and on a certain night while I was at rest and sleeping in a private room in my lodgings, they bribed one of my servants with money, and then took the cruellest and most shameful revenge.'[7] A group of men, led by Fulbert, held him down and, swiftly and mercilessly, sliced off both of his testicles.

Even by the harsh standards of the era, this was a terrible crime. The men who did it (but not Fulbert himself) were quickly hunted down and castrated in turn. This gave no comfort to Abélard, whose fame now rested upon his wrecked genitalia as much as his skill in theological debate. In his rise to the commanding heights of Parisian intellectual life he had made many enemies, few of whom now passed up the chance to mock the castrated philosopher.

Roscelin, who had never forgiven Abélard for his youthful attacks upon him, hit hard with an open letter, which spitefully made philosophical play of Abélard's mutilated body:

Since the part that makes a man has been removed, you are not to be called 'Petrus', but 'imperfect Petrus'. It is relevant to this heap of human disgrace because in the seal by which you seal your stinking letters you form an image having two heads, one a man and the other a woman . . . I have decided to say many true and obvious things against your attack, but since I am writing against an imperfect man, I will leave the work that I began incomplete.[8]

A rival called Fulco made for Abélard a list of the benefits of castration – among them the fact that he could pass through a crowd of married women or play with young girls with the utmost decorum. He then warned him to stay away from the 'secret retreats of sodomites', issuing the sarcastic and solemn statement that 'blessed are they who have castrated themselves for the sake of the kingdom of heaven'.[9]

As he had done before, Abélard retreated to a monastery, first at Saint-Denis, then as abbot at Saint-Gildas in Brittany. He returned to theology and philosophy with a vengeance, continuing to court intellectual danger, 'still laying siege to Paris'. He was eventually condemned for heresy at the Council of Soissons, largely on the grounds of his arguments over historical accuracy in the Church, and made a new and powerful enemy in the form of Saint Bernard of Clairvaux. Having sought to rebuild himself as a man with the 'weapon of dialectical reason', he found himself emasculated a second time when the Pope condemned him to silence.

He had never fallen out of love with Héloïse and, when still under the Abbot of Saint-Denis, he built an oratory called the Paraclete which he dedicated to her. This renewed the original scandal and an attempt was made on Abélard's life. At the same time, the famous love affair now reached a new level of poignancy, expressed in the famous letters – perhaps the only contact they had with each other – exchanged between Abélard and Héloïse in the final years of their lives.

The first of these is the *Histoire de mes malheurs* ('Story of Calamity'), Abélard's candid if occasionally self-pitying autobiography, which details his philosophical arguments, his wanderings, his sufferings and above all his enduring passion for Héloïse and their 'ill-starred bed'. Although addressed enigmatically to 'a friend', this text was obviously meant for Héloïse who, when she read it, was immediately prompted to write a long and impassioned reply. It is here that Héloïse reveals herself as a full sexual being, a shrewd intellect and a free-thinker unafraid to make statements which, a century later, would have had her burned at the stake for heresy. Most remarkably, for example, in response to Abélard's icy declarations about sainthood and the abandonment of worldly pleasures, she makes a plea to keep women in the same earthly domain as men, instead of elevating (or relegating them, as she saw it) to the status of martyrs or saints. Héloïse even daringly invoked sexuality as the engine of love; 'And if the name of wife appears more sacred and more valid,' she wrote, 'sweeter to me is ever the word friend, or, if thou be not ashamed, concubine or whore.'[10]

Héloïse's frank sexuality was clearly a challenge to the authorities of the era. It was inevitable that such female defiance would be met by male violence. Héloïse's punishment was to be reduced to a double exile – from ordinary human society and, most tellingly, the physical presence of Abélard.

The crime of the two lovers was, however, not that they had had sex with each other – Paris was during this period as bawdy and tingling with sex as it ever had been or would be – but that they had been caught out in public. In contemporary eyes, Fulbert's castration of Abélard was savage and morally wrong but at some level considered a right and just reward for the transgression of taboos. There was also a frisson of terror and delight in recounting the tale.

For these reasons, this period in Parisian history is unsurprisingly rich in similar stories of genital mutilation. In his autobiography, Guibert de Nogat, for example, tells gory tales of torture, as devised by the likes of Thomas de Coucy, who hung his enemies up by their penises until the organs were ripped from the body. Another popular legend was of a nun who fell in love with and became pregnant by a young canon, was forced to castrate him and then return to her cell. The *fabliau* ('moral tale') of the 'Prestre Crucifié' ('Crucified Priest') was the story of a priest who, having been discovered in bed with a sculptor's wife, tries to disguise himself by adopting the position of Christ on a nearby crucifix. The cuckolded sculptor, pretending that he did not recognize the priest, lopped off his genitalia, on the pretext of improving the wooden statue of Christ.

The tale of Abélard and Héloïse, in the same vein of delicious cruelty, was described by a southern poet of the same era as 'a story sweeter than honeyed wine'.[11]

Students and Street-fighters

Less dramatically, Abélard has also often been claimed as the founding father of the University of Paris. The chief reason for this is the suggestion that he was the first to introduce an argumentative dialectical practice into his teaching. At the risk of heresy, he blew away the mystical methods that until then had held sway and taught those who gathered on the Left Bank to think critically.

Secondly, by abandoning the cloisters of Notre-Dame for Montagne Sainte-Geneviève, he had moved philosophy away from the Church and into the secular territory it would occupy for the next millennium. It was indeed not long after Abélard's death that the various groups around the Montagne would come together as a guild to form the city's first university. In 1257, Robert de Sorbon, chaplain to Louis IX, founded the college which would eventually give its name to the whole university. The name of the Sorbonne was indeed famous throughout Europe by the end of the century.

The college was originally founded to help poor scholars. Initially it offered sixteen bursaries to support students of all nationalities, but it quickly grew beyond these quite modest ambitions as donations poured in from across Christendom. Its first buildings were on rue Coupe-Gueule ('Cut-throat street', named for its terrible reputation as a den of murderous thieves), running in front of the old Roman baths, and then in rue des Deux Portes and rue des Maçons, both of which are slightly nearer to the site now occupied by the Place de la Sorbonne. Its reputation first rested upon the rigour with which its scholars studied heresies and opposed, for example, the influence of mendicant friars upon the ordinary citizens of Paris. This made it immediately unpopular with the various abbots and bishops in and around Paris who had been making themselves rich at the expense of a gullible and deeply pious populace. The anti-clerical and insurrectionary traditions of the Sorbonne were clearly already present from its origins onwards.

More than this, however, it was the establishment of the university, no less than the construction of Notre-Dame or the ever-increasing prosperity that came from the river trade, which pushed Paris to the forefront of European affairs. Again Paris conceived itself as a rival to Rome and was jealous of the power of the papacy. But although Rome wielded the political power of theology, it was in Paris, at the burgeoning university at the foot of Montagne Sainte-Geneviève, that true intellectual power was being developed.

This was where, in an environment shaped by scholars from all over Europe, the new millennium was being defined. The students and scholars were fascinated not only by theology in traditional terms but also by questions, still unanswered from classical times, of thought and substance. More to the point, the teachers and students speculated on metaphysical matters with a freedom more akin to the ancient Greeks than the constraints of medieval Christendom. From this ferment, and in this unstructured, febrile and often overheated atmosphere, ideas and arguments were being made that would shape European thought and history for centuries to come. The establishment of the university was, however, a process of slow and gradual development, determined by economic and social factors rather than by any one great intellectual leap into the future. When the likes of Abélard, for example, had dominated the Parisian intellectual scene, it was by teaching in the open air at the foot of Montagne Saint-Geneviève in the rue de Fouarre (translated as 'the street of straw', in reference to the ramshackle coverings set up by the students). The notion of organizing such activities into a proper site with accommodation had not yet occurred to teachers or students.

Similarly, the range of subjects taught at first had changed little from Roman times. These were essentially the *trivium*, consisting of grammar, rhetoric and dialectics (usually limited to Church-approved translations of Plato or Aristotle); and the *quadrivium*, which was made up of music, arithmetic, geometry and astronomy. The Left Bank was given over almost exclusively to students and their activities, virtually all conducted in several varieties of Latin.

The growth of the intellectual classes was matched by a new social stratum of artisans and craftsmen, the *mercatores*, who were based in one fixed spot in the city, as opposed to the itinerant tradesmen who until then had been the most numerous and popular traders in the city. Along with the development of brotherhoods and guilds there came the beginnings of a specifically urban mentality, which distinguished itself from rural individualism in a collective spirit of endeavour. As these artisans settled in a semi-permanent fashion alongside the schools and monasteries, the city began to take shape as a fixed, urban entity.

This Paris was also an increasingly cosmopolitan place. The overflow from the Cathedral School of Paris created a demand for *studia generale* – a place of study for students from various countries on the model of the established institutions at Bologna or Salerno. These meeting places developed into the *Universitas magistrorum et scholarium*, which by the thirteenth century had four faculties – Theology, Canon Law, Medicine and the Liberal Arts. The students were segregated according to which 'nation' they had come from. In the thirteenth century, this meant that 'French' students included Spaniards and Italians; the English nation included German students and the Picard nation not only Picards but also students from the Low Countries.

The establishment of the university therefore introduced into the city young intellectuals who came into frequent conflict with native Parisians and the authorities. Students referred to Parisians contemptuously, nick-naming the average city-dweller 'Jacques Bonhomme', an insult with a whiff of serfdom. The first major student strike in history was launched in 1229 over the price of wine in a tavern in the Faubourg Saint-Marcel. On this occasion, the students found themselves soundly beaten, as neighbours rushed to help the tavern owner. They returned the next day, heavily armed and with a serious contingent of drunken comrades willing to smash a few Parisian heads. The incident became a major street battle, spilling out across the neighbourhood and terrifying innocent bystanders. The king's own men got involved, killing and seriously injuring a good number of students. In response, both students and teachers temporarily left the city. The situation was resolved only after a promise of protection from the university.

The students brought cash and prestige to Paris and were largely tolerated, albeit grudgingly, for these reasons. The chronicler Jacques de Vitry was wary of the foreign faces and manners which could be found all over Paris, but most especially around the university on the Left Bank. 'The English are boastful drunkards,' he wrote, describing the life of the young university. 'The French [meaning non-Parisian inhabitants of the Île de France] are proud, soft, effeminate; the Germans aggressive and bad-tempered; the Normans vain and pompous; the Poitevins treacherous; the Burgundians brutal and stupid; the Bretons light and inconsistent; the Sicilians tyrants; the Lombards greedy and wicked; the Romans seditious.'[12]

Whether or not Vitry was exaggerating for comic effect, it was true that the streets of the Left Bank around the university were not always safe and that, although Paris announced its status as a capital by projecting itself as a microcosm of the known world, it was still very much a volatile place.

8. Saints, Poets, Thieves

The thirteenth century was a time of extremes. On the one hand, the reign of Philippe-Auguste had marked a decisive turning point in the history of Paris, and therefore France, as his government, under Suger's firm control, proved successful in war and acquired territory with ease. The political prestige of France had never been higher. On the other hand, this was also the age of faith. Accordingly, in the early thirteenth century society was roughly divided between the nobility, the clergy and peasants, in imitation of the Divine order that had stood immobile since the last days of Lutetia. But this hierarchy was about to be disrupted for ever by the emergence in Paris of a new urban middle class with entirely separate interests from those of the ruling classes. The first instinct of the monarchy, confronted by this shift in power, was to retreat into the certainties of Christianity. This retreat was most clearly marked in the reign of Louis IX, or 'Saint Louis' (he was canonized in 1297), a highly strung ascetic whose dogmatism and febrile cruelty – as we have seen, he invited the Inquisition into Paris as well as financing several disastrous and murderous forays into the Holy Land – may well have cast him in the present era as a serial killer rather than being appropriate behaviour for a king of France.[1]

Still, for all his religious fervour and contempt for the material world, Paris flourished under Louis IX. Most notably, in 1242 he commissioned the construction of the Sainte-Chapelle, which is even now one of the most beautiful and mysterious religious sites in Paris, an almost psychedelic series of contrasts between delicate stonework and otherworldly painted visions of the heavens and the starry sky. Gazing at the low ceiling of the lower chapel, or the exquisite stained glass of the upper chapel, still jolts the viewer into a direct awareness of the mystery of being and non-being. Overall no work represents better than the Sainte-Chapelle the interplay between mysticism and solid matter that characterizes the prevailing mood of the thirteenth century.

After Louis's death, Paris went into a slow decline. This was partly due to the indifferent policies pursued by his successor, Philippe III, called 'le Hardi' ('the Bold'), who spent most of his time away from the city campaigning in small, pointless wars. The decline became more marked under the reign of Philippe IV, who came to the throne in 1285 and went on to bring the city to its knees.

Middle-Class Revolt

At this point in its history, Paris was divided by the Seine into three distinct districts: Le Quartier d'Outre-Grand-Pont ('The Quarter Beyond the Great Bridge'); Le Quartier d'Outre-Petit-Pont ('The Quarter Beyond the Little Bridge'); and Le Quartier de la Cité ('The City'). These names were shortly to be simplified into La Ville, L'Université and La Cité, terms that remained in use until Paris was finally divided into twenty separate areas several centuries later. The richest of these areas was La Ville, a mercantile district and home to the most well-known Parisian families, with names such as Barbette, Bourdon, Popin, Bonne-Fille and Piz d'Oë. La Ville also contained Parisians of a lower order with much more prosaic names – Le Grand, Le Gros and Boulanger were common – but few of these could rent anything grander than a single dwelling-room, and many slept with animals in the servants' rooms.

La Ville was essentially the area around Saint-Denis, where many of the streets, such as rue de Male Parole (nowadays, rue des Mauvaises Paroles, 'the street of bad words') or rue des Lombards (the Lombards were known as money-lenders), have remained more or less intact in name and structure. There were nearly a hundred Italian bankers in the district (these money-lenders were regularly expelled from the city unless, like Gandolfo Arcelli of Piacenza, notoriously one of the richest men in Paris, they could bribe and grease their way towards residency).

The district known as L'Université was quite different, however. The Right Bank was already being shaped by the demands of political power and commerce, which meant the construction of impregnable government buildings and, as far as possible, straight roads at right angles which permitted the free access of traffic and goods. The Left Bank, in contrast, was developed according to the demands of the colleges, convents, churches and monasteries who vied for students and space and who paid little attention to the public shape of the city beyond their own walls. Even the commercial life of the Left Bank was determined by academic needs. The city's only ink-maker, owned by a woman called Asceline de Roie, was at rue Saint-Victor, while the city's eight bookshops were scattered across the area from rue Neuve-Nostre-Dame, in the shadow of the great cathedral itself, to rue de la Boucherie, now rue Mouffetard, the main artery leading to the edge of the Latin Quarter.

The political and religious centre of the city was the area around the cathedral, La Cité. The richest and most important building, the Hôtel-Dieu, was here, just across from Notre-Dame, and was inhabited by thirty monks and twenty-five nuns. Only one bridge, the Petit-Pont, connected the Left Bank with La Cité, whereas the Right Bank was connected by two structures, the Grand-Pont and the Pont des Planches de Mibrai (*mi-bras*, or 'halfway' across the Seine), which connected with the Petit-Pont, providing a direct route from the Right to the Left Bank. Yet crossing from one side of the river to another was, even at this stage in history, like crossing both a geographical and a mental frontier. There were Parisians who actually refused to leave their own areas, on the grounds that those on the other side had nothing to show or teach them.

Much to the annoyance and puzzlement of the nobility, this was also the period that gave birth to the first *borjois* or 'bourgeois' classes of Paris. The term indeed was first used in a royal document of 1134, thereby rather innocently designating free burghers of the city who did not fit into any of the previously fixed social categories, neither serf, nor artisan nor noble. Paris of course now contained all manner of social classes – beggars, peasants, artisans, students, merchants, monks, knights, nobles – enough indeed for it to be described as the microcosm of the world. The 'bourgeois' were, however, a new phenomenon, which because they were unclassifiable perturbed the king's administration. Above all, the king and his nobility had no desire to concede any power to this new class, which was not constrained by the old oaths of fealty to the monarch.

By now, the bourgeoisie had grown and developed its own multifarious hierarchies, dependent on accent, manners and wealth rather than birth. Most importantly, this period saw the emergence of the *haute bourgeoisie* as a social force, a class that lay threateningly just below the nobility and which, while aping many of the nobility's manners, remained fiercely separate from its needs and demands.

The most illustrious families of Paris were all in some way allied to or derived from the bourgeois classes during this period. Paris at this stage consisted of roughly 100,000 people, a surge in population that meant that much of the city was now seriously overcrowded. Most houses were still built of wood (this is why no examples remain); they were tall and thin and quite precarious. They were also extremely cramped; the average size of a room was no more that 10 square metres, while the entire dwelling of a bourgeois family, including servants, animals and a courtyard, rarely exceeded 80 or so square metres. Even this much was largely hidden from the view of the street as the façade of a house was never more than 6–7 metres wide.

The number of influential families in Paris was never more than twenty, but they had a power entirely disproportionate to their number. They all sought alliance, however, with the burgeoning mercantile classes. The Bourdon family, for example, who gave their name to several streets in Paris, had closer links with the merchants and riverbank traders than they did with royalty. The same applied to the Arrode family, who were related through marriage to the Bourdons and who founded a chapel in their name. Even the Gentien family, one of the richest in Paris, who lived in splendour on rue Lambert de Chiele (now rue du Roi-de-Sicile), felt obliged to build and maintain good relations with the emerging middle classes rather than be subservient to royal caprice. It was dislike and fear of these emergent middle classes which best explains the bizarre new laws set up by Philippe le Bel ('the Fair') in 1294 that forbade any bourgeois from owning a carriage, wearing ermine or precious stones, owning more than one set of robes per year and decreed that they limit themselves to only locally grown food. These laws were quickly ignored and commercial Paris flourished as wine-makers, spice merchants, tailors and jewellers flocked to Paris from all over Europe to meet the ever-growing demands of its wealthy merchant classes.

Philippe le Bel was not only deeply jealous of these new Parisians but also wildly profligate with the revenue that they brought to the city. In his *De laudibus Parisius* ('Treatise in Praise of Paris') of 1323, Jean de Jandun records the magnificence of Philippe's feast thrown in honour of King Edward II of England in June 1313. Over two days, the royal party consumed no less than 380 rams, 200 pike, 189 pigs, 94 oxen and 80 barrels of wine. Paris itself, according to Jean, was 'a wondrous city', unequalled in Europe for the splendour and opulence of its royal and religious buildings.[2]

Unsurprisingly under Philippe le Bel, the city was almost constantly bankrupt. Philippe was obsessed with building monuments to himself such as the Palais-Royal – an extension of Philippe-Auguste's Palais de la Cité – which despite the money poured into it was never to be completed in his lifetime. His grandiose activities cost the city literally a fortune. Philippe's first response was to confiscate private wealth, cancel his own debts and then impose an unpopular tax, the *maltôte*, on the businesses of the city. Even these attempts to bolster the Crown's income were not enough, however, and, although private counterfeiters were liable to be boiled alive in punishment,

Philippe himself had no qualms about adulterating the gold used in minting the currency to achieve the correct weight.

The Rustic Ox

Philippe's tax census, *Le Livre de la taille de Paris* ('The Book of the Taxes of Paris'), does at least have the merit of providing a detailed and intimate portrait of the city during this period. It reveals, for example, that in the rue de Quincampoix, alongside the Temple, knights, serfs, maids and artisans all lived together in what was a presumed harmony. The names too revealed a young city where it was enough to be identified, like a peasant, as Jehanot de Nanterre (Johnny from Nanterre), Jehane la Normande (Jeanne the Norman), Robert le Maçon (Robert the Mason), Juliene de la Ruele (Juliene from the Little Street). Women had enough status to be identified independently as, for example, Dame Agnès, or Dame Agace, la Savonnière (Lady Agace, the Soap-maker).[3]

This was the Paris of ordinary people where a provincial poet known as Rutebeuf became notorious by wandering its streets and mocking its greedy citizens, crooked politicians and venal priests. It probably helped that Rutebeuf was not a native Parisian. He had been born in Champagne around 1230 but came to Paris in 1248, with the idea of studying at the university. He mingled there with the Goliardi, poor clerics who despite their high education could not find work within the Church or royal patronage and who moaned long and loud in stilted Latin verse about the misery of their condition. It was probably these bitter and disappointed sophisticates who gave the young poet the nickname 'Rude Bœuf' or 'Rutebeuf' ('Rustic Ox') to signal his position as a clumsy peasant in the big city.

Rutebeuf soon abandoned his studies and became a *jongleur* in the streets, markets and small squares around Montagne Sainte-Geneviève. The *jongleur* was a public entertainer (the term comes from the Latin *joculatores*, 'player' or 'actor'), in effect the direct descendant of the *mimi* and *histriones*, the musicians, singers, acrobats and storytellers who wandered the towns of the Roman world. Rutebeuf also functioned as a kind of itinerant journalist, satirizing and arguing with all classes as well as himself. Most effectively, he presented a clear-eyed view of the combination of selfishness and ruthlessness that made the Parisians at street level so distinctive.

In his most personal verse, the 'poèmes de l'infortune' ('poems of misfortune'), Rutebeuf paints a portrait of a harsh city, a far cry from the splendour of royal palaces. These intricate and sometimes grotesque poems were intended as begging letters or to be intoned on the streets as a pan-handler's plea for food and cash. Yet they veer brilliantly between poetry and pathos, most particularly in those passages where Rutebeuf attacks himself as an inveterate gambler who 'does not remember his neighbour's affliction but weeps only over his own'.

The poor in Rutebeuf's Paris, such as the gambler, thrive on the nearness of their own destruction. They drink ('gulping it down in torrents'), eat ('feasting on hope') and fornicate ('like rats on a haystack') with a demonic, doomed energy. But Rutebeuf can be tender too. In his poem 'Le dit des ribaux de Greive' ('Dockers on the Place de la Grève'), he pities the poor man who 'has no clothes and bare heels to walk on, stung by the black flies and then the white [snow and hail]'. Most importantly, unlike any of the scholarly verse being composed across the river at the time, the poet speaks directly to the 'docker', the poor man or the peasant, celebrating his vices as virtues. This kind of direct feeling for the Parisian poor would find its fullest and most famous expression two centuries later in the writings of François Villon; but in Rutebeuf there is already at work a distinctly Parisian lyricism, a genuine echo of the dark streets of what Baudelaire would later call the stinking shadows of the city.[4]

Policemen and Thieves

Rutebeuf's Paris was also a lawless place: murder and banditry were all too common, and prostitution an accepted part of the city's fabric. The poet often called satirically upon the king to bring charity if not justice to the 'honest men' of the city. There had, however, by this latter part of the thirteenth century already been several attempts, not all of them successful, to bring some measure of civil order to Paris.

One of Philippe-Auguste's most fundamental achievements, for example, had been to impose a crude but effective policing system upon the city. At first this took the form of appointing a series of bailiffs to impose law and order in the city while the king and his nobles were away at the Third Crusade in 1190. These were intended more to prevent the possibility of political subversion than to combat everyday crime and were really an extended version of Philippe's personal bodyguard. The bailiffs themselves were often referred to as *ribauds* or *ribauz*, a word related to the English 'ribaldry' and which was used to describe the lawless troops who followed a military campaign for the pleasures of rape and pillage. It soon became widely used in Paris as a term to denote licentious behaviour. For obvious reasons, with his arms and swagger, the 'ribald' did not inspire much confidence in the ordinary Parisian.

A slightly greater level of order and stability was brought to organizing life on the street with the establishment in 1160 of the office of *grand prévôt* ('provost marshal') of Paris, the first of whom was simply called Étienne but occupied a post of crucial significance in the development of the city. The *prévôt* was normally a non-native of the city (the post was even occupied by an alleged Englishman in the fifteenth century) in order to uphold a degree of independence from the city's criminal elements. Yet so many *prévôts* were closely allied to criminal gangs or the king's own disreputable bodyguard that the post was also unofficially designated as *roi des ribauds* ('king of the ribalds'). The *prévôt* was not above murder, as demonstrated by Thomas, *prévôt* of Paris in 1200, who was alleged to have been involved in the killing of five German students. Other *prévôts* were excommunicated or hanged for blasphemous crimes. Most grotesque and melancholy of all was the fate of *prévôt* Guillaume de Tignonville who, in October 1408, had ordered two students guilty of murder to be hanged at Montfaucon. The university and its famously litigious lawyers fought back and finally won an appeal in May the following year. The unfortunate Guillaume was ordered to take down the corpses of the students, which had been rotting in the open air through the winter, and convey them to the convent of Les Mathurins, where they were to be laid to rest. Most chilling was the punishment demanded by the university lawyer, who ordered Guillaume to kiss both students on the lips to show his contrition as the stinking bodies were taken down. The order was carried out.

Notwithstanding the crimes and other weaknesses of its incumbents, the office of the *prévôt* was part of a distinguished tradition of policing in Paris that went back to the Gallo-Roman city and the Graeco-Roman notion of *politia* as a form of civil government. In the seventh and eighth centuries, the counts in the court of the French kings performed essentially the same tasks as the Roman administrators: keeping public order, catching wrong-doers, ensuring a steady food supply to the city at reasonable prices, safeguarding public morals (in other words, controlling prostitution) and passing judgement according to the law. These functions were preserved more or less intact until 1789. The essential point was that the *prévôt*'s authority came from the king and not from the community.

Such a post was always open to corruption, which is why Louis, the neurotic religious zealot, had appointed the apparently incorruptible Étienne Boileau (sometimes referred to in documents as Boilèvre) to the post in 1261. Dressed in a black habit and a velvet bonnet, carrying a large sword and accompanied by a guard of honour, Boileau cut an impressive figure, whether in his official residence in the fortress of Châtelet or attending king's counsel at the court. One of his first jobs was to regulate, or try to regulate, the city's economy, examining corporate statutes and drawing up the *Livre des métiers* ('Book of Trades'), in 1268, which documented what was made, imported, exported and consumed in thirteenth-century Paris. This was not regarded as an unusual duty for a policeman.[5]

Boileau documented more than 120 corporations, with over 5,000 members, with apprentices and masters in guilds ranging from brewing beer to knife-making; the guilds were often split into sub-divisions with, for example, a separate section in the brewers' guild dealing with fermentation of hops, sales and distribution, and so on. It was not regarded as strange or even particularly sinister that pickpockets, hired assassins and beggars had their own guilds modelled on those of the artisans: each had an interest in making as much money as possible for as little work. The Parisian artisans were notorious in the provinces for their short hours and drunkenness. Violent strikes, provoked by an insulting word or a bad debt, were commonplace.

Below Boileau there were rows of *commissaires-enquêteurs*, junior magistrates whose office went back at least to the seventh century, and *sergents*, tough, pugnacious characters who did most of the strong-arming and occasional sword-fighting in the city. A typical police mission, mainly conducted at night, would involve a group of *sergents* sent out to investigate an allegation of witchcraft, a butcher or brewer who was charging too much for his products, or a case of adultery.

However, the king's real concern was with the prostitutes, who advertised themselves in the city with bright ribbons displayed at midriff level. Most disturbing to Louis's sensibility was the habit of such *filles publiques* of shouting after priests in the street if they refused to do business with them. The most common insult was 'sodomite'. Even Boileau could not drive these girls out, mainly for fear of inciting public disorder if he did. Otherwise both the king and the *prévôt* were happy to live with the lie that Paris was an orderly place.

By the time of Philippe IV, crime was still rife in the city. Punishments were harsh and became harsher still, satisfying less a need for justice than a bloodthirsty taste for cruel entertainment. Thieves, murderers and counterfeiters were usually hanged. Other criminals had their eyes cut out, were whipped or branded with irons (not only on the shoulder but on the cheek or forehead). There was no fixed penal code and judgements were arbitrary. Nobody had any faith in the streets at night. Ordinary Parisians disobeyed orders to keep lamps lit in front windows at night (this was an early rudimentary attempt at street lighting). They barricaded their doors and always kept weapons to hand.

There were citizen guards, who also patrolled at night, but their duties, less glamorous than those of the forces of the *prévôt*, were confined mainly to keeping the peace and preventing crime. This close association, even deliberate confusion, of police and judicial authority was to play a defining role in the nature of Parisian policing for decades to come: unlike British policing, which is mainly concerned with prohibiting, the Paris (and therefore French) police system has been, and continues to be, equally concerned with prescriptive measures, intervention and surveillance. Yves Guyot describes perfectly the ambiguous interplay between freedom and control in the policing of Paris in his remark, made in the shadow of the massacres of the Commune, that 'the Parisian can do what he likes, as long as it's under police supervision'.[6]

9. Destroying the Temple

The greatest criminal of all, at least in the mind of most ordinary Parisians at the turn of the thirteenth century, was the king himself. By 1300, Philippe le Bel's wilful cruelty and financial stupidity had already wrecked the economic stability of the region. He then made matters worse by upsetting the delicate political balance of power within Paris, turning his attention to the Knights Templar, who for the past century or so had occupied a huge enclave just outside the city walls, covering the territory of what is now the eastern part of the Marais.

This was essentially a closed environment that lasted in one form or another until 1820 when the last traces were erased in the rush towards modernity. Vestiges of the donjon of the great enclosure can still be found at Square du Temple, at the northern end of the Marais, while the enclave itself is roughly marked out by the present-day rue du Temple (originally Viae Militiae Templi in 1235), rue de Bretagne and rue de Picardie. The Knights Templar had settled here in the eleventh century, building a refuge and hospital for wounded or impoverished monk-soldiers returning from the Crusades. By the twelfth century, with royal approval, the Villa Novi Templi, a vast enclave which eventually extended towards what is now Ménilmontant and Charonne, had grown over the years into an important centre of learning and culture, forming effectively a rival city to Paris. The Knights had also accumulated great wealth which, by the late thirteenth century, was attracting more than its fair share of attention from beady-eyed outsiders.

The Order of the Knights Templar was founded in 1118, when the nine original Knights travelled to Jerusalem to offer their services to King Baldwin II in securing the passage of pilgrims, on the model of the Hospitallers of Saint John. They lived briefly in the mosque called Masjid-al-Aksa. This means in Arabic the 'most distant place' and is held to be the third holiest shrine in Islam after Mecca and Medina. It was built on the ruins of the old Temple of Solomon and was commonly held to be the centre of the world (this is how it appears on Arabic and European maps of the period). The Knights took their name from the Templum Domini, the Christian place of worship established on the nearby Dome of Rock, an astonishing act of vandalism against Islam that none the less delighted Christians across the Western world.

The Knights took a vow against owning property but in the following decades and then centuries acquired great wealth. They did this by acting as bankers, financing and effectively controlling forays into the Holy Land at will. This is how they gained such powerful enemies as Louis IX, whom they had refused to ransom from Egypt on one of his more catastrophic expeditions. The Knights also became known for their greed and vanity. Their own campaigns in the Holy Land were, in the words of one historian, both 'devastating' and 'disgraceful' (a fact which incidentally underlines the opinion of the veteran French medievalist Jacques Le Goff that the only item of benefit that the Crusades had brought to Europe was the apricot).[1]

When Philippe declared war on the Knights, he was able to draw upon deep reservoirs of ill-will towards them. The Knights were notorious among Parisians for their arrogance. It was known that the soldier-monks practised sodomy, but this was accepted as a 'standard vice' of monks and military men. The poet Guyon de Provins spoke for most Parisians when he attacked them for their *orgueil* ('pride') and for being *cruels et méchants* ('cruel and wicked').[2]

Relations between the Templars and the avaricious Philippe began cordially enough, with an exchange of letters in 1292 in which the king apparently confirmed his approval of their 'privileges'. The only warning that trouble lay ahead came in 1296, when the city of Paris was ordered to make a gift of a hundred thousand livres to the king, the total sum to be paid by the Knights themselves. The order came, naturally enough, from the *prévôt* of Paris, whose duty it was to maintain the payment of taxes, no matter how arbitrarily they had been imposed. The Knights challenged this order and after two years' argument in the *parlement* (or 'parliament', which had been in existence only since 1250 and was generally subservient to the king), they won their case.

Philippe was privately enraged but held his anger in check in public. He was in constant need of funds as his financial incompetence regularly brought the city to the brink of disaster. It was while taking refuge from one of the riots against his administration in 1305 in the Great Tower of the Temple, that Philippe's wrath was to reach boiling point. He had been offered this hospitality by Jacques de Molay, the Great Master of the Temple, who had told Philippe of the riches his men had brought back from Jerusalem and Cyprus, and which were buried beneath the tower. Philippe vowed there and then to take them for himself.

Philippe not only drew Pope Clement, a weak and easily put-upon Frenchman, on to his side (the king had a hand in the Pope's establishment at Avignon in 1309) but manoeuvred the Parisian mob against the Knights with his propaganda machine, which described how the Knights denied Christ, spat on the Cross, performed human sacrifice, gave themselves to orgies, practised sodomy and Sufism, worshipped a demon named Baphomet and had close ties to Hussan Sabah, leader of the Order of Assassins, the hashish-intoxicated martyrs who fought so fiercely against the Christian invaders in the Holy Land. It was even rumoured that the Templars had a 'cave excavated in the ground, very dark, where they have an image in the form of a man over which is a human skin and shining carbuncles for its eyes'.[3]

The name Baphomet was clearly a corruption of 'Mahomet' or 'Mohammed' and this fed the virulent Islamophobia at work in Christian Paris. The charges of buggery were also fuelled by Orientalist fantasies of 'un-Christian' sexual practices. Yet there may well have been certain truths encoded in the black propaganda. Certainly, the Knights had come into close contact with Muslim sects and the Hermetical knowledge they possessed. They may even have come across the Hermetic Nag Hammadi texts, allegedly written by God, which put forward the argument that Christ was not 'the crucified one'.[4] On a less speculative level, there is every reason to believe that as a closed order they organized rituals and forms of worship that were a direct threat to the sovereign Christian order.

The Knights considered it beneath their dignity to answer the charges made against them, but found themselves finally confounded by the king's inquisition, which, long practised in the use of torture, forced confessions from some seventy-two Knights. In one single operation, over a hundred Knights were burned alive, each of them protesting innocence of the charges laid against them.

The Pope, well aware of Philippe's true motives, wavered until 13 April 1313 when he finally ordered the abolition of the Temple. It was an abject and craven decision and a fateful moment. In response to the Pope, Jacques de Molay and his chief officers immediately retracted their confessions, for which act they were condemned to the stake. As he walked to his execution on the Îlot des Juifs, set upon what is now Île du Square du Vert-Galant, the tiny island in the dead centre of Paris, Molay launched a curse against the Pope and the king, predicting that neither would see the end of the year. The Pope died just over a month later from a mysterious disease. Philippe was killed in a riding accident a few months later.

Into the 'Sotadic' Zone

The Temple remained as the Knights had left it for another two centuries, even as the city spread around it. Its main tower was occasionally used as a garrison or a prison, but for the most part the buildings served their original functions as places of prayer or trade, while the cultivated lands, sometimes referred to as Le Marais (the marsh), continued to flourish. By the sixteenth and seventeenth centuries, the Temple had become home to three categories of people – aristocrats, artisans and debtors – who made use of its status (won by the Knights in the thirteenth century) as a place exempt from tax. The Temple was also known at this point as a decadent place where Christian morals were in severe danger: sexual orgies, gluttony and drinking were rumoured to be everyday activities.

A century later, in 1712, Philippe de Vendôme, philosopher and gourmand, follower of Rabelais and masterly libertine predator of both sexes, declared the Temple to be the world headquarters of spiritual Epicureanism, making the place doubly loathsome to those who still suspected that its inhabitants disdained and plotted against the outside world of Paris. The adage, 'boire comme un Templier' ('to drink like a Templar'), was common at this point, spat out in disgust by Parisians.

In his 1982 novel *Landscapes After the Battle*, the Spanish writer Juan Goytisolo refers to the area around the northern edge of the *quartier* now called Temple and Le Sentier as the 'sotadic zone', a term he borrowed from the English explorer Sir Richard Burton, who coined it to describe the territories to the south and east of the Mediterranean where homosexuality flourished as the norm.[5]

Goytisolo's 'sotadic zone' in Paris is far from being exclusively homosexual, however. The area traverses the historic and commercial centre of Paris but is indeed still largely unknown to the thousands of Parisians and foreign visitors who cross it every day, en route to the sex shops of the rue Saint-Denis, the shopping mall at Les Halles or the chic splendour of the *grands boulevards*. The western edges of the district are criss-crossed by the nineteenth-century passages which so fascinated Walter Benjamin and the Surrealists (see Chapters 28 and 37). The triangular formation of Le Sentier, from rue d'Aboukir to Place du Caire, is today mainly known as the heart of the Parisian textile industry. This area, stretching to the metro station of Temple, is also 'home', if that is the right word, to a permanently floating population of third-world labourers. The streets at the northern edges of the district are mainly Pakistani and Afghan, the central axes Turkish and Kurdish; any number of languages, from Albanian to several varieties of Yiddish, can be heard in the surrounding streets.

The secret traditions of this old district are clearly visible in the twenty-first century. Through the centuries, the Knights Templar have been associated with the legitimate heir to the French throne, as well as a host of secret and semi-secret networks. These include Freemasons, neo-Gnostics, Nazis, occultists of every variety and neo-medievalists who justify any and all conspiracy theories. Others, such as the Surrealists and other avant-garde groups, have found both pathos and enchantment in the legend of these doomed heretics. The Knights have been most recently represented in the best-selling book *The Da Vinci Code* by Dan Brown, which again depicts the order as the keepers of secret wisdom.[6]

There are plenty of people in present-day Paris who still believe this. The Parisian headquarters of these groups can be found today at the Bar-Tabac des Templiers, 35 rue de Rivoli, a scruffy late-night joint which doubles in the daytime as a bookmaker's. The bar is on the corner of rue de la Tacherie, once called rue de la Juiverie but renamed when Philippe le Bel, having expelled the Jews who lived here, gave it on a whim to a valet named Puvin.

Through the fog of cigarette smoke and the clattering commentary on televised horseracing, you notice with a start that every inch of the walls of the bar is lined with images and effigies dedicated to the Templar tradition, including statues of Joan of Arc, Louis XVI's last testament and photographs of the present contender for the French throne, Louis XX. It is in this incongruous environment that present-day keepers of the flame, such as the 'Milice du Christ' (*milice* meaning 'militia') and 'Ordre du Temple', meet regularly to discuss and debate the Knights' legacy. It is rumoured that this spot was formerly the headquarters of the High Command of the Knights, and that buried somewhere in the cellars is the shrine where they worshipped the devil-god Baphomet.[7]

It was also near here that in 1662 the poet Claude Le Petit, in his *Paris ridicule*, praised the Templars for defying the laws of God, remaining faithful to their own vision of a purer world; Le Petit himself was hanged shortly afterwards for atheism. Across the street, the traditions of libertinism and apparent enthusiasm for sodomy attributed to the former inhabitants of the Temple are preserved in the streets around the rues du Temple, Sainte Croix de la Bretonnerie, Vieille du Temple and des Mauvais Garçons. It is here that the international and Parisian gay scene have come together to make their headquarters, forming a closed if cosmopolitan brotherhood whose ways of love and worship evidently belong here more than in any other part of the city.

10. Rebels and Riots

Philippe le Bel, as we saw, died suddenly and at a relatively young age, in 1314. Most Parisians believed that this was the obvious and inevitable result of the Templar's curse. The shock of his death was all the greater since his control over the city of Paris and its population had never been less than firm and complete. The city had grown under his reign. Île de la Cité alone boasted more than twenty churches. As a centre for study or worship, Paris was without doubt the most important city in western Europe, perhaps only matched by Venice as a centre for trade.

All of this had been achieved despite the fact Philippe's main ambition in life had been to rob his subjects. The irony was that in order to do this he had created a variety of institutions that proved to be both solid and long lasting. Most notably, under Philippe the court was broken up into three main divisions: the royal council, which ruled over France; the *chambre des comptes*, which handled finance; and the *parlement*, which administered justice. All three of these branches of government were dominated by the king's will and remained intact and guided by this principle until 1789. Philippe's early death had only postponed the inevitable popular anger against a government so well organized and dedicated to fleecing its populace.

Philippe bequeathed his successor Louis X ('le Hutin' – 'the quarrelsome') a city that was morally and financially wrecked. This was the beginning of what Fernand Braudel terms 'the satanic century', when all the achievements of the previous century seemed to go into reverse and Paris entered a period of endless war, shattering violence, disease and hunger.[1]

Changes in the Parisian population were caused by disastrous events on a wider scale. The most pressing of these was the famine of 1315–17, which was widespread throughout Europe but which came as a profound shock to the Parisians who only a generation earlier had prided themselves on the abundance to be found in their city. The fragile economy came under further pressure from the confusion over the Capetian succession in 1317. The sudden death of Louis X meant that there was no male heir to the throne. The lawyers of Louis's brothers fought successfully to create new laws which excluded all female challengers to the throne (this was Clovis's 'Salic Law' at work, referred to in Chapter 3). But in 1328, the throne came to the founder of a new line, Philippe de Valois. The predatory English king, Edward III, the last surviving grandson of Philippe le Bel, seized his opportunity to wreak havoc in France and set in train the bloody challenge to the French king that became known as the Hundred Years War.

This apparently interminable war had many direct and indirect consequences. It provided for the English a national myth of identity founded in the victories at Crécy and Agincourt and the fact of not being French. In more practical terms, the capture of Calais, which would be held by the English for the next two hundred years, opened up the ports and manufacturing towns of Flanders to the English economy. Although England would eventually lose the war and once again become an island, the aggressive pursuit of territorial acquisition in the name of sovereignty and trade bore the hallmark of the future British Empire.

For the French, the war also created a new national mythology. This was, however, less to do with self-aggrandizement than self-defence. One of the results of the war was the breaking up of regional identities – such as Picard, Gascon and Norman – as people fled the terrors in their own part of the country. Paris, which shrank in grandeur and stature through the course of the century, was a natural home for these refugees. Most importantly, the dreadful experiences of the Hundred Years War pushed ordinary Parisians to take control of their own political destiny. The path ahead was hard and long, paved with insurrections, mutinies and small-scale revolts. These were the first direct challenges in history to royal authority. They failed in the short term, but they did play the crucial role of alerting the monarchy to the fact that it was dependent on the goodwill of the people rather than the other way around. Taxes, salaries, food shortages and strikes were the controversial issues of the coming years.

The long and deadly guerrilla war with the English also made everyday life in Paris difficult if not occasionally impossible. Many Parisians played both sides in the conflict, acting as go-betweens, collaborators, spies or profiteers. Meanwhile, the English cut a swathe across the countryside outside and around Paris, claiming territory via a scorched-earth policy that left those peasants who were not massacred or killed off by hunger with no way of earning a living. They retreated behind the city walls, hungry and disaffected. The war turned even patriotic Parisians against their rulers. 'This damned war has caused so much misery that I believe France has suffered more in the past twelve years than she has in the past sixty,' complained one contemporary observer. 'We are ruled by young men and fools.'[2] In 1330, there were riots across Paris in direct opposition to the war. The retribution of Philippe de Valois, the 'young man' on the throne, was merciless.

When the Black Death arrived at the gates of Paris in 1348 – heralded by a fireball that swept through the murky skies above the capital – its citizens cried that they could suffer no more.[3] Terrible news of the devastation the disease could bring had already travelled to the city from Marseilles, where it had first appeared in France.

The city was quickly in the grip of the epidemic and the death rate soon stood at several hundred a day. The overcrowded labyrinth around Notre-Dame was turned into a fetid charnel house: corpses lay stinking in the streets, gnawed by rats (the city's cats had been massacred by Parisians who mistakenly thought they were carriers of the plague). The disease raged for over a year, slicing the city's population by half and wrecking the busy river trade. It was exactly, as the historian Guy Bois put it, 'like a kick aimed at a human anthill'.[4]

Insurrectionists

Throughout the following century, the city simmered with plots, executions, expulsions, matched on the streets by a frightening surge in petty crime accompanied by violence. Charles V came to the throne in 1364 with the intention of controlling the unruly forces at work within and outside the city. His first step was to extend and strengthen Philippe-Auguste's original defences by establishing a new wall around the city. On the Left Bank this meant simply rebuilding and fortifying what was left of Philippe's wall. On the Right Bank, however, a new wall was built as far north as Temple, cutting through urbanized areas, stretching from the Porte Saint-Antoine to Porte Saint-Honoré (roughly matching the limits marked by the present-day rue du Faubourg Saint-Antoine and the lower end of rue Saint-Honoré). One of the present-day consequences of this wall is the shift in the north–south axis of the city from east to west; most traffic on the Right Bank in Paris below the Porte Saint-Martin therefore now roughly follows the contours of what was the wall. The Louvre was no longer the central pivot of the city's defences, but this did not stop Charles from strengthening its towers. In a climate of political unrest – as a result of war and famine, salaries in Paris for most of Charles's reign barely met the basic needs for most ordinary people – this was done in order to watch and control Parisians rather than to defend them.

The wall proved useless. The ramparts and ditches provided refuge at night to an underclass of desperate peasants, army deserters, whores, pimps, touts, thieves and professional assassins. Charles determined to rid the countryside and the city of these so-called *écorcheurs*. But by night these criminals controlled the streets on the edges and in the centre of the city.

If the streets were filthy, unlit and unmarked, they were, despite the dangers, meant to be home. What shocked Parisians, during a famous trial for rape in 1333, was the discovery that a little girl ten years of age (called 'Jehannette') had been abducted while sitting at the front of her father's house. The trusting child had been led away by a neighbour, Jacqueline, who turned her over for cash to the rapist Lombart. Most horrifying of all was that Jacqueline had previously been known as a good friend to all in the street. The tale proved that the Devil lived everywhere.[5]

There were also inevitably frequent *jacqueries*, popular revolts led by the peasants, which although often entirely unfocused – they were usually provoked by hunger or a rise in taxes – were incendiary enough to destabilize an already unsteady series of governments. None of Philippe le Bel's successors, it seemed, had either the intellect or moral strength to cope with or contain these problems, which made it increasingly difficult for them to rule the city of Paris. One of the first and most direct challenges to royal authority in the mid fourteenth century came from a notably wealthy businessman who, despite his *haut bourgeois* background, brought the city to its knees in the most devastating revolt of the period.

Étienne Marcel was in fact born in 1320 in the rue de la Pelleterie on Île de la Cité into a family of money-changers and drapers. The Marcel family were long established in the district and indeed had made enough money over the years to be considered an illustrious bourgeois dynasty with easy relations with the likes of the Barbou, the Cocatrix and the Dammartin families. Indeed Marcel's first wife was the eldest daughter of the Dammartin family. He married for a second time in 1344 (his first wife had died), this time into the Des Essars family, one of the richest and most powerful families in nearby Rouen. Well connected, politically astute and flamboyant in style, Marcel did extremely well in business, extending his commercial empire as far as Flanders and Brabant.

Marcel was also politically ambitious and deeply sceptical about the ability of the ruling monarch to deal effectively with external threats (mainly from the English) or to administer properly the complex business environment of Paris. In 1355, he was first made an alderman of the city and then elected *prévôt des marchands* ('provost of the merchants'). This was an extremely political and politically sensitive position which had been for a long time the preserve of *haut bourgeois* dynasties, including the Bourdon and the Arrode families. Marcel proved himself to be even more bold, dynamic and wilfully arrogant than any of his predecessors. His first move was to establish his headquarters on the Place de la Grève, at the heart of the city's business activities, and his second to drive through a new constitution which virtually disestablished the Dauphin, Charles, acting as regent in his father's absence (his father, Jean le Bon, was a prisoner in England).[6]

Marcel's aim was to take back the city from its lazy and ineffectual rulers and return it to the people. His first priority was to organize the citizens into militias so that they could defend themselves against the English. The humiliation of the regent was followed through with the setting up of a Committee of National Defence, backed by the bourgeois classes, which seized the Louvre, the residence of the regent. The anger of the crowd was fired by the news that Jean le Bon had signed a treaty which gave half of Paris to the English. Marcel's men killed all the regent's guards and advisers but spared the young Charles, deliberately humiliating him by parading him before the mob in a red and blue bonnet. He then fled to Picardy.

With 3,000 men under his command, Marcel began extending and building new city walls. Having established himself as the governor of Paris in 1357, he then set about trying to spread the rebellion against the king through the countryside. He found himself effectively blockaded by the king's armies, however, which had regrouped and surrounded Paris. Marcel fell back to Paris and his defensive walls were nearly complete when the regent, who had a year earlier escaped from Paris, turned up with an army, intent upon taking back his city.

This time the bourgeoisie took the part of the king. The change of allegiance was partly inspired by the fact that Marcel had become increasingly reliant on English mercenaries to defend the city and keep order in its streets. The discontent among Parisians simmered away before erupting into sudden violence. On the night of 21 July 1358, an armed mob stabbed thirty-four of the hated Englishmen to death near what is still now the rue des Anglais, the headquarters of the arrogant and usually drunken Anglo-Saxons. Another forty-seven were taken prisoner before the authorities were forced to lock up four hundred English troops in the Louvre for their own safety. On 27 July, Marcel made the fatal error of releasing these troops, only days after a party of native Parisians had been sliced to pieces by English soldiers as they marched towards the garrison at Saint-Cloud.

Jean Maillart, city treasurer and formerly a staunch comrade, finally betrayed Marcel. Maillart had switched his allegiance back to the Crown, accusing Marcel of treachery and collusion with the English. Marcel was hunted down and killed by Maillart and his supporters and his body displayed, naked and mutilated, at the church of Sainte-Catherine-du-Val-des-Écoliers. The regent then entered the city.

Marcel's revolt was an action that presaged later turmoil and exposed essential flaws in the royal control of Paris, and indeed France. Certainly its violence and challenge to the social order provided inspiration to the revolts that came in its wake. Most notably, the angry riots that spread across the city in February 1382 as a response to yet more taxes imposed by the king found their impetus in Marcel's refusal to bow down before arbitrary and unfair law-making. The rioters were called *maillotins*, after the lead mallets they had taken from the Hôtel de Ville, and which they used literally to hammer tax inspectors to death. The Florentine Buonaccorso Pitti, then resident in the city, noted that these riots were led by 'popolo minuto', ordinary people of Paris, young people, students, craftsmen, servants, the unemployed. What astonished Pitti was both their anger and daring: they attacked, and sometimes massacred, money-lenders, rich bourgeois, policemen and Jews.[7] Theft, murder and rape became commonplace as the middle classes stealthily left the city for the duration, many of them making their way to Avignon and the protection of the Pope.

The retribution of the king, who began to establish order in March 1382, was predictably savage and established a grim pattern of massacre and counter-massacre that characterized relations between the poor of the city and its ruling élite for decades, even centuries, to come.[8] More than this, as an expression of popular anger that found a focus in the pursuit of autonomy and the abolition of authority, Marcel's revolt has often been described as a premonition of Parisian troubles right through to the Commune of 1871. The statue of Marcel – cast as a noble and defiant figure – which currently stands overlooking the river from the Hôtel de Ville, certainly corroborates this view but also demonstrates a certain historical illiteracy. More to the point, although he was not above exploiting the *jacqueries* in the countryside for his own ends, Marcel was extremely conscious of his elevated position in the social hierarchy of the period and cared little or nothing for the suffering of those below him. Neither was he looking forward to a fairer and more equal world; rather he took as his model the golden age of the 1200s when Paris flourished and expanded under the control of a merchant élite who were at best indifferent to incompetent royalty. Marcel's vision was doomed from the outset as disease, war and famine cut a swathe through his own caste and reduced the rest of Paris to a spiritual and material poverty quite unlike anything the city had known before.

One of the most serious consequences of the arrival of the Black Death in the city and the warfare in the surrounding territory was that Paris was now almost permanently cut off from the great trade routes across Europe. No Genoese or other European ships called at French ports except in an emergency, while the neighbouring commercial regions in Germany, Flanders and even England continued to grow at a great pace, widening the cultural distance from the Paris basin. The insurrections in the city only made wider and deeper the division between the rest of commercial Europe and Paris.

Throughout this period, the primary motif of the city was disorder. In 1358, the university made a formal complaint to Charles V that the streets around the rue de Fouarre, where most classes were held, were being used at night by criminals, who brought with them whores and other *femmes malpropres*. Students and professors were disgusted each morning to find urine, excrement, stale wine and vomit lining the streets. Two large gates were built at rue de Fouarre, Place Maubert, rue des Deux-Portes-Saint-Sauveur and other places in the city. Students themselves favoured the bank of the Seine known as the Pré aux Clercs for fishing parties and general revelry. When the abbé of Saint-Germain tried to put an end to this in 1343, it led to bloody conflict and went as high as the Pope. No agreement was properly reached but the Parisian clergy added this to the long list of grudges it held against the university.

Charles V sought to encourage the arts, and under his reign the collection of books within the Louvre grew larger than it had ever been before. But development within Paris had shrivelled away to the extent that by 1383, as shown in the fifth 'great map' of Paris, the only buildings of any note in the past fifty years were the fortifications constructed at the gates to the city. Beyond the walls, at what is now La Villette and the Porte Saint-Martin, there was a no man's land, inhabited by the starving, lepers and deserters, which extended for some miles towards the forest.

11. The English Devils

Among the various catastrophes that afflicted Paris and France, from war and famine to revolt, was the weakness and stupidity of the monarchy. Most disturbingly, King Charles VI, who ruled the country from 1392 to 1422, veered dangerously and unpredictably between clear-eyed sanity and the most demented folly. Charles's madness was probably pathological – most likely a variant of schizophrenia or encephalitis – but either way the symptoms had severe consequences for the kingdom. He was capable of brooding, murderous rage and once on a hunting expedition ran his sword through four courtiers whom he suspected of betrayal. On another occasion, he dressed as a 'wild man' for an official banquet, shocking guests and frightening those who knew him well. In his later years, Charles thought that he was made of glass and had iron rods inserted into his clothes so he would not shatter on contact with other human beings.[1]

The most direct and unfortunate consequence of this debilitating condition was that the king's two brothers, the duc de Bourgogne (Burgundy), leader of the Burgundians, and the duc d'Orléans, who led a faction called the Armagnacs, were constantly locked into a struggle over who would control the Crown. The sibling rivalry extended into every political sphere, at home and abroad, encompassing papal politics, policy in the Low Countries and internal struggles over the size of French territories. For Parisians, the matter was complicated even further by the fact that, unlike other major centres in France, the city of Paris did not have a charter independent of the monarchy. As such, more than any other place in France, it was subject to direct rule from the Crown and, most crucially, its capricious ways.

The family divisions were clearly announced in the earliest years of Charles VI's reign. He was still the boy-king when he returned with his uncles to Paris from a successful campaign against the Flemish in 1392. More than 20,000 Parisians, armed to show their support for Charles, turned up at the city walls to hail him as a conqueror.

To general bafflement, they were told that such an open show of support had disturbed the king, and to return home. The following day, Charles's battle-hardened troops entered the city, arresting and then executing the senior civil administrators. A huge fine and severe taxes were levied on the city. The Parisians could not understand this behaviour and noted it as an aberration or a sign of the king's madness. But it was no accident that the following year saw the construction of the Bastille, a place that would be hated and feared for centuries.

Lights Out

The slow-burning rivalry between Burgundy and Orléans came to a head at half past seven in the evening on 23 November 1407. In a dark passage near the Porte Barbette, the duc d'Orléans was murdered in the street by eighteen of Burgundy's thugs in an alleyway near the convent of the Hospitaliers Saint-Gervais. The body was taken straight to the church of the Blancs-Manteaux in the heart of the Marais. When Jean sans Peur ('the Fearless') – successor to the old duc de Bourgogne, who had died in 1404 – went to see the corpse, it apparently started spurting blood, showering Jean and thereby identifying him as the assassin.

Public opinion was however firmly on Burgundy's side. He was seen as a hard man who could unite the nation in the face of external threats and bring together squabbling factions under the Crown. Charles VI, practically demented all the time, was now an irrelevance. Burgundy took effective charge of the government, promising reforms in the administration and to lighten the tax burden. Corrupt officials were sacked or executed. But Jean's ruthlessness could also quickly turn to reckless cruelty, which could have unforeseen consequences.

In 1413, the Burgundian forces murdered what was left of their Armagnac rivals in Paris. The corpses, according to one observer, 'were piled high in the streets like pigs in mud'.[2] This massacre inevitably provoked a hostile reaction from erstwhile moderates such as the *prévôt des marchands*, Jean Jouvenal, eventually leading to the resurgence of Armagnac forces, who regained control of the capital and held on to it until 1418. The return of the Burgundians in that year was heralded by a fresh massacre.

Throughout this period, the political administration in Paris teetered constantly on the brink of chaos. The only ones to gain from the situation were the English. The war between France and England was reaching its climax. The English, profiting from their alliance with the Burgundians, came to Paris in 1420. Despised by ordinary Parisians, who were also weary of the years of internecine conflict, they none the less occupied key positions on the river's edge of the Right Bank well into the next decade, when the tide of war turned against them. The Dukes of Salisbury, Suffolk and Willoughby ventured further south, owning property at what is now Saint-Michel.

Originally, the English had come with the promise of establishing stability and bringing an end to bloodshed. The English occupation was, however, one of the darkest periods Paris had yet known. The hard-fought-for authority of the *prévôt* and his four aldermen (*échevins*) started to disintegrate, along with the city police and night guards; there was little respect for legality within or outside the administration. Businesses began to collapse as the city government's jurisdiction over the sale of wine, firewood, essential foodstuffs and the business of the river itself, was seen to be failing.

The city was now dependent on English financial aid, which never came, and English law, which was sporadically applied. Few Parisians could bring themselves to swear an oath of allegiance to the English – those that did were said to be thereafter under a curse – but all were forced to bow to increasing English might, whose representatives stalked the city with a lordly swagger while its native citizens starved, or survived on dregs. The memory of the English as devils lived on in France long after the occupation in the expression *d'anglois couëz* ('an Englishman's tail'). The Parisian folk tale behind this phrase is based on the story of Saint Augustine's evangelical visit to Rochester, where he was apparently insulted and had pigs' and calves' tails tacked on to his clothes. As a Divine punishment, the English race were all given pigs' tails – the mark of a true Anglo-Saxon.[3]

The English also left behind two statues that, according to legend, destroyed themselves as if by magic when Calais was finally seized back from them in 1558. All other traces of the occupation in Paris, linguistic or cultural, have long since been wiped away in shame. The street sign on the rue des Anglais, where the English traditionally drank, sang and brawled, is still regularly vandalized some six hundred years on from the occupation.

Paris also fell into a deeper lawlessness under the English than it had known for a long time. Although various orders and laws were made throughout this period demanding that citizens leave candles in their windows at night, nobody obeyed these instructions, for fear of making themselves a target. And so by the end of the century, the only public lighting in the city was, as it had been under Philippe le Bel, three great torches, which burned at Grand-Châtelet, at the Tower of Nesle and at the cemetery of the Saints-Innocents, to the south of the city.

The darkness was so complete that the city guards could report fifteen unsolved and unsolvable killings on a nightly basis. Instead of placing their faith in government, Parisians watched the sky for omens, praying for deliverance from the nightmarish chaos of daily life in the city. In August 1400, a thunderstorm broke over the city, but it was hard to work out what God was saying to the beleaguered population. One contemporary eye-witness reported that 'such thunder was heard, between five and six in the morning, that an image of Our Lady, which was on the altar at Saint-Ladre, made of strong new stone, was broken into pieces and blown into the street'.[4] And at La Villette de Saint-Ladre, two men were struck by lightning, their shoes, stockings and tunics burnt to a crisp.

12. Machaberey's Dance

The everyday Parisian world of the early fifteenth century was dangerous, volatile and circumscribed by religious edicts that did little to control the population. The city was overcrowded and dirty. Since the time of Philippe-Auguste in the twelfth century, no great building had been constructed outside the city walls built by Charles V, and which encircled the city from Porte Saint-Martin to Saint-Germain. Despite the losses from war and disease, the population had, however, swollen to some 200,000 people. The result was a squalid and febrile labyrinth. This world is described in the anonymous *Journal d'un bourgeois de Paris*, a grim, sometimes bitter account of life written some time between 1405 and 1449 in a city at war with itself and the rest of France, and enduring the English occupation.

Although the 'bourgeois' of the *Journal* records the larger movements of civil and international war, his first allegiance is always to the city of Paris. His concerns are also relentlessly personal and domestic – harsh frosts in winter, a plague of cockchafers in the summer are all recorded for the impact they make on daily life. The same goes for his account of the Hundred Years War, which presents a worm's-eye view of history. Whenever hostile forces approach the capital, the 'bourgeois' – one of the first in a long line of Parisian middle-class moaners – grumbles that the price of bread goes up, while cheese and eggs cannot be found. This is not only the fault of the hated English who – O irreligious aberration! – boiled meat as well as killing children, but also of priests and soldiers and the likes of Joan of Arc, who far from representing a model of patriotic and religious valour, is here debunked as a nuisance and a bad influence on the young.[1] (None the less, although she appeared in the city only briefly, at the storming of the Porte Saint-Honoré in 1429, where she was wounded, Jeanne d'Arc played a pivotal role in the history of Paris by providing Charles VII with the courage and faith to be crowned at Rheims and to unify France. As a counterpoint to these facts, it is no small irony that in recent years she has been adopted as a heroine of the extreme Right, who use her statue on the rue de Rivoli as a rallying point during elections and at times of national crisis.)

It is clear from the *Journal* and other texts of roughly the same period that by the early fifteenth century the use of the term 'Parisian' to describe not only an inhabitant of the city but also a way of behaving and thinking was obviously in common and easy usage. In *Le Mesnagier de Paris* ('The Housewife of Paris') – a book written in 1393 by an *haut bourgeois* as a guide to proper behaviour for his wife in the city – she is instructed to learn the arts of dancing and singing, shown how to run a household, choose servants, dress well and know her place in society, who to look down on and who to look up to. The middle classes clearly lived well: the author discusses, for example, the best way to cook or prepare venison, oranges and exotic delicacies such as the small root vegetable known as a *carotte*. Although the wife of the *haut bourgeois* is instructed not to mingle with the nobility, she is also told that she is in no way inferior to them.[2]

Two of the chief characteristics of the 'Parisian' mentality were held to be superstition and a practical interest in bribery. The faith in Divine intervention, and the propitiating effects of ready cash, could sometimes backfire, however. In 1413, Paris fell under the control of the Duke of Bavaria and the comte d'Armagnac, who both bore sizeable grudges against the city. They could not be bought off for any amount of money. At this time, the anonymous 'bourgeois' of the *Journal* records how the city's population was laid low by a mysterious plague of coughing called the *tac* or *horion*. No one died of the disease but it was reported that the cough was so strong that men had permanently ruptured their genitals and pregnant women gone into labour prematurely; there were no priests who could sing high Mass anywhere in Paris. At first the disease was blamed on the small children who went to fetch wine or mustard in the evening in the rue Mouffetard, singing lines from a popular rhyme: 'What a cough you've caught in the cunt, old girl. What a cough, what a cough in the cunt.' Parisians joked half seriously with each other that this had displeased God who had made the air 'foul and corrupt, so that everything was rotten',[3] and who now really had given them 'a cunt of a cough' to pay them back. No physician could offer an alternative explanation, until blame shifted itself on to the greedy dukes who lay encamped at the gates of the city.

As the political situation in France shifted, and the balance of power left Bavarian and Armagnac hands and went back again towards Paris, the curse was suddenly lifted. Traders made money again, Mass was sung, prostitutes went back to whoring, bonfires were lit and the city was reborn. The 'bourgeois' happily noted that none of the wine that year 'went thick or ropy or stinking'.[4]

'A nimble knave; a pleasant theefe'

As it emerged from the Hundred Years War, like most cities in the aftermath of bloody conflict, Paris was characterized by a headlong flight into pleasure. This was a world alien to the eminently respectable 'bourgeois' – one of the most notorious killjoys in French literary history – but brilliantly described by the poet François Villon, who called Paris a 'Great Carnival' and wrote about bandits, virgins and drunks.[5]

Villon could also be tender. He describes children shopping for mustard and bread at mealtimes, old women gossiping around a fire, beggars sleeping in the warmth of a bakery, prostitutes swapping tips on professional expertise and protocol. It is a world of small sensual pleasures still recognizable to us today. This was a city that had undergone great hardship and within which most of its citizens were still on intimate terms with poverty, disease and starvation. Villon had the same relationship with his city as a peasant had with the land: nothing was out of bounds to him and through his poetry he was able to record and report how life was lived in Paris at its social and criminal edges as well as at its centre.

Nobody is quite sure when or where François Villon was born or what his real name was. Appropriately enough, the few traces of his life that he left behind are to be found in police records, which in Paris have never been a truly reliable source of information at the best of times. The apocrypha and anecdotes that are recorded almost by chance in his poetry were written not for posterity but off the cuff to amuse boozy crowds of failed students, army deserters, pickpockets and vagabonds in Left Bank drinking-shops. In the seventeenth century, Cotgrave notes the word *villon*, and he defines it as a 'cousener, conycatcher, cunning or wittie rogue; a nimble knave; a pleasant theefe; (for such was one François Villon, whose death a halter suited to his life)'.[6] Villon was an educated hustler, with a taste for crime and vice. Although he spent time in prison for murder and robbery, he was never condemned to death. Still, he feared death enormously and some of his finest lines are drawn from the fact that he was both a sinner and a believer. When George Orwell came to Paris in the late 1920s and lodged in the rue du Pot de Fer in the Latin Quarter, he brought a copy of Villon's poems with him as his guide.

Villon's Paris was in fact a relatively small area, stretching from what is now the Pont des Arts to the southern edge of the Latin Quarter, with occasional forays into the Cité or over on to the Right Bank. He was born near Pontoise, where his father died prematurely, probably of drink. His mother lived for a long time (until 1461 at least) but he was none the less adopted by Guillaume de Villon, Chaplain of Saint-Benoît-le-Bétourné in the Latin Quarter. He was educated at the university, achieving the status of *licencié* and then *maistre-ès-arts*, although he acquired a reputation at the same time as a difficult and often dissolute student.

Villon also had a shifting identity at this point, often identifying himself according to circumstance as 'maître François des Loges, autrement dit de Villon', 'Franciscus de Montcorbier' or 'Moultcorbier'. He fell out with the university and dropped out of his studies (in theology) in 1451. The most probable explanation for this was his role in a prank involving the removal by a group of drunken students of a piece of ancient stonework called the *pet-au-diable* ('Devil's fart') from the property of a Mademoiselle de la Bruyère. The authorities took this 'crime' seriously and there were violent armed assaults on the students of the Left Bank in retaliation. University professors went on strike in anger at this response in 1453–4.

Villon himself, disgusted by the stupidity and random nastiness of both the ecclesiastical and academic authorities (they were indeed barely separate in those days), slunk away into the dispossessed student proletariat. This was a vast army of young men with no trade, no visible means of support and nowhere to go. Unlike those students attached to a community or college, these students were left to their own devices once they had enrolled at the university. They were identified as drinkers, sexual barbarians and subversives and treated by the police just as harshly as any other 'marginal class', such as vagabonds or army deserters.

It was at about this time that Villon started to mix with *coquillards*, the dangerous bands of deserters, robbers and murderers, most of them economic or social casualties of the Hundred Years War, who gathered outside the city gates of French towns at night, when they were not roaming the countryside terrifying peasants. The *coquillards* spoke their own impenetrable slang and Villon became an adept at this sinuous, ever-shifting tongue, related to the Gypsy languages.

Villon had by now already begun composing *ballades*, written with considerable skill and distinction, when on 5 June 1455 he was involved in the most serious incident so far: the killing of a priest. Villon's friends, the only witnesses to the incident, argued that Villon had merely acted in self-defence, fighting off a challenge to take his purse off him. This was deemed most unlikely, although many priests in Paris at that time were known to be less than saintly figures.

None the less, Villon decided to flee Paris rather than risk a trial and certain death. He returned a year later, apparently protected by a letter from his adoptive father, another letter from a lawyer and, allegedly, the watchful eye of some of the leading *coquillards*, who by now ran riot in the Latin Quarter.

Villon never sought fame, but as a young man had a high reputation for entertaining the *voyous* ('hooligans') who were also his friends; he was effectively an entertainer who mixed tragedy, pathos and comedy in roughly equal measure. He frequented taverns like the Père Lunette, a dive on the rue des Anglais known for being all the more rowdy due to a clientèle of drunken English students. It also, most notoriously, served *rosbif*, pickles and ale in the English fashion. Other favoured drinking haunts named by Villon, and frequented by the *coquillards*, included Le Heaume at Porte Baudoyer, Le Grand Godet at Place de la Grève, Le Barillet at Grand-Châtelet and La Pomme de Pin on rue de la Juiverie, Île de la Cité.

But despite his growing reputation as a poet, Villon was still fatally attracted by crime. Towards the Christmas of 1456, with four accomplices, including two disgraced former comrades from the university, he planned his most ambitious misdemeanour yet: the burglary of the chapel of the College of Saint-Navarre.

This time, when the plot was discovered, Villon had to get out of Paris quickly and, to all intents and purposes, for ever. This was an exile he could not stand, however, and in spite of the dangers he returned a year later, at first cautiously half disguised and then flagrantly and drunkenly himself. But his rackety life caught up with him once more and he was arrested again in 1463, having been caught up in a street fight in the course of which a certain Ferrebuc had been almost fatally stabbed with a dagger. It looked likely that Villon would be hanged on account of his 'bad life', but the sentence was again commuted to banishment, this time for six years. No one knows how or where Villon died.[7]

In his life and work Villon announced the birth of a long Parisian tradition of poets, writers and singers who played the role of a suicidal clown, *le bon follastre* – the most recent of these being Serge Gainsbourg, who died in 1991 from cigarettes and booze, and whose slurred, self-knowing precision and antinomianism were all entirely 'Villonesque'. Villon is commonly described as the patron of the city's dispossessed, the deserters, the destitute or those who simply refuse to work.

Villon's city of drunks, vagabonds and misfits is still there. It is on the city's wastelands, on the banks of the river and in the despised and neglected outer suburbs. Most of all it can be found in the metro, where the Parisian *clochard* – a noble tramp celebrated in verse and song for his addiction to *gratte-gorge* (rough red wine) and freedom – has in recent years been replaced by an army of SDF (Sans Domicile Fixe). These are the Parisian homeless whose aimless journeys on the city's transport system are diametrically opposed to those of their fellow passengers, who move in fixed patterns between home, work and leisure. There is little noble or poetic here: nobody celebrates this raw world in song. But the violence and desperation in this micro-society are an authentic echo of Villon's Paris.

Carnival Scenes

The author of the *Journal d'un bourgeois de Paris* was undoubtedly a kind man – he laments convincingly the condition of the poor and he is genuinely appalled by the 'burnt carcass' of Joan of Arc. The 'bourgeois' shares with Villon a great compassion and, more than this, an active curiosity with regard to the changing face of his city.

This is why, like most Parisians, the 'bourgeois' was driven by curiosity to go and see the Gypsies who came to the city for the first time in 1427. They had not been allowed into the city but were camped at La Chapelle-Saint-Denis, several hundred of then claiming to be the remnants of a 'nation' of several thousand. They said they came from 'Lower Egypt' and gave a garbled account of their itinerary, including conversions to Christianity and Islam, visits to the Pope, who imposed on them the penance that for seven years they should go to and fro in the world without ever sleeping in a bed, while ordering every bishop to give them a one-off payment of ten thousand livres as they travelled through.

The 'bourgeois' was fascinated by these strangers, and curious most of all about their alleged mastery of the black arts. 'Their children were very, very clever, both the boys and the girls,' he noted:

Most of them – almost all of them – had their ears pierced and wore a silver ring in each ear, or two rings in each. This, they said, was a mark of good birth in their country. The men were very dark, with curly hair; the women were the ugliest you ever saw and the darkest, all with scarred faces and hair as black as a horse's tail. They had no dresses but an old coarse piece of blanket tied on the shoulder with a bit of cloth or string; under all this covering was a wretched smock or shift. But in spite of their poverty they had sorceresses among them who looked at people's hands and told them what had happened to them or what would happen. They brought trouble into many marriages, for they would say to the husband, 'Your wife has cuckolded you,' or to the wife, 'Your husband has deceived you.' What was worse, it was said that when they talked to people they contrived – either by magic arts or by other means, or the devil's help or by their own skill and cunning – to make money flow out of other people's purses into their own.

The 'bourgeois' visited the Gypsies three or four times and sounded mildly peeved and disappointed not to have been swindled himself.[8]

Obviously this sort of unchristian behaviour could not be allowed to continue and, somewhat nervously, wary of their diabolical powers, the Bishop of Paris ordered them to depart, which they did apparently without leaving their customary curse behind them. Paris was not short of novelty for long, however: within a few short weeks, the 'bourgeois' was able to report that not only had the quality of wine improved as the price dropped, but Paris was visited by a young woman of about twenty-eight or thirty from Hainaut called Margot, who was the best tennis player anyone had ever seen (tennis was then regularly played in the rue Grenier Saint-Lazare and at the Petit Temple). Margot played forehand and backhand (indicating that racquets were in use at this early date) and, the 'bourgeois' excitedly reports, was a match for all but the strongest men.[9]

The 'bourgeois' reports these events alongside accounts of public festivals, fluctuations in the price of beer and turnips and the most appalling massacres, sometimes perpetrated by the English and at other times by the vicious Armagnacs or a group of bandits known as 'the Flayers', who haunted the roads between Paris and its outlying towns and villages. He reports on 'Grand Politics' from a distance, probably informed by disdain, being more concerned with the comings and goings in the rue Saint-Martin where he lived. Sometimes politics comes literally to his door, as in 1436 when the English, about three hundred of them, swept down the Grand'rue Saint-Martin, banging on doors, crying, 'St George! St George! You French traitors, we'll kill the lot of you!' The English eventually came across two 'honourable, decent householders', Jean le Prêtre and Jean des Croustez, who were 'slaughtered ten times over'.[10]

The streets of the city during this period were more usually alive with a cacophony of travelling salesmen, beggars and shopkeepers. Although they were bound by a law of 1270 to refrain from hassling potential customers in another shop, tradesmen were still allowed to hail passers-by at random. Each trade was distinguished by its own rhyme and slang (which persisted long into the twentieth century) and by its own particularities: women traditionally sold flour, fruits, clothes, furniture and pottery; men dealt in heavier goods or those such as meat and wine that were considered to be more substantial. In each part of the city, town-criers and watchmen announced public events, executions and the time of day.

Although the city was evidently vibrant and ever-changing – in the manner of Villon's 'Great Carnival' – life was also extremely harsh. In particular, the 'bourgeois' was concerned with the sufferings of 'le menu peuple', the poor of Paris, who had no control over politics or their daily lives. He kept a regular tally of food prices across the city, reporting regularly on the sparse provisions available to the poor. 'Black and ill-flavoured bread' was their staple diet; at other times rotten fruit and even the carcasses of dead dogs were eaten to stave off famine. The 'bourgeois' laid the blame for these conditions squarely at the feet of vain warmongers in the nobility.[11] The casualness with which he expressed this view indicates that, like the easy acceptance of death, it was the prevailing attitude of the middle-class citizens of the city.

The Dance of Death

Corpses were a common sight in the city at this time. Villon wrote beautiful elegiac lines in honour of the tramps who had been frozen to death during the bitter winter nights on the edges of the Seine. Less obviously poetic were the stinking bodies of plague victims, the leprous or starving, which lay in the muddy streets to be collected up at dusk like so much waste matter by the gravedigger who carted them off to the charnel houses of Saints-Innocents.

The cemetery of the Saints-Innocents had been for a long time integral to the life of the inner city. Originally, it had been a Roman cemetery, which in the Roman fashion had been established on one of the routes out of the city. As Paris had grown outwards and around the cemetery, it had become fixed as the centre of the medieval city. The soil of the cemetery, a relatively small space at the centre of the Right Bank and not bigger than the public squares of the city, was alleged to have great powers, to be so powerful in fact that it could 'eat up a corpse', that is to say strip it of its flesh, in a matter of days.

Parisians were not afraid of death, although they did their best to avoid it, and the site, visited by Villon and countless other low-life aficionados, was well known for prostitution and other pleasant vices. This in turn attracted petty thieves, touts and itinerant wine-sellers. The authorities, partly through superstition and partly through indifference, turned a blind eye.

Less visible to the ordinary criminal or the police were the necromancers and alchemists who cited the spot as one of magical significance, or came here at night in pursuit of the raw materials needed for their 'experimental sciences' (the supposed house of the alchemist Nicolas Flamel, still covered in alchemical hieroglyphics, stands on rue de Montmorency a few steps away from where the cemetery once was).

In 1424, the 'bourgeois' of Paris also noted, again casually as was his manner, the appearance in the cemetery of the 'Danse Macabré', a series of murals of a 'dance with Death' marking the site of a plague pit. These were the first versions of a fashion that spread through England and the Low Countries, taking a particular hold in Germany. The most popular forms were paintings in churches or cemeteries, or wood cuts. Common to all versions were the representation of Death in the literal form of the Reaper, taking lives and revealing the pointlessness of finite human existence.

The origin of the term 'Macabré' is obscure. The fact that it is in the possessive form ('de Macabré' being implied) has suggested that it was the original name of either the painter of the murals, or the poet who wrote the inscriptions underneath them. Several other, more exotic etymologies, have been suggested, including derivations from the Syrian Arabic word for 'gravedigger' (*meqabberey*) or a distortion of the biblical 'Maccabée', or even a pagan god 'Machaberey' (the term which appears in English in the engravings in Paron's Yard near St Paul's, executed in 1439 and destroyed in 1539). This is unlikely to be the case, however, since the term 'Macabré' appears in a poem written about 1376 by one Jean Lefèvre. Whatever its origins, the *danse macabre* evidently addressed a need to stare death full in the face. All that remains now of this plague pit are the arches of what were once the charnel houses which lined the cemetery along the rue de la Ferronerie. Once these were piled high with indiscriminate heaps of bones and rotting flesh, to be nibbled by rats. Now there are designer clothes shops, a food stall, a perfumerie, all subsumed into the parade of Forum des Halles, the shopping mall that goes deep underground into the cemetery.

13. Maps and Legends

For the past fifteen hundred years, Paris had been copiously represented, with varying degrees of accuracy, in carvings, paintings and illuminated manuscripts. There were, however, no usable maps of the city until the 1450s. Paris was by now known to provincials and foreigners as a legendary place. But it was also full of hazards; no one could really know the city in depth. Those who needed to be guided around – merchants from the provinces or from foreign parts – relied on touts and hustlers who fleeced them, led them into the filthiest and most dangerous backstreets, or, on a few occasions, proved invaluable friends in an incomprehensible and hostile environment. If you were not from the city – this much was quickly deduced by watchful predators from your clothes, accent and manners – finding your way around Paris without being robbed, murdered or simply getting lost was largely a matter of chance.

The Romans of course had made military maps and their urban planners drew up rigorous plans, which did not survive the ravages of the post-imperial era. One of the few remaining maps of Lutetia is a police map, although this was made in 1705 and, like nearly all other maps of the Gallo-Roman city, is mostly fantasy.[1] The idea of making maps of the city also came from Italy, where map-making as an art form had been popular since the twelfth century. This activity did not necessarily have any other political or commercial function – the map of Venice made by the Milanese Hellia Magadizzio in 1110 for the doge Ordellaffo Fallio, for instance, is an exemplary version of a map that barely corresponds to reality and has only a decorative function. In 1494, however, François II, the Marquis of Mantua, came up with the project of setting a view of a great city in a similar fresco for the *camera della città* that he was building in his palazzo. The choice was between Paris and Jerusalem.

The choice was simpler than it might have seemed: Paris was nearer at hand and politically and strategically more important. The astrologer and chiromancer Paride Cesara sent François a message, promising to make a book describing not just Paris, but many other towns, along with stories and legends, and the lives of dukes and kings. This was clearly a reference to the depiction of Paris in a German volume, the *Liber cronicarum* ('Book of Chronicles') of Hartmann, published by Schedel of Nuremberg in 1493. The only problem was that this was an entirely imaginary Paris as neither the artist nor his publisher had ever seen the city.[2]

The first halfway accurate maps of Paris appeared in the 1550s, the so-called *Plans de Munster* or *de Braun*, carved on wood, representing the city roughly around 1530, and offering an aerial view of it for the first time.[3] Their publication was driven by the needs of kings and their economists to make sense of the mutable dimensions of the city. From this period onwards, the cartographers of Paris played a defining role in the culture and politics of the city. The names of the great map-makers of the next two centuries – Quesnel and de Vassalieu, de Gomboust, de Bretez and Verniquet – are as important in the history of the life of the city as any literary artist or thinker. The map-makers of Paris changed not only how Parisians and visitors thought about the city, but also how they could actively make use of its infinite variety.

The first maps of Paris represented the city as a circular or oval space; indeed, it was commonly described as being round like an egg. They also looked at the city sideways on, presenting north on the right and south on the left (hence the present-day divisions between Right and Left Bank). This was an imperfect symmetry, but it had the advantage of presenting the city as a world unto itself. The axis shifted in the next fifty years as maps were turned around 360 degrees to reflect more accurately the division of political power in the city (the mercantile Right Bank now dominates the 'intellectual' district of the Left Bank). The circular city was also preserved long into the twentieth century by the development of the *boulevard périphérique*, which encircles the city with traffic. Beyond this are the uncharted territories of the *banlieue*, which in the Parisian imagination is as dangerous now as the forests of the fifteenth-century city.

The first maps of the city were also intended to capture its greatness, its monuments, palaces and churches. There were no individual lives recorded in these maps, but rather a static representation of royal splendour. This again was clearly political, and the likes of Quesnel were admirably open about their attempts to map a city quite unlike any other in Europe or the world. The same frank ambitions to further political aims in map-making applied to the police and military maps of the city, which shifted the focus of their attention on the division between the wealthy west and the poor and potentially revolutionary east. It is, however, a truism that, on one level, all maps, past and present, are fictions, the subjective representation of a place by one or various individuals. Then as now, the only true means of capturing the city, of grasping its essence, are instinct and intuition.

The fifteenth century is commonly portrayed as a period of decline: the death of an era. This is, more specifically, the influential and sometimes brilliant argument of Johan Huizinga, who points out that the essential consequence of several generations of bitter warfare, fought mostly on French soil, was the decline and decomposition of older idealisms.[4] The final years of the Middle Ages were a 'waning', the twilight of a vast and complex part of history that presciently saw its own end in the reality of a world that was changing faster than ever before. François Villon began the *Testament* in 1461, the last great book of the medieval period as well as a precursor of the early modern humanism of Rabelais and others. In 1470, the first printing press was set up in Paris.

The two events were not unrelated: both bore witness to the speed of change as well as the profound shifts in thought and behaviour that drove history forward. In Paris, the 'waning' of the Middle Ages was also a period of reconstruction, however. A fundamental shift was taking place, as the European world felt itself turning again towards Italy and the ancient civilizations.

PART THREE
Slaughterhouse City
1461–1669

Why would I want to live in Paris?
I know not how to trick, lie and deceive.

Nicolas Boileau, 1660

In the old city of Paris
There are thirty-six streets
And in the *quartier* of Hulepoix eighty-three more:
And in the *quartier* of Saint-Denis three hundred and six.
Count them and be at your ease.
The Devil knows them all well.

Les cris et les rues de Paris, 1567

It is well known that Satan visits Paris often.
His appearance always signals disaster.
For this reason, he is at home there.

René Benoît, priest of Saint-Marcel, 1568

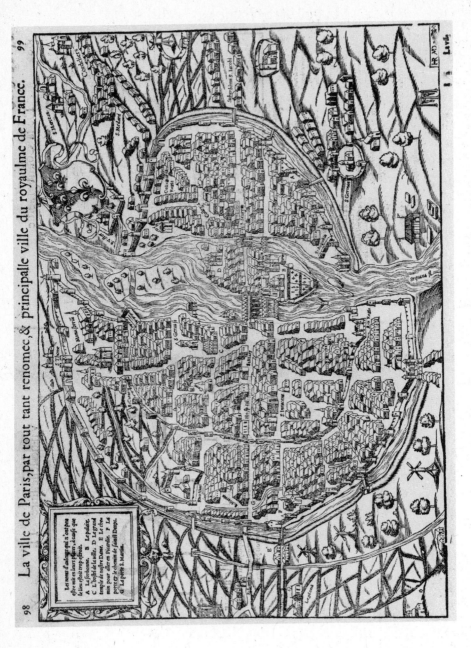

A plan of Paris, La Ville de Paris, par tout tant renommée, & principalle ville du royaulme de France, en 1548, by Sébastien Munster, 1568.

14. Dark with Excess of Light

Paris was indeed now prosperous and overflowing with people and ideas. Only Lyons, at the crossroads of Italy, Spain and Germany, stood in any way as a serious rival to growing Parisian supremacy. The southern city was indeed briefly a hotbed of literary and philosophical activity during the early part of the sixteenth century, producing figures such as Louise Labé, Maurice Scève and Louis Meigret, who were deeply steeped in Italian culture and who married the influence of Petrarch and Bembo to the French language. But Lyons did not yet have a university and the Lyonnais were famously more concerned with making money rather than cultivating ideas. The Loire Valley was equally alive with writers – Ronsard, Du Bellay, Jean Bodin and Rabelais all came from this region – and there were universities in the surrounding territories of Angers, Orléans (which taught civic law, a subject still unknown in Paris), Bourges and Poitiers. Yet cultural life remained focused on Paris.

More to the point, although Paris produced few writers of note during the sixteenth century, art, philosophy and money flowed in equal measure into the capital, attracted to the city by its growing influence beyond France. As Paris consolidated its position as an intellectual and political capital in the wake of the Hundred Years War, speculators invested in increasingly grandiose architectual visions of the city. Much of the city was conceived on neo-classical, Italian models – straight roads, ornamental squares, colonnades and bridges – and well-heeled Parisians aped Italian clothes, food, manners and speech (the French language, and particularly Parisian French, was at this time infested with Italicisms in vocabulary and accent).

The nascent Renaissance city could still be a dark and pestilential place, however. When the new bridge at Notre-Dame had been swept away by floods in 1499, it hardly augured well, so it was felt, for the coming century (the high volume of traffic in the city and the density of the population living on the bridges meant that all the bridges now had to be secured with chains). Yet this was a period of extraordinary optimism. The new mood was reflected in tiny details that improved the quality of daily life, such as the appearance of the first street signs (previously both citizens and visitors had been obliged to rely on haphazard door-signs or simply guesswork) and the reshaping of the stinking charnel houses of the Saints-Innocents cemetery into a perfectly banal fountain in the highly decorative style of the age. Given the generally wretched conditions of city life, however, it was still surprising that it should attract such high praise from apparently the most clear-sighted and rational writers of the era. 'Farewell to Paris sur Seine,' wrote Marc-Antoine de Saint-Amant in homage to the quick wit of its working classes. 'Superb city . . . where I learned to use words sharper than blades.'[1]

Most surprisingly, and uncharacteristically, Michel de Montaigne – normally the most provincial of writers – praised the gloomy and sinister city as the 'glory of France and ornament of the world'. He went on, dousing his words no doubt with liberal amounts of irony: 'I love it tenderly, with all its warts and stains. I am indeed only French through this great city.'[2]

Most importantly, however, as even the stubborn Montaigne grudgingly recognized, the seeds of the Renaissance in Paris lay as much in old native idealisms as in imported models. These writers who lived in or visited the city looked out to the 'universal' Europe of ideas and progress, but were as often determinedly Parisian in their assurance and swagger. Clément Marot praised the women of Paris – previously noted in the poetry of the medieval period (and not just Villon) for their toughness and coarse sexual manners – as surpassing those of Italy; high praise indeed in this era of the cult of all things Italian. This self-confidence was reflected in the reconstruction of the city itself: the Louvre was restored and improved, preserving some of the original work dating from Philippe-Auguste; work continued on the Tuileries palace and then the city walls. At the same time, the Sorbonne was growing in stature as the crucible of new wisdom. Indeed, it was native self-belief in this city rather than admiration for Italy which was expressed in the formula that Paris was to be the 'New Rome'.

The Spider King

Louis XI is commonly described as the last medieval king and the first of the Renaissance monarchs. Certainly his coronation was performed with a Renaissance flamboyance not entirely in keeping with the mood of the times. He was crowned in 1461 at Rheims, the traditional site of the coronation of kings of France, and was mobbed by enthusiastic crowds each step of the way to Paris, which he loudly and explicitly had declared the capital of his nation.

Although the Parisians were outwardly enthusiastic, hailing the king as he entered the city at Porte Saint-Denis on his way to Notre-Dame, they had also seen and heard all of this before and were not slow to make sarcastic remarks about the monarchy and its precariousness. The manner of Louis's entrance only served as further fuel to those who were dubious about him – he proceeded on horseback, his head covered with a blue satin canopy, accompanied by a fountain which produced wine and milk, as well as an entourage of bare-breasted young women, 'Sirens', in an artificial pond. This last sight was welcomed by a contemporary chronicler, who made a point of drily admiring the women's breasts as 'droit, séparé, rond et dur' ('elevated, separated, round and firm').[3] The king himself did not attract as fulsome a compliment.

The ridiculous scene, however, belied Louis's low political cunning, an altogether necessary skill in the murky world of the Parisian court. Louis anticipated Machiavelli by bringing to the craft of kingship the black arts of flattery, intrigue and deception. His main enemies, at least at first, were the potentially rebellious nobles of Brittany, Bourbon, Orléans, Charolais and Dunois. Equally dangerous was the clear fact, as revealed at the coronation, that the populace of Paris could not be trusted either. In his residence at the Hôtel des Tournelles (he deliberately eschewed the Louvre), Louis constantly flattered to deceive during endless dinners and banquets, winning over his enemies with his 'grace of speech'. His vision extended beyond Paris to France, and then to Europe, where he sought to establish France, via stealth rather than war, as the primary power. He was called 'the Universal Spider' for the way in which his web of intrigue extended over so many apparently diverse interests.

It was during this period that France assumed the hexagonal shape it has today: Maine, Anjou, Provence and Burgundy were all finally subdued. Louis XI's interests extended as far as Naples, establishing a relationship with Italian political culture which would prove to be a poisoned chalice for centuries to come. For now, however, it was enough that French hegemony was powerful, largely unchallenged, and enriched by the cultural treasure-house of its neighbour Italy, the true engine-room of the Renaissance. But Parisians resented these foreign adventures and the high taxes they had to endure to pay for them. It was just as well that Louis spent much of his time away from the city.

He was not altogether negligent of its cultural life, though. Most importantly, he encouraged the development of the city's first printing press, in the face of fierce opposition from the scribes' and booksellers' guilds, which had so far had a monopoly over texts sold in the city. Printed books had first appeared in Paris in 1463, brought there by two Germans, Fust and Schöffer, but these had been quickly confiscated by the guilds. Louis, on the other hand, paid the men compensation of 2,500 crowns, a substantial sum that was meant to show that he was thanking them for introducing the new technology to the city. The two Germans set themselves up in the rue Saint-Jacques at the sign of the Soleil d'Or and, although the first books to appear were in High German Gothic script (the move to Roman took place under François I), publishing was soon to become a flourishing industry. A press was established at the Sorbonne in 1470 by two Swiss printers at the invitation of Jean Heynlin and Guillaume Fichet, a scholar with rooms to spare in the college.[4]

One of the less predictable consequences of Louis XI's prolonged absences from Paris, and the absences of the kings who followed him (they too were often caught up in Italian adventures), was that the city, lacking a court life, was taken over by the bourgeoisie, who were able to afford quite palatial properties at reduced prices. The fashionable nobility, not necessarily close to the court, settled for a while on the Left Bank, rue Saint-André-des-Arts and rue de Buci, and the eastern edges of the Right Bank, rues de la Verrerie, Sainte-Croix-de-la-Bretonnerie, des Archives or des Francs-Bourgeois. Here they lived alongside all strata of bourgeois society, as well as the poor of all classes. It was here too that the sentiment was forged that Paris, and Parisian society, was something set apart from the monarchy. Certainly, the development of the city in the late fifteenth and early sixteenth centuries owed little to royalty. An 'intellectual' quarter was established at the same time between rue Saint-Jacques and rue de l'Hirondelle, while financiers and jurists favoured rue des Blancs-Manteaux and rue Sainte-Avoye, north of the river. Merchants and traders clustered around rues des Lombards, de la Vieille Monnaie and Marivaux, just north of the Tour Saint-Jacques, much admired by Parisians for its height, and whence it was claimed you could see the wicked enchantress Italy if you tried hard enough.

Indeed Italy was something of an obsession with French royalty during this period. Louis's son, Charles VIII, was as fascinated by the place as his father and initiated a series of lightning raids on the country which almost brought him Rome itself. His successor, Louis XII, was drawn into Italian politics by Pope Julius II, a confirmed disciple of Machiavelli, who sought to use French military power as a deterrent force against the Venetians; of course, when the military tide turned, as was inevitable, the Pope shifted his allegiance to the Venetians and Louis was quickly crushed. Yet Italy lingered long in the French, and particularly Parisian, imagination. The manners, style and language of the aristocracy and *haute bourgeoisie* of the coming century were all to be defined by their southern neighbours.

'Paris is not a city but a whole country'

François I cut a dash at well over six feet tall and clad in the handsomest finery available in Europe. He came to the throne in 1515, entering Paris at Saint-Denis, proceeding to Notre-Dame surrounded by the *gens de la ville* (city administrators) and *gens du roi* (the king's own men), flanked by two companies of troops and a complement of 400 archers. Every bit as flamboyant as his predecessor, Louis XI, he showered the crowd with silver and gold coins as he made his way through them dressed in a suit of silver cloth and a white hat adorned with jewels.[5]

François also fancied himself as a patron of the arts. He thought of himself as an athlete (he enjoyed wrestling contests with the tougher members of his entourage) and was also a skilled orator and a natural man of letters. Accordingly, he saw it as his duty to establish Paris as a cultural capital, which did not mean confining intellectual activity to the university quarters but, in the manner of the Italian Renaissance, establishing the court as the cultural heart of the city. With this in mind, he rebuilt and added to the Louvre, making it once again the political centre of the city. In the same vein, he invested money in restoring several châteaux around Paris and established the Bibliothèque Nationale. He spoke in Latin with university theologians, setting up the regius professorships at the Sorbonne, and encouraged a climate of humanistic tolerance, which allowed satirical writers such as Rabelais to flourish. François even stood against the Sorbonne on behalf of his sister Marguerite d'Angoulême, whose poem *Miroir de l'âme pécheresse* ('Mirror of a Sinful Soul') of 1531 was condemned as heretical.

Yet there was also a cultural naïvety at work here. François could not understand, for example, why many of his fellow Parisians could not bear Benvenuto Cellini, whom the king brought to Paris twice. François unashamedly admired Cellini as a genius, a master diarist, wit, goldsmith and sculptor. Certainly Cellini hardly endeared himself to the higher echelons of French society when he forcibly kicked the *prévôt* out of his official residence at the Petit Nesle, directly opposite the Louvre, in the armed company of his servants and students. Afterwards Cellini was attacked on the street several times and attempts were made to haul him through the courts. Still, François remained faithful to his wayward Italian friend, helping him out of the trickiest situations.

An imagined dialogue of the period has Charles Quint ask his rival, François I, which is the most beautiful city in France. 'It is Rouen, my fine cousin,' answers François, 'for Paris is not a city but a whole country.' Such civic pride did not prevent the king from falling out all too frequently with his Parisian subjects, sometimes dangerously so. As ever, the main issue was money. Like his predecessors, François was fatally drawn to Italy and taxed the city heavily to pay for his adventures there. In 1523, the king was in residence in the heavily Italianized city of Lyons, when he received an urgent plea to return to Paris. An English army was moving swiftly southwards and the terrified Parisians feared a return to the darkest days of English occupation. Diffidently, or so it seemed, the king refused to return, although pledging his life for the city. Parisians never really forgave him for that. They grudgingly paid a ransom for him when he was captured by Spaniards in 1526 and when François fell ill on his return to the capital, the false rumour that he had died was eagerly gobbled up by Parisians of all social classes. He was also regularly satirized by the actor and playwright Monsieur Cruche, who performed mainly at Place Maubert. It was prudent not to go too far, even so: Cruche was nearly battered to death by a group of courtiers who took offence at his jokes about the affair between the king and the daughter of a councillor at the *parlement* called Lecoq.[6]

The New City

It was not until after François's death in 1547 that the Renaissance style in architecture became a defining feature of central Paris. In the first half of the sixteenth century development took place on the edges of the city, where land was cheaper and less vulnerable to the political changes of Paris *intra-muros*. The first of these areas to take on a life of its own was the Faubourg Saint-Germain, stretching from rue Saint-André-des-Arts to the Porte de Buci, which had been condemned as far back as 1430, Saint-Sulpice and rue de l'École de Médecine. One of the most attractive features of this area for Parisians from every sector of the city was the fair of Saint-Germain, which was held from February onwards every year, and which occupied the crossroads between what is now rues de Buci, du Four and de l'École de Médecine. All levels of society flocked to markets and public spectacles, which brought merchants, traders and performers from as far away as Germany, Venice and England.[7]

Development was also taking place towards the west, with the establishment of houses between the abbeys and churches, although the streets were made of mud, unlike the now elegant paved passageways of central and eastern Paris. These were still marginal zones, stretching out from rues du Dragon, du Sabot and des Saints-Pères, towards Square Boucicaut, where there was still by the early sixteenth century a lepers' colony.

At the other end of the Left Bank, a new quarter was founded between the rues Gracieuse, Lacépède, Geoffroy-Saint-Hilaire and Daubenton. This had formerly been the Clos d'Albiac, a vineyard and a tangle of narrow streets: now it was renamed Villeneuve Saint-René, with its new buildings, shops and well (the Puits de l'Ermite, 'Well of the Hermit', now commemorated in the street of the same name which these days frames the Great Mosque of Paris). Towards the end of François's reign in 1545, this area had grown to encompass rue Mouffetard and the Abbey of Saint-Victor, rues Censier and La Clef. Above all, its growth demonstrated two things: that the expansion of Paris was unstoppable; and that it was possible to live an altogether metropolitan life in what had previously been considered the margins of the city.

The consequences of this growth inspired François and his successors to think differently about the organization of Paris. It was clear, for example, that the state of the city's economy was not only reflected in but also actively stimulated by the construction of clean, regular avenues, straight-sided squares and open public spaces – all of the principles of town planning in Renaissance Italy. The reconstruction of the Pont Notre-Dame and then the building of stone *quais* at the Louvre and Châtelet were the first steps towards the rational planning of the city, allowing free movement during the highest of floods and heaviest rains.

Paris was not immune from the great tensions of the age, however. Despite the enlightened views of the court and city planners, the city itself seethed with old and new hatreds, exacerbated by the rising tide of Catholic fundamentalism which was soon to erupt into mass murder at the heart of the great capital.

15. Choose Now – The Mass or Death!

The early part of the sixteenth century saw the first attempts at planning and regulating the city, which meant laying out streets with a clean uniformity of façade and designing a city of public spaces. The new aristocratic quarters of the Marais or Faubourg Saint-Germain were a far cry from the filthy and congested warren that made up the centre of the city. This opposition was emblematic, it seemed to many, of the French court, which famously combined grandeur and low life, and where, before the scandalized eyes of visitors, a dinner all too often degenerated into an orgy. Foreigners from more righteous parts of Europe (mainly Germany, the Low Countries and Switzerland) wrote scathingly of political corruption and a widespread public taste for decadence. Parisians, who prized finesse over rigour in the arts of love, war and cooking, met the attacks of Puritan outsiders with indifference.

One of the most shocking aspects of Parisian life to the outsider was the way that sex and religion were intimately linked in the very heart of the city. In the early 1500s, whores were seated decorously in the nave of Notre-Dame, mingling freely with the faithful, whispering their prices to any likely looking mark. This practice was apparently long established. The poet Mathieu, one of the most notorious misogynists in Parisian literary history, had described in his *Lamentationes* ('Lamentations'), written in the late thirteenth century, how women went to the churches of Paris pretending to be holy but were really burning to satisfy their sexual appetites. 'It is less sinful to sell a horse near a church than to take what these most pious women offer,' cautioned Mathieu. Translated into French from Latin, Mathieu's book remained popular as a guide to sexual mores long into the early Renaissance period when prostitution flourished and, according to one observer, the city could count on at least 'six thousand beautiful girls devoted to prostitution'.[1] The Italian visitor Antoine Atezan was one of many who came to Paris for the sole reason of marvelling at 'an innumerable quantity of girls whose manners were so gracious and lascivious that they would have inflamed wise Nestor and old Priam'.[2]

Paris itself also inspired fear in provincials. This was not just because the city was large, culturally complex and intimidating, haunted by hustlers, whores and heretics. During the coming century, the city would become the battleground for competing religious ideologies, the old established Catholic faith, tied to Spain, Italy and the powerful Guise family, and the new and blasphemous creed of Protestantism.

Throughout this turbulent century, Paris remained a bastion of Catholicism, however. The Parisian authorities indeed kept a close eye on developments in Germany, the excommunication of Martin Luther in 1520 being warmly welcomed by the Sorbonne. Luther had been no more than an obscure German monk when he had nailed his ninety-five theses to the door of the church in Wittenburg, protesting at the financial and moral corruption of a church led from Rome and Madrid. In just a few years, he had become one of the most influential thinkers in Europe and, as Lutheran tracts circulated around Paris, he attracted the attention of those in high political circles, including initially even François I himself, who felt constrained by the authority and arrogance of the universal Church. When François was wounded and taken prisoner by the Spanish, his mother Louise, acting as regent, took a sterner line, listening closely to the Pope, the Sorbonne and the *parlement*, which condemned Lutheran doctrines in 1521.

On his release, the king too was more inclined to contain or destroy the new thinkers. The suppression began with the banning and burning of books and the torture of the most notable heretics. It was to culminate just a few decades later in a bloody and shameful mass murder, the gory equal of any of the most wretched ethnic genocides of the twentieth century, and an act which has forever stained the Catholic tradition in Paris and France.

The Prince's Whore

It was against this background that Catherine de Médicis arrived at the court of François I, with a charged sexual presence entirely appropriate to the sensual climate of the period. She had been imported from Italy by François as a wife for his son Henri and was immediately nicknamed 'the prince's whore'.

The reason for this was that Catherine was both exotic and delicious, carrying with her an aura of wickedness. She masked her diminutive figure in elegant robes and high heels (her footwear immediately reminding the more imaginative neo-classicists of the court of the high sandals worn by the prostitutes of Old Rome – in England women who wore high heels were condemned as witches long into the seventeenth century). Most importantly, she soon became the strongest and most powerful figure in the most dissolute court in Europe.

Catherine brought with her Italian manners, cookery and a taste for the theatre, with a particular penchant for the Italian style of 'comedy' – usually adaptations of Plautus, Terence and other antique authors – which was then making inroads in France. Strolling players from Italy, such as the 'Compagnia dei Gelosi' ('Company of Jealous Ones'), performed to rapturous crowds in Paris. Catherine's own daughters acted in *tragi-comédies*. This was stopped after a performance of *Sophonisbe*, a prose adaptation by Saint-Gélais of an Italian tragedy about a queen who prefers suicide by poison to dishonour. This was deemed by Catherine to have caused her bad luck and thereafter only comedies were played at court. The farce *Pantalon* regularly had the queen roaring with laughter.[3]

Catherine was not above using sex to get her own way, which at first meant her own charms and later on those of proxies. But her real interest lay in religious matters in Rome and Madrid. She was also fascinated by politics and the deepest, darkest mysteries of statecraft; she was a disciple of Machiavelli and his doctrine that people in power are 'more prone to evil than good'. It was unsurprising that during this period the Royal Poisoner became one of the most important figures at court. Catherine's gifts were notorious and to be feared. The Protestant prince de Condé narrowly escaped death when he was presented with a basket of fruit from the queen; on the advice of his physician, he passed an apple to his dog, which immediately dropped down dead.

The court also swarmed with alchemists, soothsayers, astrologers and magicians of every nationality. It was rumoured in London a century later that Catherine made sacrifices to Satan himself. This was dismissed in France as Jesuit propaganda but certainly Catherine took the advice of occult sages seriously and even constructed a tower overlooking the Paris skyline for her most favoured astrologer, Cosimo Ruggieri, who had replaced Nostradamus when he retired to Provence. The tower is still there in the rue de Viarmes, near the stock exchange. This is one of the many sites in Paris where the Devil is said to have made an earthly appearance, and there are allegedly traces of magic at work in the surrounding area, now mostly a banal clearing of trees, shrubs and gravel lanes. Nothing remains of the glass windows that encased the chamber at the top of the tower where Ruggieri read the stars and called down supernatural forces to aid the queen.

But Catherine could be sceptical and scoffed easily at astrologers who made mistakes. ' 'Tis a pity he couldn't see his own future,' she remarked of one notorious charlatan who had been robbed and killed outside the city limits.[4] Ruggieri's tower was finished in February 1572, only a few months before the massacre of St Bartholomew's Day, an orgy of murder that, as we shall see, was largely due to Catherine's own inability to foresee or control the consequences of gambling on the entirely negative political strategies of duplicity and assassination.

Holy Wars

In truth, Paris had been shot through with terrible tensions since Luther's theses had first been introduced to the city. The Sorbonne held itself as the absolute religious authority in the city and attacked Martin Luther as the source of any heresy or deviation from official teaching. The university not only censored books but ordered raids on students' quarters, arresting those suspected of the slightest degree of religious or political dissidence. There were spontaneous attacks on those suspected of heresy; the meeting places of Protestants were well known, scattered mainly across the Left Bank, and were easily targeted by vindictive death squads. On 4 March 1557, a group of Catholic students burst into the house of a lawyer who was known to have Protestant sympathies. When they found a service in full flow, they killed everybody they could, stabbing to death even ladies from the court, and beating up those whom they could not kill. When the police arrived on the scene, they congratulated the students on their work, rounding up the 'heretics' to be tried the following day.

Punishments for those found guilty of heresy were, at first, usually prison or exile; later, as the century advanced, they became more refined and cruel. The Place de la Grève was nicknamed 'the burning chamber' on account of its almost permanent stench of burnt human flesh. Other forms of punishment included the *strappado*, an Italian device which stretched the victim's limbs to breaking point and dislocation as he was lowered slowly above a fire. The Place de l'Estrapade, now a gentle and green crossroads in the heart of the Latin Quarter, was named after this device, reflecting its popularity. (In the succeeding century, this was where small boys sold numbered lanterns to guide night-time visitors through the labyrinth of the *quartier*, boasting of its terrors and its agonized ghosts.)

Tensions were already heightened in the early years of the century among ordinary Parisians, including the most illiterate and wretched members of the population, who identified themselves and their city with the Holy Mass. The influx of Protestant refugees into the capital, fleeing random massacres such as the slaughter at Wassy in 1562, made Catholic Parisians fear for their own safety and sense of sacred identity. This was a city which had been constructed as a rival to Rome and which by the 1560s overflowed with 'heretics' who not only denied papal supremacy but actively sought to challenge it. Such Protestants were given the name Huguenots, regardless of whether or not they actually came from Geneva, the headquarters of European Protestantism and where they had been called *Eidgenossen* ('confederates', the term that became transliterated into French as 'Huguenots').

The nervousness among Parisians had already been exacerbated by the so-called 'Day of the Placards' on 18 October 1534, when the Catholic population awoke to find that Protestant propaganda, neatly delivered in High Gothic, had been posted all over the city, declaring that the Catholic Mass was a sham and a contradiction of Scripture. Parisians were seized with terror as rumours of insurrection and slaughter whirled around the streets of the city: Christians would be murdered at Mass, churches sacked and the Devil himself would appear, laughing and announcing he would kill the sovereign and rule a new city of the damned. To calm the panic, all the great panoply of the Catholic faith in Paris – from the relics of Sainte-Chapelle to the Blessed Sacraments – were brought out by the Church and paraded around the city in a procession led by the Bishop of Paris himself. A High Mass was said at Notre-Dame as six more 'heretics' were thrown into the flames at Place de la Grève.

There were by that time around 15,000 known Protestants in Paris, a significant and highly visible chunk of the population, and sectarian violence was by now a well-established part of Parisian life. Although Protestants vowed loyalty to the king, and even tried to woo him to their cause, they also published pamphlets which declared their admiration for the model of Calvin, who stayed for a short time in Paris before establishing himself in the Protestant republic of Geneva. Most importantly, they took from Calvin a deep sense of injustice and anger at the illusion of Divine power falsely invested in royalty. The Crown accordingly kept a keen eye on the Reformers' attempts to build a temple at Saint-Marcel in a house near the Bièvre, or to establish more modest places of worship in Saint-Germain-des-Prés. Catherine passed an edict in 1562 that permitted freedom of worship in private homes in order to avoid violent confrontations in the street. But by this stage, a grim pattern of murder had been established on both sides: Protestants were particularly adept at seizing churches and killing priests when tensions reached an unbearable height. The church of Saint-Médard, at the foot of the rue Mouffetard, was even set ablaze by fanatics in the name of the Reformed Church.

By the latter part of the century, the Parisian population also feared military confrontation. Some of the leading political and military figures in France, including Coligny, the Admiral of France, were sympathetic to the Reformed religion, mainly as a way of countering corruption at home and shaking off the claustrophobic influence of Rome or Madrid in foreign policy. The Huguenots in general were also good soldiers, and their armies and militias were, so it seemed, capable of seizing Paris whenever they chose. The Huguenot prince de Condé threatened to do this in 1562, and in 1567 Huguenot armies blocked all entry to Paris, until eventually driven back by a starving mob. The civil war that had been simmering slowly for decades would shortly reach boiling point.

'Kill them all'

The trigger for the massacre of St Bartholomew's Day was, ironically enough, a marriage. On the 18 August 1572, Marguerite de Valois, a Catholic, was set to marry Henri de Navarre, a Protestant aristocrat from the Bourbon family (eventually to become king as Henri IV). Invitations were sent out to all the great families of France and the festivities were expected to last several weeks; great balls were to be held in the Louvre, Hôtel de Ville and Hôtel de Bourbon.

This was a marriage brokered by Catherine de Médicis, with the obvious strategic aim of uniting the two opposed religious forces in a union that supported the Crown. Although most Protestants had declared that their only goal in Paris was freedom of worship, the royal family had long feared their growing popularity and potential to overthrow the sovereign. This threat, it was optimistically anticipated, would be dissolved in blessed marital union. The capital was packed with Protestant and Catholic nobility for celebrations organized by Catherine. The young couple were betrothed on the square outside Notre-Dame, although only Marguerite and fellow Catholics were allowed to attend Mass within the great church. Some Protestants, wary of the hidden motives of the Crown, kept a careful distance from the city none the less, lodging in quarters away from the

Louvre and the city. Within days of the marriage, the city would be littered with the cadavers of wedding guests and others caught up in a murderous frenzy which apparently erupted out of nowhere.

Catherine's deeper strategy was to get rid of Coligny, who had become increasingly confident of his growing popularity, using the wedding festivities as a screen for her plan. On the 22 August, a marksman was sent on Catherine's orders to kill Coligny as he made his way from rue des Fossés-Saint-Germain-l'Auxerrois to rue des Poulies, on his way to a meeting of the Council of the Louvre. Two shots were fired; Coligny was wounded in the left shoulder but survived. Catherine and the royal retinue were among the first to visit and hypocritically offer their condolences. But the Protestant leaders who then gathered at Coligny's residence at the Hôtel de Béthisy were unconvinced by the royal displays of sorrow, and argued for revenge.

In panic at potential Protestant retaliation, the city was closed by royal decree. It was now the turn of the Crown nervously to survey the way ahead. It was clear to all by then that the assassination attempt on Coligny could only have come from the royal family. On the evening of 23 August, Charles IX wrote to the Queen of England to reassure her that the would-be assassins would be punished. In the meantime, his own future in the face of a Protestant insurrection looked bleak.

Then, as the clock struck two in the morning on 24 August, the slaughter began in earnest. 'Kill them all,' declared the king, 'so that none shall reproach me for it.'[5]

The first task was to get rid of Coligny properly. This was done by the duc de Guise and his men, who slit his throat and then dangled his severed head from the window of his apartment with a rope. 'We've started well,' Guise said to his men, 'but now we must follow through the king's will.'[6] Guise's men did this by marching through the streets with bloodied weapons, dragging the mutilated corpse of Coligny with them, exhorting the population to rise and commit murder. Coligny's testicles were ripped off and thrown into the Seine, followed by his headless corpse. He was then fished out and hung by his feet for several days at Montfaucon.[7]

From the Louvre to the backstreets of Île de la Cité and the Latin Quarter, a madness swept through the city. The ordinary people of Paris were overwhelmingly Catholic and the Protestants their aristocratic overseers (over the years, many of the leading Parisian families had converted to Protestantism in disgust at the venality of the government and the court). It was time now to settle accounts. Most of the important murders, at least from a political point of view, took place in the opening hours of the massacre. But the blind killing, driven by blood-lust and ancient hatreds, went on through the day and night until the streets looked like a battlefield. The dead and dying were not, however, men at arms, but gentlemen come to a wedding, poor artisans and workers, the elderly, women, children and babies. There were rare pockets of resistance – a certain Tavernay, one of Coligny's lieutenants, held out for over eight hours until he was over-whelmed by exhaustion – but most were taken with ease and by surprise. Pezou, a butcher by profession and a captain faithful to Guise, prided himself on killing human beings like beasts and boasted of slitting the throats of more than 120 Protestants in a few hours, and throwing the bodies into the Seine with his own hands.

'The city was no more than a spectacle of horror and carnage,' wrote one contemporary eye-witness. 'The streets echoed to the sounds of despair, and looting and killing. From every corner one heard the moans of those who had been stabbed or were about to die. There were dead bodies everywhere, thrown through windows, into courtyards already full of cadavers. Or they were dragged through the mud. There was so much blood that it ran in torrents.'[8] Another eye-witness described the river Seine turning red with blood. Within days, the Seine was so swollen with bodies that they floated back on to the banks of the river almost as soon as they had been thrown in. It was impossible to bury this many dead and huge pits were dug instead of graves, to soak up the human detritus. The king merely laughed when his captains reported that Paris could not swallow all these Protestants.

The massacre was also the excuse for slaughtering Protestants in other French towns (in Lyons 2,000 were killed in a single day). The example of Paris brought the country to the very edge of civil war as murderous anti-Protestant riots raged in Bourges, Rouen, Angers, Orléans, Bordeaux, Toulouse and Albi throughout September and October. The few Protestant strongholds of Montauban, Nîmes and La Rochelle closed their city gates in self-defence.

But nowhere claimed the privilege of a city turned slaughterhouse as readily and with as much pride as the unholy combination in Paris of royalty and the mob united in hatred against a common enemy.

16. As Above, So Below

The St Bartholomew's Day Massacre established a Europe-wide reputation for Paris as the capital of treason and murder. News of the massacre spread fast to London, Geneva, Vienna and Madrid (where the Spanish king laughed loudly and publicly at the slaughter) and Rome (where Pope Gregory XII rejoiced with a Te Deum). This was an age of religious tensions across Europe, and Paris, still physically not much more than a medieval city, was the capital city of these great ideological conflicts. Most crucially, in the eyes of non-Catholic Frenchmen and indeed nearly all other Europeans, Parisians were either assassins, religious fanatics, or both.

The truth was, however, that there was precious little Christianity involved in the French Wars of Religion. The struggle was really about who ruled France and it was this which had set the Catholic faction, led by the Guise family, and the Bourbon–Huguenot faction (led by the kings of Navarre) against each other. From 1559 onwards, when the death of Henri II threw the succession into question, there were indeed eight wars over thirty years. The St Bartholomew's Day Massacre was only the most bloody and well known of the battles ahead. Across the Christian world, Paris acquired notoriety as a satanic place of limitless slaughter. The only redeeming feature of this horrific period in its history is that the bloodshed in the name of religion provoked disgust among all reasonable people, thereby laying the seeds for the Enlightenment.

One of the more immediate and unforeseen consequences of the St Bartholomew's Day Massacre was the rise to power of Charles IX's younger brother Henri III. Charles died not long after the massacre, in Paris, officially of tuberculosis but, it was rumoured, probably poisoned by Catherine's hand, possibly as a political gambit on behalf of unnamed Catholic powers. Even the sacred relationship between mother and son was suspect in this city.

It was therefore appropriate that Henri's brief reign in the latter part of the century was over a court notorious for its sexual intrigues, ranging from incest to homosexual orgies. These activities were, however, only the most public examples of the debased nature of life in Paris. At all levels of society, public and private moralities were increasingly blurred into a matrix of needs and self-interest that bore only a loose relation to the strictures of the Church. The obvious appeal of Protestantism, especially for those who stood closest to the bastions of power in France, was that it offered a tonic and ethically pure code of civil action. Catholicism, on the other hand, apparently stood for no more than a greedy and degenerate hierarchy whose main aim was to preserve itself in power.

In the wake of the St Bartholomew's Day murders, Paris fell into the hands of the Catholic League, created in 1576 and led by the duc de Guise, who finally took the political power which he had long believed was his due. The League was officially subservient to the Crown but in practice controlled the city with a fierce and free hand. It was also far more vicious than any previous sectarian organization had dared to be, and actively provoked rebellion and warfare among the lower classes. It functioned as a paramilitary vigilante force, provoking demonstrations and leading murderous riots against Protestants. The League numbered several thousand but, most importantly, it had the almost total support of Parisians. In a rare moment of political intervention in May 1588, Henri sought to check Guise's increasing popularity by stationing soldiers at the bridges of the city and in parts of the Latin Quarter where a pro-League insurrection might arise. Angry at this apparent check on their freedom, the Parisians rose in revolt and erected barricades around the city. Henri quietly withdrew his men, leaving the storm to play itself out.

In the meantime, the carnal licence in Paris crossed all religious, social and gender barriers. Henri preferred sex to politics and surrounded himself with effeminate young men – *les mignons*, or 'the little cuties' – who worshipped him, applauding when he appeared at court dressed as a woman, and who nicknamed him the 'King of Sodom'. The *mignons* themselves were known all over Europe for their extravagant dress sense and camp antics. Edmund White describes them as 'bisexual enough to duel over women' and 'brave enough to defend their monarch when he was attacked during the religious wars'.[1] The *mignons* were, however, also hated by the common people as the representatives of a degenerate political system where sex and money bought privilege and power . . .

Henri III was as capricious as he was cruel. His fool, Foellet, was for example whipped and sent to the Bastille for saying that Paris contained poor people as well as rich ones. The self-evident truth of this statement was perceived to be as good as a direct threat to the king. Meanwhile, as the century progressed and the city became increasingly associated with fanaticism and murder, the very word 'Parisian' became a term of abuse away from the court. In the provinces, even the meanest 'Parisians' were all too often turned away from city gates as religious lunatics and potential assassins.

Counter-Cultures

The most visible signs of the moral decrepitude of the city were the number of whores and beggars that greeted the visitor. To anybody arriving from the orderly towns of Angers, Rouen or Dijon – each of which had their own considerable population of criminal classes – the hordes of touts, petty thieves, maimed beggars, child prostitutes, drunks, shameless whores and bandits must have seemed simply staggering. Guillebert de Metz noted that in the mid fifteenth century the capital had 80,000 beggars out of a population of 250,000. This was probably an exaggeration but there were plenty of incidents which signalled that by the mid sixteenth century the underworld was larger and more dangerous than it had ever been before in the history of the city.

Many of the hustlers and vagabonds who flocked to Paris in the first decades of the century were unemployed soldiers, often from rural origins, who found themselves adrift in the city without a trade and estranged from their family background. As it had been in Villon's day, crime was simply the sole and obvious option for survival for these men. Similarly, although prostitution was a semi-respectable profession, rape, incest and pregnancy out of wedlock were entirely taboo and usually the reasons why women and girls found themselves on the street, fending for themselves in a tough, male-dominated underclass.

What shocked Parisians most of all were the frequent public clashes between members of this underclass and the salaried soldiers who spent large amounts of money in taverns or cabarets. The regulars took the side of their dispossessed comrades in 1536, when many veterans of the Italian campaigns returned to Paris to find that the Crown had forgotten to pay them. There were violent riots and respectable Parisians tried to avoid venturing out of doors after dark, or lingering by bridges or in narrow alleys in the daytime for fear of robbery and murder at the point of a bayonet.

By 1536, the criminal population had swollen to the extent that it was not only a nuisance but a genuine threat to the city authorities. In 1518, a group of criminals attacked the stocks in Les Halles and killed the city executioner; in 1525, the Port au Sel on the Seine was wrecked in a riot;

in 1534, a gang of street people broke into the Louvre and stole the King's Colours or royal flag.

The authorities oscillated between treating the problem as a social evil (in 1554, a Great Office for the Poor was established at the Hôtel de Ville to dole out food to the starving) or simply evil (it was technically impossible to distinguish between poverty and criminality: those suspected of criminal tendencies were locked up in an asylum in Saint-Germain nicknamed 'Little House' by Parisians).

It was at this time that the legend or legends of the *Cours des Miracles* ('Courtyards of Miracles') arose in Paris. These were secret places in the city where the beggars, hustlers and thieves would return at night 'miraculously' to cast off their afflictions – fake blindness, amputation, or some terrible disease. They would then run riot with drink, whores and comrades in criminality, all under the watchful eye of the 'King of Thieves'. This 'king' was called under François I 'Le Ragot' (the inverted form of this name is the alleged origin of the term *argot* or 'slang') or later on the 'Grand Coësre' ('Great Chief'). The rule was to pay a percentage of the day's takings to this 'king' (this was called *cracher dans le bassin,* 'spitting in the basin'); the rest had to be spent by daybreak on drink or whores. The 'king' wore a bonnet, a torn sheet and carried a kind of sceptre. This truly was the world turned upside down.[2]

There were at least a dozen of these schools for robbery and prostitution scattered across Paris. According to Henri Sauval, these could be found along the rues du Bac, de Reuilly, de la Mortellerie, the Marché Saint-Honoré, the rues des Tournelles, du Marsis, the Faubourg Saint-Marcel and the Butte Saint-Roch. The most notorious of these was next to the present-day Place du Caire, near the rue de Damiette. This *cour* dated back to the thirteenth century and with its stinking courtyard, accessible only by a tangled mass of tortuous tiny streets, was the model for the famous *Cour des Miracles* in Victor Hugo's *Notre-Dame de Paris*. Henri Sauval, who had read and heard enough about these places to fuel a reckless curiosity, visited it with a guide – which did not mean, as he acknowledged, that he was not taking his life in his hands.

This courtyard is situated in a square of some considerable size and in a stinking cul-de-sac. To get there you must find your way through tiny and foul streets, which twist and turn in all directions; to get into the square, you must stumble down a quite long and uneven slope. I saw there a half-buried house of mud, strikingly old and rotten, of no more than fifty square yards, but which lodged fifty women in charge of an infinite number of infants, naked or half-dressed. I was told that five hundred families, piled on top of one another, lived in the courtyard. It had been bigger in the past; nowadays, one was nourished by idleness, grew fat on brigandry, in greed and all sorts of crimes and vice. There, with no thought of the future, each enjoyed the present and ate each evening with pleasure that which had been acquired with so much trouble to others and even violence during the day; for there to earn was to rob; and it was one of the fundamental laws of the *cour des miracles* that nothing should be kept for tomorrow. Each person lived with great licence; there was neither faith nor law. Baptism, marriage and sacrament were unheard of . . .[3]

The *Cours des Miracles* not only operated under their own leaders, but also had their own language and rules of conduct, structuring criminal activity in a strict hierarchy. This included: *Courtauds de Boutange*, part-time beggars only allowed to work the streets in the winter; *Capons*, who worked the cabarets as pickpockets or with daggers, or with a few accomplices attracted the attention of passers-by pretending to have been robbed; *Francs-mitoux*, who feigned illness to a degree that fooled the best doctors; *Hubains*, who were in possession of a false certificate stating that they had been cured of rabies by Saint Hubert and now needed to make a pilgrimage to thank him for this intercession; *Rifodés*, who, accompanied by wife and children, presented unwary Parisians with a certificate which claimed that their house had burnt down; and *Sabouteux*, who terrified onlookers with fake epileptic fits, or visitations from the Devil, rolling around on the ground, frothing at the mouth with what was in fact soap.

There has been extensive debate about the extent to which the *Cours des Miracles* are a purely literary invention. According to the historian André Rigaud, Henri Sauval almost certainly borrowed his account from a writer named Olivier Chéreau. The latter had in turn most likely taken it from a certain Péchon de Ruby, who had first written about the *Cours des Miracles* in a work called *La Vie généreuse des mercelots, gueux et bohémiens* ('The Generous Life of Con-men, Rogues and Bohemians'), published in Lyons in 1596. Péchon de Ruby claimed to have spent many years on the road studying and documenting the life of these characters, their language, patron saints and the inverse hierarchy of their professional and social lives. The portrait he paints is naturally sympathetic and provides a sharp insight into a micro-society that scorns all forms of authority and disdains money as a servile snare. The 'generous life' was the freedom to be found in avoiding work or attachment to land or territory: in this way, these Bohemians were crude ancestors of the anarchist groups that would emerge in the same part of Paris in the nineteenth century, declaring war on work, family and religion.

In the same way, the most notorious streets of this period have persisted through the centuries. Since the fifteenth century, the rue de la Grande Truanderie and its small but no less sinister relation, rue de la Petite Truanderie, have been known as *coupe-gorges*, cut-throat alleyways where *truants* ('criminals') of all kinds claimed the territory as their own and beyond the law. Little in this part of central Paris has changed: on a late summer afternoon in the early twenty-first century, I watched, in the midst of a small crowd of respectable Parisians too frightened to intervene, as two hard-faced pimps slashed a victim in the face in one of these streets.

Meeting the Devil Himself

Parisian life in the sixteenth century had its own myths. One of these (as we saw in Chapter 12) was that the soil of the cemetery of the Saints-Innocents, a relatively small space at the centre of the Right Bank and no bigger than the public squares of the city, had great powers.

Even if this were the case, by the late sixteenth century the cemetery, which dated back to pre-Roman times, had become dangerously over-crowded. Human remains were constantly being exhumed and piled up in foul charnel houses lining the cemetery to make room for the freshly dead; the streets around the place, all of which were long-established commercial and residential centres, were notorious for the powerful stench which could not be dispelled even in winter; in summer, diseases could be caught from simply strolling along the rue Saint-Denis.

No less terrifying were the rumours of satanism being practised in underground caverns, a fear that many wily Parisians used to their own ends. One of these was César, who died in a dungeon in 1615 (allegedly strangled by Satan himself), and who had made a profession of making the Devil appear to young *sérapiens* (backwards slang of the period for *parisiens*), who paid him considerable amounts of money to be scared out of their wits.

'I found a deep quarry about a quarter of a league from Paris, on the way to Gentilly,' wrote César in his *Confession* in 1615. 'When I found someone who wanted to see the Devil I would take him there, but before entering he had to pay me at least 45 or 50 pistols, then he had to swear not to speak afterwards, not to be afraid, and not to invoke any Gods or semi-Divinities who might irritate the Devil.'

César had six accomplices, who were dressed up as Furies and who would whoop and yell, lighting torches as César intoned incomprehensible but apparently satanic gibberish. The climax was the appearance of an unlucky goat, as the Devil himself, who had been painted vermilion and was guaranteed to provide nightmares for the tourist in hell for the rest of his life.[4]

17. Sinister Days

The rumours and legends of Satan's presence in Paris spread across France and most provincials shunned the city if they could. Rumours of Paris as the Devil's domain reappeared in the nineteenth century, when writers such as Baudelaire, Pétrus Borel or J. K. Huysmans embraced the sinister cause of Satan in the name of underground rebellion and aesthetic revolt. The terror inspired by Satan in the sixteenth century was, however, much more visceral and certainly justified.

Fear of witchcraft, sorcery and satanism was of course widespread across Europe during this period, culminating in the witch-burning hysteria of the seventeenth century, and it was common to both Catholics and Protestants. At the beginning of the sixteenth century, the Church had made satanism and sorcery its official enemies. This much was stated in the *Malleus maleficarum* ('Hammer of Evil'), the witch-finder's manual published by the Dominicans in 1486. In Paris, this proved a useful diversion from the real political issues at stake – concerning which religious faction had the right to govern the city. For many on both sides, however, the various massacres that Catholics and Protestants inflicted on each other in Paris in the name of this debate could only be properly explained as the Devil's work.

Catherine de Médicis was portrayed as the earthly representative of the Devil in *Les Tragiques* ('The Tragic Ones'), the long and powerfully volcanic poem written by the Huguenot Agrippa d'Aubigné in the late 1500s. This poem is intended as an allegory of the civil wars which had raged in France since the 1560s, with the slaughter of St Bartholomew's Day at its centre. In it Catherine is accused of witchcraft, devilry, the sacrifice of innocents (she was indeed rumoured to have attended a black Mass at Vincennes). But most important of all, at least from the view of Calvinist theology, is the fact that she incarnates a principle of constant change ('change en discord avec les elemens') that is the very essence of human evil. When she died in 1589 at the age of sixty-nine, Parisians swore that if they could get hold of her body they would throw it in the Seine. She was buried quickly and crudely at Blois. Yet her death, appropriately enough, did not mark an end to the agonies of Paris but the beginning of yet another murderous cycle.

This was heralded by the killing of Henri III in the same year. By this time, the population of Paris had been under the control of the Guise family and the Catholic League for some twenty years. Ordinary Parisians hated the king for his effeminacy and profligate ways and it was not hard for the League regularly to whip up a crowd to march through the streets railing at the court. The Sorbonne was also beyond royal control and effectively in charge of the changing moods of the city, determining what was both 'heretical' and politically expedient. This included praying for the death of the king and the final victory of the League. In the wake of the death of Catherine de Médicis, it seemed that the whole of Paris was organizing a war against the king.

The Catholic League and Henri were deadly enemies right up until the instant that Henri was stabbed by Jacques Clément, a monk in the ancient convent of the Jacobin friars in rue Saint-Honoré (these monks were called 'Jacobins' because their first house had been in the rue Saint-Jacques: the name was later transferred to the political club of the 1789 Revolution, which also used to meet in the ancient convent of the first 'Jacobins'). Clément had been persuaded by Bourgoing, the senior priest of the convent and an intimate of the Guise family, that angels would come down from heaven to help him kill the king, or that at the very least he would enter heaven as a glorious martyr to the Catholic cause.

Clément had gone to see the king at his château at Saint-Cloud, to the south-west of the city, on Tuesday 1 August 1589 in the pretence that he was carrying important letters from dissidents held in the Bastille. He was at first refused entry by the king's guards but when he saw the monk arguing with his soldiers, the king gestured him forward, declaring loudly that he was not 'an enemy of monks' nor did he seek to avoid them. As the king began to read the letters, Clément drew his dagger and plunged it into Henri's belly, leaving the broken blade inside his entrails. 'I am being killed by an evil monk,' cried the king. 'Kill him before he kills me!'[1]

The news of Henri's death was greeted with unrestrained delight in Catholic Paris. The duchesse de Montpensier – a leading figure in the League and a sworn enemy of the king, and who had encouraged Clément – embraced the messenger who brought her the news. 'Ah, my friend,' she said, 'can this really be true? This wicked and perfidious tyrant, is he really dead? God has given us a great gift! I am only angry at one thing: that he did not know before he died that I had this done to him!' Together with the duchesse de Nemours, she went into the streets of Paris, running, dancing and shouting loudly with gleeful spite: 'The Tyrant is Dead! Good

News for All!'[2] Declaring that the king's death should be celebrated with green ribbons, she distributed them throughout the city.

The duchesse de Nemours, meanwhile, went into the church of Les Cordeliers and spat at the corpse of the dead king. Lamps were lit every night in celebration across Paris throughout the mourning period. On a more political level, priests wrote and published apologia and polemics in favour of Clément, or distributed images of him at their altars as if he were a martyred saint.

For a brief moment, it seemed as if the Crown would fall into the hands of Charles de Lorraine, duc de Mayenne, a prominent member of the Catholic League and the idol of the zealous Parisian mob. Public emotion had already been heightened by loose talk of murdered Catholics and martyred priests in London. Mayenne had sworn to empty Paris of Protestants and loyalists who had supported Henri III, restoring a pure Catholic ascendancy to the throne. For the time being, Mayenne was content to take the governorship of the city. There was, however, a serious and convincing challenge from Henri de Navarre, a Huguenot from Gascony who claimed lineage to Louis IX and had been named by Henri III as his successor. (His marriage with Marguerite de Valois had been the fateful union that sparked the St Bartholomew's Day Massacre.)

Within weeks of the murder of the king, Henri had moved from his bases in the south to Normandy, where he could count on allies against the Catholic League and its Council of Sixteen, a ruling body made up of the most fanatically pious papists, who now held the city in its tight grip. Henri waited out the winter months, studying all movements in and out of Paris, waiting for the right moment to take the city. His first strike was at Ivry, just a few days' march from the capital. But by now, Mayenne had bolstered his forces with reinforcements from friendly Spain. With a new ruthlessness, Henri cut his way through them and, with most of his forces intact, he found himself at the gates of Paris in March 1590. His men set fire to the surrounding fields and settled down for what they anticipated would be a brief siege before Henri finally entered the city, cheered on by a grateful and naturally subservient population.

'The bread of Madame de Montpensier'

The reality turned out to be quite different, however. Paris was a wealthy and well-stocked city and not ready yet to give up easily. The first two raids launched by Henri were weak and dismal affairs. As he surveyed the city from the heights of Montmartre, it was reported that the population laughed at his daring and stupidity.

But Henri was also stubborn. Realizing that the city was isolated both politically and militarily, he prepared in around early March for a long siege. It was easy enough to capture Saint-Germain-des-Prés and the surrounding villages of Montrouge, Issy and Vaugirard. What was left to conquer lay within Philippe-Auguste's walls and was controlled by the League. These authorities, reasoned Henri and his generals, could not survive for longer than six months, even if they did believe God was on their side.

It was easy enough, at least at first, for the Leaguers to maintain their grip on political power. The homilies of priests were loaded with anti-Protestant propaganda – Henri was no less than the Anti-Christ, they claimed, come to wreak vengeance for St Bartholomew's Day and lay waste to the city. Dissenters and suspected spies were thrown into the Seine or strung up in public squares for mutilation and humiliation. The League raised militias in each *quartier*, some numbering 3,000 men, few of whom had the stomach for a fight but feared the priests even more. It was, however, much harder for the League to control the anger and despair of a population that was slowly starving to death. The monasteries, convents and churches were still well supplied with food, but by June most of the city was locked into a famine.

The first signs of this were clear enough. Domestic animals, goats, horses and donkeys, were slaughtered and sold in butchers at high prices. Then even cats and dogs were seized by the authorities and roasted on huge spits in public squares. The meat was handed out to the poor of the city with a portion of bread. Wealthy people who had bought expensive fur clothes as an investment against hard times found these too were requisitioned and devoured by their hungry fellow citizens. This was a long way from the worst that Parisians would suffer. An eye-witness who was also a member of the League reported that, in this early period of the siege,

the poor ate dogs, cats, rats, vine leaves and other herbs and grasses. Throughout the town all that could be seen were boiling pots of gruel leavened with donkey meat or the flesh of mules. Even the cooked skins of these animals were being sold and eaten with great appetite. In the taverns and the cabarets, instead of wine the people drank potions of bitter herbs. If white bread for a sick person could be found, it cost more than an *écu* a pound. I have seen with my own eyes, poor people descend on the corpse of a dog in the gutter of the streets, and others eating entrails thrown into the sewers, or eating dead rats and mice, or the brains of a dead dog.[3]

As the death toll began to rise through the early part of the summer, the streets were piled high with rotting corpses. Between 150 and 200 bodies were found each morning. Then came the various sicknesses – the swollen stomachs of dropsy victims, both living and dead, were now a common sight in the city. There were no more songs and parades in favour of the League, only the moans of the dying and diseased. A delegation of poor Parisians slipped out through the trenches to see Henri and petition for his mercy. Moved by the condition of these starving Parisians, he gave permission for some 3,000 of the worst afflicted to leave the city. The next day, almost 4,000 attempted to get out of Paris; 800 or so were rounded up by Henri's troops and sent back to starve.

Conditions were rapidly disintegrating. The poor and hungry began to forage in the cemetery at night. They began by digging up bones and crushing them into dust, in the belief that was a kind of flour that could be made into bread. The most famished ate this dust, which they called 'the bread of Madame de Montpensier', the fanatically pro-Catholic zealot who had danced through the streets of the city to celebrate the death of Henri III.

There were strange portents of further disaster. As the duc de Nemours left his mansion early one morning to visit sentries at the city walls, he was warned by a guard not to walk down towards the rue des Francs-Bourgeois; 'there is a dead woman being devoured by serpents and venomous beasts,' hissed the frightened guard. Such hallucinations were commonplace.[4] Cannibalism was reported to be widespread throughout Paris. Most melancholy of all was the tale of a noblewoman, a widow, whose two children had died of hunger. Unable to buy bread, she had roasted the children with the aid of her housekeeper and over two weeks eaten them every evening, tears streaming down her cheeks. Unsurprisingly, the woman and her servant died within days. 'Parisians had begun the siege with pride and dignity,' reported another contemporary eye-witness, 'but they were soon in a state of extreme desolation, eating their furniture, their goods, each other. Over one hundred thousand died in three months. The grass grew in the streets, the shops stayed shut, nobody moved. All was horror and solitude.'[5]

Too Much Blood

Many if not all Parisians were convinced that a miracle would save them. In the late September of the first year of the terrible siege, it almost came in the form of a Spanish army that had been dispatched under orders from Madrid to rescue Catholic Paris. Boats carrying grain reached the city for the first time in months. The Sorbonne guaranteed the martyrdom of those who had died in the worst months of famine and, despite thirty thousand dead, the priests were able to pronounce that a great victory had been won.

In truth, this was no victory but only a way of prolonging the battle for the city. Henri withdrew his men but did not concede defeat. There were various attempts to take the city by subterfuge. In February 1591, a troop of Henri's men tried to enter it at the Porte Saint-Honoré disguised as flour merchants. The Catholic die-hards who were guarding the city showed no weakening of resolve and massacred the soldiers and stole the grain that they were carrying. Similar incidents were repeated throughout the coming months.

The League was, however, less competent at judging the mood of the people. Despite the best efforts of the Council of Sixteen to 'purify' the *parlement* and other offices of the city, there was a growing tide of discontent with the city authorities, who seemed immune to the suffering all around them. In November, the discontent became a rebellion and then a genuine revolutionary force. The trigger was the trial of two clerics, Magistri and Brigard, who were found guilty of royalist sympathies. Brigard was acquitted and Magistri given a light sentence. But the League was outraged by the lack of severity in the trials and punishments, and called upon priests to denounce the action. The priest of the church of Saint-Jacques declared that it was time to 'play with knives'. Denunciation led swiftly to murder and, in defiance of the city judiciary, Bresson and the other magistrates who had led the trial were lynched and hung from the windows of a building at Petit-Châtelet.

Catholic unity was not broken, however. Mayenne came down hard on the 'ultras' who had lynched Bresson but, wary of the popular mood, did not yet set about hanging priests. In the meantime, the bourgeois classes no

The Gaulish leaders in league against Julius Caesar (100–44 BC), led by Vercingetorix (d. 46 BC), from a protective sleeve for school books, late nineteenth century.

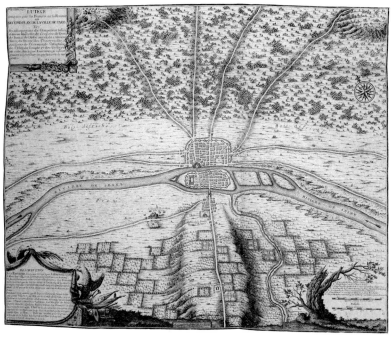

Lutetia or the second plan of Paris in the fourth and fifth centuries AD, French School, 1722.

Sainte Geneviève gardant ses moutons, French School, sixteenth century.

Book-buying in the shadow of Notre-Dame cathedral.

Epitaph of François Villon (1431–?)
from *Le Grant Testament Villon et le petit,
son codicille. Le jargon et ses balades*, 1489.

Epitaphe dudit Villon
Freres humains qui apres no⁹ viues
Nayez les cueurs contre no⁹ endurcis
Car se pitie de no⁹ pouurez auez
Dieu en aura pluftoft de vous mercis
Vous nous voies cy ataches cinq six
Quât de la char q̃ trop auôs nourrie
Elle eft pieca deuource et pourrie
et no⁹ les os deuenôs cêdres a pouldre
De noftre mal perfonne ne fen rie
Mais priez dieu que tous nous vueil
le abfouldre
                                g iii.

'Weighing of Souls', French fifteenth-century stone carving.

Engraving of the *danse macabre*, artist unknown, 1493.

Portrait of Catherine de Médicis (1519–89), French School, sixteenth century.

'La Cour des Miracles'

Engraving of the St Bartholomew's Day Massacre, Paris, 1572, by de Soligny.

'Le Cimetière des Innocents et le quartier des Halles, 1750',
engraving by Fedor Hoffbauer, nineteenth century.

Garden and Cirque at the Palais-Royal, Paris, by Fedor Hoffbauer, *c*.1885.

Scène grivoise by François Boucher (1703–70).

'The Sans-Culotte', French School, nineteenth century.

'A Meeting of Artists, Mudscrapers and Rag Merchants', caricature of a popular café at the Palais-Royal in Paris, French School, *c.*1800.

longer recognized themselves in the fanatical speeches of clerics and began to drift away from religion and murder. Peace was a long way off, but the process was under way as a result of an inevitable mood of weariness and exhaustion. Paris, for the time being, had seen too much blood.

A breakaway faction of the Parisian population naming themselves *les politiques* decided that negotiation was the only way out of the impasse. Even Mayenne accepted this and in March 1592, despite the threats of excommunication from the Abbot of Sainte-Geneviève and the priest of Saint-Eustache, a delegation led by Mayenne went to parley with Henri. There was only one major item on the agenda: Henri's conversion to Catholicism.

Henri did not hesitate long over his decision. He was persuaded not only by Mayenne's arguments that this would be a great and irrevocable gesture of love towards his Parisian subjects, but also by the arguments of his lover and companion Gabrielle d'Estrée, who wanted more than anything to be queen of Paris. There was also the threat of the Spanish imposing a foreign but Catholic king on Paris, a fate that both Mayenne and Henri wanted desperately to avoid. Theologians were consulted and finally by 10 May Henri was able to declare himself ready to convert with the famous words that 'Paris is worth a Mass'. On 25 July, Henri could be seen in Montmartre receiving Communion. The Leaguers had prepared an assassination plot, however. A monk from Lyons called Barrière travelled to Paris to meet with monks and priests and offered himself as the martyr who would kill the king. Mayenne's men unmasked the plot and arrested Barrière and his fellow conspirators, who were tortured and killed in the prison at Melun. 'Is it not a strange thing which demonstrates the wickedness of men's hearts that so many religious men want me dead,' the king is said to have mused to himself.

Henri did not enter Paris until March the following year. By then the ground had been laid for a triumphant but not triumphalist entry into the city. The city was now firmly in the hands of the 'propitious', led by the charismatic and moderate *prévôt des marchands* Jean Lhuillier. To avoid a direct confrontation with the king, Lhuillier had sent those Spanish soldiers still in the city and faithful to the League deep into the countryside in pursuit of a non-existent regiment of Huguenot troops. On 22 March, at four in the morning, Lhuillier himself opened the Porte Neuve on the Quai du Louvre. At the very same moment, the alderman of the city, Martin Langlois, opened the Porte Saint-Denis. An hour passed and then the army of the King of France silently filed through. As dawn broke,

Henri IV himself entered the city as his troops handed out a tract declaring a general amnesty.

The crowds gathered as the king made his way down rue Saint-Honoré, rue des Lombards and rue des Arcis. It took him nearly two hours to reach the Pont Notre-Dame, which had not been seen by royalty in five years. Spanish soldiers, Leaguers and religious zealots were told to leave Paris, which most of them did at once. There would be no prisoners in the city nor any more blood spilt. Henri was sure of his friends in the city but wanted to pacify or neutralize his enemies. The ordinary people applauded his generosity and were delighted that he loved them enough to spare them more conflict. After half a decade of starvation and war, Paris again had peace, bread and a king.

18. Making Paradise Visible

As the civil war in Paris slowly drifted into memory, the first concern of Henri IV and his advisers in the late 1590s was to rebuild the city. This was as much a political imperative as anything else. Parisians would never have forgiven him if he had not fulfilled the faith that they had placed in him as sovereign by restoring Paris to its earlier eminence. More to the point, Henri and his advisers were aware that his power was still fragile and needed to be quickly consolidated in the formerly great capital in order to ward off future challenges. Henri himself seemed genuinely to love the city and wanted to make it great again for the simple reason that he wanted to live somewhere that was busy and vibrant.

Endless street warfare, sieges and larger battles fought across the city landscape had left Paris physically wrecked and financially ruined. Churches and state buildings lay destroyed. Even the most prosperous streets in the central part of the city were no more than muddy tracks and only the wealthiest Parisians were able to cross the city, on horseback or in one of the few working carriages, without being covered in muck and excrement. New houses had been poorly built with the cheapest materials, while even the grandest *hôtels* were half in ruins, having been neglected for decades. For the visitor new to the city, the most striking aspect of this dereliction was the stench from stagnant or flooded sewage systems. 'Il tient comme boue de Paris' ('It sticks like the mud of Paris') was a saying used all over France to describe the black, stinking stuff. 'Variole de Rouen et crotte de Paris ne s'en vont jamais avec la pièce' ('You can never get rid of pox from Rouen or dung from Paris') was a similar saying forged in the filth of the city. Houses and streets were alive with rats and almost as many Parisians died from plague or other diseases as from violent conflict during the three decades of civil war.

One of Henri's first actions on seizing power was to announce a series of building projects that would reinstate Paris as the jewel of Europe. This was also the advice of Maximilien de Béthune, later known as the duc de Sully, who had been one of Henri's closest confidants and chief strategists throughout the most difficult years of the recent conflict. Sully was a Protestant with a clear-eyed vision of Henri's destiny, and with it that of

Paris and France. Most notably, unlike his contemporaries in England or Spain, he was not eager to grab land or riches in the New World but saw the future of France as the leader of Europe, or at least that part of it – Flanders and the Rhineland – standing at the furthest remove from Madrid or Rome. Sully was also a shrewd and careful administrator who saw that the financial investment in restoring Paris to its former pre-eminence would be easily paid back when the city assumed its true position as the cultural and economic capital of northern Europe. The growth of Paris under Sully and Henri can be measured in the maps made in 1609, when the king's projects were first underway, and in the size of the city on the maps drawn by Jacques Gomboust in 1652, which reveal the early modern city grown to almost half its size again, swollen with immigrants and boasting the most splendid public architecture in Europe. Paris would not undergo such a radical transformation again until the Second Empire of the nineteenth century, when Napoleon III set himself the task of creating the most spectacular city in history.

Remaking Paris was no easy task, however. By the late 1590s, despite the attempts at town planning in the early part of the century, this was still essentially a medieval city, albeit one in ruins. Henri handed out commissions to architects and builders with express instructions to wipe away the past and its memories and to build a city on classical lines such as he had admired in Italy. Timber was to be banned and the houses of the new city were to be made of brick and stone.[1] The model was the elegant colonnaded square of the Place des Vosges, finished in 1605 on the site of a former horse market and named the Place Royale until 1800. The square was soon a popular duelling venue, a pick-up spot for whores and a fashionable promenade in the city, a step away from the smart but pestilential *quartier* of the Marais. Henri had originally conceived of the square as a way of alleviating the condition of the Parisian poor by providing low-cost housing, but the Place des Vosges was always, from its first days, an irredeemably stylish and fashionable address. Henri had even grander plans to build a huge public square, the Place de France, at the entrance to the Marais and the city at what is now rue de Turenne. This was, however, still in the planning stage by the time of his death in 1610.[2]

'The clitoris of Paris'

The same modernizing influence was applied to the bridges over the river, which were swept clean of the houses and shops that made them such death traps in times of flood or fire. In 1607, Henri declared that work on the Pont-Neuf, the broad stone bridge across the Seine which had been planned since 1566, was finally complete. Parisians had been reluctant to fund it themselves and had tried to force Henri's hand by refusing to pay for it unless other towns and regions in France paid their share. Henri simply levied a further and higher tax on every barrel of wine which entered Paris and the work was completed within six years of his original plan[3]. As the bridge was being built, it became a popular sport for young men to show their daring by leaping across the unfinished ramparts, risking drowning in the Seine if they fell short. The king was fascinated enough by the game to leap across himself. When it was pointed out that many had drowned in this way, he replied: 'This may be so, but none of them were kings' – a baffling if, to most Parisians at least, impressive piece of bravado.[4]

When it was finally finished and opened, the Pont-Neuf immediately became a magnet for Parisians, who flocked there to buy and sell all manner of goods, or stroll about aimlessly or in search of sex or money. On the bank facing the bridge there was originally a stone carving of Christ and the Good Samaritan, the memory of which was preserved in the nineteenth century when the Cognacq-Jay family took the name of 'La Samaritaine' for their department store which stands there to this day.[5]

Henri also developed the wastelands which stood on either side of the bridge. On the right-hand side facing the Right Bank, he commissioned the construction of the Place Dauphine (named for Henri's son), a triangle of garden and red-brick houses built according to the 'rustic' style then popular in the provincial cities of Rouen and Orléans. This was intended to provide a deliberate counterpoint to the clean, neo-classical lines of the Marais and a more village-like atmosphere in the mercantile heart of the city. The Place Dauphine now stands half hidden from the busy life of central Paris and, behind the grim Palais de Justice, with its picnickers, boules players and idling smokers, has a genuinely dozy, provincial air.

It has also had accordingly, at least since the nineteenth century, a secret, erotic allure. This is one of the places where André Breton pursued Nadja across Paris in a frenzy of desire; André Malraux, usually the most staid and discreet of writers, wrote that the Place Dauphine was like a vagina, 'with its triangular formation with slightly curved lines, and the slit which bisects its two wooded spaces'.[6] Another poet has described the Place as 'the clitoris of Paris'.[7] Baron Haussmann died before he could accomplish his project of wiping the Place Dauphine from the map of Paris.

The true erotic centre of Henri's Paris, however, was to be found below the bridge, on the left-hand side facing the Right Bank. This is where the king ordered the construction of a small park at the water's level, where he could linger and cavort with his pals, entertainers, courtesans and women of even lesser virtue. The island was originally known as the Îlot aux Juifs but was soon unofficially named by Parisians the Square du Vert-Galant (the *vert galant*, or 'gay blade', was Henri's nickname, earned by his taste for high living and erotic flamboyance).

The name persisted long into centuries to come, as did the island's reputation as the site of nocturnal sexual adventure. This was precisely the sort of degenerate version of the city that Protestants had railed against so long. It was also the beginning of a long Parisian tradition of semi-clandestine, semi-public sexual play enjoyed out of doors, a tradition that persists in the city to this day, from the gay cruising areas of the Tuileries and the bridges beneath Austerlitz to the pan-sexual carnival of the Bois de Vincennes or the Bois de Boulogne.

Moralists and Cynics

One of the most astonishing facts of Henri's reign was that Parisians so easily accommodated themselves to it after decades of apparently unstoppable and unending violence. In part, this was due to war-weariness and a desire from all sections of the population to move on from the destruction of earlier years. Secondly, Henri himself was by all accounts an extremely disarming figure whose love of sex, music and wine and disregard for the strictures of religion or Machiavellian political manoeuvrings endeared him quickly to the general public. His weakness for women was well known and his chief mistress, Gabrielle d'Estrée, something of a star in her own right.

Parisians laughed at the king's goat-like smell and generally dishevelled appearance and how he still managed to satisfy the fastidious Queen Marguerite (whom he none the less divorced in 1599) and conquer such well-known beauties as Gabrielle. Parisians were also appalled at Gabrielle's sudden death in 1599; she was most probably poisoned by a certain Sebastiano Zametti, a crony of the king and possibly one of her lovers.

It was the mark of the man that, although genuinely heartbroken by Gabrielle's death, he eventually recovered enough to marry Marie de Médicis, a far homelier figure than Gabrielle, whom he named the 'fat banker' but who went on loyally to provide him with sexual and emotional stability in the years to come.

Under Henri, Paris thrived and became a relaxing place where European visitors came to taste the freedoms that Parisians themselves had not enjoyed for nearly a century. Surprisingly, despite the political turbulence of the late sixteenth century, life in Paris had also been marked by a curious cultural unity. The Wars of Religion were complex and bloody, but the guiding principles of the conflict had been quite simple: an opposition between the growing influence of Protestantism and the difficulties within the Catholic Church, which had yet to emerge from a medieval vision of the world and society.

The murderous events in Paris were the epicentre of this conflict. At a political level, the crisis of central government in Paris foreshadowed the absolutist monarchy that would be so revered and vilified in the eighteenth century. On a cultural level, however, Parisian life was strangely enriched by the sectarianism and even the most crazed violence. In the first instance, this was the result of the emergence of Calvinism as a literary and political force. It had always been notoriously difficult to work out exactly who was Protestant and Catholic according to social class (although roughly speaking, peasants and nobility were Catholic and the hard-headed middle classes Protestant). With their contempt for priests and a passionate belief in their own virtue, Calvinists were, however, easily distinguishable in politics and literature. Calvin himself wrote with an unforgiving, steely brilliance which sliced the arguments of his opponents into pieces and emphasized that God was intelligible and not mysterious. In Paris, where Calvin had lived and studied, and which had been torn apart by the collision between the Catholic Church, with its fanatical medievalism, and its Reformist enemies, this extreme form of rationalism was met with both outrage and applause in equal measure. Its importance and influence were beyond dispute.

The Calvinists excelled at a moralizing form of theatre (*Le Pape malade*, 'The Sick Pope', is a fairly typical title of a play from the 1560s) and what they termed 'scientific poetry', which aimed at the study of man in historical, political and theological contexts. Agrippa d'Aubigné and the Gascon follower of Henri IV Guillaume du Bartas are particularly good examples of this tedious genre, much admired by Milton, among others. The likes of Rabelais and Montaigne, who espoused a liberal Christian humanism and were sympathetic to the Church in all its fallen glory, stood as polar opposites to Calvin and his followers. This tradition found its fullest expression in the *Satire Ménippée*, a compendium of anti-Catholic texts produced by a variety of humanists, who were united in their belief in a moderate 'third way' out of the impasse that they had been brought to by Calvin and his fanatical Catholic enemies.

The book is composed of three parts: a burlesque introduction that ridicules the pan-European ambitions of Catholic Spain; a second part containing imaginary speeches by the rapacious and witless Leaguers; and a final section of fake epigrams. The text was named after the philosopher Menippus of Gadara and aimed at turning reality upside down in the manner associated with the philosophical school known as the Cynics, who flourished in Greece in the third century BC. It circulated freely in manuscript form in Paris after 1593 and was received with glee by ordinary Parisians, who identified with its heightened sense of the ridiculous and lack of reverence for any pure theological principle. The fact that a priest, Leroy of Rouen, had probably collated the text only underlined to most readers the subversive nature of the book. Most notably, it offered not only a coherent case for the accession of Henri IV, but dared to liken his Paris with Jerusalem, a comparison which was not so much heretical as ludicrously hyperbolic in a city that had yet to scramble free of the wreckage left by the sectarian hatreds of the sixteenth century.

A Visionary Killer

It was an undoubted fact, apparent to visitors and citizens, that under Henri IV Paris was immediately an easier and more attractive place to live. Crime was still a problem and the king himself intervened to strengthen the city guard, increasing salaries and doubling its numbers. In 1607, a barracks was established at Châtelet and Henri oversaw the setting up of a small headquarters for the guard in each *quartier* and constant patrols throughout the city. Robbery and murder were common but less frequent or casual than they had been in the final years of the previous century. There were several assassination plots against the king, but these were shrugged off as part of the job. Henri, who was as immodest as he was charming, explained how and why he had transformed the city as another part of his kingly duty. 'It is simple,' he explained to his retinue. 'When the master is not in his house, there is disorder; but when he comes back, his presence is an ornament and everything is to be gained from it.'[8]

However, there were still those in Paris who nurtured resentment and hatred of what Henri, the former Protestant heretic and now loose-living degenerate, had done to the city since his conversion. The Leaguers, who were still at work in a semi-covert fashion in the city, never stopped agitating against him, drawing faithful priests, dissident monks and even sympathetic members of the nobility into their operations. Paris was still a Catholic city, they argued, the spiritual inheritor of Rome's glory and its mission. It was now in the hands of a diabolical liar, thief and anti-Christian monster.

One of the fanatics who believed this was a certain François Ravaillac, a wiry and frighteningly ascetic, devout would-be monk and failed teacher from Angoulême. He claimed to be in direct communication with God and to see visions of God's enemies bloodied, dead or in flight. His hatred of the king and his new city – which was not Jerusalem but Hell! – was fuelled by the theatrical comedies performed in the cabarets of his home city, which, in the now well-established Protestant tradition, were heavy on moral argument and light on leavening humour, irony or wit. In the April of 1610, in Étampes, at a performance of *Ecce Homo*, a set-piece of Protestant propaganda, it occurred to Ravaillac what would be his life's work: to kill the king and save Paris. He set off to the city at once.

Ravaillac had been to Paris before, seeking in vain an audience with the king to tell him to expel all Protestants from the country. He went again to the king's residence at the Louvre, where he chatted to royal servants and loafed around for several days. On 10 May Ravaillac bought a large carving knife.

The morning of the 14 May was unseasonably warm and, as he travelled from the Louvre to the Arsenal to visit the ailing Sully, Henri pulled back the blinds in his carriage. Ravaillac, knife in hand, had been following the king's entourage from the rue Saint-Honoré. As the king's carriage made its way down the rue de la Ferronerie and through the stench of the adjoining cemetery of the Saints-Innocents, it was forced to stop by a cartload of straw which blocked its passage. As Henri bent over towards the duc d'Épernon to make a remark, Ravaillac thrust himself through the guards, into the carriage and plunged the long knife three times into the king's chest.

Even under the most severe torture, Ravaillac claimed that he had acted alone. When the king died, just a few hours later in his library, the entire country was distraught. The fanatics of the League were restrained in their joy. But still it seemed that once again the history of Paris and France was doomed to be determined by a lone murderer and his fanatical backers. The fear of civil war once again paralysed the city.

Still, some Parisians were able to find a little comfort in the brutal nature of Ravaillac's execution – he was scalded, ripped into pieces and part of his torso was roasted and eaten by the mob before the rest of him was reduced to ashes.

19. A Marvellous Confusion

' 'Tis a strange thing,' wrote the diarist and lawyer Pierre de L'Estoile in his journal of 1584, 'that in the town of Paris there are committed with impunity thefts and acts of brigandry that would best suit a darkened forest.' L'Estoile's anger was in fact aimed at the random and deadly violence which had become a staple of everyday life in the city. 'Assassinations, armed robberies, debaucheries and all forms of excess reign supreme in this extra-ordinary season,' he wrote in January 1606:

There are all forms of insolence from lackeys, including murder . . . two assassins who tried to kill baron d'Aubeterre were broken on the wheel at the Place de la Grève; a soldier was hanged for killing his landlord over 10 francs; a merchant on his way to the fair was slashed through the throat and found in the ditches of Saint-Germain; this is all without mentioning the nineteen other killings in the streets of Paris, committed by parties unknown. The year starts badly, and promises worse to come.[1]

In the space of a single day – 4 May 1596 – in the parish of Saint-Eustache, seventeen people died of hunger. This kind of statistic was soon to become commonplace in the new century as the city was swept by new waves of famine and disease. Henri's city was monumental and sometimes magnifi-cent but it was certainly no paradise, especially for the poor, the old or the sick. Paris was also infested with murderous criminals, nicknamed *coupe-bourses* ('purse-cutters') or *tireurs de laine* ('wool-grabbers'), who in full daylight slashed purses open or pulled the fanciest cloaks from the shoulders of terrified citizens.

It was rumoured that nearly all of them were linked to the city guards. Most vicious and feared of all were the *barbets* (the 'setters' – so called because the length of their hair resembled that of the long-haired dogs which were then fashionable). These dagger-wielding youths would simply march into the houses of the rich and, with a knife to the throat of the unlucky householder, demand money or other items.

The response of the clergy to the city's evil fortunes was to order processions of penitents through the city, and trails of barefoot men and women, traipsing to one or other of the churches even in the depths of winter, were a common sight. On the 14 February 1589, over a thousand penitents, semi-naked and shivering in the icy east wind, gathered in the parish of Saint-Nicolas-des-Champs to march to church. The fact that this day was normally given over to masquerades and other carnivalesque activities only heightened for so-called 'good Catholics' the holiness of their devotions, and for more sceptical Parisians the gullibility of the laity and the manipulative powers of God-crazed priests.

This spectacle was not only mocked by Protestants but also the small number of atheists in the city, who had now dared to reveal themselves in the wake of the Edict of Nantes, the declaration of religious tolerance signed by the king in 1594. Ordinary Catholics too knew that the Catholic clergy was now more dissolute than it had ever been before; even the meanest Parisian was aware of the fact that many priests carried arms, often led private militias and were involved in sacrilegious magical practices. Both nuns and priests were worldly and aware of their power over the lives of ordinary Parisians. To the disgust of laymen such as L'Estoile, they were not shy about wearing the most fashionable clothes, aping the nobility who then favoured fine lace from Venice, spectacles, powdered wigs and the use of elaborate watches, worn around the neck, known as *montre-horloges*. The wearing of long beards had long been a mark of style from the days of François I onwards. L'Estoile was shocked by all of this obvious decadence, which he took as an affront to his own piety, especially when he spied two nuns in the street wearing make-up, their hair curled and powdered. But still, as he noted, despite the obvious corruption of the Church, the sheer amount of visible wickedness in the city – from robbery to rape and murder – kept the churches packed.

Visible Gods

Henri IV was succeeded by his wife, Marie de Médicis, as regent. With a steady hand she reassured Parisians that the future was safe until Henri's son, the dour young Louis XIII, came of age in 1612.

Marie hated the Louvre, which she found gloomy and full of bad memories. In the wake of Henri's assassination, she set out to construct a new royal city on the Left Bank. She began by acquiring the private mansion of the duc de Luxembourg-Piney and ordered her architect, Salomon de Brosse, to build her a palace to equal the Palazzo Pitti in Florence. The result was the Luxembourg palace and its gardens, which she never saw in its complete form, finished in the mid part of the century, long after she had died in exile at Cologne (where Richelieu had driven her).

The other great changes which the city underwent in this period were no less tangled up in the political manoeuvrings of the ruling classes. The volatile nature of the city and the instability of the recent past had made the monarchy both frightened for itself and always ready to stamp on dissent with maximum violence. When he came to power, Louis XIII distinguished himself by his aloof manner, casual cruelty and the distance he maintained between himself and the pestilential city, which he abandoned at every opportunity to go hunting in the countryside. Louis was happy to leave the exercise of real power to his chief adviser, the Cardinal de Richelieu, the arrogant but shrewd son of a gentleman from Poitou who would soon be effective ruler of Paris.

Richelieu had three main priorities: to wreck the Protestant cause in France, to deepen the absolute power of the monarchy, and extend the frontiers of France at the expense of the house of Austria. Richelieu had started out as a priest for the Concini, a wealthy and influential family who were rumoured to have been involved in the murder of Henri IV and who were wiped out by Louis XIII when he came of age. After the assassination, the wily Richelieu retreated to the Church but he was soon back in favour and eventually effectively in charge of the court and its ministers. He prided himself on his cruelty: 'When I have made a resolution,' he said, 'I go straight to the goal; I overturn everything; I strip everything bare; and then I cover all in my red cassock.'[2] Enemies mysteriously disappeared on a regular basis and there were rumours of torture and mutilation in the châteaux of Bagneux and Ruel. Most of Richelieu's victims died on the scaffold, usually without trial and mostly because of suspected conspiracies against him. He was vain and prickly and personally came to watch the decapitation of the famous and distinguished historian Jacques-Auguste Thou, who had written approvingly of the Reformation and made some mildly disparaging remarks about the cardinal's antecedents.

The eventual consequence of this form of state tyranny was an abject kind of deference that soon became the prevailing modus operandi of the political classes. The king himself, a cold and treacherous figure, held absolute power and was described in the *parlement* as 'inspired by Divinity' and a 'visible God'. Richelieu, as God's right-hand man, soaked all of this up without comment.

Although a clumsy writer, Richelieu fancied himself as a patron of the arts, writing books of theology and plays, and founding the Académie Française. The books were written mainly in order to impress his mistresses (the most famous of these was Marion Delorme, duchesse de Comballet, who was also Richelieu's own niece). The Académie Française had begun as a literary group – including such distinguished names of the period as Jean Ogier de Gombault, Antoine Godeau and Jean Chapelain in their number – who met in semi-secrecy to discuss literary and philosophical matters. It was Richelieu's idea to turn this into an official body to give authority to the French language and its productions. The Académie's ability to function autonomously was hindered from the outset when Richelieu imposed on it the task of publishing an attack on Pierre Corneille's *Le Cid*, in which the cardinal had discerned an attack on himself (the Académie's final condemnation of the play was in fact no more than a mealy-mouthed and pompous critique of Corneille's grammar and style).

In Paris, Richelieu's ambitions were centred on projects to further his own glory. He founded the Jardin des Plantes, it is true, partly on the advice of the royal physician Labrosse as a source of herbal medicaments. His lavish funding of the restoration of the Sorbonne was, however, entirely in the service of his own vanity, as he was seeking a suitable setting for his own tomb. In the same way, the Palais Cardinal, which would become the Palais-Royal, was built in his honour as the centrepiece of a so-called 'aristocratic quarter', designed to house the rulers of the city in the splendour they deserved.

The territory of Paris was at this stage mostly under the control of clever and rich speculators – men like Louis Le Barbier, who kicked out the whores and touts from the Île aux Vaches and the Île Notre-Drame, bringing the two islands together to make the much more salubrious enclave of the Île Saint-Louis. Le Barbier was commissioned by the king to knock down the old walls to the north of Paris, extending the capital's reach with several new districts. Contracts were drafted and re-drafted but little was done without direct payment (Le Barbier's priority was to build up sizeable dowries for his daughters). Richelieu hated Le Barbier and his colleagues with a vengeance as his ambitions for the city were directly at odds with their opportunism and entrepreneurial energy. Still the cardinal could find no pretext for simply killing these men. Instead, he set out to ruin them with a long war of financial attrition that he was always bound to win, even at the cost of almost destroying the royal finances.

The area immediately north of the river, stretching towards the far end of what is now rue de Richelieu, was the epicentre of the cardinal's urbanist dreams and accordingly given the name of 'Quartier Richelieu'. It was hard to tell how ironic Corneille really intended to be when he praised this 'new Paris' in *Le Menteur* ('The Liar') of 1643 as 'a whole town, built with pomp, and which seems to have come, as a miracle, from a rotten old ditch'.[3]

The Theatre of the Street

The advance of the political culture of absolutist government was in direct opposition to the life of most ordinary Parisians, who under Louis XIII's regime had certainly not lost any of their sense of irony, or their appetite for the earthy pleasures of the fairs and markets which were now established as a central part of Parisian popular culture. During the early years of the new century, and despite opposition from religious authorities, comedians, jugglers and strolling players had once again become regular fixtures at street markets and fairs, much as they had been in the medieval period, before Puritanism and civil war had wiped the streets clean of *ménestrels*, *trouvères*, *jongleurs* and their harmless fun.

Parisian favourites included 'Gros Guillaume' (he was in fact a native of Normandy called Robert Guérin), who, at least according to Henri de Sauval who regularly watched him perform, was 'so fat, so lardy and fat-bellied' that 'he walked in pursuit of his stomach'. Gros Guillaume's act was to appear on stage dressed in a barrel and with his face covered in flour (reminding his audience that he had been a baker). He joked, sang and grimaced his way through a repertoire that veered between acid political satire and the most coarse sexual ribaldry, targeting both men and women with equally scabrous wit.[4]

Gros Guillaume was usually to be found in the late afternoon or early evening at the Pont-Neuf, which was the epicentre of the city's cultural life, a busy throng of hawkers, touts, whores, shoppers, beggars and respectable middle-class Parisians. The bridge, at 28 metres wide, was not only broader than any existing bridge in Europe, but also wider than any avenue or street. It was a natural stage for the city's performers, providing a site for spectators to sample the essence of the city and its endless, shifting activity.

Guillaume was often in the company of Gaultier-Garguille and Turlupin, two other well-known comedians with whom he would team up to make a trio. All three of them had worked in Faubourg Saint-Laurent as bakers, a trade mysteriously associated with that of the street player (this tradition had arrived in Paris from the Midi). The comedy gang even briefly enjoyed royal patronage, until Gros Guillaume fell foul of the magistrates with a joke too far. He died, hungry and mirthless, in prison. All three are buried in Saint-Sauveur, the patron church of Parisian street performers.

Other street players enjoyed less harsh fortunes. These included a legendary master of the three-card trick, Maître Gonin, whose sly dexterity with cards or goblets made him famous, admired even by royalty, who recognized similarly adroit manoeuvring in their ministers of state ('Maître Gonin' was later one of the nicknames popularly applied to the notoriously slippery Richelieu). Two of Gros Guillaume's greatest rivals were the clown Tabarin and his master Mondor, who worked the Pont-Neuf over the same ten-year period (roughly 1620–30) as Guillaume. Tabarin was most famous for the sketch in which he played a gormless oaf or a hypochondriac (or both at the same time) pestering Mondor, dressed up as a physician or some other man of science, who answered him in the most earnest and entertaining gibberish. Other set pieces invariably involved Tabarin as a gullible idiot easily duped. None of this prevented him practising his other profession as the maker and vendor of medicines of all kinds, which he plugged relentlessly between sketches. Tabarin is credited with more or less single-handedly inventing the commercial break – he would regularly stop to expound the virtues of some product or other – as well as providing the inspiration for Molière's farce *Les Fourberies de Scapin* ('The Swindles of Scapin') of 1671, the tale of a deceitful and unscrupulous valet. Tabarin's act only came to an end when he introduced a mildly pornographic flavour into his work, which immediately brought the city authorities crashing down on him (pornography, although widely enjoyed, was then as now regarded primarily as a private form of entertainment).

The Pont-Neuf was where the *coupe-bourses* and *tireurs de laine* lingered and thrived. Both sides of the street were lined with con-men, whores, entertainers, charlatans and tricksters whose main aim was to distract passers-by on their way to the rue Dauphine, the newly created passage down into the heart of the Left Bank, or the markets and docks of the Right Bank. This new and vibrant addition to the street life of Paris under Louis XIII was celebrated in a song, 'Les Filouteries du Pont-Neuf' ('Frauds of the Pont-Neuf'), which entered immediately into the city's already rich store of folk memory.

You, meeting-place of charlatans,
Tricksters, tarts,
O Pont-Neuf, theatre of the street!
Sellers of unguents and suppositories,
Home of teeth-pullers, rag merchants, booksellers, show-offs,
Singers of new songs,
Panderers, purse-cutters,
Smart-arses and masters of filthy trades.[5]

The Pont-Neuf was also a cauldron of anti-government, anti-royal and anti-religious activity. Most of the time this was expressed in criminality and vagabondage, but the real guiding spirit of life at street level here was to be found in the quick-witted satire of the entertainers and the slick patter of the salesmen. This naturally subversive quality was soon allied to political causes. The Pont-Neuf was, for example, where Paul de Gondi, who was not yet known as the Cardinal Retz and nephew of the Archbishop of Paris, came in 1648 to whip up a mob against the absolutist government of Louis XIV and the wily Giulo Mazarin, the king's chief adviser.

The trigger for Gondi's anger was the arrest of Pierre Broussel, the loudest member of Mazarin's opposition in the *parlement* and a vehement opponent of the disastrous fiscal policies pursued by the government to support pointless wars with Germany and Spain. Parisians were justifiably incensed at this waste of money and it was not hard for Gondi to find a sympathetic audience among the hard-bitten street dwellers and petty criminals of the Pont-Neuf. The first response of the crowd, made furious by Gondi's speech, was to launch an insurrection, erecting barricades in rue de l'Arbre-Sec and then across the city. There were soon a thousand or so barricades, made of timber, steel and the paving stones of Paris. The atmosphere was festive – taverns provided free drink and meat to the rioters – but likely to turn very quickly into shocking violence. The royal family sheltered in the Palais-Royal and, as soon as they could, made for their refuge outside the city at Château de Rueil. Meanwhile, the insurrection became a full-blown revolt against the Crown, as the prince de Condé, an opportunistic young princeling with proven military acumen, made for the city.

The rioters were called *frondeurs*, after the *fronde*, a slingshot used by Parisian urchins to pelt well-off passers-by. These same slingshots had been used by rioters to smash Mazarin's windows, and the revolt itself soon became known as 'La Fronde'. There were in fact two insurrections that went by this name. The first, which took place in 1648, was the 'Fronde des Parlements' and was primarily a reaction against Mazarin's taxes. The second, in reality a series of minor riots throughout France lasting from 1651 until 1653, was known as the 'Fronde des Princes' and mainly centred on rival bids for the throne. Both were provoked by disgust at the wilful policies of the Crown. There was, however, no full-scale revolutionary movement, mainly because it was impossible to impose any coherence on what was essentially a disordered show of fury rather than a revolutionary programme. The first and second movements of the 'Fronde' were imitated in the countryside and in provincial towns but similarly lacked any co-ordination. It was also soon clear that Gondi, whose revolutionary ire ebbed with the promise of a cardinal's hat, was in love with trouble itself rather than social justice. The *esprit frondeur* ('slingshot wit'), with its origins in the street life of the newly built Pont-Neuf in the early seventeenth century, has now passed into Parisian folklore as part of the verbal armoury of any self-respecting Parisian.

PART FOUR

New Rome and Old Sodom

1670–1799

Palermo has Etna:
Paris, *la Pensée*.

Victor Hugo,
Littérature et philosophie mêlées, 1834

The Good Parisian drinks all,
devours all, swallows all.

Louis-Sébastien Mercier,
Le Tableau de Paris, 1782–8

View of Paris by an unknown artist, seventeenth century.

20. Splendour and Misery

The use of the term *le grand siècle* ('the great century') still causes argument. The expression was first used by French historians in the nineteenth century to describe the period that began and ended with the one-person rule of Louis XIV, who came to the throne in 1643 and governed France until his death in 1715. Louis took sole control of the government following the death of Mazarin, his adviser and chief minister, in 1661. This was a period of French cultural and political ascendancy that led to two hundred years of almost uncontested French supremacy in mainland Europe, and only ended with capitulation to Bismarck's Germany in 1871. Dissenters have argued instead that the term 'the great century' should only really be applied to the eighteenth century. This was when royal power declined and the face of France and Europe began truly to change. This was the period when, as Michelet put it (on reading Rousseau), 'things began to happen', when religion was forced to retreat in the name of Reason and the old order began to break up.[1]

Most of the seventeenth century, in contrast, was a confused and messy era, when the French were still bound up in old religious conflicts and largely unaware of their political potential or destiny. For many historians concerned with twentieth-century Leftist movements, the so-called *grand siècle* was at best no more than an illusion of cultural power, and at worst a hubristic myth of greatness that still poisons the French body politic.

From the mid-part of the seventeenth century onwards, it is none the less an undeniable fact that Paris was effectively the European capital of politics, fashion and the arts. High society in Rome and Vienna aped Parisian manners, dress and even speech (to be a good Parisian, it was considered elegant to be as circumspect and ironic as possible at all times). Only chilly England, it seemed, was in any way indifferent to the spell the city cast over the rest of the continent.

Parisian politics was indeed even more alien to the English than Parisian high fashion. This was an era when French domestic and foreign policy, all emanating from Paris, was dominated by the pursuit of *la gloire* – a word that meant in this context not only 'glory' or 'majesty' but also a God-given destiny, and which was reflected in the literature of the period.

Military success was important, but so also was the magnificence of the court and state that made these victories. The king was, for a while at least, attributed with almost superhuman powers: absolutism was the most perfect of all forms of government. For the citizens of seventeenth-century Paris, the 'great century' was characterized above all by a coming together of government and monarchy into an almost indissoluble whole. The king stood as the incarnation of the state itself and the representative of God on earth.

The clearest physical manifestation of this political belief was made visible in the heart of the city in the form of the triumphal arches, at the Porte Saint-Martin and Porte Saint-Denis, the old toll-gates, in 1670. These were commissioned by Louis XIV to honour his victories abroad. At the same time, as Paris was no longer under serious threat of siege, the fortifications around the city's edges were finally removed, making avenues that would become the first boulevards in the city (the French word *boulevard* has its origins in the German-derived word 'bulwark'). The Porte Saint-Denis carried particular historical significance as the royal gateway to Paris (ironically enough, the last sovereign to pass this way was Queen Victoria during a visit to the 'universal exhibition' of 1855).[2]

The model for the city, in form and mission, was its Roman inheritance. Writers of the period did all they could to stress the antique origins of Paris and its mission as a classical city reborn. In accordance with this apparently Divine destiny, art, literature and science, as representations of French greatness, were all eventually under state control. The state also kept a beady eye on 'scandalous' or subversive texts that contradicted or contravened the limits that it had fixed as part of its programme for a new and better society. Yet, despite the controlling hand of the state, the shifts in the legislative and religious framework of power were matched by several extraordinary generations of artistic or literary talent who came to or from Paris and found there ready and sophisticated audiences who appreciated their wit, subversion, melancholy and brilliance.

The most popular mode of expression was the theatre: an art form that, even in the hands of a master *comédien* like Molière, confirmed the prevailing view that the cultural life of Paris was a spectacle without equal in Europe. Audiences flocked to see his plays alongside those of Pierre Corneille and Jean Racine. Their works were often savaged in the literary journal *Le Mercure galant* but Parisians still came in their hundreds to watch, drink, get into fights, pick up members of the opposite sex or mock the actors, as well as imbibe culture. The Comédie Française was formally constituted in 1680, but its players, who included Molière, a long time favourite of royalty and the public, performed mostly in the Palais-Royal and then the Théâtre Guénégaud near the Pont-Neuf. Louis XIV was prudish and occasional attempts were made at censorship, especially of the ribald Italian farces, but his efforts were feeble and generally ignored.

Indeed a night at the theatre was judged a disappointment if it did not contain dangerous, even erotic, thrills for the wealthier classes. The *parterre*, or pit, in all theatres was well known for its dangers and its population of drunken servants and soldiers. This was a source of titillation and entertainment for the rich Parisians who often took up seats on the stage to watch both audience and spectacle. One audience in 1673 had famously tried to burn down a theatre. In the 1690s, the theatres were packed with soldiers on leave or just discharged from the battlefield, and hooliganism reached new peaks of idiocy and terror. One evening at the Comédie Française an overly grim performance of a Racinian tragedy was halted by the antics of a Great Dane, brought to the theatre by a marquis. The crowd encouraged the dog to howl at the actors before the play was abandoned. Two aristocrats were arrested an hour or two after the performance for having beaten up a coach driver. Their excuse was that they 'had not had a good enough time at the Comédie Française'.[3]

This kind of random violence was also a reminder that the real city of Paris was still filthy, disease-ridden, a good place to be stabbed or raped, or to starve to death. If it was at the centre of European history, few Parisians sensed that they occupied a privileged and unique position.

Inner-City Hobgoblins

The myths and legends of Parisian prestige indeed rarely reached the lowest levels of society. Louis XIV and his people kept a wary distance from each other until the king finally retreated to Versailles. From that point on, for ordinary Parisians, the king was no more than an abstract representation of the country. Everyday life in the city was filthy and dangerous and far more absorbing and important than the life at court.

A mark of Parisian contempt for the court at Versailles was that none of the kings who lived there ever entered Parisian folklore. Until now, it had been common for kings to be celebrated or satirized in a Parisian song, satire or saying. With the court at Versailles, Parisians considered the king to be an irrelevance. This status was a long way from Louis's original ambition, which had been to make the capital his political and cultural base, fusing sovereign, state and city. Louis XIV had come to the throne at the age of five under the regency of his mother, Anne of Austria, and grew up under the steadying hand of Mazarin. On the death of his wily adviser in 1661, he fully assumed power at the age of twenty-three, convinced of his Divine destiny to lead France and Europe. This was the same youth who, ten years earlier, according to popular myth, had galloped six miles back from a hunt and swaggered into the Palais de Justice when he heard that the *parlement* was meeting without his authority. Without hesitation, and allegedly cracking a whip, he had declared: 'I am the State!'

This kind of behaviour was entirely in accordance with Louis's love of show and spectacle. He was nicknamed the Sun King after an emblem on the shield he wore while parading around the city as part of a great pageant held to celebrate the birth of his first-born son. Yet although he was apparently popular with his subjects at this stage, Louis was already suspicious of Parisians; from an early age he spent as little time as he could in the city. As soon as he could, he removed himself permanently to Versailles, where he felt both safe and able to construct a palace that reflected what he considered to be his exalted fate. He hunted fairly well and as often as he could, and planned the palace and grounds as an ordered and thoroughly rational estate, in complete contrast to the disordered but vibrant streets of the nearby capital. He would return to Paris only twenty-five more times throughout the next forty years or so.

Louis's dislike of the citizenry had been mainly fuelled by the insurrections of the Fronde. He was also driven by a sense of his own glorious status and was wary of either contact with the people or any intimates who might rival his own eminent position. One of these was a certain Nicolas Fouquet, a brash and arrogant former superintendent of finance who fancied himself as prime minister in the wake of Mazarin's death. Fouquet made the fatal error of inviting the king to a lavish banquet followed by an outdoor torch-lit performance of Molière's latest play, staged by none other than the great playwright himself. Fouquet's mansion was magnificent and outshone the king's own residence in terms of luxury and ostentation. Louis was outraged by such display but waited three weeks before having Fouquet arrested on trumped-up charges of embezzlement and treachery and smearing him as a pornographer (Fouquet was rumoured to be the co-author, with a certain Madame de Maintenon, of *L'École des filles*, 'The Girls' School', a spicy stew of Sapphic erotica that did the rounds at all the best *salons* in Paris). The man was also a hero of the Paris street, which was all the more reason for Louis to keep his distance from the city as Fouquet was sentenced to life imprisonment in the Bastille.

Meanwhile Jean-Baptiste Colbert, former secretary to the court and assistant to Fouquet himself, took Mazarin's position. He was a cold and calculating figure (nicknamed 'le Nord' by Madame de Sévigné, a sharp-eyed if not always reliable witness to life at court) and utterly ruthless in the execution of his various strategies. Colbert's greatest plan was to extend Paris further and build it better than ever before, finally overtaking Rome as the capital of European civilization. He devoted time and energy to the arts, founding academies, building his own library and encouraging erudite publications like the *Journal des savants*. Above all, Colbert believed passion-ately in the destiny of France as the great nation that would lead Europe. His careful planning was undone by Louis's endless wars, however, which regularly emptied the treasury and angered Parisians, who paid the bills in taxes. Like Louis himself, Colbert became increasingly estranged from Paris and was finally hated by its people.

Among themselves, Parisians noted that a sinister hobgoblin, called the 'little Red Man', had been seen again haunting the Tuileries and the Louvre. This sighting can be attributed to a familiar mixture of popular superstition and insurrectionist fervour – the 'little Red Man' was held to presage the death of a regime – and his appearance had been justifiably feared by the likes of Catherine de Médicis and Richelieu. The 'little Red Man' would surface again in Parisian history, on the eve of Revolution in 1789 and the massacres of 1793. He made his final appearances, legend has it, to Napoleon on the edge of disaster in Egypt and Russia. When he appeared in 1648, to herald the troubles of the Fronde, Parisians welcomed him, believing that he represented the true spirit of the city.[4]

A Spectacular Society

The age of classicism and grandeur was also an age of irony and indifference. The corpse of a murder victim (a common enough sight in the city) was neatly stepped over on the Pont-Neuf by any right-thinking and fashionable gentleman or lady, who ignored with the same blank weariness the cries of a starving infant or a *cul-de-jatte* ('limbless beggar' – the Pont-Neuf was a favoured headquarters for this sort of person) as they perhaps hailed a *haquet* – the new form of carriage for hire, invented to navigate the muddy streets.

Appearance was all. Even in the early years of the era, well before the city had been properly beautified, a new fashion emerged for kissing hands with as much ostentation as possible. The practice, called *baise-mains* ('hand-kissing' or 'hand-fucking' – the double meaning of *baiser* stood then as now), was shockingly most prevalent among effeminate young men, who performed the ritual on the street as much as possible. These young men were almost always deeply in debt and flamboyantly careless about such matters: 'Mais il n'est pas bon gentilhomme, qui ne doit rien à ce jourd'hui' ('He who owes nothing these days cannot be called a gentleman'), wrote Claude d'Esternod in a satire of the period.[5] Esternod was himself a gentleman and a thief. Robbery had recently become a fashionable sport for the well-heeled and stylish young men who drank in the taverns around the Pont-Neuf and parts of the Marais. The aim was to steal the finest luxury items – cloaks, gowns, hats and purses – and then hide yourself in the crowd. The new street lights and the occasional strolling policeman were usually a deterrent to Esternod, but he still admired the guile and skill that went into this 'noble project'. Men and women alike admired the most artful street thieves, with names like baron de Veillac and chevalier d'Odrieu.

The real dangers for women in the city were kidnap, rape and forced marriage. It was common for a *gentilhomme* without a fortune to abduct a widow or young girl from a wealthy family and, in a solitary spot outside the city, marry her under the orders of a bought priest. The prelude to this act was often rape, which destroyed the last shred of respectability for the unfortunate woman. The practice was widely accepted among the aristocracy. The fathers of these abducted brides usually coughed up some sort of dowry and, although principally devised as a money-making racket, many marriages strangely flourished from these unlikely beginnings.

Despite the turbulent nature of city life, Paris was changing shape to reflect the growth in public confidence. Most notably, by the first decade of the seventeenth century the last medieval houses had either fallen down or been destroyed. For the first time, the organization of life in the city was being planned according to the logic of finance and trade rather than royal whim and the random chaos of medieval urbanism.

Paris was indeed thriving in many ways. The first street lamps did not appear until 1667, but by then the streets had been widened and light now flooded certain city streets and bridges in the early morning. By night the city was still dangerous, but within a few years the chief of police, Nicolas-Gabriel de La Reynie, had made the streets safer, if still not entirely free of bandits and thieves. La Reynie's guards meted out rough justice to anyone who broke street lanterns or otherwise interfered with his plan to bring security to the city. Duelling was banned and no one, not even the most distinguished *gentilhomme*, was allowed to carry weapons into a theatre.

Posters appeared for the first time, advertising public fairs and political meetings. The first newspaper, *La Gazette*, was newly established in the 1630s, appearing soon on a regular basis with news from all the European capitals. Parisians flocked to see visitors from even further afield, packing the streets for a glimpse of the Turkish ambassador, captured slaves from Senegal or the Moor Matheo Lopez, a black man and a Muslim from Morocco.

A politician called Jean-Jacques Rounuard de Villayer, tired of sending servants to deliver messages and money across the expanding city, came up with the idea of a postal service and postboxes began to spring up in the well-heeled parts of town. The first properly run public transport systems had appeared earlier in the century – a carriage for hire by several citizens at once and called a *carrosse* had been invented by an enterprising carpenter called Nicolas Sauvage in around 1654. By the 1660s, more than twenty or so of these carriages could regularly be found lined up for hire at the church of Saint-Fiacre (they were nicknamed *fiacres* thereafter) and a decade or so later, following itineraries devised by the philosopher and mathematician Blaise Pascal, for 5 sous, the Parisian could travel in some comfort from the Palais de Luxembourg to the Pont-Neuf to the Louvre and back again.

Professions and classes now clustered in various distinct parts of the city and the notion arose of neighbourhoods made up of like-minded individuals, even if the idea of neighbourliness remained then as now an alien concept. The term *quartier* entered common usage to describe these areas of the city. A great deal of money was invested, particularly in the Marais and the Île Saint-Louis (formerly ignored and left without bridges), and architects vied with each other to create residential housing that was both beautiful and practical. They began by imitating the Renaissance ideal of the Italian city-state of colonnaded passageways and open piazzas. This was the age of stone, and houses were often more solid than their Italian models had been. There was also a certain democracy at work: the Parisian bourgeoisie were determined not be excluded from the elegant life of the city and commissioned the construction of houses called *pavillons*, which were only slightly less grand than the great mansions known as *hôtels* that were fashionable among the urban aristocracy.

Houses in central areas of the city were now being constructed horizontally rather than vertically and the streets and squares built around them, lined with arcades and avenues, were ideal for promenading or parading the latest fashions. The term *flanner* ('to wander without purpose') arrived in Paris from Normandy and was a perfect description of the elegant idleness that so many young men feigned as their primary purpose in the city. As we shall see, the *flâneur* would become a stock figure in the nineteenth and twentieth centuries. The cult of idleness in this period was a pseudo-aristocratic response to the utilitarian demands of work and industry. The *flâneur* would thus, ironically enough, become a key element in the defining of modernity. But already in the seventeenth century he (and it was always a 'he') was a familiar figure on the Parisian landscape, straying at random in pursuit of sexual or alcoholic pleasure. As the city was developed and became denser throughout the century, this landscape seemed to grow infinitesimally more complex and diverse on a daily basis.

The Arts of Pleasure

Paris had always been a drinkers' terrain. Lutetia had been famous across the Roman world for its vines and taverns, and the medieval city was notorious throughout northern Christendom for the quality of its alehouses and the lavish quantity of wines and beers they offered. By the latter part of the seventeenth century, nearly every street in the city boasted at least two or three taverns of varying cost and quality. Although, in the eyes of the court, the Church and the police, these places were illicit and the crucible of potential disorder, they were for most Parisians a staple of everyday sociability. It was where ordinary people went to eat, drink, find sex or a fight, quarrel, make plans and mingle with their neighbours, each of whom belonged first to the *quartier* rather than to Paris. The taverns were hard to control and impossible to police effectively; the debauchery and idleness that they promoted was an ever-present threat to the moral order of what priests commonly referred to as 'this city, most Catholic'.

The rumbustious world of the drinker was also a clear threat to social order in the most practical terms: it was where political and religious dissidents were able to find their support, and from the earliest days of the city, the authorities made regular interventions to control it. In 1350, the king, Jean le Bon, had fixed the price of red wine at 10 deniers a pint, white wine at 8 deniers, and ordered that wine could be sold only by registered *marchands de vin*. This, and subsequent efforts to control the flow of alcohol through the city, did little or nothing to stop the growth of an anarchic drinking culture that regularly opposed or undermined the official city authorities.

Everyday life in the taverns and backstreets of the city offered a bracing counterpoint to the sterile grandeur of Versailles during the reign of Louis XIV. Some of the most famous drinking places had now been there for several centuries – longer than any royal dynasty. Some of the most distinguished figures of the *grand siècle* could be found drinking in places like the Pomme de Pin ('The Pine Cone'), on the corner of rue de la Cité, a former haunt of Rabelais and Villon and now a regular meeting place for Racine, Molière, Chapelle and Boileau (who was on one occasion so famously drunk that it was claimed he would have to change his name in order not to be recognized).

Other famous drinking holes of the period included La Corne ('The Hunter's Horn'), at the edge of Place Maubert, Le Berceau ('The Cradle') on the Pont Saint-Michel, La Fosse aux Lions ('The Lions' Ditch'), rue Pas-de-la-Mule, Le Cormier Fleuri ('The Sorb Tree in Bloom'), near Saint-Eustache, or La Croix de Lorraine ('The Cross of Lorraine') near the Bastille. The names were originally intended to provide a guide to the type of atmosphere and clientele, evoking most often a rural idyll or a pseudo-patriotic or pseudo-religious significance, or a pun (Au Lion d'Or, '[At] The Golden Lion', also meant 'au lit où on dort', 'a bed to sleep in', and was usually a lodging house). Meaning and reality were, however, often quickly separated (the patriotic-sounding Croix de Lorraine was famous for its fights between released prisoners from the Bastille and drunken Musketeers, the king's guard, who were known for their hard drinking as much as for their valour). Drinking was also a badge of local patriotism: the most popular wines came not only from Burgundy or Bordeaux, but also the Paris region, from Montmartre, Suresnes or Argenteuil.

The first cafés – places that specialized in coffee rather than ale or wine – were established in the city in the 1660s without much success initially. These were brought to Paris by two Armenian brothers, Pascal and Grégoire Alep, who had the idea of devoting establishments to the sale and ingestion of the newly fashionable drink. The café itself was an Eastern import which, like the croissant, had arrived in the city in the wake of the siege of Vienna, when the Turkish armies were finally broken and driven out of Europe. Parisians regarded these Oriental imports with great suspicion at first and even greater circumspection (tea from China, which arrived in 1636, was by contrast immensely popular from the moment it arrived).

Most Parisians were, however, deeply enthusiastic about food and drink from Italy. Lemonade, orangeade and sorbets were long-familiar staples of street life from the period of Catherine de Médicis onwards. It was little surprise, therefore, that the first truly successful café in Paris was run by a Sicilian, Francesco Procopi. The Café Procope sold wine, but prided itself on its coffee and on being a place to talk in a reasoned manner, away from the boozers, whores and gamblers of the traditional taverns. It would soon become famous as the cradle of Enlightenment coffee-drinking, attracting figures such as Voltaire, Rousseau, and Jean-François Marmontel, and indeed, after several changes of address, now stands in the rue de l'Ancienne Comédie flogging over-priced *steak-frites* to tourists on the back of this heritage. In 1689, when it first opened, it appeared to be no more than an intriguing fad that, one wag predicted, would soon pass – its new-fangled coffee and croissants and all – into memory like 'a shooting star in the blackest night'.[6]

Paris was still wretchedly poor during this period of expansion, and Colbert was occasionally driven to ship in cheap food from places like Poland and the lower Rhineland. The staple diet of the poorest Parisians was beans, bread and herbs. For those who could not afford the new and exotic pleasures of cafés and *limonadiers*, the streets were still alive with rogues, poets, whores and thieves, who provided a daily and (since the introduction of street lighting) nocturnal parade. These included the self-styled 'mathematician' Vaulesard, an austere, haggard figure ('a skeleton in rags', according to the writer Marc de Maillet, himself a vain and bumptious man)[7] who was given to expounding incomprehensible poetry without warning.

Most disturbingly, at least for the monied classes, was the fact that Vaulesard was a known political zealot (or potential madman) who spent hours staring into the new *rôtisseries* and restaurants around rue Visconti and rue de Buci, glaring reproachfully at all those bourgeois and aristocrats who could eat their fill in full view of the starving thousands of the city.[8]

21. Shadow and Stench

Despite its continued growth in the early part of the eighteenth century, Paris was still physically close to the countryside and even true wilderness. Fields of barley stood no more than a five-minute walk from the *barrière* Saint-Jacques. The cobbled streets of the Faubourg Saint-Marcel became leafy country lanes in the same space of time. In his memoirs, Des Essarts, a wealthy and urbane Parisian lawyer, records how glad he is to escape from the city and find himself, within fifteen minutes' walk from the École Militaire, leaning on a fence chatting about homely country matters with friendly farmers for whom Paris was a rarely visited place far away.[1] The royal road to Paris was often frightening for provincials and country folk. You could hear the roar of the city long before you could see it. This was a marvel and a terror to those who lived their lives according to the gentler rhythms of the seasons and the fields: Paris was all noise, confusion, disorder and violence of the soul. Those who made the journey to the city also risked robbery or worse from the armed bandits and drifting gangs of ex-soldiers who haunted the route.

The most famous sounds from the city – known to most provincials also – were those of the 'criers' of Paris. These street hawkers were a long-established part of Parisian folklore. From the early medieval period onwards, Parisians had been variously entertained by the puns, poems and songs of the hawkers.[2] By the early 1700s, the social grouping of the hawkers was as carefully stratified as any other part of Parisian society. Brandy vendors (they sold it by the cup to cold and weary artisans on their way to work) and coffee sellers enjoyed a special prestige during this period. Fishmongers, who were usually women, were traditionally of low status, despite the Parisian love of seafood (which was brought to the city faster than any other imported foodstuff, usually arriving from the coast within one or two days). Porters, carriage drivers, whores, drunks, soldiers and charlatans all contributed to the incessant noise of the streets.

Above the clattering cacophony, town criers from the Hôtel de Ville barked municipal orders (to stay off the frozen river or watch out for thieves). These were announced in the main squares or at the dockside and always to the sound of drums. The day was measured by the sound of bells, from churches or the clock towers at Hôtel de Ville, where Minerva held the city's coat of arms in her hand, or at the pumping station of La Samaritaine, carrying over to the far edge of the Pont-Neuf. The Parisian working class soon became accustomed, even attuned, to the shouting, quarrelling, snoring, farting and belching that rattled through the thin walls of cheap new buildings. Parisians were famous for shouting or screeching at the slightest provocation and it was the custom of the aristocracy, and then the bourgeoisie who aped them, to lower their voices to distinguish themselves from the lower classes. Everybody in Paris, no matter what their position in society, grew quickly used to the smells of bodies, food, excrement, coffee, animals, and the very mud of the streets of the rapidly expanding city.

Panoramas

In the quest for precision and order within the city itself, Parisian planners and geographers during this period set about producing a wealth of maps of the city. Between the end of the seventeenth century and the Revolution of 1789, more than a hundred maps were made – an unprecedented number but all, despite the best efforts of the most rigorous and determined map-makers, consistently inaccurate.

The first reason for this was that in their drawing map-makers deliberately exaggerated the width of city streets in order to show off the façades of buildings. Most Parisian streets of the period were in fact no wider than four and a half metres, and often narrower, and if paved, slanting towards a gutter. The right of way of carriages in such streets was usually resolved with violence, usually at the point of a sword.

The second reason why map-making was such a difficult and imprecise art was simply because the city was growing at such a fast rate, regularly spilling over into the countryside, that it was impossible to chart.

In the heart of the city, the building boom that had accompanied Louis XIV's reign had made the streets denser and more impenetrable than ever. The engineer Edmé Verniquet drew up the first truly accurate map of the city between 1785 and 1790. He had worked in the dead of night, measuring and mapping the streets with an eye for every detail. Yet the real life of the streets, the engineer concluded, was in the end unknowable to science.[3] Map-making was, none the less, a noble and dignified art (as indicated in Chapter 13), which charted not only the present but left its own mark in the creation of the future city.

But even though Parisians in the early seventeenth century lacked a panoramic vision of their city, they could still see the signs of change and possible decay. One of the clearest symbols of the end of the 'great century' was for many the unfinished triumphal arch at the Place du Trône (now Place de la Nation), which was eventually knocked down in 1716. Originally, Louis XIV had commissioned five of these *portes* to surround the city; only two were completed, at Saint-Denis and Saint-Martin.

There were, however, other more pressing concerns in the early years of the century. The Seine was still the life-blood of Paris, but it also regularly carried disease into the city – dysentery and typhus were commonly imported from smaller hamlets along the Seine, lapping into the city at its eastern edges. In addition, Paris was vulnerable to bad weather and the great frost of 1709 had made the river impassable for weeks at a time. Little grain was brought into the city, and when the price of bread rose to a previously unthinkable 2 sous a loaf, the lieutenant-general of police, René d'Argenson, was compelled to place troops around bakeries.

The Seine was, during this period, congested at the best of times. Wine and grain were transported into the city in small vessels known as *flettes* or, most commonly, in large convoys of boats 16 to 18 metres long. These had to be pulled by two dozen horses. It was a common occurrence for such convoys to be robbed or their passage blocked by thieves.

The death of the king himself in 1715 was shrugged off by Parisians, who had long since grown either bored or weary of the cult that had formed around him. The funeral was appropriately sombre; but along the streets just outside the city, peasants and Parisians drank, danced and sang bawdy songs. The child who would become Louis XV, on the orders of his uncle Philippe, duc d'Orléans, the regent, moved back to Paris, installing himself in Richelieu's Palais-Royal.

'Marked by licence'

Philippe in many ways was the very opposite of the austere figure that the Roi Soleil had become in his latter years. He was witty and possessed of an easy charm. He had a taste for gossip, drink and sex, and by the age of forty-one, when he took up the office of regent, he was said to look much older. He was unpopular among the Catholic hierarchy, however, who whispered that he was a *libertin* (a term first used to describe free-thinkers of the period but which quickly came to mean a sexually voracious predator – see Chapter 22).

Rumours circulated that Philippe had seduced his own daughter. Another story took hold that once, even drunker than usual (two bottles of champagne was a standard breakfast) on returning from a feast at the Palais de Luxembourg, Philippe had lurched over to his captain of the guards, La Fare, and asked him to cut off his right hand. 'Can't you smell it?' slurred the regent. 'It's rotten and has a smell that I can't wash away, and I can't put up with it any longer.' The captain gently ushered him into his bedchamber. Philippe's mother did not believe this or any of the other, similar stories that circulated around the court. She did reproach her son, however, for bedding ugly drunken women who, she said, may well have been lesbians.[4]

Contemporaries were not always kind to Philippe either. Among those who took against him was Voltaire, who, at this point, still loved the city with all the fervour of the native Parisian (he was born there in 1694 into a family that came originally from Poitou). In many ways, at least at this stage in his career, Paris represented a kind of perfection for Voltaire as the place where the great tensions of the age met in conflict and contradiction. Above all, Paris offered to Voltaire the *philosophe* a grandstand view of the movement of history. He was less enthusiastic about Parisians, whom he described as 'idle a lot of the time, always keen to get involved in futile matters, sticking noses in where they shouldn't be'. Later, exiled from the city, he looked on Paris with a mixture of melancholy, anger, regret and the banished Parisian's keen nostalgia for 'the shadow and stench of the streets'.[5] This much was presaged in the era of Philippe, described by Voltaire in accordingly acid terms: 'Herewith the time of the easygoing Regency / A fine time marked by licence.'[6]

In reality, Philippe was an urbane and well-read individual whose only real failing as he took up office was that he had little experience of how to wield power and make politics work. He was, however, shrewd enough to see that a successful economic policy would ensure the survival of both the monarchy and the capital. To this end, he finished the wars that Louis XIV had started and which were bringing the country sporadically to its knees. He opened the prisons, freed galley slaves and set about dismantling many of the quasi-feudal structures still in place in the city and elsewhere.

Philippe was also an optimist and had a somewhat naïve belief in progress. This accounts for why he made the disastrous mistake of inviting the Scotsman John Law to Paris to advise him on how to run the Royal Bank of France. Law had a reputation as an innovative financial thinker and Philippe was delighted with his first suggestion to set up a 'general bank' that had the state as its principal shareholder. This initial success encouraged the king and his advisers to extend their field of operations to the newly acquired wastes of Louisiana (New Orleans had been named after the regent). Parisians flocked to throw money at what seemed to be a foolproof get-rich-quick scheme.

Inevitably, the bubble burst more quickly than anyone could even have guessed. Families were ruined; there were suicides and murders. Disgusted bourgeois Parisians who had lost their capital in what was no more than a hare-brained pyramid scheme burned money and paper shares in the streets to show their anger. John Law had been a canny Edinburgh lawyer but was now identified by Parisians as a 'wretched Englishman'. He got out of Paris as quickly and furtively as he could, narrowly avoiding a lynch mob on his trail. The regency itself would never recover from this monumental failure. When Philippe died, it was reported that one of his favourite animals, a Great Dane, had leaped on to his deathbed and gobbled up his heart. In the taverns and cafés of Paris this was considered a deliciously amusing and appropriate end for the debauched fool of a regent who had bankrupted the city.[7]

The popularity of the monarchy was not enhanced by Philippe's successor, Louis XV. An austere figure with no interest in people, books or politics, he did, however, have a large sexual appetite and after the death of his chief adviser, Cardinal Fleury, in 1742, was all too often ruled by his desires and mistresses. The monarchy was still, despite Philippe's best efforts, far removed from the people of the city, and the gap between the king and his subjects would in fact grow far wider and deeper in the coming years.

Secret City

The wild speculation on international markets was matched in the back-streets of Paris by an equally fevered enthusiasm for gambling. The police easily tolerated the *jeux de société* popular among the aristocracy and other people *de qualité*. What was rather less tolerable, and a clear threat to the social order, was the proliferation of illegal gaming tables that spread across the capital through the first years of the eighteenth century, and which indeed endured well into the Napoleonic era. One of the most notorious of these places in the back alleys of the Marais was called L'Enfer (Hell) and was famed for a ruthlessness that left families of all classes destitute. Police reports of the period note also that women of a certain age ('probably former whores', according to one sergeant) were 'unduly excited' at these tables, gambling and wasting even larger sums than men.[8]

The political philosopher Charles de Secondat Montesquieu, ever a keen and acid-tongued observer of public morality, pointed out that many of these women took up gambling 'expressly to ruin their husbands, and that they are of all ages, from tender youth to the most decrepit old age. I have often seen nine or ten women at table, showing fear, hope and fury and seeming never to be at peace. A husband who wants to control his wife is seen as a disturber of public joy.' These same women were unrepentantly promiscuous, in his view. One such woman, found by her husband in the bed of his son's valet, fired a volley of abuse at the dumbfounded spouse. 'What do you expect, sir?' she shrieked with self-righteous venom. 'When I have no knight, I take his lackey.' Gambling obviously drove women mad, Montesquieu remarked gravely, and led inevitably to murder.[9]

More threatening and more sinister still, at least in the eyes of the police and other public authorities, was the growth of secret and semi-secret societies in Paris. It was believed that between 1700 and 1750 more than a dozen sects loosely affiliated to the cult of freemasonry were installed in the centre of the city. The adepts of this cult, drawn in the first instance mainly from the artisan classes and the lower reaches of the bourgeoisie, believed that they were initiates to sacred mysteries that pre-dated the Flood. Occultism and paganism were nothing new in Paris – indeed they were, and continue to be, two of the deepest veins of historical knowledge in the city – but these movements were a threat because they were also explicitly political. More precisely, in a discreet and clandestine fashion, they aimed at occupying the strategic positions of true power in the capital, finally displacing the monarchy itself. To this extent freemasonry, as a society beyond the control of central government, offered a straightforwardly political response to absolutist power.

The most important Masonic temple in Paris was built on the rue Cadet, which in the early eighteenth century was still called rue de la Voirie ('waterway'), a place known as much for the general stench of its sewers, which were diverted further east. Philippe, duc d'Orléans, made the area fashionable by commissioning a private mansion at number 24. The street now houses a museum devoted to artefacts and medals relating to the long history of freemasonry in the city.

Despite its semi-official status, freemasonry was for a long time a radical movement in Paris, if not quite the authentic medium for spiritual transmission that its early adepts held it to be. The Freemasons were unequivocal in their support for the Commune of 1870, sending delegates to wave banners declaring 'Love One Another' at flashpoints such as Porte Maillot and Porte Bineau. Other Freemasons took up arms and were summarily executed in the wake of the Commune's defeat.

For the duration of the German Occupation of Paris from 1940 onwards, the offices of the rue Cadet were under the control of Jean Marquès-Rivière, a Nazi collaborator and self-styled expert on the occult. It was a signal act of poetic justice that a Freemason, Charles Boileau, an officer in the Free French Forces, liberated the offices in 1944. He also happened to be a Communist and a Jew.

22. Porno Manifesto

There has always been a powerful tradition of bawdy or plainly erotic writing in Paris. This genre flourished particularly from the twelfth century onwards. From then on, Parisians of all social classes were familiar with humorous poems such as *La Damoisele qui ne pooit oïr parler de foutre* ('The Girl who Wouldn't Hear of Fucking') or *La Veuve* ('The Widow'). The authors of these poems were either forgotten or anonymous, but the tales themselves entered deep into Parisian folklore. Many of these poems, such as *Le Chevalier qui fist parler les cons* ('The Knight Who Made Cunts Speak'), were admired not only for their ribald content but also for their sophistication and cheeky wit.[1]

Indeed the latter poem (penned by a Parisian called Garin in the thirteenth century) was the inspiration for the tale *Les Bijoux indiscrets* ('The Indiscreet Jewels', 1748) by Denis Diderot – the story of a king who possesses a magic ring which makes the genitals of his ladies at court speak. As a man of reason and science, a *philosophe* and an atheist, Diderot decided that he had a moral duty to attack all forms of superstition, including that of royal power. *Les Bijoux indiscrets* is a barbed allegory satirizing the lies, duplicity and sheer venality of life in the court of Louis XV at Versailles. As such, it is also a good example of how the popularity of erotic writing in the eighteenth century lay in the fact that it was often explicitly political.

Paris now had cutting-edge facilities for book production and distribution and, most importantly, a market of educated and semi-educated readers who were hungry for knowledge, enlightenment and entertainment. The rise in literacy did not lead necessarily to a rise in book ownership, but even the meanest servant could read his master's newspaper or magazine at home or in a café. Hence reading pornography, in the café or at home, was an activity open to all classes of society.

The newly established Parisian bookshops of the early eighteenth century were noisy and sociable places. As reported by one commentator, groups of readers stood 'as if magnetized around the counter; they are in the way of the shopkeeper, who has removed all the seats in order to force them to stand; but that does not stop them remaining for hours bent over books, busy perusing pamphlets, making advance judgements of their merit and their fate'.² The most famous bookshops were fashionable and charged with sexuality. The most notorious were those in the arcades of the Palais-Royal, which provided a focus for much intellectual preening and discreet flirtation in the daytime. These included establishments such as the Librairie Pierre-Honoré-Antoine Pain, whose bestsellers comprised the likes of *Le Parnasse des poètes satyriques* (an anthology of erotic poems), *Thérèse Philosophe* (a young girl's introduction to sexuality) or *L'Enfant du bordel* ('Child of the Brothel'), one of whose heroines is 'gifted with a clitoris which would shame the fairest ankle in France'.³

Many of these bookshops stayed open late into the night, when the Palais-Royal was flooded with whores, dandies and several varieties of sexual adventurer. Reading an erotic text by candlelight in one of these shops was for many young men and women of the era the eighteenth-century equivalent of a sexual apéritif, a sharpening physical stimulant before venturing out into the blackened streets of the city in pursuit of gratification.

The Literary Underground

Accompanying the growth of reading as a fashionable activity came the *bouquinistes*. These were the poorer and more desperate booksellers who first made their appearance in Paris in the sixteenth century, selling their wares in the open air along the Pont-Neuf. Initially referred to as *estaleurs* ('street merchants'), they were notorious for selling clandestine Protestant pamphlets during the Wars of Religion. The authorities regularly clamped down on them as thieves or subversives. By the eighteenth century, they had become semi-respectable, their stalls frequented mainly by students, and were known as *boekinistes* or *bouquinistes* (from the Flemish term *boekin*, 'little book'). They had also spread out along the Seine, occupying the positions that they roughly occupy now. Regular attempts were made by the authorities to stamp them out, but each successive wave of troubles in Paris, from famine to the riots of the Fronde, gave them a ready market of Parisian readers keen to devour illegal pamphlets denouncing the king or attacking the government of the day. By 1732, the banks of the Seine were packed with over 120 *bouquinistes*, feeding the Parisian appetite for politics and porn.

Paris was indeed home to a large body of underground literature during this period. Much of it was imported from Amsterdam or Brussels, but a great deal was also home-grown and scandalized readers with detailed and knowledgeable accounts of life in the city. Politics (or sometimes places) and erotica often went hand in hand, and the municipal and royal authorities found it almost impossible to keep track of what was being sold where and to whom. If a book was not on sale in the Palais-Royal, it could usually be found *chez les bouquinistes*; failing that, it could be bought from the *colporteurs*, itinerant booksellers and scribes, who were not settled in one spot like the *bouquinistes*, and who distributed their wares throughout the city, in cafés, taverns and *salons*.

The *colporteur*, like the *bouquiniste*, had indeed been a staple of Parisian life since the sixteenth century, as literacy rates rose and reading became an everyday activity rather than the mark of a privileged élite. He was basically a wandering salesman, a street hustler ever alert to the authorities. *Colporteurs* could be found on most Parisian street corners selling books on a tray, with the most incendiary or sexual texts hidden under a *papier bleu*. As one contemporary eye-witness observed:

Police spies wage war on the colporteurs, a race of men who trade in the only good books one can still read in France, which are consequently banned. They are horribly treated; all the police bloodhounds pursue these poor creatures who do not know what they are selling and would hide the Bible under their cloaks if the Lieutenant of Police took it into his head to ban the Bible. They are put in the Bastille for selling silly pamphlets that will be forgotten tomorrow.[4]

Parisians devoured all manner of texts from the *colporteurs*: books on magic, almanacs, comedies (*Les Adieux de Tabarin* – the versified text of the act of the street performer Tabarin was a bestseller), burlesque guides to Paris (*le Déjeuner de la rapée* – literally 'The Grated Lunch' – was a famously scatological version of the city), dictionaries of slang or a guide to farting.

The public also had a taste for facts that were freakish or just plain grisly. Events reported in newspapers between 1716 and 1717 included, for example: a wedding in the church of Saint-Eustache between a groom of a hundred and five years old and a bride of ninety-five; the upturning of a boat and the drowning of its cargo of washerwomen in the frozen Seine, their heads poking through the surface and their bodies trapped below; the body of a girl tied to a stake, frozen to death, in the vicinity of Saint-Denis; and the discovery in a street in the Faubourg Saint-Marceau of a girl roasted on a spit, 'the spit being through her head'.[5] Most popular of all, however, with all classes of reader were the erotic texts that opposed all public morality in the name of freedom.

Much early pornography was entirely functional, however, both as guidebook and entertainment. They provided addresses and the menu of services at well-known brothels, such as Le Gros Millan on the rue du Beaujolais or Le Grand Balcon on the rue Croix-des-Petits-Champs. The genre soon became an entertainment in its own right and a great deal of police energy was wasted on pursuing printers, publishers and readers of work that was deemed to be anti-Christian and anti-social but which most Parisian found as life-enhancing as any of their other pleasures.

The Tender Pervert

The link between pornography and politics is one of the oldest Parisian traditions still alive in the modern city. It has been argued that the erotic writing of the early eighteenth century is the source of all subsequent forms of political and artistic liberty in Paris – from the carnivalesque Terror of 1789 to the joyous revolutionary festival of 1968. This is the view of the film director and porn actress 'Ovidie' as expressed in her book *Porno Manifesto*, a polemic in defence of porn in which she makes a case for the contemporary porn industry on the grounds that it reflects Utopian desires.[6]

And this is why, on a chilly September morning, I arranged to speak to her in a café near the rue Saint-Denis, the tawdry heart of the Parisian sex industry. Above all, I wanted to ask what connections could be made between the oldest traditions of sexual libertinage in Paris and the heartless present-day spectacle of porn supermarkets and peep shows.

Ovidie was tiny, body-pierced and dressed in black pyjamas, with the hard stare of a junior Maoist. She began to answer my questions by quoting the contemporary thinkers Jean Baudrillard, Georges Bataille and Guy Debord, who in different ways have made the case that total freedom means total sexual freedom, with all the existential difficulties that this position implies ('Who do we fuck and why?' as Ovidie put it). She cited the popularity of porn in pre-Revolutionary Paris, before explaining her notion that because it is based on a universal need – if it is literally placed in the right hands – 'porn can set you free'.

Ovidie went on to tell me how she had herself discovered pornography in early adolescence in the company of her sister. She said that it came to her as a revelation at the same tender age that mere physical events could be the source of so much delight and anguish. She went on: pornography is about nothing more than the promise of human happiness. The physical and economic exploitation that are undeniably involved in the sex industry are, in her view, wrong only because they are a betrayal of this original, quite innocent trust. The exploitation of women in particular, she said, is a betrayal of the original liberating aims of eighteenth-century pornography. It is this original egalitarian philosophy that Ovidie claims to recapture in her work. This does not preclude payment: indeed quite the opposite. 'I fuck for money,' Ovidie said to me. 'And of course that demands respect.'

Any self-respecting eighteenth-century man or woman of reason would have understood this argument straight away. The guiding theory of the age was that the ascertained facts of mathematics or natural science offered forms of knowledge superior to those of the hierarchical institutions of monarchy or religion. More than this, it was the moral duty of every intelligent being to act on this principle and debunk all previous and harmful ideas and general codes of behaviour. It was therefore possible, and indeed on occasion even necessary, to be an ardent moralist, while opposing all forms of traditional morality.

It was therefore no accident that the age of mathematics was also the age of pornography. The relation between the two forms of thought is closer than it may seem. For one thing, the pornographers of the eighteenth century, as good avatars of reason and science, were obsessed with numbers and geometrical precision to an unintentionally hilarious extent. This obsession surfaces not much later in the works of the marquis de Sade, whose icy fictional gang-bangs are punctuated by severe commands for 'an extra two or three cocks' or, most revealingly, 'some order in these orgies, please'.[7]

To this extent, pornography was intricately linked to the rise of a new class of thinkers, the *libertins*, who were avowedly atheist and sceptical about all other entrenched beliefs such as the absolute power of the monarchy. The original sense of the term *libertin* indicated a radical humanist and free-thinker, and prominent 'libertines' under Louis XIV, such as M. de Vauban and Pierre de Boisguillebert, were held to be the spiritual descendants of Rabelais, Montaigne or even Boccaccio. By the time of Louis's death, however, under a relentless assault from sophisticated religious thinkers like Pascal and Bossuet, the term *libertin* was used as an insult.

It was indeed difficult to defend with any great dignity such titles as *The Nun in Her Nightdress* or *John the Fucker, Debauched*. The imprint of such books was often equally precise in its language and clear in its intent ('À Anconne, chez la veuve Grosse-Motte' – 'At Incunt, at the house of the big-cunted widow' was, for example, a popular and extremely well-known fictional address). The *libertin* (or indeed libertine) was, however, a tender pervert, an atheist who fought superstitious piety by embracing the pleasures of the flesh and earth. Pornography was a literary representation of this combat and was indissolubly associated with other struggles against political and philosophical irrationalism.

'Love must be reinvented'

Individual Parisians are on Ovidie's side. They indeed take a chauvinistic pride in their horror of prudery, and still lament how people's pleasures have been ruined by town planning in more ways than one.

As the city was made more 'modern', for example, public prudery took over. The first and clearest sign of this was the changing of street names in the brothel-ridden streets of Les Halles. In 1809, rue Tire-Boudin ('Sausage, or cock, Puller Street') became rue Marie-Stuart; rue Trousse-Nonain, or 'Tumble-Nun Street', already disguised in official documents as Tasse-Nonian, became rue Beaubourg; rue de la Pute-y-Muse, or 'Idling Tart Street', became Petit-Muse, while the scatological collection of rues Merdeuse, Merdelet, Chieur and Chiard all disappeared from Haussmann's new maps of the rational and hygienic city. The rues du Petit et du Gros-Cul ('Big and Little Cunt'), Gratte-Cul ('Scratchy Cunt' – this street contained some of the favourite brothels of Casanova) and du Poil-au-Con ('Hairy Cunt') also disappeared at the same time although, as drily noted by a contemporary observer, the establishments that had inspired the street names continued to offer their customers the democratic tradition of freedom of choice.

The last traces of this tradition are only just visible in central Paris. One of these, according to Ovidie herself – Le Beverly, the only porno cinema left in the middle of Paris – was preparing to close its doors for the last time. This cinema stands at the top edge of the red-light district of rue Saint-Denis, almost but not quite in the rapidly gentrifying area of Montorgueil Saint-Denis. Over the door there is a photograph of the poet Rimbaud and his famous line 'Il faut réinventer l'amour' ('Love must be reinvented'). A poster in felt-tip pen offers special rates for couples on Thursday nights. There is a tender pathos at work here, as well as an unashamed, perverse exhibitionism.

Most of the old-style porno cinemas in Paris were swept away in the 1980s, victims of the booming video trade and the regular appearance of hard-core porn on mainstream television. Le Beverly somehow struggled through the 1990s. Most of the customers who now come are visibly die-hards. Some of them look too old to be even interested in sex – perhaps they come just for companionship and out of loyalty. Others look sinister and sheepish in equal measure. A handful of third-world immigrants sit back in their seats, smoking.

Le Beverly was never respectable – the atmosphere in the pitch-black *salle de spectacle* was tense and fervid, with more than a hint of real physical danger. But to visit this place, in all its sleazy glory, was to take a trip to a bygone era: a time when showing sex in a public space was a real transgression. These days, as a short stroll down the rue Saint-Denis or through the backstreets of Pigalle reveals, where porn DVDs are on sale at knockdown rates, the opposite is true. I left Le Beverly intrigued but not quite convinced by Ovidie's argument that writing or screening sex is in itself a genuinely subversive statement of wilful and unrepentant erotic intent. This may have been the case in the eighteenth century, or even the 1970s, but nowadays I felt the vision of the writer Michel Houellebecq – who in one of his poems brilliantly describes with appalled precision how the deadly routine of the hand-jobs and peep-shows fits in with the office hours of the central city – was indeed a more grimly accurate version of 21st-century Paris.[8]

'Our civilization suffers from vital exhaustion,' Houellebecq writes elsewhere:

In the century of Louis XIV, when the appetite for living was great, official culture placed the accent on the negation of pleasure and of the flesh; repeated insistently that mundane life can offer only imperfect joys, that the only source of true happiness is in God. Such a discourse . . . would not be tolerated today. We need adventure and eroticism because we need to hear ourselves repeat that life is marvellous and exciting; and it's abundantly clear that we rather doubt this.[9]

As I walked away from Le Beverly, it seemed to me that this theory explained, if it did not justify, the strangely drab and haunted faces on the girls I passed on the rue du Caire.

23. Night-Vision

Paris grew bigger in the eighteenth century but it was still not a well-defined geographical space. One of the problems faced by government and police was that nobody knew precisely where the city began or ended.

By the early 1700s, the perimeter firmly marked on Jouvin de Rochefort's map of 1674 had been made obsolete. There were, however, pressing reasons to make sure that the city limits remained intact or at least recognizable. The first of these was the need to ensure that the population could be fed, measured and controlled. Until this point, monarchy and government had more or less disregarded the existence of the *petites gens*, the ordinary people of Paris, considering them merely as subjects and potential cannon-fodder.

The huge increase in population in the seventeenth and eighteenth centuries meant, however, that even if the king did not love or even like his subjects, he could not afford to ignore their well-being. There were also specific exigencies: the need to limit the number of Parisians exempt from tax; anxiety about potential insurrectionary movements such as the Fronde; the military desire to safeguard the city walls.

If anything, the political commitment to development on the part of monarchy, administrators and speculators had made the city denser than ever. The oil lamp replaced candles, streets were numbered, police and spies monitored daily life, and new streets – straight and precise – cut through the most ancient *quartiers*, radically reshaping the urban landscape into a place of ever more flourishing exchange, traffic and trade. Economic expansion meant that the city was packed with migrants from the countryside. These people were physically different from the native Parisians. They were thin, sunburned, often deformed from a life of hard labour and usually in rags. By contrast, Parisians were pale and often lardy – they avoided the sun, which anyway hardly penetrated the narrow streets and certainly not the brothels or taverns. They looked down on these bronzed immigrants as primitives, fools and chancers. They also often feared them. Unlike the exotic visitors from the Orient or the New World, these immigrants were recognizably Frenchmen and occupied therefore a strictly predetermined place in the city's rigid class structures.

The newcomers to Paris met a city of subtle and complex hierarchies. Most of them were stunned by the lavish consumer goods on offer, the noise and energy of the markets and taverns. Less important in the everyday life of the immigrant and indigenous poor was the sumptuous architecture – the new buildings of La Monnaie ('Mint'), the Panthéon, the École de Droit ('School of Law'), the new theatres. None the less, these rapid and dramatic developments on the cityscape announced a clear and powerful vision of a new social order for the coming century.

In his book *Le Tableau de Paris*, the writer Louis-Sébastien Mercier describes the newly cosmopolitan, even exotic, city as 'a Temple of Harmony'. It is a place where, to the writer's delight, different moments in history meet and sometimes overlap each other.

A man in Paris, who knows how to think for a moment, has no need to go beyond the city walls to know men from other climes; he can perfectly well get to know the whole human species in studying the individuals who swarm in this great capital. You can find there Asiatics propped up all day on sequinned cushions, and Lapps who vegetate in narrow huts, Japanese who will slash open each other's stomachs at the slightest dispute, Eskimos who do not know what era they are living in, negroes who are not black, and Quakers who carry a sword. One finds there customs, habits and characteristics of the most distant peoples; the alchemist who worships fire, the vagabond Arab, beating upon the ramparts of the city, whilst the Hottentot and the Indian idle in the boutiques, the streets, the cafés. This is where you'll find the charitable Persian who gives remedies to the poor, and on the same floor a cannibal debt-collector. The Brahmans and Fakirs are no rarer than the Greenlanders who have no temples or altars. Antique and voluptuous Babylon is made again here each evening in a temple dedicated to harmony.[1]

Geographical precision mattered little to Mercier. As we shall see, he began his career as a dramatist, and his description of the city owes much to his ability to set a scene and move characters around upon it. He was also a fierce believer in reform and part of his intention in writing this work was to move the ordinary people to the centre stage and highlight the disparity between poverty and wealth in the city.

But it is of great significance to Mercier that, as the above extract shows, Paris offers a stage to all-comers from all points of the globe – Eskimos and Japanese simply add colour and life to the 'theatre' of the street. He is equally struck by the incongruous juxtapositions the wanderer could find at random in the city streets: non-violent Quakers who carry arms and pale and wan blacks (probably albinos). Most of all, he exults in the presence of 'Orientals', from the Middle East or North Africa, here in the former capital of Christendom now become the capital of Enlightenment and Reason.

The Parisian relationship with the Islamic world would subsequently pass through many difficult stages, from the conquest of Algeria in 1830 to the wave of Islamist-inspired bombings which terrified the city in the 1980s and 1990s. But in the eighteenth century, Parisians welcomed the Orientals who came on business. Arab maps of Paris (often more precise than their French counterparts) were printed in Arabic script and distributed in Baghdad, Damascus and Cairo as early as the 1750s. The translation of *Thousand and One Nights* by Antoine Galland in 1704 had set in motion an Orientalist vogue that accelerated through the century. Arab travellers to the city found themselves the objects of both curiosity and hospitality. Parisians called these visitors Turks, Moors, Berbers, Kabyles and Maronites. Words such as *bicot* ('young goat' or 'filthy Arab'), *bougnole*, *sidi*, *raton*, *salopard*, *tronc*, *melon* – all offensive terms for an Arab – had yet to be coined. In the Muslim world, Paris attracted young intellectuals who were drawn to the city of Voltaire, Diderot and Rousseau. Their presence signalled that the city dominated not only Europe but the world.

'A rapid and noisy whirlwind'

The major changes that were taking place in the urban landscape of Paris during the eighteenth century – the neo-classical buildings, avenues, bridges and streets – were not, however, truly new developments. Rather they were the extension of the civic ideals of the previous century – order and commerce – into a new century of unprecedented technological advances. The great works of the period aimed above all at organizing the city. Fewer churches were built as energies were diverted into civil and military institutions on the Left Bank. In the early seventeenth century, it had still been possible to see the remains of Philippe-Auguste's wall south of Saint-Germain-des-Prés. This was soon demolished as the city pushed beyond its limits at the Carrefour de l'Odéon and the rue des Fossés-Saint-Bernard. Parisians of the period were not in any way interested in the past and visitors to the city in search of sights or 'curiosities' were directed to the strictly utilitarian tanning factories at Gobelins or the Observatoire.[2] On the Right Bank, the wealthy and powerful continued to invest in private mansions in the Marais, stretching developments westwards.

The contradictions and inequalities of the previous century were further deepened: no ordinary Parisian could fail to see this on a daily basis as the monarchy continued the task of transforming the city into a magnificent and monumental capital while, in the streets away from the royal quarters, squalor reigned everywhere and at every social level.

This fact was indeed the reason why Mercier had set himself the task of capturing the complexity of Paris in *Le Tableau de Paris*, a long work composed between 1782 and 1788. Mercier started out as a dramatist and journalist. He satirized the governments of the day, and railed with particular spleen against war and the military life – the subject of his early work *Jeunesse* ('Youth', 1768). Although Mercier enjoyed a relatively distinguished academic career (he was professor of rhetoric at the Collège de Bordeaux and then chair of history at the École Centrale in Paris), he identified with ordinary Parisians against the ruling classes. He attacked the classical ideals of the age and classical literature (referring to Racine and Boileau as the 'plague-bearers of literature').[3] In constant disagreement with all governments and authorities, he considered himself a true prophet of revolution.

He was not well regarded by many of his contemporaries, however, who found him shallow and sentimental. But he had a sharp eye for detail and the stamina to match his literary ambition. *Le Tableau de Paris* is a fascinating work, ranging over topics as diverse as the higher politics of Parisian law-making, where to buy the best (and least expensive) clothes for men and women, where to overhear the best conversations, the disposal of corpses, the art of the pickpocket (and why Parisian pickpockets display more guile and craft than their London counterparts), the fetid air of the city, the poverty of the Faubourg Saint-Marcel, water-sellers, spies, prisons, body snatchers and the anatomists who fund them, street hustlers and charlatans, the best places to walk, fireworks, *filles publiques*, the police (cruel, lazy, scared and corrupt), tobacco, beggars, hospitals, the erotic life of the crowd at the opera, and the best time and place to grow mushrooms.

One of the most detailed insights into the intricate fabric of Paris is provided by Mercier's evocation of a typical day in the life of the city. He describes Paris as a 'rapid and noisy whirlwind', which began at seven every morning with cab-drivers, gardeners and shopkeepers setting out their stalls. By nine o'clock, the city streets were jam-packed with carriages conveying lawyers and civil servants to their offices, ladies on their way to visit each other, and all the business of commercial life high and low. The movement abated at three o'clock, when the moneyed classes sat down to dine. Five o'clock was the hour of promenading in the fine, new parks of the city. Paris then fell quiet at dusk, the most dangerous hour according to Mercier, when thieves and footpads lurked in every darkened passage. This was when all good Parisians went to bed, with the exception of those who had the money and time to pursue their pleasures into the night.[4]

The opera was a central focus for this activity. The streets surrounding the theatre were swarming with prostitutes, known as *vulvivagues* (the word suggests an itinerant vagina), who pursued any likely mark with entreaties and insults. Mercier noted drily that the incidence of rape was by now hardly known in Paris and explained this by the relative cheapness of commercial sex. Mercier was on the side of the poor and dispossessed, and this included whores. He also emphasized the homely side of city life, writing admiringly of the peasants who trudged through the city in the early hours, bringing fruit, bread, vegetables and meat from the furthest provinces to the ever-hungry Parisian population. He marvelled at how hard they worked, how much they drank and their scorn for the finery of well-heeled city fops. Among Parisians, Mercier prized the ordinary workers and their families; those who kept the city alive through hard work and determination. He noted the guile and sexual appetite of the native Parisian who, when roused by the noise and clatter of the carriages of the rich leaving the theatre, woke up his wife to make lazy, delicious love, and – God willing! – maybe even a new little Parisian.[5]

The Nocturnal Spectator

A counterpoint to Mercier's earnest, reformist spirit is found in the writings of his contemporary Restif de la Bretonne, the son of a peasant, a novelist, printer, occasional spy and erotomaniac. Mercier expressed admiration for Restif, but was careful to distance himself from his relentless reporting on the Parisian underworld, noting that life in the city was a movement between light and dark and it would be wrong to place undue emphasis on either of these conditions.

Restif worked tirelessly and ceaselessly on his novels and dramas (by the time of his death in 1806, he had completed and published 250 books). He liked to think of himself as a moralist and his most famous works – *Le Paysan perverti* ('The Corrupted Peasant', 1775) and *La Paysanne pervertie* ('The Corrupted Countrywoman', 1776) – are grim tales of healthy countryfolk brought low by evil Parisian manners. The problem was that Restif himself was so obviously in love with the blacker side of the city that his didactic tales failed dismally in their attempts to convince the reader of the wickedness of Parisian life. As with the philosophical fables of the marquis de Sade (himself an avid reader of Restif), the reader of Restif's tales is usually quite delighted when the wholesome (and irritating) provincial is intoxicated and overwhelmed by the spicy scent of sexuality and vice. (For his part, when the opportunity arose, Restif hypocritically denounced de Sade – 'if he were read by soldiers he would cause the death of 20,000 women' – while alleging in his romance *Monsieur Nicolas* that the Jacobin Revolutionary hero Danton had used the marquis's novel *Justine* as an aid to masturbation.)[6]

Restif may have been a hypocrite but he was also a keen and shrewd observer of the city's night-life. He called himself 'the owl' or 'nocturnal spectator' and set out in a spirit of scientific inquiry, prurience and barely concealed erotic excitement to explore Paris at night. To better conceal himself he wore 'an old blue cloak and a broad felt hat', boasting that he had not needed to buy any fresh clothes between 1773 and 1796.[7] Dark clothes were the habitual costume of the lower classes. Such attire immediately sent out danger signals to the well-heeled members of society, but it allowed Restif to drift wherever he wanted from midnight to dawn in the darkened city.

He documented his adventures in a series of tales he called *Les Nuits de Paris* ('Paris Nights'), published in 1788. These owed a great deal to the *poissard* genre of literature that was enormously popular in the eighteenth century (*poissard* was a sixteenth-century word for 'thief' or 'varlet': the novels themselves were packed with low-life slang and colour). Restif was melodramatic, self-obsessed and prone to lofty, moralizing statements. He fancied himself as a champion of the people: 'Of all our men of letters, I am perhaps the only one who knows the popular classes; by mingling with them, I wish to paint them, I wish to be the sentinel of good order. I have mingled with the lower orders in order to observe all abuses.'[8] This was a ludicrous statement, of course: *Les Nuits de Paris* is every bit as contrived and staged as Mercier's *Tableau de Paris*. But if Restif cannot really claim to speak for the lower classes, which was his overriding desire, he is at least a compelling writer if not always truthful witness.

The nocturnal spectator's favoured cafés were, in the rue de la Montagne-Sainte-Geneviève, the Café Procope, or Manoury's, where he went to watch games of draughts, the Café Aubry in rue Saint-Jacques, or the

Régence, where he regularly observed Jean-Jacques Rousseau locked in an impossible chess game with his artisan friend Ménétra. These were relatively ordered places where Restif went to overhear conversations, read the newspapers and generally take the pulse of the city's literary and political life. He occasionally noticed spies up to the same tricks as himself but shrugged this off as a necessary evil in a city where hatred of the authorities was so clearly and tangibly on the rise.

Restif was fascinated by the new practice of sustained idleness that had become fashionable in the more elevated classes and was seemingly promoted by these cafés. Workers could not afford to stay idle, but lived from day to day and took their sexual, alcoholic and gastronomic pleasures with a fierce intensity. A poem from 1773 by an anonymous *poissard* is a complicit evocation of these delights, describing the poorer Parisian's appetite for mindless, sensual fun:

> From every *quartier* of the city,
> On Sundays and holy-days, there's a procession
> Of decent folk from every trade,
> Cobblers, tailors, wig-makers,
> Fish-wives and patching women,
> Vegetable peelers and laundry maids,
> Serving-girls, lackeys and scrubbers,
> Dandies from the harbour or porters,
> And here and there soldiers
> And their whores
> Who with no fear of the Devil
> Turn their backs on the sermons
> And gallop off to the pleasure-gardens
> Where the cheap wine is drunk.[9]

Restif was both puzzled and attracted by such easy and everyday activities. In order to explain them, he lingered in the lower depths of the city – the taverns, cabarets, gambling dens and whorehouses – where he became a familiar figure, stalking the edges of every scene in the shadows, watching, listening. 'I hate drunkards and gamblers,' he grumbled.[10] But this did not prevent him spending nights on end in their company.

People drank at all hours of the day. The day started – as it still does in some parts of Paris – with a cold and clean white wine. Mid-morning was the time for artisans, market traders and their assistants to knock back a few bottles at a tavern, often with oysters bought from an itinerant oyster-seller on the door. They came in waves throughout the day, downing tools to drink a bottle as a tonic for fatigue before returning to work. The police were less concerned about everyday inebriation than the systematic drinking that lasted over a week and led to madness, suicide and abandoned families.

Violence was never too far away in these places. With the precision of the easily shocked, Mercier had noted that the murderous brawls that were a regular feature of tavern life were preceded by a series of ritual insults: 'slut', 'bugger', 'nark', 'old cunt' and 'dog' were commonplace. At this point, the tavern owner would usually intervene, defending the honour of his establishment. This was when knives or daggers were drawn and the place erupted into a free-for-all.[11]

Restif reported on all of this with what he hoped was the cold eye of a scientist. His original impulse in composing *Les Nuits de Paris* was Utopian: like Mercier, under the influence of Enlightenment values, he believed that the chaotic world of the city could only be made orderly by rational planning in favour of the public good. The stated aim of his book was to uncover the dark side of the city so that it could literally be moved towards the light. Many of his recommendations were common sense, from his suggestion for planting fruit trees to curtailing traffic and banning the sale of bad wine.

Restif planned at first that *Les Nuits de Paris* would consist of texts covering 366 nights – 365 to cover a whole year, and an extra day to mark the beginning of a new annual cycle. The advent of the Revolution compelled Restif to add another fourteen sections to document the city in 1790, but the precision with numbers was important. Gérard de Nerval, a poet who wandered the city in an hallucinatory daze some fifty years later, for this reason described Restif as 'one of the first Communists', determined to fix the world with mathematics.[12] But Restif's legislative frenzy was also obsessive; his compulsive need to classify and codify his experiences belied a secret appetite for drink, sex and crime. Every evening, at a fixed time, he began the same promenade around the city from the eastern edge of the Île Saint-Louis, descending into the hellish miasma of city life in the hope of revelation. 'This is how I began the beautiful nights of the summer,' he wrote, 'in walking meditation, with visions of Paris, waiting for the dawn.'[13]

The City in Shadow

Now the dominant cultural force in Europe and an economic power-house, Paris – as observed by Mercier and Restif – was a dynamic and volatile place, fraught with social and financial contradictions and seething with political ideas which quickly turned into political discontent. Yet the catastrophe that was about to destroy the monarchy was not inevitable.

The chief reason for making this argument is that as late as the 1780s Paris was still a stable and ordered city where even those who petitioned hardest for change – the journalists, *philosophes*, writers, artists and *libertins* – had a clear notion of the fixed limits of their ambitions. The looming crisis, which came to many Parisians as an enormous surprise and shock, was really a failure of government at the highest levels. The responsibility lay with Louis XV who, by the time he died in 1774, had thrown away any goodwill he had inherited from the previous regime due to a mixture of financial incompetence, extravagance and arrogance and a disastrous foreign policy which had culminated in petty and humiliating defeats in war.

His successor, Louis XVI, was a man without qualities. His rather pathetic main ambition was, as he put it, 'to be loved'. His silly Austrian wife, Marie-Antoinette, gushed with frivolous gaiety on their accession to the throne. Louis XVI himself was not immune to stupidity. 'We are so young!' he announced to a baffled group of advisers as he established himself at court.[14] It was true of course that he was only twenty years old, poorly educated, of mediocre intelligence and with little idea of the demands of his office.

The new king's first major decision was whether or not to accept the so-called Turgot plan. Turgot, who had been navy minister, was Louis's controller-general. A tough-minded pragmatist with a keen political sensibility, he alone among the king's advisers understood that the political discourse in the 1760s and 1770s had shifted (he had, for example, advised the king against the extravagant and archaic coronation in 1775 that had enraged Protestants and *philosophes*, while alienating him from ordinary Parisians). Turgot pledged himself to 'no bankruptcy, no increased taxation, no further borrowing'. He produced a plan to save France, abolishing forced labour as an alternative to taxation and simultaneously wiping out the privileges of the medieval guilds. He advocated free circulation of grain, rigorous accounting practices, a budget and tight control of the royal finances. However, Turgot's plan was thrown out by a court devoted to preserving its own wilful control over France and its destiny. 'Turgot wants to run France like a slave plantation,' sneered one courtier.[15] The king was sympathetic to Turgot but caved in to his other advisers.

Louis XVI further enraged Parisians with the establishment in 1784 of a new customs barrier – the wall of the Farmers-General. The original aim of this was ostensibly to stop smuggling, increase revenue and reinforce the city limits that Louis XV had tried to establish with his decree on restricting the size of Paris in 1724. The Farmers-General were private officers who had the right to set and collect indirect taxes. Parisians loathed them, quite justifiably, as members of arbitrary and greedy organizations whose only allegiance was to themselves. Now the barrier forced Parisians to pay tax in areas that had been exempt until then. Worse still, construction was expensive and the wall itself too grand and severe. Rumours circulated that it caused disease, sheltered bandits and encouraged crime. In short, it represented everything bad about the monarchy.

In the past two centuries, Paris had developed at a breakneck pace. By the 1750s, the energy and optimism that had carried the population and the government through the *grand siècle* had long since dissipated into cynicism and a sense that somehow ordinary Parisians had been tricked into lending their support to the government. These were the arguments that swilled around the city in pamphlets, debates, jokes and anecdotes. Many people lived well, possibly better than anyone in the city had lived before. The population of Paris was now 600,000, a good proportion of whom were comfortably housed. The rich dwelt in private mansions designed by architects in neo-classical or baroque mode. Middle-class Parisians more commonly lived in rented accommodation in buildings six or seven storeys high. All of these buildings were built of stone and had their own stoves. All those who were not workers, peasants or vagrants slept in their own beds.

The increasing wealth of the city of course only heightened the gap between the rich and the poor, who were legion. The view on the street in Paris, when the wall of the Farmers-General was built, was that the king was laughing in the face of increasing poverty and hardship. In the taverns, cabarets, dives and dockside eating houses documented by Mercier and Restif, the bitterness was palpable. In manners, language and style, these places were the very opposite of the Enlightened Paris of cafés and *salons*, where anti-government tracts and pamphlets were composed and distributed. But it was in the lower depths of society, the so-called 'dangerous classes', where truly insurrectionary hatred simmered. It was this anger that would soon explode into so much bloody violence in the name of revolutionary justice.

24. From Revolt to Revolution

By the 1750s, the largest and busiest districts in Paris were no longer to be found at its historic centre around Île de la Cité, the university and the Marais. They were rather to be found to the east of the central axis on both sides of the river, stretching to the perimeter of the city just beyond what is now Place de la Nation.

This was the result of steady developments since the early 1700s. The city had simply grown in population around its industrial and commercial axes. The most important areas were now the Faubourg Saint-Marcel on the Left Bank, home to a filthy tannery and the polluted waters of the Bièvre, and, on the Right Bank, the Faubourg Saint-Antoine, populated mainly by carpenters, joiners, builders, journeymen printers, *traiteurs-aubergistes*, butchers, knackers' yards, market traders and a whole assortment of other minor tradesmen. This place was neither rich nor poor – although it did have its own population of what was by now called *la canaille*, a shifting low-life army of hustlers and whores. It was, however, the busy and teeming workshop of Paris – a place where the rich rarely dared to venture.

It was just as well that this was the case because when Paris suffered – and in the eighteenth century disease and famine were never far away – it was hit hardest and most disastrously in this district. The rich were always to blame. Most importantly, the people here saw the rich not just as parasites but as outsiders to the city, a place that by right belonged to those who both lived and worked within its boundaries. The distance between rich and poor was not simply a physical one but also a cultural divide. Daniel Roche describes how 'the wits, the aristocrats, the drawing-room dilettantes, the mistresses in the boudoirs . . . in their little theatres' of the Marais and the Palais-Royal laughed at the lower classes as savages who were barely human.[1] Upper-class males in eighteenth-century Paris accordingly sought to distance themselves from the lower orders by adopting manners and clothes that bordered on effeminacy. Wigs had become popular from the 1760s onwards and were adopted as fashion by the Parisian bourgeoisie as well as the aristocracy, as had the parasols sold to both sexes at either end of the Pont-Neuf during the summer months to keep them from the sun and preserve their fashionable pallor.

There were inexplicable crazes among these classes, such as the fashion, again in the 1760s, for the style-conscious Parisian to carry with him a small marionette, a *pantin*, which would be taken out and fiddled with nonchalantly in public as a mark of urban style and refinement. The comedian Ramponneau, who had a *guingette* on the Île aux Porcherons was a fashionable figure and all things admirable were said to be *à la Ramponneau*, when they were not *à la grecque* (Greece and all things Greek were incomprehensibly modish: a fact preserved in the unappetizing dish *champignons à la grecque*, which still appears on restaurant menus). Frivolity and irony were the prevailing modes of behaviour and response among the upper classes; any other sentiment was said to be *ridicule*. To appear *ridicule* was of course an unforgivable social sin.

These bewigged fops did not dare to say any such thing out loud on the rare occasions that they ventured into the heart of Faubourg Saint-Antoine. The lower orders of Paris had their own moral code and their own anti-heroes, such as Louis Dominique Cartouche, a stylish outlaw and murderer, whose execution in 1721 was mourned by thousands. Cartouche was admired most of all for the insouciance with which he slaughtered the rich. As such, his cult was a premonition of the popular fantasies that would become reality in 1789.

In the literature of the period, the Paris of the popular classes inspired disgust: mud, filth, darkness were omnipresent. Most feared of all were the *sans-culottes*, the lowest of the Parisian proletarian classes, who did not wear breeches (*culottes*) but long trousers instead as a badge of their social status. Those intrepid upper-class explorers who visited the lower regions of the city reported on these Parisian proles as 'savages', as exotic and threatening as any to be found in the burgeoning colonies of the New World.

Much of this fantasy was provoked by fear of the lower classes, but it was also true that working-class Paris was indeed a warren. The Faubourg Saint-Antoine was, for example, criss-crossed by thirty-eight main streets and thirty other minor passageways. Most traffic centred on the rues du Faubourg Saint-Antoine, de Charenton, de Reuilly, de Picpus, de Montreuil, de Charonne and the arteries to the Quais de la Rapée and de Bercy. Many craftsmen and artisans had settled here to take advantage of the nearby warehouses and ports. It was a densely packed area where families lived on top of one another in poorly maintained apartment buildings.

But still the workers made a kind of living here most of the time. The shops and market stalls were usually well stocked and the Marché d'Aligre, established in 1777, was known all over Paris for the quality of its merchandise. Despite the difficulties of daily life, the people prided themselves on their good humour and generosity to others. They hated policemen, aristocrats, clerks, tax inspectors and spies, and grumbled at price rises and salary cuts, but otherwise the area was generally known for its homely if occasionally tense atmosphere. This was where, for example, Restif came to observe the lower orders at play and marvel at their capacity for innocent fun.

It was also where, in April 1789, the first shots were fired that would change the world for ever.

Storming the Bastille

The riot had been set off by a garbled comment from a wallpaper-maker in the district, a certain Réveillon, who had apparently remarked in public that it would be better for all if wages were lowered. In a game of Chinese whispers, this comment had swilled around the district, passed from bars to cafés, to workplaces and homes, from brothels to taverns, until it became 'fact'. It then provoked the noisiest and most dangerous riot yet in the city of Paris, a place that in 1789 was almost visibly vibrant with angry emotion among the poorer classes, who were all too often starving when not coping with mere malnutrition.

The starting point of the real violence was a fusillade fired by troops as they tried to end the riot. They were trying to finish off a series of minor street battles in the area around the bottom end of the rue du Faubourg Saint-Antoine. Battle had been raging throughout the day between workers, the unemployed and government troops, who by the evening were exhausted, confused and frustrated. Within minutes of the fusillade, as emotions tore through the crowd, expressed in a loud roar of anger, it was clear to all observers that this disturbance was far from over.

The disturbance was made doubly effective by the fact that the rioters of Saint-Antoine had made an alliance with the tanners of the Faubourg Saint-Marcel (who really were among the most wretched poor of the city), who came charging as a mob over the bridges to the Right Bank to hammer the police and the king's soldiers in the name of social justice. Nervous and exhausted from a day of hand-to-hand combat, the *gardes françaises*, loyal to the king but also poorly led and with no clear idea of how to empty the streets – which were now filling with drunks and drunken rioters – opened fire from the corner of rue de Montreuil at around dusk. Hundreds of workers and their allies were killed, their broken and dismembered bodies strewn in the mud of the streets.

The incident was dismissed by the king as bloody but insignificant (Louis himself blamed professional agitators in the *parlement* for the disturbance). The real significance of this event was that it took place against the background of France in turmoil, racked by unemployment and the fear of famine. By 1788, workers were standing idle in the big towns all over France (it was estimated that there were 25,000 silk workers without a job in Lyons alone). The countryside was flooded with vagrants and beggars moving from village to village looking for the most basic forms of sustenance. Fourteen years earlier, riots due to bread shortages in Brittany – known as the so-called 'Flour Wars' – had forced the government to deploy troops regularly across this region, to keep the peace. Now, as the impact of civil bankruptcy really started to hit home, as starving peasants and workers regularly attacked priests, nobility and bourgeois across the country, France stood on the very brink of disaster. No one close to the monarchy seemed to be aware of this, or if they did, they said and did nothing.

The events that transformed the revolt into a full-scale political revolution began properly on 17 June 1789, when the delegates of the Third Estate – the commoners – declared that they alone constituted the *parlement* or National Assembly of the French People. This was a direct challenge not only to the First and Second Estates (the nobility and the clergy), who always outvoted the Third Estate, but also to the king. The first response of Louis XVI was to send guns and troops to Paris and Versailles, where the streets were packed with the disaffected, starving and unemployed allied with workers whose voices were to all intents and purposes disregarded. The next few weeks were a fervid time of pamphlets, noisy public debates and, on the orders of the Third Estate deputies, the recruitment of a people's army in every area of the city.

The rebellion suddenly took on a momentum of its own when on 12 July the king sacked Jacques Necker as his chancellor, replacing him with the authoritarian baron de Breteuil. Necker was one of the few members of the government still popular with the people and his dismissal was seen as an insult and an affront. Almost immediately people formed militias and started equipping themselves with guns and pikes for street-fighting. Thousands walked to Versailles to clamour for the reinstatement of Necker, only to be loftily ignored by the king.

The search for arms by the people now became desperate. On 14 July, a mob looted the museum on Place Louis XV, finding only ancient and unworkable weapons from the time of Henri IV. A raid on the Invalides garrison was more profitable, however; the crowds seized over 30,000 muskets. Now armed, and more enraged and dangerous than ever, the Parisian crowds set off for the prison of the Bastille, the hated symbol of royal tyranny that stood at the bottom end of the district. The prison's governor, the marquis de Launay, at first tried negotiating his way out of trouble. But in the late afternoon, he ordered his men to fire on the insurgents, killing two hundred. In response, the crowd battered their way into the prison (they crossed the moat around the prison on planks before being thrown the keys to a drawbridge by a friendly guard). De Launay's head was sliced off by a kitchen boy called Desnot, who severed it with a pocket knife, and paraded it around the streets on a pike. When he heard all of this, Louis XVI, who had believed the previous day that all was well in Paris, asked one of his chief advisers if this was just another revolt. 'No, sire,' the adviser is said to have replied straight away. 'It is a revolution.'

Killing the King

The crucial factor that turned these incidents from a series of insurrectionary movements for reform into a real revolution was a desire for the abolition of the monarchy. Violating this taboo had previously been thought of as impossible in French history. Kings had been killed before, but these were normally the actions of mavericks or renegades acting on behalf of marginal groups. The British Civil War a century earlier, when Oliver Cromwell had ruled as lord protector in place of the monarch, offered no real precedent as it was considered in France and elsewhere in Europe to be no more than a regional dispute with no ideological significance. In France, the king was the sole and central binding force in society. Without him the very existence of France as a nation was in danger.

To arrive at the decision to do away with the monarchy was therefore no easy matter. In the first instance, the abolition of the monarchy had never been an aim of the Third Estate even in its most fiery mood. The decision to kill the king was reached in several stages, each more radical than the preceding one, and in a series of movements driven by groups who had previously been peripheral to or excluded from the political process.

Women of the Parisian working classes were, for example, from the outset and for the first time in French, indeed European, history a powerful and influential force for radical change. Histories of the Revolution have endlessly demonized these women as brutal harridans, caricaturing them as the sour-faced *tricoteuses*, perversely entertained by the spectacle of suffering and death during the worst days of violence.

In reality, women, who ran the family budget and fed their children, were often more in touch with the grim consequences of everyday politics than men. Certainly, women were not afraid to make the connection between economic reality on the street and decisions made in government. In October 1789, a baker was nearly lynched on Place de la Grève by a group of women who found him guilty of using false weights. The baker was saved by guards, but the enraged women found it impossible to check the angry force they had set in motion. The mob swelled and turned its invective first of all on the Hôtel de Ville, before the women who had started the row led a march over the river to Île de la Cité, turning back across the Pont-Neuf, marching past the Louvre and the Tuileries towards Versailles, where they laid siege to the Assembly and the king. They waited all night before breaking into the royal palace at daybreak.

This was now a crowd of several thousand women, armed with pikes, swords, pistols and muskets. The king had little choice but to allow himself to be escorted to Paris wearing a Revolutionary red, white and blue cockade. Along the way he was saluted by laughing women, who lifted their skirts to show their backsides or genitals, and made bloodcurdling gestures to the queen. The royal pair would never see Versailles again. It seemed to the people of Paris that they could make anything happen now.

It was only a matter of time before republican fervour turned to regicide. Louis did not help his own cause by resisting reform and plotting with foreign forces in an ambitious scheme to retake Paris by force. He made a badly organized attempt to escape Paris on 20 June 1791 to join up with the foreign allies, but was spotted by an alert revolutionary at Varennes and returned to the city. The escape attempt destroyed any vestigial faith of Parisians in the king and the only real question now asked in the streets, the cafés and the revolutionary clubs was what was to be done.

The strongest appeals yet against the king were made on 20 July 1790, when a crowd of some 50,000, again mostly made up of workers and citizens from Saint-Antoine and Saint-Marcel, marched on the Champ de Mars, calling for the head of the man they now called 'Louis Capet' (all French kings since Hugues Capet were now deemed false). A nervous regiment of guards opened fire, killing fifty or so. Inevitably, the anti-monarchist sentiment only spread further.

The king's position was made even more precarious by the threat of Prussian invasion and then the manifesto of the allied forces under the command of the Duke of Brunswick, who declared he would destroy Paris if any harm came to the sovereign. This was exactly the excuse needed by the extremist group known as the Jacobins, led by Maximilien Robespierre, to state that 'the fatherland was in danger' and that it could only be saved by the abolition of the monarchy. The Jacobins, who were also known as the 'Société des Amis de la Liberté et de l'Égalité', took their name from the headquarters of the club in a building that had been a Dominican convent on the rue Saint-Honoré (as noted previously, the Dominicans were nicknamed 'Jacobins' because they had once been based on rue Saint-Jacques). They numbered no more than 3,000 members but soon controlled all of Paris. Most prominent among them were Georges Danton, Camille Desmoulins, Jean Marat, Antoine Saint-Just and their leader, Robespierre. The group argued for total democracy and advocated revolutionary violence and dictatorship to defend this principle. The mass killings began in earnest in late summer. On 10 August 1792, the king's Swiss Guard were slaughtered by a mob in the Tuileries. In September, thousands of prisoners taken by the Revolutionaries were killed without trial, the king unseated and the first French republic declared over a heap of corpses.

The king was finally decapitated in the Place de la Révolution (formerly the Place Louis XV) on 21 January 1793. The violence in Paris that year reached a peak that has never been matched, the background to this being the so-called 'second revolution', which had been triggered by the massacre of 10 August.

There were essentially three conflicting groups in Paris at this stage: the *sans-culottes*, who represented the people, the Girondins, who represented the bourgeoisie, and the Jacobins and Montagnards (so called becaue they occupied the steepest seats in the Assembly), factions on the extreme Left who promised a 'regime of virtue'. By the autumn of 1792, after a bloody period of infighting, intrigue and assassination, the Jacobins stood unopposed as the leaders of the Revolution.

In March 1793, the Jacobins formed the Committees of Public Safety, initially created in order to control the movements and activities of foreigners. These committees quickly became a law unto themselves, randomly pursuing the innocent and conspirators alike. The thirst for blood reached its notorious peak in the autumn when a group of *sans-culottes* broke into the National Convention at the Hôtel de Ville, demanding bread and the suppression of all the internal enemies of the Revolution. This was the trigger that sparked the Terror, a wave of executions during which some 20,000 were killed in the name of freedom. The very streets around what became Place de la Révolution were stained dark red, while the city was haunted by rumour, denunciations and counter-rumour. 'While Robespierre reigned, blood flowed and no man went short of bread' was an adage of the day. In truth, the harvests of 1794 were wretched and Paris was soon on the brink of yet another famine. Potatoes were sown in the Tuileries and Luxembourg gardens, but disaster did not seem far away.

The killing went on. It only stopped when, sickened by the carnage, a group launched a counter-plot against Robespierre, the 'incorruptible' grand inquisitor and chief terrorist. The pale assassin, who had been personally responsible for 6,000 severed heads in Place de la Révolution, was himself marched to the scaffold and beheaded on 28 July 1794. Crowds noted that his face was bloodied and deformed, the result of an abortive suicide attempt that he had made in panic and fear the night before his arrest.

25. The Bloody Path to Utopia

One of the first ambitions of the Revolutionaries was to make a complete break with the past in order to usher in a new world. On the streets of Paris, the *sans-culottes* set out systematically to destroy traces and symbols of what they would soon call the Ancien Régime. One of their first actions was to break down the wall of the Farmers-General, an undertaking that was both symbolic and immensely practical. There was a popular punning rhyme that blamed the wall for the rise of revolutionary sentiment – 'Le mur murant Paris rend Paris murmurant' ('The wall surrounding Paris has left Paris murmuring') – but the general feeling was larger than this; it was in fact a hatred directed towards all symbols of the past. This was the role played by the Bastille, which like the wall of the Farmers-General was smashed to pieces and used to rebuild the Pont de la Révolution (formerly the Grand-Pont and now Pont de la Concorde).

Christianity was now suspect if not hated altogether. In 1792, the Revolutionaries had already abolished the Christian calendar, replacing it with the names of months based on the seasons (May was renamed 'Floréal' (flowers), July 'Thermidor' (heat), for example). Now it was time to re-invent the city itself. Plans for this ranged from declaring Notre-Dame a 'temple of Reason' (even the most die-hard atheists among the Revolutionaries could not find it within themselves to order its destruction) to attacking churches and colleges. The statues of what were believed to be the kings of France on the façade of Notre-Dame were beheaded (these were in fact the heads of the kings of Judah and were replaced; the originals were found in a cellar in 1975).

The most prestigious institutions of the University of Paris were closed down, sold off or renamed or used for some other more demeaning role. The Sorbonne itself was briefly turned into a factory, while other colleges were made into prisons or workshops. The Revolution similarly declared that all churches had to be wrecked or changed to some other designation. The word 'saint' was obliterated from street signs. However, although nearly all churches in Paris suffered some form of desecration – the relics of Sainte Geneviève were burned at Place de la Grève and the Sainte-Chapelle turned into a flour warehouse – only fourteen churches were in fact burned down. The most common alternative to burning down a church was to give it a new Revolutionary meaning. The church of Sainte-Geneviève was called the Panthéon and dedicated to the great men of France. The church of Saint-Germain-des-Prés became the* headquarters of various Revolutionary groups. The *corps de ballet* from the Opéra staged 'a dance of Reason' on the high altar of Notre-Dame.[1]

The life of the city continued as normal during the Revolution but the public mood was visibly more sombre. This much had been the case anyway in the period leading up to the Revolution, when even drunkenness and the use of prostitutes were in a marked decline. As France edged towards crisis, it was observed that few songs were now sung in taverns or on the street, and those that were sung were usually mocking or sardonic. During the Revolution itself, everyday life was defined by extremes. The private and public morality of the Revolution and the Revolutionaries was all too often contradictory. It swung from an extreme form of permissiveness, in the name of revolt and subversion, to an excessive public prudery that condemned all forms of pleasure as a match for the debauchery of the Ancien Régime. At the height of the Terror, the city was consumed with a febrile sexuality and even the hardest-working whores reported that they were exhausted and could not keep up with trade. At the same time, the Jacobins condemned drinking, whoring and other forms of pleasure as, at best, counter-revolutionary frivolities or, at worst, a betrayal of the Revolution.

The worst years for ordinary Parisians were yet to come, however. This would be the period in the immediate aftermath of the Revolution when famine and disease would return. But in the meantime the tension between liberty and libertinism was still unresolved.

'One more effort . . .'

One of the most unlikely heroes of the Revolution was therefore the marquis de Sade, who had nearly been one of the prisoners liberated during the storming of the Bastille. De Sade had been in prison since 1778, first in Vincennes and then the Bastille. He had originally been arrested on charges of poisoning and sodomy but was cleared. Since then, he had been held without trial, gorging himself, masturbating and writing the scroll of *Les 120 jours de Sodom* ('The 120 Days of Sodom'), the massive compendium of sexual perversions published in 1787 that would become his masterpiece. De Sade had been moved from the Bastille to the prison of Charenton only ten days before the storming of the Bastille had ignited the firestorm that swept across Paris. The marquis's library of six hundred books, his paintings and manuscripts were all slashed, burned or stolen by the Revolutionaries.[2]

When he was finally freed in 1790, the marquis turned on his own class, the aristocracy, and became a mere citizen, a man of letters and a pious Revolutionary. After a brief spell in an asylum, de Sade turned to the theatre (one of the few arts officially encouraged under the Revolution as an historically subversive force). The marquis's works were notorious but only properly known to a few who were able to get hold of them. On the basis of this reputation, he was generally admired for his attacks on the hypocrisy of the aristocracy and the Church. His actual practices – which ranged from organizing small-scale orgies to attempted murder – were more problematic. De Sade's most direct intervention in the political debates of the day was the sermon 'Yet one more effort to be Republicans', which was inserted among the scenes of buggery and coprophagy that otherwise make up most of his text *La Philosophie dans le boudoir*, written in 1795.

The aim of this book was to demonstrate the illusory nature of all religion-based morality and to encourage individuals to abolish all super-natural forms of authority. Only when humanity began to act on this, argued the marquis, could individuals properly describe themselves as free men and women and therefore the republican avatars of liberty. Most important of all to his contemporaries, however, was the vision of the terrors of absolute freedom – the polar opposite of absolutist government – that this book and others by de Sade opened up. It was this aspect of his thinking that has fixed his image then as now as the master theorist of transgression, the bloated figure in Man Ray's famous Surrealist portrait of 1938, who gazes with a piercing eye into the blank infinite and empty space of the future.

The venue for most Parisian transgressive pleasures during the Revolution was still the Palais-Royal. There were rumours that it now played host to sex shows on a nightly basis, organized by whores who worked for free and invited former clients to participate while they had group sex in public in the name of Revolutionary secularism. The reality was no less compelling for many Parisians of all classes, who flocked to the Palais-Royal in pursuit of sex. One eye-witness reported that

at the height of the Revolution more than two thousand girls were to be found at any time of day strolling in the gardens. Some of them had come from afar, others lodged in the buildings there. The doors of their lodgings are decorated with shop signs that are more than suggestive. The merchandise itself is available on the balcony. And if the passer-by neglects to pay attention to them, the ladies amuse themselves by emptying their chamber pots out of the window. At the Palais-Royal, it is wise to be always looking upwards.[3]

One of the special amusements in the brothels of the Palais-Royal was the availability of *sosies de vedette*, whores who looked like or dressed up as famous women of the day. These whores were also sometimes referred to as *sunamites* (a term borrowed from the name of the Bride in the biblical Song of Songs). The favoured models were stars of the theatre or the opera. Sexual activity here only intensified during the height of the Terror, when the girls wore red, white and blue bonnets and offered a special price to top members of the Assembly.

Despite the air of carnival ('truly a new Sodom!' wrote one visitor to Paris approvingly), the taverns and brothels of the Palais-Royal were strictly organized.[4] The most expensive and sophisticated girls frequented the Café de Foy (the place where Camille Desmoulins, an unemployed lawyer and propagandist, had made a coruscating speech to a crowd on 12 July 1789 which culminated in the storming of the Bastille). Some of the most elegant prostitutes occupied apartments on the second floor, where they offered other entertainments such as dinners and piano recitals. Other transactions were more primitive and commercial. The *Almanach des adresses des demoiselles de Paris de tout genre et de toutes les classes* ('Almanac of addresses of the unmarried women of Paris of every type and class') gave full descriptions of who and what was on offer; these included 'Bersi', a mulatto of voluptuous figure, smiling face, a cute little 'jewel', and all the suppleness and vivacity of an American, at 6 livres (a moderate sum). An Italian brunette with 'soft skin, provocative breasts, without a veil' came in at 12 livres for a *demi-nuit*. Foreign girls were always more expensive than the native Parisians, especially those like 'Georgette', who was 'dainty' when sober, but 'debauched and shameless' when she had drunk 'punch'. 'Georgette' cost just 3 livres a night, if you could stand the drinking and possible abuse.[5]

Sodomites

The Revolution, like the marquis de Sade, gave licence to nearly all material human pleasures, from sex to drink to gluttony (food and drink were not, however, as readily and regularly available as sex). One of the few taboo areas of experience was homosexuality. The marquis de Sade praised sodomy as the highest and most delicious form of vice, but this was nearly always between men and women or, if practised between men or boys, in the context of a bisexual orgy. Exclusively homosexual sodomy was considered to be a purely aristocratic vice, despite the fact that – as de Sade's texts confirm – many of those who enjoyed it were from the lower classes.

The Parisian police authorities had long considered sodomy to be a scourge on the city. As far back as 1715, a chief of police called Simonnet had orchestrated a campaign to do away with homosexuals in Paris. The most popular technique for entrapment was to send spies, called *mouches* ('flies'), to linger and flirt with homosexuals in parts of the city where they were known to meet – the Tuileries or the Luxembourg gardens at dusk, for example. After 1738, police records began to refer to 'sodomites' as 'pederasts', a term that, deriving from the Greek, was thought to be more scientific and secular ('sodomy' had biblical connotations and was associated with sin rather than crime; a tricky theological point for the police). This did not stop the apparent growth in popularity of same-sex assignations. Most disturbingly for the authorities, many married men were found to be indulging in mutual masturbation in well-known 'pederastic quarters', although many of these claimed not to be 'sodomites' or 'pederasts', that they disliked anal or oral sex and were simply saving money that they might have spent on whores. Much of this was also blamed on drinking in places like the Cabaret du Chaudron in the rue Saint-Antoine, which played host to a private club where 'men took women's names and made marriages together'.[6]

This sort of activity was impossible to police properly, mainly because it was cheap and widely popular. Throughout the eighteenth century, hundreds of 'sodomites' were arrested but punishments were generally not harsh – a short prison term or fine unless, like the marquis de Sade, the prisoner could be held without trial on some other pretext. Few homosexuals were executed during this period and most of those that were had usually committed other crimes.

Homosexuality made the authorities anxious precisely because it was so difficult to police, and because it was so widespread, concerning hidden sections of society that presented an apparently moral front. On the eve of the Revolution, one police record notes that 40,000 people in the city of Paris were under surveillance for 'immorality'. This is an extraordinary figure (the population of Paris was then roughly 400,000). It demonstrates, if nothing else, that the greatest concern of government was not how it fulfilled its functions of governance but who it actually governed. The anti-sodomy laws were finally abolished in 1791 as part of the Revolution's rejection of Christianity. The sexual morality of private citizens was thus no longer an issue in the century of de Sade and in the city of Danton and Robespierre.

Changing the World

The chronology of events and the personalities of the main actors in the French Revolution of 1789 have long since passed into the collective memory of the world. Events such as the execution of Louis XVI and Marie-Antoinette, the assassination of Marat by the peasant girl Charlotte Corday, the massacres and the Terror, and then figures such as Robespierre, Saint-Just, Danton and Mirabeau, are the stuff of legend rather than history.

But interpretations of the Revolution provoke arguments and contain politically loaded messages. For the French themselves, the Revolution has provided a national myth and identity for their nation as the founding state of the modern age. This was the version of the Revolution that was, for example, commemorated so noisily in the streets of Paris in the bicentenary in 1989 (by chance, I was in Paris for this event and recall mainly scepticism on the part of Parisians towards the official celebrations). Notwithstanding this, the Revolution has given every generation of Parisians since 1789 a world-historical role as radicals and rebels and, perhaps a self-fulfilling prophesy, every insurrection since 1789 has in part been fuelled by the obligation to play this role.

The myth of the Revolution has also been frequently challenged. This was done most recently and effectively by the historian François Furet, and a team of researchers, who, in his work *Penser la Révolution française* (published in 1978), argues against the orthodox Marxist view that the Revolution was about class struggle. Most importantly and most bracingly, Furet argues that Revolution was of its era and its influence is now finally over.

This may or may not be so − it is essentially a philosophical statement rather than a statement of empirical historical fact − but it is none the less the case that historians still fiercely contest the origin, impact and consequences of the Revolution. These debates range over the influence of the *philosophes* in undermining the political will of the government, the extent to which the Revolution was the product of grievances against the excesses of Church, nobility and court or complaints against the injustices of absolutist government, or whether, as in the view of Jules Michelet, it provided the necessary corrective to 'the miseries of the people'.[7]

The central conflict, still unresolved despite Furet's work, is between the view of the great Socialist historian of the Revolution, Georges Lefebvre, who sees the Revolution as the victory of the *sans-culottes*, of the slaves over the masters, and therefore as an emblem of future social change, and the Englishman Alfred Cobban, who squints more narrowly at facts rather than theories and has concluded that the Revolution was the victory of bourgeois interests.[8]

The Revolution made Paris itself into a mythical place. Names of sites such as the Bastille, Place de la Grève, Saint-Antoine, Place de Louis XV (soon to become Place de la Révolution and then Place de la Concorde and home of the guillotine) became known all over Europe. Even those hostile to the Revolution, such as the Englishman Thomas Carlyle, who greeted it as a 'Destiny dim-brooding',[9] grudgingly conceded that the historic events had given the city an unprecedented prominence and major symbolic significance in the world.

This was no time for building − money, materials and plans were all lacking − and the Revolution did little to change the physical shape of Paris. The events of the Revolution, which spanned only a few short years, did, however, change the status of Paris for ever. Paris was no longer a mere material reality but also represented a new idea of what humanity could be. 'Happiness is a New Idea in Europe,' declared Saint-Just, a dedicated champion of the people and a ruthless 'terrorist'.[10] Across the world, opinion was divided over whether this meant the noble pursuit of liberty at all costs, the culminating point of the project of the Enlightenment, or the pointless slaughter of innocents in the name of an unattainable abstraction.

The term 'revolution' was itself coined and defined in the Enlightenment. It had indeed been commonly used in French and other European languages since the early Renaissance as part of the growing lexicon of science (most often used to describe the movements of the stars or, in geometry, the complete rotation of a cylinder around its axis). It was only in the late sixteenth century, as the old political structures of the Middle Ages fell apart for good, that the term, used by historians and chroniclers, took on a metaphorical usage to describe changes in society or a sudden change in the perception of the world, or both experiences at the same time. When, however, the idea of revolution finally became a reality in 1789, it was individuals and their actions, rather than the guiding theories of philosophy, that would finally define its meaning for Parisians.

Furet was right about one thing: in reality, the events of the Revolution were driven as much by psychological as political factors – that is to say, by the emotions that were encountered and experienced on the streets of the city. This is what explains, for example, the kind of visceral fury that, on 14 July, drove a crowd of hundreds and then thousands of the 'people' to march on and destroy the Bastille. The most powerful primary motive for this seismic event was the fury of ordinary Parisians when they realized that they had been lied to and taken for fools.

As the century drew to a close, as the army gathered strength and the fireworks of Revolution faded into memory, Paris buzzed with more rumours, counter-rumours and outright propaganda. The stage was being set for a drama that in the space of just a few years would bring the newborn nation to its knees.

PART FIVE

Dream House, Dream City

1800–1850

July 27, 1830. Outside the school, men in shirtsleeves were already rolling casks; others brought in paving stones and sand by wheelbarrows; a barricade was begun.

G. Pinet, *Histoire de l'École Polytechnique*, 1888

Each epoch dreams the one to follow.

Jules Michelet, *Avenir! Avenir!*, 1847

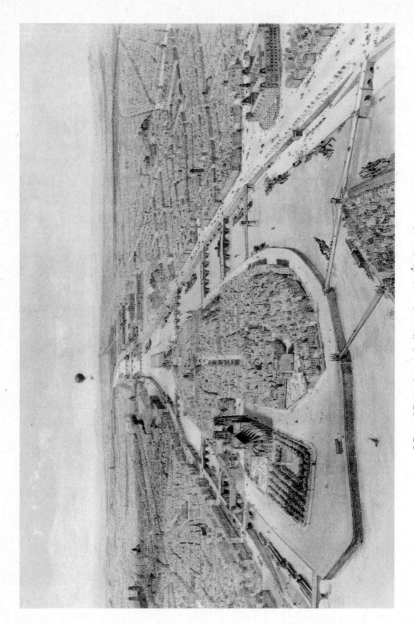

View of Paris from a balloon above the Île Saint-Louis, 1846.

26. Empire

The year 1800 was not in any official sense a meaningful date for Parisians. It did not, for example, mark the beginning of a new century as it did elsewhere in Europe, as Parisians were still under the Revolutionary calendar, in the year VIII. Neither was there any sense that the Revolution was over or even moving into a new phase. The 18 Brumaire year VII (10 October 1799), when the young Napoleon Bonaparte seized power for the first time, did not seem to be especially significant either. Most Parisians saw this as just one of a long line of political convulsions that had taken place regularly since 9 Thermidor Year II (17 July 1794) as moderates sought a way forward between royalists on the Right and Jacobins on the Left. Bonaparte promised stability and security but these promises had been heard many times before in the preceding years. Nobody was truly convinced that he could make them effective. Still less did anyone imagine that within the next fifteen years Paris, under the control of this young and sallow-faced adventurer, would become the epicentre of a military and political drama that would engulf Europe in its entirety and change the world for ever.

This was the beginning of the century in which Paris would become unquestionably the most beautiful and important city in the world. Parisian ideas, style and manners – in political revolution, literature, art, sex, fashion and gastronomy – would have an immeasurable influence across Europe, the New World and the colonies. Its status would be underlined and enhanced by ambitious projects for urban planning and architecture that reinvented the classical ideals of harmony and precision and recast the city as a paradigm of order and beauty. So much of our present-day idea of the physical nature of Paris – the arcades, the hidden passages, the great boulevards, the flat, grey façades of apartment buildings, the elegant squares, the ornate and delicate street furniture of fountains, cobbles and street lamps, the bridges and the sometimes strange and secret gardens – dates from the next hundred years that it commonly seems as if the nineteenth century must have progressed smoothly and effortlessly towards modernity.

The reality was, however, that in the coming century Parisians would encounter destruction and death on a scale entirely unprecedented in the city's history. The historian Jules Michelet, one of the thinkers who is partly responsible for this mythologized version of Parisian history, recalled that in his childhood in the 1800s the streets of Paris stank of corpses and rotten meat, and that if you stamped on a paving stone hard enough, congealed blood would rise to the surface.[1] Over the next hundred years, the city streets would again flow with blood, mostly that of ordinary people who would be locked into a deadly cycle of insurrection and counter-insurrection, in pursuit of the liberties claimed by the Revolution but which were all too often obscured or ignored by venal politicians, vengeful aristocrats or ambitious charlatans on the make. This was to be the age of huge technological progress, but it was also an age of great hatreds and contempt for the way in which commodities and capital were reshaping everyday life beyond the control of ordinary people. The enormous con-vulsions of the time were not simply violent outbursts in the name of theoretical or abstract definitions of liberty, equality and fraternity, but rather volcanic eruptions of forces driven underground by politicians and power-brokers but which could not be long kept in check.

The nineteenth century in Paris has attracted more historians, critics and historiographers than any other period in the city's history. Some of these, such as Karl Marx, found there in the most direct form the contradictory forces of thesis and antithesis, between progress and freedom, which explained, even if they did not quite justify, the very meaning of history itself. 'And so – to Paris, to the old university of philosophy and the new capital of the new world,' wrote the 25-year-old Marx to a comrade in Germany during his first exile in the city. '[This is] the nerve-centre of European history, sending out traumas at regular intervals which shocked the world.'[2]

Writing in the 1930s, Walter Benjamin, another German exile in Paris and an unruly disciple of Marx, devoted hundreds of pages of notes to deciphering the secrets of the nineteenth-century city. His key notion was that this was to be found in tracing the movement and meaning of places and objects in the city against the unfolding background of everyday life in Paris. It was in the interplay between ordinary people and the city that was being created around them, Benjamin stated, that the past, present and future of the city could be glimpsed as a continuum. Once this much was understood, or rather experienced, he argued, the nineteenth-century in Paris would be revealed as the most dynamic and convulsive in human history.[3]

Historians of nineteenth-century Paris are also often shocked by the extreme nature of violence in the name of justice which, from the revolutionary days of 1830 to 1848 to the Commune of 1870, brought fire, gunshots and more dead bodies to the city streets. This was an era of plotters, pamphleteers and ruthless Utopian fanatics. Parisian political violence was, in this sense, only the demon brother of the wild and unstoppable capitalist energy that coursed through the city itself, through banks, businesses, theatres, brothels and cabarets. It is the collision between these two forces which ushered in the city's most glorious and deadly age.

Dreams of Empire

By 1800, most Parisians were exhausted by war, revolution and politics. What most ordinary people wanted by now was food, work, political stability and domestic security, all of which were in conspicuously short supply in the early days of the new century. Since the early 1790s, the French Republic had faced new enemies on all fronts, from rebellion in Brittany, counter-revolutionary forces across the countryside and a series of coalitions of European nations hostile to Revolutionary ideas and practice. The result of these struggles was a wrecked economy, an irregular food supply and a countryside alive with murderous partisans. In the cities, and in Paris in particular, there were plots and counter-plots, denunciations and assassinations. The Terror had abated but in its wake life seemed harsher than ever. The very existence of the republic may have been all too often in danger, but ordinary people soon began to clamour for a life without shortages and the threat of random violence.

If war was an unavoidable burden, however, worst of all was the return to a state of near-famine. The Revolution had destroyed the aristocracy and crushed the Church but it had also reduced Parisians to an everyday misery that they had not known for over a hundred years. There were food riots and attacks on food hoarders and speculators, mainly from the bourgeois classes. In 1795, the Revolutionary authorities were superseded by the Directory, an executive committee of five citizens that partially restored authoritarian rule of Paris. The city no longer had its own central administration and was carved up into separate districts under the control of the Directory. The real problem with the Directory was that it did not have any clear idea about the way forward after the Revolution. More specifically, it offered no political or administrative mechanisms for resolving disputes between law- and policy-makers, who were anyway a swiftly changing cast of chancers and demagogues. Paris was trapped in a political stalemate. In the meantime, inflation spiralled out of control at a truly dizzying rate. The Directory made feeble efforts at reining in the economy, but found it easier to reform institutions, such as the Institut de France (whose scholars accompanied Bonaparte on his adventures to Egypt, thereby founding Egyptology and, inadvertently, laying the foundations for what Edward Said has termed 'Orientalism' – a misguided and Eurocentric method of studying and representing non-European cultures).[4] Financial divisions in Paris grew ever sharper. The era of the Directory proved to be miserable, depressing years for Parisians.

It was then hardly surprising that against this background the figure of Napoleon Bonaparte made such a popular and positive impact on the public imagination of Parisians. Bonaparte spoke French with a noticeable accent and often with difficulty (his mother tongue was a Genoese dialect), and was an outsider to political intrigues in Paris. But since the early 1790s, he had been cutting a swathe in foreign territories in the name of France. Life at home was wretched but, as Napoleon's mass conscript army, soon to be known across Europe as 'La Grande Armée', took on and overcame the military might of Europe's most advanced states, Parisians were still able to believe that they were possessed of a unique destiny.

The Corsican

Napoleon's real name was Nabulione Buonaparte and he was born in Ajaccio in 1769, a year after Louis XV had bought the island from the Genoese authorities. He was sent to France for his military education but never lost the sense of being a foreigner. Napoleon had been in Paris in 1792, as a young major of artillery, and he watched with a dispassionate eye the chaotic storming of the Tuileries gardens, when the masses launched an uprising against the Assembly, pushing the Revolutionary government even further to the Left. Bonaparte paid lip service to the ideals of the Revolution – and indeed personally he had no respect for social graces or inherited rank – but he also remained perpetually wary of the power of the Parisian mob. When the king was made to wear a red bonnet by the exultant crowds, he turned away and refused to celebrate. Even at this early stage, his real concerns were to establish order and discipline.

He first came to the fore in 1794 in Toulon, the southern seaport that had been occupied by the English counter-revolutionary forces. Bonaparte drove the English into the Mediterranean with an astonishing combination of guile, courage and tactical skill. He was by then already friendly with Robespierre, who had him promoted to brigadier-general and made him a hero of the Parisian Revolutionary classes (he was also dissuaded by Robespierre from applying for a commission with the Ottoman Sultan).

In 1795, Paris was again in turmoil. The catalyst for the widespread disorder was inflation and in particular the exorbitant price of bread. In May that year, Jacobin insurrectionists seized the hall of the National Convention in protest but were driven out at bayonet point by the National Guard, the defenders of the working class now become the allies of the bourgeoisie. As political power shifted once again towards the bourgeois classes, Napoleon who was then in Paris was, as a confederate of Robespierre, the object of suspicion as a possible 'terrorist'.

The authorities needed to crush the Jacobin rebels. They were, however, equally fearful of the counter-revolutionary forces that had been gathering in Paris, awaiting their chance to reverse the victories of 1789. In October, the royalists took their chance and lay siege to the Convention with the aim of bringing down the Revolutionary government. The army was called in and General Barras put down the uprising with ruthless efficiency. His second-in-command, Bonaparte, did not flinch from ordering his troops to shoot Parisian civilians in the Tuileries. This moment has entered history as the famous 'whiff of grapeshot' that ended a rebellion. In fact, over two hundred people were killed.

In 1797, Bonaparte returned to Paris from a successful campaign in northern Italy to find himself met by the members of the Directory kitted out in full Roman-style regalia to greet the general as a conquering hero. This was obviously partly a distraction to turn the attention of the Parisians away from the visible misery in the streets, but it also gave Napoleon political inspiration. In 1799, on 18 Brumaire, he stepped up to take control of the Directory, Paris and France, as one of three consuls (another idea filched from Roman practice). Within a few short months, after another successful victory in Italy, Napoleon was, by popular acclaim and his own ambition, effectively in charge of the city, and France, as First Consul and virtual dictator.

Bonaparte may not have been likeable but he was charismatic. Most of all, he offered Parisians internal security without a return to the monarchy. In the days leading up to his seizure of power, posters appeared all over Paris, declaring, 'Citizens, Bonaparte must be in Paris if we are to have peace!' Peace was indeed brought to Paris but this was at the price of a chain of wars fought across Europe in the name of the Revolution. It was during this period that the term *gloire*, which had become prominent in the seventeenth century, meaning a combination of militarism and patriotism, became widespread once again.

Bonaparte's wars were not only a diversion from domestic miseries in France, but also provided a justification for his most ambitious policies of territorial conquest and political domination. Between 1800 and 1814, France would be involved in forty battles led by Bonaparte, all ostensibly fought in the name of 'defending the Revolution' and 'self-defence' but in reality aiming at strengthening his hold over the country and those territories in Europe under the control of his mass conscript armies.

'The Emperor – that World-Soul'

In the meantime, the ideals of the Revolution were gradually eroded away piece by piece. In 1801, Bonaparte came to an agreement with the Pope – the 'Concordat' – that restored and relegitimized the Catholic religion in France. This was celebrated by an Easter Te Deum, held in the presence of the Pope in Notre-Dame, which during the Revolution had been used as a wine warehouse.

Bonaparte also sought to modernize and make the city more stable and effective as a capital. He founded the Bank of France and encouraged private enterprise. Within just a few years, the economy began to recover and the city to rediscover a taste for luxury that had not been seen since the last days of the Ancien Régime. Napoleon himself had no real interest in the aristocracy, except when it suited his political ends, but he did not place any obstacle in the way of returning émigrés to Paris, who brought with them some of the manners and refinements of the old order (as well as a certain sniffy disdain for the provincial Corsican who had allowed them to return).

The slide towards authoritarian control in Paris was swift and inexorable, and seemed to many almost as if it had been planned as Bonaparte's first real intention. On 2 December 1804 (most people had by now ceased to use the impractical Revolutionary Calendar), Bonaparte crowned himself Emperor of France in the cathedral of Notre-Dame. The coronation was performed in the presence of Pope Pius VII (who had married Napoleon to his mistress Josephine in a secret religious ceremony in the Tuileries chapel the day before his coronation – Josephine had already been married to Napoleon in a civil ceremony in 1795). Most famously, it was Napoleon and not the Pope who placed the crown on his own head and who crowned Josephine, signalling to the watching world that power lay entirely in his hands.

The reaction of the Parisian masses was initially enthusiastic, despite the misgivings of journalists and intellectuals such as Pierre Simon, François-René de Chateaubriand (who had at first found favour with Bonaparte with *Le Génie du christianisme* ('The Genius of Christianity', of 1802, a work of Catholic propaganda that served Bonaparte's purpose in the years of reconciliation with the Church) and Madame de Staël; all writers who would soon become sworn enemies of the whole Napoleonic system of government.

The cult of Bonaparte was both mysterious and intoxicating. The use of the terms 'consul' and 'emperor' was not initiated by Bonaparte but simply part of the classical vocabulary then in vogue as a way of reinventing structures of government and administration on Enlightened, and therefore usually Roman, models. Soon, however, these terms began to take on their own meaning and prestige as the apparatus of government itself was shaped on classical lines. Having crowned himself 'emperor', Bonaparte was henceforth to be known simply as 'Napoleon'. This shift alone indicated how much of the destiny of Paris, France and Europe was to be invested in one single name and just one man.

On the night of 12 October 1806, as Bonaparte's troops were about to enter Jena in southern Germany, the philosopher G. W. F. Hegel wrote to his friend F. I. Niethammer in homoerotic awe that he had seen 'the Emperor – that World Soul – riding out to reconnoitre the city; it is truly a wonderful sensation to see such an individual, concentrated here on a single soul, astride a single horse, yet reaching across the world and ruling it'.[5] Hegel wrote these notes in the wake of finishing the first part of his *Phänomenologie des Geistes* ('Phenomenology of Mind'), the dense and magisterial work, published in 1807, in which he laid out his vision of history as a narrative that could only be given meaning by powerful individuals who incarnated a great sense of purpose. For Hegel, as for the Parisians who had cheered him at his coronation at Notre-Dame, Napoleon was the very incarnation of this visionary being.

The City in History

The physical shape of Paris began to change to reflect the dreams and ambitions of this new era in history. Bonaparte himself had declared that he wanted to make Paris more beautiful than any city had ever been. To this end, he commissioned the architects Fontaine and Percier to create new landscapes, destroying the old mansion houses that stood between the Tuileries and the Louvre, to reveal the Champs-Élysées as the widest and most magnificent avenue in Europe, symbolic of the nation's destiny and the military paths to glory.

Above all, the emperor wanted a city that matched his own ideas of France and himself. This was to be a monumental city, again on the Roman model, of arches, statues and great political architecture celebrating the greatness of the French Empire. Although ludicrously grandiose, Napoleon's reshaping of the urban landscape was also immensely practical: he made the city work better and more efficiently than it had for nearly a hundred years. Five new bridges were built to ease movement around Paris. Five new slaughterhouses were installed to feed the city (the most important of these were at Ménilmontant, between rues Saint-Ambroise and Saint-Maur, at Montmartre, at Place d'Anvers, and Villejuif, between rues Pinel and Stéphen-Pichon). Eight covered markets were built, including the flower market on Île de la Cité (the only other remaining market from this period is along the exterior wall of the Marché Saint-Germain, which has been a market since 1176).

One of his greatest and most durable projects was building the Canal d'Ourcq, which brought new trade and life into the heart of Paris. The relationship between Parisians and the river Seine was still deeply ambiguous; in 1801–2 a series of floods had taken lives and soaked the city from the Champs-Élysées to Les Invalides, and from Place de l'Hôtel de Ville to Saint-Antoine. By contrast, during the Revolutionary period and its aftermath, the river had also been one of the few sites for recreation away from the blood-soaked city streets. The *riverains* who plied their trade between the provinces and the city were famous for their indifference to the world-shattering events taking place all around them, and for many Parisians this subversive individualism offered a source of comfort and pleasure. The Seine was a magnet for swimmers, seducers and sometimes also suicides.

The construction of the Canal d'Ourcq was Napoleon's way of showing

Parisians that he understood the importance of water in the life of the city. Like the installation of fifty-six ornamental fountains across the city (some of these, such as the Fontaine de Mars at rue Saint-Dominique or the Fontaine du Palmier at Place du Châtelet, are still impressive sights), which were fed by the canal, this was both a practical and poetic gesture.

Napoleon's signature is these days still to be found all over Paris, literally inscribed into the great projects he personally commissioned, such as the bridges of Austerlitz or Iéna, named for famous victories on the battlefield, or into the very shape of the city, in the form of great avenues such as the rue de Rivoli. His mark is to be found most dramatically in the vast perspective of the Arc du Carrousel between the Louvre and the Tuileries, and the huge and monstrous Arc de Triomphe (work started in 1806 and finished in 1835). Constructed at precise angles to reflect and heighten a visitor's sense of awe in the city, this remains, despite its association with tyranny and despotism, the most profound symbol of French (if not especially Parisian) patriotism.

In the years immediately after the Revolution, however, Paris was a shabby and dilapidated place. Efforts during the early part of the eighteenth century to straighten roads, widen bridges and thoroughfares, and direct movement through the city in a free and orderly fashion had long since ground to a halt. The population had actually shrunk to 500,000 as Parisians abandoned the broken city in search of food and security elsewhere.

Recovery began properly in 1802 and 1803, years that both saw successful harvests. The city began to look forwards. In 1803 in the wake of a temporary peace settlement with England, Paris was briefly a fashionable destination for British visitors. They found (often to undisguised relish) a city that was far less developed in every way than London – the streets were often unpaved and the roads sometimes no more than muddy passages littered with carriages, people and animals. But these tourists were none the less fascinated to find themselves in a city that in the past twenty years had been demonized as the fulcrum of all of the evils of the modern world. It was not hard to seek out forbidden pleasures, from the elegant bare-breasted ladies at the theatre, the *filles de joie* of the Palais-Royal, to the rougher trade of both sexes clearly visible at the various impromptu fairs and markets held at the edges of the city.

Visitors also thrilled at visiting Place Louis XV, where it was said that the stench of blood was still so strong that cattle and horses refused to cross it. Bonaparte was himself an attraction as an object of fascination.

Parisians were often baffled or perturbed by their Anglo-Saxon visitors, whose looks and manners seemed to be deliberately cultivated to offend. Sweaty Englishmen were booed at the opera for watching a performance in their shirtsleeves. Other caricatures around this period are consistent in portraying Englishmen as red-faced boors, usually drunk, ready for a fight or gawping with awestruck lust at the whores on parade. Often – as is still the case in the British stag parties that infest present-day Paris and other European capitals at weekends – all three of these activities were combined into one single, low-level debauch. The English visitors, in turn, were sceptical about the new city being built around them. They noted that much of the magnificence was stolen plunder, whether in the form of the Renaissance masterpieces (as well as books, manuscripts, statues) looted from northern Italy, which were now making the Louvre the most import-ant art museum in the world, or the bronze horses that stood aloft on the Arc du Carrousel. The new empire could not last long, they speculated, if it was to be built on burglary abroad and tyranny at home.[6]

It turned out that they were right. The end of the empire began, in truth, around 1810, when defeat in Spain and a financial crisis in Paris sent the government reeling. Within months, 270 banks had folded. Unemploy-ment and then food shortages followed. It only took a poor harvest in 1811 for Parisians to sense that their destiny may not have been as glorious as Napoleon had promised.

The first universally acknowledged sign of impending disaster was Napoleon's retreat from Moscow in 1812. The sense of gloom and panic increased in the wake of his defeat at Leipzig in October 1813 at the so-called 'Battle of Nations', when Russian, Prussian and Austrian troops had reduced the 'Grande Armée' to tatters. Parisians now feared that they would pay the price for the Corsican's hubris. Above all, they were terrified by the Russians, regarded as ruthless, bloodthirsty and, inspired by the burning of their capital city (the burning of Moscow had in fact been ordered by their own government), who knew only two words of French: 'Brûler Paris!' ('Burn Paris!').[7]

In the wake of Leipzig, Paris had been prey to fearful hearsay, the bulletins from the front coming in a fragmented and distorted form from the emperor's headquarters as his ragged and broken army zigzagged back across the plains of Poland and eastern Prussia. From January 1814 onwards, the city was swollen with refugees and deserters from the Grande Armée who begged in the streets, robbed passers-by when they had the strength or the chance or, if especially badly wounded, lay dying, bleeding in the gutters.

Most terrifyingly for Parisians, they also brought with them terrible and grisly rumours of the violence to come. The city was gripped with near-hysteria. By March, the streets were jam-packed with the carts of peasants seeking refuge in Paris from the battles about to happen in eastern France. The asylums and hospitals were emptied of their inmates to make way for the wounded; lunatics and the terminally ill wandered the streets, braying, drinking, screaming and generally adding to the rising cacophonous tide that was fast engulfing the city as Paris waited to be destroyed. The mortuaries were also emptied and hundreds of bodies thrown into the Seine, the authorities promising Parisians that these fresh corpses were not contaminated and could cause no disease.[8]

The spectacle of the dozens and then hundreds of bloated and purple cadavers that were thrown up on to the banks of the Seine in the warm days of late March 1814 did little to reassure Parisians about their continued health or their future fate.

27. Occupation and Restoration

The army that finally arrived at the gates of Paris in late March was composed of over 100,000 men, a coalition of Prussian, Austrian and Russian troops led by the Austrian marshal Prince Schwarzenberg, the victor at Leipzig. Against this force stood no more than 12,000 members of the Paris National Guard, troops that were well disciplined and largely loyal to Parisians if not the authorities which governed the city. As news of Napoleon's defeats reached the city, this body had been infiltrated by royalist supporters hopeful of finally crushing the working classes in whatever conflagration might ensue from the coming collapse of the tight authoritarian government of the emperor.

Royalists were both encouraged and alarmed by the simmering class hatreds of the Revolutionary era, which, never too far away at any point in the history of Paris up until then, were now once again rising to the surface. One of the main reasons for Napoleon's humiliating defeat, so it was argued in the cafés and drinking-halls of working-class Paris, was that, out of fear and contempt, he had refused to arm the workers of the Faubourg Saint-Antoine, who might or might not have come to his aid. One Parisian eye-witness, the historian and journalist Juan-Antoine Rodriguez, described how middle-class Parisians shivered in fear as 'individuals with no religion, no morals and leading an abject and degraded life' pointed out the houses they would rob and the individuals they would slaughter when the Cossacks came.[1]

On the night of 30 March, in the hours before battle, Parisians clambered up to the heights of Montmartre (which during this period had been briefly renamed Montnapoléon: on the summit of the hill, amid the windmills and vineyards, was the famous telegraph machine that Napoleon used to transmit news and orders to the city) and with a mixture of awe and trepidation watched the movements of these foreign troops as they sat eating and chatting at campfires outside the walls of the city, listening to the exotic sounds of Russian music and preparing for the bloodbath to come.

The battle came at dawn. The worst of it lasted five hours, during which smoke from artillery fire buried the northern heights of the city in a dense cloud. Some Parisians watched the battle as if it were a sporting event from rooftops or through telescopes from their windows. Meanwhile most of the city's population made for the safety of the centre. On the boulevards, the atmosphere was relatively calm, and upper-class Parisians took coffee or ices at Café Tortoni and other fashionable *terrasses* with as much feigned insouciance as they could muster in the face of heavy gunfire and the bloodied soldiers returning from the front.[2] The working classes were more agitated, however, and even as a ceasefire and an allied victory was declared at half past three in the afternoon, waves of panic swept through the muddied lanes and tenements of Old Paris. The news was that the dreaded Russians had taken Montmartre and were poised to punish the city for Napoleon's mistakes in their own country. The prefect of the Seine, the comte de Chabrol, reported back from negotiating a peace settlement that he had seen Russian troops throwing campfire ashes into the air with clearly ominous intent, shouting with glee, 'Paris! Paris!'

The Russian tsar, Alexander I, had come to Paris to supervise the campaign personally and was determined to be generous in victory. He declared that his only enemy was Napoleon and ordered his men to post on the walls of the city an order that Paris was now under his 'special protection'. At eleven o'clock on the morning of 31 March, the tsar entered the city through the Barrière de Pantin, accompanied by his Cossacks and his Prussian and Austrian generals. Relieved that there would be no massacre, Parisians now flocked to meet the incoming army, crying, 'Down with the emperor! Death to the Corsican! Long live peace! Long live our liberators!' The cries grew louder and more intense as the victory parade entered the boulevard des Italiens and the richer western edges of the city. Women seemed particularly glad to see the Russians, declaring to one English observer that 'Napoleon had killed all our lovers'.[3]

The occupying army swept through the city and camped finally on the Champs-Élysées, which was then still mostly a large wooded park, and in the Bois de Boulogne. The city was carved up into three distinct military zones under Russian, Prussian and Austrian command. Parisians drew breath and resumed everyday life with renewed vigour. Fuming in retreat in Fontainebleau, where he had withdrawn with what was left of his support, Napoleon referred to Paris disdainfully as 'la Grande Cosaquie' and the treacherous Parisians as 'monstres cosaques' ('Cossack monsters').[4]

The Cossacks were indeed made welcome by Parisians of all classes. At first they had inspired fear – tales had travelled with them of how they enjoyed rape and savage games such as whipping men as they stood naked in the icy cold. Parisian men respected their conquerors' discipline and military bearing; women were easily seduced by their exotic manners and looks. The Cossacks themselves disdained the luxuries of Paris, but drank deep of its earthier pleasures. The term *bistro* – the Russian word for 'quickly' – is said to have come into usage at this point to describe the kind of no-nonsense restaurant favoured by Cossacks. Brothels also reported brisk and improved business.

The occupation of Paris in 1814 was none the less a profound shock to its inhabitants. Even those Parisians who still scorned religion and super-stition could not help but see this new disaster as a uniquely cruel punish-ment for the Revolution sent by whichever Divinity ruled over the tragic destiny of the city.

For this reason, Parisians embraced their temporary rulers with a pro-visional enthusiasm rather than love. The general feeling was that Napoleon had brought them to the brink of disaster. The tsar, on the other hand, quickly became a hero in Parisian eyes, admired for the way in which he had spared the city and established order and stability with minimum cost to the city's population. Parisians gathered to watch him with a mixture of fear and admiration as he made his way to worship in the morning and in the evening at the Russian Orthodox chapel on the Place Louis XV (soon to be renamed Place de la Concorde). It was not long, however, before the occupation began to inspire melancholy in Parisians – a nostalgia for the autonomy and revolutionary momentum that they had lost, rather than elation at simply getting rid of a tyrant.

Burying the Dead

One of the chief causes of Parisian gloom during this period was the wretched state of the city by the time Napoleon had abandoned it. The emperor had sought to make the city a monument to his glorious destiny and had cut great swathes through the central and western axis of Paris to shape the urban landscape into a contemporary version of imperial Rome, with great triumphal arches, avenues for military parades and streets cut into straight lines with military precision. The medieval alleys and passages of the old heart of the city, stretching from Les Halles to the east and south, were relatively untouched by these developments, although those who lived there grumbled long and loud about the rotten sewers and the cost of building Napoleon's dream capital.

The stench of central Paris was notorious. The reason for this was that by the early nineteenth century the cemeteries of Paris, many of which dated back to pre-Roman times, were dangerously overcrowded. The most ill reputed of these was that of the Saints-Innocents in the heart of the city. This place had long been famous, at least by night, as the haunt of necromancers, whores, drinkers, thieves and, throughout the eighteenth century, grave-robbers who sold the freshest corpses to students and professors in the École de Médecine across the river. The cemetery of the Saints-Innocents was, as we have seen, a part of Parisian folklore but it was also a place to be avoided whenever possible. It had reached a gory apogee during the Revolutionary Terror when baskets of severed heads and headless bodies were regularly and unceremoniously dumped at its edges. Its very smell – rich, deadly and overpowering – was the foulest reminder of the recent, murderous past.

In 1776, the common grave, into which the poor of Paris had been flung like so much garbage over the centuries, began to subside; dead bodies began to appear in rotten lumps, breaking through the cellar walls of nearby houses alongside flesh-eating rats. Many of these houses were on the point of collapse and their inhabitants were suffocating in the foul, sulphurous air. In 1780, several people died in rue de la Lingerie of a mysterious pestilential infection caused by 'bad air'.

It was not until the early 1800s that the decision was taken to destroy Saints-Innocents, along with all the other smaller local cemeteries of Paris, and to open three large spaces for the dead, of which the largest was Père-Lachaise, on the outskirts of the city. The bones of Saints-Innocents were to be removed to Denfert-Rochereau, the old quarry that had provided the stones for the new city. The early years of the nineteenth century, the so-called 'century of light', were marked by the night-time manoeuvres of corpse-carriers, shifting the bones of the dead from one end of the city to another, trailed by a retinue of priests intoning prayers for the dead. A journalist who protested that this was a desecration of the city's deceased ended up in prison, indicating that there was also a specifically political aspect to these activities.

More to the point, the old quarries and underground tunnels that were revealed at the end of the eighteenth century were rumoured to be harbouring revolutionaries and insurrectionists, a literal underground force that might rise up at any time and seize the city. Better to block the gaps with the useless dead.

Restoration

Parisians of all classes were relieved that the occupation was short-lived. On 4 May 1814, the Bourbon monarchy was restored in the form of Louis XVIII, brother of the king who had been decapitated in 1793. This did not mean, however, an immediate return to the pre-Revolutionary order, which was now both impossible as well as undesirable. Rather, the restoration was an interim response to the unsolved problem of the political cast of Parisian life. The Russian allies had left the city soon after signing the Treaty of 30 May, which left the city in Louis's hands. The statue of Henri IV that had been destroyed during the Revolution was repaired with plaster and erected once again on the Pont-Neuf. This patched-up monument was to prove a useful metaphor for Louis's government, which never truly had a hold on the city; his government lacked focus and direction, other than a vague yearning for the past.

During the first months of the restoration, Paris was a cauldron of political discontent. In the wake of the collapse of imperial discipline, the city was home to a wide range of political opinions from the likes of Catholic monarchists, *sans-culottes* egalitarians, liberals and Jacobins to melancholy Bonarpartists. The working classes were angry at the return of the king and the succession of empty promises which he made. The unemployed soldiers, including 12,000 former officers of the Grande Armée, gathered in the streets and cafés, lamenting the lost dream of imperial glory and complaining bitterly about the meagre pensions they had received.

This mood had been predicted in 1813 in a prescient pamphlet, *De l'esprit de conquête et de l'usurpation* ('The spirit of conquest and usurpation'), by Henri-Benjamin Constant de Rebecque. The Swiss novelist and journalist Benjamin Constant, as he was known in Paris, was a sworn enemy of the mysticism of Napoleon's authoritarian rule. His pamphlet was published in Hanover but widely distributed in Paris, especially in the days leading up to the emperor's first downfall in 1814. Above all, Constant attacks the worship of patriotism and power as political abstractions, opposing them with the common-sense values of everyday life. 'While patriotism exists only by a vivid attachment to the interests, the ways of life, the customs of some locality,' he writes, 'our so-called patriots have declared war on all of these. They have dried up this natural source of patriotism and have sought to replace it by a factitious passion for an abstract being, a general idea stripped of all that can engage the imagination and speak to the memory.'

This description of the underlying psychology of Napoleon's will to power would become for future readers of Constant a powerful and prophetic statement about the true nature of twentieth-century totalitarianism.[5]

Constant, like many intellectuals of the period, was both enraged and unsurprised when Napoleon returned to Paris and to power in the spring of 1815. With bold simplicity, as news of the political chaos in France reached him, the emperor had decided to leave his exile in Elba in March, landing in the south of France and marching towards Paris, collecting supporters along the way. When Napoleon finally reached the capital, the government of Louis XVIII melted away as if it had never existed. The fat old king did not wait for the arrival of Napoleon but fled in the night for Ghent long before the emperor's troops were first sighted.

When he entered the city again, Napoleon was cheered in the Tuileries but the working-class districts were subdued and cautious. Nobody really believed that any good could come of this reliving of the past. Napoleon himself seemed to be aware of the mood and even summoned Constant, the sceptical Swiss Protestant (who had gone into hiding when he heard of the emperor's return), to meet him and to advise him on how to become a born-again liberal ruler. Constant agreed to help draw up legislation for a constitutional government but did not believe for a minute that Napoleon could change.

Nor did anyone else, least of all the Parisians who had lived through the promises of glory and the bruising trauma of siege and occupation. Wellington's victory over Napoleon at Waterloo, which finally crushed the dream of a pan-European state stretching from Spain to Germany and Egypt, was greeted by most Parisians with a mixture of sadness and relief. Similarly, most were glad to see the emperor leave for the final time on 21 June, when he said his last farewell to the city en route to his definitive exile in St Helena.

It was not quite so easy, however, to wipe away the traces of glory and catastrophe that had marked the early 1800s. The century that had begun with a frenzy of patriotic warmongering among all Frenchmen, and Parisians in particular, soon crashed into humiliating defeat and the end of the imperial dream.

Napoleon's final defeat had a shattering impact on the city. The treaty signed by the French authorities in November 1815 was far harsher than the one forced on the city by the allied armies the previous year. Worse still was the arrogance and naked desire for revenge which now characterized the allied authorities as they established themselves in Paris.

Louis XVIII returned from exile on 8 July, accompanied by 300,000 soldiers who set up camp in the heart of the capital. These troops were despised by Parisians but they would stay for the next two years, functioning almost as the king's private police force, rounding up suspected 'Reds' (Jacobins and Bonapartists alike) and executing summary royalist justice. There was a constitutional government but it was often ignored. Louis thought that he had been betrayed by Parisians and did all he could to revenge himself on them. He delighted in offending even the mildest elements in the Parisian middle classes by insisting on restoring the clergy to its pre-Revolutionary prominence in society and the government. His death in 1824 was little mourned in Paris, although his successor, Charles X, a former libertine who had become a fanatical Catholic, promised to be even lazier and more vengeful.

Charles indeed committed the capital error of seeking to restore the monarchy to its pre-Revolutionary position. He was also stubborn. In 1827, the Parisian electorate (which Charles had reduced to the property-owning classes) voted liberal in protest at his ultra-conservative government. Streets were barricaded and working-class mobs from the eastern part of the city patrolled the avenues of central Paris calling for 'Death to the government!', 'Death to the Jesuits!' and 'Death to the bigots!' The insurrection was suppressed, but in the stifling summer heat of July 1830 Parisians returned to the barricades.

This time the provocation had come directly from Charles, who in June had passed four unconstitutional laws, which included abolishing the Chamber of Deputies (which had refused to co-operate with Charles) and controlling the freedom of the press. Memories of the heavy hand of government under Napoleon were not too far away. Discontent continued to brew steadily throughout July, culminating in a demonstration against the king outside the Palais-Royal on 26 July. The unease was heightened by the fact that Charles asked Marshal Marmont, an unpopular former favourite commander of Napoleon's regiments, to police the crowds. Barricades went up in eastern Paris on the 27th. Shots were fired; a young woman was killed and her body placed symbolically in the Place des Victoires as an incitement to revenge.

There followed three days of street-fighting – *les trois glorieuses* as they were called in revolutionary folklore – with the working-class insurrectionists once again leading the way from the eastern *quartiers* of Saint-Antoine. The conflict took the form of running battles with troops (many of whom were soon sympathetic to and fraternizing with the workers) in the narrow streets of Old Paris. These streets were impassable; the troops were at a serious disadvantage, quickly losing the conflict.

In the next day or so, fighting spread westwards. Soon the rioters found themselves in charge of Paris, drinking themselves stupid on the fine wines of the newly captured Tuileries and wrecking the palace of the Archbishop of Paris. Amid panic and confusion among the city authorities,[6] Charles X made one last stubborn attempt to save the Bourbon dynasty by proposing his grandson, the duc de Bordeaux, as Henri V.

Paris was in no mood for compromise, however, and Charles X headed for exile. The Parisian underclasses congratulated themselves that they had done with inherited monarchs once and for all and therefore finished the project of the Revolution. Yet events over the next fifty years would demonstrate in the most violent terms that this conclusion was entirely misguided.

28. The Bourgeois World of Louis-Philippe

Despite the ferocity of the rioting during the events of the *trois glorieuses*, there had been relatively few casualties in comparison with previous conflicts in the city (the death toll amounted finally to some 600 rioters and 150 troops). Most importantly, the insurrection had not led, as some commentators thought it would, to a Bonapartist restoration or a full-blown republic. Rather, a third way had been found which was to install a new monarch, who was from the house of Orléans rather than the by now thoroughly discredited house of Bourbon (the rivalry between the two contesting families for the throne had not really diminished despite the Revolution).

Charles X was thus succeeded by a new king, Louis-Philippe, the last king of France and an Orléanist. Although he had in fact been nominated to the post by Charles, in a manoeuvre to save the monarchy if not his own throne, Louis-Philippe did all that he could over the next eighteen years of his reign to distance himself from the ultra-conservative excesses of his predecessor. This was a constitutional monarchy with none of the trappings of the mysticism of absolutism, which had repulsed liberals and extremists alike during the reign of Charles. To this extent, Louis-Philippe cultivated the image of a plain and honest middle-class businessman. It followed from this that the reign of Louis-Philippe announced an era during which the values of bourgeois individualism held sway as the supreme form of public morality.

Louis-Philippe was indeed a banker by trade and even as king was often to be seen walking in the Tuileries gardens in a frock coat and with a green umbrella like any bourgeois gentleman of the day. He had served with distinction in the republican army of the 1790s and was keen to disassociate himself from the pairing of Crown and clergy that had been the mark of the last Bourbon restoration. The philosophy of his government was defined in the words his first minister and chief adviser, François Guizot, an Anglophile and a shrewd political operator, whose maxim was '*Enrichissez-vous* (make yourself rich) and leave the politics to me'. Despite his nonchalant appearance, Louis-Philippe lacked faith in those who claimed to support him and accordingly held on to power with a tight rein. The authority of the police was increased and he kept a watchful eye on political movements and the mood of the press.

Louis-Philippe's Paris was, for all his attempts at public order, still a violent place. A cholera epidemic in 1832, which claimed the lives of several thousands, provided a temporary hiatus in the long-running battles between the forces of order and the so-called 'dangerous classes' of Paris. These included not only underpaid or unemployed workers but also itinerants, drinkers, beggars, thieves and whores: all those who had no connection whatsoever to Louis-Philippe's ideal bourgeois state. Riots and mutinies were never far away, all too often culminating in the slaughter of innocent bystanders (which is what happened in 1834 in the rue Transnonain when twelve men, women and children were killed in a raid on a building where there was alleged to have been a sniper; the incident was famously immortalized in contemporary fiction by Flaubert in *L'Éducation sentimentale*, whose characters recalled a gory scene of blood and bayonets, and recorded by Stendhal in *Lucien Leuwen* and Victor Hugo in *Les Misérables*).

Paris was also dirty, crowded and poorly maintained. Street lighting was rudimentary or non-existent and the streets of any Parisian *quartier* at night were an excellent place to be robbed and killed. The popular novelist Eugène Sue, a bestselling writer of the period, produced melodramatic potboilers that were set among Parisian low life and provoked an almost pornographic shiver of fear and delight in bourgeois readers. The most famous of these was *Les Mystères de Paris* ('The Mysteries of Paris'), a compendium of tales from the slums published in 1842–3. Many of Sue's characters, such as 'Rodolphe', the enigmatic prince who frequents the Parisian underworld in disguise, or La Mère Pipelet, the archetypal concierge of the rue du Temple, have now passed into folklore. The books themselves have often been dismissed by critics on the Left as sensationalized accounts of working-class life into which the intrepid bourgeois steps seeking vicarious excitement.

There is evidence, however, that the substance of Sue's accounts of the city is true, even if his tales are often overwrought and exaggerated. One nineteenth-century commentator, Charles Louandre, noted that 'in certain neighbourhoods of the capital, no one doubted the existence' of all the main characters.[1] Certainly, there was no love lost between the social classes in Paris. At times, the conflict between the poor and the forces of order made Parisians feel that they were locked into an unending civil war. The reasons for rioting were not always economic; in 1831 the church of Saint-Germain-de-l'Auxerrois was besieged by an angry mob trying to disrupt a Mass that was being said for the duc de Berry and which was rumoured to be in honour of 'Jesuitical Bourbons'. The same crowd marched on the palace of the Archbishop of Paris and burned it down. Clashes between republicans and Bonapartists in the eastern edges of the city left 800 dead in the streets in 1832.

It was one of the paradoxes of the era that, in spite of the continuous political and social upheavals, Paris produced a remarkable number of writers, artists and thinkers during this period. This had not been the case during the Revolution, when daily life for even the most prominent and distinguished Parisians was dominated by the ever-present demands of hunger and fear. Similarly, the atmosphere of Napoleonic Paris had hardly been conducive to free thought and expression (although the likes of the Parisian poet and satirist Pierre-Jean de Béranger enjoyed great popular support; his relative freedom was no doubt due to the fact that he was also a shameless propagandist for Napoleon).

The new historical dynamic was incarnate in the Parisian barricades, even the substance of the streets themselves. In 1830, it was said that there were 4,054 barricades across the city, made up of over 800,000 *pavés*, or cobblestones – good weapons to throw at troops or the police. The *pavé*, along with the barricade, would now enter history as an integral part of the enduring myth of revolution in the city (only to be finally discarded in the wake of the events of May 1968, when the cobbles of the Latin Quarter were covered in asphalt).[2]

Victor Hugo famously described the *pavé* as 'the quintessential symbol of the people . . . You tread upon it until it falls on your head.' This was a direct reference to the July Revolution during which a German observer, Friedrich von Raumer, noted, 'Fewer were felled by bullets than other projectiles. The large squares of granite with which Paris is paved were dragged up to the top floors of the houses and dropped onto the heads of the soldiers.'[3] Hugo also praised the mutinous and seething city that inspired fear in kings and where 'the lava of events' shaped human destinies as a 'human Vesuvius'.[4] Praised by poets and feared by governments across the globe, in the slipstream of 1830, Paris now became properly famous as the world capital of revolution. Parisians themselves also started to believe the myths of the city. When they looked back, they saw a tradition of riots and insurrections, from the *jacqueries* of the Middle Ages through to the troubles of the Fronde. The very word *parisien* had long been a synonym in French for 'troublemaker', while 'barricade' had its origins in the word *barriques*, earth-filled barrels that were used as defensive walls in the days of the League in the sixteenth century.[5]

Passages of Desire

The shape of Paris was relatively stable throughout this period. By 1817, the population had swelled to 700,000 and would reach the one million mark by 1844. Urban planning was, however, remarkably unambitious, reflecting the tentative mood of markets and speculators in a volatile political climate. The major new buildings that appeared in Paris were either religious, such as the Chapelle Expiatoire constructed on the exact spot where Louis XVI and his wife had been killed and intended as atonement for their murder (working-class Parisians hated it straight away for this reason), or had a strictly commercial function (the Bourse, or 'Stock Exchange', that had been started in the Napoleonic era was also finished during this period). There were, however, much to the relief of most Parisians who by now were both weary and broke, no great new monumental avenues, buildings or boulevards to the glory of great men or the destiny of France to tax the pockets of ordinary people.

There was, in contrast, a frenzy of private speculation, beginning in the early 1820s, over developing sites in hitherto ignored or unknown parts of the city. In 1819, a private holding company in the charge of a certain La Peyrière set out to develop the area between rues de La Rochefoucauld, de la Tour-des-Dames and Saint-Lazare. The original intention had simply been to build apartment blocks sufficiently far apart to allow the free flow of fresh air between them. The developers were not concerned with constructing new roads or ways into the city, but envisaged instead a healthy place to live in at some distance from the fetid streets of the city centre. When it was finally finished, the area was described as 'La Nouvelle Athènes' and was immediately sought after, attracting well-known figures from the worlds of politics or the arts who thought it fashionable to live at a certain remove from the city (the writers George Sand and Alexandre Dumas and the actor Talma were among the first inhabitants of the area for this reason).

Investors and entrepreneurs quickly realized that they could make money by developing the edges of Paris, and building projects soon extended across the northern boundaries of the city to places like Batignolles and to the south at Grenelle. The new apartment blocks, while smaller and less ornate than before, frequently aped the late Renaissance styles of the sixteenth century that had come back into fashion (this did not mean, however, that the Marais, which had long since fallen into a decline, was a fashionable place to live). Few private householders could afford these indulgences, however, and most investors were reluctant to spend more than what was strictly necessary on style and decoration.

The greatest novelty for Parisians and visitors to the city was the proliferation of covered passages on the Right Bank, linking streets and boulevards and forming a matrix of routes across the city that were not subject to the traditional network of paths across Paris, or indeed even the weather. The notion of covered passageways in the urban environment was not new to France – in the south-west, most towns and cities had some form of covered market dating back to the thirteenth century and perhaps influenced by the great souks of Arab cities. What was remarkable about these new passageways was first of all their construction and design. They were built out of wrought iron and stone, and combined light, graceful, often highly convoluted patterns with a solid and unbreakable structure, presenting a totally new departure from the structures of classical or neo-classical architecture. Most importantly, the passages were entirely dedicated to commercial activity and leisure. As such, the *passages de Paris* were harbingers of the modernity that the city would both incarnate and define in the nineteenth century. Ferdinand von Gall, a German in Paris, noted that people smoked in the passages during a period when it was still considered unseemly to smoke in the street; the passageways were 'the favoured haunt of smokers and strollers, theatre of operations for every kind of small business. In each arcade there is at least one cleaning establishment. In a salon that is as elegantly furnished as its intended use permits, gentlemen sit upon high stools and comfortably peruse a newspaper while someone brushes the dirt off their clothing and boots.'[5]

The first passageway proper was the passage du Prado, established in 1785 to link the rue du Faubourg-Saint-Denis with the boulevard. In 1786, work started on the so-called *galeries de bois* ('wooden galleries') linking the Palais-Royal to the *galeries* of Valois and Montpensier; they were an immediate success, with booksellers and fashionable clothes merchants hurrying to set up business there. The passage du Caire (adjoining the rue Saint-Denis) and the passage des Panoramas (linked to rue Saint-Marc) were in business by 1800.

Between 1820 and 1845, thirty-four passages were built across the Right Bank (the Left Bank was considered by investors as less commercial and, with its semi-intact medieval street plan, more difficult from an architectural point of view). By the 1870s, there were more than 150, but they had already begun their decline, superseded by the activity of the boulevards and the improvements in urban transport which made them less important as a refuge from rain, mud and dangerous horse-driven carriages.

In the twentieth century, the passages were venerated by the Surrealists in the 1920s (see Chapter 37), who adored the way in which they made a mysterious labyrinth out of the city, and, in the 1950s, by the Situationists, a tiny sect of artists and intellectuals who dreamt of a future Paris dedicated to idleness, pleasure and poetry rather than the demands of money and work. Both groups admired the writings of Walter Benjamin, a German émigré to Paris in the 1930s, a Marxist intellectual and a passionate historian of Paris. In his unfinished study of the city in the nineteenth century, Benjamin devoted thousands of words to the passages, describing them as 'temples of commodity capital'.[7] Having sprung up during the mercantile excitement and high-risk speculation of the 1820s and 1830s, the passages were emblems of the energy of capital and also its quasi-Utopian belief in the future. As cosy and intimate interior spaces in the city, they were also intricately linked to the values of Louis-Philippe's fantasy bourgeois society, which prized the domestic comforts of work, family and hearth as the highest values.

Benjamin was also fascinated by the way in which the range and quality of commodities on offer in these places stood as the visible manifestation of the collective desires of society. He called them 'dream-houses' and argued that, since past and present occupy the same continuum, in reading carefully the most obscure desires of past generations, as encapsulated in the *passages de Paris*, we can also glimpse our own possible futures. It is hard to see how this remains true in the many newly gentrified passages of 21st-century Paris, such as the Galeries Vivienne, which have been remodelled and resurrected as classy and expensive museum pieces. But in dustier, more neglected parts of the Right Bank, such as the passage du Caire, where the textile business, the sex trade and a thriving underworld of people-smugglers and dope dealers (all peddlers of several varieties of human desire) collide, it is still possible to see what Benjamin meant by 'historical scenes . . . a dialectical exchange between carnal pleasure and the corpse'.[8]

'A new moonlight'

One of the most sharp-eyed visitors to Paris in the 1830s was a certain Mrs Trollope, mother of the distinguished English novelist and herself a writer of travel books. Following in the footsteps of other tourists, she visited the famous Café Tortoni on the boulevard des Italiens and gushed over the exquisite fancies on offer and the 'brilliant light within, the humming crowd without'.

She also noticed among the well-heeled and fashionable Parisian youths who gathered there a 'wild, bold eye that turns from every passing glance'. She had been told by someone who knew Paris well that there had been a significant rise in suicides among young men in recent years, and that this was usually attributed to 'light literature', which praised death and scorned the everyday values of Louis-Philippe's society for a more transcendent world view. With superb Anglo-Saxon high-handedness, Mrs Trollope dismissed such stories as feckless and melodramatic nonsense, although she did confess that she was troubled by her encounters in the Café Tortoni with 'such picturesque individuals'.[9]

The young men who had disturbed Mrs Trollope's peace were no doubt admirers or members of a sect called 'Les Bousingos'. This group, which included the poets Gérard de Nerval (a pseudonym for Gérard Labrunie), Philothée O'Neddy (an anagram of his real name: Théophile Dondey) and Jehan du Seigneur (a medievalized made-up name; his real one is lost to history), had been founded by the poet, novelist and professional eccentric Pétrus Borel, aged twenty-one, in his rented room on a corner of the boulevard de Rochechouart. They named themselves first of all 'Le Camp des Tartares' (a provocatively pro-Russian nomenclature) and then, to demonstrate their progressive outlook, 'Les Jeunes-France'. The group set out to insult and attack all aspects of Louis-Philippe's society with a series of serious pranks, including strolling around naked, or leaving a dressmaker's dummy in the street wrapped in a shroud and claiming it to be a corpse freshly dug up from the cemetery. They were forced to leave their head-quarters in the boulevard de Rochechouart after police intervention (the police had been called to prevent angry neighbours lynching them after it was thought they were shouting 'Vive Charles Dix (X)!'; they had in fact been singing 'Vive Bouchardy!', in reference to a novelist who was one of their own number). They decamped, appropriately enough, to the rue d'Enfer, where they held an inaugural feast during which cream was eaten out of hollowed-out skulls and most guests were knocked unconscious by the lethal punch.[10]

They named themselves 'Les Bousingos' during a party at a cabaret called the Petit-Moulin-Vert, dancing around a bowl of alcohol that had been set alight, and making up verses ending in 'go' or 'goth' (in praise of Victor Hugo). They soon became famous in the popular press as their antics – spending a day in a cemetery or dissecting room – were recorded in the likes of *Le Figaro*. They made up songs celebrating cigarettes ('Let us smoke, smoke! Like cigarettes, all things are brief in a useless life') and celebrated the virtues of idleness, orgies, drugs, suicide and murder.

There was, however, a serious, even political, aspect to this playful behaviour. More specifically, the Bousingos detested the 'stupidity' and bovine nature of the world as it was organized under Louis-Philippe. They were children of the 1830 revolution who had been desperately disappointed by its aftermath. Their founder, Borel (who occasionally styled himself as a 'werewolf'), had described the insurrectionary Paris of July as 'a crater' in which 'new moonlight' revealed the horrors of a decaying clergy.[11] His rebellion was the direct consequence of society's collective inability to assume responsibility for making the true revolution.

The same sense of disappointment touched intellectuals from all social strata. Indeed, another reason why Louis-Philippe's reign was doomed was his inability to understand, let alone resist, the march of ideas in the nineteenth century. The memory of the 'Grande Révolution' had never been too far away among the so-called 'dangerous classes' of the city. But in the late 1830s it was no more than a fading nostalgia for a promise of freedom that successive governments had failed to honour. During this period, when Louis-Philippe's government was consolidating power with guns as well as low taxes, the Revolutionary tradition was only properly held intact, it was claimed, by young radical intellectuals with interests in literature and philosophy as well as politics.

This was not exactly true – it was a claim made by the young intellectuals themselves and never believed by the working classes – but it was true enough that in Paris, as elsewhere in Europe, a new spirit of liberty was at large in the *salons* and minds of the intelligentsia. The term *romantisme* first entered the French language in 1822, although the term *romantique* had long been in use as both noun and adjective. Loosely speaking, the word described a mood in European thought which since the late eighteenth century had taken on the cast of a movement. The central principle of French Romanticism, inspired by the writings of Jean-Jacques Rousseau and, more recently, Madame de Staël, as well as the political upheaval of the Revolution, was that the classical standards of the beautiful were insufficient to represent life truly in thought or art. Romantic theorists, who by the 1830s included such names as the poets Alphonse de Lamartine, Alfred de Vigny and Victor Hugo, called for 'liberté dans l'art', and argued for total freedom in the choice of subject matter and language. Splinter groups, such as the Bousingos, were considered extremist outgrowths of this movement and even praised by mainstream figures for what was termed their 'frenetic Romanticism'.

In Paris, the new mood had been confirmed as the guiding theory of the day in February 1830 in the wake of the so-called *bataille d'Hernani*. This was less a battle than a cultural clash in which traditionalists and young Romantics had come to blows in the Comédie Française over the play *Hernani* by the young but soon to be famous Victor Hugo. Although the play itself was essentially mediocre, it provoked outrage over its subject matter (a weak and indecisive king). Most significant and politically contentious was the free and frank use of language and tragic form (the traditionalists hissed to hear a king speak in less than perfect poetic diction and use everyday locutions). The *romantiques*, who during the two controversial evenings of the play's performance featured professional rabble-rousers such as Borel and the future poet Théophile Gautier, howled down the traditionalists and were not afraid of landing a blow or two in the name of 'the art of liberty'.[12]

Ordinary Parisians were indifferent to or ignorant of such squabbles in the name of high art. But the 'battle', which was a conflict of generations as much as anything else, did mark a turning point in the career of Louis-Philippe. It signalled, most importantly, that his values were unacceptable to the present and future generations of thinkers and opinion-makers. The poet Alphonse de Lamartine, an infinitely more respectable and politically influential figure than Borel, when asked why he did not support the government of Charles X, responded with: 'Does the lion grant pardon when his tongue has tasted blood?'[13] This was unusually emotive language for a poet known for his humanity and moderation. No less than the Bousingos, Lamartine and the world he represented had been disappointed by the gap, ever widening, between the myth of revolution and the reality of its aftermath.

29. Balzac's Mirror

Nobody could undo the Revolution, however. Throughout the next seventy years, the myth of Revolutionary Paris, reawakened in the events of 1830, would play a central role in the imagination of all Parisians, dominating the decisions they made and leading ultimately to the key moments of convulsive violence in 1848 and 1871.

It did not seem to matter very much that, until 1830, the Parisian population had also enjoyed long periods of passivity and inertia, and even collaborated with ineffectual rulers and despotic regimes. The changes that actually occurred under the 'July Monarchy' were in fact more in line with Louis-Philippe's belief in a nation of shopkeepers rather than glory-seeking warriors. The first *grand magasin*, the precursor of the department store, had appeared in Paris as far back as 1824 (this was La Belle Jardinière on the Quai aux Fleurs on Île de la Cité, which introduced the revolutionary concepts of fixed prices and payment at the counter). In 1828, the entrepreneur Stanislas Baudry had founded the Compagnie des Omnibus, the first integrated transport system for the Parisian region, with 100 horse-drawn carriages with 18–25 seats. By the mid-point of Louis-Philippe's reign, these carriages were moving more than two and a half million travellers across the entire city. In 1836, there appeared two new daily newspapers, *La Presse* and *Le Siècle*, which aimed at the burgeoning bourgeois market and attracted a massive circulation, heralding the twin novelties of a subscription service and high-paying advertisers to Parisians. A new street-numbering system (incidentally introducing the blue steel number signs that are still in use today) was inaugurated in 1847. Paris was quickly becoming more domesticated and modern at the same time.

Despite the improvements in the quality of everyday life, Louis-Philippe's government never enjoyed any real popular support, however. This left the way open for royalists, Bonapartists and a rising tide of groups on the Revolutionary Left to subvert his cosy ideal of a state ordered principally around the comfort and well-being of its middle classes. It was no accident that it was during this period, and particularly as conditions for the poor in Paris visibly deteriorated in the wake of the economic crisis of 1846–7, that Karl Marx and Friedrich Engels began to present the city as the capital of all coming revolutions in the name of social justice. Anyone who in the 1840s walked from the west to the east of the city, crossing the rues Saint-Denis or Saint-Martin with the trepidation of someone crossing a dangerous, invisible border, could not fail to see the real, direct meaning of the Marxian definition of history as the angry exchange of blows between social classes. Paris was a divided city where the two populations, the rich and the poor, did not even speak the same language, let alone breathe the same air, eat the same food or wear the same clothes.

It was against the background of this rising tide of discontent that France launched into an overseas adventure which would have long-term and eventually calamitous consequences. This was the French conquest of Algeria, a vast and unknown territory on the other side of the Mediterranean, rumoured to be rich in plundered loot and Oriental treasures and, so it was thought, easy prey for the superior technology and military might of the French army.

The First Battle of Algiers

The French had indeed long coveted Algeria, which was considered to be one of the weakest links in the Ottoman Empire. The inspiration came from Napoleon's partial success with an expeditionary force to Egypt in 1798, which had triggered a vogue in Paris for all things Oriental, from rugs, carpets and furnishings to jewellery and hashish. The catalyst was an insult delivered to the French consul Deval in 1827 by the Dey of Algiers, or El-Djezair as the city was then known, who had swiped at the consul with a fly-swat when the latter had demanded excessive interest on a French loan made to the Algerian nation.

Three years later, France took its revenge. The idea was first publicly mooted by Charles X in March 1830, with the stated intention of recovering an unpaid debt from corsairs and pirates. Even at this early stage, Charles's enemies saw this as a cynical ploy to recover rapidly diminishing popularity at home with a foreign adventure in pursuit of *la gloire*. Notwithstanding, on the 14 June 1830, French troops landed at Sidi Ferruch, a beach some twenty miles to the east of Algiers. The enterprise was launched as an entertainment as well as a war, with fashionable Parisians watching the bombardment of Algiers from hired pleasure boats. The Dey capitulated after five weeks of fighting, by which time Charles X had also fallen and gone into exile.

Louis-Philippe inherited the adventure, pursuing it with as much vigour as he could, mainly on the grounds that he could not afford to lose face in Paris or be seen to be conceding any ground to the English, who had been observing all French manoeuvres with predatory eyes from the outset. Parisians themselves were largely indifferent to the project. It was only when the fighting moved deeper into the interior, and French troops were slaughtered in ambushes or froze to death in the mountains, that Parisians took any notice at all of what was happening as it was reported to them in the popular journals of the day. The war was never simple, however. Much to the dismay of French generals, the tribal structure of the Algerian nation became organized under the strong hand of the 25-year-old resistance leader Abd-el-Kader, who won extraordinary victories against the colonial power. French retaliation, in a pattern that would become grimly familiar in the twentieth century, was tough and remorseless. Louis-Philippe had declared that all methods for winning the war were justified. 'What did it matter,' he said, 'if a hundred million shots are fired in Africa. Europe does not hear them.'[1] The Parisian public was deeply shocked in 1843 by the tactics of the French army, which had killed almost five hundred Algerian men, women and children by lighting fires at the entrances to the caves where they lived and letting them choke to death.

Parisians were even less inclined to sympathize with their own government when they learned that the general with responsibility for such massacres was Thomas Bugeaud, the butcher in charge of the slaughter at the rue Transnonain in 1834. None the less, the drive towards colonization went ahead. By the late 1840s, working-class Frenchmen, mostly from the south, with a sprinkling of Italians and Spaniards, began arriving in Algeria, settling in farms and establishing trading centres. The Algerians called them *roumis*, based on one of the oldest words for 'Romans', and then *pieds-noirs* (or 'black feet', most probably on the grounds that they wore black, polished shoes – although another school of thought held that the settlers were given this name by metropolitan Frenchmen because their feet were blackened by the sun). Bugeaud himself was sceptical about the value of the adventure, predicting as far back as 1837 that Algeria would prove to be an onerous possession that the nation would find difficult to shed. When violence erupted into the streets of Algiers and then Paris in the 1950s and 1960s, as *pieds noirs* fought both the French government and the indigenous population to hold on to their territory, Bugeaud's words would come to seem doubly prophetic.

'A most delicious monster'

It was no accident that the words *chauvin* and *chauvinisme* entered the Parisian lexicon at this time. The terms were a reference to songs and stories about the archetypal figure of Nicolas Chauvin, a Napoleonic ex-soldier and fierce patriot, enemy of all foreigners, and especially Algerians. As Louis-Philippe entertained the heads of Europe in the Tuileries throughout the late 1830s and 1840s, working-class Paris simmered with slow-boiling hatred towards outsiders. English men and women, regarded as the source of all France's troubles, were often attacked in the street. Other foreigners kept a low profile outside the cosmopolitan enclaves of the Champs-Élysées and Palais-Royal.[2]

The feverish atmosphere of this period is captured with great precision within the many tales, novellas and novels of Honoré de Balzac. These stories hardly celebrate the age into which Balzac was born, but they do give the true flavour of a society coming to terms with the birth of modern capitalism, the urban machine and the cult of the individual: all the hallmarks of nineteenth-century modernity. More than anything else, Balzac is a writer whose universal appeal is rooted in his local and intimate knowledge of his adopted city.[3]

Despite his reputation as the supreme chronicler of Parisian life, Balzac was in fact a provincial. He was born in 1799 in Tours to a modest family who had their origins in Provence (the aristocratic 'de' in his name was his own invention). He began his academic career badly, impressing his teachers mainly with his idleness and disdain for authority. He was, however, a voracious reader and when he arrived in Paris in 1814 (his father's business had brought the family to the city), he quickly displayed enough wit and guile to land a position in a lawyer's office (the knowledge of the intricacies and nuances of law he acquired there was to serve him well in his later fiction). He was also attending lectures at the Sorbonne, most notably those given by the idealist philosopher Victor Cousin and the literary critic Abel-François Villemain, an expert on French eloquence from the Renaissance to the Revolution. Balzac was already setting out to be a writer himself, living alone in Paris where he wrote appalling poems and unreadable histories and tragedies. In the 1820s, he devoted himself to becoming rich, publishing a series of sensationalist novels in the 'frenetic' fashion of the day and concocting useless and doomed investment schemes. By the age of twenty-nine, he was hopelessly in debt and laughed at as a serious writer.

At the age of thirty, however, Balzac published *Les Chouans*, an historical tale in imitation of Sir Walter Scott about the royalist insurgents of Brittany (the insurgents were called 'Chouans', or 'owls', because of their practice of calling to each other at night with owl-like cries). The book was an immediate success, partly because of its subject matter, which tapped a rich vein of royalist nostalgia during the last tottering year of Charles X's reign, but mostly because it announced a new sort of novel where characters acted according to real human motives rather than abstract notions of liberty, freedom or justice. Balzac's reputation was further enhanced by the stories, aimed at a mainly female readership, he published as *Scènes de la vie privée* ('Scenes from private life'), in the popular journal *La Presse*. This relative success was followed in 1832 by *La Peau de chagrin* ('The Wild Ass's Skin'), a semi-autobiographical fable of ambition, failure and lust set in the heart of heartless Paris. The novel was read avidly by a generation of Parisians and provincials just arrived in Paris who recognized themselves in its pages. His appeal lay precisely in the fact that he described ordinary Parisians in a manner that made them both believable and extraordinary.

In one fell swoop, Balzac had heralded the death of Romanticism and the beginning of the modern novel. He was lucky to have been born in an age of revolution and counter-revolution, which seemed to him to be confirmation of the principle of perpetual motion underlying all human development. Balzac grew to maturity during the Bourbon restoration, and although most of his novels were written under Louis-Philippe, his works are most often set in the period of the restoration, with a sense of its impermanence and looming catastrophe.

Once his writing career was properly underway, Balzac's ambition grew even more massive. He dosed himself with extraordinarily strong coffee, wrote through the night for weeks at a time, producing works of breathtaking energy and vitality in order to make an impact on a world he saw as deeply rotten but also endlessly improvable (it was the coffee and overwork that eventually killed him at the age of fifty-one, with an ulcerated stomach and shattered heart). Balzac was both enervated and crushed by his ambition to bring the city to life in his books; his nervous, skittering energy and melodramatic imagination make him, in many ways, the perfect example of the lower-middle-class Parisian in the early nineteenth century, caught between nostalgia for the stability of the past and fascination for an unknowable future.

Between 1832 and 1834, he began sketching out a plan to bring all of his writings together as a whole under a collective title, *La Comédie humaine*

('The Human Comedy'), which would sum up his singular purpose. His aim was no less than to present Paris to the reader as a totality, mapping all of its complexities, nuances and details. By the time of his death in 1850, he had published more than ninety novels or novellas, featuring more than two thousand characters drawn from the provinces or the streets of Paris.

He was an admirer of the American novelist James Fenimore Cooper and set out to make maps of Paris in much the same way that Cooper mapped the uncharted territories of the New World. Paris for Balzac, as it was shaped under the harsh dynamics of the early capitalism, was thus a jungle, a forest, a labyrinth. For nearly all of Balzac's characters, Paris is an entire world, often *the* entire world. Even if – like the seditious criminal mastermind Vautrin – they dream of a bucolic Utopia in the Americas, they are condemned to Paris, its monuments, palaces, fetid squares and muddy, unpaved streets. Survival in the city depends on wit, guile and the ability to read the invisible signposts that point the way out of poverty to the dream-life of the *beaux quartiers* of the western edge of the city. Paris contains streets that are 'noble', 'honest' and 'honourable'; other parts of the city are simply 'murderous' and 'ridden with infamy'. It is the mark of the successful Parisian that he or she knows how to negotiate between the alternating movements of shadow and light.[4]

Balzac judged himself a failure, but even before his death critics and admirers acknowledged that he had not only painted a vivid and lasting portrait of Parisian life but done a great deal to contribute to its cultural and political substance. Most significantly, the books of *La Comédie humaine* are unified by geography and genealogy. They nearly all take place in or near Paris, and the same characters, at different stages in their careers or development, take minor or principal parts depending on the issues and debates of the book. Balzac's great theme, reflecting the ethos of both the restoration and the July Monarchy, is that money can do everything. This is, however, understood in its most literal sense; evil all too often prospers over those who – like Balzac himself – have no business sense or are too greedy or witless to understand the dangers of Paris.

In reality, Balzac's Paris was essentially divided up into three separate zones – the Faubourg Saint-Marceau, an impoverished and broken-down area on the Left Bank, directly facing the Faubourg Saint-Antoine; the Faubourg Saint-Honoré, a well-heeled area of *arriviste* businessmen and bourgeois bankers flush with new money; and the Faubourg Saint-Germain, the domain of the old aristocracy. In the *Histoire des Treize* ('Story of the Thirteen'), a trilogy published in 1833–5, he calls the city a 'great courtesan', 'a fat queen with irresistibly furious desires'. Paris was also variously 'a most delicious monster', 'a volcano', 'a jungle', 'a marshy region' and an 'ocean'. In all of his books, Balzac counsels against the destructive force of passion in excess – not just lust for sex and money, but also avarice, as in *Eugénie Grandet* (1833), or overwhelming paternal love as in *Le Père Goriot* ('Father Goriot', 1834). It is Paris itself which incarnates this excess.

Crosstown Traffic

Politically, Balzac was a reactionary with little interest in what he called the 'nebulous theories' of the Utopian socialists who were gathering in Paris in the 1840s, as the bourgeois monarchy was feeling the strain and the world capital of Revolution was preparing for another violent turn. Balzac was sharp enough to see, however, that the restoration was doomed to failure from the outset. This was not because of any inherent flaw in the monarchical system, but because the monarchs themselves were small-minded men with no sense of the national interest or any real ambition. This explained to him the 'decadence' that gripped the best of young Parisian intellectuals after 1830, immobilizing themselves in ironic poses and works of art that sought to please rather than instruct. Balzac himself worked ferociously in opposition to what he saw as this sterile posturing.

In the aftermath of 1830, when Paris was commonly described in the most masculine terms as victorious in combat, Balzac, always a stubborn nostalgic, was unusually faithful to the oldest images of Paris as a woman (all French cities are traditionally feminine and are represented by statues of women). In *La Peau de chagrin*, he describes the grey sky that 'lends Paris a menacing air, in the same way that a beautiful woman is given to inexplicable caprices of ugliness and beauty'. Balzac's Paris is a demonic and haunted site where, more than in any other place on earth, these energies are concentrated in the filth and noise of the city streets. We meet his characters as if by chance, as if they emerge from the crowd only to merge with it again; the real character is indeed the pulsating throb of the urban machine – 'the delicious monster' itself. It is this aspect of Balzac's work that makes him most modern. His politics may have been reactionary, but the mirror he holds up to his city and his age reflects, with unflinching detail, a portrait of a society shaped in equal measure by glory and disaster.

Balzac lamented the loss of Charles X and with him the departure of all law and discipline. He fantasized about a city and country united in faith and values but which he knew already to be a lost cause. He was intelligent enough to see this departure as a turning point in Parisian history from which there could be no going back. The image of Parisian political and cultural unity was indeed by the early years of the 'bourgeois monarchy' an optical illusion.

In reality, the working classes and bourgeoisie were already travelling in opposite directions, a fact which would have terrible consequences for the city before long.

30. The Age of Contempt

Long before the killing started, everyone in Paris had known that Louis-Philippe's reign would end in violence. Certainly, from the early 1840s onwards even the most well-disposed opinion-mongers could see no future in a government predicated upon the patently fake premise of reconciling republican desires with Royalist nostalgia. The growing unrest in the streets – the almost tangible contempt which people felt for the government – and Louis-Philippe's unwillingness or inability even to begin to heal the sharp social divisions in Paris were also major factors in his downfall.

Parisians of all classes saw the reign of Louis-Philippe through the eyes of the cartoonist Honoré Daumier. In the political and satirical magazine *Charivari*, Daumier drew Louis-Philippe as a corpulent and gormless figure – an egg-shaped fool, topped off with a mane of curly hair. Daumier was funny and savage and, no less than Balzac, he summed up the age in his drawings. In particular, Parisians loved his character Robert Macaire, a rogue and thief who later became a huge hit in a stage adaptation by the actor Frédéric Lemaître. Most damagingly, Daumier captured in Macaire the chiselling and unscrupulous love of financial chicanery which most people held to be at the heart of Louis-Philippe's government.[1]

Louis-Philippe ruled for eighteen years, a fact that seemed both unbelievable and shocking to most Parisians of the period. This was mostly because, throughout his reign, Paris was an extremely tense place, made all the more so by both the brittle nature of Louis-Philippe's regime and the harsh measures he employed to crush dissent. Insurrections and mutinies were never far away from the surface of daily life. Louis-Philippe himself was constantly the assassination target of one group of conspirators or another. Parisians hated most of all the way that he surrounded himself with foreigners – especially the hated English – while they themselves did all they could to survive in the muddy, squalid streets of a capital whose pretensions to monumental grandeur, the Napoleonic arches and statues, were hardly matched by the wretched state of most of the east end of the city.

The nervous nature of the regime had been cruelly exposed in 1840 by the funeral of Napoleon – a magnificent and moving affair attended by most Parisians who, whatever their real views of the Corsican, could not fail to feel some nostalgia for a glorious past that was now fast receding into the distance. The fragility of Louis-Philippe's regime was underlined by the fact that the only truly ambitious projects that were completed had already been commissioned and planned under Napoleon Bonaparte as part of the emperor's vision for the capital of Europe and, by extension, the world. The Arc de Triomphe, the church of the Madeleine and the Obelisk, which was installed on Place de la Concorde during Louis-Philippe's reign, were tribute to an earlier, more ambitious era and no Parisian associated them directly with the 'citizen-king'. Even the Colonne de Juillet, which Louis-Philippe had installed at Place de la Bastille to commemorate the days of July 1830 that had brought him to power, was somehow seen as a practical mark of devotion to the people rather than monarchical vainglory.

A New Idea in Europe

In the meantime, a new word and a new idea had entered the everyday vocabulary of Parisians in the 1840s. The word was 'Communism' and the idea associated with it was the creation of a new and perfect civilization where all social classes and hierarchies were dissolved in the realization of total and absolute freedom.

This form of Communism, according to its propagandists, had been the original dream of the true Revolutionaries of 1789, before the Revolution itself had been compromised by the Terror and corrupted by bourgeois liberals. The visible failure of Louis-Philippe's regime, it was argued, only provided further proof that the ideal Communist society was both near at hand and more desirable than ever. Violent sacrifice was but a necessary prelude to the new world. In the streets of Paris, where poverty and starvation were the daily experience for most of the population (the corpses of starving proletarians were by now a common sight on the corners of the most fashionable boulevards), such arguments not only gave hope but also promised vengeance on a society which was so clearly bent on preserving the privileges of a small élite.

Communist ideas had indeed been part of the currency of radical thinking in Paris since the 1780s (the theory and the word were known to such disparate thinkers as Restif de la Bretonne and François-Émile Babeuf, for example). The year 1840 saw many of these ideas enter daily usage and debate with the publication of Proudhon's *Qu'est-ce que la propriété?* ('What is Property?'), Louis Blanc's *L'Organisation du travail* ('The Organization of Work'), Pierre Leroux's *De l'humanité* ('On Humanity') and Agricol Perdiguier's *Livre de compagnonnage* ('Book of Trade Guilds and Corporations'), each of which contested the present organization of money, work and society. In the same year, working-class Parisians attended for the first time the so-called 'Communist banquets' held in Belleville and Ménilmontant. These were open-air debating circles, organized by radical intellectuals as well as artisans, illiterate labourers and modern-style proletarians. The meetings were lubricated by plenty of wine and reported on by Léon Faucher on 3 July 1840, who for the first time in history described the apparently spontaneous organization of what he called a 'Communist Party'.

The term 'Communist' was, however, first properly disseminated in Paris by the lawyer and journalist Étienne Cabet, a native of Dijon and briefly an émigré to England where he had come under the influence of the Utopian industrialist Robert Owen. Cabet had also been influenced by the Utopian communalist philosophies of Charles Fourier and Babeuf, who both argued that the work of the Revolution had yet to be realized in practical human terms (for Fourier this took the form of imagining a whole human society run on proto-Communist lines; Babeuf, a man of action as well as ideas, had conspired to hijack the Directory to take the Revolution in the right direction).

Cabet took from Owen the notion that environment influenced mankind, and that if only the perfect environment could be shaped, the perfect society would follow. On his return to Paris, Cabet was briefly a lawyer serving in Louis-Philippe's regime but he became even more radical after his direct encounters with the Parisian working classes. He set up a newspaper, *Le Populaire*, to spread his ideas, wrote a popular history of the Revolution and a 'Communist' novel, *Voyage en Icarie*, a semi-autobiographical account of a Utopia in which eternal happiness for all is the direct consequence of abolishing all economic systems based on profit. This book, published in 1840, became a bestseller and the word 'Communism' became both an emblem of defiance for the Parisian poor and a spine-tingling threat to the bourgeoisie. Cabet himself set off for the United States in 1848 to found his own 'Icarian community', which ended in rancour and squabbles over unpaid bills.

But by then Cabet had done more than enough in Paris in the early 1840s to ignite a flame that would soon engulf the city. In 1848, as the government of Louis-Philippe collapsed when confronted with Parisians fighting in the streets, and a chain of revolutions spread across Europe, from

Paris to Milan to Vienna, it seemed briefly that the 'spectre of Communism', defined by Karl Marx in London but with its origins in Paris, would soon shake the world to its foundations.

Reading and Writing History

As the discontented voices of those who hated the regime rose in a crescendo, newspapers, magazines and journals of all kinds flourished in Paris. It was estimated that readership of the press increased in the city from 60,000 to over 200,000 between 1830 and 1848. This indicated not only a high degree of literacy but also a thirst for news and ideas. Most importantly, the press both reflected and influenced the very nature of Parisian anger.[2]

Aware of the enormous potential for subversion, the government kept a wary eye on all of these publications and, as far as they could, on their readers. They had much to fear. By 1830, it had become an established fact among the intelligentsia that the Parisian press, from its origins in the seventeenth century with *La Gazette* and *La Muse historique*, *Le Mercure galant* and *Le Journal de Paris*, had made a significant contribution to all the great convulsions of the past century, from the Revolution to the Terror, to the Directory, Bonaparte and the two restorations. Under the July Monarchy, the press had gained a popularity and importance which it had not known since the early days of the eighteenth century, when *colporteurs* had distributed new ideas, information, theories and jokes across the city. The popularity of the press was hardly touched by the laws of 1834 and 1835, which controlled the activities of street vendors selling pamphlets and other potentially incendiary writings. Indeed, this nervous, half-hearted attempt at suppression only increased the prestige of editors and the writers they commissioned.

The leading publication, at least in terms of sales, was *Le Constitutionnel*, founded in 1815 during the Waterloo campaign and intended as a progressive, anti-clerical newspaper. It had been shut down for a short period by Louis-Philippe for its rumoured Bonapartist sympathies but was always eagerly devoured by the public, who enjoyed its regular columns of literary gossip (its vehement attacks on the Romantics were also appreciated by its determinedly middlebrow readership). It published the literary big guns of the period, from George Sand to Alexandre Dumas and Eugène Sue (it would later be the headquarters of the acerbic critic and commentator Sainte-Beuve). The nearest rival to *Le Constitutionnel* was *La Presse*. This was much cheaper, largely because it was the first newspaper to carry advertisements (other editors railed long and loud about this but soon followed suit). By the end of the century, *La Presse*, which also practically invented the notion of a foreign correspondent, was the most widely read newspaper in Paris and France.[3]

At one stage, Paris supported twenty-six daily newspapers. Literature and politics were inextricably linked. At the same time, the sale of all forms of published books reached an all-time peak. The corollary of this was the huge advances given by booksellers to the likes of Balzac, Victor Hugo and Chateaubriand (it was rumoured that the lordly Chateaubriand – whose *Mémoires d'outre-tombe* ('Memories Beyond the Grave'), an autobiography and elegy to a lost France, published in 1849–50, was a favourite across classes – had ruined his publisher with his demands). Bestsellers such as Eugène Sue's *Mystères de Paris* or the most popular of Balzac's novels also touched the non-reading public, being read aloud for entertainment at street corners or in cafés and taverns.[4]

Above all, Parisians were fascinated by Paris. Among the bestsellers of Louis-Philippe's era was *Paris ou le livre des cent-et-un* ('Paris or the Book of a Hundred and One'), a fifteen-volume compendium of essays and poems on Parisian life published in 1831–4. The subjects included the life of the streets, legends and history, public monuments and private houses, as well as Parisian folklore. In 1835, Jacques-Antoine Dulaure, a native of Clermont-Ferrand who had spent most of his life in Paris as an engineer and convinced republican, published a monumental eight-volume history of Paris from its origins. The tale of the city was told in a gossipy and entertaining mode and immediately became the source for countless other histories of the Parisian Middle Ages, the Parisian tradition of insurrection, everyday life, the bad habits of kings and so on. Other popular volumes included, in 1844, an illustrated guide to the city, *Les Rues de Paris* ('The Streets of Paris'), edited by Louis Lurine, and the *Nouveau Tableau de Paris comique, critique et philosophique* ('New *Tableau de Paris*, Comical, Critical and Philosophical'), a variety of popular texts assembled by the comic novelist Paul de Kock (who briefly also had a following in England including the likes of Macaulay and Elizabeth Barrett Browning).[5]

Parisians had for a long time thought of themselves as a unique species. The boom in publishing allowed them to read about themselves at length in literature, Unsurprisingly, it was during this period that many of the clichés of Parisian life entered into wide circulation, from the *gamins de Paris* to the stock figure of the *parigot*. There was, however, a clear political dimension to this fascination with the city and its history. Most importantly, in the tales of Eugène Sue or the histories of Dulaure and his ilk, Parisians came to see that they were not mere passive spectators in the narrative of the city, but rather active agents of transformation with an historical destiny.

The Banquet of Life

During the early part of the nineteenth century in Paris radical changes were also afoot in the way that Parisians ate and drank. It was due to these changes that Paris began to acquire its reputation as the European capital of gastronomy. The reputation of fine cooking in Paris had been forged in the late eighteenth century with the establishment of its first restaurants (rather than cafés, taverns or mere drinking-holes). Until then, the highest arts of the table had been the exclusive preserve of the aristocracy. The impossible standards that cooks for the aristocracy set themselves were exemplified in the story of François Vatel, cook to the prince de Condé at Chantilly, who stabbed himself to death in 1671 in despair at 'two failed roasts' at a dinner and the slow delivery of seafood for a lunch party. In her memoirs, Madame de Sévigné recounts with the steely gaiety usual to the upper classes that the disaster was happily repaired for the prince's party and that, despite the loss of the chef, 'the dinner was excellent, so was the luncheon. They supped, they walked, they played, they hunted. It was all enchanting.'[6] (Vatel's suicide was recalled by the French press in 2003, when the chef Bernard Loiseau shot himself at his house in Burgundy in despair at losing a Michelin star at his restaurant in Saulieu. Suicidal chefs, it was argued, were no more nor less than a part of a long French tradition, which demanded the ultimate commitment.)

In reality, until the eighteenth century and well into the nineteenth, most French people of even moderately prosperous means lived on black bread and greasy soups made from what was most easily available. Paris was the exception and peasants and provincials all marvelled at the produce on offer – white bread, fresh meats and dairy products that did not always give you tuberculosis. The invention of the restaurant was part of the drive towards modernity and democracy characteristic of the eighteenth century. The earliest and most famous restaurant with an *à la carte* menu was Beauvilliers's in the Galerie de Valois, which opened its doors in 1782. The success of Beauvilliers's, which prided itself on offering dinner as a theatrical performance accompanied by the finest wines of France, was followed by some fifty or so establishments by 1789. The restaurant flourished during the Revolution and its aftermath, and by 1820, Paris boasted over 3,000 places offering luxury food.[7]

One reason for the high quality of such restaurants was that they were often set up by the chefs of the aristocracy, now out of work in the post-Revolutionary period and looking for a way to make an honest living. Another reason for their popularity was that eating expensive food – previously the preserve of the aristocracy – in a public place immediately announced to the world one's democratic principles. The Jacobins had no time for the elaborate manners of the upper classes, but they were notorious gourmands and drinkers (with the exception of the abstemious Robespierre).

Restaurants quickly became an integral part of political life. This was confirmed as a tradition in 1793, when the leaders of the Revolution drafted the Constitution in a restaurant called Chez Méot, hosted by the former cook of the prince de Condé. Politics also meant fashion: the restaurant Les Trois Frères Provençaux, which was known to be frequented by Bonaparte in the 1800s, was visited by tourists and Parisians alike and saw its takings go up to 15,000 francs a day. In contrast, in the Latin Quarter, where whole streets were given over to cafés and restaurants, it was possible to be fed for less than a franc at Viot's or Flicoteaux's. A five-course meal was on offer at Chez Dufour on the rue Molière for 1 franc and 80 centimes (the best place to get a taste of such establishments in contemporary Paris is either the *bouillon* Chartier near the Folies-Bergère – a *bouillon* was a cheap kind of chop-house – or, at the other end of the scale, Lapérouse on the Left Bank).

By the mid 1840s Paris, more than any other city in Europe, was a capital of very public pleasures. Restaurants and cafés were refuges from the abject conditions in which most people lived and accessible to all but the poorest classes. They were the perfect forum for the spread of ideas in the booming press and literature of the period and the ideal stage for rehearsing the future society that would wipe away all traces of the past. The city was indeed alive with citizens' clubs, revolutionary circles, Utopianist societies and all manner of talking-shops, all fuelled by increasingly bold and incendiary journalists.

By 1847, all of Paris could see that the touch-paper was ready to be lit.

'Vengeance on Louis-Philippe!'

As the gossip columnist Madame de Girardin put it in *La Presse*: 'The sky is darkening. A *feast* on a volcano! All this can only end in revolution, we are in 1830–92–89!'[8]

The bad harvests of 1846 and 1847 only heightened the already apparent tensions in Paris. Yet strangely enough, when the revolutionary violence did come, in early 1848, the press had only an indirect influence on events, and certainly did not trigger or control them as it had done in earlier insurrections.

The catalyst was a 'reform' banquet, organized in Paris for 20 February. These outdoor feasts were arranged by middle-class radicals in the spirit of the earlier 'Communist banquets' of Belleville and in opposition to government efforts to forbid public meetings. They offered an opportunity for influential writers, journalists, deputies from the National Assembly and other disaffected members of the bourgeoisie to tear into a government that had lost all sense of purpose or direction. During the days leading up to the banquet in February, tensions had been building in Paris. On the 12th, songs from 1789 were sung by the crowd in a Paris theatre. Nervous of growing public hatred of the monarchical system – a hatred exacerbated by events in Milan where Austrian royalty was being openly challenged by the people – the government cancelled the banquet at the last minute.

Complacency still reigned, however, and the authorities, perhaps misled by republican informers, did not at first order any troops into the streets, despite the visible and noisy discontent that for now took the form of demonstrations. On 22 February, in pouring rain, students and workers flooded into the Champs-Élysées and Place de la Concorde, singing the *Marseillaise* and chanting, 'Down with Guizot!' Barricades were being built across the city, and not just in the traditional hotbeds of dissent. On the morning of the 23rd, the leaders of the various revolutionary clubs and secret societies declared that it was now 'time for action'. By the afternoon, soldiers were openly challenged by stone-throwing youths and children. Fighting broke out by early evening at the Porte Saint-Martin.

Louis-Philippe's regime had been built on a falsehood. The *roi-bourgeois* lived in the Tuileries with his wife Marie-Amélie and his five children, and appeared the very incarnation of domestic tranquillity. The fantasy of Louis-Philippe's regime was that true happiness lay in the simple pleasures of family, home and hearth. This was deliberately set against the prevailing, destructive myth of Bonapartism, which promised death and martyrdom in the name of the glory of France. As we have seen, no great monuments appeared in Paris during this period. Few churches were built, and those that were were constructed to relatively modest proportions (Notre-Dame de Lorette at rue de Châteaudun is a good example of this tendency). The truth was of course that Louis-Philippe was indeed no simple family man, but a king with sophisticated and expensive tastes. All Parisians knew this and regarded him with contempt, not so much for his tastes – which all right-thinking Frenchmen aspired to anyway – but because, like Pétain a century later, he lied about them.

Louis-Philippe's immediate reaction in the wake of these first signals of revolution was to sack Guizot. Most Parisians, including the monarchist Balzac (who commented that these were Louis-Philippe's first steps on the road to exile), saw this as a cowardly and fatefully stupid move, reminiscent of Charles X's stubbornness and inability to take responsibility. Events then took on a swift and remorseless logic, as barricades appeared across Paris on both sides of the river. At about ten o'clock that evening, a crowd carrying torches tried to break into the Ministry of Foreign Affairs on the boulevard des Capucines, the headquarters of Guizot and a focus of resentment against foreigners in the city. At least fifty rioters were shot dead. Their bodies were loaded on to carts and carried through the city to the cries of 'Vengeance on Louis-Philippe!'

At the same time, the most radical newspapers joined in the fray. The staff of *Le National* and *La Réforme* printed posters calling for Louis-Philippe's head and posted them around the city. In desperation, the king called on Marshal Bugeaud, the butcher of Algeria, to take control of the situation. Bugeaud swore to restore order by shooting 10,000 or so of the city scum who, he alleged, were causing the trouble. His troops were less convinced that this was appropriate and many of them began to desert, handing out weapons to their friends among the insurrectionists. There were now 1,500 barricades in Paris, often manned by women, who spread glass and broken china around them to break the hooves of cavalry. Ordinary Parisians slipped through a small passage at the side of the barricade. Troops, soldiers and other figures in authority were either abused, set upon or showered in excrement, mud and bricks.[9]

Within hours, realizing that the city hated him, the king was gone, fleeing to England under the name of 'Mr William Smith'. A mob broke into the Tuileries palace where, among other effects, they looted the throne, which was tossed around by drunks and hooligans in the courtyard. It was finally burnt at the foot of the Colonne de Juillet. The reign of the last king of France was over.

The 'June Days' and Another Bonaparte

For all the fighting and heroic talk, the 'February Revolution' was a failure. A Second Republic was announced at the Hôtel de Ville, comprising the likes of the poet Alphonse de Lamartine among its leaders. A new pro-gramme of reform was launched immediately – including universal male suffrage, the abolition of slavery in French territories and a ten-hour work-ing day. The problem was the hard core of Parisian radicals, concentrated in the east of the city, who refused to acknowledge any advances made by a so-called 'bourgeois republic'. The regime slammed down hard on these groups and effectively crushed them during the 'June Days' of 1848, when Paris again erupted into random street-fighting and battles were fought on barricades. This time the radicals and proletarians were the losers. Over 1,500 'Reds' were killed – the streets around rue Blanche stank of the rotting, unburied corpses. Thousands more were throw into jail or sent to Algeria.

Fear of unleashed anarchy had already driven voters to return a conservat-ive government in the elections of April 1848. In December that year, France elected Louis-Napoleon Bonaparte, the nephew of the first and greatest emperor, as president. This was seen as the revenge of Catholic, rural France on Paris and as a vote inspired by the first Napoleon's restor-ation of Catholicism and generosity to the peasantry. The Parisian political élite at first refused to take this new Napoleon seriously. Worse still, they did not heed the warning signals – the grandiose postures and the vaunting ambition – that would once again bring back imperial dreams to Paris.

PART SIX

Queen of the World

1851–1899

Reveal the truth to these depraved fools,
O Republic, by foiling their plots!
　　Then reveal your Great Medusa face,
All ringed by red lightning!

Pierre Dupont, 'Chant des ouvriers', 1851

These are your fruits, O bloodthirsty Commune,
Yes, you wanted to annihilate Paris!

Les Ruines de Paris,
pamphlet circulated in Paris, 1871

When your feet, Paris, danced so hard in anger!
When you had so many knife wounds . . .

Arthur Rimbaud, 'L'Orgie parisienne', 1871

Road development in Paris between 1850 and 1914.

important routes up to 1850

main development of roads between 1850 and 1870

main development of roads between 1870 and 1914

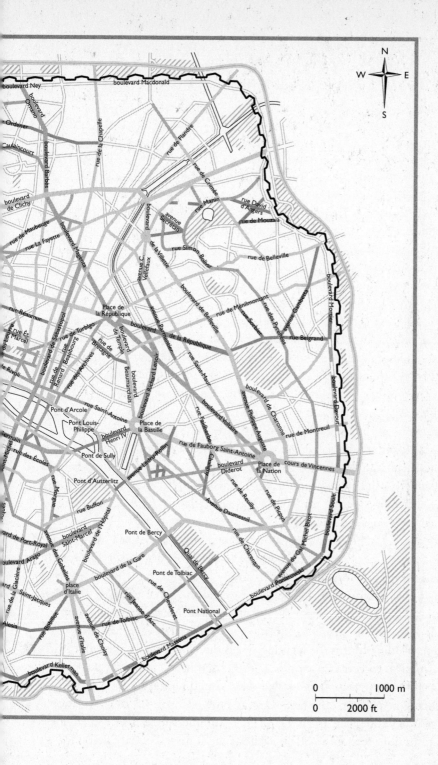

31. The Cretin's Empire

Even the most deluded bourgeois could see that by the late 1840s Paris was a city in deep crisis. In the past, catastrophe had usually been attributed to God or nature (the poor harvests of 1846 were indeed still seen in this way by the peasantry). The present crisis in Paris – at least according to those free-thinkers who claimed to understand the new, harsh dynamics of the capitalist city – had solely economic origins, however; the overproduction and wild financial speculation of the era of Louis-Philippe had led directly to a city at war with itself, where two classes, the rich and the poor, stared at each other hard over the barricades in the streets.

In Paris itself, rickety, newly built structures were artificially grafted on to an urban infrastructure that had barely been touched or improved since the late medieval period. A third of the city's population was crammed into the narrow streets of the eastern quarters on the Right Bank, lodged in five-storey houses. Only one house in five had running water. The Seine, the Bièvre and the stream of Ménilmontant were still in use as sewers. There were no straight roads through Paris, whose centre, Île de la Cité, was a dark and muddy labyrinth, rank with infection and crime.

The conflicting realities of the mid nineteenth century in Paris met in the Cité Cazeaux in passage Denfert, which is still to be found near the boulevard Raspail at the top end of the 14th *arrondissement*. This passage is formed by two rows of four-storey buildings facing each other across a cobbled street. The buildings were designed and constructed by a certain M. Pigeory in 1855 and, with their singular lack of adornment and austere charm, they represent a desire for harmony and calm in the dead centre of the city that is typical of this period. Beyond the gated entrance, the city moves swiftly and endlessly in all directions. The Cité Cazeaux, in contrast, was and is a still point in a fast-turning and turbulent universe.

More to the point is the fact that when the Cité Cazeaux was built, Paris was caught between two worlds. On the one hand, the city's population had grown from 786,000 in 1831 to over a million in 1848. Its industry was advancing at a remarkable rate. This, combined with the city's traditional role as the centralized focus of finance, commerce, culture and political administration, seemed to augur well for the future. The city described by

Balzac as 'the rushing stream',[1] an ever-flowing current of ideas, commerce and culture, was also set to live up to its other title as 'the queen of cities' or even 'the queen of the world'. The reverse side of this inexorable rush to progress was growing discontent among those who were excluded from its benefits.

The pace of change in Paris during this period was also measured by the development of new wide avenues in the city, which permitted the free flow of horse-drawn traffic and provided an ever-changing spectacle for idling Parisians. It was not, however, quite so easy to travel from Paris to other points in Europe. Walter Benjamin noted that as late as 1847 a daily coach service left Paris for Venice each morning, arriving in Venice some six weeks or so later.[2] The railway, which had galvanized the economy of the dreaded rival, Britain, was slow in coming, partly due to the volatile nature of political life in Paris, and partly because it was mistrusted as an Anglo-Saxon invention.

None the less, from 1837 onwards, when it was decreed that railway lines should be built to reach all of France's frontiers, the network grew at an unprecedented rate, allowing Parisians to enjoy for the first time day-trips to the countryside, and linking the major industrial centres (the increase in the railway network had also fuelled the speculation which led to the financial crisis of the 1840s).

The new technology demanded a new architecture to celebrate it. The first railway stations in Paris (the Gare Saint-Lazare was built in 1836, the original Gare du Nord was started in 1846 and redeveloped in 1860) reflected the modern fascination with machinery, movement, glass and iron, light and air. Parisians were at first reluctant travellers – partly through fear (the speed of these new machines was often described as lethal) and partly because they thought it was expensive. The traffic soon began to flow into Paris from the provinces, however, and to meet the needs of these travellers, as well as the burgeoning trade in international travel (Brussels, London and Amsterdam were all brought nearer to Paris by the railway), the streets around the stations were filled with hotels, *brasseries* offering groaning tables of seafood and beer, hustlers, pickpockets and grinning provincials on their first day in the city.

'A throw of the dice'

Louis-Napoleon Bonaparte took control of this divided, volatile and busy city with all the swagger he could muster. He had been born in Paris, the third son of Louis Bonaparte, the King of Holland and younger brother of Napoleon. His early years were spent in Switzerland after the collapse of the First Empire and he served in the Swiss Federal Armies. In the wake of the death of Napoleon's first son, the duc de Reichstadt, Louis-Napoleon laid claim to the throne of France in the name of Bonaparte and launched regular conspiracies against the government of Louis-Philippe. He was exiled in 1836 to the United States but soon returned to Europe, settling in London, which he used as his base to publish his manifestos for a France that would fully bring about the glorious reforms of the first Napoleon. He was again captured and tried for treason and this time sentenced to the fortress-prison of Ham in northern France. He escaped and returned once more to London, where he published propaganda and bided his time until the February revolutions of 1848 brought down the government. Much to the surprise of observers on both the radical and moderate factions of the Left, who had hoped for a return to unmitigated republican values, Napoleon III (as he now styled himself) was swept to power by popular acclaim as representing a middle way between a harsh revolutionary government and the sickly, dying conservative regime.[3]

Despite his Swiss-Germanic accent, deepened by long years in exile in England and Germany, he was a favourite of the crowds, who chanted, 'Poléon, nous l'aurons' ('We will have Napoleon') at every public appearance. Many of the ruling classes at first took him for a fool (General Rochefort described him as looking like 'a melancholy parrot')[4] and it was the view of the political élite that he was a 'cretin' who could be easily controlled (a description attributed to Adolphe Thiers, a leading journalist and ambitious politician who would go on to play an important role in later wars in the city). But, despite his reputation and the appearance of his entourage, and as events would soon reveal, Louis-Napoleon was no clown but a Machiavellian adventurer whose only weakness was an inflated sense of his own destiny.

From the outset, despite a much-flouted belief in universal suffrage, Louis-Napoleon displayed a thinly disguised contempt for democracy. He launched a military intervention in Italy in 1849 to preserve French influence in the region and to prop up the power of the Church, which was facing a liberal insurrection. He protested that he 'did not send an army to Rome to smother Italian freedom' but nobody in high political circles in Paris was convinced.[5] Louis-Napoleon was, however, a shrewd manipulator of public opinion. Amazingly, he rose above the Italian adventure, portraying himself to the Left as a moderating influence on reactionary violence while presenting himself to the Right as upholding the traditional values of property, family and religion.[6]

It was the conservatives who misjudged him most seriously. They believed that they would be rid of him in 1852, when his office as president came to an end. At the same time, they launched plans to restrict suffrage, hoping to win a big enough majority in the Assembly to restore a proper monarch rather than the Bonapartist usurper. Unwittingly, they played into Louis-Napoleon's hands by giving him the justification for the *coup d'état* that he had been plotting since his arrival in Paris in 1848.

The plot, nicknamed Operation Rubicon by the president and his fellow conspirators, was revealed on 2 December 1851. The preceding months had been tense, with rumours of insurrection and counter-insurrectionary violence swilling around the highest offices of power and the meanest backstreets. On the evening of 1 December, the president held a reception at the Élysée Palace and chatted about the problems of slum clearance, funding sanitation programmes and other mundanities. Later that same night, seventy-six leading Parisians, including leaders of the Socialist and radical groups, were arrested in their beds and taken to cells at the prison of Vincennes. In the meantime, groups of policemen took over printing works across Paris to oversee the publication of an 'appeal to the people', alleging a conspiracy by Thiers and other leading dissenters to 'overthrow the Republic'. Parisians woke on the morning of 2 December to find troops lining the boulevards and both banks of the Seine and occupying Place de la Concorde, the Tuileries, the Palais-Royal and the Champs-Élysées.

At first, the prevailing sentiment in the streets was relief, even in the traditionally working-class areas where the coup was perceived as a lesser evil than returning a pro-monarchy assembly. There were, eventually, in the following days, barricades and demonstrations in the areas of Saint-Antoine, Saint-Martin and Saint-Denis, and inevitably shootings. The bodies of 400 working-class Parisians lay strewn for days in the cobbled streets of eastern Paris.

Less than a mile away, troops marched as if in a pageant down the *grands boulevards* to the applause of well-heeled crowds at restaurants or simply strolling the streets. There was an order to stay away from central Paris and not to impede the work of the military, but the working-class districts were another world from the smart shops, passages and cafés. The massacres taking place there were like a blood sport for the rich.

When a referendum was held on 21 December, the population of France overwhelmingly endorsed Louis-Napoleon's coup in the general belief that his action had saved France from a far worse fate. A Te Deum was sung at Notre-Dame on New Year's Day 1852 and Louis-Napoleon installed as absolute monarch of all France. This was the moment when, as Karl Marx drily remarked in an essay on the subject, the republican slogans of 'Liberty, Equality, Fraternity' were replaced by 'infantry, cavalry, artillery'.[7]

The Demolition Artist

The story goes that Louis-Napoleon had arrived in 1848 at the Gare du Nord with a map of Paris in his hands and a grandiose vision to remodel the city in his own fashion. This may or may not have been true, but it was certainly made clear as soon as he seized absolute power after the coup of 1851 that the city was his and that he intended to make it into a monument to his power. Louis-Napoleon's model city of the imagination, like that of his uncle before him, was ancient Rome and he set out methodically to make Paris the modern equivalent. He was also much impressed by the energy and magnificence of London and saw Paris as dirty, cramped and squalid in comparison to the English capital.

In 1853, Louis-Napoleon appointed Georges-Eugène Haussmann prefect of Paris. Until then, Haussmann had been an obscure figure known, if at all, in Paris as the prefect of the distant region of the Var in the south of the country. He was born in Paris in 1809, at 55 rue du Faubourg-du-Roule (which is now rue du Faubourg Saint-Honoré), ironically enough in the kind of *hôtel particulier* – a small mansion with a private courtyard and garden – that his later projects would condemn to history. His family were well to do and had connections with the imperial family. He studied at the Lycée Henri IV in Paris but also spent a great deal of time at his father's factory in Colmar, which gave him a reputation as heavy-handed and brutish. Certainly, few of Haussmann's contemporaries had any kind words for him (George Sand was alone in describing him with something like affection as 'an earnest young man with a passion for general ideas').[8]

It is unclear how Haussmann came to the attention of Louis-Napoleon,

but the emperor was evidently impressed both by Haussmann's administrative efficiency and his unwavering devotion to the imperial cause
(Haussmann indeed served Louis-Napoleon for almost the entirety of his
reign). Louis-Napoleon also admired the way in which Haussmann had
tackled the twin menaces of republicanism and Socialism head on in the Var
region and gained thereby a reputation as an uncompromising negotiator as
well as a fervent monarchist. Like Louis-Napoleon, Haussmann was also a
relative outsider to Paris (Louis-Napoleon had only ever lived there as a
baby) and had no sentimental attachment to the city's streets or to its people.

The reconstruction of the city began in earnest within the first weeks of
Haussmann's appointment, when he drew up a plan that would bring
together the local services of each part of the city under centralized control.
At the same time, Haussmann began to develop a plan of attack. This would
soon be revealed as what was termed the *percement* of the streets – literally
'piercing' whatever confused and confusing warren lay in the path of
development with a straight road through it. The overall aim was to establish
at the centre of Paris a great crossroads pointing to north and south, east
and west. From this crossroads, a series of wide roads, boulevards and
avenues would be constructed to link up with railway stations and the main
exits to the city. These arteries would also be designed with an eye to
permitting the best views of the city's new monuments. At the centre of
the city, and the real beginning of the Haussmann project, was the construction in 1851 of the 'Fort de la Halle', consisting of eight buildings of iron
and glass built on the site of the traditional city-centre markets of Paris.
This would later be described by Émile Zola as the 'stomach of Paris', 'a
modern machine beyond all measure', which represented the true axis of
the city.[9] Les Halles would, ironically enough, give rise to its own myths
and legends, every bit as potent as stories from the older parts of the city;
when it was first conceived, however, it was designed along the same
utilitarian lines as any part of Haussmann's Paris.

From this point on, the plan was executed with ruthless efficiency,
financed by a complicated alliance between private investors, speculators
and government funding bodies. On 26 March 1852, a law was passed
permitting the 'Ville de Paris' to buy any land or property standing in the
way of the project, and over the next seventeen years Paris was turned into
one vast building site. Historic quarters that had stood intact for centuries
were ripped down. Countless thousands of Parisians were forced to move
to what were alien parts of the city. Haussmann acquired the title of the
'Alsatian Attila' (his family had come from Alsace) and unselfconsciously

described himself as a 'demolition artist'. Meanwhile, property developers grew rich by buying up areas scheduled for demolition at the cheapest prices and selling them at several times their original value to builders and architects.

Louis-Napoleon and Haussmann also shared a vision – of a city planned first of all on purely functional grounds. Louis-Napoleon's monument to empire had to be beautiful and magnificent but above all, as the exemplary capital of nineteenth-century modernity, it had to work. The construction of a city that dealt effectively with sanitation, sewage and the free flow of traffic was a priority over any aesthetic concerns. Paris would be made beautiful, but first of all it had to smell good and its citizens had to be able to breathe fresh air.

Louis-Napoleon and Haussmann were also both either indifferent to or contemptuous of the past. In the early years of the nineteenth century, Paris was considered a great city by foreigners and visitors alike because it was the European centre of culture, commerce and politics, and also because, almost everywhere in the busy streets, you could make out traces of the past; often several distinct periods could be glimpsed at once in the architecture, fashions and manners of a single street. The warren of alleyways, narrow streets and passages was already written about in terms of an idealized folklore in the early nineteenth century, and described affectionately as 'le Vieux Paris'. This process was much accelerated by the writings of Victor Hugo and Eugène Sue, who represented Paris as variously a prison, a hell, a muddy inferno and sink of vice, but always too as the home of a witty, combative and endlessly inventive population. In his poem 'Le Cygne' ('The Swan'), Baudelaire describes Paris changing for ever and mourns the end of a whole swathe of the city's history; 'Old Paris is no more,' he writes. 'The form of a city changes faster, alas, than the heart of mortal man.'[10]

Haussmann is still a controversial figure in Paris. He is generally regarded with scorn and contempt as a brutish Alsatian whose major contribution to the life of Paris was to destroy several centuries' worth of accrued meaning in the streets of the old city within less than two decades. He is also accused of serving the political aims of Louis-Napoleon in his organization of the city: the great boulevards and avenues that cross the city from west to east, it has been argued by Leftists of all tendencies, were built not just to ease access across the city but also to ease the passage of troops and guns in times of insurrection. This may or may not have been true, but Haussmann himself took no profit from his work. He retired in 1870 with nothing but his pension of 6,000 francs (this was in a period when property speculators could make a killing of several million francs on a single house). He left the city with a sound sanitation system (drinking the water in Paris was no longer to risk cholera), with a properly organized street-lighting system and better able to face the technological demands of the century. Sharing the Anglomania of Louis-Napoleon, he introduced the first public parks to Paris on the Anglo-Saxon model (the Parc des Buttes-Chaumont and the Bois de Boulogne were the fruits of this passion).

What had been lost was the spontaneous life of the streets – the intimate Parisian worlds of the *petites gens* who made a precarious living in whatever way they could, from water-sellers to itinerant carpenters, scribes to marionnette-sellers. Louis-Napoleon commissioned the photographer Charles Marville to document the death of 'Old Paris'. This was not done, however, in a spirit of elegiac reflection but rather in accord with the desire to provide a cold-eyed scientific witness to progress on the march.

32. Ghosts in Daylight

The Paris that emerged from the early part of the nineteenth century had little to touch the emotions or affect the daily life of Parisians, apart from making them feel out of pocket (monumental Paris did not come cheap and at one stage an 80 per cent tax was levied on certain parts of the population in order to finish building projects). This much could not be said of the rebuilding of Paris during the Second Empire, when Napoleon III and Haussmann set out to make Paris the most spectacular city in the world, a project that Haussmann implemented with a notorious ruthlessness and contempt for the intimate and intricate world of Old Paris.

The transformation of Paris under Haussmann was little short of miraculous. In the chaos of noise, dust and destruction, as streets and old buildings were torn down, Parisians could see a new world emerging before their very eyes. Order was laid upon disorder. A wide new avenue stretched from Gare de l'Est south across the river to the Observatoire. On the Right Bank, a whole new network of boulevards – including Pereire, Malesherbes, Strasbourg, Sébastopol, Richard Lenoir, Magenta – was laid between Porte Maillot in the west and Porte de Vincennes in the east (despite this, no fashionable Parisian would live east of boulevard de Sébastopol). On the Left Bank, the boulevard Saint-Germain cut a curved and ruthless line through areas known for their fine examples of Renaissance architecture, and in particular the *grands hôtels* that had been such a fundamental part of the Parisian urban landscape.

One of Haussmann's most notable 'massacres' was on Île de la Cité, where he swept away the medieval houses clustered around and in front of Notre-Dame. This area had been the inspiration for Hugo's novel *Notre-Dame de Paris* (see Chapter 6) and over the centuries had been the source of countless myths and stories, and hence a defining part of Parisian folklore. Under Haussmann's dead hand, this totemic site became instead the meeting point of three main roads through the city, while the streets that had once thronged with convicts, thieves, hustlers, whores and murderers were now the location of the most important police station in the city, as well as a large and stultifying administrative complex housing law courts and lawyers.

The most prominent aspect of Haussmann's legacy in contemporary Paris is not, however, his contribution to making the traffic flow, or ensuring that the government held political and military control over the 'storm-centres' of the eastern part of the city, but rather the establishment of a common style for the apartment blocks built along his miraculously straight roads. The aim was to create an effect of grandeur through the uniformity of decoration and a long, horizontal perspective, fixed by the line of wrought-iron balconies running together down the street. Individuality was much less important than the impression of the street as a continuous and harmonized sequence. The interior décor of a typical bourgeois apartment was, in contrast, heavy and rich, often loaded with Romano-Byzantine trappings or Orientalist paraphernalia. This pointedly contradictory aesthetic – an interplay between external severity and internal opulence – is still a defining feature of French-inspired urban planning, from Rabat to Bucharest. In mid-nineteenth-century Paris, it not only represented a new form of modernity in which urban spectacle took prominence over individual style, but also indicated, in its refinement of the art of paradox, the great uncertainty that lay at the centre of Louis-Napoleon's regime.

This also explains in part the deep mediocrity of much of the architecture that is termed 'Second Empire'. The city built by Haussmann was both superb and chilling, representing a triumph of organization and technology over the past. The architectural design of churches and other public monuments of the time was, however, chiefly backward-looking when it was not simply a copy or pastiche of past styles.

One of the best places to see the 'Second Empire' at work in all its monumental and strangely impressive vulgarity is gazing at the new Opéra, built by Charles Garnier from the doorway of Brentano's bookshop on the avenue de l'Opéra. The avenue itself is magnificent and inhuman, too long to walk without boredom or fatigue and too wide to cross without serious risk of being run down. Crowned by the Opéra in all its absurd and ornate exoticism – a Romano-Byzantine temple crammed into a busy city intersection – it conveys all the grandeur, ambition and folly of the Second Empire. It seems all the more appropriate that construction of the Opéra was not finished until the empire had collapsed, by which time even its architect had to pay for his own seat in the theatre.

Wanderers

One of the most notable aspects of city life during the Second Empire was the way in which the city's *grands boulevards* were soon filled with *grands magasins*. These temples to the new religion of commerce made Paris the first truly modern city in the world. Paris was also now a city of street signs and posters, some of them political but most of them advertising some new marvel of the age. It was here that the death of Old Paris was most clearly visible. The Parisian tradition of the seditious placard or subversive graffitti was not yet dead, but the destruction of the old *quartiers* had also broken up the working men's guilds and associations in whose cafés private pleasure and revolutionary agitation went hand in hand. Parisians were encouraged to leave the political past behind and admire the new world that Haussmann's boulevards spread before them.

Yet for all its great tensions, the Paris of the Second Empire was also a city of great pleasures. Indeed the city now had a reputation across the world as the capital of all forms of hedonism. In the *Paris Guide* of 1867, the anonymous writer 'X' could barely contain his almost sexual excitement when it came to describing the seductive nature of the avenue de l'Impéra-trice (now the avenue Foch). 'The woods! The lake! Authentic barouches, hired coupés, smiles everywhere, people dressed to the nines . . . But what elegance, too, and what splendours! Dowries to be had for the asking, and love bobbing on the tide. All the world's seductiveness is here, hard at work, armed for battle.'[1]

It was around this time that the terms *bohème* and *bohémien* entered the French language to denote a generation of young men who hated money and work and the mediocre comforts of the bourgeoisie. These young men were variously vagabonds, drunks, misfits, poets, journalists, satyrs, narcissists, philosophers and often all of these at the same time.

The term *bohémien* was first popularly used to describe the young Romantics of the 1830s. Among these was the poet Théophile Gautier, who rented rooms in the impasse du Doyenné, a run-down collection of buildings opposite the Tuileries and only a few steps from the Louvre. This place was at the centre of the city, indeed it directly faced the monuments and buildings of the bourgeois monarchy. But to Gautier it had a totemic value, as a half-broken and abandoned relic of the past, representing the very opposite of the notions of rational progress and economic development promulgated by the mercantile and ruling classes. 'The impasse ends in a plot of land partitioned off very roughly by a fence of weather-beaten planks salvaged from boats,' wrote Gautier. 'The ruins of a church (a demi-cupola, two or three pillars, and the end of an arcade are still standing) help to make the place wild and sinister . . . it was possible there to lead a Robinson Crusoe life, not on the island of Juan Fernandez, but in the very heart of Paris.'[2]

One of the new pleasures available to those city-dwelling *bohémiens*, who, like Gautier, sought the strange, the uncanny, the poetic and the mysterious that lay around them, was the art of wandering pointlessly through the city. This activity, termed *flânerie* – a word that dated back to the sixteenth century and which had originally been used to mean 'wander' or 'drift' – was already apparent in the seventeenth century (see Chapter 20). By the early nineteenth century it was very much in use by *bohémiens* such as Arsène Houssaye, Camille Rogier and Célestin Nanteuil to describe their strolls around the city in pursuit of adventure, stimulation or, if possible, pleasure.

At first the activity was associated in the popular press simply with idleness – the journalist Jules Janin described in 1829 a provincial newly arrived in Paris as 'lazy, without cares and a loafer [*flâneur*]' – before becoming an end in itself. In 1837, Balzac describes one of his characters 'wandering [*flâner*] the whole day on the boulevards, returning home only to dine. For the Parisian wanderer [*flâneur*] is often a man driven by despair as much as idle desire.'[3] Oddly enough, however, this description also applied to Balzac himself, who was frequently to be found stalking the boulevards at strange and ungodly hours. The journalist Gustave Claudin, who wrote a well-regarded and popular column for *Le Figaro*, recalled an encounter between a famous gambler called Méry, who kept running into Balzac on consecutive nights at four and five in the morning:

On the third day, he [Méry] asked Balzac why he always found him there at such an early hour. Balzac felt in his pocket and produced an almanack which stated that the sun did not rise until 4.55. 'I'm being pursued by *gardes de commerce* [debt collectors],' Balzac explained, 'and I'm being forced to hide during the day; but at this precise moment I'm free. I can take a walk, and no one can arrest me. The sun hasn't risen yet.' 'When I suffer from the same inconvenience,' answered Méry, 'I don't go into hiding, I go to Germany.' On which they both shook hands with each other, and went their way.[4]

When he was not being pursued by creditors, Balzac enjoyed strutting along the boulevards in the afternoons and early evenings cutting a dash among the crowds with his gilt-edged drum-major's wand. Such public ostentation on the boulevards and in other public places had long been typical of a class of Parisian males who scorned politics, business and family life in the name of art, freedom and self-conscious displays of narcissism. In the late eighteenth century, these elegant young fops had been known as *Muscadins* or *Incroyables*, and distinguished themselves with effeminate clothes, exaggerated hairstyles and musk perfume (the *Incroyables* were so called because they affected not to be able to pronounce the letter 'r', producing sentences in French such as 'En véité, c'est incoyable!'). The female equivalents were called *Merveilleuses* and adopted Greek dress and espoused a neo-classical nostalgia. The young dandies were all reactionaries and in 1793, in Lyons, and in 1796 in Paris, they took part in anti-Jacobin demonstrations. They despised the working classes and resisted troops with a determination that surprised the stout soldiers who thought them all homosexuals.

By the time of Louis-Philippe, the life of the boulevards had become far more democratic. For dandified *boulevardiers* the enemy was no longer the working classes but the bourgeoisie, whose timid manners and hypocritical lifestyles had to be confronted at every turn. None the less these parts of Paris were still mainly the domain of the well-heeled. Fashionable dandies were called *lions* and behaved with aristocratic insouciance on the *terrasses* and on the street. In the *Physiologie du lion* ('Physiology of the Lion', 1840), a timely piece of Parisian culture-spotting by the hack journalist Félix Deriège (with illustrations by Honoré Daumier), the modern *boulevardier* or *lion* 'strides down the boulevard as if he owned it, puffing bursts of smoke from his pure Havana cigar into women's faces. He has spurs screwed to the heels of his boots; he only takes them off to go to bed or to mount a horse.' One of the favoured sites for public display was the boulevard de Gand (later renamed boulevard des Italiens), which was home to some of the best restaurants in Paris, such as the Café Anglais, the Maison d'Or and – at the corner of the boulevard and rue Taitbout – the Café de Paris, where the writer and socialite comte Horace de Viel-Castel famously ordered a dinner for 500 francs, including a *pyramide de truffes entières* washed down with a bottle of 1819 Clos Vougeot.

The distance between the classes was marked in the daily timetable: whereas the worker started work at six o'clock, the dandy of the boulevard was already considering his *déjeuner* – a long alcoholic lunch – at eleven. Dinner then followed between six and seven. Theatres scheduled performances from eight onwards and cafés stayed open until midnight. For the determined noctambulist there were specialist places, such as the Café des Variétés, a favoured spot of journalists and actors, and *boulangeries-pâtisseries* on the boulevard Montmartre and rue de Richelieu, which served roast chicken and a variety of *assiettes* through the early hours.

By the time of Napoleon III, as the city grew and was developed in a way that invited witnesses to the urban spectacle, strolling aimlessly through Paris was no longer confined to the artistic or Bohemian classes and had become a distinctly bourgeois activity. In Haussmann's Paris, the *flâneur* became a stock archetype of the male stroller (*flâneurs* were at this stage predominantly male) through the urban scene. What characterized the *flâneur* during this period was the fact that he remained always detached from the pleasures he observed and indulged in.

The poet Charles Baudelaire, despite his nostalgia for Old Paris and sympathy for the poor, was the supreme *flâneur*. Baudelaire had become truly famous in 1857 when he was prosecuted for his collection of poems *Les Fleurs du mal* ('The Flowers of Evil') on grounds of blasphemy and obscenity. Six of the poems were banned (and stayed banned until 1947) and the book could only be sold without them. One of the most remarkable aspects of this work, however, is Baudelaire's visions of old and new Paris. Most notably, he has, to say the least, an ambiguous attitude to the new 'spectacular city'. On the one hand, for many of his admirers, the most interesting fact about his poems is that – charting as they do the alienation and bleak ugliness of city life – they establish Baudelaire himself as the premier poet of Parisian modernity.

On the other hand, Baudelaire also reveals himself to be half in love with the modern city that torments him, and takes himself on endless wanderings through its half-forgotten corners, its past and present. In a poem dedicated to Victor Hugo, who was implacably opposed to Louis-Napoleon, and whom Baudelaire saw as his only true rival, he describes Paris as 'city of swarming, city full of dreams, / Where ghosts in daylight tug the strollers' sleeves!'[5] Hugo was in self-imposed exile in Guernsey from a regime he deplored as venal and criminal in equal measure; Baudelaire was no less an enemy of Louis-Napoleon but saw in the city itself the possibility for resistance and rebellion by reawakening the old ghosts of the streets in active opposition to the sleek city of modernity which was being built all around him.

The central ambiguity of Baudelaire's writing on Paris is that the hashish-intoxicated poet (it was rumoured that at the height of his notoriety he ate hashish or, when available, opium every day for breakfast) none the less embraced with relish the city's boulevards, department stores, art galleries, music halls and brasseries as inspiration, plunging into them as into an 'immense reservoir of electricity'.[6] Baudelaire's Paris is a city of fragments, intimate drama, old myths, displacement and exile – in this sense, unlike the magnificent panoramas of Hugo, it is recognizably a living city to the contemporary reader.

The View from the Café Momus

In his later years, when his looks were sagging and it seemed ridiculous for him to stalk the city in his dandified finery, Baudelaire was a regular at a tavern called Au Petit Rocher at the corner of rues de Navarin and de Bréda, not far from the building site of Garnier's Opéra. This place was known familiarly as Chez Dinocheau after the original owner, Madame Dinocheau, who left the business to her son Jean-Édouard. A modest dinner here cost only 2 francs, including limitless quantities of burgundy which, according to one patron, 'smelt strongly of the earth'.[7] The restaurant was popular with writers, artists and architects and its Bohemian atmosphere – Jean-Édouard often played the violin to entertain his clients and accepted payment in the form of drawings or poems – attracted visitors from even the distant Left Bank.

By now, Baudelaire was a legend in Paris due to his fearless baiting of the bourgeoisie. His provocative manner extended to ordering dinner, occasionally disturbing even the patrons of a louche establishment like Chez Dinocheau. One of these was Maxime Rude, who in his *Confidences d'un journaliste* ('Secrets of a Journalist') recalled Baudelaire with 'long, fine, greying locks which Potrel, that bantering Parisian, used in his wild moments to call soufflé hair'.[8] He also noted that the decrepit poet had lost none of his facility to shock with language, recounting that

Baudelaire was one of those refined men who spend two louis on a cutlet. He sometimes went to a restaurant in the Faubourg Saint-Germain, and had one cooked between forks in kirsch, over flaming punch . . . One evening, in a restaurant where he was known, Baudelaire ordered a well-done fillet steak. When the steak was served, the proprietor, a good family man, came upstairs himself to see if his customer was satisfied. 'It's just the fillet I wanted,' answered Baudelaire. 'It's as tender as the brain of a little child.'[9]

One of Baudelaire's celebrated instructions for poets, as a method and technique, was 'to get drunk and stay drunk forever!'[10] Among *bohémiens*, drinking to excess and with total disregard for the consequences was indeed thought to be a supreme virtue. This much was celebrated by the drinker and philosopher Fernand Desnoyers in the song 'Les rôdeurs de nuit' ('The prowlers of the night'), included in his collection *Chansons parisiennes* ('Parisian Songs'), but most well known to those who heard him sing during his regular sessions at Chez Dinocheau. Desnoyers's song is an amusing testimony to the salutary qualities of an evening lost in this cellar a few yards away from the boulevards:

> Quand le bourgeois dort,
> Il fait soif encore,
> Passons la nuit à boire!
> La rue est toute noire;
> Mais les vitraux des boulevards
> Sont en feu, comme des regards.
> Atmosphère enflammée,
> Filles dans la fumée,
> Eau-de-vie et bruit,
> Voilà notre nuit!
>
> Boire est le vrai bien!
> Après, il n'est rien!
> Rien, sinon boire encore,
> En attendant l'aurore!
>
> [When the bourgeois sleeps
> We are thirsty, still;
> Let's drink the night through!
> It's quite dark outside;
> But the windows on the streets are
> Ablaze like people's glances.
> Burning atmosphere,
> Girls in the smoke,
> Brandy and noise,
> This is our night!

> Drink is the real pleasure!
> There's nothing after!
> Nothing except to drink again,
> While we wait for the dawn to rise!][11]

Another favoured point of retreat for *bohémiens* from the spectacular carnival of the Second Empire was the Café Momus in the rue des Prêtres-Saint-Germain-l'Auxerrois, between the rue de l'Arbre-Sec and rue du Louvre. This was an enclave of free-thinking and free-living at the heart of the commercial city, where the novelist Henry Murger and his friend Alexandre Schanne held court in the smoking room, driving out bourgeois customers with an unrelenting stream of venom and sarcastic invective. The life of the Café Momus was later made legendary by Murger in his book *Scènes de la vie de Bohème* ('Scenes of Bohemian Life') of 1848, first published in serial form in the journal *Le Corsaire* (Murger was paid 15 francs an episode) before finding wider acclaim as a play and the source of Puccini's opera *La Bohème*. Murger's Bohemia was a picturesque world of wit, free-living and high drama. In its literary form at least, it was most notable for the way in which an invented world, based in reality, gave Parisians a glimpse of an alluring alternative lifestyle.

The success of this work was mainly due to the fact that the world described by Murger had great appeal even for those Parisians who did not dare broach the entrance of the Café Momus for fear of ridicule and humiliation. The point was that the café and its denizens stood as a symbol of resistance to the prevailing ethos of bourgeois self-gratification which, as Haussmann's project advanced, seemed to find concrete expression in the restructuring of Paris. The life of the Café Momus stood as a radical counterpoint to the conventions and standards of a regime that promised a return to the glory of the first Napoleonic era but was in fact buried under absurd and mediocre ambitions.

Most crucially, Louis-Napoleon wanted to think of himself as a 'good tyrant' without ever realizing that, under the economic and social conditions of the era, it was impossible to reconcile the interests of a comfortable bourgeoisie and those of the disaffected working classes who, as the economy boomed, were only further separated from the political mainstream. Haussmann's Paris, shaped as it was by the twin demands of bourgeois comfort and capitalist utilitarianism, was emblematic of the division between the bourgeois and the worker in the so-called 'liberal empire'.

Louis-Napoleon promised reforms, and earned the title 'the well-meaning' for his various projects aimed at improving the lot of the poorer classes. He introduced shorter working hours, health care, destroyed the old, stinking prisons (as late as 1830, convicts were paraded through the city of Paris in chains), built rest homes and hospitals. He was, however, as aware as anyone else of the difficulties he faced, commenting with a self-deprecating shrug to the English politician Richard Cobden that 'in France we make Revolutions not Reforms'.[12] For their part, the working classes had their political views formed by the recent chain of revolutions in which, from 1789 through to 1830 and 1848, they had given their blood but received little or nothing in return.

33. Red Lightning

Louis-Napoleon's main weakness, from the point of view of history, was his inability to understand or control foreign affairs. His greatest crime in the eyes of most Parisians who lived through his regime was, in contrast, to have ignored the reality of misery and poverty that lay beneath the surface of his spectacular but hollow empire. These two failings were clearly visible – for those alert enough to see them – during the second 'universal exhibition', which Louis-Napoleon organized to demonstrate the power, opulence and achievements of his regime. The first of these exhibitions had been held in 1855, and had been visited by Queen Victoria (who, to the surprise of her courtiers, had uncharacteristically flirted in girlish fashion with the ever-gallant French emperor).

This visit was regarded as a great moment, since the original intention of the exhibition was to demonstrate that French culture could easily rival or exceed anything dreamt up by the industrious but dreary English. The London exhibition of 1851 paled into insignificance, at least in Louis-Napoleon's eyes, when compared to the great shifting city of tents and pavilions built on the western limits of the Left Bank. The second exhibition, intended to exceed the grandeur of the first, was installed in April 1867 on the Champ de Mars and visited by thousands, with visitors coming from all over the globe. Baffled proletarians from Belleville and Ménilmontant came too, gazing with awe and often contempt at the opulent wonders of a world far removed from their own lives.

The Paris of the Second Empire was indeed a deeply divided city. For a small section of Parisian society, the aristocrats who had returned to Paris with Louis-Napoleon, the years of imperial reign were little short of being one long, extravagant party. One of the first reactions of the *haut monde* to the bourgeois sense of thrift and moderation characteristic of Louis-Philippe's Paris was deliberately to ape the manners of the pre-Revolutionary society of Louis XVI. This took the form of public spectacles, more often than not meant as a deliberate provocation rather than staged out of nostalgia. Moneyed aristocrats thought nothing of organizing elaborate hunting expeditions in the Forest of Fontainebleau kitted out in the lace and finery of the late eighteenth century. The city itself became the capital of *haute couture* (a term that dates from this period) as dressmakers, costumiers and designers vied with each other to win the attention of royalty and their imitators. The fashion of the day for women was tumbling curls, deep cleavages, narrow waists and yards of rich material. Men favoured dark suits and discreet but expensive ornaments – tiepins, cufflinks, silk ties.

Even the city streets were beginning to be well dressed, at least in the *beaux quartiers* of the west. By the 1860s, Paris was attracting visitors from all over the world, who came to sample its pleasures and to marvel at Haussmann's new city. The first of the so-called *colonnes Morris* – the circular green columns advertising theatrical performances – appeared in 1868. These were the brainchild of a printer of the rue Amelot called Gabriel Morris who spotted a gap in the market for his poster business. The sinuous and elegant green fountains, called *fontaines Wallace*, were to appear shortly afterwards: these were named after the English philanthropist Richard Wallace, who donated fifty of them after watching the population dying from thirst in the wake of the siege of 1870. By 1900, there were more than a hundred of these fountains, which had become as integral a part of Parisian street furniture as the blue street signs, the *colonnes Morris*, the triangular green newspaper kiosks, *buvettes* (stands selling food) or *vespasiennes* – the open-air urinals notorious as the haunt of thieves and homosexuals. It seemed at the time that the whole city was being turned over for public pleasure and consumption.

During the Second Empire, the masked ball was quickly established in elevated circles as the most fashionable form of gathering (Louis-Napoleon himself would usually dress up as a seventeenth-century Venetian noble). At these balls, the very air was alive with the musky odours of sex. At a famous ball held in the Ministère de la Marine in 1866, guests admired *tableaux vivants* of the five continents consisting mainly of nude or semi-clad 'natives' in suggestive poses. In the antechambers of the main ballroom, the scene had already descended into an orgy. Such balls were typical of the era and shocked only foreign visitors, who none the less noted the heaving bosoms of the women and the stamina of the men at these occasions.

The sexual energy of the upper classes was contagious. Police records in 1866 note that there were 5,000 prostitutes registered in the city of Paris. There were alleged to be another 30,000 more part-time whores, who were called by various names, including *comédiennes*, *lorettes*, *grisettes* and *cocodettes* – all politer terms for members of the 'oldest profession'. These were usually tough girls from the working classes who offered sex in return for an opportunity to have dinner, visit a theatre or sample any other of the city's new pleasures.

The appetite for ever richer and more luxurious foods matched the sexual voracity of these Parisians. It was during the Second Empire that the best Parisian restaurants acquired their reputation for exquisite excess. The soundtrack to all this urban hedonism was the frenetic noise of Offenbach. The cancan – the explicitly sexual dance originally described as an import from exotic and savage Algeria – was performed nightly in theatres and cabarets across the city and represented, in many ways, the Second Empire's apotheosis.

Omens

The revenge side of these excesses was syphilis and hunger. The twin evils of public prudery and political hypocrisy had demanded the censorship of Flaubert's *Madame Bovary* in 1857 and impelled journalists to condemn Manet as a perverted and corrupting swine for his works *Olympia* and *Déjeuner sur l'herbe*. Meanwhile men and women from all social castes were devoured by syphilis, their ulcerated, broken bodies a common enough memento mori at the liveliest cabarets. Prominent victims included Maupassant, Jules Goncourt, Baudelaire and the 'immoral' Manet. Across the city, at its northern and eastern edges, in Belleville, Ménilmontant, Saint-Antoine, and in the new areas of immigration founded around the Gare du Nord and the Gare Saint-Lazare, the biggest killer was not disease, venereal or other, but simply starvation.

It was against this background that the exhibition of 1867 closed with a military review – over 30,000 troops were aligned at Longchamp – and an assassination attempt. This was made not against Louis-Napoleon but on the life of Tsar Alexander II, who was in attendance. The tsar, who was not oblivious to the radical discontent brewing in Russia but had not expected it to follow him to Paris, was deeply shaken by this. The reaction of Louis-Napoleon to the incident was, by contrast, non-committal. He had himself been the target of a serious assassination attempt in 1858 – a bomb thrown by the Italian patriot Felice Orsini who saw Louis-Napoleon as a bar to Italian unification – and refused to read any real meaning into what he saw as the work of a lone fanatic. The tsar, however, saw this as a mark of Louis-Napoleon's essential frivolity. He became, as a result, uncertain about the durability of Louis Napoleon's government and refused to sign an agreement with France.[1]

This dealt a severe blow to the confidence of a regime that had until then prided itself on its stability and popularity. In truth, however, Louis-Napoleon's unpopularity had already been rapidly accelerating during the 1860s. One of the catalysts for this was the doomed military campaign he launched in Mexico from 1864 to 1867. This imperial adventure was purely opportunistic. Louis-Napoleon had originally sought to recover debts from the Mexican government but settled instead on imposing an imperial monarchy, which ended in disaster and humiliation for France. Most Parisians had no interest in foreign affairs, but they did notice when failure in such campaigns hit them in the pocket.

There was worse to come, however. In 1870, Louis-Napoleon was provoked and tricked by the arch-statesman Bismarck into declaring war on Germany. The source of the conflict – a dispute over the succession to the Spanish throne – was a matter of profound indifference to all Parisians, but it triggered a catastrophic war that not only destroyed the empire but brought terror and destruction once more to the streets of the capital.

On 19 July, when the French government declared war, the news was met by the exultant cries of 'À Berlin!' from the bars, cafés and on the boulevards. But the French army, as Bismarck had quietly noted during his visit to Paris in 1867, was totally unprepared for any serious conflict. The emperor himself not only lacked the tactical skills of the first Napoleon but indeed suffered so badly from pain from his gallstones that he could barely sit on his horse. This was to prove a cruel metaphor for the excess and hubris that were to bring his empire crashing down. Within six weeks of the exchange of insulting words that launched the war, the French army had been defeated by the Prussian war machine at Sedan and Louis-Napoleon himself captured. Soon German troops would surround Paris, training their guns from the heights around the city at its citizens.

It would have been almost impossible to imagine three years earlier, during the exhibition of 1867, that the site of the exhibition would be littered with the bodies of battered French soldiers and that the population of Paris would be reduced to eating rats to survive. It was Louis-Napoleon who, through a lack of guile and an over-inflated sense of France's military strength, had brought this about. Within just a few years of declaring Paris to be the 'queen of the world', he had all but wrecked the capital. In nine short months, from September 1870 to May 1871, at the height of its development and prestige in the great century of progress, the city and its people would suffer more than anyone had done within living memory.

The Siege

Louis-Napoleon had fallen stupidly into Bismarck's trap and few Parisians were inclined ever to forgive him for this. But even his harshest critics were taken aback by the demands that the Prussian chancellor was now deliberately making of the Parisian authorities, and which could not possibly be met. Bismarck's response was to encircle the city and see what happened. On 4 September, the Chamber of Deputies deposed the emperor (who fled to exile in London) and announced a provisional government. At the same time, a disaffected crowd occupied the Tuileries palace, calling for a republic. This was quickly established but it was a long way from providing anything like a real solution to the crisis. By 25 September, the city was in the tight grip of the Prussian armies.

Parisian confidence was high during the first few weeks of the siege. The city was packed with 350,000 fighting men of the National Guard and its walls – which had been fortified back in 1840 during a moment of prudence entirely uncharacteristic of the Second Empire – were solid, thick and easy to defend. The Prussians, however, had no intention of storming the city. They watched impassively during the first weeks of the siege as balloons left Paris to communicate with the outside world. One of these transported Léon Gambetta out of the city in a doomed effort to raise an army of provincial conscripts to come to the aid of Paris. Gambetta's feat of daring looked frivolous but was extremely brave, not to say foolhardy. The balloon was an unsteady and unreliable craft at the best of times and a tempting target for any bored Prussian sniper. The combination of extravagant courage and wasteful bravado involved in this kind of activity seemed to sum up the mood of the Second Empire in its decline.[2]

It soon became clear that the Prussian tactic was to starve the city. At first this presented most well-off Parisians with very little hardship; many Parisian bourgeois had hoarded food since before the defeat at Sedan in any case. Top restaurants continued to offer the best fare throughout the siege and the richest customers complained only at the lack of fresh seafood and the poor quality of the vegetables. It was also an amusing novelty at the best tables to order an elephant steak, camel kidneys or stewed beaver freshly slaughtered from the zoo. Gourmands discussed the relative merits of different species of rat, the plumpest of which were sold by butchers as a cross between 'pork and partridge'. There was always a steady stream of the finest wines, champagne and liqueurs to wash such delicacies down. The mood in the city was caught between high tension – expressed in a 'spy-fever' that imagined German agents everywhere – and an almost maniacal self-belief. A contemporary Anglophile witness, one M. Dabot, recorded a typical scene in a bootmaker's shop in the city in the late autumn:

'I should like to read your English newspapers now,' said one. 'Your *Times* told us we ought to cede Alsace and Lorraine, but its editor must now acknowledge that Paris is invincible.' I told him that I felt convinced that he did so regularly every morning. 'No peace,' shouted a little tailor, who had been prancing about on an imaginary steed, killing imaginary Prussians. 'We have made a pact with death; the world knows the consequences of attacking us.' The all-absorbing question of subsistence then came up, and someone remarked that beef would give out sooner than mutton. 'We must learn,' observed a jolly-looking grocer, 'to vanquish the prejudices of the stomach. Even those who do not like mutton must make the sacrifice of their taste to their country.' I mildly suggested that perhaps in a few weeks the stomachs which had a prejudice against rats would have to overcome it. At this the countenance of the gossips fell considerably when the bootmaker, after mysteriously closing the door, whispered: 'A secret was confided to me this morning by an intimate friend of General Trochu. There is a tunnel which connects Paris with the provinces and through it flocks and herds are entering the town.' This news cheered us up immediately.[3]

Away from the wealthy parts of town and the *terrasses* on the boulevards, the poor of Paris were nearly always half-starving anyway. As the siege hardened, the most desperate among them took to digging up corpses in various cemeteries around the city, mincing the bones to make a thin sort of gruel, which offered little nutritional value but at least kept them warm. The city began really to feel the pain of the siege in mid-October, which heralded the beginning of an unusually harsh winter. Fuel was low and trees on the Champs-Élysées and other great boulevards were soon chopped down for firewood. The lack of food stopped being a joke and became a real hardship for all but the most wealthy Parisians. On 10 November, Dabot's prophesy came true: he noted that rats were being sold in Les Halles at 25 centimes each. An American, Wickham Hoffman, stationed at the American Legation, also recorded that 'dogs sold from 80 cents up, according to size and fat. There was a refinement in rats. They were known as the brewery rat and the sewer rat. The brewery rat was naturally the titbit.'[4]

Worse still, Bismarck was swiftly growing impatient to take this proud and arrogant capital. On 5 January 1871, as the winter cold hit hardest, he ordered his artillery to begin terrorizing Parisians with a non-stop bombardment. The city was under assault for three weeks. Streets and buildings were wrecked and at least four hundred Parisians were killed by the same model of Prussian gun that had been proudly displayed in the heart of the city at the exhibition of 1867.

Despite the privations of the siege, the ordinary people of Paris only grew more defiant in the face of Bismarck's onslaught. The wealthier classes, on the other hand, were becoming increasingly nervous at the prospect of losing everything in a long war and a vengeful Prussian peace. In early February 1871, the National Assembly was returned with an over-whelmingly bourgeois and conservative majority, which immediately began brokering for peace. On the 21st of that same month, this government signed the Treaty of Frankfurt with the German imperial government in the Galerie des Glaces at the Palace of Versailles. The terms of the treaty were a devastating insult to France. They included conceding Alsace and Lorraine to Germany and the payment of crippling war reparations. Thirty thousand German soldiers marched down the Champs-Élysées in a final act of lofty Prussian disgust and contempt, and what would be a chilling premonition of further humiliation in the century to come.

The ruling classes breathed a sigh of relief, however, and began to dream of restoring something of the pre-war prosperity and exuberance to the city. But the divisions opened up by the war and the siege were a long way from being healed. Most notably, the working classes were suspicious of the fact that the newly conservative republic continued to maintain its headquarters at Versailles, away from the city and its tensions. In the streets of Paris, hatred of the government was heightened by its high-handed fiscal policies, which included raising taxes and interest on debts and abolishing the daily allowance to the National Guard. Every Parisian who had shivered through the winter, surviving on vermin and crusts and the bone-meal of cadavers, now felt suddenly and bitterly betrayed once again by those who profited from the city but who had no real stake in its fortunes.

Parisian War Songs

The explosion of violence that overwhelmed the city in the ten weeks of spring 1871 was sparked off by an apparently insignificant argument in Montmartre. On 18 March, a party of government troops marched up to the main square – which in those days was still a bucolic semi-rural affair – to commandeer some 200 heavy guns. These guns had been bought for the defence of Paris by public subscription and it went against the grain for every patriotic Parisian to see them being practically stolen by the lackeys of the hated bourgeois, Versaillais government. A crowd quickly gathered around the troops, most of whom were sympathetic to ordinary Parisians. Stones were thrown and a riot began, the mob growing in size with every hour and moving where it wanted to through the city. Two generals were shot dead in the rue des Rosiers and their bodies strung up to public delight. The guns were reclaimed and the rioters jubilant. Adolphe Thiers, who had risen to head of the new government, immediately ordered all troops out of Paris. They were quickly followed by functionaries and the wealthier classes. The city was now, surprisingly and terrifyingly, once again in the hands of the people.

This new insurrection hardly came as a surprise. Throughout the siege of Paris, the city had been effectively without government and boiling with revolutionary tension. The first popular uprising against the government had taken place on 31 October 1870 in response to rumours that the Prussians had captured Metz and that Thiers was set to sell out the city. On this occasion, a demonstration that began at Place de la Concorde went on to the Hôtel de Ville, where the demonstrators called for a commune to control the city. The notion of a 'commune' was not really linked to the 'Communism' of the day but rather an idea of a collective form of urban self-government that dated back to the Middle Ages and the earliest revolts against kings and taxes. It was, in truth, an ill-defined concept, but in the late nineteenth century the word itself carried enough revolutionary and patriotic potency for its use to have a galvanizing effect upon the populace. 'Commune' was used as a rallying cry during the second insurrection, on 22 January 1871, when, after a failed breakout of the city by government troops, angry and disaffected Parisians marched on the Hôtel de Ville, demanding the release of those imprisoned after the October rebellion, and control of the city. Shots were fired again.

The decisive moment came on 28 March 1871, ten days after Thiers had evacuated the city, when sixty-four representatives of the people stood on the steps of the Hôtel de Ville and announced that henceforth the city of Paris was in the hands of the Commune, a self-constituted council whose duty was to serve the people. Nineteen of the members of the Commune had formerly been in the National Guard, others were Jacobins – an extreme Revolutionary position that still held currency in certain circles – followers of the radical Auguste Blanqui or anarchist followers of Sully Proudhon. They also included eccentrics, oddballs and mystics, such as the clairvoyant Antoine Arnaud and Jules Allix – author of a work called *La Vie humaine correspond à la vie des astres* ('Human Life Corresponds to the Life of the Stars') – a vet, a brothel-owner, a concierge and a well-known drunk.

The culture of the Commune – which was anarchic and spontaneous and defined by an almost mystical hatred of all forms of authority – entirely matched the poet Arthur Rimbaud's call for unlimited subjectivity in art and life. In the works inspired by his experience (admittedly brief) of the Commune of 1871, Rimbaud had tried to incorporate into his work propaganda, overheard conversations, snatches of popular songs (the Communards were constantly making up songs – one of which, 'Les trois cerises' ['The three cherries'], has persisted down the years and is still a popular Parisian tune) and street sounds. The most notable examples of this can be found in the poem 'Chant de guerre parisien' ('Parisian war song') – which celebrates the 'bare arses' of the city – and the poem 'L'Orgie parisienne' ('Parisian orgy'), a cruel celebration of the 'city in pain':

> When your feet, Paris, danced so hard in anger!
> When you had so many knife wounds;
> When you lay helpless, still retaining in your clear eyes
> A little of the goodness of the tawny spring,
>
> O city in pain, O city almost dead,
> With your face and your two breasts pointing towards the Future
> Which opens to your pallor its thousand million gates,
> City whom the dark Past could bless:
>
> Body galvanized back to life to suffer tremendous pains,
> You are drinking in dreadful life once more! You feel
> The ghastly pale worms flooding back in your veins,
> And the icy fingers prowling on your unclouded love![5]

The Communards might have had no leader but they did have a shared programme: to restore the true values of revolution to the streets of Paris. The real violence began on 2 April when the Communards set out to Versailles to crush what they saw as an oppressive and unpatriotic government. The cry of 'À Berlin!' was now replaced in the streets of Paris by 'À Versailles!'

The march to Versailles began at midnight. Hundreds set off from Paris, often drunk or half drunk, and all fired up by the belief that once their proletarian 'brothers' understood the true nature of the conflict – the war of the poor against the rich – they would immediately drop their arms and join up with the forces of social justice. The walls of the city were plastered with posters announcing this along with other heartfelt propaganda predicting victory and vengeance. One such poster read:

Workers, do not be deceived! This is the great struggle. It is parasitism and labour, exploitation and production that are at stake. If you are tired of vegetating in ignorance and coughing in misery, if you want your sons to be men and not animals raised for the battlefield, if you no longer want your daughters – whom you cannot raise and protect – to be the instruments of pleasure in the hands of the aristocracy of wealth, if you would like to see the reign of Justice – Workers Arise![6]

The Communards might well have achieved a decisive victory if, as Karl Marx pointed out later, they had marched on Versailles straight away with the 200 hundred recaptured guns. As it was, the Commune had wasted valuable time in making largely irrelevant pronouncements – abolishing the night shift in bakeries, establishing workers' co-operatives, calling for the 'liquidation of property', fixing the highest salary of any functionary at 6,000 francs (the same as a mason or carpenter) – instead of taking the initiative and attacking the disorientated and lightly armed Versaillais troops. In the event, the Versaillais forces were given precious time to recover and regroup as the Communards pontificated and prevaricated. The assault from Paris was easily beaten back – Thiers, who had been responsible for the fortifications built around Paris in 1840, knew well the difficulties in storming them from within and without. As the wine and euphoria faded in the grey light of early morning, the workers were cut down in tens and then hundreds as they sought to break out of the city. Hundreds of captured Communards were marched off to the prison camp at Satory near Versailles, where they were summarily executed as an example to all future insurgents.

Fighting continued sporadically over the next few days, and particularly bloody skirmishes took place at Issy and Vanves. As news of the brutal treatment of prisoners by the Versaillais made its way back to Paris, the women of Paris began to organize themselves. Dressed in black with red rosettes in their caps, they planned a march on Versailles to parley for peace. The National Guard – on the side of the Communards – determined that victory was still possible, put a stop to such 'nonsense', however.

Instead, attitudes and actions in the city hardened. This was partly in response to the slaughter at Vanves and other vulnerable points south of the city and partly due to the actions of the Communard prefect of police, a 24-year-old former Bohemian, a former denizen of the Café Madrid and a friend of the poet Paul Verlaine, one Raoul Rigault, who would prove to be as fascinating and repulsive as any twentieth-century fanatic. Rigault had been a brilliant student, indulging in all the usual excesses of the Bohemian student lifestyle before transforming himself into a piercing political journalist. He was a follower of Auguste Blanqui, 'le Vieux', who preached total freedom and uncompromising violent resistance to the state. Blanqui was voted as a representative to the Commune but was in prison for the duration of the conflict; Rigault swore to carry out his theories in practice.

Rigault was by then already known to the right-wing press variously as a *fanfaron de perversité* ('braggart of perversity'), *bambin méchant* ('wicked child'), *canaille* ('scum') and an *aristocrate de la voyoucratie* ('aristocrat of the hooligan élite'). He revelled in provocative jokes, such as claiming to have invented a guillotine which could slice three hundred heads an hour. In his new office as prefect and then *procureur de la Commune* (an office with almost unlimited powers), he sported an extravagant uniform he had designed himself (it was a scarlet suit, fringed with gold and matched by yellow gloves). He seduced women efficiently and without mercy ('I want sexual promiscuity; concubinage is a social dogma' was one of his favourite maxims).[7] At the same time, he was given to chilling aphorisms, such as 'revolutionary laws are never strong enough', or advocating a new system of justice under which 'sons would judge fathers, convicts the judges'.[8] Rigault's response to the failure of the Communards to overcome the Versaillais was to order the immediate arrest of several dozen prominent figures in Paris, most of them clergymen, and including the Archbishop of Paris, and declaring them hostages. The archbishop, Monseigneur Darboy, was held in solitary confinement in the prison at Mazas.

Rigault, as a severe and uncompromising political aesthete, had no time for those liberals, including Victor Hugo, who objected to such actions. But his black sense of humour, a relic from his Bohemian days, and his lingering admiration for the marquis de Sade, had not quite abandoned him and he relished interviews with clergymen in which he declared God 'a vagrant' and threatened to issue a warrant for his arrest. It was with the same icy sense of humour that he ordered the killing of any prisoners who displeased him, including finally the unfortunate archbishop himself.

'Fire from heaven'

Paris under the Commune was neither the floating free festival imagined by nostalgic libertarians and anarchists during the 1960s, but neither was it, as countless reactionary historians have argued, the direct precursor of the deadly totalitarian governments of the twentieth century. The government, such as it was, consisted of disparate factions – Jacobins, anarchists, Communists, eccentrics, sadists, adventurers, mercenaries – whose social programme was incoherent and whose military knowledge was laughable. There was, however, no doubt that the Commune was a genuinely popular movement. This much was demonstrated not only in the enthusiasm with which the ordinary men, women and children of Paris rushed to their deaths in its name, but also in the way in which daily life was transformed and embraced by ordinary citizens with a vigour that had never been known under any previous regime and certainly not in the recent terrible times. It may well have been true, as so many historians have argued, that the simplest explanation for the Commune was that the working classes of Paris, brutalized and alienated from the city by the twin forces of burgeoning capitalism and Haussmannism (the two were of course interlinked), wanted to reclaim their own space in the city.

Paris indeed seemed to many observers to be permanently *en fête* (in a festive mood). On 16 May, a party of Communards blew up the column of the Place Vendôme, a glorious act of political blasphemy performed under the watchful eye of the artist Gustave Courbet and in an atmosphere of gleeful nastiness, accompanied by the sound of marching bands and watched by eager crowds.[9] Just after midnight that same night, a party of some three hundred Communards broke into the cellars of the Grand Hôtel du Louvre and drank themselves into a stupor in the name of liberty, all the while smoking huge and expensive cigars or gorging on the hotel's food stocks. On Sunday 21 May, the Communards organized a huge musical concert, with over 1,500 musicians, in the Tuileries gardens. In the late afternoon, not far away in Place de Goncourt, the diarist and socialite Édmond de Goncourt noted that a huge crowd had gathered around a carriage carrying a man who claimed to have seen the Versaillais troops entering the city.[10]

The report turned out to be true. As Parisians drank, slept or caroused late into the night, Versaillais troops had entered the western edge of the city and marched through Passy and Trocadéro as far as the Arc de Triomphe, meeting limited resistance and no barricades. The following day, they slipped into the city through the gate at the Point du Jour, which had been left unguarded and unattended. They advanced towards Saint-Germain-des-Prés and the boulevard Saint-Michel, fanning out towards the Faubourg Saint-Antoine, the traditional cauldron of revolution. The next few days saw slaughter on a scale quite unprecedented in a city that had already seen so many massacres.

One of the reasons for this was that the Versaillais troops were under express orders to show no mercy. A second reason was that the Communards, who lacked both a coherent strategy and any sense of organization, mounted a shambolic and disordered defence. As key areas of the city fell to the Versaillais without any effective armed response, the Communards launched a scorched-earth policy. Even at this late stage no one seemed quite sure who gave the orders or why they were given, but as the Versaillais drew closer to the centre of Paris, the city's main buildings and monuments were set on fire. The amazing sight was reported across the world. It had little or no military value but was none the less an extraordinarily dramatic climax to the struggle.

The confusion gave rise to many conflicting rumours, including the story that working-class women − or possibly even orphan girls − known as *pétroleuses*, were responsible for the fires. There were reports of groups of shabby, middle-aged women, usually dressed in black with a red bandanna around their heads, who for 10 francs would firebomb a building with a milk can full of burning kerosene. No woman was ever convicted, but the press was full of wild rumours and caricatures of ugly, wild-eyed women slinking in the shadows, ready to toss a bomb at any moment. The actress and courtesan Maris Colombier described the city under the shadow of the bombers in suitably apocalyptic terms:

As dusk fell, during the days of exile, we used to gather on the terrace at Saint-Germain, which looked over Paris; it appeared in the distance like the promised land. One evening, we saw a light appearing, and gradually growing; it spread out into jets of fire, stretched out and in reddening sheets, and filled the whole of the horizon, the sinister dawn of a conflagration. We looked at each other and understood: 'My God! Those madmen have just set fire to Paris!' It was in fact the Commune which was hoisting its red banner over the capital. The fire rumbled like a continuous bass, punctuated at intervals by crackling sounds. The light became so bright that it lit up the whole terrace: a fearful apotheosis . . . After eighteen hundred years, a crime as terrible, as fearfully radiant as the sack of Rome, blazed out under the starry calm of heaven: Paris was burning . . . nothing now, but the saraband of the *pétroleuses*.[11]

No doubt the fear these fantasies inspired in the middle classes had been fuelled by the participation and leadership of real women in the Commune – this indeed was one of its most striking achievements. The most notorious of these women, at least in the mind of the right-wing press, was Louise Michel, the so-called 'Red Virgin'. Michel was in fact a poet, teacher and anarchist who, during the 1850s, had opened free schools to spread her republican beliefs. This had made her the target of police harassment and drew her closer to dissident groups around the likes of Jules Vallès. During the days of the Commune, she was a member of the National Guard, fighting as hard as any man, and organized a central committee of the Women's Union. Michel's sustaining belief was that women were basically more revolutionary than men because they suffered from greater oppression. Michel was called the 'Red Virgin' because she refused to marry, but this did not stop her enjoying a long list of lovers, whom she took in the name of total freedom. She became a legend on the barricades of the 18 March, defying cannon and bullets to wave the Red Flag before the Versaillais troops.

Such gestures were in vain, however. As the centre of Paris burned, the Communard troops fell back, retreating in a ragged movement towards the east of the city. Along the way, the Versaillais were executing all who crossed their path. These included the street kids, who had fought bravely in their hundreds at Château d'Eau only to be gunned down until the streets ran black with blood. The massacres were all the more disturbing for the casual and mechanical manner with which they were carried out; hundreds and then thousands were dragged before firing squads all over the city and shot, their bodies piled high until they could be removed.

The smoky streets now stank of charred flesh, dried blood and rotting meat.

The pro-Versailles press urged the troops on in their deadly task. 'Paris has morally ceased to be the capital of France,' thundered *Le Soir* on 24 May. 'If at present it escapes the biblical fire from heaven, it cannot escape the pity and contempt of men.' There was plenty of contempt but little pity as the killing went on through the last days of the month. The marquis de Gallifet, already known in pre-war days as a sadistic dandy, excelled himself in his cruelty, making jokes to his mistress on his arm as he pointed out apparently who whould live and who would die.

The Commune's last stand was in the cemetery of Père Lachaise, at the centre of the working-class district of Belleville. The last defiant but doomed defenders were cut down in the passageways between the tombs of the writers Balzac, Nerval, Nodier and Delavigne. The surviving Communards were lined up against the eastern wall of the cemetery and shot. This spot became a favoured place of execution for 'suspects', who were rounded up over the next few days and months and sliced up by the new technology of the machine-gun, which could kill hundreds a day without unduly fatiguing the executioners. Across the city, behind high walls and in public, the bodies of Communards were heaped without ceremony. Sightseers who could stand the stench tripped over nearly a thousand bodies laid out in the Trocadéro. It had been raining for days and the streets were now muddy, dangerous labyrinths, still obscured by smoke and home to the last fugitive Communard snipers or patrolling Versaillais death squads. The atmosphere among the supporters of Versailles was loud and smug with triumph: Charles Louandre, a journalist and 'enemy of the people', declared that it was a blessing to see an end to 'this orgy of power, wine, women and blood known as the Commune'.[12]

The last barricade was broken in the rue Ramponneau in Belleville on 28 May. One lone sniper held off the Versaillais troops for several hours before disappearing, unknown and still free. 'Today, the struggle is terminated,' declared Marshal MacMahon, commander of the Versaillais counter-insurgency that had delivered such grim vengeance.

34. After the Orgy

The years that stretched from the 1880s to the First World War were first termed *la belle époque* in the wake of the mass slaughter of the Great War. The expression was used by French journalists and historians who had been traumatized by the savagery of total war and were nostalgic for the apparently innocent and idyllic life of Paris before the massacres began. The city itself was idealized as the centre of art, sex, music, poetry, food, literature, philosophy and unrelenting and unbridled hedonism. One of the reasons for this was that Paris during the last decades of the nineteenth century was beginning to look uniquely beautiful. The cultural life of the city was also highly sophisticated and its cabarets, bars, theatres and restaurants attracted intellectuals, artists and pleasure-seekers from all over the world.

It is this depiction of Paris that has helped to create the fantasy version of the city that still fuels the tourist imagination worldwide. But even at the height of the so-called 'beautiful epoch' – when the 'Ville-Lumière' did indeed dazzle the world with its style and glamour – this was a place shot through, as ever, with terrible tensions. More to the point, it was not easy to wipe away the burden of over a hundred years of violence in a few short decades. The reputation of these years as an innocent era was based upon an illusion and a dangerous myth. In truth, the catastrophe that lay in waiting for Paris had its origins in this era of unresolved conflicts and poisonous grudges.

The first and most historically significant of these was the heavy price paid by Parisians for the Commune. In the weeks and months after the Communards' final stand, more than 40,000 people were arrested and summarily tried as 'suspects' or 'insurgents', of whom 20,000 were shot. Nearly all of the rest were imprisoned or transported to rot in tropical prisons such as the infamous Devil's Island. The government forces had lost no more than a thousand men in the conflict. None the less, Thiers pushed on with a fierce ruthlessness, ordering that all opposition should be wiped out.

Many of the mass executions took place in the Luxembourg gardens or the Parc Monceau, areas that had been specifically designed to illustrate the benefits and convey the message of modernity but which now were transformed into sites of massacre and terror. A Third Republic was declared, but the people were not to be trusted and, under the presidency of Marshal MacMahon, who had been wounded at Sedan, the government stayed at Versailles until 1879, and even then returned carefully and slowly to the centre of the city.

The authorities called for repentance, but this was met by sullen resistance, even by many of those who had not actively supported the Commune. In spite of this, and as an act of atonement, the government ordered in 1873 the construction of the basilica of Sacré-Coeur on the hill of Montmartre. The Parisian working classes may have been beaten but they refused to forgive the bourgeoisie that easily. The builders who came to work every day to start the construction of the cupola were met by the regular cry of 'Vive le Diable!' from passers-by. Another popular song of the period was 'L'Bon Dieu dans la merde' ('The Good Lord in the shit'), a jaunty refrain that urged workers to spit in the faces of 'bosses, bourgeois and priests', before leading them to 'la lanterne' ('to hang from a street lamp').[1] The Sacré-Coeur was not completed until well into the twentieth century and it remains a controversial monument, despised by many Parisians not only for its sickly pastiche of the Romano-Byzantine style, but because it represents the grim victory of the forces of social order over the oppressed. Despite this, the church has become one of the key totems of Parisian identity for provincials and tourists alike.

The aftermath of the Commune was rich in similar historical ironies. The most visible of these was that the scorched-earth policy of the Communards in their retreat towards the east of the city had accidentally helped finish the urban project of Haussmann. In the years leading up to 1870, this had been running out of both money and momentum. In 1876, by contrast, it was decided by the city authorities that the great project of urban development would be an appropriate way to help heal divisions in the city. The city council had negotiated a massive loan for this and other projects and work resumed on the avenue de l'Opéra (linking with the rue de Rivoli) and the boulevard Henri IV.

The execution of these plans was even more ruthless and expensive than it had been before 1870: the avenue de l'Opéra was built by slicing down the incline of the Butte de Moulin, and demolishing hundreds of old buildings, whose owners had to be compensated. In all, this one avenue cost the city some 45 million francs, a previously unthinkable sum for the period. The costs were roughly half of those in the much poorer Arsenal district, where boulevard Henri IV met the boulevard Saint-Germain. The street lines were straightened across the Right Bank; rue de Franche-Comté was connected with boulevard du Temple; rues du Louvre, Réaumur and Jean-Jacques Rousseau were all widened, providing better access and sanitation but destroying in one blow the historic *quartiers* of this part of central Paris. Thousands of buildings in the now familiar grey and anonymous style appeared all over the city. Paris was finally assuming its role as the most advanced and best-designed city in the world but, as artists, writers, engineers, architects, as well as ordinary Parisians protested, this was at the expense of the city's unique identity.

The 'beautiful epoch' saw outbreaks of irrationalism in all fields of experience, from politics to poetry. This was one of the aspects of the civilization of the city that made Paris a uniquely fertile territory for artists, poets, writers and political activists from France and throughout Europe, who embraced all forms of extremism as the way towards the new century. This was a city of sharp, conflicting but endlessly creative contrasts. The new 'religions' of Communism and Socialism were accompanied, for instance, by a Catholic revival among the middle classes in the years after 1870. The contradictions at work in the city's cultural life also took a physical form. The Seine was, for example, no mere decorative frontier between the Left and Right Banks but also a busy channel through the centre of the city, packed with *bateaux-lavoirs* (floating wash-houses), and *bateaux-mouches* carrying suburban commuters, barges and fishing boats. The Champs-Élysées was grandiose but also an ideal place for strollers, idlers or even horse-riding. Montmartre was definitely still rustic and home to windmills, vineyards and as many animals as human beings. The centre of the city, in contrast, was an endlessly churning machine of industry and commerce, vehicles and people.

The quick pace of change was caught by a generation of painters – Claude Monet, Auguste Renoir, Edgar Degas, Berthe Morisot, Mary Cassatt – who captured reality as a blur of light and movement rather than as a fixed image. They were named by critics who saw their first exhibitions in 1874 as 'Impressionists' on the grounds that their works consisted of an 'impression' rather than a static scene; they themselves at first resented the label, arguing that their paintings were both 'finished' (as opposed to being 'impressionistic' sketches) and that moreover they represented reality as it was. As ideas, technology and experimentation accelerated across all fields of human endeavour, the greatest challenge for the Impressionists and the artists who followed them was how to keep up with the speed of progress as the century advanced.

A State Funeral

On the night of 31 May 1885, the atmosphere in Paris was strangely festive and as the darkness thickened it became peculiarly orgiastic. The cafés were full to bursting; even respectable gentlemen were drunk much of the night.

The occasion was the state funeral of Victor Hugo, a moment that would later prove to be one of the great turning points of the history of Paris in the late nineteenth century. For reasons that were unclear but deeply felt by most Parisians at some obscure level, his funeral marked the death of one era while heralding the birth of another. From the point of view of history, the death of Hugo signalled the shift from the dead certainties of the nineteenth century towards the uncharted territory of the twentieth. For Parisians who had lived through the era, Hugo's funeral was both a tragedy and liberation.

Hugo had managed to occupy at the same time the role of a thundering prophet, the greatest chronicler of the Parisian dispossessed, and that of a sickly, sentimental old fool. Most importantly, he was seen by all Parisians – even those who had not read him – as the very incarnation of the city's recent past. He had been born in an age of imperial glory, lived through revolutions, massacres and uprisings in the name of liberty, and finally made his peace with God and the world. His will was simple, clear and as great a statement as he had ever made: 'I give fifty thousand francs to the poor. I desire to be carried to the cemetery in one of their hearses. I refuse the prayers of all churches. I ask for a prayer from all living souls. I believe in God.'[2] His remains lay in state for twenty-four hours in a huge urn on top of the Arc de Triomphe, watched over by a phalanx of young poets dressed in the robes of the ancient Greeks. Whores had stopped working in honour of the great poet and amused themselves instead by picking up strangers for free in obscure corners of the Champs-Élysées ('A strange orgy took place,' noted one foreign observer, 'which was both wholly Parisian and entirely unprecedented'). The following day, over three million people packed the streets and the funeral cortège took almost six hours to reach the Panthéon, originally built by Jacques Germain Soufflot as a church in 1764 but now unconsecrated for the funeral, and draped in black as a mausoleum for the great men of France.[3]

In the days after the funeral, it was as if the burden of the past had been lifted and the future was revealing itself in the frenzied and theatrical street life of the new city. Most importantly, these changes were taking place at the level of everyday life. All Parisians were, for example, impressed by the spectacular shop-fronts that were being developed along the *grands boulevards*, and which were transforming Paris into the first modern commercial city.

The first true *grand magasin* was Au Bon Marché, which opened on the rue du Bac in 1876 in a building designed by Louis-Charles Boileau and Gustave Eiffel. The construction was a work of art in itself – wide, monumental staircases, a match for those in the Opéra, connected galleries and multi-layered floors, all flooded in light from the glass ceiling. The goods on sale were at a fixed price and appealed, at least in theory, to every level of income. By the end of the 1870s, the store was a roaring success and by the 1880s department stores on similar lines spread across the Right Bank, from rue du Louvre to the bottom end of Belleville. These included names now long familiar to Parisians, such as Au Printemps, La Belle Jardinière (this was in the working-class *quartier* near the Gare de Lyon) and Galeries Lafayette.

The argument of many on the Left was that the expansion of commercial activity 'democratized' the boulevards, turning them into a place where all classes mixed. It was, however, a second and singular irony that these irreversible commercial developments had been born out of the wreckage of the Commune. Despite the best efforts of politicians and merchants to embrace a future where class differences would be dissolved in consumerism, after the Commune the divisions between the classes became irreconcilable. The reinvention of Paris by Haussmann may have been a blow to nostalgics, revolutionaries and all manner of poetic dreamers in the tradition of Victor Hugo, but it could not be denied that, unlike 'Old Paris', it did work. From its sanitation systems to the shops, theatres, newspaper offices, cafés and restaurants on the boulevards, Paris was now a fully functioning, model environment. This was quite simply something that had not been seen before in human history. Even its fiercest detractors had to concede that in its ruthless energy and creative life, the new city that was established in the 1880s was both savage and magnificent.

The Rise of Low Life

Only slightly earlier, Arthur Rimbaud, boy poet, sodomite and patron saint of a generation of so-called 'Bohemians', had hailed the coming generation as a 'wild parade' of anarchists, idlers and drunks, who opposed the 'bourgeois' century of science with magic, art and revolutionary contempt for the shibboleths of progress and reason.

One of the myths of the *belle époque* that was not wholly untrue was that Paris was now the world capital of pleasure. In part this was a purely economic phenomenon linked to the rise and growth of the city. There were approximately 30,000 cafés or drinking-shops in Paris in 1789. By 1885, when Second Empire regulations on café life had been long since abolished, there were nearly 30,000 establishments licensed to sell drink. This was more than any other city in the world (London boasted little more than 5,000 pubs and New York only 10,000 bars). These places were known by a variety of names: as well as the names that have come down to the twentieth century (bistro, café, cabaret, brasserie), *boc, bibine, boîte, cabremont, caboulot, cargot, abreuvoir, assommoir, bastringue, boucon, bouffardière, bousin, cabermon* and *troquet* were all in common usage. What they all shared, from the most respectable bourgeois establishment to the *tapis franc* ('thieves' den'), was a zinc bar, an all-powerful *patron* and a thirsty clientele.[4]

Cafés also played a variety of roles in the life of the city; they offered not only food, drink and (in most places) commercial sex, but also ideas, arguments, companionship, a refuge from work, a meeting place, somewhere to get hired or sacked, not to mention warmth and light. The cafés of Paris were, quite rightly, regarded with suspicion by all governmental authorities, who were all too aware of the role they had played, from 1789, as carriers of the virus of revolution. Leading hygienists, medical men and easily shocked social philanthropists fulminated against the evils of alcohol and the deadly dangers of sexual licence, but nobody who enjoyed either of these pastimes was ever listening. The disease called 'alcoholism' was invented in 1853 by the Swedish doctor Magnus Huss, who first isolated drink as the chief cause and origin of a whole range of pathological disorders and alcoholism as a chronic ailment in itself. This theory was, however, loudly discounted in Paris by the highest medical authorities, who claimed alcohol as a life-preserving tonic for the working man and a life-enhancing pleasure for the well-off. Alcoholism, it was argued, if indeed it existed at all, was a problem for chilly northern populations who drank dangerous spirits and who, anyway, were given to gloom and introspection on account of the climate. In 1873, a society against the 'abuse of alcoholic drinks' was launched at the Académie de Médecine, which became, under the patronage of the likes of Hippolyte Taine, Louis Pasteur and Baron Haussmann, the 'Société Française de Tempérance'. This was, however, no more than a group of cranks. The favoured drink of the moment continued to be the famous *fée verte* ('green fairy'), absinthe in other words, which was available all over Paris often at more than 72 per cent proof.

The police did not care about morality or health, but none the less kept a close eye on drinkers and drinking-shops, especially in working-class districts. Much of the spying was concentrated on straightforward criminal activity. Notorious dens such as Chez Paul Niquet at 36 rue aux Fers and the Lapin Blanc on the rue aux Fèves were wiped out by Haussmannization, much to the relief of the local gendarmerie. Politics was another matter. During the Second Empire, a series of legal measures aimed at reducing public drunkenness had been adopted, including fines, warnings and imprisonment. They did little to stem the tide of alcohol that was the essential lubricant to Parisian life.

Most importantly, the café was the meeting place of Leftist intellectuals and the 'dangerous classes' whose historic mission was to make history. Unsurprisingly, much of the damage done during the Commune was blamed on the widespread drunkenness that spilled over from the café to the street. The burning of Paris during the *semaine sanglante* was thereby reduced in the eyes of right-wing historians to no more than an act of 'alcoholic pyromania'. Accordingly, the café life of working-class Paris was perceived by the ruling classes as both a threat and a source of fascination. Both of these responses had sexual undertones. It was, for example, widely believed that all women in working-class cafés were prostitutes, but this was simply not the case. In fact, such women were able to drink, smoke and argue politics in their local cafés in a way that would have shocked their bourgeois sisters in the *terrasses* on the boulevards (where every woman was indeed most likely to have been a professional or amateur whore).

Paris by Night

Above all, Paris was now a city of conflicting febrile energies, all of which were reflected and represented in its rich and dense night-life. At the heart of this was the old village of Montmartre, which during this period became the main playground for Parisians of all classes in the pursuit of drink, sex and the vicarious thrill of brushing shoulders with the real *canaille* and criminal classes of nearby Belleville and Ménilmontant. This was where the cabaret was invented, denoting a place for drinking, eating and sharp, usually political and satirical, entertainment. One of the first of these was Le Chat Noir on boulevard de Rochechouart, opened in 1881 by the failed painter Rodolphe Salis. The origins of the cabaret lay with a group of Bohemian poets and students briefly prominent in the late 1870s who called themselves the 'Hydropathes' (on the grounds that they were always 'thirsty' for drink or culture). Among the leaders of this groups were the poet Charles Cros, a friend of Rimbaud and Verlaine who was also famous for his sarcasm, and the writer Alphonse Allais. The Hydropathes were both customers and the entertainment at Le Chat Noir, offering a variety of skits, songs and 'events' (which took the form of crude shadow plays or short dramas) for patrons, who were insulted by Salis as they entered and lampooned by the resident clientele. The atmosphere was intensely patriotic and nostalgic (the bad-tempered waiters wore the green palms of the Académie Française; on the cobwebbed walls of the establishment, Salis had hung 'the very cups' used by Villon, Rabelais and Julius Caesar). This was the opposite of the well-meaning Leftist atmosphere to be found on the Left Bank but was all the more popular for it. Le Chat Noir even had its own newspaper, edited at first by the Hydropathes and then by a whole galaxy of short-lived stars of the literary firmament.[5]

The massive success of Le Chat Noir spawned a generation of imitators, including Le Mirliton, hosted by Aristide Bruant, who wandered provocatively among his audience and whose scabrous songs and stories of Parisian life both mocked and exploited the moods of the period. These were followed by a dozen or more similar establishments, including Le Moulin Rouge in 1889, and a host of lesser dives, all offering art, drink, ideas and danger in roughly equal measure.

It was at this time that the term 'avant-garde' first entered the Parisian lexicon. The expression originally had a military meaning, referring to a small group of infantrymen whose job was to make a breach in the defences of the enemy. It was already being used as a political metaphor in the wake of the events of 1848, when it was adopted as a masthead by a variety of journals who all claimed to be leading the revolutionary Left to its historic victory. It became associated with art in 1863 under Napoleon III, who promoted an exhibition of artists (including Manet, Cézanne and Pissarro) who had been excluded from the official Salon de Paris. By the 1880s, 'avant-garde' had come to refer to small groups of artists and writers whose work, even if not explicitly political, represented a challenge to the established order.

Many of the self-styled 'avant-gardists' of this period also called themselves *décadents* – the term was probably first used pejoratively by the poet Jules Laforgue – and formed tiny literary societies known as 'Les Hirsutes', 'Les Zutistes' or indeed 'Les Hydropathes'. In literature and philosophy, they argued for novelty over boredom, horror over the banalities of beauty. Their heroes were Baudelaire, Rimbaud and every other writer who was for revolt and against orthodox society. The diverse and apparently unrelated writings of J. K. Huysmans, Lautréamont or Stéphane Mallarmé – none of whom were *décadents* in the sense that they belonged to no single movement – were all drawn together by this same purposeful iconoclasm. It is a singular irony that this mood, which would become a defining force of Paris in the twentieth century, had its origins in the cultural upheavals of the 'beautiful epoch'. The Parisian night-life of that period, and in particular that of Montmartre, has become a tourist cliché; the spirit of defiance founded there is none the less still one of the most potent mythologies of contemporary Paris.

Class Wars

The volatile mood was, however, caught not just in the furious pleasure-seeking that preoccupied great swathes of the city, but also in random terrorist violence. The figure of the anarchist bomber, who killed bourgeois and worker without apparent rhyme or reason, haunted the imagination of all Parisians and in most of the press became an archetype of the still-feared current of proletarian violence which coursed through the city.

The geographical separation, between the revolutionary working classes in the eastern part of the city and the bourgeois classes in the *beaux quartiers* of the west, had indeed now become a chasm. (Despite the recent partial gentrification of the east, these tensions persist today. I stayed in Ménilmontant for a short while and as I scuttled to the metro on my way to an office in the bourgeois heartland of the 16th *arrondissement*, all too often nursing my own hangover, I was frequently struck – and impressed – by the *quartier*'s resident wino who, at 6.48 in the morning swigged back his plastic litre of *rouge* with dandified nonchalance, and whose fierce beard and defiant glare could have come straight out of the pages of *Le Père Peinard*, a bloodthirsty anarchist propaganda sheet of the 1880s. The *quartier* belonged to him, not to me.)

In reality, the anarchist revolution had its origins in the southern towns and cities of France and flourished most notably in Lyons, where a united and powerful working-class movement had regularly collided (and won occasional victories) against state and financial authorities. The movement had spread towards the north through the mid-part of the century but had grown best of all in the fertile ground of Paris after the Commune, where anti-militarism, anti-capitalism and anti-clericalism had fused into the single force of the anarchist movement.

Anarchists were most at home in Belleville, which was now the unofficial headquarters of revolutionary movements in the city. Intellectuals such as Jean Grace and Émile Gauthier, both anarchist leaders, founded their journals on the Left Bank, respectively near the rue Soufflot and rue Mouffetard, but the real work of propaganda took place in eastern Paris. There was a variety of groups at work in Belleville in the 1870s, with names such as 'Les Libertaires', 'Les Travailleurs Communistes', 'Le Drapeau Noir' or 'Le Groupe Anarchiste du Père-Lachaise'. They lacked any central organization or guiding theory but were none the less united in a philosophy that advocated controlled disorder as the way towards an ideal society composed of 'autonomous communes', organized by workers for the workers, which made capitalism and the social hierarchies it produced irrelevant. This had particular appeal for the craftsmen and artisans of this part of Paris, who were aware that their labour and products were systematically being exploited by capitalists and who favoured the local, intricate economies of their own *quartier* over the impersonal machine of the commercial city that they called 'New Babylon'.

The anarchist was an integral part of the social fabric of this part of the city, as yet untouched by Haussmannization and its heartless mercantile mentality. Still, police spies kept a careful eye on the movements of known anarchists, watching and taking notes as they manoeuvred in cafés and bars on the rues Ménilmontant and Belleville, boulevard Charonne (the Café de la Nation was a favoured haunt here) and rue du Faubourg du Temple. This was a hard, tough world, far removed not only from the lights of the boulevards but also from the easy-going frivolity of the Left Bank and its Bohemian and student population. The anarchist prophets targeted misfits, drinkers, vagabonds, criminals – all members of the so-called 'dangerous classes' who were excluded from the glittering life of the city and who had nothing to lose and everything to gain in promoting a political philosophy that advocated destruction as the prelude to the creation of a new world.

The most famous anarchist of all was François-Claudius Ravachol, also known as Koenigstein and Léon Léger. Ravachol gave his name to a new verb, *ravacholer* ('to wipe out'), which was briefly popular among young Bohemians. He was notorious for five murders and several attempts to kill prominent magistrates, and was sent to the guillotine in 1892. The poet Stéphane Mallarmé, whose work was admired in the most rarefied circles for its severe and uncompromising abstraction, defended Ravachol in court, aligning him with a burgeoning literary avant-garde whose aim was the elimination of bourgeois morality. The writer Octave Mirbeau, who declared himself openly as a supporter of anarchy, went one step further, defending Ravachol's violence as the only way of wrecking the capitalist civilization and supporting him against those who described him as no more than a common murderer (among Ravachol's least poetic or impressive transgressions was hammering to death the hard-working female owner of a hardware store and her daughter). According to Mirbeau, the anarchists had the right to 'do what they may to deliver themselves from the reactions of fear . . . governments will not prevent the inevitable. We are at a decisive moment in human history. The old world collapses under the weight of its crimes. It is that world itself which lights the bomb which will destroy it.'[6] Such sentiments were reduced to a formula by the literary critic Laurent Tailhade, who was famously quoted as saying at dinner 'what do a few human lives matter, when the gesture is beautiful [*le geste est beau*]'. Despite being blinded in one eye two years later by an anarchist bomb thrown into the same restaurant, Tailhade stubbornly refused to concede that he may have been mistaken in his earlier opinion.[7]

Ravachol's actions were imitated by other determined and impressionable young men, including a young bourgeois called Émile Henry who was caught by the police as he placed a bomb in the Café Terminus of the Gare Saint-Lazare. Despite the apparently pointless and murderous nature of most of these actions, there was a groundswell of support in Paris in the anarchists' favour. This was partly the natural reaction of the working classes, who saw the anarchist bombers as foot soldiers in the long, revolutionary war against the ever-mutating but apparently unstoppable might of capitalism. The terrorist bombings were applauded in the bars and cafés of Belleville as 'brave gestures' and songs were sung in honour of Ravachol and other 'enemies of order'.

The Promethean aspect of the terrorist enterprise also attracted support from literary quarters – not just semi-prominent figures such as Mallarmé but also a generation of young men and women who embraced futility, terror and crime as the only logical responses to a society in a state of collapse. For this reason, the mass trials of anarchists – who included the writer Félix Fénéon, a supporter of the Impressionists – in 1894 attracted a good deal of popular support among Parisians. The trial reached a comic finale when the government lawyer opened in court a package sent to him, and which he believed to contain explosives but actually was packed with a slippery and foul-smelling turd. As the lawyer retreated to wash his hands, Fénéon cried out that 'never, since Pontius Pilate, has a lawyer washed his hands with such show!' He was greeted with loud applause from the viewing gallery.[8]

In the 1890s, the anarchist threat disintegrated almost as quickly and suddenly as it had emerged. But while it lasted it introduced a fine thread of fear and disruption into the fabric of a city that otherwise tended to congratulate itself on having eradicated the grubby and squalid aspects of everyday life in the name of reason and progress.

'The comedy is over!'

This city of conflicting ideas and interests provided much of the inspiration for the novelist Émile Zola, who had arrived in the Faubourg Saint-Marcel from Aix-en-Provence as a young man, and spent a lifetime determined to understand the subterranean cultures of Paris.

Zola thought of himself as a kind of scientist and developed the theory of *naturalisme* to justify his minutely observed but often ponderous novels. Between 1871 and 1893, he set out to publish the twenty novels of *Les Rougon-Macquart*, with the subtitle *Histoire naturelle et sociale d'une famille sous le Second Empire* ('Natural and Social History of a Family under the Second Empire'), aiming to document in every detail the 'true life' of Second Empire Paris (the city being the main setting in ten of his novels). Zola is at his best, however, when he forgets his theories and his stories take on a feverish life of their own that captures something of the essence of the turbulent, teeming city.

Zola's best descriptions of the city are in the novels *Le Ventre de Paris* ('The Stomach of Paris') of 1873 and *Au Bonheur des dames* ('The Happiness of Women') of 1883, set respectively in the food halls of Les Halles and a fictional department store on the boulevards. Zola is unashamedly a man of the Left and his novels portray the city from the point of view of those it oppresses or destroys. Paris is depicted as a machine, an all-consuming monstrous engine of destruction in the service of capitalism. The city itself is threatened by internal forces of commerce and capital that are more powerful than history. 'Paris lay out stretched below,' he writes at the end of *Au Bonheur des dames*, 'but it was already a diminished Paris, consumed by this monster. The houses, as humble as country cottages, disappeared in a welter of indistinguishable chimneys. Even the monuments seemed to melt away: on the left were two dashes for Notre-Dame, on the right a circumflex for Les Invalides, and off in the distance the Panthéon, ashamed and abandoned and not even as big as a bean.'⁹

At the opposite end of the political spectrum from Zola, the major preoccupation of all parties of the Right was revenge against Germany for the humiliation it had inflicted on France in 1870. The fact that France, and Paris in particular, had flourished since then was no compensation for the lingering sense of injustice and shame that could only be expiated in war. The exhibition held in Paris in 1878, when the triumphs of French industrialization and colonialization were paraded before the world, had gone some way to restoring faith in the country's potential. But it was no substitute for lost territory or wounded self-esteem.

Nationalists found an unlikely hero in the form of General Georges Boulanger – patriot, republican and an ardent believer in the mission of the army as saviour of France. Boulanger was also notorious as a philanderer and a populist politician who was unafraid to win votes by calling for the destruction of the Prussian enemy. Boulanger was appointed minister of war in 1886 and impressed Parisians with his beard (the mark of a full-blooded republican), his coal-black charger and by making resounding statements such as 'the army doesn't take sides'. Boulanger entered folklore in the popular song 'En revenant de la revue' ('Coming back from the review'), a tune in celebration of 14 July: 'Moi, j'faisais qu'admirer, / Not'brav' général Boulanger.' ('All I could do was admire, our brave general Boulanger'). In 1889, Boulanger was elected to the National Assembly and increased his popularity even further, mixing with Royalists, Bonapartists and radicals in turn. Wary of his incomprehensible but undoubted popularity, the government of Georges Clemenceau engineered the deportation of Boulanger's mistress, Madame de Bonnemain, to Belgium, knowing that he would follow her. The crisis point came on the evening before her departure, as crowds gathered in the streets calling for Boulanger to march on the Élysée Palace to take power. Boulanger was famously dining in the Durand restaurant, where he could hear the cries from the streets. He hesitated and the next day followed his mistress to Belgium. She died a year later. A year after that, the body of Boulanger was found on her grave, where he had stabbed himself to death.

Parisians relished the combination of melodrama and intrigue in such a tale, which was ultimately a farce. On hearing of Boulanger's death, Clemenceau put it well in his characteristically apt but brutal style when he said, 'Now the comedy is over.'[10] A far greater tragedy was, however, at work throughout the 1890s. This was the so-called 'Dreyfus affair', which began to unfold in 1894, when an unsigned letter containing French military secrets and apparently on its way to the German military attaché in Paris was intercepted by French intelligence. The letter was attributed to Captain Alfred Dreyfus, a hitherto blameless officer in the French army whose only mistake was to be Jewish at a time when 'Jew hatred' was at its height among Parisians of all political persuasions (there were many deputies to the National Assembly who had, for example, been elected for their unashamedly anti-Semitic policies).

When it later emerged (in 1896) that the letter had been written by a Major Esterhazy, an officer of documented dubious integrity, the War Office suppressed the information. When details of the way in which Dreyfus had been framed emerged at Esterhazy's court martial (where he was acquitted), France was engulfed in a crisis that revealed how deep the divisions between those who believed in the infallibility of French government and those who saw it as irreparably flawed really were.

Against Dreyfus were all those who stood for the rule of law and military order. His supporters, on the other hand, argued convincingly that the law could not stand if it was not based on truth and natural justice. The culminating point of the conflict was the pamphlet *J'Accuse!*, published by Émile Zola in 1898. In this text, the novelist called for a retrial and launched a brilliant polemic against the rottenness of a country that had lost all its belief in its ability to withstand the truth about itself. The pamphlet made him so unpopular – indeed it placed his life in danger – that he was forced to spend a year in exile in London. Since then, Zola's polemic has been hailed as the birth of the twentieth-century notion of the 'intellectual' as a writer or thinker whose historic duty is to engage with his or her era, and if possible, or if necessary, to transform it. In this sense, Zola is the father of the 'committed' generation of Sartre and Camus. The Dreyfus affair itself was a precursor to the poisoned political atmosphere of Paris in the 1930s, where Jews were regularly vilified as 'traitors' and 'betrayers of the republic'.

Portents

The construction of the Eiffel Tower was intended to give the world the supreme symbol of the century. It had been planned as the prime exhibit at the exhibition of 1889, which was itself meant to mark a hundred years of French achievements since the Revolution of 1789. Less obvious to foreign visitors, but a clear source of disquiet for Parisians, was that the exhibition and the tower were also meant to signal a return to the world eminence which Paris had claimed for itself before the 'terrible years' of 1870 and 1871. For this reason alone, Parisians were sceptical and often loudly unhappy about the 'metal asparagus' or 'suppository' being built in their midst. Others made objections on aesthetic grounds, arguing that it was an eyesore, a 'steel monster', which wrecked the Parisian skyline. The most common opinion, aired in the lowest dives and the most respectable *salons*, was that it was an act of hubris and almost certainly a bad omen.

It was not wise to underestimate the power of such superstitious thinking in a city that, as it approached the last years of the century, had embraced revivals of occultism, fanatical Catholicism and a widespread belief in the end of the world (even the vogue for Symbolist poetry could be said to be part of the widespread faith in irrationalism and the fatal qualities of chance). Other signs of imminent catastrophe, or at least a stark recognition that modernity carried with it its own dangers, were to be found in the streets of the city itself. Probably the most famous of these, and one which brought together the twin marvels of the burgeoning society and the new technology of the filmed image, was the disaster of the Bazar de la Charité in 1897.

The Bazar de la Charité was a cloth, wood and canvas structure on the Champs-Élysées that had been founded and was organized by upper-crust ladies to show every kind of fashionable attraction to visitors of all classes, but especially the well heeled and well connected. On 4 May 1897, the ladies of the Bazar arranged a showing of the Lumière brothers' *cinématographe*, which had recently been invented and was the talk of Paris. Lighting came from a faulty ether lamp, which shot flames across the room when an attendant tried to relight it. The canvas walls caught fire straight away and within seconds the whole flimsy construction had become an inferno. Hundreds of men, women and children were trapped in turnstiles or found their way blocked by burning walls. The final body count was never properly known – over two hundred people is a conservative estimate.

The shock and horror were all the greater because the dead included dozens of members of Parisian high society, most of whom were women.

The disaster had no particular political meaning, but it did appal Parisians from all walks of life who had already had enough reason historically to be scared of fire, crowds and machines. It also gave rise to a grotesque and thoroughly bizarre anecdote about comte Robert de Montesquiou, whose wife had been killed in the fire. Montesquiou was famous for his dandified elegance and over-refined wit. He was said to have inspired the character Des Esseintes in Huysmans's novel *À Rebours* ('Against Nature', 1884), the epitome of the 'decadent' aesthete who rejects objective reality for the 'higher' realities of beauty in perversity. Montesquiou was most definitely also the model for the degenerate figure of Proust's Baron de Charlus.[11]

Des Esseintes is quite possibly one of the most sickly and repugnant characters in all world fiction, but well matched in reality by Montesquiou, who was seen to have poked his wife's body with a cane, lifting her charred clothes off with its tip in order to recognize her. The Symbolist poet Henri de Régnier later alleged that Montesquiou had fought his way out of the bazaar with the cane, leaving his wife to perish in the flames. A duel was fought, but the argument was unresolved. The fact that most Parisians of all classes believed the poet's insinuation, however, illustrated the extent to which they had a clear view of the excesses of their century and the monsters it had produced.[12]

PART SEVEN

Magnetic Fields

1900–1939

In the end you are weary of this ancient world
  O Eiffel Tower

shepherdess the flock of bridges bleats this morning
You've had enough of living in Greek and Roman antiquity

I love the grace of this industrial street
Located in Paris
between the Rue Aumont-Thiéville and the Avenue des Ternes

Guillaume Apollinaire, *Zone*, 1917

A Landscape haunts as intense as opium . . .

Stéphane Mallarmé, 1888

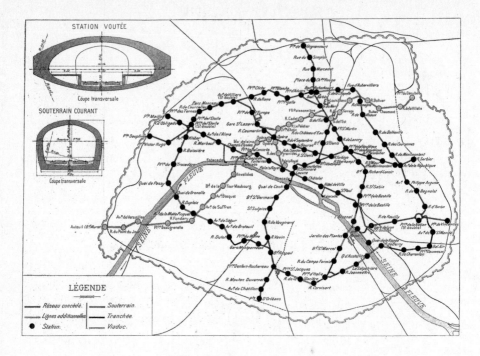

Plan of the Paris metro in 1900.

35. New Spirits

Over the next hundred years, Paris would grow denser and richer than ever before in its history. It would still be locked, however, into the tight circle defined by the outer ring road, the *boulevard périphérique*, 'le périph', which marks it as a city, unlike Los Angeles or London, of essentially medieval dimensions. In the same way, the history of Paris in the twentieth century would be defined by a series of conflicts – between rich and poor, progress and tradition – that were firmly rooted in the past but which were so deeply entrenched as to be immovable.

This was to be an age of great traumas. From the horrors of the battlefields of the First World War, the diseases that ravaged the city in the war's aftermath, the riots and near-civil war of the 1930s, to the Nazi Occupation of the 1940s, Parisians were all too often betrayed and humiliated by their political leaders, who told them lies and were indifferent to their suffering. The revolutionary promises of the working and 'dangerous classes' of the nineteenth century were lost in the clamour of argument between a Communist Party that for far too long into the century saw Moscow as the only beacon of hope for humanity and the various parties of the Right who embraced quietism, cynicism and occasionally Fascism in the name of a republic they did not really believe in. Paris was the world capital of ideas and ideologies and also a place where intellectuals of all sides made excuses for some of the greatest crimes ever committed in the name of advancing humankind. Hitler, Mao and Stalin were all heroes here at some point during the century.

The early part of the twentieth century also saw the rise of the avant-garde movements, from Cubism to Surrealism and Existentialism, and all their offshoots. These groups thought of themselves as providing cultural and political resistance to the cruelty of the historic forces that at times threatened to engulf the city. Yet for all their promises of redemption, the avant-gardists only ever belonged to an élite, and failed time and again to connect with the masses.

Such issues, however, were far from people's minds during the winter of 1899, as Parisians entered the new century in a distinctly subdued mood. The autumn had been cold and wet and the population shivered and sneezed its way through the darkest months. There was little sense of an historic break with the past in politics, literature or everyday life. Most Parisians were indeed mainly concerned with surviving and making a living in a city that regularly proclaimed itself as the model for the future, but which in many ways was mired in the divisions of the recent past.

Arguments still raged around the Dreyfus affair and the Panama Canal scandal of 1893, a financial con-trick that had impoverished many Parisians and only deepened the visceral anti-Semitism coursing through the city. Anti-Semitism was indeed matched only by anti-British sentiment, and the papers delighted in reporting on the British difficulties in South Africa (the death of Queen Victoria in 1901 was also the target of much comic satire. In the wake of her funeral, fashionable Parisians took to wearing felt hats in what was taken to be a mildly pro-Boer stance).[1]

The city authorities intended that the turning of the century would be announced by a dazzling blur of art, technology and fantasy. The Eiffel Tower glistened in the grey and humid air, newly washed by winter storms and standing as the proud symbol of the meeting of design, engineering and Utopian desire. Sometimes all these three elements came together. This indeed was the theme of the Paris exhibition of 1900, which was intended to exceed all other previous achievements – including the 1889 exhibition, which had introduced to a goggle-eyed public not only the Eiffel Tower but also an incredible moving walkway. It did this quite easily by celebrating the city of Paris itself as the world capital of modernity and progress, a fact that was demonstrated in the supreme craftsmanship and daring that went into the iron and glass constructions of the Grand and Petit Palais and the Pont Alexandre III, all built especially for the exhibition. The status of Paris as the centre of world civilization was underscored by its colonial conquests, which were represented in numerous exotic exhibits around the exhibition site, bringing the world to Paris rather than the other way around.

The exhibition was open until November and was viewed by over 50 million visitors, which was more than the population of France. The entire site of more than two and a half miles was powered by electricity and at night the Palace of Electricity was lit up by more than five thousand fairy lights, drawing gasps from all who saw it. 'Old Paris' now properly left history and entered folklore in the form of a fake *quartier* of artificial houses, spires and gables on the Right Bank of the Seine. This was meant to show Parisians what they were leaving behind and what their future could be. In the same way, Parisians and others came to marvel at the Orientalist fairyland of souks, coffee-houses, minarets and harems that had been constructed to depict French colonial acquisitions; they left breathless at the other, alien worlds that Paris had conquered, and infused with an even deeper sense of patriotism and pride in their nation.

Or at least that was the intention. It was undoubtedly true that life in Paris and the provinces had improved immeasurably since the mid-part of the nineteenth century. The country as a whole was richer than it had ever been before and even the meanest peasant or most wretched city-dweller had access to work, food, wine, decent clothes and a reasonable standard of health and hygiene. Paris still had its slums – indeed they seemed to be growing and spreading as the city extended beyond its nineteenth-century boundaries towards the unknown and uncharted areas known as *la banlieue* – but it also contained the promise of social advancement, or at the very least the prospect of a job and a full belly for most. Political passions, although as virulent as ever, were temporarily contained in the Dreyfus debate, which, fierce and divisive as at it was, never seemed likely to arouse the revolutionary fervour that had so regularly convulsed the capital in the past hundred years.

Instead, Parisians gave themselves to the arts of leisure and consumerism. The city was a temple to the new world of commercial advertising, with whole streets devoted to the passive delights of wandering through a forest of publicity materials, which incited the spectator to 'lécher les vitrines' ('go windowshopping', or literally, 'lick the glass display cases'). Among the popular new forms of entertainment was the cinema, firmly established as one of the great attractions of Paris by the end of the 1890s. The cinema was rivalled in popularity only by the popular theatre of the boulevards, which, with the likes of the comic playwright Georges Feydeau leading the way, exulted in high and low farce. By 1913, there were already thirty-seven cinemas in Paris, including the Pathé Cinema at Les Invalides, which claimed the largest screen in the world; by 1920, there were more than 200 cinemas in central Paris, often built to elaborate and grandiose designs to capture the 'new spirit' of the age (a remarkable leftover from this era, Le Grand Rex, is still a busy commercial film theatre, standing at the corner of boulevard Poissonnière). No less extraordinary was the construction of the Paris metro, which was started in 1898 and the service fully functioning by 1900 (the first line ran from Vincennes to Porte Maillot, including several stops along the Champs-Élysées for visitors to the exhibition).

Work on the metro had been much delayed as the city authorities had squabbled over finance for the project, losing ground and prestige to

London and New York, which both had underground train systems in operation by the 1870s. The Paris métro distinguished itself from the outset, however, not only as a feat of engineering but as a miracle of design. This was the work of the architect Hector Guimard, who was awarded the contract for the project in 1898 and who was a slavish and passionate follower of the fashion then called *le style moderne* and now known as art nouveau. The central tenets of this design philosophy were to oppose the cold impersonality of monumental art and to strive for an artistic unity defined by the individual artist. To this extent, the art nouveau movement in France and Europe (where it was known as *Jugendstil* in Germany and *Modernista* in Spain) had much in common with, and indeed had been directly influenced by, the English Arts and Crafts movement spearheaded by John Ruskin and William Morris. Guimard's famous designs for metro stations had the flowing contours of plant life as their central motif and as such were in direct opposition to the stark, mathematical lines of the Haussmannized city. Parisians welcomed them at once, admiring the way in which they gave the life of the city streets an almost domestic sense of harmony and individuality. The uses of the new technology encapsulated by the metro were similarly Utopian – Parisians imagined a future city of easy speed and unstoppable momentum – but its direct application was hazardous. In 1903, the newly installed line between Étoile and Nation short-circuited after a surge of power. At least eighty-four people were entombed in the dark, smoky tunnels, poisoned by gas, their corpses unburied and gnawed at by rats.

Such accidents were easily shrugged off in the name of progress and the promise of a new century when human happiness would be achieved through rational and scientific principles. This vision of the twentieth century had been formulated in Paris as far back as 1863 in Jules Verne's novel *Paris au vingtième siècle* ('Paris in the Twentieth Century'). These days, Verne is popularly known as the writer of adventure stories and the father of modern science fiction, whose tales are generally of a positive and positivist bent. He had, however, serious literary ambitions (his works are packed with allusions or quotations from the likes of Hugo, Baudelaire, Diderot and Edgar Allan Poe, among others) and could be suitably gloomy about the fate of mankind. This was the principal reason why Verne's publisher Hertzel rejected the manuscript of *Paris au vingtième siècle* – it presents a future dream of the city in the 1960s as a loveless dystopia organized around the needs of capital and industry. However, the book does contain strange truths: it predicts, among other things, the fax machine, modern transport systems and the fact that Parisian writers in the 1960s would devote themselves to penning unreadable books which even their authors could not decipher.

To view the future as a potential catastrophe was indeed a powerful heresy in the nineteenth century. This was most markedly the case at the turn of the century when Parisians of all classes seemed to have an uncontrollable need to believe that the future had to be better than their own immediate past.

Lords of Terror

The reverse side of the relentless optimism that fuelled the 1900 exhibition and gave rise in the papers to talk of a new Parisian 'golden age' was an increased fascination with crime in the city. Much of this was associated with Montmartre, which enjoyed a dual role as the city's 'pleasure' centre and the focus of all transgressive activity, from revolutionary politics to commercial sex.

Paris had never been short of celebrity criminals from the days of Villon or Cartouche. From the Enlightenment onwards, the most famous criminals were admired for their 'genius' and their ability to outwit bourgeois authorities. This tradition began properly with the gangster and police informer Eugène Vidocq, notorious in the 1790s for his numerous disguises and talent for blending in with all social milieux, from high society to the *canaille* of the slums. In 1836, Pierre-François Lacenaire, self-styled poet, assassin and dandy, bewitched a court with his rhetoric and style, declaring himself above the law and the enemy of all society (he was none the less convicted of killing a transvestite and his mother and a botched bank robbery). Lacenaire would later reappear as one of the central figures in Marcel Carné's 1945 film *Les Enfants du Paradis* ('The Children of Paradise') and was the most likely prototype of the master criminal Vautrin who appears throughout Balzac's *Comédie humaine* (covered in Chapter 29).

There were dangers in the city which were much more real and threatening, however. One of these was an apparent surge in crime led by organized and semi-organized gangs of street thugs called *apaches* (the name was inspired by the appearance of Buffalo Bill at the 1900 exhibition). These were soon the stuff of legend, known for the red scarves they wore around their necks, the knives they carried in their pockets, their capacity for drink and a tendency to knock their women about (apparent in the *apache* dance that lingers forlornly in a heavily diluted form in the present-day tourist cabarets of 21st-century Montmartre).

In reality, these were working-class toughs who avoided work and revenged themselves on a bourgeois world with theft and violence. Their aggression was also real enough. A report in the US-based *National Police Gazette* of 21 October 1905 describes the boldness and techniques of the *apaches*, including the celebrated *coup de Père François*, which involved half strangling the victim before pillaging his pockets. The reporter also notes how the *apaches* had once been the stuff of songs celebrating the 'eccentric' edges of the city, but had now become a menace in the centre of Paris:

For a full hour the Place de la Bastille in central Paris was a bloody ground on which the police did the bleeding. They fight with knuckle dusters, called 'American punches', with blackjacks, leaded canes, sword canes and revolvers. But their really favourite weapon is the long, thin, sharp knife called the 'zarin'. Which they handle with a ripping stroke. An American darky stranded in Paris, who saw the battle from the windows of a wine shop, where he worked, quit that day without asking for his wages. 'Dat's too sporty for Dan,' he confided to a friend, 'dah kick 'em in dah groin wit dah big boots and tramps on dah haid and shoot and slash scandalous.' Should a battle half this size take place in the Park Row district of New York – or should we say Union Square? – the papers of all Europe would ring with the tidings. Here the incident will be forgotten because, for one thing, there is a new one every day.

The fight is reminiscent of the street battles that have been taking place on a regular basis between rival gangs of *banlieusards* in Les Halles and Charles de Gaulle-Étoile, terrifying shoppers and tourists in the twenty-first century. Indeed, when it comes to containing the violent energies of those excluded from the commercial spectacle of the city, little seems to have changed over the past hundred years (including the policeman's ludicrously clichéd rendition of Black American speech).

The *apaches* in fact belonged to an old tradition of neighbourhood gangsters and thugs dating back to the early Middle Ages. In the new century, Paris was more shocked by the likes of the 'Bande à Bonnot' ('Bonnot's gang'), the so-called 'tragic bandits' who brought crime up to date by carrying out for the first time ever bank raids with automatic weapons and the newly invented motor car. The gang were also explicitly political, declaring themselves to be anarchists and winning admiration from disaffected workers for the bold glamour of operations such as the robbery of the bank of the Société Générale in rue Ordener in 1911. The leader of the gang, Jules Bonnot, a native of Montbéliard, had washed up in Paris via stints in Geneva, Lyons and a brief period as the driver for Arthur Conan Doyle in London. He was an avowed enemy of bourgeois society and justified his killings as 'revolutionary propaganda'.

Bonnot was finally cornered by police in a 'safe house' in Choisy-le-Roi. Thousands came from all over Paris to watch the five-hour siege, which ended with Bonnot's quasi-heroic death, with the house dynamited and his escape into a hail of police bullets. He was rumoured to have cried out the word 'Salauds!' ('Bastards!') as he was finally gunned down. Bonnot was soon installed as a Parisian folk-hero, whose influence filtered down through the twentieth century (during the attempted insurrection of May 1968, for example, an amphitheatre in the occupied Sorbonne was named after the doomed anarchist, while his activities were brought back to life that same year in a film starring Jacques Brel).

Rising Tides

It rained steadily through the winter of 1909 and 1910. By 29 January, the waters of the Seine had risen to some eight and a half metres, the highest ever recorded level, at least since the last great flood of 1740. The swollen river could not be contained for long; the courtyard of the École des Beaux-Arts and the railway station at the Quai d'Orsay were both impassable. It was not long before the metro, the pride of the modern city, was paralysed along with all other forms of transport. Bridges were under water and the population was terrified by press reports of deadly crocodiles swimming out of the zoo. When the waters finally receded in the spring, over 200,000 homes had been wrecked. The cost to the city's self-esteem as well as its pocket was enormous.

That same year saw the return of political passions which had long been dormant. In 1905, a decree had been finally issued which separated the Church from the state. The result of this was to harden opposition between Right and Left, already bitterly separated by the Dreyfus affair, over where ultimate authority lay. Most damagingly, the army was effectively taken over not by hard-headed professionals who had an essentially secular vocation, but by practising Catholics on the Right.

The Left accordingly preached a virulent anti-militarism which resulted in an overall weakening of the army to the tune of some 100,000 troops. German adventures in Morocco in 1905 and 1911 rattled the government, but life in Paris for most people still went on, oblivious to the dangers from the east or the illusory nature of the prosperous society that complacent Parisian politicians claimed as a model for the world.

For the most part, Parisian political life was thoroughly stagnant. Each successive government from the turn of the century onwards was primarily concerned with scoring points and playing off the domestic tensions aroused by the Dreyfus affair rather than with building on the economic growth that had occurred almost by accident at the end of the nineteenth century, or with forging a coherent foreign policy. Although the parties of the Right had only a limited mass appeal, fear of internal agitation – with memories of the Commune never far away – and the twin demons of xenophobia and anti-Semitism guaranteed a conservative consensus that stifled any truly radical voices on the Left and encouraged complacency in the centre and elsewhere. France was sleepwalking towards disaster.

Inventing the Twentieth Century

The greatest changes taking place in Paris were therefore neither in politics nor engineering but in the arts and particularly in literature. In music, the first performances in April 1902 of Debussy's opera *Pelléas et Mélisande*, based on the Symbolist play by Maurice Maeterlinck, introduced a new spirit of adventure into the traditionally linear structures of operatic theatre. Initial responses ranged from the lukewarm to the openly hostile (Maeterlinck himself was so incensed by Debussy's choice of the Scots-American singer Mary Garden that it actually provoked him to violence), but in its rich and elaborate forms, although in debt to Symbolism, the opera also represented an original way of conceiving musical theatre as not merely spectacle but living poetry, and as such it was a genuinely new departure. A less portentous but no less subversive note was struck in the popular novel, with the appearance in the same year of Colette's *Claudine à Paris*, which recounted the mildly Sapphic adventures of Colette herself, then one of the most energetic and daring lesbians at large in a male city which still did not really believe such exotic creatures existed.

In the 1900s, Parisians fell in love with a new anti-hero. This was the fictional character Fantômas, created by the writers Pierre Souvestre and Marcel Allain. Fantômas first appeared in a series of short stories published in a monthly serial by Arthème Fayard. The Parisian public devoured these tales in which the elegant and debonair genius (Fantômas was rarely depicted without a morning suit, top hat, cane and mask) sowed terror in the city for the sheer sake of it. His evil antics included placing sulphuric acid in the perfume dispensers at a luxury Parisian department store, sending a horde of plague-carrying rats on to an ocean liner, murdering an unfaithful disciple by hanging him as a clapper in a huge bell and allowing him to be smashed to pieces and showering the streets below in blood. Fantômas's daughter, 'la belle Hélène', was of uncertain sexuality, wore men's suits and smoked opium day and night. Unforgettable scenes from these tales included Fantômas stripping the gold from the dome of Les Invalides, wrecking passenger trains and steamships, or pursuing a carriage driven through the streets of Paris at full gallop by a hollow-eyed corpse.

Fantômas was also an early hero of the Parisian cinema, appearing in a series of five films made by Louis Feuillade in 1913 and 1914 (and also a television series in the 1970s). Crowds flocked to watch a celluloid Fantômas perform outrageous and sinister tricks on the plodding bourgeoisie and police, who were constantly on his trail. Part of his appeal to readers (and viewers) was that these adventures took place in a recognizably Parisian setting. Mostly, this was in the eastern or northern edges of the city, in Belleville, Ménilmontant or Montmartre. Favoured locales included the rue de Mouzaïa, rue Compans, Place Clichy, Barbès-Rochechouart, Place Pigalle, rue des Saules and Place du Rhin. By placing the fantastical Fantômas in these ordinary settings, which could be visited by Parisians any time of the day or the night, the authors introduced a theatrical quality into the mundane décor and patterns of everyday life. It was this opposition, as well as the disguises and implausible plots and escape plans, that fascinated a present and future generation of Parisian avant-gardists, from Max Jacob to the Surrealists. The poet Robert Desnos described Fantômas as the 'grey-eyed spectre, who arises from silence'.[2] A Fantômas paperback lies on a café table in a 1915 still life, *Parisiana*, by Juan Gris.

For a variety of reasons, literary commentators have often regarded 1913 as the turning point in the early history of the century, the year when the twentieth century really began. This was the year in which Marcel Proust's *Du côté de chez Swann* ('Swan's Way') was published, André Gide was putting the finishing touches to his first masterpiece, *Les Caves du Vatican* ('The Vatican Cellars'), and the poet Guillaume Apollinaire saw the publication of his collection *Alcools*. Each of these works seemed to announce a new sensibility that prized the subjective vision of the individual over the fixed and immobile narratives of the nineteenth century, which, from Hugo to Zola, were predicated on the omniscient presence of the author (this 'new spirit', in part at least, temporarily blinded readers to the homosexuality of Gide and Proust). For Léon-Paul Fargue, the meaning of modernity was to be literally in the streets of Paris: the city was a dream world made up of intricately nuanced and related sensations. This way of seeing was close to Symbolism, but Fargue was also in real life an indefatigable walker in the city and his Paris is intensely alive with what Baudelaire called the 'anarchy of detail' to be found in a city street. This is Fargue in one of his best prose poems on the city: 'On the pavement swilling with brothels, their windows opaque, whores apparently on guard before an appalling wall of advertisements cross themselves when the lightning flashes. The blaring strip of light of a music tavern illumines waiting phantoms . . . ragged image of an evening.'[3]

For Guillaume Apollinaire, modernity meant doubting the authenticity of all previous literary forms of expression. The poems of *Alcools*, like the Cubist paintings that were their direct contemporaries, did not describe the world in conventional terms (or in the case of painting, depict the world with representational figures) but instead tried to render the world in a new way. Apollinaire, born in Rome to a Polish mother, none the less centres his vision on Paris, where he had arrived penniless in 1898. The cityscape he evokes as a newcomer to the city is no longer recognizable as the homely clutter of 'Old Paris'. Rather, Apollinaire describes a city of margins, industrial landscapes, wrecked buildings, workers' quarters: each section of the city alive with its own ghosts and its own myths:

> Now you are walking in Paris all alone among the crowd
> Bellowing herds of buses roll past you The anguish
> Of love catches at your throat
> . . . Today you are walking in Paris The women are stained with
> Blood It was and would I could forget it was at the twilight
> Of beauty[4]

All of this is determinedly anti-realistic and constructed with reference to myth and the geography and history of Europe and indeed Christendom. Paris is the capital of modernity but, as demonstrated not much later in T. S. Eliot's *The Waste Land* (1922), the very meaning of modernity is called into question.

Most crucially, the hallucinatory energy and distorted logic of the poem perfectly captures the mood of French political and cultural life at the end of the 'beautiful epoch', when the world was spinning all too quickly off its axis, and Paris, once again, heading towards war.

36. New Wars

The arrival of war in August 1914 came as a massive shock to nearly all Parisians. It was as if nobody in Paris had been paying attention to the political strategies rapidly disintegrating across Europe and the dangers of the dubious alliances and game-playing that had been set up to outdo colonial rivals. More to the point, nobody even wanted war or properly understood why it had to be declared. On 31 July, the Socialist leader Jean Jaurès was gunned down as he dined at the Café du Croissant in the rue Montmartre. Jaurès was a noted opponent of militarism, an enemy of France's pact with Russia and a fervent believer that his German Socialist brothers would never again launch a war on France. Jaurès's killing inevitably helped fuel the mounting crisis.

The papers and ordinary Parisians in cafés and bars called the outbreak of war *une bavure* ('an administrative cock-up') and grumbled about the stupidity of their leaders. But once Austria had invaded Serbia as revenge for the assassination of the Austrian Franz-Ferdinand, it was as if a madness had been let loose in Europe. Troops were made ready across the continent, as France mobilized as a response to Germany's mobilization, which was in itself a response to Russian advances, made entirely out of fear. In Paris, the population, at first unsure, cheered the first troops out of the Gare du Nord in a gay mood, heedless of the catastrophes that had always come in the wake of such adventures. Some older Parisians remembered 1870, the meals of rat-stew and the bullets, and began to hoard food. Others, exhilarated by the possibility of combat, ran amok in the rue Montorgueil, smashing any shopkeeper's sign with a vaguely 'Teutonic' ring to it: these included the soup-maker Kub in the nearby rue Tiquetonne, whose wares were said to be poisoned. The tailor Yarf, in the same street, hung a flag from his shop declaring that he was really called 'Fray' and was set to join up as soon as possible.[1]

One of the immediate fears of the government in the wake of the declaration of war was a general strike. There had already been several surges of worker discontent in the Paris area in the years leading up to 1914, but the government was unsure whether this was due to legitimate or semi-legitimate trade unionism, anarchism or Communism. Surprisingly, many of even the most anti-government workers were motivated by an atavistic hatred of the enemy, and the fears of revolution dissipated as workers joined up for the Eastern Front, leaving the Gare du Nord or the Gare de l'Est to the sound of a regimental band. There were minor mutinies and attempts at insurrection in the trenches, but military discipline was both harsh and effective.

For all Parisians, the first truly terrifying moment of the war came on 26 August 1914, when German outriders were spotted on the outskirts of Paris and German forces reached the Marne. German cavalry captured the racing grounds at Chantilly and moved towards the city until they could be seen from the Eiffel Tower. The city was seized with panic and hysterical outbursts were common in the streets, in the shops and the markets as it looked as if the dreaded siege of 1870–71 was about to happen all over again.

Paris took to arms. The Eiffel Tower was surrounded by machine-gun nests. Over 300 heavy guns were deployed across the city. The *portes* were barricaded and cattle and other provisions brought into the heart of Paris. As in earlier centuries, the city was swarming with refugees, many of them foreigners whose heavy accents made them suspect as German spies. On the 2 September, the government left the city for Bordeaux. Another train carried off the gold reserves of the Bank of France to a secret location. In bourgeois circles, the family silver was buried in gardens. Parisians of all classes flocked to offer up prayers once again to Sainte Geneviève for a miracle to save them from the monsters from the east.

It was clear to all military minds that Paris could not stand another siege. What was left of the old fortifications of 1870 was in a bad state of disrepair and visibly disintegrating. The population of the city had swollen to the extent that sufficient food could not be guaranteed for even a few weeks. There was no option for General Galliéni – the veteran commander of the French forces in Paris, who had been captured at Sedan and lived through the Commune – but to launch a counter-offensive. Yet the questions remained: when and how?

The so-called 'Miracle of the Marne' that saved the city was really a combination of accident and good fortune. The first piece of luck was the discovery on the body of a German cavalry officer of a bloodstained map of the German plan of attack. French intelligence seized on this and took it to Galliéni, who worked out that the German advance intended to swerve to the east, missing Paris, and cornering the remaining French forces against the Swiss border. Most crucially, this left an important section of the

German flank exposed. Galliéni determined to hit this hard and on 6 September commandeered the entire Parisian taxi fleet to move his troops to the most vulnerable German positions. The manoeuvre saved the city, slowing down and eventually turning the German advance. Few Parisians were able to forget, however, that for all their undoubted bravery, many of the Parisian *taxistes* had still insisted on full fares for transporting men to this moment of heroic self-sacrifice for the nation.

'Century of speed'

The feverish mood in Paris leading up to and during the initial stages of the war is caught perfectly in the opening pages of Louis-Ferdinand Céline's epic novel *Voyage au bout de la nuit* ('Journey to the End of the Night'). This book was published to great acclaim in 1932 and won the previously unknown Céline a reputation as the 'new Zola'. Céline's real name was in fact Destouches and he made a living as a medical doctor in the poorer parts of northern Paris, where he acquired both a deepened sense of compassion and a hatred for all forms of state power. Having been wounded in the trenches (where he had earned medals for gallantry), Céline was a virulent pacifist with a visceral antipathy towards war. This position would later be compromised when, in the 1930s (as we shall see in Chapter 38), he published lengthy (and beautifully composed) tracts against the Jews and the 'Anglo-Saxons', arguing in favour of a Greater Europe under Hitler.

The *Voyage* begins with a furious and hilarious conversation between two medical students, the main character Bardamu and Arthur Ganate (who swiftly disappears from view), in a café on the Place Clichy in the summer of 1913. Both of them have anarchist leanings, typical of the period, and they try to outdo each other in denunciations of the state, God, capitalists and warmongers, reading aloud anti-capitalist, anti-war poems. 'That's how it all started,' says Bardamu. 'I'd never said nothing. Nothing.' Ganate launches into a generalized attack on the complacency and torpor which characterized Paris in the years before the war:

'The people of Paris always look busy', he says, 'but in fact all they do is walk around from morning to evening. The proof of this is that when the weather is no good for walking, too hot or too cold, they're all inside drinking café-crèmes or bocks. That's the way it is. Century of speed? Where's that then? Great changes, they say! How so? Actually nothing has really changed. They continue to admire each other and that's your lot! And there's nothing new about that either. Maybe there's a few little words which change, and not many of them either. Two or three here and there . . .' Proud of having declared these useful truths, we sat back, delighted with ourselves, looking at the ladies in the café.[2]

No twentieth-century writer has been able to better Céline's grasp of the elliptical, staccato and untranslatable rhythms of everyday Parisian speech. With the same pace and the jerky, speeded-up illogic of an early silent film, the scene at the café shifts imperceptibly to 1914. Suddenly Bardamu, who a page earlier has poured scorn on the French nation, signs up to throw his life away in the trenches. He is 'caught like a rat'. He watches in horror as a colonel's head is blown off, the blood in his severed neck 'gurgling like warm jam'. The shell-shocked Bardamu is sent back to wartime Paris, which is now shrouded in darkness and where ordinary life has been abolished and replaced by a permanent mood of unreality which pervades the city.

The confusion at the front was indeed matched by the volatile moods of the city during this time. For most of the war, Paris was both a city under siege – although this was nowhere near the level of pressure that the Germans had exerted in 1870 – and a point of retreat for wounded, shell-shocked and exhausted troops as well as refugees from all over France. The city was also caught up in a wave of anti-German hatred which reached even the most sophisticated and urbane sections of the intelligentsia. André Gide, a disciple of Nietzsche among others, called the Germans 'brutish'. Marcel Proust wrote of 'devious' Prussians. The former Symbolist Octave Mirbeau, himself no stranger to arcane sexual practices, described Berlin homosexuality to scandalous effect. At less elevated levels of the city, ordinary Parisians spoke of the hideous pig-faced *Boches*, baby-killers and cannibals, who represented the antithesis of civilized values. The theatres, cabarets and cinemas were all packed whenever they showed anti-Hun propaganda. The Opéra-Comique cancelled a performance of Puccini's *La Bohème*, an opera suspected of pan-German sympathies. Even children participated in the anti-German fervour; the popular cartoon characters called the 'Pieds Nickelés' blew up German arms factories while Bécassine, a sweet but dim Breton schoolgirl, nursed the wounded. On the boulevards, street vendors sold toy soldiers, flags, rings and scarves made by the *poilus* ('conscripts') from spent ammunition. Easter eggs and yule logs were made in the shape of cannons, and groups of fresh-faced innocents at school sang out loudly anti-German propaganda such as 'La chasse aux barbares' ('The hunt for barbarians') and 'Culot d'Alboche' ('The cheek of the Boche').[3]

As the pressure on the city relented, life in Paris picked up something of its usual rhythm. There were shortages – mainly of oil, butter and other staples – but nothing to compare with the previous attacks on the city. The population was, above all, hungry for news, and all magazines and journals saw their sales and circulation rise during this period. The bestseller was *Le Parisien*, but the appetite for newspapers was so voracious that crowds would often gather at the intersection of boulevard Poissonnière and rue Montmartre to grab the first editions of whatever was available (this was where most newspapers had their offices and printing presses). Parisians did not take easily to censorship, however, and they were amazed and outraged in January when, in the name of secure intelligence, the papers did not report on houses and buildings bombed by the Germans. Other falsifications, such as the claim made by *Le Matin* that no one served more than a week in the trenches, were so obvious and easily rebutted that they presented a serious challenge to the government's credibility. At one stage, the government even banned fortune tellers and astrologers from making bad predictions. The satirical journal *Le Canard enchaîné* (a rough equivalent of *Private Eye*) was established in 1916 as a direct response to this heavy-handed approach.[4]

The atmosphere in the streets was notable for its disorientating mixture of sombre intensity and frenetic gaiety; the boulevards, cafés and theatres were always busy with men on leave and women eager to comfort them, but there was also a desperate air about seeking pleasure only a few hours from the savagery of the front. On 21 February 1916, the worst battle of the war began, at Verdun. This would last until December that same year and cost over 400,000 French lives. Yet behind the lines in Paris there was a calm, even smug air. Most of the bad news from Verdun was suppressed and soldiers returning from the front were shocked to find a city that was all but fully functioning, offering food, drink, sex and fun. The baking of croissants had been briefly banned in 1915 – to save on precious butter – and the government instructed citizens to do without meat for at least one day a week (few heeded this stricture), but black-market goods and profiteering were rife. Many soldiers were bitter about this state of affairs, but this did not stop them taking advantage of the pleasures and comforts of the capital for the short time available to them.

The effects of the war really started to bite in the winter of 1916–17, in the wake of the massacre of Verdun and as supply lines to the city became ever more strained. The battle of Verdun was announced as a great and glorious victory, but too many of its survivors knew the truth about the squalor, the mud and the endless lines of corpses mowed down in what was no more than 10 square kilometres of wasteland. The winter that year was unusually cold and harsh and, as Parisians tasted for the first time some of the privations of the rest of France, the bad news from the front introduced a new edge of despair into the war effort. The defeatist arguments from Left and Right now started to grow louder and gather pace. Most strident of all was the voice of the journal *Bonnet Rouge*, which had first supported the war but had long since espoused pacifism. In 1917, it was revealed that the paper was in the pay of German backers who were also encouraging it to support the various mutinies that were breaking out across the front. The scandal deepened when the radical minister Louis Malvy was unmasked as a key supporter of the paper's line and directly linked to its German financiers. Malvy was charged with treason, but narrowly escaped the death sentence handed out to his accomplices in betrayal.

The political will in Paris was visibly disintegrating, but the most dangerous moments were yet to come. This was in early 1918 when, as Russia retreated from the war, the German forces were able to concentrate their efforts directly on Paris. Under General Ludendorff, the German armies marched to the west, ripping through British lines and advancing swiftly and apparently inexorably upon the city.

Paris was now also under steady bombardment from the aeroplanes known as 'Gothas' and soon the heavy cannon nicknamed Big Bertha. Parisians could be blown up in the heart of the city and with no warning. On Good Friday, a shell was aimed at the church of Saint-Gervais during Mass. It killed seventy-five people in one blow; over a hundred more were injured (the church is still marked by shrapnel). For the first time since 1914, Parisians started talking about leaving the city. Only the steady hand of Georges Clemenceau, who had lived through the Commune and who at seventy-six years of age had assumed command of the city, was able to calm Parisian fears.

The war turned in the summer, as the momentum of the Ludendorff advance came to a halt. With the support of the Americans, new to the war and not yet weary of its rigours, and the British, who on 8 August, smashed the German lines, the French broke out of the trap they had been held back in for two years and, under Marshal Foch, suddenly and dramatically advanced. By late October, the German army was shattered and about to fall to pieces. At eleven o'clock precisely on 11 November 1918, the Great War was over.

Interzone

Parisians reacted to the news of the ceasefire with a mixture of relief and jubilation. The first 'total war' of the twentieth century had been devastating for France, but Paris had been spared the worst of its horrors. The city was still intact and had neither been occupied nor destroyed by siege and bombardment. In Paris itself, the morning of 11 November was dank and cold. As the bells started tolling for the Allied victory, the streets began to fill with Parisians from all parts of society and soldiers of all nationalities. The crowds flocked down rue de Rivoli to Place de la Concorde and the National Assembly to see Clemenceau, shaking with emotion, declare victory and pay homage to the dead. This speech was followed by days and nights of furious, drunken celebration.

The euphoria was short-lived, however. The war had wrecked the lives of millions. One and a half million Frenchmen had been killed – more than any other country had ever lost in a conflict in human history. Widows and virgins were plunged into endless, deep mourning. An epidemic of Spanish flu was killing hundreds and thousands more, including the poet Guillaume Apollinaire, who had expired in a feverish delirium only days before the end of the war, believing that the crowds in the streets crying 'À bas Guillaume!' ('Down with Kaiser Wilhelm!') were really calling for his own demise.

Clemenceau's government was, with some justification, worried about the vengeful mood of men returning from the trenches and, with an eye on events in Russia the previous year, decided to keep soldiers under military discipline for at least another twelve months. Rationing continued for the same period and there were continual shortages of fuel and food. The harsh peace terms imposed on Germany by the Treaty of Versailles in 1919 went some way to assuaging public anger in Paris in the short term, although it famously did little to resolve the rancorous disputes that lay at the heart of this and the next war. Even in Paris, the Versailles treaty was regarded with deep scepticism: the day of the signing was marked by a transport strike led by Communists but supported by all the important factions of the dissident French Left, whose ranks were now bolstered by disaffected *poilus* and civilians. The argument of many on the Left was that the war was not really over but had opened up a new period of transition, which logically could only culminate in revolution. The war only had any meaning if it could be seen to have cleared the way for the future. These

'Gargantua', caricature of Louis-Philippe I by Honoré Daumier, 1831.

Aerial view of Paris, *c.*1871, showing public buildings, many of which were destroyed during the Paris Commune.

'The Occupation of Paris, 1814 – English Visitors in the Palais-Royal', English School, nineteenth century.

The bombardment of Paris, German School, *c.*1870.

The siege of Paris, bombardment by the Prussians, 1870–71, French School, nineteenth century.

The construction of the avenue de l'Opéra, Paris, 1st and 2nd *arrondissements*, 1878.

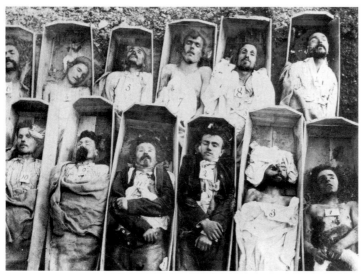

Unidentified dead insurgents of the Paris Commune, 1871.

Barricade on a Paris street during the Franco-Prussian War or during the Paris Commune, *c.*1870–71.

Illustration by Jacques Tardi
from *Voyage au bout de la nuit* by
Louis–Ferdinand Céline, 1932.

André Breton, *c.*1930.

'Une maison close monacale, rue Monsieur-le-Prince (couple s'embrassant)', photograph by Gyula Halász Brassaï, *c*.1931.

Scene from the film *Hôtel du Nord*, directed by Marcel Carné, with Arletty and Louis Jouvet, 1938.

Liberation fighters in Paris, 1944.

French women punished for collaborating, 1944.

A policeman throws tear gas to disperse crowds during student riots in Paris, 17 June 1968.

Riots in Paris suburbs, 28 October 2005.

were arguments which also found a receptive audience in the likes of André Breton, Louis Aragon, Robert Desnos and others, who in just a few years would lead the Parisian avant-garde movements forwards to made their most daring and uncompromising confrontation with the forces of control and order.

The immediate problem for the municipal authorities in Paris was how to reconstruct the city in a way that would restore public confidence and give Parisians some kind of faith in their future. France had squandered more than a quarter of its financial reserves during the war, and it was clear that major investment in heavy industry would be difficult or out of the question. Paris had, in fact, not been terribly damaged during the war, but it was shabby and run down and barely recognizable as the gleaming model city of the *belle époque*. The decision was taken to beautify the city once again – tidying up public spaces, adding street furniture and polishing existing monuments – a far cheaper and more politically expedient option than risking long-term investment and inflationary policies to support it.

The main areas for development were *les fortifs*, the old fortifications around the city that had proved useless in warfare and which since the mid-nineteenth century had provided shelter and home to the marginal, the poor and the dispossessed of the city. The 'Zone', as the old belt around Paris was called, was also the source of much powerful Parisian folklore. This was the home, for example, of the *chiffonniers*, the itinerant rag pickers celebrated by Baudelaire and Walter Benjamin, who lived proud and separate lives away from the city-dwellers below (the precise geographical angle is important here: much of proletarian Paris, from Zola to Céline, is described as gazing down from the heights of the city's edges to the city centre). The Zone was also feared as the home of the legendary and dreaded *apaches*, the working-class hooligans who, even if they did not really exist any more by 1918, were the stuff of a great deal of anti-proletarian propaganda in bourgeois Paris. Notwithstanding, a law was passed in 1919 that imposed a compulsory purchase order on the military (who owned the Zone in name) and opened it up for development.

Many 'Zonards' (inhabitants of the Zone) refused to move out or into the ugly new HBM (*habitations à bon marché* – 'cheap housing') that were being built to accommodate them. Instead, they clung on to their old ways of life, their own dialects. It would take another war to destroy them completely and clear the ground for the construction of the deadly roads and flyovers of the *boulevard périphérique* that now encircles Paris. The Zone of rag pickers, hoodlum 'angels' and poets has long since become a tragic space, populated mainly by dead-eyed whores waiting at the kerbside for their marks.

37. Paris Peasants

The end of the war brought mixed emotions. On the one hand, Parisians were delighted that Alsace and Lorraine had been reclaimed and that the humiliation of 1870 had been wiped away. But as the second decade of the twentieth century drew to a close, it was clear that the victory had been bought at a great price. The war had wrecked a generation. The mood of anger and disaffection was perfectly expressed in Abel Gance's film *J'Accuse!* of 1918, in which the corpses of those killed at the front are brought back to life by a poet and ask why they have been killed. The film's impact was all the more devastating given that many of the slaughtered soldiers were played by real survivors of the war.

The dead could never be replaced, and thousands of Parisian women reconciled themselves to early widowhood or middle-aged virginity. 'Make me still pretty when the boys come back' had been a frequently voiced prayer from young women to Sainte Geneviève: now there were no more young men to come back, and those that did were all too often psychologically damaged or mutilated by bullets and bombs.

On the economic front alone, it would take France several decades more to restore the general quality of life to anything like what it had been at its pre-war level. Politically, only the *grande bourgeoisie* – the professional and élite classes at the top of the social scale – enjoyed any real power. The successive governments that attempted anything like real reform were hamstrung by investors who immediately withdrew holdings in government bonds. The Left and the Right stared each other down in 1924 over a programme set out by the Cartel des Gauches, a moderate Socialist coalition led by Édouard Herriot and Aristide Briand that proposed to revoke one by one the failed policies of the right-wing Bloc National, which had been in charge until then and signally failed to collect any war reparations from Germany. The Cartel des Gauches collapsed in 1926, opposed by capitalist businessmen and undermined by extremist Left factions, who argued revolution instead of reform. Raymond Poincaré was returned as prime minister with a groundswell of centre-right support. The aim was consensus government: in reality, there was little coherence or authority. In this way, France stumbled towards the Depression and the stark polarities of the 1930s.

The Left was also divided over the unfolding adventure in the Soviet Union. The centre-left and moderate alliances clung to the wreckage of the *union sacrée* (the 'sacred union' of all political parties that had held throughout the war, despite the break with the Socialists in the wake of the Russian Revolution of 1917). This left the way open for *Boche*-hating nationalists and other suspect forces to set the political agenda, much to the disgust of old-style liberals such as Clemenceau. The consequence was a bitter division – which would grow deeper and more violent over the coming decade – between those who controlled government and business and a floating coalition of leftist dissidents who saw the war as a Pyrrhic victory and who pressed with increasing determination for much-needed social reform. These were the forces that would regularly clash in the streets of Paris in the 1930s.

Yet, despite these clearly visible divisions in society, everywhere the talk was of liberation. It was as if the war had provided a release for uncontrollable negative energies, which, now discharged, had cleared the way for real progress. It was the firm belief on the Right and the Left that Paris, the world capital of Western civilization, had once again triumphed over the barbarian hordes from the east and would now demonstrate its true potential. In the press, it was a commonly announced shibboleth that Paris would become the capital of the twentieth century as it had been the 'queen of the world' in the previous one.

The most visible change at street level was a shift in the pace of life: this was now a city where everyday life was dominated and accelerated by the motor car, the bus and the metro. In line with this spirit of modernity, women claimed new freedoms (although none of these included the vote): they smoked in public, played sports and lived openly with lovers (some of whom were other women), wore short, angular skirts and shorter, closely trimmed hairstyles. The architecture of the period expressed a naïve belief in geometrical design as the mark of modernity (the overpoweringly ugly monuments at the Musée de l'Homme at Trocadéro are testimony to the appeal of this neo-Fascist aesthetic).

These were, however, only surface changes. For most Parisians in 1919 the future looked decidedly uncertain. The news from Moscow, the new capital of the international working class, often provoked strikes and a slow-burning unrest in the areas of Belleville and Ménilmontant and other working-class districts that the government could do little to control.

Paris had, in truth, not been so badly damaged in the war, but it did look neglected and wounded. Working-class and *petit-bourgeois* Parisians lived in conditions that were hardly any better than those of the 1850s, and in some cases – such as the Faubourg Saint-Marcel, where industrial pollution brought its own devastating illnesses such as lung disease – considerably worse.

As politicians of all political hues argued loftily about speed, technology and the civilizing mission of France, the poor of Paris continued to die as they always had done: unknown and unlamented, usually in pain and with little hope of redemption in this or any other world. The consecration of the Sacré-Coeur in 1919 and the canonization of Joan of Arc in 1920 were taken as a double insult by those Parisians who had been betrayed by the lies of their political and religious leaders.

Revolutions of the Mind

A further consequence of the Great War was to throw into question the very nature of the meaning of 'civilization'. This was not just a question for intellectuals. Those who had been in the trenches and seen the slaughter at first hand never forgot the raw and bloody experiences they had undergone in the name of the so-called higher values of French culture. There was no cult of death in the French military, as there was in the German regiments, and no ordinary French soldier could identify with the quasi-mystical outpourings of the likes of the German warrior-intellectual, who exulted in destruction like a modern-day Teutonic knight.

In contrast, French soldiers returning from the front to Paris felt little patriotism, reserving their energy for hating their military commanders and bosses, and placing their faith in the only true homeland of international labour. The French Left was all too often divided and split into factions, but the bitterness that united workers against all 'civilized' values was real and potent enough. *Untergang des Abendlandes* ('Decline of the West'), by the German philosopher Oswald Spengler – a long and turgid wail of disappointment in Western civilization, predicting its eventual overthrow by hordes from the Far East – became a central text throughout the next few decades from its publication in 1918 for everyone who had been disillusioned by the war.

The word 'civilization' had indeed been a guiding article of faith among Parisians since the Enlightenment and was considered an integral quality in

French life: a non-negotiable value on a par with liberty, equality or fraternity. The Revolution had been made for all in the name of all of these values. The war had, however, cruelly exposed the supposedly noblest values of humanity as a lie. The capitalist 'civilization' of the nineteenth century, the great project of progress and improvement that flowed directly out of the republican belief in man-made Utopias, had in fact produced nothing better than machines for the mass killing of workers to protect vested interests.

This rhetoric was common to all parties of the Left throughout the 1920s. It was also of central importance to the burgeoning avant-garde groups who were beginning to emerge as the most powerful and influential dissi-dent voices in Paris in the aftermath of the Great War. The most strident of these voices during and immediately after the war was that of the Dadaist movement, which had been founded in Berlin and Zurich in 1916 and brought to Paris in 1918. Dada (the name was essentially meaningless, although it could mean anything from a rocking-horse to 'Daddy') was conceived as a negation of the entire system of moral values underpinning Western thought. It opposed reason, order, meaning and hierarchies in equal measure, while being in favour of limitless irrationalism, transgression and anarchy. Dadaism was not meant as an art movement but as a political weapon, carefully calibrated and loaded, and aimed directly at the beating heart of the rotten capitalist order that had murdered so many millions.

When Dada arrived in Paris, in the form of the Romanian poet Tristan Tzara, it found a ready audience among a generation of young men who had grown up despising everything around them. Tzara's *Dada Manifesto 1918*, published in the third edition of the *Dada* bulletin, indeed spoke directly to all those who had lost faith in their homeland and its civilization:

I'm writing this manifesto to show that you can perform contrary actions at the same time, in one continual, fresh breath; I am against action; as for continual contradiction, and affirmation too, I am neither for nor against them, and I won't explain myself because I have common sense . . .

No pity. After the carnage we are left with the hope of a purified humanity . . .

Let each man proclaim that there is great destructive work to be done . . .[1]

Among those who were listening most closely to Tzara were the likes of Louis Aragon, André Breton and Philippe Soupault, all young conscripts who had hated the war and were now setting out on careers as poets and intellectuals with a programme for revenge against the society which had tried to kill them. The Dadaist group such as it was (Tzara and a few allies) held performances, organized debates and published freely. Soupault, Breton and Aragon took it upon themselves to found the journal *Littérature* to publish this new poetry of negation (the editorial line of the journal was firmly *anti*-literature, its title having been sarcastically borrowed from a line by Verlaine, 'tout le reste est littérature' – 'everything else is just literature').[2] As the negative force of Dada burnt itself out, its spirit was carried over into a new movement, *Surréalisme*, founded by Breton, Soupault and Aragon, which would remain faithful to Dada's destructive sensibility but this time with the aim of founding a new society.

The word 'surrealism' had actually been coined in 1917 by Guillaume Apollinaire to describe his proto-Dadaist 'play' *Les Mamelles de Tirésias* ('The Breasts of Tiresias'), which had ended in a mini riot in the tiny space of the Salle Maubel in Montmartre. Under the leadership of Breton, the Surrealists announced a programme for reinventing society according to the laws of the unconscious, replacing reason with desire. Their aim, following from this, was no less than the transformation of the totality of human existence – the revolution of the mind which the poet Arthur Rimbaud had called for a generation earlier amid the wreckage of the Commune.

Appropriately enough, the Surrealists seized on Paris as the battleground for what they saw as the true meaning of modernity, where they would oppose the rational demands of the 'machine civilization' with dreams, poems and plays. In his short but dense compendium of Surrealist experiences in the city, *Le Paysan de Paris* ('The Paris Peasant'), published in 1926, Louis Aragon called for a new mythology of the city that would install it as the capital of a Utopia of untrammelled subjectivity and vision.

This was a ludicrously grandiose demand (and as such entirely typical of the Surrealist group as a whole). But Aragon did none the less compose an effective and convincing picture of Paris in the early twentieth century, a place where capitalism stood opposed by all those who still dared to dream of freedom. Above all, Aragon, like the other Surrealists, understood its human scale to be the defining quality of Parisian urban experience.

The Surrealists were obsessed with images and objects that were just about to become out of date and lose their original meaning or function. They endlessly patrolled the covered passages of the Right Bank (see Chapter 28), now a network of dusty arcades and passageways with greenhouse roofs that ran between Haussmann's great boulevards and which were still cluttered with specialist shops, selling anything from a truss to a mannequin. The passages are still pretty much intact in this form: you can still walk for hours without ever entirely being sure where you are in the city or what you are looking for.

This was indeed the whole point about Surrealist activity as it was theorized and practised in the early 1920s: to create visionary experience out of the everyday; to make the city, in the formula of André Breton and Philippe Soupault, a 'magnetic field' where the detritus of modern life is magically transformed through the power of the individual mind.[3]

Foreigners

One of the best and most famous photographs of André Breton was taken in the early 1920s, and shows him standing in a characteristically imperious pose on the boulevard Montparnasse, just in front of the *bar américain* of the restaurant La Coupole. The photograph is fascinating for a variety of reasons – it is, for example, despite the much-vaunted Surrealist faith in the poetry of the urban dialectic, one of the few portraits of Breton in a Parisian street. It also captures him at the cusp of the Surrealist adventure, before fame and politics had wearied him. It also signals the post-war shift from Montmartre to Montparnasse as the centre of Parisian pleasures and literary politics. Most importantly, the photograph places in close proximity two emblems of Parisian life in the 1920s – the flashy and newly fashionable *bar américain* and a hero of the revolutionary avant-garde. Despite their close and frequent contact, the cultural distance between these two icons could not have been greater: Breton was a determined enemy of all forms of American culture in Paris; the *bar américain*, in contrast, not only was a new invention in the city but introduced new, freewheeling forms of behaviour to Paris (jazz, exotic dances and cocktails) which, even at this early stage in the twentieth century, were identified as the enemies of the city's traditions.

The same was often said of the American exiles who came to Paris during the 1920s. The first Americans had come to France as soldiers in 1917. They took back with them to the United States stories of unbridled hedonism and a thirst for the good life that seemed to be absent from their uptight Protestant homeland. The whores of Paris became Doughboy legends from New York to the most isolated Midwest hamlet. Black Americans noted that they mostly were free from the legal and social constrictions that made the United States seem in comparison a divided and unjust nation. Black musicians who stayed on in Paris after the war found themselves admired for their art and in great sexual demand from *Parisiennes* of all classes who fancied a taste of the exotic. The *Revue Nègre*, starring the singer and dancer Josephine Baker, the orchestra of Claude Hopkins, which included the likes of star saxophonist Sidney Bechet, and dancers such as Joe Alex, who specialized in *danse sauvage*, opened on the Champs-Élysées in 1925 and drew crowds from all across the city, swiftly becoming the great hit of the season. Baker's cabaret on the rue Fontaine enjoyed a similar success in the years to come. In the wake of these successes and the cult of 'negrophilia' that grew out of them, *le jazz nègre* (it was only later transmuted into *le jazz hot*), as Parisians called it, invaded Paris. The main venues were the Caveau de la Gaîté on rue de la Gaîté in Montparnasse or, on the northern side of the city, Le Pigall's or Le Palace. In 1927, the impresario Hugues Panassié introduced Louis Armstrong and Bessie Smith to stunned audiences. In 1928, Duke Ellington and Fats Waller performed for the first time in Paris. A musical review, on the model of the *Revue Nègre*, called *Black Birds*, played to packed houses at the Moulin Rouge (among the audience was the writer, philosopher and erotomaniac Georges Bataille, who thrilled to the vibrant sexuality on display).[4]

It was no accident that this passion for contemporary Black American culture coincided with the avant-garde discovery of 'primitive' African art, promoted first by Picasso and later praised by the Surrealists for its authenticity and wild charm (Philippe Soupault published a text called *Le Nègre* in 1927, while André Breton famously collected African art). However, far from feeling patronized or humiliated, most American Blacks savoured for the first time the taste of artistic freedom and social equality. Over the years, this fact has given rise to the lie that Paris is a 'city without racism'. This indeed was a phrase used repeatedly at the celebrations of the fiftieth anniversary of the liberation of Paris at Place de la Bastille in 2004. It did not seem to mean much to my then neighbours in the rue de Vertbois, asylum seekers from Rwanda and Congo whose decrepit hotel was regularly firebombed or otherwise vandalized by packs of weasel-faced white youths throughout that summer and autumn.

In truth, life for the 5,000 or so blacks, mainly from colonial Africa, who settled in Paris in the 1920s was extremely difficult. Many of these were single men who had been discharged from the French army but had yet to found a family and make their mark in French society. Others were students or servants brought back from the colonies by families who had retired from their postings abroad. Most of the blacks in Paris were workers, brought in to work long hours for low wages at the car factories of Renault or Citroën, the chocolate factory of Amieux or other utilities. Parisian women of all classes flocked to the cabarets on the rue Blomet in the 15th *arrondissement*, which were known haunts of the Caribbean population (there was a certain antagonism between Caribbeans and Africans, who were often seen as colonial lackeys). But the reality was that there was little that was 'exotically sensual' about sleeping in the slums of the Zone and rising at dawn to grind out a living in this way.[5]

The first American exiles to Paris were followed in the early 1920s by a wealthy, upper-class crowd. The motivation was really not so different: the social and pan-sexual freedoms of Paris were much more advanced and widely available than in the United States. Lesbianism was, for example, increasingly fashionable (one of the most famous lesbian bars was Le Monocle in Montparnasse). Bisexuality and homosexuality were practically the norm in other parts of town. The trickle of exiles became a flood in the late 1920s as a generation of young exiles came to Paris to slake their thirst for drink, culture and sex in roughly equal measure. As the Prohibition laws in the United States reached their absurd apogee, Paris became not only a place of refuge for the Bohemian and the dissident but, for many wealthy Americans, the ideal combination of a richly stocked cocktail bar and a brothel. The most famous names included Ernest Hemingway, Scott Fitzgerald, John Dos Passos and Gertrude Stein, whose apartment on the rue de Fleurus functioned as a kind of literary American embassy. The true headquarters of literary American exiles was, however, the bookshop Shakespeare and Company on rue de l'Odéon. This was maintained and run by the formidable Adrienne Monnier, who did not flinch from funding and promoting the works of James Joyce when all English-speaking authorities had condemned them either officially or unofficially as unreadable or obscene.

From the literary exiles' point of view, Paris in the 1920s was a veritable palace of modernism. The centre of all this activity, in painting, literature, drinking and sex, was Montparnasse. No one could quite explain why the avant-garde groups had abandoned Montmartre – whose indigenous life was as lively as ever – and even now there are conflicting theories about demographic shifts (Montparnasse was packed with eastern Europeans, including Lenin and Trotsky at one point), changing tastes in food, drink and manners (Montparnasse had – and indeed still has – some of the most elegant and cosmopolitan bars in Paris at La Coupole or Le Sélect). The most important fact was that Montparnasse seemed physically right for the high point of twentieth-century modernism; Montparnasse is less villagey, not so twee and less nostalgic than Montmartre. It was then, and is now, a place of sharp angles and an uncompromising and determinedly metropolitan culture.

The impact of the American presence in Paris was minimal, and indeed barely if ever noticed by ordinary Parisians of the period. Few Americans spoke anything more than basic French and their engagement with the real culture of the city – as opposed to the in-crowd gossip of a wealthy élite – was mainly limited to waiters, prostitutes or pimps. In this, the American community had all the trappings of a colony, although unlike the French they did not have the empire to match. Among the small number of Americans who made any effort to understand the political and intellectual currents of the period was the young writer Paul Bowles, who was then at the beginning of a career that would take him across the world in pursuit of the feeling of always being the outsider. In Paris, Bowles, at that point still unsure of his sexuality, was introduced to the coterie around Gertrude Stein; his real interest, however, was in the Surrealist adventure and he made efforts to make contact with the group, even publishing a few modest poems in a proto-Surrealist journal called *transitions*. Bowles even managed an interview with the great Tzara, and marvelled at his collection of African masks. To the young writer Tzara looked, however, more like 'a doctor than a surrealist poet'. The disappointment for Bowles was slight, but it was the starting point for his drift towards the genuinely strange and challenging lands of North Africa rather than what he perceived as the empty wastes of grey, intellectual Paris.[6]

38. Darkness Falls

The frenetic gaiety and hedonism of the 1920s lasted only a few years, and were in any case only enjoyed by a privileged élite, most of whom were neither Parisian nor French. Beyond the chrome and steel of fashionable Montparnasse brasseries, the nude models, the alcoholic artists and the free-living exiles, the predominant mood in Paris by the end of that decade was fear. This was most commonly the justified fear of another war. But there were other dangers closer to hand, which seemed to present a no less direct threat to the precarious and hard-won well-being of working-class Parisians.

The most widespread anxiety was inspired by the radical changes in the Parisian population since the turn of the century, which had been accelerated by the war. In the late 1920s and early 1930s, Paris was filling up with many more different races and languages than ever before, even if these were nigh well invisible to well-heeled cultural tourists. At the beginning of the century, France had been a largely underpopulated country and – certainly compared to London or New York – Paris was a relatively spacious and racially homogeneous city. The generation cut down by war had to be replaced somehow and immigrant labour was the easiest and cheapest way to achieve this. It was indeed the only solution. The impact of massive immigration to France was seismic. In Paris in 1921, foreigners represented 5 per cent of the population. By 1930, this figure had doubled. Crime rates soared in the same period and the police delighted in reporting that over a quarter of all crimes in the city were committed by foreigners.

Working-class Parisians, whose way of life and livelihoods were often deemed to be in danger by political parties at both ends of the political spectrum, often felt under a genuine threat. This was partly an instinctive and pointless response to the shifting cultural mix of the city, but also frequently manipulated at street level by political leaders seeking to make a cheap point about the fragility of the French nation. The rise of Fascism in Italy and an uncertain climate across Europe did nothing to allay Parisian fears of an impending collision with the wider forces of capitalism and government. 'The scum of the world is arriving in France and has come to take over Paris' was a view widely aired in the streets and in the papers.

A word that was also widely used in the press at this time was the term *métèque*, a neologism from the ancient Greek word *metic*, which was used for aliens who had no citizenship in a Greek city. It was introduced into French by the right-winger Charles Maurras in the 1890s, at the height of the Dreyfus affair, and it became commonly applied to foreigners in France. Its use was always pejorative if not strictly speaking racist. On the Right and the Left, as the economic crisis deepened in the wake of the Wall Street Crash of 1929, the finger was increasingly pointed at the *métèques* as the cause of all of France's ills. Racist violence was common across the country as well as in Paris: Italians were regularly attacked in Lyons, Moroccans were killed in Marseilles. In Saint-Denis, in the by now hard-core Communist enclave outside Paris, there were loud cheers in bars, cafés and cinemas in early 1931 when the government announced that foreign workers would from now on pay higher taxes than French workers. The slogan 'La France aux Français' ('France for the French') became a catch-all rallying cry for the Left, although Maurice Thorez, the tough and wily Communist leader, would later explain it as merely a formula to rid the country of spies and other foreign agents.[1]

The first sizeable group to settle in Paris during this period were the Italians, many of whom were fleeing Mussolini's regime (the rate of immigration picked up sharply after Mussolini's march on Rome in 1922). These were known as the *fuorisciti* (literally 'those on the outside') by other Italians and they wore their exile as a badge of honour. Others arrived from Italy with an opportunistic eye for the good life and had less noble political views. They all made their way to the north-eastern edges of the city, where they met Russians, Poles, Armenians (most of whom arrived in 1923 fleeing the Turkish massacres) and Jews from all nations. Work was precarious and money was in short supply: still, Paris was a base and a haven. The Italians were not universally welcome – nor were any group of immigrants to Paris, for that matter – but at least they were Latins and perceived as part of a larger family of Romance-language nations, extending from Liguria to Romania, and with therefore some legitimate claim to civilized values.

The largest and most politically contentious group who settled in Paris in the 1920s were the North Africans. Life was particularly difficult for Algerians, who strictly speaking were French citizens but who were treated as *métèques*, or outsiders, on the grounds of race, language and religion. Algerians were generally associated with criminality, as were many southern Italians; the difference between Algerians and Italians, it was argued, was that Italians were only vicious through economic necessity, while Algerians were capricious and sly and given to random violence. Fortunately there were charismatic leaders among the North Africans – Hadj Abdel Kader, for example, was a former Communist who set up the 'Étoile Nord-Africaine', a nationalist movement that supported Algerian workers employed in industry.

North African attitudes in Paris hardened during the Rif War of 1925–7. This was essentially an insurrection against French rule in Morocco led by Emir Abd-el Krim, whose courage and daring quickly made him a hero to disaffected North Africans in the metropolis. The rebellion was crushed by devastating French air power and no small amount of cruelty. The loudest dissenting voices on the Left were those of the Surrealists, who objected to any civilization assuming superiority over another. It was no accident that the year of Abd-el Krim's humiliation also saw the construction of the Grande Mosquée de Paris at the top end of the Jardin des Plantes. This is a genuinely beautiful version of the Hispano-Moorish mode of religious architecture and its courtyard is one of the loveliest spots in Paris to take tea on a hot city afternoon. (It is also treated with contempt by many hard-line Muslims in 21st-century Paris, who see it as a grotesque colonial pastiche and a betrayal of the true freedoms they have yet to gain.)

New Zion

In the early 1930s, most Parisians had never knowingly met a Jew – this was because many Jews preferred to remain in their own enclaves, or had become thoroughly assimilated. But nearly all Parisians had strong views on what was commonly described as the 'Jewish problem' and its many potential solutions.[2]

Most of the political parties of the Right were unashamedly anti-Semitic and indeed, since the 1890s and the Dreyfus affair, wore their anti-Jewish credentials as badges of honour and patriotism. The main organ of debate was the journal *La Libre Parole*, a long-discontinued, formerly Dreyfusard rag, which was relaunched to a wide and enthusiastic, mainly Catholic, readership in 1930. Among its contributors was Georges Bernanos – a former leading light in Charles Maurras's 'Action Française', the key activist movement on the Right – who had turned to a form of melancholy nostalgia for the Middle Ages that included literature condemning the Jews. If not entirely acceptable to many, this version of anti-Semitism was at least understandable as a tradition almost as old as Paris itself, dating at least as far back as the pogroms of Philippe-Auguste.

More troubling, at least for those who proclaimed themselves supporters of the Revolutionary Left and the artistic avant-gardists (these two factions were more or less indistinguishable by 1930), was the virulent growth of Jew-hatred among the working classes and in the parties of the Left – the twin forces that, in the eyes of radical thinkers, were supposed to be shaping the form and content of Parisian modernity. In 1920, a new wave of Jews had arrived in Belleville at the same time as a cholera epidemic: the Communist newspaper *L'Humanité* and the Socialist newspaper *L'Œuvre* were not slow to echo the voice of the worker in the street that Jews were bringing poison and disease to Paris. When they were not portrayed as plague-carriers or vermin, Jews were seen as bloated and greedy capitalists whose only aim was to subdue and exploit the native Parisian worker.

None of this seemed of undue significance in the early years of the 1930s. Hatred of foreigners was a common and usually admirable virtue and Jews were not at first especially hated more than any of the other races who had found their way to Paris. The novelist and diplomat Paul Morand, whose anti-Semitic prejudices had been finely honed by a prolonged stay in Romania, objected just as loudly about the presence of Cubans and Brazilians in Paris. Many other so-called respectable writers, including André Gide, Romain Rolland and François Mauriac, wore their anti-Semitism lightly. It was a prejudice that, as one commentator put it, had an entirely 'innocent air'.[3]

All of this changed in 1933, when Germany fell suddenly and tragically under the dark shadow of the Nazi Party. By the end of that year, more than 20,000 Germans had fled to France. By the end of the decade, over 55,000 exiles from Germany would pass through the country. Most of these were Jews and the term 'refugee' immediately became synonymous with 'Jew'. The successive governments of the Third Republic grew increasingly fragile as pressure on them mounted to defend the French worker and bourgeois against what seemed to be an unstoppable tide of aliens.

'Paris has become the New Zion,' wrote Morand. 'First one, then ten, then a hundred, then fifty thousand.'[4] The word 'invasion' now became common currency in even relatively moderate circles. Another fear was that these new aliens would make an alliance with 'resident Jews' – Jews who were already long established in France – in a conspiracy against the country. Two Jews speaking Yiddish near the Gare de l'Est were attacked by a mob who claimed they were praising Hitler. Another pair of Jews were nearly battered to death in Belleville by a working-class crowd who accused them of chanting 'Long Live Hitler! Long Live Germany!' in a foreign tongue. When the novelist Louis-Ferdinand Céline, now famous as a bestselling author, produced in 1938 his long (and brilliantly written if thoroughly evil) diatribe *Bagatelles pour un massacre* it was hailed as great if deliberately provocative. This text is a torrential outpouring of sneering, sarcastic venom directed against Anglo-Saxons and their paymasters the evil Jews. It is ferociously anti-Jewish and pro-Nazi. Even some seventy-odd years on from its publication, it has lost little of its power to disgust the reader. Yet on its publication it was met mainly as a compendium of common sense and wit from a master writer. 'War for the bourgeoisie was shitty enough,' wrote Céline, 'but now war for the Jews! . . . half-negroid, half-Asiatic, mongrel pastiches of the human race whose only desire is to destroy France.'[5]

Riots and Conspiracies

Such nihilistic passions could hardly be held in check by any government and there was a certain sense of inevitability when, in February 1934, they spilled over on to the streets of the capital in days and nights of street-fighting that were the most dangerous moments any government had known since 1871.

The background to these events was an increasing disillusionment with the short-lived government of Camille Chautemps provoked by a long-running affair known as the Stavisky scandal. Between 1932 and 1933, there had been five different governments but little change in the personnel, who were uniformly as cynical as the public they were elected to serve. Serge Stavisky himself was no politician but a financier who was variously alleged to be of Hungarian, Polish or Romanian background, and certainly Jewish (he was in fact the son of a Ukrainian Jewish dentist). He was known to have close links with many prominent figures in the worlds of property, politics and the law, and in 1933 came under police investigation for alleged corruption.

The rumours and allegations turned out to be true but the police investigation was mired in incompetence, and in the press and on the streets it was argued that the police themselves were party to the web of evil woven by the high-living Stavisky, who was, it emerged, not only a hated *métèque* but also a Freemason. The Chautemps government fell at the end of January

1934, having barely survived two months, to be replaced by a coalition led by Édouard Daladier that proclaimed republican unity. The Parisian public were by now heartily sick of all forms of elected government, however. The stage was set for a dramatic confrontation between forces on the Right and the Left, who both believed that a strong and steady hand was needed to steer France away from conflict with Germany and disaster. Memories of the *bavure* that led to the carnage of the First World War were never far away.

Leading the way on the Right was a loose coalition of *ligues* ('leagues'), none of whom were strictly 'Fascist' in the terms set by Mussolini in Italy and who had little in common with the revolutionary ideologues of the Nazi Party in Berlin. The *ligueurs* were indeed an echo of the older Catholic League that had brought so much agitation to Paris during the Wars of Religion (see Chapter 16). They included the 'Camelots du Roi', fiercely Catholic and Royalist militants associated with Action Française; 'Jeunesse Patriote', who had a mainly anti-Bolshevik agenda; and 'Solidarité Française', an organization led by the *parfumier* François Coty, whose members marched around in a neo-Fascist outfit of blue shirt and black beret in a somewhat camp imitation of Mussolini's crack guards. The most convincing and popular league was the 'Croix de Feu', a group of war veterans led by Colonel Casimir de la Rocque whose only stated aim was to clear out the corruption at the heart of the French Republic in the name of the common soldier.

It was de la Rocque who co-ordinated the other leagues into a march on the National Assembly on the 6 February, ostensibly to demonstrate against the weakness and instability of government and its corruption as demonstrated by the Stavisky affair. Stavisky had by now committed suicide – or been 'suicided': no one knew for sure – but his ghost was still causing trouble.[6]

There had been skirmishes between *ligueurs* and the police throughout January, but the police had applied a relatively light touch to groups whose aims they basically shared (the prefect of Paris, Jean Chiappe, was anyway known to be a crony of Stavisky, a fact that enraged left-wingers). There had been a mini riot at the Gare du Nord over delays on commuter trains and the press was actively looking for a fight, with headlines such as 'End of the Regime' and 'Time for the Necessary Purge!' But still the mood on the late afternoon of 6 February, as distinguished and be-medalled veterans led the first waves of *ligueurs* across Place de la Concorde, was relatively calm. For two hours or more, the crowd stood still before a lightly armed line of guards, which was all that stood between them and the seat of power. In the days leading up to the demonstration, the press had shouted wildly about government aggression, predicting tanks, machine-guns and squads of savage Negro soldiers who would be sent to run amok among patriotic Frenchmen. Since nothing of the sort happened, or looked likely to happen, the vacuum had to be filled.

The violence came from another source altogether; this was between the most rabid *ligueurs* and factions from all the Leftist parties who had come to protest at 'Fascists' launching a potential *coup d'état*. The police lost control: kiosks and buses were overturned, street lamps turned into weapons, paving stones were once again ripped up and thrown at the forces of order in the name of human dignity. All of a sudden, as the tune of the *Marseillaise* was replaced by the *Internationale*, for a joyous moment it seemed to the rioters of the Left that an insurrection or even revolution might once again be on the cards.

There was of course no such thing. Daladier's government resigned the next day, but despite the demonstrations and counter-demonstrations which erupted sporadically across the city, there was no real, generalized will for a violent transformation. In all, sixteen people had been killed out of a crowd of some 40,000 rioters. Throughout bourgeois Paris, there was as much bemusement as excitement: the real tensions of the city – the class divisions which had not been repaired since the Commune – could not be avoided for much longer.

The Great Illusion

Paris was quickly running out of political solutions to the permanent sense of crisis that paralysed its governments. In the days after the February riots of 1934, the Left was terrified most of all by the spectre of a right-wing coup led by de la Rocque and his 'leagues'. As a response, the Communist Party called for a united front to fight the menace. Surprisingly, the various factions of the Left were able to make common cause and even declared a general strike later that month. In July, the leader of the Socialist Party, Léon Blum, and the leader of the Communist Party, Maurice Thorez, signed an agreement of political unity. The two groups came together most magnificently in a force of nearly half a million, which gathered at the Bastille on 14 July 1935 as a counter-demonstration to the show of strength by Croix de Feu on the Champs-Élysées a mile or so away. Under the

banner of 'Front Populaire', Socialists and Communists launched a movement with the slogan 'Peace, Bread, Freedom'. There had been rumours
of civil war, but as the Red Flag flew once again, the talk was rather of
revolution – this time for keeps.

The historic moment arrived less than twelve months later when the
Front Populaire swept to power in the May elections of 1936. This was a
bloodless coup, but Parisians were not slow to understand its significance.
The cries of 'Vive le Front Populaire!' immediately gave way to 'Vive la
Commune!' and some 400,000 Parisians flocked to the Mur des Fédérés at
Père-Lachaise to salute the slaughtered Communards they saw as their true
ancestors.

Everything changed in France more or less overnight. A maximum
working week of forty hours and paid holidays were introduced for the
first time in the history of Europe. Workers began to sense that at last they
were in control. The problem was that all too often they did not understand
what they were in control of. The usual bargaining weapon was the strike.
Just a few weeks after the election of the Front Populaire government, a
series of strikes spread across the country, bringing production in important
military and civilian factories to a halt and threatening to inflict more
damage on the economy than even the most corrupt minister could achieve.
The strikes, which were often festive and drunken occasions, did not stop
even when government conceded to workers' demands and despite stern
warnings from Thorez to his own Parisian Communists.

Still, much of the disorder was genial – workers were as likely to sing
a popular hit such as 'Auprès de ma blonde' as the *Internationale* during a
demonstration – and working-class Parisians delighted in the new concept
of leisure. Folk memories of the Front Populaire usually conjure up images
of cycling trips to the countryside, expeditions by train to the sea, huge
soccer crowds, Sunday picnics with wine and flirting and, above all and at
last, a sense of dignity for the working population. There were new products, such as sun-tan lotion by l'Oréal or the fizzy drink Orangina, which
brought what once were luxury goods into the hands of the masses. Paris
was declared a workers' paradise on a par with Moscow.[7]

It was of course no more than an illusion, and it was not long, as inflation
and depressed wages began to bite, before the workers' demands were
creating real hardship for the workers themselves. The right-wing press,
ever alert to the 'Red Terror' in Paris, began publishing cartoons of workers
raping rich old ladies in the name of 'rights'. Fear returned as the dominant
leitmotiv of everyday life. As Franco lay siege to Madrid, it was rumoured

that de la Rocque was plotting to take Paris. The anti-Semitism that had destroyed Stavisky transferred itself to Blum, a Jew and a vociferous supporter of Dreyfus who – again it was rumoured – was planning to wreck France and take refuge with his co-conspirators, the deadly and hypocritical English. The gutter press was alive with the wildest allegations, which no one dared refute or challenge in case the attacks became worse. The same press also regularly carried dire predictions of a devastating future war that would destroy France once and for all.

In the meantime, most Parisians wanted to have a good time. Despite the rise in unemployment and the slump in wages, the bars, cabarets and restaurants were still packed most of the time. This was also when cinema-going became popular among the masses, not just for the reason that French and American cinema was reaching new heights, but for the ample opportunities for licit and illicit sexual liaison that were offered in the darkened spaces of the elegant and flashy new cinemas on the boulevards. Parisians wanted to laugh or be thrilled and the products of Hollywood, from Fred Astaire to Disney via the Marx Brothers, were always popular. French films were now both popular and intelligent, and movies of the late 1930s such as Julien Duvivier's *Pépé le Moko* or Marcel Carné's *Hôtel du Nord* or *Quai des Brumes* ('Port of Shadows') easily matched any of their Hollywood rivals in popularity and wit.

What characterized these films above all was a sentimental view of Paris that most Parisians could already sense was slipping away from them. Audiences were moved to tears by the singer Fréhel's rendition of 'Où est-il donc?', a hymn to Old Paris sung from the bottom of the heart and from the depths of the Algiers casbah to Jean Gabin's Pépé, a Parisian gangster on the run in Algeria and nostalgic for his home city. They rocked with the laughter of self-recognition when in *Hôtel du Nord*, Arletty – the supreme working-class *parigote* (in contemporary English terms, a cross between the young Barbara Windsor and Twiggy) – disgustedly rebuffs her lover's suggestion that they should move to the countryside for its 'atmosphere' with a famous phrase that has now become part of Parisian folklore: 'Atmosphere? Atmosphere? Listen, mate, do I look like the kind of girl who goes for atmosphere?'

Most controversial of all was Jean Renoir's masterpiece *La Grande Illusion* of 1937, an anti-war parable that was at first censored. It played to packed houses and crowds sang along with great emotion to the scene when the prisoners sing the *Marseillaise*. It was with no sense of irony that many in the crowds did this while making a Fascist salute.[8]

'A rising tide of murder'

It was, however, a common enough position among even so-called patriotic Parisians to declare that they had lost all faith in their own politicians and political systems and to welcome the scourge of Hitler as a necessary purge. This was indeed the position of Céline who, despite the bluster of *Bagatelles* and his other 'pamphlets', expressed the commonly held view that catastrophe was preferable to the present state of inglorious humiliation. There were other intellectuals, more nuanced and finely mannered than Céline (including the likes of the influential novelists and critics Robert Brasillach and Lucien Rebatet), who were lining up on the Nazi side for their own complicated reasons, ranging from an aesthetic sympathy with Fascism, high-bourgeois anti-Semitism or simple leader-worship. Bizarrely, the French translation of *Mein Kampf*, in circulation in Paris at this time, omitted the sections in which Hitler defines France as Germany's historical enemy by force of geography and destiny. The result of this kind of intellectual blindness was a hardening of positions on Left and Right, a process accelerated by the Spanish Civil War, which erupted in 1936, abolishing all possibility of dialogue between two sides now describing themselves as revolutionaries.

Among the few on the Left who sought to penetrate properly the mysteries of Fascism was the writer and critic Georges Bataille, who has since become famous as an influence on the generation of Michel Foucault and who is often described as the bridge between the modernist avant-garde groups of the early twentieth century and the melancholy scepticism of the post-modernist era. At this stage in his career, Bataille was an obscure figure who worked as a librarian and was known, if at all, for a pornographic novella – *Histoire de l'œil* ('Story of the Eye'), published in 1928, a classic tale of adolescent mutual masturbation and murder – and public arguments with the Surrealists, with no less than André Breton himself (who denounced Bataille as a 'sexual pervert').

In 1935, Bataille began writing a novel called *Le Bleu du ciel* ('The Blue of Noon'). The main character in this novel is a disaffected Leftist named Tropmann (a name borrowed from the nineteenth-century murderer who had also fascinated Rimbaud). Tropmann spends most of his time drunk or recovering from the effects of drink in a hallucinatory Europe that seems on the brink of collapse. He travels from London to Paris to Barcelona and finally Trier, the birthplace of Marx, where in a suicidal and necrophiliac frenzy he has sex with his lover Dorothée (nicknamed 'Dirty'), who pretends to be dead in a graveyard as a detachment of Nazi youth march past.

Le Bleu du ciel is still worth reading now as a relatively straightforward premonition of a Europe bent on self-destruction. In particular, Bataille brilliantly captures the sinister, unstable atmosphere in Paris, where the revolutionary Left has been wrecked by splits and is unable to confront the historical forces which are leading civilization to destruction. Tropmann careers drunkenly through Paris, from the most fashionable Montparnasse bars, where the empty chatter of intellectuals is a kind of white noise that makes him feel sick, to the lowest brothels where he seeks self-annihilation in a toxic mist of whisky and whores.

Bataille argued that Fascism was a religious rather than a strictly political problem. To this end, in 1935, with his friend the artist André Masson, he founded the journal *Acéphale*, and a secret organization of that name, which would be dedicated to understanding a society that replaced its faith in ritual and religion with slavish adoration for the cult of the leader. What Bataille did not properly reveal to other than the highest initiates in the group was that his real plan – deadly and deadly serious – was to perform a real human sacrifice. One of the members of Acéphale would be elected, or elect themselves, to be killed by Bataille's hand in a ritual held before the rest. This crime would bond the society in silence and secret sorrow, the origins, as Bataille saw it (leaning heavily on J. G. Frazer's *The Golden Bough* – then staple reading for intellectuals of all political backgrounds), of all organized 'religion', including Fascism.

No murder was ever actually committed. Later, in the 1950s, when he was the editor of the influential journal *Critique* and a name to be reckoned with in Parisian intellectual circles, Bataille explained his actions as an attempt to found a religion. This was the only way, as he understood it, in which the psychology of Fascism could be properly understood: as a real experience of holy terror rather than pseudo-scientific theories based on philosophical speculation.

It was no accident that during this period Bataille had also attended – along with Jean-Paul Sartre and others – the lectures given by the Russian émigré Alexandre Kojève on Hegel. Kojève's reading of the German philosopher is often what is termed the 'terrorist' version of Hegel – the philosopher who embraces negativity and destruction as absolute and necessary values in the historical dialectic. Marxism and Nazism, it was argued from this basis, thus shared the same basic ethical values. Bataille's dangerous experiment with the Acéphale secret society was an attempt to test in real, lived experience the limits of this notion. The Acéphale project was obviously, as Bataille put it himself, 'insane'.[9]

But in the context of the late 1930s, as Europe once again raced towards catastrophe, Bataille's plans did not seem any more insane than the so-called rational actions of politicians, generals and financiers who were responsible for what Bataille described as 'a rising tide of murder sweeping across Europe'.[10] By the end of the decade, like most of his generation of Parisian intellectuals, Bataille despaired of politics and abandoned the project of a community or any other collective work. Instead, he turned in on himself, practising yoga and seeing visions of 'a world in flames', an inner vision that would all too soon become a grimly accurate prophecy.[11]

PART EIGHT

The Capital of Treason

1940–1944

Paris is most beautiful when one is about to leave it.

Robert Brasillach, 1945

German street signs in Paris, 1942.

39. Night and Fog

Ordinary Parisians were of course largely ignorant of or indifferent to the comings and goings of the Left Bank intellectual élites. But it was their world too that was about to be ruined for ever by war and occupation. As the decade wore on, and as the skies blackened with the coming conflict, the predominant mood in Paris for everybody, alongside fear, was a sense of unreality. From the mid 1930s onwards, it was clear to everybody on all sides that war with Germany was imminent and inevitable. It was simply a question of when it would happen, and which side you would be on.

The complaints against the government reached a peak in 1938, when the Germans invaded Austria. The Front Populaire, which had already long been crumbling from within, now seemed out of date and irrelevant in the world of realpolitik. Nobody in the French cabinet had the skill, guile or courage to confront the Germans properly as the population now steeled itself for a war it didn't want. In September, Daladier, who had again assumed control of the government, signed an insulting deal with the Germans at Munich that effectively conceded the French right to respond to German aggression. The Munich agreement had its fans among the Fascists, but most Parisians thought of it as a gross humiliation. It also put the country on a war footing and for weeks afterwards the roads outside the city were swarming with cars and wagons carrying whole families out of the city.

The year 1939 was a time of strange tensions in Paris. One of the indirect effects of the workers' legislation brought in by the Front Populaire was a lack of investors' confidence in France; the franc went into free fall and inflation began to soar. Meanwhile, Mussolini and Hitler were carving up great swathes of European territory apparently at will. The response of the Parisian press was either to ignore these acts of aggression as meaningless provocation, to blame Anglo-American and Jewish conspiracies or to call for appeasement. Not a single voice was raised that acknowledged French responsibility for the rise of a newly venomous Germany from the ashes of the Versailles treaty of 1919. Shamefully, even before a shot had been fired, there was already open and active collaboration between the German authorities and leading intellectuals such as Pierre Drieu la Rochelle, Robert

Brasillach and Abel Bonnard. Cinema-goers were starting to get used to a steady stream of propaganda about 'la patrie' and gloomy newsreels about arms sales and distribution; this was two years before the collaborationist Vichy government truly set to work dismantling everything that the Parisian Left had fought for since 1789. The fact that 1939 was the hundred and fiftieth anniversary of the revolution that had ushered in the modern world passed most Parisians by.

In the summer of 1939, as much news space was given in the popular press to the trial of Eugène Weidmann, a German con-artist and murderer, as to the fast-disintegrating European order. Weidmann's crimes were unspectacular: he had operated on tourists in Paris during the exhibition of 1937, and had stabbed to death an American, an Alsatian, a fellow German and others. He had not made much money from his crimes but fascinated the public – women in particular – with his cool demeanour and predatory sexual manner. Women were barred from wearing short skirts in the courtroom during the trial, although they turned out in their hundreds, gasping as Weidmann went to the guillotine in what would be the final public execution in France.[1]

For all those who hoped that war could be averted, even at the price of another humiliation on the same level as the Munich agreement, there were many more who knew that war was inevitable. One fact united the two sides: this was a war that nobody wanted. Those who feared it most of all were the senior officers in the French military who knew full well that for all the bluster about the Maginot Line – an apparently impressive line of defences running down the eastern border of the country – their forces had neither the will nor the means to cope effectively with the unstoppable might of the Nazi war machine.

The Great Fear

The month of August in 1939 had been unseasonably dismal – grey skies and a leaden, stagnant atmosphere. As usual, those Parisians who could afford it decamped to the sea or the countryside. Those who stayed behind remarked on the heavy and airless atmosphere in the city streets. Then, on 22 August, the announcement of a pact between Nazi Germany and Stalin's Soviet Union shattered the calm. Barely a week later, Hitler's divisions crossed the Polish border. By 3 September, Britain and France were at war with Germany.

The first reactions to the war in Paris were stunned disbelief then an ironic shrug as business returned to normal, or as near normal as it could be. Amazingly, the squabbles and incidents of petty corruption that had eroded public faith in elected officials continued. Through the winter and spring of 1939 and 1940, there was a strange kind of stasis as, for good or ill, Parisian life continued pretty much as usual, while most people either downplayed or ignored the threat from the east. Theatres and music halls went on playing to packed houses, only occasionally running on past the ten o'clock curfew, which was in any case imposed only in January 1940. High culture, for the time being, affected a lofty indifference: the critically acclaimed producer Gaston Baty put on *Phèdre* at the Théâtre Montparnasse. *Cyrano de Bergerac* and *Madame sans gêne* ('Madame without Shame') were successfully staged at the Comédie Française. The poet Paul Valéry, known for his high aestheticism and indifference to the material world, gave a well-received lecture on the philosophy of French art to representatives of the five central academies in Paris. Restrictions on the consumption of meat were belatedly imposed (citizens were asked to go vegetarian for two days a week), but again this was mostly ignored (the concept of a meat-less meal was then as now something of a puzzle to Parisians). Petrol consumption was, somewhat recklessly, still unrestricted and excursions to the countryside remained a common weekend pastime.

Most of Paris, from the working classes upwards, buried their fear of the war in heedless hedonism. There were popular songs, such as Ray Ventura's 'On ira pendre notre linge sur la ligne Siegfried' ('We'll hang out our washing on the Siegfried line') and Maurice Chevalier's 'Paris sera toujours Paris' ('Paris will always be Paris'), which promoted the crudest form of defiance. The most popular arguments still ran: 'Why should we die or suffer again for people we don't know and will never meet?' or 'Let Hitler have Europe if he wants it that much'. There was no shame in muttering such defeatist platitudes in even the most radical circles of the Left. A tract called *Paix immédiate* ('Immediate Peace') was produced by the anarchist Louis Lecoin, signed by respectable friends of the working man, such as Jean Giono, and passed around the cafés and bars of Belleville.[2]

The mood among the troops was, if anything, more defeatist. There were perceptive and energetic senior officers such as Charles de Gaulle who saw the flaws in the Maginot Line and called for the retraining of troops to deal with the new and devastating blitzkrieg tactics of the Germans (this form of warfare was essentially a highly mobile and totally ruthless subjugation of enemy territory). No one listened to them and nothing could galvanize the troops. Alongside defeatism, drunkenness was a major problem on the front lines. The Parisian railway stations even set up special *salles de deséthylisation* to dry out the new recruits who were setting off for the front so inebriated they could barely stand. Meantime, along the front itself, troops passed the time playing cards, soccer or listening to friendly German voices on the other side of the lines who implored them, 'Don't die for Danzig! Don't die for the Polish or British! We won't start shooting if you don't.'[3]

This was of course famously all a feint. In early May 1940, the German divisions advanced through Holland and Belgium, clearing everything that stood in their path. As the Germans moved relentlessly towards Paris, the theatres and restaurants none the less continued to operate as usual. With more and more refugees arriving in the city, the government, now a coalition led by Paul Reynaud, issued constant instructions, confused and contradictory for the most part, insisting that the government would stay in the capital, that everyone should be patient and that Paris would fight.

Many Parisians and those passing through the city saw flight as the only realistic option, however, and in the final weeks of May the roads out of the city started filling up with cars, wagons, buses and handcarts as those who could get out started to move. The panic was called *la grande peur*, ('the great fear') by the press. Over a quarter of the population were on the roads out of the city at any one time: they were often shot at for sport by German aircraft and, if they could, they returned to the city chastened and fearful about what would happen next. Thousands of children were separated from their families in the confusion. Many of them would never see their parents again.

On 16 May, Winston Churchill, the English prime minister heading an emergency coalition government that was only a few days old, came to the city to meet the French government and high command. He was amazed at the chaos that prevailed. While Churchill returned to London, Reynaud led the prayers to Sainte Geneviève in Notre-Dame. By the end of the first week of June, and despite their earlier protestations to the contrary, the government had left for Tours.

Within days, heavy German bombardment began. Until 10 June, as the number of refugees fleeing Paris became a swarm, the military command debated whether to defend the city. Finally, on 11 June, General Maxime Weygand announced that Paris was an 'open city'. His decision was taken on sound military grounds – there was no way that the city could possibly have withstood any serious attack by air or artillery and it is clear that massacres and much suffering were prevented by this brave tactic. The troops of General von Kuchler's 17th army entered Paris on 14 June at 5.30 in the morning. Two divisions advanced in tandem on the Eiffel Tower and the Arc de Triomphe. By noon, General Bogislav von Studnitz had taken up residence in the Crillon Hotel on Place de la Concorde. There had been no battle, or even the slightest sign of resistance. To the Germans, and especially to Hitler, this was direct proof of the generally held theory of the morally degenerate nature of the French.

'DEATH to the Jew!'

There were, however, more pressing racial problems for the Germans to deal with in Paris than the perceived weakness of the French. The persecution of Parisian Jews started almost as soon as the Germans had taken control of the city. The Germans found willing allies in the city authorities and especially the Paris police, who were more than happy to deflect the mixed emotions of humiliation and self-hatred induced by the Occupation on to the invented enemy within.

The German presence announced itself suddenly and powerfully at the level of the street with a plethora of street signs in the hated Teutonic tongue, directing German-speakers to military and leisure facilities across the city. One of the first German visitors to Paris was Adolf Hitler himself, who made a three-hour tour of the capital on the morning of 24 June in the company of the Nazi architect Albert Speer and the artist Arno Breker, both of whom were great admirers of the city. To further humiliate the French, Hitler had arranged for the surrender of the city to be made in the railway carriage in the forest of Compiègne where the Germans themselves had previously been humiliated by the Treaty of Versailles over twenty years earlier. A British propaganda film was carefully edited to portray Hitler dancing like a madman; viewers in Germany saw a more authoritative version of the same scene in which Hitler stamped his foot hard on the floor of the carriage, assuming his historic stance as the greatest military commander of all time.

This was in fact Hitler's only visit to the city. As a mark of his triumph, a photo was taken of Hitler in the empty expanse of the Trocadéro, framed by the Eiffel Tower – the great nineteenth-century symbol of modernity alongside the very incarnation of twentieth-century fanaticism. A few days after his visit, Hitler recorded his views on the city. 'I was grateful to fate to have seen this city whose aura always possessed me,' he said. 'It is our responsibility at several levels to preserve undamaged this wonder of Western civilization. We have succeeded.'

The transformation of the city under the Germans was swift and apparently unstoppable. During the early period of the Occupation, the Germans installed several garrisons throughout Paris as well as a Gestapo headquarters. The centre of all operations was the Majestic Hotel on the avenue Kléber, the 'Militärbefehlshaber in Frankreich' ('French High Command') under the control of Hans Speichel and the urbane but ruthless figure of the writer, soldier and mystic Ernst Jünger. Their specific mission was not only to establish the strategic importance of Paris from a military point of view, but to begin the larger operation of wiping out the cultural presence of France in Europe. This particular aspect of strategy was devised and implemented from the 'Propagandastaffel der Gross Paris' ('Propaganda Division of Greater Paris'), a bureau under the steady hand of Helmut Knochen at 57 boulevard Lannes.[4]

Knochen was a sophisticate and a witty gossip, and much of his time in Paris was spent organizing elaborate dinner parties during which he would flatter collaborationists and non-collaborationists from industry, the arts and journalism into sharing wine, food and information about French politics and the economy. The hard work of torture and murder was left to his deputy, Kurt Lischka, a native of Breslau, who had acquired a reputation in Nazi circles for the rigour and effectiveness of his methods. One of Lischka's favourite torture methods – and one that provoked much laughter at Knochen's parties for its novelty and inherently comic style – was to feed prisoners nothing but salted herring for days on end. Lischka prided himself on the fact that even the toughest prisoner could not stand more than two days of this. Lischka was also admired for his attention to detail. His first task on taking up the position was to order more supplies for his own headquarters at 11 rue de Saussaie. These included: fifty coffins to be added to the present supply; 150 pairs of handcuffs; thick curtains for vans taking prisoners to execution; 2,000 litres of fuel for burning the corpses of the executed in the Père-Lachaise cemetery; whisky, wine and snacks for the execution squads.

One of Lischka's first major jobs in Paris was to start sorting out the so-called 'Jewish problem'. Within weeks of the Occupation, cinema-goers were informed that the collapse of their country was entirely due to the conspiracy of Jews, Freemasons and Anglo-Saxons, whose only interests were greed and the destruction of the way of life of the ordinary French working man. These films, with titles such as *Le Péril juif* ('The Jewish Peril', regarded as a masterpiece at the time), *Les Corrupteurs* ('The Corrupters') and *Forces occultes* ('Occult Forces'), were highly sophisticated mini dramas that pulled no punches in depicting sinister hook-nosed Jews cackling over the destruction of Christian civilization. They were well scripted, beautifully shot and damningly accurate in the use of Parisian geography (the rue Cadet, headquarters of the Parisian Freemasons since the eighteenth century, is a recurring motif). In the autumn of 1941, an exhibition called 'The Jew and France' was organized by the French and German authorities on the boulevard des Italiens. It attracted thousands of visitors but little or no public or private censure. The exhibition was billed as 'of great educational importance' and visitors were quickly guided to the enormous spider hanging over the entrance. They were informed that 'the spider represents Jewry feasting on the blood of our France'. The other projected image in this exhibition and the accompanying films was of the Jews as an unscrupulous and unbelievably rich élite of non-Europeans ('like insects, like parasites') feeding off the labour of decent Frenchmen.[5] One of the reasons many Parisians had never seen a Jew, it was often reasoned, was because Jews all lived in palaces or on the French Riviera.

In reality, most Parisian Jews lived in the Marais – the Pletzel ('little place' in Yiddish) – where they had come in successive waves from 1880 onwards, fleeing poverty and oppression in eastern Europe. The Marais was a home for some, and for others a stopping-off point for emigration to the Americas or Palestine. It was then one of the most neglected and filthy parts of Paris, but until the early 1930s at least, it was a relatively free place and, as far as it could, the community remained immune from the anti-Jewish sentiment that occasionally swilled around the city. Most 'Gentile' Parisians, whatever their thoughts on the Jewish question, had no business in this part of the city and rarely if ever came into contact with anybody who lived there.

Yet the collaborationist Parisian press railed against these 'poisonous aliens'. Typical of such rhetoric was an article in *Au Pilori* in March 1941 that all but screamed for the extermination of the Jewish race:

DEATH to the Jew! Death to all that is false, ugly, dirty, repulsive, Negroid, cross-bred, Jewish! Death! Death to the Jew! Yes. Repeat it. DEATH! D.E.A.T.H. TO THE JEW! For the Jew is not a man. He is a stinking beast. We defend ourselves against evil, against death – and therefore against the Jews!

It is significant that this was written not by a German but by a native Parisian. In August, the first laws against Jews were passed, arousing little comment from other Parisians. Jews were banned from swimming pools, allowed to shop only during certain hours and forced to ride in the last car of the metro. They were not allowed to use telephones, queue for food, run businesses or ride bicycles; nor could they move home, teach in higher education or otherwise take part in public life. On 29 May 1942, they were forced to wear the Yellow Star of David. A French company called Barbet-Massin, Popelin Ltd was more than happy to provide 5,000 metres of material necessary to make at least 400,000 stars, which all Jews over the age of six had to wear in public – 'quite visible on the left side of the chest, carefully sewn onto the item of clothing', according to the ordinance.[6]

The level of public tension had already been ratcheted up a notch further on the night of 2 October 1941, when the calm of the Parisian night was shattered by a series of explosions in the early hours. The bombs exploded across the city – in rues des Tourelles, Notre-Dame-de-Nazareth and de la Victoire; they were all aimed at synagogues. There was no proper explanation for the bombs. The Germans – who had of course orchestrated the incident – explained it as a spontaneous pogrom by Parisians angry at the damage that the Jews had done to the city. In the bleak dawn, Jewish Parisians shivered and waited for the situation to get worse.

They did not have long to wait. SS-Hauptsturmführer Theodor Dannecker had been based in the city since September 1941. A mere twenty-seven years old, Dannecker came to Paris with high recommendations from no less than Adolf Eichmann, Hitler's most favoured bureaucrat. He was a hard-headed and ruthlessly efficient manager of Jewish affairs who would soon play a key role in the development and implementation of the 'Final Solution' in France. It helped that Dannecker had a visceral hatred of Jews, which must have made the huge logistical task of planning and carrying out mass-murder that much easier.

Effectively Dannecker had not come to Paris to make propaganda but to kill. Under his steady hand, anti-Jewish activities in Paris quickly moved from exhibitions, newspaper articles, films and jokes, to organizing deportations to the east. There was, by late 1941, a reasonable groundswell of public anti-Jewish feeling in the city – an optician, Lissac, had posted up a slogan which said 'Lissac is not Issac' and the popular Café Dupont in the Latin Quarter had a jocular sign declaring that it was closed to 'dogs and Jews'. The first 'round-ups' or *rafles* had started in early 1941, when poor, immigrant Jews to Paris were 'invited' to signal their presence to the police. They soon found themselves in the prisons of Beaune-la-Rolande or Pithiviers.

'Spring Wind'

For Dannecker, this was an amateurish and painfully slow way of dealing with the problem. He was concerned not only with the 'exotic' Jews from eastern Europe who clustered in the Pletzel but also the Gallicized professional classes, the 'integrationists', who were working away in the body of French life like an insidious cancer. The real solution to this problem was to act on a larger and more ambitious scale. In the offices of the Gestapo building on the avenue Foch, Dannecker put to his superiors a plan that he called 'Vent Printanier' ('Spring Wind'). The aim of this operation was, with the co-operation of the Parisian authorities, to round up 28,000 Jews and to send them east or deal with them in other ways. Nothing on such a scale had ever been attempted, but, if successful, it would provide a blueprint for dealing with Jews in other parts of Nazi-occupied Europe.

Dannecker was driven by ambition and a genuine love for his work. When he received the approval of the German High Command for operation 'Spring Wind', he set to with an unprecedented enthusiasm which even his colleagues noted was beyond the call of duty. His first major problem was to convince the Parisian and military authorities of the importance and feasibility of the plan; he would then watch as it swung into place. Nobody in the Parisian authorities raised any objections in the first or subsequent meetings with Dannecker, although it was pointed out that the first projected date for the *rafle* – the night of 13–14 July – might be tricky as people would be celebrating Bastille Day and might not be either sober or co-operative. Reluctantly, on the advice of French colleagues, Dannecker shifted the date to 16 July.

Many in the various Jewish communities of the city had long been aware that a major operation was being planned. Partly this was common sense and intuition; others such as the underground Jewish resistance group 'Solidarité' had concrete information from informers and sympathizers. But no one knew the exact dates, or what would happen precisely. The events in the streets of Paris on 16 July came as a shock to Parisian Jew and Gentile alike.

Dannecker was clear that, if it was to work, 'Spring Wind' had to be seen to be a French operation. To this end, he had set up nearly 900 teams of arresting officers. Altogether the whole city judiciary of about 9,000 men was involved. The arresting orders were clear: 'As soon as the identity of a listed Jew has been confirmed, guards proceed with the arrest, taking no notice of any protest or argument'; 'Every Jew is to be brought to the preliminary collecting centre, no notice being taken of the state of health of prisoners.'[7] At four in the morning, the homes of Jews all over Paris were invaded by French police. At first, Jewish families were relieved to hear the French voices of the arresting officers. Then they saw the buildings being systematically emptied, the forlorn Jewish families carrying whatever they could down staircases, the buses and vans from the Compagnie des Transports waiting ominously at the corner of the street. The few non-Jewish Parisians awake at this hour – workers, waiters, maids, concierges – watched helplessly and mostly with pity.

By noon, there were nearly 7,000 people – 4,000 of whom were children – thronging into the Vélodrome d'Hiver, the cycling arena on the rue Nelatour known to Parisians as the 'Vél d'Hiv'. For several weeks this was to be the staging camp for families with children. Others were driven straight to Drancy, a railway station in the northern suburbs and the starting point for the cruel journey east. Despite Dannecker's best efforts at organization, the scene at the Vél d'Hiv was mostly chaos – buses were arriving overloaded from all over Paris every ten minutes. There was no food and little sanitation (ten toilets for 7,000 people). There were attempted suicides – including ten successful ones: most of them simply leapt from the top of the grandstand. Some women gave birth. Diarrhoea and dysentery arrived quickly; death for many was not far behind. The French and German authorities ordered that only two doctors should be available at any one time. In a rare moment of clemency, André Baur, secretary-general of the 'Union Générale des Israélites en France', was allowed to visit the Vél d'Hiv on the night of 16 July. He later described a scene from an apocalypse: 'The nurses have tears in their eyes,' he wrote; 'the policemen are heartsick.' A doctor from the same organization was reduced to tears by the sight of a young girl pleading to see her parents: 'She was sick. With her eyes glued to my face, she was begging me to ask the soldiers to let her go. She had been a good little girl all year; surely she didn't deserve to be put in prison.'[8]

It was not long before Pierre Laval, the head of the government now at Vichy, signed the order that sanctioned the deportation of Jewish children: in this, the French collaborationist government sickeningly demonstrated that it had not only the stomach but the requisite sense of purpose to carry out themselves the 'Final Solution'. Amazingly, operation 'Spring Wind' was considered to be a relative failure – too many of the projected 28,000 Jews had either escaped or committed suicide. Adolf Eichmann commented to Hitler that he had always doubted the Parisian will to get the job done properly. Dannecker himself was recalled to Berlin and replaced by one Heinz Rothke, who arrived in Paris with the express brief to let the French programme of deportations carry on so long as the French authorities themselves showed a commitment to the cause. Still, it was not long before the machinery Dannecker had set in place began to work and the trains started moving all Jews to Drancy – nicknamed 'Pitchipoi' by children who thought they were travelling to a playground – and then to the east, to death by starvation or the gas chamber.[9]

The round-up at the Vél d'Hiv is one of the most dreadful moments in Parisian history. Reaction in Paris at the time was muted. It is true that few Parisians could really have known what was going on – and that the rumours from the Jewish underground were discounted as Jewish propaganda, but the smell, the cries, the urine trickling down the concrete sides of the stadium should have been more than enough to alert the outside world to the crime that was taking place inside. In the same way, the empty streets of the Marais, where only the crack of jackboots on cobbled stones made any noise in an area notorious for its over-population and commotion, were an obvious signal to anybody who knew the city that something terrible was happening. Worse still, 9,000 French men and women took part in 'Spring Wind'. They all knew what they were doing; the simple fact is that they all preferred to look the other way.

Equally disgraceful is the way in which successive French governments and governmental authorities since the Occupation seem to have suffered severe bouts of amnesia about what happened in the city between 1942 and 1944. The fact remains that the French authorities, aided by significant numbers of their countrymen, willingly and enthusiastically sent tens of thousands of innocent people to their deaths in the camps in the east. Even as the Allies were closing in during the last days of the war, the death trains were still running with chilling efficiency and precision. By then nearly 80,000 Jews, from all over France, had passed through Paris on their way to starvation, torture and annihilation.

Not least of the traumas of the period for Parisian Jews has been the reluctance of the authorities to own up to the crimes committed in their name. René Bousquet, the prefect of police during the Occupation, and the man therefore directly responsible for the round-ups and deportations, was arraigned for trial only in 1993 (he was shot by Christian Didier in an apparently motiveless crime – depriving Jews of a trial). In his 1955 film about Auschwitz, *Nuit et brouillard* ('Night and Fog'), Alain Resnais brought home to Parisian cinema-goers the reality of what lay at the journey's end to the east, and condemned 'those who do not see, who do not hear the cry to the end of time'. It took far longer than that to awaken Parisians to the enormity of the crime committed in their midst. The memorial to the deportations that now occupies the eastern end of Île de la Cité is a formal acknowledgement of the darkest days in the city. Even on a balmy summer afternoon it is a grim place, and rightly so.

Underground

Until 1942, the suffering of the Jews was largely a matter of indifference to most Parisians. The inhumanity of the round-up of the Vél d'Hiv and the terrible scenes at Drancy, which were witnessed but rarely discussed by neighbours in the surrounding high-rise apartments, marked a turning point in that for the first time among Parisians Jews provoked a sympathetic response. There was from that point on a small minority who whispered words of support or sympathy to Jewish friends or colleagues in the street or the metro, and even a bold few – including a Catholic priest – who wore the Yellow Star as a mark of defiance. Even so, a combination of residual, instinctive anti-Semitism and a preoccupation with their own difficulties kept nearly all Parisians at arm's length from the brutal events taking place before their very eyes.

Parisians were indeed more visibly shocked in the winter of 1940 by the shooting of Jacques Bonsergent, a student of engineering, who was caught up in a brawl with a German infantryman outside a bar. Originally from Brittany and one of ten children from a poor family in Lorient, Bonsergent had come to Paris in 1939 to make his fortune. He had been arrested after a drunken brawl near Gare Saint-Lazare and refused to give the names of his companions, who had already fled the scene. Bonsergent gave the Germans as good as he got with reciprocal insults and was immediately arrested and charged with terrorism. The young engineer laughed at the charges and told one of his brothers, who came to visit him from Lorient, that he was sure that he would be released soon as his crime was not political and he believed in the correctness of the Germans. He was unaware, however, that the Germans were using him as a pawn to blackmail the Vichy government to reinstate Pierre Laval, the very model of collaborationism, to power. Marshal Pétain had summarily dismissed Laval for his duplicity and further offended Hitler personally by refusing to come to Paris to receive the ashes of Napoleon's son, the duc de Reichstadt, otherwise known as L'Aiglon. These had been removed from Vienna, where L'Aiglon had died, and sent to Paris on Hitler's orders as a gesture of collaboration.

The 'terrorist' Jacques Bonsergent went before the firing squad in the early hours of Christmas Eve, to the astonishment and disgust of nearly all Parisians. On the morning of 24 December, posters appeared all over Paris announcing that 'the engineer Jacques Bonsergent was condemned to death by a German military firing squad for an act of violence against a member of the German army'. Spontaneously, women brought flowers and laid them beneath the posters; every time the Germans removed the flowers, women brought more. Parisians acknowledged this as a small but brave act of open defiance against the bullies and murderers who had taken over their city.

That winter was as tough as anyone could remember. It was bitterly cold and food shortages were now starting to hit hard. Rationing had been introduced in August and meat and butter had long since been in short supply. Cycling became the most widely used form of transport across the city. To the annoyance of concierges and fastidious neighbours, many households began breeding rabbits and pigeons as an insurance policy against future food shortages.

This was when most Parisians began to resent the Germans properly. It could be seen, for instance, in the jazz-addicted youth of Paris, who hated the Germans with the same venom that they had traditionally directed at teachers or priests. The most fervent disciples of the American jazz masters adopted the baggy zoot suits and greasy, lank hairstyles they had seen in those Hollywood movies that made it through the German censor, and called themselves 'Zazous' – apparently a Gallic corruption of the 'zah-zuh-zah' phrase used by the much-cherished band-leader Cab Calloway. As far back as 1942, a journalist called Raymond Asso had written in the collaborationist newspaper *Le Globe* of the 'Zazou menace', referring to distinct groups of young people whose main aim in life seemed to be irritating the German authorities as much as was humanly possible.

They were mostly under twenty-one (the Zazous also nicknamed themselves 'J3' – a reference to the ration books assigned to those Parisians who had not come of age) and haunted the *terrasses* of the Champs-Élysées – at the Pam-Pam or La Capoulade – or the Latin Quarter, at the Dupont-Latin, Le Petit Q or Café Cluny. They were distinguished not only by their American suits and tendency to invent slang out of the remnants of English that they took from jazz songs, but also in dandified details, such as wearing a minuscule knot in a necktie or always carrying an umbrella. Female Zazous were unashamedly sexy, sporting the reddest lipstick, thin dresses adorned with big modernist squares, short skirts and high heels. Both sexes adopted incomprehensible but modish fads as a mark of tribal belonging. These included drinking beer with grenadine (a disgusting concoction, known as a 'Monaco', that is still a favourite with students) or, most bizarrely of all, ordering *carotte râpée* ('grated carrot') with every meal.[10]

The Zazous were pranksters and teenage rebels a decade before these attitudes were properly codified in the pop culture of post-war Europe. It would be a ludicrous exaggeration to say that they represented anything like a true threat to the occupying forces, but they were a genuine nuisance and a rallying point for disaffected youths who, precisely because they were below the age of majority, were harder to police and control than other sections of the population.

Occasionally, much to the disgust of the middle-class families from which they generally came, young men and women accused of 'social delinquency' by the authorities would be sent to the countryside, to work alongside peasants who were supposed to knock the metropolitan edges off these urbanites. But this experience usually had the opposite effect, by hardening attitudes. Unsurprisingly, as the war dragged on, many of these city youths made their way into the fledgling resistance movements, where they often became dedicated 'comrades' with a real sense of history and purpose.

Resistance

In the same way, the Nazi Occupation shattered the city but did not destroy it. If anything, the Occupation did a great deal to harden French resolve against the Germans – the very quality which had been lacking in the pre-war period – and, as the resistance movements gained momentum, it turned ordinary citizens into skilled snipers, saboteurs and insurrectionists.

The Occupation had been at first a massive blow to morale across France and Europe. In a single movement, it had reduced the world capital of the Rights of Man – a city whose ideas and whose intellectuals had been a beacon to the planet – to a shadowy nest of liars, traitors and murderers. But as the initial shock of the Occupation receded, to be replaced by the trauma of subjugation and subordination, apart from those collaborators who had long since thrown their lot in with the Nazis, even the most pacifist Parisian began to see the current situation as intolerable. Resistance and rebellion seemed to be the only possible options.

The moral vacuum of Paris in the first months of the Occupation could not last for ever. The first serious blow against the occupying forces was struck at nine o'clock in the evening of 21 August 1941 in the metro station at Barbès. This was the shooting of Alfons Moser, an officer in the German navy, on the *quai* of the station as he waited for a train to the west of the city. The killer was 22-year-old Pierre Félix Georges, a Communist militant who was henceforth to be known by his nom de guerre 'Le Colonel Fabien'. Georges shot Moser through the chest and walked away, apparently protected by the crowds at the station, into history and legend. This was the moment, according to official Communist Party sources, that France lifted its head and began to fight back against the occupier. The murder angered the Germans and shocked collaborationist Paris; other Parisians were delighted that at last the real work of fighting back had begun.

The background to this moment was not, however, as clear and simple as it seemed from the killing. Despite his youth, Pierre Georges had considerable experience of the Communist Party at all levels and was considered a first-class militant, capable of outrageous violence and daring. Previous actions had included throwing bricks through the window of a collaborationist headquarters on the boulevard des Filles-du-Calvaire, experience as a republican infantryman in the Spanish Civil War and participation in a series of violent demonstrations against the Occupation. The trigger for his action was Hitler's invasion of Russia in June 1941, a move that had done a great deal to relieve tension on the French and European Left and opened the way for the kind of armed struggle against the Nazis that many Communists had thought the only possible strategy since the late 1930s.

The changes were also determined by the twists and turns in the war outside Paris, and the way in which, with every cruel and ruthless manoeuvre within the city, the Germans drove a deeper and deeper division between themselves and ordinary Parisians. The real shift in the mood of Parisians at this stage in the war was not provoked by the rumours of the deportations of Jews and others to the death camps, or indeed the everyday experiences of bullying and privation that became more frequent and harder to stomach through the bitter winter of 1940–41, but by the increasing certainty – revealed as the German grip tightened on the city – that a whole culture was in peril.

40. Patriots and Traitors

Not all Parisians found the German presence a burden, however. The Germans behaved at first with an over-mannered correctness that was entirely agreeable to bourgeois Parisians, who much preferred the stiff elegance of these real soldiers to the scruffy and drunken conscripts, French and English, who had just passed through the city in retreat. There were other, darker reasons why some Parisians admired the Germans. In Jean-Paul Sartre's novel *Le Sursis* ('The Reprieve', 1945), one of the principal characters, Daniel, has an erection as the German troops enter the city, marching in formation down the Champs-Élysées. He stares in a lustful trance at the *Wehrmacht* troops, who are all hard muscles, blue eyes and blond hair. He fantasizes about rape and being raped, and finds that this gives him a pleasure he can't explain. But it is a pleasure all the same.

The character of Daniel had been explicitly based on Jean Genet, an orphan, thief, rent boy and writer, whose character and texts greatly pre-occupied Sartre during this period. In particular, Sartre was fascinated by Genet's notions of 'treason' and 'betrayal' – values Genet held high in a direct inversion of those of the bourgeois society that he hated. In his account of vagabondage in Europe in the 1930s, *Le Journal du voleur* ('The Thief's Journal'), published in 1949, Genet wanders down to the southern edge of Spain and gazes over the straits of Gibraltar at the city of Tangier, a distant, glimmering jewel on the North African coast. He brings to mind its reputation as a vicious den of gangsters, traitors, pederasts and murderers, and is sexually excited by the thought of finally reaching the place which he calls with awe 'the Capital of Treason'.

By 1940, Genet had no need to travel to North Africa: Paris was by now already swarming with would-be traitors, both petty and on a grand scale, who would go on to fulfil his most dramatic masochistic fantasies. Sartre's Daniel also had his real-life corollaries in the emergence of notable pro-Nazi intellectuals as the leading lights of the Occupation. These writers – including Robert Brasillach, Lucien Rebatet and Pierre Drieu La Rochelle – often styled themselves as 'true voices of Paris' but their ideological line had been determined in Berlin, where many of them had moved to at the outset of the war. At least, Genet and Sartre's Daniel had the merit of self-knowledge, admitting that their dreams of power and humiliation were at root no more than twisted sexual fantasies. These collaborationist intellectuals, in contrast, saw themselves as launching a moral crusade that would lead white, heterosexual Europeans towards the new world order as dreamt up by the Nazi High Command.

The way forward had already been shown by the establishment of the Vichy government under the stewardship of Marshal Pétain and Pierre Laval in the sleepy spa town to which the French government had retreated. The Vichy government, set up as the true French government disintegrated amidst the chaos of 1940, exhorted collaboration as a patriotic duty. It had, bizarrely, an 'embassy' on the rue de Grenelle in Paris that was supposed to encourage good relations between French intellectuals and the Germans. Among those who had already led the way towards intellectual and political collaboration was Jacques Doriot, a former Communist leader who had been one of the founders of the pro-Nazi 'Parti Populaire Français' and had violently opposed the war in the name of the working man.

This, at least, was a shift based on principle; many journalists and writers were easily flattered by the German ambassador Otto Abetz and his proxy Ernst Jünger, who dazzled them with promises of cash and the editorships of widely circulated journals. The journal *Je Suis Partout*, under Robert Brasillach, had been one of the loudest pro-German voices in pre-war France. It now came to the forefront, alongside the newspaper *Au Pilori*, as the leading organ of the Right and remnants of the self-hating French Left. Among those journalist intellectuals who came over to the collaborationist side without shame or hesitation were the writers Abel Bonnard, Fernand de Brinon and Jean Luchaire.[1]

The 'patriotic' argument common to all of these writers was that since the First World War France had been in severe decline and that, given the European and indeed world prominence of French culture, this 'decadence' would have a disastrous effect on European culture as a whole. Fascism was also the only solid defence against the threat of Communism. The Munich accords of 1938 had damaged this argument somewhat, but the alliance between the Nazis and the Soviets was only a temporary measure against the more dangerous threat of 'Anglo-Saxon' democratic liberalism, regarded as no more than a stalking horse for savage, unbridled capitalism.

It followed from this that the strategy of Abetz, the German ambassador, was not simply to deal with the French Right or extreme Right – factions that had fallen quickly in line with the Germans in any case – but to court those writers, intellectuals and politicians who had formerly been or indeed were still associated with the Left, but who were disillusioned by the wreckage of the Parisian political and cultural landscape. This explained the apparently anomalous situation in 1941 and 1942 when well-known writers of left-wing sympathies – including the likes of Raymond Queneau, Marguerite Duras, Simone de Beauvoir, Albert Camus and Jean-Paul Sartre – found themselves published and even lauded in Occupied Paris. The former Surrealist turned Communist Louis Aragon now even came properly to national prominence with his 'patriotic' poems which, both reactionary in both form and content, echoed Victor Hugo's thundering calls for national solidarity against the oppressor. In the 1943 poem 'Du poète à son parti' ('The poet to his party'), Aragon presented, for example, a peculiarly Parisian marriage of Communism and patriotism that, brought out by the leading publishing house of Gallimard, both evaded the censor and had genuinely popular appeal:

> My party has restored my eyes and my memory
> I had forgotten what every child knows
> That my blood was so red and my heart a French heart
> . . . My party has restored my belief in heroism
> I see Joan of Arc I hear Roland's horn[2]

Aragon was no exception: although a handful of intellectuals chose not to publish at all during the war (these few included the poets René Char and Tristan Tzara), most writers and artists were able to function almost as if nothing was happening. Sometimes this was because the censor had genuinely failed to grasp anything truly anti-German in the work (this was said to explain the positive critical reaction to Sartre's play *Les Mouches*, 'The Flies', of 1942 – German critics turning a blind eye to its clear allegorical reference to the Occupation). Courting French writers was also a useful tactic on the part of the Germans for preventing the emergence of potential literary martyrs, reducing much of the literary output of the period to mere impotent rage: political and philosophical debates centred on issues of defeat, suffering and silence, but rarely engaged directly with the enemy. This was proof, it was argued on the Right, that the French model for civilization – democracy and egalitarianism – had been no more than a dangerous illusion that had brought the country to disaster.

A Prophet

The most heady spice in this poisonous stew of ideas was of course raw anti-Semitism. The pro-Nazi novelist Louis-Ferdinand Céline had written in a pre-war pamphlet that 'a dead million stinking Yids was not worth the fingernail of an Aryan'.[3] He had declared that the arrival of the Germans was 'a necessary tonic'. His only disappointment now was that the war had not been devastating enough.

Since the success of his first novel, *Voyage au bout de la nuit*, in 1932, Céline had been seduced by fame, money, the five-star hotels and opportunities for travel that went with his new status. His voice, and his hatred, remained, however, the authentic sound of the Parisian slums; his anti-Semitism came from the same source. It was undoubtedly useful to the Germans as propaganda but as impossible to rein in and control as the writer himself.

Céline was a genuine nihilist. As such, he proved a problem for the Germans, who preferred their anti-Semitic ideologues to have at least a veneer of culture and nuanced sensibility – Nazism was, for example, often favourably compared to Greek or Roman values by the likes of Lucien Rebatet or Robert Brasillach. Similarly, Jean Cocteau, while never an active collaborator, was equally effete in his references to 'European culture' and blended in easily with those other wits, cynics and bons vivants who dined at Otto Abetz's grand residence on the rue de Lille. Céline was regarded as not only uncultured but also an active enemy of *haut bourgeois* culture.

Still, Céline had supporters among the Germans. Most prominent among these was Karl Epting, who admired Céline as a stylist as well as a thinker, and who had written to the author as far back as 1938 to express admiration for *Bagatelles pour un massacre*, and again in 1941 in praise of his polemic *Les Beaux Draps*. Epting was then a junior cultural attaché and *Les Beaux Draps*, with its wild and fierce denunciation of a European society bleeding to death, seemed a long way from official Nazi dogma. Epting wrote that he admired Céline as the writer who had re-awakened the language of Rabelais; he also praised Céline as a thinker and regarded both *Bagatelles* and *Les Beaux Draps* ('The Fine Bed-sheets' – a reference to the French government lying down and allowing itself to be 'taken' by the perfidious English and American governments with their Judeo-Masonic conspiracies) as wise and astutely prophetic. 'If you really want to get rid of Jews,' Céline had written, 'then there are not 36,000 remedies, 36,000 grimaces: racism!

That's the only thing that Jews are afraid of: racism! And not a little bit with the fingertips, but all the way. Totally, inexorably. Like complete Pasteur sterilization.'[4]

When Epting rose to the directorship of the German Institute of Paris in 1941, he brought Céline and the urbane Jünger together in the belief that these were the two writers who best understood the nature and consequences of modern war (Jünger's *Der Kampf als Innererlebnis*, 'War as Inner Experience' – originally published in 1922 – had been recently translated into French as *La Guerre, Notre Mère*, 'The War, Our Mother', and was widely read in Paris). But Jünger kept his distance from Céline, describing him as a maniac and an irrational Celt (Céline loudly claimed Breton ancestry), and the latter's role in the Institute of Jewish Affairs – the anti-Semitic propaganda organization – was only as an adviser. None the less, Céline was an enthusiastic Jew-hater and impressed major collaborationist figures such as Henri Poulain, Marcel Déat and Pierre Constantini by the virulence of his arguments at a meeting he had organized in 1941 at the offices of *Au Pilori*, the anti-Jewish newspaper. Unsurprisingly, he was one of the chief targets of the resistance, who posted small black coffins to his Montmartre flat to warn him that he was under sentence of death.

In spite of his rampant anti-Semitism, Céline is today regularly placed alongside Proust as one of the best prose stylists of the century. His testimony to a city under bombardment proves him to be a vivid, sometimes mesmerizing writer, his curious elliptical and staccato prose conveying exactly what it must have felt like to experience the nerve-shredding tension of a city under siege. Despite the comparison with Proust, his is a style of writing far removed from the elegiac tone of the author of *À la recherche du temps perdu*, as this description of the bombing of Montmartre clearly shows:

Baroom! . . . Vroom! . . . They're razing the city! . . . The whole street caving in at the shore . . . thunder at the Grand Café! . . . A table sails by and slices the air! . . . it twirls, smashes the window across the way into a thousand splinters . . . Everything meat! It's a horrible mess . . . the world is crumbling! The mud from the river spatters everything . . . churns, tosses the mob shrieking, gasping . . . the bridge totters . . . It's the saraband of terror . . . a carnival amid the rumble of crawling disruption! . . . But we don't die . . . still turning, twisting, moaning . . . We're death's acrobats . . . ![5]

In real life, Céline was capable of malicious actions that could have deadly consequences. He accused, in print, a certain Menckietwickz, a senior figure in the medical establishment, and even his own doctor of being Jews. This was not only untrue (Menckietwickz was a Catholic Pole and Céline's unfortunate medic an Armenian Christian) but directly provoked a visit to both of them from the German police that almost culminated in a one-way ticket to a death camp. After the war, Céline himself barely escaped a French firing squad, retreating back to his lair just outside Paris after a spell in prison, both snarling and unrepentant, muttering still about Jewish conspiracies and the end of the world. His hatred of Jews was clearly more pathological than political.

But this precisely is why it is essential to read him, in order to understand something of the emotional climate of Paris during the Occupation. This argument – which is not an apologia for Céline but rather a condemnation – was made by Saul Bellow in 1983 on a nostalgic return to Paris, a city he had not visited since a stay there as a student some thirty years before. Bellow, a Jew and a believer in liberal humanism, noted that the English-speaking countries had never taken seriously the deep reservoirs of poison that had eaten away and destroyed French political life. Yet the signs had all been there in the art of the period: indeed, the atrocities of the 1940s were already foretold in the terrors and hatreds of the 1930s. More than anything else, says Bellow, this made Céline not only a great writer but a prophet. 'A great European literature had told us what to expect,' he wrote. 'Céline had spelled it out quite plainly in his *Voyage*.'[6]

'Only one enemy, the invader'

As the reality of war was revealed in the first year of the Occupation, there were the first stirrings of organized resistance and rebellion against the German authorities. Paris was ideally suited for this sort of activity: Parisians were by instinct subversives and had been all but bred for the demands of clandestine insurrection; the city itself, with its alleys, labyrinths and double-entry buildings, was large enough to disappear in. The first waves of insubordination came in the summer of 1940 from schoolchildren and students, who were able to call strikes, launch demonstrations and chant for General de Gaulle with – at that point at least – relative impunity from the Germans, who did not yet want to be seen as thuggish child-haters. Graffitti appeared across the city, normally in the form of the 'V' for victory sign or the Croix de Lorraine.

Among the first resistance networks proper was a cell called 'Configuration Notre-Dame' and grouped around a 'Colonel Rémy', who had come from Nantes to Paris on orders from London. This was quickly broken up by informers but was swiftly followed by the 'Réseau Saint-Jacques' and 'Réseau Nemrod' (*réseau* meaning 'network'), both led by the impressive and charismatic figure of 'Capitaine d'Estienne d'Orves', who was finally assassinated in 1941.

Most important of all was the cell operating out of the Musée de l'Homme at Trocadéro, under the overall control of Boris Vildé, a linguist and academic. The activities of the group involved helping British and French airmen escape, minor acts of sabotage and publishing in 1942 a clandestine tract, *Résistance*, which called on all French men to assert themselves against 'one enemy, the invader', as well as disseminating news from the BBC and the Free French government from London. The Musée de l'Homme group were appalled by the laziness and cowardice of their fellow Parisians and to counter this published in the same year a famous tract, *Conseils aux occupés* ('Advice to the Occupied'), on how to behave towards the conqueror. The advice included a wide range of everyday acts of insubordination deigned to infuriate and baffle the enemy: 'You do not know their language or have forgotten it,' ran one piece of advice. 'If someone addresses you in German, make a sign of ignorance and be on your way without remorse.' Or: 'They parade in your dishonour. Study the signs in the store window instead of watching' and 'The voice that gives you courage is that of Dr Goebbels'. One of the most daring members of the group, the head janitor of the museum, amused himself by cycling behind German trucks and pasting stickers in favour of de Gaulle on to them.[7]

The Musée de l'Homme group survived until 1942, when they were infiltrated and betrayed by a Vichy official. All of them were executed or deported, but their legacy was to encourage further groups that they could defy and outwit an ostensibly more powerful enemy.

Despite the obvious difficulties of operating in a city where every neighbour could be a traitor and the dangers of torture and execution all too real, the next wave of *résistants* were hardy and dedicated to the cause, fired up by the patriotic propaganda from London or, as Moscow entered the war against Hitler, from the capital of the workers' paradise. The German authorities liked to overplay their hand, describing all *résistants* as Communists, but it was also a fact that many of the boldest and most effective operatives were indeed Communists and were driven by their belief in the founding of a new post-war world based upon truly Socialist freedoms. This was for many not only an internationalist position but also an attitude entirely in accord with the oldest Parisian traditions of revolution in the name of human dignity.

In the spring of 1942, as Hitler advanced through Russia, the Soviet-backed cells sanctioned the use of *francs-tireurs*, or snipers, against the occupying forces. With every new move in the war, the Communist *résistants* took strength from their vision of the new world close at hand. More than 700 so-called Communists were slaughtered by the Germans at Mont Valérien in an attempt to frighten Parisians, but the Parisian Communists only took heart from this as they did from the epic battle of Stalingrad, which was being fought hundreds of miles away but was felt as an everyday reality in the working-class neighbourhoods of Ménilmontant and Belleville whose inhabitants identified with their 'comrades' in the east. In 1943, as the battle for Europe began to turn against the Germans, the number of *résistants* inevitably swelled to match the turning tide of the conflict. There was an unspoken civil war between the Communist forces and the Gaullist cells, who each envisaged a very different post-war Paris, but for the time being the common cause of making life impossible for the German occupiers was the central concern of most Parisians.

Paris Fights Back

The guerrilla war against the Germans reached its climax on the 18 August 1944. The Allied landings in Normandy in June were led by mainly American and British forces and the American commander-in-chief General Eisenhower had at first decided to ignore Paris as he pushed his forces to the east, estimating that it was of little strategic value and that its resistance forces were probably negligible. As the Allied troops drew nearer the city, the Free French Forces of the Interior – which was what the various resistance forces at work in France now called themselves (they were nicknamed the 'Fifis') – decided to launch an uprising in the city against the German authorities.

The main inspiration behind the insurrection came from the Communists at work in the resistance, whose ultimate aim was not merely the liberation of Paris but a full-blooded revolution in France, with Paris as its epicentre. The revolt began properly on 15 August with a strike launched by the Paris police force. This had been provoked by the German move to disarm the police but was also, more cynically, an attempt by those policemen who had acted with craven subordination to the Germans to rescue something of their honour. Many policemen, bizarrely, now began to claim themselves as Communists, gambling that such an association would help them out of a tricky spot in the post-war city.

The police strike soon became a general one as other public workers joined in. Armed insurrection began with shots fired on the morning of 18 August, as Communist fly-posters appeared all over Paris. Resistance snipers had been placed ready for the call to action as barricades began to be set up across the city. As the fighting started and gained momentum, the Gaullist *résistants*, who had been placed in the city on de Gaulle's express orders to monitor and if possible control events, had no option but to join in with Communist-led insurrection.

There was vicious street-fighting in nearly every part of Paris over the next few days. The conflict was particularly intense around Place Saint-Michel, where German vehicles were ambushed and set alight. In the nearby rue Saint André-des-Arts, a field hospital was set up. The Germans had a straight line of fire down the rue de Seine. On the orders of the Fifis, barricades were to be set up across the city in order to stop the Germans moving around (this was a lesson that Communist insurrectionists had learned from street-fighting in Madrid and Barcelona in 1936). Such barricades were conspicuously absent in the wealthier areas of the 16th and 8th *arrondissements*, but in the traditionally left-wing *quartiers* of Belleville, Ménilmontant and Saint-Marcel, whole neighbourhoods came out to block the streets with cobblestones and whatever else came to hand, to drink and to celebrate what felt like a revolutionary festival.

The Germans, under General von Choltitz, fought desperately to control the city. The resistance fighters were lightly armed and poorly trained. (Although it was estimated that there were some 15,000 of them in the city, opposing a fixed German garrison of some 16,000, there were barely enough arms and ammunition for 2,000. In the days before the uprising, the main activity of resistance cells had been attacking individual German soldiers for their weapons.) For many in the resistance, this was their first experience of combat. More than 2,000 were killed in the first few day of fighting alone.

The Germans were no match, however, for the city that had now turned against them with such hatred and venom – qualities which were all the deeper for the humiliation that had accompanied the craven way in which it had initially surrendered. Even the measured minds of the likes of the novelist and philosopher Albert Camus – who had spent the war as a committed *résistant* and who was staunchly opposed to the kind of hatred that drove the likes of Céline – now understood the pull of vengeance. In his final letter to 'a German friend' – an internal dialogue and diary that Camus had written in the last days of the war – he stated that he was writing from Paris, a city known throughout the world as an upholder of human rights, but which during the dark days of the Occupation had betrayed humanity. The blame for this, argued Camus, lay squarely at the feet of the Nazis, the cruel yet elegant monsters who 'mutilated souls and destroyed the world'.[8]

The bravery of many young *résistants* was contagious. German patrols of fewer than five soldiers were likely to be surrounded and quickly over-whelmed by bands of young men, often armed with no more than revolvers and clubs, but whose anger gave them an especially ferocious energy in combat. The German response was to move around the city in armoured vehicles and tanks; five armoured vehicles and an infantry squadron were, for example, sent up the rue Soufflot to deal with snipers at the Mairie of the 5th *arrondissement*. The battle for Paris was also a free show for those who preferred to watch from windows and balconies; many of the most foolhardy acts of bravery – stealing a German vehicle or attacking an individual soldier – were also deliberate displays for an applauding audience.

The insurrection was two days old when de Gaulle, newly arrived in France from exile in Algiers, was told the news of what was happening in Paris. He had two main concerns: first that this would lead to Communist control of the city and, secondly, that lack of Allied support for the insurrec-tion would lead to its failure and inevitably to massacres in reprisal. He urged the Allies to make for the city, which they finally did on the 22 August. At the same time, he determined to lead the uprising himself as soon as he arrived in Paris.

The other priority for the Gaullist forces was to establish the fact that the recapture of Paris had been an entirely French event. Ignoring American orders to hold the line, the French army under General Leclerc entered the city from the south on 25 August. The troops made straight for the Hôtel de Ville, still under fire. As they advanced through the city, soon to be followed by Americans, the church bells began to peal. The radio played the *Marseillaise*, which had been banned in public for the past four years, the cacophony completed by the occasional burst of gunfire or shelling. Von Choltitz surrendered to the Free French Forces in the Meurice Hotel on the rue de Rivoli on 25 August. His one claim to historical honour was that he had ignored Hitler's crazed command to burn Paris to the ground as a final act of wilful revenge. As he was led away to sign the formal act of surrender in the Hôtel de Ville, a crowd gathered to hurl abuse. Later that same day, de Gaulle took control of the War Ministry in the rue Saint-Dominique and gave a rousing speech at the Hôtel de Ville, declaring famously that Paris had now been finally 'liberated by itself'. As usual, de Gaulle had an instinctive sense of the deeper currents which lay beneath political events. The liberation of Paris by the resistance probably was, as Eisenhower had it, of no military value in the longer game now being played out across northern Europe. But the fact that Parisians themselves could be seen by the world to have recaptured their city was of massive psychological and symbolic importance.

PART NINE

Society of the Spectacle

1945–2005

Beauty is in the street!

Street poster, Paris, May 1968

'La Beauté est dans la rue', graffito, May 1968, Paris.

41. Landscapes After the Battle

In the weeks and months after the Liberation, Parisians began to realize that their home was almost unique among the great cities in post-war Europe in that most of its physical features had been left intact. The city had been bombarded by the RAF and the Germans – mainly on the outskirts – but few of the famous monuments in the central part of the city had been touched. In the same way, the layout of the streets had not been affected by either artillery or street-fighting. The city in 1945 would have been immediately recognizable to anybody who knew it in 1918, and even a Parisian from the 1870s would have had little trouble in navigating the complex urban landscape that was the legacy of nineteenth-century town planning.

What the city did have in common with other European cities, however, was that it looked neglected and half wrecked. Buildings were riddled with bullet-holes and covered in filth. The streets were dark and dirty. During the final battle for the city in late August 1945, the lightly armed teenagers who had flocked to the resistance had exulted in the blood of fallen German soldiers that had once again stained the city's cobblestones red ('Chacun son Boche!' – 'A German for everyone!' – had been the battle-cry of Colonel Rol-Tanguy, Communist leader of the militias). Now, in the aftermath of conflict, the city was scarred. The air itself was thick with choking dust, which caught at everyone's throat, and unnamed poisons which, it was rumoured, the Germans had left behind as a final act of revenge.

In truth, the bitter divisions that polluted the cultural and political atmosphere in the city were created entirely by Parisians. In the immediate wake of the Liberation, the waves of anger against so-called 'collabos' were quickly translated into arrests and attacks on those who had collaborated or were perceived to have collaborated. This was the *épuration sauvage* ('wild purification'). The first acts of revenge, launched through the autumn and winter of 1944–5, promised justice, or so they purported. In fact, they formed part of a grim orgy of self-hate and vengeance. The first targets were known spies and police informers and black marketeers, who may or may not have been in the pay of the Germans.

Most were summarily executed without trial. In the first three months after the Liberation there were rumours that up to 100,000 known collaborators had been killed across France – this was later dismissed as being an exaggeration by victims who wanted to heighten their sense of martyrdom and discredit the 'Liberationist' forces as bloody savages. Further accusations came from the Right that the disorder and mob violence were echoes of the Terror of 1793. This was not entirely untrue – most of the purges were carried out in a spirit of cold vengeance that had much in common with the icy revolutionary mentality of the 1790s. There were at least 10,000 killings (as stated by the government).[1]

The real problem in post-Liberation Paris was in deciding what the word 'collaboration' meant. This should have been an easy task: it was clear enough who the most active collaborators were – they had public profiles and reputations. They also had a clear ideology: they were sincere Fascists through conviction, who dreamt of a European master-race and, if they were French, were seeking revenge for the Dreyfus affair and the myriad other crimes that, as they saw it, had been carried out against European civilization in the name of Socialism or democracy. To be a collaborator in this sense was an active decision taken in 1940, at the moment when Marshal Pétain, in a radio broadcast on 30 October, had declared it the duty of all Frenchmen 'to make a sincere collaboration. It should include a patient and trusting effort.' In 1940, the vast majority of Parisians had been 'Pétainist', if not actual partisans of the Fascist cause.

The course of the war had, however, altered all these earlier fixed meanings of the term 'collaborator'. The ambiguities over the meaning of collaboration had indeed become apparent only as they deepened during the period of the Occupation, when nearly everybody at some stage was forced into a compromising situation, usually petty, with the occupiers. It subsequently became less clear to all in Paris what was meant by passive collaboration – was it a crime to sleep with a German soldier, for instance, especially if you were in love? Was it 'political collaboration' smilingly to serve drinks to a polite and well-meaning group of German officers? To sing or perform in public, or to publish a book? To denounce a suspicious neighbour who may or may not be a Communist *résistant* or a Jew? It was a commonplace to say that by late 1943 'everybody collaborated'. There was no sliding scale of evil.

The Spectacle of Justice

The terrible scenes from this period included the spectacle of hundreds of women having their heads shaved as a punishment for so-called 'horizontal collaboration' – literally 'sleeping with the enemy'. In Paris, especially in the working-class districts, it was a common sport to join in with the crowd who attacked such women and jeer at their miserable fate. A whore who had serviced German infantrymen was kicked to death by an exultant crowd in the 18th *arrondissement*. The same rough justice was meted out to homosexuals who were known to have sold themselves to their blond conquerors. Railway workers, who were usually strongly Communist, took revenge on the petty overseers who had supervised and bullied them for the past four years, smashing their testicles or otherwise mutilating them so that they couldn't work. It was a widely believed rumour that Arletty – the archetypal *parigote* who had publicly consorted with the *Boches* in the finest salons and hotels – was to have her breasts sliced off by a group of young *résistants*. In the event, she was arrested and wore a turban in public, fuelling rumours that she had had her head shaved (she was temporarily released from prison to appear in Marcel Carné's *Les Enfants du Paradis*, then being filmed in Paris). Other women were tarred and feathered, daubed in swastikas, paraded in the streets and publicly tortured. The gaiety that accompanied such human suffering quickly became a taboo subject among 'Liberationist' groups and on the Left in general.

The 'purification' was no less savage among intellectuals and politicians, the only difference being that most of the official trials that took place did so under the aegis of the proper government authorities rather than the rackety kangaroo courts run by the wildest and most vengeful *résistant* groups (many of whom had their own dubious criminal pasts). The trials began in the spring of 1945, which was warm and sunny, and a direct counterpoint to the dark and gloomy atmosphere hanging over the *cours de justice*, the hastily assembled courts that had been set up to arraign as many people as quickly as possible. The taste for vengeance in Paris had been sharpened by the return in that spring of the deportees who had survived the death camps. They were immediately recognizable on the street by their twisted gait, blackened teeth, and limbs shrivelled to sticks. Many Parisians collapsed uncontrollably into tears at the sight.

In the weeks and months after the Liberation, those who had supported the Germans found themselves stranded in a city which had become a potential death-trap. There were mysterious suicides and disappearances. Others shuttered themselves away in darkened flats, hoping for the storm to pass. When the trials began, it was almost with a sense of release. The most anticipated trials of all – those of Marshal Pétain and Pierre Laval – which took place in the summer and autumn of 1945, felt almost like an anticlimax. For many Parisians, who watched with mixed feelings of anger, betrayal and shame, Laval's attempted suicide and execution and Pétain's life sentence hardly seemed to match the magnitude of their crimes.[2]

Many of the arch-collaborators relished the chance at least to put their case to the court – a moment that was always dangerous for a government-led judiciary that had yet to establish its own authority. Among these was Robert Brasillach, who still had many friends in high places in Paris, including the Académie Française (among those who signed a petition protesting against his death sentence were Paul Valéry, François Mauriac and Paul Claudel). But Brasillach's demise was mourned by few. Jacques Benoist-Méchin, aesthete, homosexual, Arabist, intimate of Proust and fellow collaborator (as well as a fanatical Hitler-supporter nicknamed 'la Gestapette'), made the bizarre defence of Brasillach 'One doesn't kill a poet!'[3] For his own part, Benoist-Méchin avoided the firing squad and re-emerged into political life in the late 1950s as a discreet adviser on Arab affairs to de Gaulle's government.

There was no doubt that Brasillach was a war criminal. His hard line on the Jews in Paris had shocked even senior Nazis (he had loudly worried to Dannecker at the time of the round-up at the Vél d'Hiv that not enough Jewish children had been captured). He was tried for treason and shot on 6 February 1945. 'Paris is most beautiful when one is about to leave it,' he is said to have remarked when he was finally arrested.

Brasillach may have been an obvious villain, but his analysis of the politics of the *épuration* was sharp and perceptive. While still in hiding and on the run in the months after the Liberation, he recalled the uprising and the recapture of the city as a 'betrayal of History'. 'I had few illusions about the military valour of the so-called "week of glory",' he wrote:

I knew that there were only a few thousand Germans left in the city. I never put much stock in the myth of the heroic uprising of Paris . . . I read some books of Aragon, including one in which he said 'shit to the whole French army' and at the same time to his recent patriotic poems . . . The papers told me that the liberation of Paris was a feat of arms glorious above all, but they kept under cover the murders, the acts of personal vengeance and the abominable crimes.[4]

Brasillach's hostile remarks on Louis Aragon – who had cynically fashioned himself into the patriotic poet of Paris during the Occupation – were well founded. Having long since abandoned the libertarianism of his Surrealist period, Aragon was now a ruthless Stalinist who was quite clearly trying to use the purges to turn the post-Liberation period in the Communists' favour. To this end, in his journal *Les Lettres françaises*, Aragon argued for bringing the full wrath of *résistant* justice on anyone who criticized the Communist Party. This included running campaigns against André Gide, the veteran novelist whose anti-Nazi credentials were every bit as solid as his dislike of the Soviet Union. It was matched by a sinister and distasteful campaign to smear the posthumous reputation of Paul Nizan, a novelist and staunch Communist until the Nazi–Soviet pact of 1939. Nizan had also been a brave soldier killed in the retreat to Dunkirk in 1940. Aragon's attempts to portray him as a police spy antagonized powerful figures on the Parisian literary scene, including André Breton and Jean-Paul Sartre, but still the hard core around Aragon persisted with the lie.

Aragon quickly acquired a fearsome reputation as the 'Robespierre of the Liberation'.[5] His tough, Stalinist credentials were beyond question, but his sympathies could be unpredictable. He had, for example, defended Drieu La Rochelle as a writer whose political ideas had been distorted by history and circumstance. In despair at a Europe now to be torn apart by Russians and Anglo-Saxons, Drieu La Rochelle killed himself on 15 March. The frenzy of the purges seemed to abate somewhat in the wake of his funeral, which was attended by prominent and distinguished anti-Fascists such as André Malraux. Other notable Fascists somehow managed to avoid the death sentence. Both Lucien Rebatet and Charles Maurras (now nearly ninety years old) were given life imprisonment instead.

The justice dealt out during the period of the 'purification' of Paris has been condemned as both 'harsh and weak'.[6] There is a great deal of sense in this judgement: even the most hate-filled *résistants* quickly grew bored or sickened by the atrocities being carried out. Official justice was all too often hasty, disorganized or corrupt and it is as a result of these factors that many of the principal figures responsible for some of the blackest crimes in Parisian history received light sentences or escaped punishment altogether. Faith in subsequent governments was never truly established as a result of this failure. At the time, the savagery and arbitrary nature of revenge in the post-Liberation city served only to heighten tensions, without bringing any sense of completion or true justice. Parisians were also so hypnotized by the spectacle of vengeance that many of them, including the most important intellectual and political power-brokers of the period, lost any sense of proportion or of the world outside the dusty, grey, impoverished streets of the capital.

Modern Times

The *épuration* provoked mainly self-disgust and melancholy and, as the trials came and went, few Parisians, on the Right or the Left, cared to delve any more deeply into the recent past than was strictly necessary. The alternative to looking backwards was of course to look to the future, and it is this impulse that in part explains the feverish pursuit of modernity which, in the years after 1945, seemed to be taking on ever newer forms on the Left Bank of the city.

The focus of activity was no longer in Montparnasse, which was now associated with pre-war melancholy and disaster, but at the *terrasses* of the great cafés located around the crossroads of Saint-Germain-des-Prés, where rue de Rennes met the boulevard Saint-Germain. The most famous of these were the Café de Flore, the Café Deux Magots and the Brasserie Lipp, which were known as the haunts not only of Jean-Paul Sartre, Simone de Beauvoir and Albert Camus, but also of the powerful editors and publishers of the journal *Nouvelle Revue française*, the publishing house Gallimard and myriad other reviews, journals and other para-literary activities. It was here that the post-war generation – which of course had yet to define itself as such – was experimenting with new forms of thought and behaviour, and making political and philosophical theories from these experiences. Anybody who wanted to engage with what was happening intellectually in Paris in the late 1940s made immediately for this small geographical triangle a few minutes' walk from the Seine.

The new word on everybody's lips was 'existentialism'. This word had first been used before the war to describe the kind of philosophy propounded by Germans such as Martin Heidegger or Martin Husserl that argued that existence in itself was essentially meaningless and morality a material fiction. The generation of Jean-Paul Sartre and other so-called 'Existentialists' had first encountered these ideas in Paris and Berlin as part of a general introduction to metaphysics. In the post-war period, Sartre had distinguished himself by trying to marry this fundamentally nihilistic philosophy with strands of traditional French ethical thought. This was the original premise of the journal *Les Temps modernes*, which de Beauvoir and

Sartre founded in 1945, and which they intended as a forum for debating the way forward from the wreckage of the Second World War. Another was the result of a lecture called 'Existentialism is a Humanism', which Sartre gave at the Club Maintenant on 29 October 1945. Much to Sartre's surprise, the hall that had been hired for the event on the rue Jean Goujon was overflowing and he gave his lecture to a rapt audience made up of eager young women and serious-looking young men.[7]

This lecture was the first demonstration of the extent to which Existentialism had left the university seminar and become the defining mood of a generation of young people who had survived the war but who were deeply sceptical of the so-called benefits of Western civilization. They flocked from all over France to Saint-Germain-des-Prés to be part of a cultural explosion that would become one of the first manifestations of post-war pop culture. To this extent, Existentialism had as much to do with style as with philosophy. For the hard core, the 'Germano-pratins' in the argot of the day, the often unisex clothes were mainly black and casual. For males, *la canadienne* – a heavy felt coat designed for harsh Canadian winters – and *Montycoat*, or duffel coat, were permissible in winter. Girls sported fringes and ballet shoes; both sexes wore polo necks. The soundtrack to the cultural, sexual and political activity was jazz, the music of those enslaved by American capitalist culture. The most popular band of the day was Claude Luter's band Les Lorientais, a favourite of the Zazous during the Occupation, and who had a residency in the cellar of the Carmes Hotel. Jazz was intellectually respectable and the writer Boris Vian – who wrote among other things a very funny satire on 'Jean-Sol Partre' and his cult – was as proud of his prowess on the trumpet as on the typewriter.

The spiritual headquarters of the 'Existentialist generation' was a nightclub called Le Tabou on the rue Dauphine, originally used by messenger boys for the local newspaper offices, which was where everyone ended up in the early hours after a night spent at the Bar Vert, the Montana, the Mabillon, Chez Cheramy or any of the other cafés of the district. It was not long before newspapers and magazines came to report on the new youth phenomenon that was sweeping the Left Bank. In May 1947, the news magazine *Samedi Soir* published a shock report entitled 'This is how the troglodytes of Saint-Germain live!', which described the 'gigantic orgies organized by filthy young existentialists' who spent their time 'drinking, dancing and loving their lives away in cellars, until the atom bomb – which they all perversely long for – drops on Paris'. It was this version of the Existentialist lifestyle that was broadcast across the world and gave rise to the myth of freewheeling Saint-Germain-des-Prés as a proto-beatnik paradise of glittering nightlife populated by hard-drinking literary young men and pliant, winsome, free-loving student girls. This world was also celebrated in song. Stéphane Golmann sang affectionately, 'Quand vous passez sur Saint-Benoît, renseignez-vous elle est là, pantalon noir et souliers plats, de l'écossais pas de falbala, elle a le regard fataliste, la petite existentialiste' ('When passing Saint-Benoît, take note that she's there, in black trousers and flat shoes, no frills and flounces, the look is fatalist, of the little Existentialist'). The scene was not above satirizing itself: a popular jazzy tune also carried witty and knowing lyrics sung by Juliette Gréco:

> J'ai lu tous les livres de Jean-Paul Sartre
> Simone de Beauvoir et Merleau-Ponty
> C'est tout le temps le même désastre
> Même pauvre t'es libre, tu te choisis
> J'ai bien essayé autre chose
> Maurice Blanchot et Albert Camus
> Absurde faux pas!
>
> [I've read all the books by Jean-Paul Sartre
> Simone de Beauvoir and Merleau-Ponty
> It's always the same disaster
> Even if you're poor you are free, you choose yourself
> I tried some other stuff: Maurice Blanchot and Albert Camus
> Absurd faux pas!][8]

Yet behind the sensationalist stories and jokes, the truth was that Existentialist philosophy contained a moral seriousness that had been inspired by the recent crises of war and occupation. The great debates and arguments of the day centred above all on the question of responsibility. More particularly, what were the responsibilities of the writer or intellectual in a landscape which appeared to be a moral wasteland?

These were the great themes, for example, of the novelist Albert Camus, whose novel *L'Étranger* ('The Outsider') had been published in 1941 and was hailed in France and abroad as the model Existentialist novel. Camus had been born and educated in Algeria and was something of an outsider himself in Parisian society. Although he enjoyed the lifestyle of the Left Bank, he was also quick to establish that he was not at all an Existentialist, at least not in any modish sense. The story of *L'Étranger* is simple: an aimless young man, part of the colonial community in Algiers, shoots dead an Arab for apparently no reason. The philosophical core of the book is 'existential' in the sense that it addresses the fundamental issues of moral action and responsibility which writers such as Sartre were already claiming as their own territory. The book has long outlived its merely fashionable status precisely because it offers no easy answers or solutions to the questions which it asks. Another important aspect of *L'Étranger* is its setting in colonial Algeria, a fact that was often overlooked by its early admirers but of deep significance to Camus himself. The random murder of the colonized by the colonizer would, within a few short years, as the Algerian crisis turned into a full-blown war, become one of the recurring and most damaging motifs in French life in Algiers and Paris.

Culture Wars

In some ways, the Liberation did little to change the quality of daily life. The French economy was wrecked, and beyond the noisy night-world of Saint-Germain-des-Prés most people lived at a subsistence level that had not improved since the worst days of the Occupation. In the working-class areas of Belleville and Ménilmontant, crippled and mutilated war veterans were a common sight, drinking in corners, incapable of working at whatever few jobs were available. The standard household meal was boiled cabbage and whatever scraps of food that could be had at the irregular markets on the rue de Ménilmontant. When the fashion designer Christian Dior misguidedly organized a photographic session of his new clothes – the so-called 'New Look' – in the 'typically Parisian' street markets of Montmartre, working-class women flew at the models, ripping the clothes to shreds in anger and disgust.[9]

In 1947, the United States implemented the Marshall Plan, diverting hundreds of millions of dollars into France to shore up its battered industries. The relief was immediate, but most people knew also that this was essentially a thinly disguised attempt to prevent a Communist revolution. By this time, Europe had been divided into East and West, between the Communist-led sphere of influence with its headquarters in Moscow and those countries under the influence of the former Allied powers. For those in the West, the freedom of Paris stood as the guarantee of future freedoms in a continent which had just emerged from the bloodiest conflict in human history. The totemic significance of the city was severely tested again in the autumn of

1947, when France endured the greatest wave of Communist-led industrial unrest it had known since the 1930s. The fears and tensions provoked by the strikes and confrontations only served, however, to establish France even more firmly in the Western camp of the Cold War.

It was a severe irony that the political uncertainties of the period also helped make this era rich in cultural activity. French writers, from Sartre and Camus downwards, held a prestige across the world unmatched since the days of Voltaire and Rousseau. This was partly due to the acquired heroism of belonging to a nation that had been initially defeated but had fought back against a more powerful and wicked political war-machine, and to the sheer glamour of Parisian theory-making, which from Existential-ism to Marxism via Freudianism and the new science of 'Structuralism' was yet again making the hubristic claim to be laying bare the very foundations of human knowledge.

42. The Seventh 'Wilaya'

The prevailing sense on the Parisian political scene throughout the 1950s was, in contrast to the intellectual confidence surging through the Left Bank, one of drift and humiliation. The Fourth Republic, a shaky series of governments first established in 1946, lurched from one crisis to another under a constitution that had hardly moved on from the 1930s. This was due in large part to a volatile mix of political nervousness, foreign crises and the unstoppable exigencies of internal economic growth. There was consequently a succession of governments, none of whom had either a full mandate or a real plan for France. De Gaulle himself, who had briefly assumed command in the wake of the Liberation, resigned in fury in 1946, effectively stepping back from the political chaos for the next thirteen years.

The period was also characterized by a dramatic change in the population, which was growing in the aftermath of the war, and the emergence of a consumerist culture that would grow ever more demanding and complex as the war-ravaged French economy began its slow recovery. French governments quite visibly failed to keep pace with these developments and the country occasionally teetered on the edge of disaster as a succession of unstable administrations came and went. The feelings of discontent common to Parisians of all classes during these years were often channelled into a crude and confused anti-Americanism, which was itself fraught with contradictions: although, for example, most Parisians, of every political persuasion, declared themselves vehemently opposed to nearly all American foreign policies in the late 1940s, they were also deeply in love with American culture, from jazz to movies to clothes. On the Left, in particular, this kind of schizophrenia produced a young generation of Parisian intellectuals who, while in thrall to all forms of American cultural production, could also proudly announce their allegiance to Moscow as a badge of philosophical and moral superiority. Other Parisians, bored by politicians and disillusioned by their policies, retreated into complacency and indifference. The brief popularity of 'Poujadisme' – essentially a right-wing protest movement led by newsagent Pierre Poujade – was a clear demonstration of the lack of moral and political guidance during this period. The supporters of Poujade had no discernible agenda, except that they disliked foreigners and mistrusted all professional politicians.

Meanwhile, on the other side of the Mediterranean, from 1945 onwards there were the first stirrings of a war that would shake France to its foundations. The future of France and Paris would indeed shortly be determined by what was happening not in Paris but in Algiers. For the time being, most Parisians cared very little about events far away from their city. They were not able to sustain this position for long, however. All too soon, the convulsions in Algeria would find their violent echo in the streets of Paris.

The fresh catastrophe began in 1945 with vague reports that slowly reached France of a massacre in the quiet market town of Sétif in the Constantine area of Algeria. It was reported that Algerian Muslims had turned a demonstration for independence into a riot. An Algerian flag was produced amidst the British, French and Russian flags on parade. When the police tried to grab this flag, shots were fired. The demonstrators then turned with axes and knives on to the local European population, the so-called *pieds noirs* (see Chapter 29). Over a hundred Europeans were killed in five days of fighting – many of them had their throats slit and were horribly mutilated. Men were castrated and women were raped. The local religious leaders had called it a 'Jihad' and declared that it was the religious duty of all Muslims to kill all unbelievers.[1]

It was bad luck, but no coincidence, that this uprising started on 8 May, which also happened to be VE Day, the day after German forces had stopped fighting in Europe. In Paris, understandably, all news from abroad was lost in a seemingly endless swirl of drink, kisses and celebrations. No Paris newspaper thought it necessary to send a correspondent to Algeria. De Gaulle himself shrugged off the events as a 'beginning of insurrection, occurring in the Constantinois . . . snuffed out by Governor-General Chataigneau'.[2]

Despite the quiet mood of the press, the French response in Algeria was in fact merciless. Over the next few weeks, nearly 6,000 Muslims were slaughtered by the French army, who wished to show their might (and possibly avenge recent humiliation at the hands of the Germans). Cairo radio reported that more than 45,000 were killed – a figure then fixed as a fact by Algerian nationalists. After Sétif, the conflict in Algeria was conducted at a fairly low level and limited mainly to skirmishes between French troops and the rival nationalist forces of the 'Parti du Peuple Algérien' (PPA) and the new and more potent force of the 'Front de Libération

Nationale' (FLN), the armed wing of the Algerian independence movement. The relatively small scale of the conflict allowed the Algerian nationalists to organize and plan a longer and tougher war. They were also able
to overcome most of their internal differences. By 1954, funded by other
shadowy forces in the Arab world, and armed with new guns and a Marxist-
Leninist ideology, it was the FLN who called the shots in Algiers and nearly
everywhere else across the country.

The Algerian war was officially launched on All Saints' Day when the
FLN – in a flurry of bombs, pamphlets and radio broadcasts from Cairo –
declared their objective of 'restoration of the Algerian State, sovereign,
democratic and social, within the framework of the principles of Islam'.
The methods included 'every means until the realization of our goal'. For
operational purposes, the FLN divided Algeria into six 'Wilayas' – an
Arabic term meaning 'under government (or military) control'. It was also
the stated aim to bring 'the war home to France', and in doing so to make
Paris the 'seventh Wilaya'.[3]

The Battle for Paris

The fresh outbreaks of violence in Algeria coincided with new waves of
immigration in Paris, mostly from North Africa. Between 1947 and 1953,
the official figures note that 740,000 immigrants arrived in Paris from
Algeria alone. The real figure was, of course, very probably much higher
than this.

At first the North Africans settled in parts of central Paris already known
to the pre-war generation of North Africans who had come here in the
1920s and 1930s – Place Maubert, rue des Anglais, Les Halles, or the suburbs
of Clichy and Gennevilliers (where there was a well-established community
of Moroccans). This pre-war generation had already long been the object of
suspicion and the target of police surveillance. The prefect of police Jean
Chiappe had indeed set up a special brigade in 1925 to control the North
African population with its headquarters at 6 rue Lecomte in the 17th
arrondissement. It was dissolved in the wake of the Liberation – its staff of
ex-colonials had been suspiciously close to the Gestapo and to Vichy.

North Africans in Paris were quick to realize that many of the promises
of the Liberation regarding racial toleration were never going to be met or
had already been broken. They encountered prejudice on a daily basis and,
like the Jews before them, they began to cluster in groups around the city

as much for their own security as anything else. They also organized themselves politically into groups, which were immediately banned. In 1952, Messali Hadj, leader of the banned nationalist group 'Mouvement pour le Triomphe des Libertés Démocratiques' (MTLD), had been condemned to house arrest in Paris, and Parisians were reminded in the press of the fact that Algerian nationalists such as Abderrhamane Yacine, Si Djilani and Mohamed el-Maadi had collaborated with the Germans. There were public complaints on the Left and Right about the hygiene of these foreigners, the incompatibility of Islam and 'European civilization' and, most commonly, the North African propensity for violent crime.

Many of the newly arrived immigrants found that life in Paris was in fact more dangerous and strictly controlled than under the colonial order at home. The great fear of the Parisian police force was the spread of the influence of pan-Arab nationalism, then incarnated in the charismatic figure of President Nasser of Egypt. Radical pan-Arab publications were constantly being set up and immediately shut down. Tension became more clearly visible on the streets of Paris in the early 1950s in the form of regular and popular Arab demonstrations that often erupted into violence. On 14 July 1953, a group of Algerian militants, members of the MTLD, were shot dead by police as they made up part of a wider demonstration of some 4,000 nationalists at Place de la Nation demanding the freedom of Messali Hadj.

As an act of solidarity, more than 20,000 Arabs of all nationalities gathered at the Cirque d'Hiver a few weeks later to mourn their dead. The secretary-general of the prefecture of police, Maurice Papon (who had been involved in the deportation of the Jews at the Vél d'Hiv), immediately set up a special unit, the 'Brigade des Agressions et Violences' (BAV), specifically to deal with 'the Algerian problem'. This was the moment when the colonial war started properly to be imported into the streets of the capital (this was also when the term *bavure*, 'a cock-up', previously applied to the events leading to the outbreak of the First World War, became a common expression of contempt for the activities of Papon's special brigades, the 'BAVs').

The task of the police was made even more complicated by the turf war being fought in the streets of the 13th, 15th and 18th *arrondissements* between the FLN and other rival nationalists. There were also regular shoot-outs in the 19th *arrondissement* in the rues Petit and Meaux between the FLN and the MTLD or PPA. Maurice Papon had to rely on inside information from native Algerians for intelligence and installed in these areas a network of *harkis* – Algerians with an allegiance to Paris rather than Algiers – whose task was to monitor and inform on the activities of their compatriots. Despised by Algerian nationalists as traitors and collaborators, *harkis* were a shameful secret of the French forces, renowned not only for their access to sensitive information but also their vicious interrogation of fellow Algerians.

For most of the time, however, the police were pleased to let the rival Algerian factions fight it out between themselves. Throughout the final years of the 1950s, there was effectively a secret civil war taking place in Paris, fought between the FLN and rival nationalist Algerian factions. The newspaper *L'Aurore* noted in 1957 that the district of La Goutte d'Or, nicknamed the 'Medina of Paris', was effectively a no-go area for Europeans and a place where FLN and MTLD militants flaunted machine-guns in broad daylight. Most deadly of all were the rues de la Charbonnière, de Chartres, Myrha and Stephenson in northern Paris, a step away from Barbès metro station; these were parts of Paris 'where the police did not dare to tread'.[4]

The French Left was generally sympathetic to the Algerian cause and many intellectuals developed the position that the only proper response was to participate actively in the struggle. Most notably, the philosophy teacher Francis Jeanson, an intimate of Sartre, organized a support network for the FLN in Paris that led to his arrest and trial in 1960. A campaign headed by Jean-Paul Sartre led to the famous 'Manifesto of 121', a petition against the Algerian war signed by prominent intellectuals of the day. The greater argument ran that the French in Algeria were now acting like the Nazis had done ten years earlier in France. As allegations of torture and murders perpetrated by the French army became widely known and corroborated, it was hard even for moderates to justify the war in Algeria.

By the time that Charles de Gaulle was returned to government, as a result of the emergency provoked by the spreading disorder of the Algerian crisis – a disorder that almost threatened to turn into civil war – the authority of the government of the day, led by René Coty, had simply melted away. It was no small irony that it was the crisis in Algeria that eventually restored de Gaulle to power. The catalyst was a mass strike and the seizure of the governor-general's building in Algiers in May 1958 by a coalition of right-wing officers and ordinary *pieds-noirs* who had entirely lost faith in the Parisian political classes. De Gaulle was careful to keep his distance from the *putschistes* but none the less engineered a constitutional return to power that enabled him to take control of the government and the situation. By 1959, much to the disappointment of those on the far Right who had supported his return, he was already indicating that the only honourable course for a 'great nation' such as France was to offer the Algerians self-determination.

The return of de Gaulle brought authority back to the French government but it did not bring order to the streets of Paris. Indeed, the war suddenly became tougher and more brutal in the wake of the so-called 'battle of Algiers', a terrorist campaign launched by the FLN in 1957, which included random bombings and shootings intended to frighten the French population out of the city. The instinctive reaction of the Parisian police was to crack down on all Algerians, and indeed any North African who might be a potential terrorist. Disastrously, Maurice Papon imposed a curfew on all French Muslims of 'North African appearance'.

This policy had terrible consequences on 17 October 1961, when tens of thousands of Algerians gathered in the centre of the city to demonstrate for peace and independence. The police response was harsh and ruthless, and in a terrible reminder of the evacuation of Jews to the Vél d'Hiv, Papon organized police trucks and wagons to take away demonstrators without trial to the Stade de Coubertin, the Palais des Sports and the Château de Vincennes, where they were savagely beaten up. On the Pont de Neuilly, a skirmish between demonstrators and police became a riot, at which point the heavily armed police forces charged into the crowd, killing two and wounding many more. The police then began to kill Algerians, throwing their bodies into the Seine.

This conflict was later dignified with the name 'the battle for Paris', but it was really just another massacre in a long line of Parisian mass murders. Papon's priority was to cover up all evidence of police wrongdoing. However, the morning after the demonstration a small group of Communist militants – all Europeans – under the guidance of the writer Arthur Adamov and the actor Jean-Marie Binoche, set out to paint the slogan 'This is where we kill Algerians!' on the bridge before retreating to the bar The Old Navy on the boulevard Saint-Germain. The slogan was quickly wiped away, but the police could not destroy all the evidence of the killings. Bloated corpses of Algerians washed up by the Seine were regularly found by ordinary Parisians over the coming weeks and months.

There was more to come: in February 1962, a demonstration against the violence of the OAS ('Organisation Armée Secrète' – a right-wing terror organization set up by *pieds-noirs* in Algeria) and for peace turned violent as police again charged demonstrators. Nine people were killed and hundreds injured in the crush at the Charonne metro station. By this time, the

Algerian war had arrived properly in Paris, as OAS terrorists claimed responsibility for bombing the new 'Drugstore' on the Champs-Élysées, the offices of the newspaper *France Soir*, the foreign office in the Quai d'Orsay and Jean-Paul Sartre's apartment in the rue Bonaparte. Other plans included blowing up the Eiffel Tower and assassinating de Gaulle himself (there was indeed a botched OAS-led attempt on de Gaulle's life at Petit-Clamart in 1962). The Parisian public were soon heartily sick of this endless and apparently unstoppable cycle of violence. When de Gaulle finally granted Algeria its independence that same year, most Parisians greeted the move with relief more than any sense of justice having been done.

'The form of a city . . .'

Indeed, as the Algerian cauldron continued to simmer away throughout the 1950s, the attention of politicians and ordinary people alike had all too often been fixed on other, less dramatic issues.

The first and most pressing of these was the increase in population and the housing problem that went with it. The shortage of suitable housing stock in French cities, and in particular Paris, was partly a legacy of the war. Almost a quarter of all housing in France had been wrecked or destroyed altogether between 1940 and 1945. The first priority of the government in the immediate aftermath of the war was to begin rebuilding the infrastructure of the country – the roads, the railways, the ports.

This meant that in the early 1950s, almost 90 per cent of homes in Paris lacked basic amenities – including shower, toilet or bath. Many parts of what is now the fashionable centre of Paris – great swathes of the Left Bank close to the Seine as well as the outer *arrondissements* on the Right Bank – were virtual slums and inhabited by the poorest of the working classes or immigrants. Apartments were rare in these parts of town: most people lived in dingy cheap hotels or hostels. Soup kitchens were commonplace, and not just in proletarian districts. Most shameful of all were the *bidonvilles* or shanty towns, made out of concrete and corrugated iron, set up outside Paris in the shadow of what had been the Zone, at Noisy, Ivry, Villejuif and Nanterre.

The shanty towns were a disgrace and there were regular calls from the Left to do something about the situation. There was no solution, however, that did not involve either the wholesale reconstruction of central Paris – which would have been disastrously unpopular on both aesthetic and political grounds – or evacuating the working classes out to the dreaded *banlieue*, a move vehemently opposed by every Leftist group in the city, which saw its true capital in the myth of 'Red Paris'.

As far back as 1948, the government had drawn up plans for social housing in the form of what were called *habitations à loyer modéré* ('housing for a moderate rent') or HLM. These were high-quality buildings, often constructed in central or desirable parts of the city, but they were in desperately short supply and often still too expensive. The HLM programme was revamped and relaunched in the early 1950s, but this time the city authorities aimed at developing what were called *grands ensembles*, the high-rise estates beyond the ring road around Paris and the suburban villas that flanked it. The most notorious of these estates was at Sarcelles to the north of the city. It was finished in 1954 and soon home to some 10,000 people. It also quickly gave rise to the disease of *sarcellitis* – a peculiarly twentieth-century form of anomie entirely rooted in the boredom and despair generated by living in a high-tech environment that left no space for cafés, bars, small streets, shops, street markets or any of the other ornamental aspects of daily life that had made Paris so rich in every detail. The 'success' of Sarcelles encouraged the city-planners, however, and by the end of the 1950s, Paris was encircled by more than ninety ugly and cheaply built estates, which depressed inhabitants and visitors alike. The population of Paris was being reduced, but at a price.

In this unstable cultural climate, older Parisians noted that the Liberation had destroyed many aspects of Parisian life, which would now never come back. Baudelaire's poems from the nineteenth century about the death of 'Old Paris' could apply equally well to the transformations that were currently taking place when he refers to 'the form of a city which changes, alas, more swiftly than the heart of mortal man'.[5]

These changes included, most famously and controversially, the demise of the old-style, semi-official brothels of the city which had been operating in the capital since anyone could remember. The campaign to close the brothels was led by one Marthe Richard (who had herself been a whore and a spy in her youth), who mobilized the press against the brothels, which, in the harsh post-war climate, were seen as a mark of the kind of decadence that had led to the fall of France in the first place. It did not help that brothels had reported thriving business during the Occupation and that they famously welcomed Germans with the same favours as Frenchmen. At a stroke, when a law was passed in 1946, more than 180 establishments were shut down in Paris, including famous names such as Le Chabanais (which dated back to 1820), Le Sphinx and Le One Two Two.

These places were not only deeply inscribed into Parisian folklore – and that of the foreigners who had come to Paris to taste their legendary pleasures – but had stood as elaborate and rich monuments to all forms of human sexual activity. Somewhere like Le Sphinx or Le One Two Two not only offered the regular forms of coupling that could be bought all over the city, but specialized in 'shows' and 'spectacles' constructed to the whim of clients, who dined well in the attached restaurants as a prelude to more carnal pleasures. The hypocrisy of those senators who voted for the closure of the brothels was not lost on Fabienne Jamet, the famous *patronne* of Le One Two Two. Having recognized the embarrassed features of several regular clients among those who voted for the closure, she pitied their wives, who could never expect their men to reach such heights of ecstasy again.[6] The business of prostitution did not of course go away, but spilled over into the streets. Prostitutes could be found all over the city but favoured especially the rue Saint-Denis, the backstreets of Pigalle, and the short, narrow streets around the Opéra. The closure of brothels was proposed as a step away from the old France that had so conspicuously failed and towards the Anglo-Saxon model of modernity, which had prevailed. Their closure was quietly mourned by all those who saw in their passing the death of an intricate, centuries-old and uniquely wrought form of Parisian entertainment.

Strangely, Paris was never more picturesque or photogenic than during this post-war period when it was simultaneously being destroyed and rebuilt. The wrecked streets and newly opened vistas made the city an ever-changing and endlessly fascinating spectacle for photographers such as Robert Doisneau and Henri Cartier-Bresson, whose main interest as artists was to capture the shifting variety of everyday life in the capital. Like Eugène Atget or Georges Brassaï before them, these photographers mapped the changing cityscape, as it moved from the past towards the uncharted territory of its future. Their photographs abound with the obscure events of life in the city against a chiaroscuro backdrop of war-damaged buildings, half-ruined *quartiers* and blackened interior scenes, which are more often than not illuminated by a tiny detail – the smile of a young girl, a tramp playing with a dog, a woman singing in tears in a café.

The same unflinching observation of everyday life inevitably influenced the *nouvelle vague* cinema of the likes of François Truffaut and Jean-Luc Godard, whose own revolutions in art began in the same city streets. The cinema they invented was an art of intimate details – from the clattering cobbled alleys and claustrophobic interiors pictured in Truffaut's *Les Quatre Cents Coups* ('The 400 Blows') of 1959, to the inviting theatricality of cafés and backstreets that feature in Godard's *Bande à part* ('The Outsiders') of 1964, the scenery of Paris seemed to offer endless potential and adventure. One of the keys to understanding the new cinema was that it was driven by a spirit of improvisation which itself sprang from the setting of a scene. The aim, as theorized by François Truffaut in the journal *Cahiers du cinéma*, was to make intimate, detailed scenarios, where the director was also an author (an *auteur* in the truest sense, in fact), and therefore a participant in the film. The result was often breathtaking and indeed breathless in its dash and verve – certainly the earliest and best examples of the *nouvelle vague* genre (again usually from Godard or Truffaut) are simultaneously daring and inventive visual masterpieces as well as high examples of poetic modernism in the city.

Most importantly, in the early 1960s, as Paris began finally to emerge in cultural and political terms from the wreckage of the first part of the century, the city streets that provided the backdrop to the mini revolution in cinema were now seen as sites for new forms of drama and beauty rather than as simply the setting for war. They would, however, also soon be the setting for a far more dramatic and wide-ranging attempt at revolution.

43. An Obscure Conspiracy

There was indeed little to suggest in the early years of the 1960s that by the end of the decade the French government would be paralysed and almost brought down by a hard-fought insurrection in the streets of Paris. But that was precisely what happened in May 1968, when a series of demonstrations and street disturbances led by young people on the Left Bank sparked a wave of similar protests across the country. The consensus at the time was that the riots and disturbances had come out of nowhere. None the less the events of May 1968 would come to mark a turning point in the cultural history of Europe in the twentieth century.

This was also a moment that had many precedents in Parisian history: the 'Front Populaire' of 1936, the Paris Commune of 1871, the revolutionary insurrections of 1831 and 1848 and even the Revolution of 1789 were all cited as models. Its distinguishing feature was, however, that for the first time this was not the revolt of an impoverished and half-starved underclass, nor a concerted guerrilla campaign fought by organized subversives, but a rebellion by middle-class students, the sons and daughters of those who had profited most from France's post-war economic recovery. For many on the traditional Left, who had fought for improvements of salaries and living conditions, it was this fact that made the revolt both so incomprehensible and shocking.

This was not the case, however, for those in Paris who were close to the various remnants of the revolutionary avant-garde movements that had survived the many upheavals of post-war development. These included members of the Revolutionary Surrealist Group, the Revolutionary Communist Party, anarchists and other minuscule factions still operational in Saint-Germain-des-Prés and the Latin Quarter, publishing pamphlets, tracts and denunciations mainly of each other. What these groups had in common was that they had decided that the Utopian promises made by the avant-gardists in the early part of the century still had to be honoured. They had long since identified underground subversion as the guiding principle of Parisian history – a theory confirmed by activities of the resistance in the not so distant past – and were determined to act upon this insight. The revolutionary vision of these groups was summed up in famous graffito of May 1968: 'Be Realistic, Demand the Impossible!'

There were, in truth, few other signs that a storm was brewing. The decade had begun with de Gaulle firmly in charge of a government whose authority, despite the difficulties of the Algerian war, was largely unchallenged in the mainstream political arena. The occasional student disturbances, such as the strikes at Strasbourg or Nantes in the mid 1960s, were largely explained even by sympathetic Leftist commentators as aberrations, the fruits of too much material comfort and boredom rather than any serious political confrontation. The new underground cultures of jazz, rock 'n' roll and beatnik literature were similarly dismissed as mere American imports that could not compete with or replace the folk wisdom of native Parisian performers – although the funeral of Édith Piaf in 1963 was said to mark the death of home-grown popular culture in the city. The sociologist Edgar Morin coined the term *musique yéyé* to describe the dissonant new sounds that were invading Paris from New York, San Francisco and Liverpool. French youth culture – as exemplified by the 'phoney Elvis' Johnny Hallyday and winsome France Gall – was in itself mainly a weedy, imitative and submissive phenomenon (this state of affairs would not last long; the likes of Serge Gainsbourg and Michel Polnareff, as well as former pop puppets such as Françoise Hardy, would soon set about inventing a uniquely effective Gallic vocabulary for pop and rock).

The main facts of Parisian life for the younger generations in the 1960s were anomie and boredom. Most young people still lived at home, or in deadly dull university residences, and the life of the city – aside from the student ghetto of the Latin Quarter – was either financially or culturally at an untouchable distance from their lives and desires. Unlike their counterparts in the English-speaking countries, where youth was taking on the mantle of cultural political power, young people in France were still dominated by a heavy-handed paternalism and a rigid social hierarchy. The revolutionary moment of the 1968 revolt was, as we shall see, clearly inspired by reaction against these constraints, as articulated by some of the wildest avant-garde groups and far-Left sects, as much as any reading of Marx and Hegel.

Instant City

Physically, Paris was still a dirty and drab place in the early 1960s. This was partly due to the fact that since the end of the war the authorities had been occupied with more pressing concerns than cleaning the city. The façades of most public buildings and even the grandest hotels were now black with soot. The Parisian love affair with the car had obviously made matters much worse and it was hard to cross any of the great boulevards that were still the main arteries of the city without suffering near-asphyxiation. Another part of the problem was that the re-organization of the city that had taken place under Haussmann in the nineteenth century was badly suited to the twentieth. In some ways, it was as if Haussmann had only half completed the job: most notably the great boulevards across Paris still left untouched a labyrinth of small streets, passages, dead ends and covered streets too narrow for traffic, which rendered movement through the city painfully slow.

Architects and city-planners dreamt of refashioning Paris using the new technologies of the era; they fantasized about underground tunnels, skyscrapers and huge shopping arcades where the pedestrian glided painlessly from home to metro to shops to work and then to home without coming into contact with the 'real' world.

This is the Paris satirized in Jacques Tati's comic masterpiece *Playtime*, a film that depicts the hero lost in a dehumanized dystopia of plate glass, moving pavements and traffic, where his only human contact is with herds of American tourists who wander pointlessly through the unreal city. Unsurprisingly, *Playtime* was a critical and commercial flop when it first appeared in 1967; many Parisians still wanted to believe that their city was a harbinger of a bright future as well as a monument to the past.

Alongside the passion for the new was an instinct to preserve and restore what was left of the old city. In the late 1950s, a process of cleaning-up and modernization had begun in the areas around rue Lafayette and Gare Saint-Lazare. This was the initiative of the minister of construction, Pierre Sudreau, who had seen the tourist potential of a cleaner and more beautiful city. Landlords doubted that the project was worthwhile and hesitated to pay the meagre local taxes funding the restoration work. The Parisian press and public was, on the other hand, unusually keen on the project and encouraged Sudreau to extend it to sand-blasting Notre-Dame, the Louvre and Les Invalides, revealing complexities of colour in the stone which had not been seen for centuries.

In 1962, de Gaulle's minister of culture, André Malraux, drew up a law that identified areas in the central city to be preserved as *secteurs sauvegardés* ('conservation sectors'), selected on grounds of historical merit. The law was first implemented in the Marais, at that time one of the most decrepit, unhealthy and dangerous parts of the city. Many of the buildings in this district had been untouched for a hundred years or more; most streets were a jumble of neglected, formerly magnificent *hôtels* from the *grand siècle*, rickety sheds and workshops, and tiny boutiques and studios. This was all very picturesque, but it stank to high heaven and most buildings lacked even the basic necessities of running water and electricity. The first job was to scrub clean the façades and remove the improvised, shambling constructions, revealing open courtyards, elegant archways and the sense of grandeur that had originally belonged here.

Other plans for developing the city were less successful and certainly less popular. These included the demolition of Les Halles, the very emblem of old Paris or at least the Second Empire city. Les Halles was not just a food market but even as late as the tail-end of the 1950s contained its own micro-worlds of whores, thieves, peddlers and hustlers whose very language was a direct link to a quickly fading past. On a less nostalgic note, the streets around Les Halles were home to a large working-class community who did not want to be evacuated to the high-rise estates outside the city, but who could not afford to stay anywhere else in central Paris. The government priority was to reduce the population of Paris in order to preserve what it designated as historic worth; there was inevitably a high human cost entailed in this plan.

There were also inevitably the first complaints that Paris was being made into a film set or a museum. In his satirical novella of 1965 *Les Choses* ('Things'), the writer Georges Perec describes the lives of two young Parisians, Sylvie and Jérôme, who wander aimlessly around a Paris that they can admire in visual terms – and which provokes their fantasies of an ideal life – but which they can neither touch nor own. The complaints about Paris as an urban spectacle did not always come from established intellectuals or artists, however. They came from the working classes themselves. But even the Communist Party dismissed many of these objections as reactionary and a backward-looking refusal to embrace progress.

Paris Underground

There were, however, in the early 1960s already various hard-headed elements in Parisian society that refused to be guided by the heavy hand of Gaullist or Communist paternalism. These included student groups and anarchists – whose ideas were in resurgence for the first time since the 1890s – as well as disgruntled working-class and immigrant communities who felt they had little in common with their alleged superiors in parties of the Right or Left.

Paris at that time was also home to a burgeoning underground scene that was influenced by similar movements in the United States and Britain. Certainly, the Parisian underground and the outside world had many of the same heroes, from Miles Davis to Jack Kerouac to the Rolling Stones. Paris itself had also briefly been a counter-cultural capital in the late 1950s for the American Beats, attracted both by the city's intellectual prestige and its louche pleasures. The headquarters of the Beats in Paris was a little hotel, nicknamed the 'Beat Hotel', run by a certain Madame Rachou in rue Gît-le-Coeur. This was where William Burroughs and Brion Gysin ate raw opium and smoked hash, performed magical experiments and invented a 'dream machine' that would unleash the fierce powers of unlimited subjectivity on to the world.

Parisian drug culture was not, however, a mass phenomenon, as it was soon to become in the English-speaking world, but mainly limited to a small élite with close links to the dying avant-garde movements in the cafés of Montparnasse and Saint-Germain-des-Prés. The drug-taking was therefore, at least at the beginning of the 1960s, a rather more calculated intellectual exercise than it was soon to become across the Western world. For young would-be intellectuals and actors, such as the fledgling writers Jean-Pierre Kalfon and Jean-Claude Bailly, the model was 'Le Grand Jeu' ('The Great Game'), an offshoot of the Surrealist movement that had conducted a long exchange with André Breton in the 1920s over the viability of hallucinogenic drugs as a short-cut to the Surrealist experience. Breton finally disagreed with them, but the group continued to experiment with asphyxiation and opium as mystical projects. The aim for those taking drugs in Kalfon's group was instant enlightenment, a new way of seeing the city that bypassed all traditional routes towards illumination.

The most widely used drug was cannabis, in the form of Algerian or Moroccan kif, which was occasionally adulterated with opium, and easily obtainable in well-known haunts such as the rues Xavier-Privas or Mouffetard. LSD arrived with the return to Paris of Jean-Pierre Merle, a long-time associate of the American 'acid guru' Timothy Leary. The headquarters of the small psychedelic scene in Paris was the shop Mandala on the rue Vavin, where LSD was passed around to a soundtrack of English or American R&B or, just as often and as familiar, music from the Orient. There were also Parisian attempts at psychedelia in the forms of the bands Mahjun and Red Noise. The American Center on the boulevard Raspail would become another 'free space', devoted to drugs, sex, political protest and transcendental philosophy in roughly equal measure.[1]

The drug scene crossed over to the world of cabaret and *chanson*. One of the more intriguing and unusual fruits of this union was the work of Brigitte Fontaine – a singer, artist and free spirit who, under the guiding hand of her friend the songwriter Jacques Higelin and the Algerian musician Araski Belkacem, was nicknamed 'the Juliette Gréco Freaky'. Fontaine had begun her career in the tradition of *la chanson française* – a genre whose most famous exponents were Jacques Brel, Georges Brassens and Léo Ferré, who prized words as much as music, creating literate, witty mini dramas or comedies in their songs. Brigitte cultivated an ironic, sarcastic style that brought comparison with Serge Gainsbourg. The album *Brigitte Fontaine est folle* ('Brigitte Fontaine is Mad') is probably the best example of this style and the song 'Cet enfant que je t'avais fait' ('This child I gave to you') was an essential part of the soundtrack of Parisian life in the 1960s.

Fontaine also experimented with a form of world music with Araski, bringing Arab and other Oriental influences into her music, and collaborated with the Art Ensemble of Chicago, who were then based in Paris, and regular players at the floating free festival at the American Center on the boulevard Raspail. She was temporarily forgotten in the 1980s but rediscovered by a new generation of performers including Noir Désir, Étienne Daho and Les Rita Mitsouko (who are probably her most successful progeny), and is now venerated as the diva of the Parisian underground and a heroine of the psychedelic era in the city.

Like Anglo-American rock music, psychedelic drugs were, however, not an immediate success, even among the most 'advanced' sections of the Parisian underground. The journal *Le Crapouillot*, usually a reliable friend of all things subversive, produced an 'anti-LSD' issue, while others denounced LSD as an 'American fad for cretins'. The way forward, it was argued in obscure, hard-edged journals like *Groupe Artistique Révolutionnaire* and *L'Internationale situationniste*, was political and in conflict.

The Dreamers

The distinguishing feature of the revolt of May 1968 was that it was a total negation of everything that Western society had to offer. Western society was sick and dying, it was argued in the seminar rooms and on the *terrasses* of the Left Bank; the only cure was a total transformation of society, a total revolution. This would not come from culture alone – movies and music were anyway only part of the 'civilization of the image' that had to be destroyed – but from a radical break with the past and all its taboos.

This intransigent, wilful and bold position is one of the central themes of the 2004 film *The Dreamers*, directed by Bernardo Bertolucci, which describes and analyses the incestuous and bisexual *ménage à trois* formed by a brother and sister from a bourgeois Left Bank family and an American student. This film has been much criticized, particularly in France, for its slick and sanitized account of the agitated street disturbances.[2] But the film none the less contains a lingering and mysterious resonance, which is in great part derived from the way in which the adolescent pursuit of absolute and impossible freedom is set against the backdrop of riots and street-fighting on the boulevards Saint-Michel and Saint-Germain. Most importantly, Bertolucci seems to be saying the eruption of violence on the streets of the Left Bank was a pathological as well as a political event – that is to say that the revolutionary ardour of the students had as much to do with an overflow of adolescent sexual energies as it did with genuinely radical demands.

One of the groups who claimed to have understood this instinct as a central part of making the revolution was 'L'Internationale situationniste' ('The Situationist International' or SI). This was a tiny band of hooligan intellectuals led by the 36-year-old Guy Debord, who published a journal of the same name from its shifting headquarters in the bars and cafés of the Latin Quarter. The SI were largely unknown at the time, and if they were read at all it was by a small coterie of like-minded Left Bank intellectuals.

Guy Debord himself was a witty, charismatic and daring troublemaker, given to hard drinking and the development of impossibly intransigent theoretical positions. Inspired in roughly equal measure by the poetry of Baudelaire and Lautréamont, the critical writings of Marx and Hegel and the practice of the Dadaists and Surrealists, Debord saw himself and the Situationist International as leading the final revolutionary vanguard of the century, an 'obscure conspiracy' that would leave the 'old world' behind for 'the new art of the future, the creation of situations'.[3]

What Debord meant by this call to arms was concentrated political and artistic activity that resisted the controlling powers of the 'spectacle' – the notion that all human relations are mediated by images from television, film, advertising, newspapers and magazines. The 'spectacle' is the enemy of impassioned human existence: 'All that once was directly lived has now become mere representation,' Debord wrote in the first thesis in his book *La Société du spectacle* ('The Society of the Spectacle'), which he published in Paris in 1967 with the express intention of 'damaging the spectacular society'.[4] This book would become one of the most famous and influential works related to the events of May 1968.

The theory of the 'society of the spectacle' was an immediate and popular success in radical Paris. It is important to understand, however, that the 'spectacle' does not refer merely to false images refracted through media. It is also, and most crucially in Situationist theory, a nexus of signs and images, which, when extended across all social relations, leads to what Debord called the 'colonization of daily life'. It followed from this that the Situationists held a relentless and implacable hostility to all forms of pop culture, the very site of the separation between spectator and spectacle. This hostility was matched by their conviction that it was disaffected youth, the very section of society that consumed the cheap gifts of the 'spectacular' society in the form of records, clothes and drugs, who would spearhead the revolutionary moment.

This much had been announced as far back as the late 1940s by the 'Letterist' figurehead Isidore Isou in *Traité d'économie nucléaire: le soulèvement de la jeunesse* ('Treatise on Nuclear Economics: The Youth Uprising'). In this text Isou, who was a crucial influence on the original Situationist group, declared that youth was excluded from the economy because it had no exchange value: without employment, family, capital, 'youths' were not people but 'luxury items' or 'utensils'.[5] Isou's call for a Letterist revolution had been based on the movement's principles of negation, which demanded that all be reduced to its most essential elements and then totally transformed.

Rather than submit to the false demands of the 'cultural spectacle', the Situationists chose to live as freely as they could, spurning family, work, study, leisure and money in favour of drunkenness, unlimited sex and a floating existence in hotels, cheap apartments and dosshouses. They hated the cleaned-up and modernized city and sought through the practice of what they termed 'psychogeography' to turn the organization of the city upside down. 'Psychogeography' was a game, or series of games, in which the participants set out to create an atmosphere that had the power to upset the routine and functions of everyday life. Drink, drugs, music, boredom, despair, fear and awe all had a role to play. The first objective of these 'psychogeographical' techniques was to blur the distinction between meaning and function in the city.[6] At one point, the Situationists urged in their journal that the metro should be open to pedestrians, that pharmacists should sell cigars and that street-lighting should have an on/off switch. The aim was to disrupt the organization of the city, awakening it to new and more passionate meanings.

One of the key Situationist books was Raoul Vaneigem's *Traité de savoir-vivre à l'usage des jeunes générations* (translated into English, somewhat incorrectly, as 'The Revolution of Everyday Life'). This book was published in 1967 and rivalled Debord's own work for its influence and popularity. Most significantly, in this book Vaneigem casts his gaze backwards towards Surrealism, which he praises for similarly esteeming transcendental anxieties (the death of God), hallucinatory violence and eroticism over the demands of rational systems. The problem with Western society was that it denied all these 'irrational' experiences in favour of order, discipline and 'meaning'. Vaneigem himself pronounced that, as a Situationist, he was in favour of total freedom, especially in the sexual domain, and including the breaking of the incest taboo. 'This is why the present state of affairs tends to favour Situationist agitation,' Vaneigem helpfully explained.[7]

But, despite their claims to the gift of prophecy, neither he nor the other Situationists could possibly have anticipated that the revolutionary events in Paris they dreamt of were so close at hand.

Freedom Now!

The seeds of the revolt were in fact sown outside Paris at the University of Nanterre. This grim set of buildings had been opened in 1964 as a 'model university', which meant that it aimed to train the future generations of technocrats who would oversee the smooth running of the cogs and wheels of French society. The suburb of Nanterre was a long way out of central Paris and could only be reached after a long metro journey to the end of the line, or an even more complicated bus route that took students through the slums and rotting makeshift buildings of the area. By 1967, the campus of Nanterre was wildly overcrowded with some 12,000 students. Student strikes against the draconian house rules of the campus were fast becoming a regular feature of university life, and pamphlets from the far Left, including the Situationists, which railed against all forms of authority and called students to take action, were eagerly devoured.

The tensions in Nanterre rose to boiling point on 22 March when a group of pro-Situationist students who called themselves 'Enragés' (in homage to the extremists of 1789 who frightened even Robespierre) launched the occupation of the main building. The take-over was quickly repulsed but by now was attracting international media attention. At the same time, Situationist slogans – 'Never work!', 'Boredom is counter-revolutionary!', 'Everything is possible!' – began mysteriously appearing all over the campus.

The focus moved to central Paris on 3 May when disciplinary charges were brought against the Nanterre activists at the Sorbonne. A hearing was set for 6 May, but by noon on 3 May there was already the promise of serious violence in the air. The atmosphere was heightened by the presence around the Sorbonne of members of 'Occident', an extreme right-wing student movement who were spoiling for a fight with 'the bolsheviks'. The Enragés and their fellow-travellers began smashing up tables to use as clubs as 'self-defence' against the members of Occident. This was when the nervous authorities decided to call in the police. By four o'clock that afternoon, the university was surrounded by the CRS – the 'Compagnies Républicaines de Sécurité', who were well known for their violent methods in breaking strikes.

The CRS wasted no time in arresting militants, or anyone who looked like they might be a militant, giving them a good hiding in the process. The students who had watched all this happen in front of their very eyes began to pour out of cafés, bookshops and bars to defend their comrades. As the stone-throwing and fighting in the boulevard Saint-Michel became a full-scale riot, the decision was taken to shut down the Sorbonne. This had happened only once in the 700-year history of the institution – in 1940, under the Nazis. It presaged a terrible moment for the government.

As fighting continued in the streets of Paris throughout the weekend of 4 and 5 May, it was obvious that de Gaulle himself, at least at first, severely underestimated the nature and the strength of the threat to his government. None of his politicians could agree to a solution, leaving power effectively and disastrously in the hands of the police. From the outset, police officers behaved with a consistent brutality and a disregard for the watching world. Young men and women were viciously battered in full view of their friends and comrades as well as the world's press. A nurse recalls her arrest and detainment at Beaujon over that first weekend:

We got out of the bus and were beaten up; then going between two ranks of CRS, I reached a stadium surrounded by barbed wire . . . A CRS man said to me: 'Come along, I'll shave you, curly locks.' He hit me. An officer intervened but the girl ahead of me had all of her hair cut off. I was taken to a cell, three metres by six. After five hours it contained 80 of us. We had to stand up. I could see the courtyard; a young man went by half naked, legs lacerated with baton blows, bleeding, holding his stomach, urinating everywhere. A young woman who'd been with him told me that the CRS beat him till he fainted, then undressed him and hit his sexual organs until his flesh was in ribbons.

The Café de la Mairie on Place Saint-Sulpice, a student hangout, was invaded by police who rained down blows indiscriminately on customers. Protesting that he was an innocent foreigner, a young man was smashed in the face by a CRS man and told, 'Yes, and you've come to shit on us in France.'[8]

The fighting was harder and more frightening than anyone might have thought possible. The students, in league with the far-Left groups who had come to join them (including the likes of the Situationists), barricaded streets and eventually occupied the Sorbonne itself. In response, the police began to use CS grenades on the rioters, weapons that had only ever been previously used in Vietnam. Still the rioters refused to surrender – setting fire to cars and hurling Molotov cocktails at the police lines. Students – female as well as male – foreigners, workers, all joined in the battle. As the dawn broke after the first nights of fighting, the streets of the Latin Quarter were revealed as an empty, scarred war zone. Situationist and anarchist graffiti encapsulated the motivating forces behind the fighting. These included: 'TAKE YOUR DESIRES FOR REALITY', 'THE IMAGINATION TAKES POWER' and 'LET US BE CRUEL!' The Situationist leader Guy Debord gloated over the furies he had helped to unleash and predicted a future of unlimited liberty. 'We are not afraid of ruins,' he said.[9]

'Run, comrade . . .'

This uncontrollable situation was serious enough but, at least according to the police, there was no question that the student revolt could become a full-blooded revolution.

Then events suddenly took an even more dangerous turn when, on 14 May, a wave of strikes among workers looked set to bring the country to a complete standstill. This was the moment that the government had dreaded, as workers and students stood poised to make an unprecedented alliance that could bring the government down. As postal workers, teachers, shopworkers, civil servants all joined in the strikes, it seemed that Paris was about to descend to a level of anarchy and lawlessness unseen since 1871. This fact was celebrated in the optimistic graffito: 'Cours, camarade, le vieux monde est derrière toi!' ('Run, comrade, the old world is behind you!').

For much of this time, de Gaulle had been away on a presidential visit to Romania; rumours circulated that he was scared to come back to France. But on the night of 24 May, as he had done in so many previous crises, the French leader decided to address the nation. He spoke to the strikers directly and contemptuously, accusing them of 'shitting in their own beds'. He did not concede to any of their demands – which were anyway so incoherent as to barely deserve a response – but he did admit that the old stranglehold on power had to be broken, and that there was a need for 'a mutation in our society . . . a more extensive participation of everyone in the conduct and result of the activities which concern them'.[10]

This rousing speech did nothing to stop the momentum of the conflict, however. The night of 24 May was indeed the most frightening and violent yet. Barricades went up in Bordeaux, Nantes and Lyons, where a police officer was killed. In Paris, some 30,000 demonstrators marching towards Place de la Bastille found their path blocked by police. They began tearing up paving stones, grabbing café chairs and tables and anything else they found in their path, and hurling them at the police. With a severely overstretched force, the police and CRS surrounded the Hôtel de Ville, the Élysée Palace and other main buildings of state. Having learned some-how that the Stock Exchange was unguarded, a group of heavily armed rioters set off towards the building, which was duly set ablaze to the chant of 'Temple of Gold'.

The disturbances could hardly get any worse, it seemed. All economic activity in France had come to a dead halt and appeared to be on the brink of being destroyed altogether. The government realized that a deal had to be made with the unions to avoid the nightmare scenario of students and workers in a continued alliance. At three o'clock in the Châtelet Hotel on the rue de Grenelle, union bosses and government representatives hammered out a wages deal that they thought would signal the end of the conflict. It was, however, almost unanimously rejected when union bosses sensed they had the upper hand. No less opportunist were the parties of the parliamentary Left, led by François Mitterrand and Pierre Mendès France, who proposed a coalition of the Left, with themselves at the helm. In the meantime, de Gaulle had left the country again. As fresh rumours of his resignation began to circulate, he was in fact meeting with his generals stationed on the Rhine to reassure himself of their support if the true revolution ever came.

The moment never arrived. Instead, at 4.30 p.m. on 30 May, de Gaulle spoke again to the French nation. This time he announced there would be elections within forty days, stating there would be 'civic action against subversion' and warning the people about the threat of 'totalitarian communism'.[11] With a huge sense of relief and triumph, the patriotic France that was de Gaulle's natural constituency rose as one: there was a triumphant parade of thousands up the Champs-Élysées, waving *tricolores* and chanting, 'France back to work', 'Clean out the Sorbonne' and, more notoriously, 'Algérie Française!'

In the occupied Sorbonne, the 'revolutionary festival' had long since degenerated into a nightmare. The filthy corridors now stank and were crawling with rats. They were also strewn with acid-tripping, lice-ridden hippies. The hard core of 'political' students who had set the rebellion in motion were baffled and slightly frightened to find themselves rubbing shoulders with every petty drug-dealer, minor criminal and whore attracted to the university by its lawlessness and the ever-hungry market for cheap dope and sex. A group of mercenaries called the 'Katangais', made up of army deserters and underclass thugs, organized a 'defence committee' and tried to impose some kind of order on the chaos, but their violence was soon too much for the freewheeling students to stomach and they were expelled in the first weeks of June.

The defenceless 'commune' was eventually taken over by police on 16 June. The historic battle for Utopia was suddenly finished, the dream of total freedom finally over.

44. The Killing of Paris?

One of the first actions of the city authorities in the aftermath of the riots was to lay tarmac over the historic cobbles of the Latin Quarter. This was done partly in the name of economic expediency, so the authorities said, but the symbolism of the action was not lost in a city where so many historic moments had been defined by barricades and weapons made out of the bricks and cobbles of its oldest passages and alleyways. One of the most widely seen graffitti slogans of May 1968 had been 'Sous les pavés, la plage' ('Beneath the paving stones, the beach'), a witty and provocative suggestion that Utopia could be found by ripping up the streets themselves. In the new, mechanized Paris of the 1970s, this would no longer be possible or conceivable.

The cultural and political life of Paris in the last two decades of the twentieth century was in fact defined by retrenchment on the Right and then disillusionment on the Left. De Gaulle himself left office in 1969. Despite the imprint he had left on French history, he departed a disappointed man. He had just lost a national referendum, which went against him partly because of his association with the chaos of May 1968. Although at his funeral a year later he was accorded all the great honours France could give him, he was still considered a reminder of the past. His successor as president, the phlegmatic and wily Georges Pompidou, and his prime minister, Jacques Chaban-Delmas, vowed to embrace modernity in all its forms. In practice, however, most of their policies were the same as or formed in direct response to those already formulated under de Gaulle.

As a consequence, Paris drifted further and further away from the global mainstream, while emphasizing its centrality in the European political arena. The right-wing governments of the 1970s were accordingly mainly centrist and the eyes of their leaders, from Pompidou to Giscard d'Estaing, were on their place in European history, rather than the quality of life for the average Parisian.

The development of Paris in the last two decades of the century closely reflected these trends. The first impulse in the 1970s was – following the model of Manhattan and the theories of Le Corbusier – to make a radical break with the past and to pursue modernity at all costs, building ever upwards to make Paris a city of skyscrapers. This project was aimed mainly at helping to renovate the *îlots insalubres* – the run-down areas mainly in outer Paris, from the 12th to the 20th *arrondissements*.

The plan was halted in 1974 by Valéry Giscard d'Estaing, who objected to skyscrapers on aesthetic grounds, citing how the Place des Fêtes in the 19th *arrondissement* had previously been charming but was completely overwhelmed by the towers which surrounded it from 1971 onwards. In central Paris, only the Tour Montparnasse and the Tour Zamansky at Jussieu survive from this period. Giscard d'Estaing also called a temporary halt on plans to renovate Les Halles.

The developments at Les Halles and the Beaubourg are the most famous and visible examples of the mania to embrace the future at all costs which defined Parisian urban planning in the late 1960s and 1970s, but the city is in fact studded with equally hideous and disastrous attempts at modernity. These include the business district of La Défense and the Tour Montparnasse. It was almost as if, in the wake of 1968, the city authorities were trying deliberately to wipe out the real life of the streets and replace it with buildings that dominated and controlled city space with their sheer power and volume.

'Paris Las Vegas – a city which only Americans could love'

The project to remove Les Halles from the centre of the city began again in earnest under the aegis of Jacques Chirac, mayor of Paris in 1977. The old 'stomach of Paris' was covered over by a series of glass and iron balustrades which parodied the original nineteenth-century structures – the Baltard Pavilions – where generations of Parisians had come to taste the gritty substance of proletarian life. A shopping mall was dug deep into the centre of the development – this was, as its architects, Claude Vasconi and Georges Pencréa'ch, smugly reassured themselves, a clever trick: an inverted skyscraper in the heart of Paris. The ugliness of this construction is matched only by the depressing and alienating effects it induces in Parisians and casual visitors alike. Similarly, the Centre Georges Pompidou (sometimes called the Beaubourg – an area identified as an *îlot insalubre* as far back as 1932), although a short walk away, is also most notable for its defiance of any architectural rigour or artistic sensibility. Designed by the English architect Richard Rogers and the Italian Renzo Piano, it will no doubt last well into the twenty-first century – if it manages to survive the pollution, the tourists and the traffic – as a monument to the arrogance of architects who prize cheap effect over beauty or style.

The prevailing opinion among Parisian intellectuals at the time of the developments was that the forces of capital and order were taking revenge against the disorderly city which had come to the surface in the 'revolutionary festival' of May 1968. This was, for example, one of the reasons why a short text called *L'Assassinat de Paris* ('The Killing of Paris') by Louis Chevalier became so popular in the late 1970s. In this book, Chevalier insisted that Paris had started a rapid decline in the late 1960s and early 1970s when de Gaulle and then Pompidou had straightened roads, tidied up rotting *quartiers* and evacuated the working classes out of the city. Since then, the city had entered its death throes and was unrecognizable even to those who had been born less than a generation ago. Chevalier was at this point in his career best known as the historian of the 'dangerous classes' in nineteenth-century Paris – the vagabonds, immigrants and alcoholics as well as the traditional labouring classes – insisting that it was the dynamic and ever-changing relation between central Paris and these marginal figures that had defined the history of the city.

Now, he said, one looked in vain for them in parts of the city that had traditionally belonged to these classes – newly gentrified Belleville or Barbès. Paris, in his view, was being murdered in front of our eyes. This was, argued Chevalier, the direct result of corrupt deals and a concerted plan to destroy the city's political heritage, and he quoted from an article in the *International Herald Tribune* which describes the city being built in the 1970s as 'Paris Las Vegas – a city which only Americans could love'.[1]

Chevalier may have been a nostalgic, and indeed it was an obvious exaggeration to say that the whole city was being cleaned up and sanitized: a short visit to La Goutte d'Or in the early 1970s would have disabused anyone of that idea. But he was not altogether wrong about the way in which the central parts of Paris were losing their unique identities. The proof of his arguments can in fact be seen on any day in an area like the Marais, a formerly run-down part of the city, where the crush of traffic, tourists and shoppers in the designer shops along the rue des Francs-Bourgeois gives the lie to the notion that this is in any way an ordinary Parisian district, somehow still intact and in touch with its past. The practice of *façadisme* – an architectural technique in which an old building is knocked down save for the front, giving the illusion of the presence of the past – became commonplace in the redevelopment of the Marais and other ancient areas in the 1970s. The term then started to be applied to the whole concept of rebuilding Paris, which had long since lost the 'dangerous classes' who had originally made its history, as an empty museum. These days, the Marais is a district that caters for those in pursuit of expensive clothes, art galleries, kitsch furniture or gay sex. But it is important to remember that this is primarily an entertainment district – offering a spectacle with no connection to real life. The food is accordingly nearly always mediocre and the bars are alive with a predominantly international clientele who could be in any big Western city in the twenty-first century. The particularity of the Marais has now been mostly lost for ever.

The Modern Look

It was no accident that the migration to the 13th and other less central *arrondissements* coincided with the political stagnation of the 1970s. By the end of the decade, the central part of Paris, focused on the Seine from the Right or Left Bank, was steadily becoming too expensive for all but the wealthiest classes. For many of the post-'68 generation (the so-called *soixante-huitards*), who demanded access to the pleasures of city life as a fundamental right but had no money or interest in making money, the only alternative was to live communally in shared co-operatives or buildings usually reserved for immigrants and lower-grade workers. Various 'auto-nomist' groups occupied empty or disused buildings, much to the chagrin of the city authorities. Most of these were in the 19th, 20th or 13th *arrondissements* and soon became established as the headquarters of a counter-culture which may have lost the battle of 1968 but which considered itself the true inheritor of the city's identity.

The impact of punk rock also changed the cultural geography of the city. The movement, which caught fire most dramatically in the mid-1970s as a cultural phenomenon in New York and London, had part of its roots in Paris. Paris-based entrepreneurs such as the record producer Marc Zermati and early bands like Shag Nasty and Stinky Toys were indeed an integral part of the European punk scene (the Situationists were also claimed as an influence by the Sex Pistols' manager Malcolm McLaren). In line with the nihilist punk philosophy of the era, it became the fashion to disdain the centre and move to the margins. The popularity of squatting, alongside the rise of hard drugs, also helped to determine a deliberately self-destructive, 'outsider' aesthetic. The archetypal artist of the period was Robert Malaval, a charismatic fan of Keith Richards and Picasso, admired and encouraged by Dalí and a flamboyant 'suicide of the art world'. Malaval lived (on borrowed money) in some style – he had an apartment on the rather swish rue du Pont-Louis-Philippe. He died in 1980 of a deliberate overdose while listening to Richard Hell's classic punk anthem 'Blank Generation' – it was, he wrote in a suicide note, his only gift to the future.

This kind of melodramatic gesture was not, however, universally appreciated by Parisian punks, who were often more political and demanding than their Anglo-American peers. One of the reasons for this was that the Parisian punk scene was influenced by the highly politicized art scene as much as mere rock music. A key driving force was, for example, the 'Bazooka' group, a self-styled collective of 'art terrorists' founded in 1975 with the express aim of disrupting as much of the media spectacle of modern Paris as they could. They included in their number Olivia Clavel, Lulu Larsen, Bernard Vidal, Jean Rouzaud and Kiki and Loulou Picasso. All veterans of various squats and collectives, they none the less hated hippies (known in French as *babas cool*) with a vengeance. In their early photos, from 1975, clearly influenced by the New York Dolls and the generic New York 'trash' style, they look like sexy and stylish, drug-addled versions of the early Manic Street Preachers.

Bazooka were, in fact, not real punks (and certainly not hippies), but rather the true heirs of the Situationists, declaring in a manifesto that they were 'a Free Republic in the heart of the Media. That is why we are threatened.'[2] They were wilfully provocative: 'We refuse to recognize the state of Israel' was an early, deliberately insulting statement. Among their more celebrated activities were the satirical attacks on the world in the mini magazines *Un regard moderne* and *Sandwich*. These were given away free by the daily newspaper *Libération*, which had been established in 1973 as the standard-bearer of post-'68 liberalism. The Bazooka group collapsed in 1978 – in best rock-band fashion, drug problems and attempted suicides were the causes of the break-up.

Their influence was immediate and widespread, however, embracing such bands as the Parisian punk feminists LUV ('Ladies United Violently'), led by artist Dominique Fury, who declared that 'Marx, Hitler and Mao were all ridiculous and all men'. Feminism was already high on the agenda at this point in Parisian cultural history. The MLF ('Mouvement pour la Libération des Femmes') was founded in 1968 by Antoinette Fouque, Josiane Chanel and Monique Wittig; now it occupied a position of political authority which affected all the parties of the Left. The works of Simone de Beauvoir had provided the initial impetus in the 1940s; the MLF also claimed new radical voices such as that of Christine Delphy, who argued for a total transformation of women's daily lives.

Other bands, with names such as Métal Urbain and Skydog Commando, were no less political than LUV, taking from Bazooka a contempt for the media and the official language of culture. The artwork for record sleeves by these bands was often almost directly borrowed from the Bazooka style, with motifs of typescript incorporating images and Situationist-style collage. The fly-posters for clubs such as Rose Bon Bon and Gibus also adopted the same typographical mannerisms. The style has persisted into the contemporary mainstream via the satirical weeklies *Hara Kiri*, *Charlie Hebdo* and *L'Écho des savanes*.

Above all, Bazooka and the groups they influenced introduced a hard-edged dissident style into the heart of a city that, to many of its inhabitants, was becoming a showcase of the past and an empty monument to capitalism. In this, Paris was at least keeping step with New York, Berlin and London, even if it was not quite assuming its traditional role as the cultural leader.

The Real Last King of France

When François Mitterrand came to power in 1981, Paris rejoiced in the arrival of a Socialist president and the return of its radical heritage. The ghosts of the Front Populaire, the Commune, even May 1968, were evoked by Parisians eager to see their city once again restored as the world capital of revolutionary politics. They were soon to be disappointed, however. Mitterrand was a master of double-dealing and doubletalk whose only real loyalty was to himself and his position in power. Most of Mitterrand's energy during the 1980s was consumed by his desire to direct events at all costs, even if that meant abandoning nearly all of the promises and principles with which he had come to power. Critics of the Mitterrand government were not slow to realize this, and the president was commonly described as the 'last king of France' both for the way in which he ran his inner entourage like a court and for his manner and attitudes; he often assumed the lofty prestige of a sorrowful man of destiny presiding over a country in a decline not of his making and which he could not stop.[3]

Still, the French accepted him as an avuncular figure (they commonly called him *tonton* – 'uncle') who – they had to assume – had their best interests at heart. Towards the end of his period in office, as he lay ill with prostate cancer, details emerged of his right-wing past and allegations of collaborationism which had dogged him from 1945. Whatever the actual truth of these rumours, they cast a long and dark shadow over the French political élite, while most ordinary people felt only shame and betrayal. The weakness of Mitterrand's Socialist successors, and then the attempts at centrist coalitions which followed from their electoral defeats, can arguably be attributed to these revelations. The electoral success of Jacques Chirac, arch-manipulator and opportunist cynic, hero of the *haut bourgeois* Right and enemy of the rest of France, can also be explained by the political vacuum which was Mitterrand's real legacy to his country.

The corollary of the mixture of hubris and icy *hauteur* that characterized Mitterrand's last years in office were the so-called *grands travaux* ('great works') which he commissioned to be built across Paris, and which were designed as lasting monuments to his government. These involved significant changes to the Parisian landscape, including the renovation of the Tuileries gardens and the Louvre and the addition of a glass pyramid to its courtyard, the construction of the Grande Arche de la Défense, the Opéra de la Bastille and the new Bibliothèque Nationale at Tolbiac. All of these projects were dogged by controversy and scandal, ranging from accusations of murky financial affairs to managerial incompetence. Worse still, they are almost universally disliked on aesthetic grounds by ordinary Parisians who have to live alongside them. Far from celebrating the 'popular' Paris of the people – those who have really made the history of the city – they are soulless, abstract constructions which could please only the cold eye of the architect and bureaucrat.

In Theory

The year before Mitterrand came to power, Jean-Paul Sartre died at the age of seventy-five. Like the funeral of Victor Hugo almost a century earlier, this was seen as a pivotal moment in the history of the era, even by those who had never read a line of one of Sartre's books. More than 50,000 people thronged the streets of the Left Bank as he was laid to rest in the cemetery of Montparnasse on a gloomy April morning. Newspapers proclaimed this as the demise, real and symbolic, of the French intellectual – that quintessentially Parisian figure whose purpose was to intervene in cultural and political life, who had been created by Zola at the cusp of the early twentieth century and reborn through successive decades with every fresh crisis and catastrophe.

Sartre had come to prominence during the Occupation but his intellectual trajectory had carried him through several generations of intellectual engagement, through the various crises of the Algerian war, Vietnam, May 1968, and the terrorism of the 1970s. His death, it was claimed, presaged the end of Paris as the intellectual capital of the world. The same lament was heard over the next decade or so, with the subsequent deaths of Roland Barthes (1980), Raymond Aron (1983), Simone de Beauvoir (1984), Michel Foucault (1984), Louis Althusser (1990), Guy Debord (1994) and, most recently, Jacques Derrida (2004).

There is some truth in this. Certainly from the early 1980s onwards, few French intellectuals held any of the commanding positions in public life or public opinion that they might have occupied in previous eras. This was partly to do with the rise of the mass media – which of course gave intellectuals a greater public but diminished their control over editorial positions and even the marketing decisions made to promote books. Alongside the popularity of mass-market 'intellectual' television programmes, such as *Apostrophes*, came mass-market intellectuals like Bernard Henri-Lévy, the leading guru of the self-styled 'new philosophers', whose silk shirts and glamorous girlfriends were accorded equal importance in the press as his views on the Hegelian dialectic or Bosnia. Serious figures, such as Jean Baudrillard, himself a critic of the 'spectacle' or 'simulacrum' of contemporary life which the media encourages, were inevitably caught in the glare of this same media coverage, even when they tried to sidestep it.

With the 'death' of the intellectual has come the decline of areas like Saint-Germain-des-Prés or Montparnasse, which in the mid-part of the twentieth century offered the democracy of the café table to all-comers. The young, the poor, the creative and the dissidents who previously defined these *quartiers* have long since moved on, unable to afford either the rents or a coffee at the *terrasses*. Contrary to the received wisdom, however, intellectual Paris is still alive and well; it has simply changed address. Previously 'marginal' areas such as the 12th, 13th, parts of the lower 14th, the 18th and the 20th *arrondissements*, or even Saint-Denis and Gennevilliers, are home to a new generation of intellectuals who are writing, painting, publishing and arguing in the traditional manner. The arguments are now over the challenges of post-colonial Europe or trans-sexual politics rather than dialectical materialism and one's relationship with the party. Derrida is still read, as are Debord, Deleuze, Blanchot and Bataille and the other masters of twentieth-century thought; but they are read alongside Alain

Badiou, Giorgio Agamben, Edward Said, Fatima Mernissi or younger thinkers such as Mehdi Belhaj Kacem.

The most powerful recurring motif in current debates is the question formulated by Jacques Derrida at the beginning of the 1990s about the ethics and meaning of 'hospitality'. In a world where the binary thinking that separates 'self' and 'other' has become the rationale for the most murderous aggressions, the importance of Derrida's question is self-evident.

It has been fashionable for a long time in the English-speaking world to proclaim either the death of the French intellectual or his/her irrelevance and ineffectuality in the modern age. Few contemporary French intellectuals will actually concede this, and with some justification. In the late 1990s, I attended lectures in Paris by Jean Baudrillard, which were always in pursuit of the ethical or ontological truth behind catastrophes such as the genocide in Rwanda or ethnic cleansing in Bosnia or considering the future of terrorism. Baudrillard is now an ageing figure but his 'children' – a new generation of intellectual dissidents – are everywhere.

What has changed is that the ideas, opinions and especially the theories of the new dissidents are as likely to be discussed in the pages of a fashionable magazine like *Les Inrockuptibles* – another descendant of the Parisian punk scene – as in the more august pages of *Le Monde*; what these cultural arenas have in common, though, is that they both take philosophical theory as seriously as any previous Parisian generation once did.

Black Years

The 1990s were in many ways a difficult decade for Parisians. The period began with the city under the shadow of a dying president and a sense of historical drift. Jacques Chirac was elected to the presidency in May 1995, but his authority was immediately undermined by a series of strikes, corruption scandals and the clumsy manoeuvres of his prime minister, Alain Juppé, whose arrogance and taste for nepotism made him massively unpopular. The return of the rightist parties to power also triggered strikes in the public sector – led by the transport unions of Paris – which grew increasingly acrimonious with each failed wages agreement brokered by Juppé. By late December 1995, after weeks of unrest and sporadic, low-level violence, Paris felt like a ghost town; on the busiest shopping days of the year, the streets were mainly empty, save for the few tourists who could afford the high prices and who were not menaced by the twin spectres of unemployment and high taxation. The press reported on the sense of depression and dread which permeated the city and began to use the term *la morosité* to describe the universally 'moribund' nature of Parisian life. Even now, cultural commentators usually point to 1994 and 1995 as 'black years', when Parisian identity was in serious danger of being subsumed under yet another series of crises.

The atmosphere in the city was also muted as a consequence of the wave of terrorist attacks in 1995. Paris was by now already long familiar with terrorism and its instigators. The steady flow of city life had already been regularly punctuated by terror attacks in the 1980s. Among the most notable of these actions had been the killings carried out by the anarchist group 'Action Directe', whose activities had culminated in the shooting by two young masked women of Georges Besse, the chief executive of Renault, in his home on 17 November 1986.

The city had been previously shocked by the shooting of six innocent diners at Goldberg's Deli in the rue des Rosiers in 1982, apparently in the name of Palestinian freedom. There were further Islamist attacks in 1986, including one at a shopping centre on the Champs-Élysées in March: two people were killed and twenty-eight were injured. In September that year, a veritable firestorm swept through the city. Bombs were placed in the Hôtel de Ville, La Défense, the Renault offices and at Tati on the rue de Rennes. With its low-price policy and easygoing atmosphere, Tati was long established as a favourite shop of immigrants and the Parisian poor. The attack seemed all the more shocking for this casual indifference to the city's poorer classes: the bomb killed seven people and injured fifty-seven more.

The bombings in 1995 announced, however, a new level in the war between factions in the Arab world and Paris. On 25 July, a bomb on the line to the suburbs at the Saint-Michel metro station killed seven and injured eighty-four people. Another bomb on 17 August at Place de l'Étoile injured seventeen more. There were further bombings – at Maison Blanche, Orsay and Saint-Michel, until the cell of Islamist Algerians responsible, led by one Khaled Kelkal, was hunted to Lyons, where Kelkal was shot by police. The attacks on Paris were almost certainly an overflowing of terrorist energies from the Algerian civil war, then at its bloodiest climax. As hundreds of thousands were being slaughtered in Algeria – by Islamist terrorists or government forces: no one is entirely clear about what happened – the Islamist militias, composed of returning veterans from the Afghan wars, blamed France for supporting their secular government and for all their previous colonial ills. These groups also predicted the attacks on New York and London in the early years of the twenty-first century. It was later revealed that, among the Islamists' chiliastic plans for Paris, one was to crash an aeroplane into the Eiffel Tower.

Sexy Boys (and Girls)

As violence and terror dominated the streets, sex and love somehow still remained central to the ethos and mythology of Paris. But this was also in a strangely mutated form. The spectre of AIDS, which had first become part of city life in the 1980s, now hung heavy over Paris. The wild nights at the Palace night-club near the Folies-Bergère, which had been drenched in LSD, cocaine and amphetamines for most of the 1980s in a pan-sexual frenzy, now gave way to a harsher, harder scene. Edmund White called the Palace 'the Studio 54 of Paris' – it was certainly the main hangout for would-be media stars and young literati. (Personally, I have fond memories of the Palace: it is where I first took LSD in 1984 and fell in love with a kohl-eyed secretary from Feyzin called Françoise Bailly, dancing to Dalida, Prince and Les Rita Mitsouko.)

The feeling of the end of an era was caught in Cyril Collard's film *Les Nuits fauves* ('Savage Nights') of 1992, a self-indulgent yet affecting journey through bisexual Parisian nightlife. Collard himself did not live to see the film or receive the awards it earned as he died of AIDS while it was being finished. The death of the writer Hervé Guibert in 1991 was an even greater public spectacle if less of a shock. Guibert had been the intimate of Roland Barthes and Michel Foucault (it was Guibert who in fact 'outed' Foucault as a sado-masochist in his memoir *À l'ami qui ne m'a pas sauvé la vie* – 'To the friend who did not save my life' – of 1990) and played on his connections to boost his own standing. He made a film of himself dying (*La Pudeur ou l'impudeur* – 'Shame and Shameless'), but by then many in the gay community found him guilty of the worst kind of self-pitying exhibitionism. To die of AIDS was a grim destiny; turning it into reality TV was an insult to all those forced to die obscurely and alone. Other gay writers, such as Renaud Camus, shunned such cheap publicity and argued instead for a new, plural 'queer' identity which left ideas like shame and fear in the past, alongside the 'superannuated priest' Jean Genet (for the likes of Camus, Genet incarnates the 'old-style homosexual' in that he is in thrall to a religion and moral order which his homosexuality negates but leaves intact).

In the 1990s, Paris emerged as not only the gay capital of Europe but also the world capital of *échangisme*, or wife swapping. This was not, as it was in most European countries, a seedy suburban activity, but a distinctly urban spectacle which took place in fashionable and exclusive clubs such as Bambou or Chris et Manu and was celebrated in glossy magazines such as *New Look* and *Interview*, which offered soft porn, politics and culture in the same package. For the more adventurous and exhibitionist there was always the *échangisme sauvage* which took place at Porte Dauphine or the Bois de Boulogne. The mainstream success of Catherine Millet's sexual adventures as described in her bestselling 'autobiography' confirmed the public's appetite for this material.[4]

The bestselling novels of Michel Houellebecq, an admirer of and heir to Céline, were often set in this world. In 1995, Houellebecq was living in an HLM near the Boucicaut metro station, working as a computer operative in the National Assembly. He had by then acquired a minor reputation as a poet whose work was unusual for its combination of realism and melancholy; indeed his poems from this period are much more in the vein of an English poet like Philip Larkin than the self-conscious experiments still popular in Left Bank coteries. Most striking of all was the fact that Houellebecq wrote brilliantly on contemporary Paris, capturing the contradictions of the city in all its tatty glamour, from the industrial erotica of Saint-Denis to the long, dreary boulevards wet with rain.

It was in 1996 that Houellebecq began work on his most ambitious novel, *Les Particules élémentaires* (translated as 'Atomized' in English). This is when I first met him (we drank and watched football together in his council flat – England and France were both knocked out of the Euro '96 semi-finals). I had no idea that this book, which lay in dog-eared sheaves in the ugly side-room Houellebecq called an office, would become a hit in France and across the world. 'It will either make me famous or destroy me,' Houellebecq said, waving drunkenly at the clump of papers he called a novel. I thought it was a joke.

In 1998, the English translation of his book crashed into the bestseller charts all over the world. The soundtrack to that summer was the cartoon disco music of the Versailles band Air, who admired Gainsbourg, Pink Floyd and German techno to roughly the same degree. Their first hit, 'Sexy Boy', was a sophisticated synthesis of all these elements and, most importantly, revealed to the outside world that cerebral Parisians could think and dance at the same time. Along with the new international popularity of Houellebecq, they seemed to announce a renaissance in Parisian popular culture.

This was all the more bizarre given the deeply sarcastic and despairing tone of Houellebecq's work. The novel is indeed conceived of as an attack on the liberal values of the 1960s that, Houellebecq says, are the source of the current moral and cultural chaos within contemporary France. The most dangerous and damaging of all of the freedoms won by the liberal Left in the 1960s, he says, was free love. Houellebecq points out that there is in fact no such thing. Free love is indeed like a free market; there has to be, through force of necessity, winners and losers. Total sexual freedom not only is impossible but comes at a very high price. Suicide, nervous breakdowns, alcoholism, eating disorders are all too often the fate of those who, perhaps because they lack good looks, charm or luck, are excluded from the sexual marketplace.

All this has given Houellebecq a reputation in the English-speaking world as a sex-obsessed libertine. (He didn't help his own cause by famously leering at the interviewer who came to see him from *The New York Times*, inviting her to appear in his erotic movie.) But in fact Houellebecq documents the Sadean underworld of *échangisme* with an unsettling mixture of scientific precision and touching pathos. His vision of 'swinging Paris' is simultaneously scabrous, hilarious and tragic. Most significantly, Houellebecq – a former Communist and self-confessed admirer of Stalin – is a stern moralist whose gloomy descriptions of sex as a commodity are matched only by his pessimistic prognoses for the future of humanity (he declares himself in *Atomized* to be in favour of cloning as a way out of the difficulties and snares of human sexual desire). His popularity as a writer is undoubtedly linked to the fact that his bleak vision reflects in some way the narcissistic but limited view that Parisians had of themselves during the last years of the twentieth century.

This is why one of the greatest surprises of the 1990s, in every sense, was the outburst of popular sentiment which greeted the victory of the French football team in the World Cup of 1998. In a decade that had so far been dominated by talk of cultural decline, this was a rare flash of colour and light.

The victory over Brazil in the Stade de France brought a normally indifferent French public on to the streets in a whirlwind of national celebration. Even the loftiest intellectuals, who kept a firm distance from football and other 'prolo' activities, claimed this as possibly the greatest event since the Liberation. The image of Zinédine Zidane, the mid-field player of Algerian origin who had scored the winning goals, was lit up in red, white and blue across the Champs-Élysées under the rubric 'Zidane

Président'. Even the most cautious figures on the French Left – including the venerable Jean Daniel in the *Nouvel Observateur* – began to talk about 'l'Effet Zidane' – a new, racially mixed and tolerant France.

The illusion lasted no longer than the hangover left by the party celebrations of the match. Prior to the competition, the right-wing demagogue Jean-Marie Le Pen, leader of the National Front, had complained of the racial composition of the French team, which was made up of Africans and Arabs as well as Europeans. When I had the opportunity to ask the French coach Aimé Jacquet about this during an interview I conducted for the BBC on his famous victory, he shrugged, stating that he had himself fought in Algeria, but could not see the significance of this any more. I was also able to pose the same question to Zinédine Zidane himself, who had recently been voted the 'most popular Frenchman of all time'. His response was a blank face and silence: in the volatile world of Parisian racial politics in the late 1990s, it was probably better to say nothing at all rather than be caught up in a struggle between forces you could neither control nor understand.

Clair-Obscur

This obviously did not apply to Michel Houellebecq, who in September 2001, days before the attack on the Twin Towers in New York, declared drunkenly in an interview with the magazine *Lire* that 'Islam was the most stupid of all religions'. Houellebecq's latest novel, *Plateforme*, which he was trying to promote in this interview, offers a grim diagnosis of the mutual hatred which defined relations between East and West at that point in the century, and which was visible in the streets of central Paris as well as its suburbs. His words were matched several weeks later by the fiasco of a friendly football match between France and Algeria, which was abandoned after Algerian youths invaded the pitch, chanting in favour of Bin Laden. Zinédine Zidane, the captain of France on that occasion, described the incident as the 'worst moment' of his professional career.

Everywhere in Paris that autumn, it seemed that Parisian tolerance was being stretched. The press and television complained regularly that the city was strangled by traffic and pollution, and threatened by a new influx of outsiders from Eastern Europe or other dangerous parts of the world. Parisian culture was being undermined and destroyed by globalization – which brought Starbucks and basketball to the city, wiping out the traditional spaces of old-style urban intercourse. Parisian culture was being replaced with 'Parisiana' – the kitsch tourist version of the city. Social commentators began to talk and write despairingly of 'Paris désemparigoté' – Paris without Parisians.

Partly as a reaction against this process, it became the craze that autumn for black and Arab youths from the poor parts of the city, or just beyond its periphery, to come into the shopping districts of the city centre – Les Halles, La Défense – to cause trouble. Dressed like Black Americans, but with accents and manners from the Maghreb, these kids staged pitched battles, terrifying both shoppers and workers. Like the rhetorical violence in rap music – at which these Parisian suburbanites excel – the aim was to shock the jaded spectator into feeling something, anything. The same instinct was the driving force behind the spectacular riots that convulsed the Parisian suburbs and then France in the autumn of 2005. The car-burning and attacks on heavily armed police had been regular events in these housing estates for over twenty years. It seemed that Louis Chevalier was wrong after all: the dangerous classes had not quite gone away, but simply left central Paris for the *banlieue*.

The social theorist Marc Augé has tried to explain this shift by writing that the city is now made up of 'non-spaces', shopping malls, car parks, business districts, which contradict everything that Paris, in its eclectic intimacy, has always represented. The only appropriate response, he says, is alienation or violent rebellion.[5] The architectural historian Paul Virilio wittily but despairingly describes how Paris is no longer defined by its outer ring road but rather by anti-terrorist devices at the airports.[6]

On a rare literary excursion to the city, the English writer Peter Ackroyd described Paris as a 'spectacular city', but it was not a compliment.[7] Paris is indeed all too often concerned with image and illusion, from the huge mirrors that gleam in every café to the endless reflections in the shop windows of the great boulevards. The most powerful illusion of all is that of its history as a repository of all that is finest and most magnificent in the human spirit. For this reason, contemporary Paris is often held up as the model of a great city that is dying, crushed under the weight of its past.

The real history of Paris is, however, as the poet Jean de Boschère puts it, a movement between the 'clair' and the 'obscur'; it is visible in the streets, he writes, as the endless play of polarities – shadow and light, past and present.[8] In strictly political terms, the history of the city has also been made by the movement between the abstract space of state and government control, and the real, inhabited space of the dreamer, the dissident, the subversive, the agitator. Paris has literally been made by the dynamic interplay of ideas and desires.

This explains the passion, bloodshed, glamour and fanaticism which are, and always have been, an integral part of daily life in this ancient place. New lifestyles, new politics, new forms of violence and pleasure are, as I write, shaping the 21st-century city. Paris still offers all the delicious and exhausting extremes of modern life.

But then, of course, it always did.

Epilogue:
Paris Underground

In the summer of 2004, when I was still writing this book, living in a tiny flat in the Temple district, I travelled to Tangier to meet up with the Spanish writer Juan Goytisolo, who now lived there. The reason for this was that I had been reading a short essay of his called 'Paris, capital del siglo XXI' ('Paris, Capital of the Twenty-first Century').[1] Despite its brevity, this essay was one of the most disturbing and provocative texts I had read on the city. In essence, the argument was that Paris had to be completely destroyed in order to emerge as the capital of the twenty-first century. I wanted to ask Goytisolo whether, in the post 9/11 world, he really meant what he had said.

We met in the wonderfully named Café Maravillosa in a 'Spanish' quarter of Tangier that was made up mainly of exiles from Franco's Spain and, by extension, Europe ('Filthy Stepmother' is how Goytisolo described the European mainland). Goytisolo was now in his seventies but, although lauded across the Hispanic world as the pre-eminent figure in Spanish letters, he had evidently lost none of his combative style or his contempt for middle-class values. He had been a close friend of Jean Genet and had inherited from the old thief a visceral suspicion of all forms of authority. He had also spent decades of his life in Paris, mostly living in the Sentier district. This is where the revelation had come to him that the idea of a European capital – made by and inhabited only by Europeans – is not just an anachronism but a dangerous myth that must be destroyed. The reason for this, he said, is that a purely European idea of the city does not correspond to the reality of the streets. Paris is, for example, the biggest African city in the world. It just happens not to be in Africa. The languages he heard outside his window in the Sentier were Swahili, Arabic, Kurdish, Hindi, Chinese as well as several varieties of non-European French. This polyphonic noise of the living city was, he said, the true sound, in fact, of contemporary Paris – the underground city which lies just below the surface of the 'society of the spectacle'.

Goytisolo commented that he had always loved the city because he believed that its oldest and truest tradition was the instinct for cultural and political subversion – this was why he himself had come to Paris as a dissident from Franco's Spain. It was this tradition, he also said, which had been temporarily lost at some point towards the end of the twentieth century, and which needed to be re-awakened. When he walked the streets of Paris now, he saw only a sanitized version of the past and no longer experienced the excitement or illuminations that he had known in his earlier life. The city had to be 'de-Europeanized' in order to make space for these new, dissident voices. That was what his short essay was about.

I returned to Paris, to my flat in Temple four floors above a Berber coffee shop, next to a building populated by mainly West Africans, and in the heart of what was known as a working-class Chinese district, and wondered whether Goytisolo was right. I also thought about how strange and distinctive Paris still is. In the world of cheap international travel, where everybody travels everywhere whenever they want, it's all too easy to forget this. Paris is, however, even in the globalized twenty-first century, a total and unique experience. The proof of this is, I concluded, in walking the streets. Goytisolo was a nostalgic émigré, homesick for a Paris he had known years ago, but he was also wrong. It's all still there. The trick is in knowing how to see – more precisely, it depends on the realization that its past and future are contained in the one singular experience of its present-day, everyday streets. This is, I decided, the secret to understanding Paris, in its infinity and all its detail.

One of my favourite walks in Paris provides a demonstration of this notion. It begins at the corner of rue d'Oran and rue Léon in the 18th *arrondissement*. From here you can take any number of directions towards the city centre – towards the market at Doudeauville, or the rue Myrha or rue Polonceau. At any point, depending upon the angle of your vision, you could be in Casablanca, Algiers, Dakar, Tirana, Beirut, or the backstreets of Bucharest. But you always know that you are in Paris – in the long, grey Haussmann streets, or the cobbled alleys, or the back lanes with their medieval curves and edges; you could never really be anywhere else.

And as you continue to walk, down towards the heart of the city, making your way through the crowded and smelly streets of Barbès, dodging Bosnian beggars, French junkies and African clairvoyants, picking your way through the Oriental squalor towards the Gare du Nord or the Eurostar Terminal, only one thing is sure: the city is changing again.

Andrew Hussey, Paris, November 2005

Notes

The literature on Paris is as vast and unknowable as the city itself. This section and the bibliography that follows are not even the beginning of a beginning to any ordered catalogue of the city. Rather they are intended as the preliminary sketch of a map that charts my own various trajectories into and through the city and its history. The books relating to Paris are clearly important in this context, but no more so than the gangster novels, histories of popular music, comic strips, albums of photographs, volumes of poetry, rap, raï and rock records, personal interviews, random encounters, lost evenings in cafés, bars, nightclubs, film videos and maps from all periods that make up the rest of the list.

Other important archives that inform this history are at Bibliothèque de Documentation Internationale Contemporaine (Nanterre), Bibliothèque Nationale de Paris, Bibliothèque Georges Pompidou, Bibliothèque du Cinéma André Malraux (Paris), Vidéothèque de Paris and John Rylands Library (Manchester).

The true text is of course to be found in the streets of the old city.

References to J.-A. Dulaure's monumental *Histoire physique, civile et morale de Paris*, 12 vols. (Paris, 1837), consulted in Parts 1–5 of this book, have been shortened throughout to 'Dulaure' plus the relevant volume number. Translation of quotations from French texts is my own unless otherwise acknowledged in the endnotes.

Introduction: An Autopsy on an Old Whore

1. Jean-Jacques Rousseau, *Les Confessions*, in *Œuvres complètes* (Paris, 1962–9), vol. 1, p. 154.
2. Interview with the author, Manosque, 2000.
3. Peter Ackroyd, *London: The Biography* (London, 2000).
4. Edmund White, *The Flâneur* (London, 2001).
5. Walter Benjamin, *The Arcades Project*, trans. Howard Eiland and Kevin McLaughlin, ed. Rold Tiedemann (Cambridge, MA, 1999).
6. See Patrice Higonnet, *Paris: Capital of the World* (Cambridge, MA, 2002); see also Andrew Hussey, 'Like a Pack of Bastard Dogs: Agitators, Rebels and the Revolutionary Mentality in Paris', *Parallax*, 37, pp. 23–31.

7. For a fuller description of the role of these terms in the creation of a Parisian mythology of revolution, see Patrice Higonnet, *Paris: Capital of the World*, p. 46. See also Éric Hazan, *L'Invention de Paris* (Paris, 2003); Christopher Prendergast, *Paris and the Nineteenth Century* (Oxford, 1992), pp. 23–7; Adrian Rifkin, *Street Noises: Parisian Pleasure, 1900–1940* (Manchester and New York, 1993), pp. 12–15; Michael Sheringham, 'Introduction', *Parisian Fields* (London, 1996), pp. 1–8.

8. François Rabelais, *Gargantua*, ed. R. Calder, M. A. Screech and V. C. Saulnier (Paris, 1961), p. 53.

9. Honoré de Balzac, *Œuvres diverses*, vol. 3 (Paris, 1841), p. 228.

10. One of the best accounts of the historical evolution of the *parler parisien* is Anthony Lodge, 'Histoire sociolinguistique du français de Paris', in *Paris: université de tous les savoirs* (Paris, 2004), pp. 257–87.

11. *Le Journal illustré*, 1867.

12. François Villon, 'Le Testament', in *Selected Poems*, trans. Peter Dale (London, 1978), p. 169.

13. Rifkin, *Street Noises*, p. 49.

14. Louis Chevalier, *L'Assassinat de Paris* (Paris, 1997).

15. Louis-Ferdinand Céline, *Entretiens avec le Professeur Y* (Paris, 1955), p. 10.

Part One: The Old Ocean: Prehistory to AD 987

The information in this section comes from Marie-France Arnold, *Paris: ses mythes d'hier à aujourd'hui* (Paris, 1997); J.-A. Dulaure, 'Du Culte des pierres', *Revue de l'École d'Anthropologie*, May–June 1902, *Histoire physique, civile et morale de Paris* (Paris, 1837), vol. 1; P. M. Duval, 'La Bataille de Lutèce', *Paris Militaire: traditions et souvenirs militaires*, no. 103 (Marseilles, 1956); Edward James, *The Franks* (London, 1988); C. Lelong, *La Vie quotidienne en Gaule à l'époque mérovingienne* (Paris, 1963); Bernard Rouleau, *Paris: histoire d'un espace* (Paris, 2003); L. Thorpe, *Gregory of Tours: History of the Franks* (London, 1974); C. Valence, 'Les Traces du culte d'Isis sur les portails mystiques de Notre Dame de Paris', *Le Goéland*, 52.

1. Dirty Water

1. For an account of this period see, for example, Arnold, *Paris: ses mythes d'hier*, pp. 34–5. See also R. and M. Barroux, 'Les origines légendaires de Paris', *Paris et Île de France: mémoires publiés par la Fédération des Sociétés Historiques et Archéologiques de Paris et de l'Île de France*, 7 (1955).

2. This version of the prehistory of Paris is generally accepted in most accounts and sourced in Dulaure's *Histoire physique, civile et morale de Paris*.

3. See Chapter 2, p. 19, for the origin of the word *seine*.

4. Diodurus Siculus, *Bibliotheke historica*, book V. 28. 1.

5. Dulaure, vol. 1, pp. 74, 76, 78.

6. E. de Ménorval, *Histoire de Paris* (Paris, 1889), p. 17.

7. This etymology is accepted, for example, in an anonymous scholarly article in the official journal of the International Olympic Committee, *Revue Olympique*, 102 (June 1914), pp. 83–4.

8. Guy Breton, *Les Nuits secrètes de Paris* (Geneva, 1970), p. 90.

9. Pierre-Yves Lambert, *La Langue gauloise: description linguistique, commentaire d'inscriptions choisies* (Paris, 2003), p. 38.

10. François Rabelais, *Gargantua*, ed. R. Calder, M. A. Screech and V. C. Saulnier (Paris, 1961). See also G. Corrozet, *La Fleur des antiquitez de Paris* (1532) (Bibliothèque Historique de la Ville de Paris), p. 134.

11. Quoted in Dulaure, vol. 1, p. 56.

12. Abbon, *Le Siège de Paris par les Normands*, ed. Henri Waquet (Paris, 1942).

13. Héron de Villefosse, *Histoire de Paris* (Paris, 1955), p. 28.

14. Quoted in G. Lafaye, *Les Divinités alexandrines chez les Parisii* (Paris, 1904), p. 227.

15. For Villon's 'Parouart', see his *Ballades en jargon*, quoted by Jean Dufournet in *Magazine littéraire*, May 1995, pp. 22–3. For Rimbaud's 'Parmerde', see his *Lettre à Ernest Delahaye, juin 1872* (Paris, 1961).

16. Jean-Pierre Goudailler, *Comment tu tchatches! Dictionnaire du français contemporain des cités* (Paris, 1999), p. 184.

17. See 'Notes de F. G. de Pachètre' (Imprimerie Nationale, Paris).

18. Quoted in 'Histoire sur le terrain', in Marcel Poëte (ed.), *L'Enfance de Paris* (Paris, 1908).

19. Baron Haussmann, *Mémoires*, introduction by Françoise Choay (Paris, 2000), p. 21.

20. 'Témoignage de Geneviève Dormann', in *Si le roi m'avait donné Paris sa grand'ville . . . Travaux et veilles de Michel Fleury* (Paris, 1994), p. 448.

21. Honoré de Balzac, 'Lettre du 21 Juillet, 1831', in *Correspondance: textes réunis, classés et annotés*, ed. Roger Pierrot, vol. 1 (Paris, 1976), p. 461.

22. Charles Baudelaire, 'Moesta et errabunda' ('Sorrowful and wandering'), *Flowers of Evil*, trans. James McGowan (Oxford, 1993), p. 129.

2. Severed Heads

1. Julian, 'Misopogon', in *Works*, ed. W. C. Wright (Cambridge, MA, 1913), pp. 428–31.

2. Danielle Chadych and Dominique Lebrogne, *Atlas de Paris: évolution d'un paysage urbain* (Paris, 1999), pp. 10–11.

3. The following account of the legend of Saint Denis is based on the account given in Thorpe, *Gregory of Tours*, and the thirteenth-century text by Jacques de Voragine, *La Légende dorée*, which is the basis for all subsequent variations. The edition I refer to here is Jacques de Voragine, *La Légende dorée* (Paris, 1911).

4. Camille Julian, *De la Gaule à la France: nos origines historiques* (Paris, 1922).

5. P. M. Duval, *La Vie quotidienne en Gaule pendant la paix romaine (1er–11ème siècles)* (Paris, 1952), pp. 34–6.

6. Suplicius Severus, 'On the life of St Martin', trans. Alexander Roberts, in *Suplicius Severus, Vincent of Lerins, John Cassian* (Cambridge, MA, 1994), pp. 3–17.

7. Sidonius Apollinaris, 'Letter to Ecidicius', trans. O. M. Dalton (London, 1915), book 3, pp. 68–86.

8. Lambert, *La Langue gauloise*, pp. 10–11.

9. See Chadych and Lebrogne, *Atlas de Paris*, p. 15.

10. For a comprehensive overview of the Gaulish languages and their relation to French see Pierre-Yves Lambert, 'Les mots français d'origine gauloise', in *La Langue gauloise*, pp. 187–212. See also Georges Dottin, *La Langue gauloise: grammaire, textes et glossaire* (Paris, 1918), pp. 72–9; W. Meyer-Lübke, *Romanisches etymologisches Wörterbuch* (Heidelberg, 1935); Rudolf Thurneysen, *Keltoromanisches* (Halle, 1884).

11. Rouleau, *Paris: histoire d'un espace*, p. 35.

3. Sea Gods

1. Henri, comte de Boulainvilliers, *Histoire de l'ancien gouvernement de la France* (Amsterdam, 1727).

2. Michel Foucault, *Society Must Be Defended*, trans. David Macey (London, 2003), p. 36.

3. Gustave Flaubert, *Correspondance*, ed. Jean Bruneau, 3 vols. (Paris, 1973–91), quoted in M. Yourcenar, *Carnets de notes des mémoires d'Hadrien* (Paris, 1952), p. 313.

4. Jack Kerouac, *Satori in Paris* (London, 1974), p. 23.

5. See Robert Cole, *A Traveller's History of Paris* (New York, 1998), p. 33.

6. Quoted in Dulaure, vol. 1, p. 174.

7. Quoted in ibid., p. 178.

8. The following account of the life of Sainte Geneviève is based on the account given in Thorpe, *Gregory of Tours*, and Dulaure, vol. 1, pp. 97–101.

9. Jules Michelet, 'Paris et ses légendes', *Cours au Collège de France: I, 1838–1844* (Paris, 1995), pp. 101–23.

10. Quoted in Edward James, *The Franks* (London, 1988), p. 157.

11. Foucault, *Society Must Be Defended*, p. 148.

4. Infidels

1. See James, *The Franks*, pp. 108–17. For a description of the geographical and political boundaries of 'France' during this period, see Elizabeth M. Hallam, *Capetian France* (London, 1992), pp. 1–6. See also P. Courcelle, *Histoire littéraire des grandes invasions germaniques* (Paris, 1964); P. Périn and L. C. Feffer, *Les Francs* (Paris, 1987).

2. Rouleau, *Paris: histoire d'un espace*, pp. 44–7.

3. A useful account of this battle is given in William Stearns Davis, ed., *Readings in Ancient History: Illustrative Extracts from the Sources*, 2 vols. (Boston, 1912–13), vol. 2, *Rome and the West*, pp. 362–4.

4. *Cronica Mozarabe de 754*, ed. Jose Eduardo Lopez Pereira (Zaragoza, 1980), pp. 100–101, quoted in William E. Watson, 'The Battle of Tours–Poitiers Revisited', *Providence: Studies in Western Civilization*, vol. 2, no. 1 (1993).

5. Interview with the author, Saint-Denis (Paris), 23 April 2004. See also Andrew Hussey, 'The Most Dangerous Man in Europe?', *The New Statesman*, 21 June 2004, pp. 25–7.

6. Fernand Braudel, *L'Identité de la France*, vol. 2 (Paris, 1987), p. 137.

7. Michelet, *Cours au Collège de France*, p. 549.

8. Dulaure, vol. 1, pp. 317–19.

9. *Annales de Saint Bertin* (Paris, 1964), p. 41.

10. Dulaure, vol. 1, p. 317.

11. Hallam, *Capetian France*, pp. 32–5.

12. Rouleau, *Paris: histoire d'un espace*, p. 44.

Part Two: City of Joy, 988–1460

Among the works consulted in this section are *À la découverte des plans de Paris du XVI au XVIII siècle* (Paris, 1995); Fernand Braudel, *L'Identité de la France*, vol. 1 (Paris, 1986); G. Duby, *Les Trois Ordres ou L'Imaginaire du féodalisme* (Paris, 1978); John Fox, *A Literary History of France: The Middle Ages* (London, 1974); Jacques Le Goff, *Les Intellectuels au moyen-âge* (Paris, 1985); Colin Jones, *Paris: Biography of a City* (London, 2004); *Journal d'un bourgeois de Paris*, ed. C. Beaune (Paris, 1990); J. Verger, *Histoire des universités en France* (Paris, 1987); K. Weidenfeld, *La Police de la petite voirie à la fin du moyen-âge* (Paris, 1997).

5. A Cruel and Brilliant Place

1. Dulaure, vol. 1, p. 339. See also Robert Cole, *A Traveller's History of Paris* (New York, 1998), p. 33; A. Horne, *Seven Ages of Paris* (London, 2002), p. 7.
2. Bernard Rouleau, *Paris: histoire d'un espace* (Paris, 2003), pp. 74–6.
3. Dulaure, vol. 1, pp. 355–6.
4. Braudel, *L'Identité de la France*, p. 127.
5. Quoted in Cole, *A Traveller's History of Paris*, p. 35.
6. Horne, *Seven Ages of Paris*, pp. 28–31.
7. Ibid., pp. 34–5.
8. Simone Roux, *Paris au Moyen-Âge* (Paris, 2003), pp. 25–9.
9. Ibid., pp. 72–5.
10. Jacques Hillairet, *Connaissance du Vieux Paris* (Paris, 1962), p. 239.

6. Sacred Geometry

1. Hillairet, *Connaissance du Vieux Paris*, p. 143.
2. For an introduction to the 'philosophy' of Notre-Dame, see Alain Ponsard, *L'Art de visiter Notre-Dame: le mystère dévoilé* (Paris, 1986).
3. Victor Hugo, *Notre-Dame de Paris* (Paris, 1992), preface by Louis Chevalier, p. 40.
4. One of the best and most recent introductions to the 'mystical' aspect of Surrealism, although it is also an attack on the movement, is Jean Clair, *Du Surréalisme considéré dans ses rapports au totalitarisme et aux tables tournantes* (Paris, 2003).
5. 'Fulcanelli', *Le Mystère des cathédrales* (Paris, 1926). See also Luis Miguel Martinez Otero, '*Fulcanelli*' (Paris, 1987).

6. For an account of this, see, for example, *Guide de Paris mystérieux* (Paris, 1985), p. 559.

7. Conversation with Alain Jouffroy, 14 March 1997. See also Alain Jouffroy, *Notre-Dame de Paris*, collection 'Monuments en parole' (Paris, 1992), p. 52.

7. Lovers and Scholars

1. Dulaure, *Histoire de Paris*, vol. 2, p. 138.

2. See John Fox, *A Literary History of France: The Middle Ages* (London, 1974), pp. 105–6.

3. There are innumerable accounts of the story that follows. This particular one is based upon the volume in modern French, *Abélard et Héloïse: correspondance*, trans. from the Latin by Octave Gérard, ed. Étienne Gilson (Paris, 1938; reprinted Paris, 2000).

4. Ibid., p. 234.

5. Ibid., p. 303.

6. Ibid., p. 87.

7. Ibid., p. 88.

8. Ibid., p. 132.

9. Ibid., p. 138.

10. Ibid., p. 176.

11. Jehan de Nisa, quoted in Fox, *A Literary History of France*, p. 56.

12. *The Historia Occidentalis of Jacques de Vitry: A Critical Edition*, ed. John Frederick Hinnebusch (Fribourg, 1972), pp. 90–93.

8. Saints, Poets, Thieves

1. For an account of the period see Dulaure, vol. 2, pp. 324–8; Jean Favier, *Paris* (Paris, 1997), p. 667. See also A. Hellot (ed.), *Chronique parisienne anonyme des années 1316 à 1339* (Paris, 1884); *Mémoires de la Société de l'Histoire de Paris et de l'Île de France*, vol. 11 (Paris, 1884).

2. Jean de Jandun, 'Treatise in Praise of Paris', in R. Berger, ed. and trans., *Old Paris* (New York, 2002), pp. 1–16.

3. *Le Livre de la taille de Paris de l'an 1296*, in Karl Michaelson (ed.), *Romanica Gothenburgensia* (Gothenburg, 1958).

4. The best edition of Rutebeuf is E. Faral and J. Bastin, *Œuvres complètes de Rutebeuf*, 2 vols. (Paris, 1959–60). See also N. F. Regalado, *Poetic Patterns in Rutebeuf: A Study in Non-Courtly Modes* (Yale, 1970); A. Serper, *Rutebeuf, poète satirique* (Paris, 1969).

5. Jones, *Paris*, p. 61.
6. Yves Guyot, *La Police* (Paris, 1884).

9. *Destroying the Temple*

1. See Amin Maalouf, *Les Croisades vues par les Arabes: la barbarie franque en terre sainte* (Paris, 1983), pp. 31–5, and Jacques Le Goff, *L'Europe, est-elle née au Moyen Âge?* (Paris, 2003).
2. Dulaure, vol. 2, pp. 349, 358–61.
3. A. Bothwell-Gosse, *The Knights Templar* (London, n.d.), p. 43, quoted in Peter Marshall, *The Philosopher's Stone: A Quest for the Secrets of Alchemy* (London, 2001), p. 267.
4. See Tobias Churton, *The Gnostics* (London, 1986), p. 67.
5. Juan Goytisolo, *Landscapes After the Battle* (New York, 1987). See also Andrew Hussey, 'Forbidden Territory: Juan Goytisolo's Maps of Tangier', in 'Writing Tangier', ed. Kevin Lacey and Ralph M. Coury, *Journal of Middle Eastern and North African Cultural Studies*, 3 (2005), pp. 35–47.
6. Dan Brown, *The Da Vinci Code* (New York, 2003).
7. *Guide du Paris mystérieux* (Paris, 1985), p. 223.

10. *Rebels and Riots*

1. Braudel, *L'Identité de la France*, p. 35.
2. Quoted in *Guide du Paris mystérieux*, p. 321.
3. See Horne, *Seven Ages of Paris*, p. 66.
4. Quoted in Braudel, *L'Identité de la France*, p. 89.
5. Dulaure, vol. 3, p. 345.
6. Ibid., pp. 14–18.
7. Buonaccorso Pitti, *Cronica* (Bologna, 1905), p. 156.
8. Dulaure, vol. 3, p. 367.

11. *The English Devils*

1. Dulaure, vol. 3, pp. 220–24.
2. Quoted in ibid., pp. 220–21.
3. Ibid., pp. 230–34.
4. Quoted in ibid., vol. 3, p. 107.

12. Machaberey's Dance

1. *Journal d'un bourgeois de Paris*, p. 45.
2. *Le Mesnagier de Paris*, ed. Georgina E. Brereton and Janet Ferrier (Paris, 1994), pp. 345–8.
3. *Journal d'un bourgeois de Paris*, p. 134.
4. Ibid., p. 156.
5. François Villon, *Ballades en jargon*, quoted by Jean Dufournet, *Magazine littéraire*, May 1995, pp. 22–3.
6. Randle Cotgrave, *A Dictionarie of the French and English Tongue* (London, 1611).
7. The best account of the intellectual context of Villon's life is to be found in Goff, *Les Intellectuels au moyen-âge*.
8. *Journal d'un bourgeois de Paris*, pp. 217–20.
9. Ibid., p. 123.
10. Ibid., pp. 115–17.
11. Ibid.

13. Maps and Legends

1. 'Lutèce ou premier plan de la ville de Paris, tiré de César, de Strabon, de l'Empereur Iulien, et d'Ammian Marcellin par M. L. Commissaire de La Mare, Antoine Coquart, 1705', *Les Plans de Paris*, ed. Jean Boutier (Paris, 2002), p. 197.
2. Alfred Bonnardot, *Études Archéologiques sur les anciens plans de Paris* (1851; Paris, 1994), p. 51.
3. *À la découverte des plans de Paris*, p. 5.
4. Johan Huizinga, *The Waning of the Middle Ages* (London, 1924).

Part Three: Slaughterhouse City, 1461–1669

Among the key works consulted here are L. Bernard, *The Emerging City: Paris in the Time of Louis XIV* (Durham, NC, 1970); R. Briggs, *Early Modern France, 1506–1715* (Oxford, 1977); G. Erlanger, *La Vie quotidienne sous Henri IV* (Paris, 1958); A. Franklin, *Journal du Siège de Paris* (Paris, 1876); Colin Jones, *The Great Nation* (London, 2002); A. Trout, *City on the Seine: Paris in the Time of Richelieu and Louis XIV* (London, 1966).

14. Dark with Excess of Light

1. Marc-Antoine de Saint-Amant, *Adieu à Paris* (1653).
2. Montaigne, *Essais, II* (Paris, 1998), p. 67.
3. Quoted in Robert Cole, *A Traveller's History of Paris* (New York, 1998), p. 64.
4. Ibid., p. 65. See also A. Fierro, *Mémoire de Paris* (Paris, 2003), p. 88.
5. Cole, *A Traveller's History of Paris*, pp. 70–71.
6. Ibid., p. 73.
7. Bernard Rouleau, *Paris: histoire d'un espace* (Paris, 1997), pp. 158–9.

15. Choose Now – The Mass or Death!

1. Quoted in Dulaure, vol. 3, p. 254.
2. Quoted in ibid., p. 255.
3. Ibid., vol. 4, pp. 30–32.
4. Quoted in ibid., p. 63.
5. Quoted in *Mémoires de L. Geitzkofler, tyrolien (1550–1620)* (Geneva, 1892), p. 64.
6. Dulaure, vol. 3, p. 460.
7. Ibid., pp. 454–7.
8. Jacques-Auguste de Thou, quoted in ibid., p. 459.

16. As Above, So Below

1. Edmund White, *The Flâneur* (London, 2001), p. 149.
2. Jean Riverain, *Chroniques de l'argot* (Paris, 1963), pp. 49–63.
3. Quoted in Paul-Yves Sébillot, *Folklore et curiosités du vieux Paris* (Paris, 2002), pp. 421–3.
4. Dulaure, vol. 5, pp. 34–5.

17. Sinister Days

1. Dulaure, vol. 4, pp. 70–80.
2. Quoted in ibid., p. 25.
3. Quoted in ibid., pp. 156–7.
4. Ibid., pp. 158–9.
5. Quoted in ibid., p. 159.

18. Making Paradise Visible

1. Alistair Horne, *Seven Ages of Paris* (London, 2002), p. 92.
2. Rouleau, *Paris: histoire d'un espace*, p. 312.
3. Horne, *Seven Ages of Paris*, p. 92.
4. Dulaure, vol. 4, p. 219.
5. Rouleau, *Paris: histoire d'un espace*, p. 123.
6. André Malraux, *Œuvres complètes*, vol. 1 (Paris, 1962), p. 143.
7. André Breton, in his novel *Nadja* (Paris, 1927), p. 53.
8. Quoted in Dulaure, vol. 4, pp. 184–5.

19. A Marvellous Confusion

1. Quoted in Dulaure, vol. 4, pp. 304–5.
2. Quoted in ibid., p. 305.
3. Quoted in ibid., p. 307.
4. L. Dupont, *Les Célébrités de la rue* (Paris, 1972), p. 89.
5. Quoted in ibid.

Part Four: New Rome and Old Sodom, 1670–1799

Among the key works consulted here are L. Bernard, *The Emerging City: Paris in the Time of Louis XIV* (Durham, NC, 1970); Richard Cobb, *The French and Their Revolution* (London, 1998), *The Police and the People: French Popular Protest 1789–1820* (Oxford, 1970), *Paris and Its Provinces* (Oxford, 1972); D. Godineau, *The Women of Paris and Their Revolution* (Berkeley, CA, 1998); Alistair Horne, *Seven Ages of Paris* (London, 2002); R. Isherwood, *Farce and Fantasy: Popular Entertainment in 18th Century Paris* (New York, 1986); Colin Jones, *The Great Nation* (London, 2002); J. Laver, *The Age of Illusion: Manners and Morals, 1750–1848* (London, 1972); Daniel Roche, *The People of Paris: An Essay in Popular Culture in the 18th Century* (New York, 1987); G. Rudé, *The Crowd in the French Revolution* (Oxford, 1959); Simon Schama, *Citizens* (London, 1989); A. Trout, *City on the Seine: Paris in the Time of Richelieu and Louis XIV* (London, 1966).

20. Splendour and Misery

1. Jules Michelet, *Cours au Collège de France* (Paris, 1987), p. 688.
2. Bernard Rouleau, *Paris: histoire d'un espace* (Paris, 2003), p. 167.

3. Dulaure, vol. 5, p. 67.

4. *Folklore de Paris* (Paris, 1998), p. 87.

5. Quoted in Dulaure, vol. 5, p. 63.

6. Quoted in ibid., p. 231.

7. Marc de Maillet, *Épigrammes* (Paris, 1620).

8. A description of Paris at this point is given in Dulaure, vol. 5, pp. 480–82.

21. Shadow and Stench

1. Roche, *The People of Paris*, p. 9.

2. *Les Cris de Paris* (Paris, 1986), p. 67.

3. Dulaure, vol. 5, p. 59.

4. Ibid., p. 57.

5. See *The Works of Voltaire: A Contemporary Version* (New York, 1901), trans. William F. Fleming, p. 341, and Voltaire, *Advertisement to the reader: An essay upon the civil wars of France [. . .] and also upon the epick poetry of the European nations* (London, 1727).

6. Voltaire, 'La pucelle d'Orléans', quoted in Jean Mohlsen Fahny, *Voltaire and Paris* (Oxford, 1981), p. 45.

7. Dulaure, vol. 5, p. 71.

8. Ibid., p. 313.

9. Quoted in ibid., p. 189.

22. Porno Manifesto

1. Alfred Fierro (ed.), *Fabliaux érotiques* (Paris, 2003).

2. Louis-Sébastien Mercier, *Le Tableau de Paris*, vol. 12 (Paris, 1997), pp. 151–5. For histories of the rise of literacy in Paris, see also Roche, *The People of Paris*, pp. 197–233.

3. Quoted in Marc Lemonier and Alexandre Dupouy, *Histoire de Paris libertin* (Paris, 2003), p. 23.

4. Mercier, *Le Tableau de Paris*, pp. 188–9.

5. Arlette Farge, *Subversive Words: Public Opinion in the 18th Century* (London, 1997), p. 12.

6. Ovidie, *Porno Manifesto* (Paris, 2002), p. 98.

7. Francine Plessix du Gray, *At Home with the Marquis de Sade* (London, 1999), p. 78.

8. Michel Houellebecq, 'À l'angle de la FNAC bouillonnait une foule. Très dense et très cruelle . . .', in *La Poursuite du bonheur* (Paris, 2001).

9. Michel Houellebecq, *Whatever* (London, 1999), pp. 29–30.

23. Night-Vision

1. Mercier, *Le Tableau de Paris*, p. 95.
2. Rouleau, *Paris: histoire d'un espace*, p. 242.
3. Mercier, *Le Tableau de Paris*, p. 108.
4. Ibid., pp. 145–53.
5. Ibid., p. 135.
6. Restif de la Bretonne, *Monsieur Nicolas* (Paris, 1797).
7. Louis-Sébastien Mercier and Restif de la Bretonne, *Paris le jour, Paris la nuit* (Paris, 1986), p. 260.
8. Ibid., p. 621.
9. Quoted in Roche, *The People of Paris*, p. 265.
10. Mercier and Restif, *Paris le jour*, p. 953.
11. Roche, *The People of Paris*, p. 259.
12. Gérard de Nerval, *Œuvres complètes* (Paris, 1961), p. 134. See also the correspondence between Restif and Victor d'Hupay of 1785, cited in J. G. Bouchon, *Histoire du communisme and du socialisme* (Paris, 1989).
13. Mercier and Restif, *Paris le jour*, p. 134.
14. Jones, *The Great Nation*, pp. 293–5.
15. Ibid., p. 262.

24. From Revolt to Revolution

1. Roche, *The People of Paris*, pp. 38–9.

25. The Bloody Path to Utopia

1. Robert Cole, *A Traveller's History of Paris* (New York, 1998), pp. 136–7. On Revolutionary festivals in Paris, see Marie-Louise Biver, *Fêtes révolutionnaires* (Paris, 1979), and Mona Ozouf, *La Fête révolutionnaire* (Paris, 1976).
2. For a colourful but accurate account of de Sade's time in prison, see Plessix du Gray, *At Home with the Marquis de Sade*.
3. Quoted in Lemonier and Dupouy, *Histoire de Paris libertin*, p. 31.
4. Ibid.
5. See Lemonier and Dupouy, *Histoire de Paris libertin*, pp. 56–7.
6. See, for example, Antoine de Baecque, 'Dégénérescence et régénération ou comment le livre licencieux juge la Révolution française', in *L'Enfer de la Bibliothèque Nationale*, vol. 6 (Paris, 1987), pp. 247–63, reprinted in Roger Chartier and Daniel Roche (eds), *Livre et révolution* (Paris, 1989), pp. 123–32.

See also Michel Rey, 'Police and Sodomy in 18th Century Paris: From Sin to Disorder', *Journal of Homosexuality*, vol. 16, nos. 1 and 2 (1988); Andrew Wikholm, 'Police Entrap Pederasts', *Gay History*, unpaginated (1998).

7. Quoted in 'Les Septembriseurs', *L'Humanité*, 18 September 2002.

8. Useful overviews of the key arguments concerning the Revolution can be found in Cobb, *The Police and the People*; Alfred Cobban, *The Social Interpretation of the French Revolution* (Cambridge, 1999); William Doyle, *Origins of the French Revolution* (Oxford, 1999); François Furet, *Penser la Révolution française* (Paris, 1978); Godineau, *The Women of Paris*; Lynn Avery Hunt, *Politics, Culture and Class in the French Revolution* (Berkeley, CA, 1994); Georges Lefebvre, *The Coming of the French Revolution* (Princeton, NJ, 1971).

9. Thomas Carlyle, *The French Revolution* (1837), section 4, 'The States-General'.

10. Saint-Just, *Sur le mode d'exécution du décret contre les ennemis de la Révolution*, speech to the National Convention, 3 March 1794.

Part Five: Dream House, Dream City, 1800–1850

Key works consulted here include P. Berthier, *La Vie quotidienne dans la Comédie Humaine de Balzac* (Paris, 1998); K. Bowie (ed.), *La Modernité avant Haussmann* (Paris, 2001); P. Corcoran, *Before Marx: Socialism and Communism in France, 1830–1848* (London, 1983); Jean Favier, *Paris* (Paris, 1997); H. Frégier, *Des classes dangereuses de la population dans les grandes villes* (Baillère, 1840); David Harvey, *Paris, Capital of Modernity* (New York and London, 2003); Alistair Horne, *The Fall of Paris: The Siege and the Commune, 1870–1871* (New York, 1965), *Seven Ages of Paris* (London, 2002); Colin Jones, *Paris: Biography of a City* (London, 2004); Armand Lanoux, *Introduction to Les Mystères de Paris* (Paris, 1998); Peter Mansell, *Paris Between Empires 1814–1852* (London, 2003); C. Prendergast, *Paris and the Nineteenth Century* (Oxford, 1992).

26. Empire

1. For Michelet's thoughts on the Revolution, see his *Histoire de la révolution française* (Paris, 1952).

2. Letter from Karl Marx to Arnold Ruge in the *Deutsch-Französische Jahrbücher* (1844). First published in English in *Writings of the Young Marx on Philosophy and Society* (New York, 1967).

3. Walter Benjamin, *The Arcades Project*, trans. Howard Eiland and Kevin McLaughlin, ed. Rold Tiedemann (Cambridge, MA, 1999).

4. Edward W. Said, *Orientalism: Western Conceptions of the Orient* (London, 1978) p. 31.

5. Quoted by Peter Singer in Ted Honderich (ed.), *The Oxford Companion to Philosophy* (Oxford, 1995), p. 919.

6. An entertaining and scholarly account of the histories of British visitors to nineteenth-century Paris is to be found in Roger Clark, 'Threading the Maze: Nineteenth-Century Guides for British Travellers to Paris', in Michael Sheringham (ed.), *Parisian Fields* (London, 1996), pp. 8–30.

7. See Mansell, *Paris Between Empires*, p. 2.

8. For a full account of these events, see ibid., pp. 2–3.

27. Occupation and Restoration

1. Quoted in Mansell, *Paris Between Empires*, p. 4.

2. Ibid., p. 7.

3. Ibid., pp. 12–13.

4. Ibid., p. 13.

5. Benjamin Constant, *Political Writings*, ed. and trans. Biancamaria Fontana (Cambridge, 1988), pp. 161–3. For an interesting description of the literary life of the period, see Denis Hollier (ed.), *A New History of French Literature* (Cambridge, MA, 1994), p. 616.

6. Mansell, *Paris Between Empires*, pp. 310–11.

28. The Bourgeois World of Louis-Philippe

1. Charles Louandre, *Les Idées subversives de notre temps* (Paris, 1872).

2. Patrice Higonnet, *Paris: Capital of the World* (Cambridge, MA, 2002), p. 60.

3. Friedrich von Raumer, *Briefe aus Paris und Frankreich im Jahre 1830* (Leipzig, 1831).

4. For the quotations from Hugo, see Pierre Citron, *La Poésie de Paris dans la littérature française de Rousseau à Baudelaire* (Paris, 1961), p. 433.

5. Higonnet, *Paris: Capital of the World*, p. 32.

6. Quoted in Benjamin, *The Arcades Project*, p. 26.

7. Ibid., p. 311.

8. Ibid.

9. Joanna Richardson, *The Bohemians: La Vie de Bohème in Paris 1830–1914* (London, 1969), pp. 16–17.

10. Ibid., pp. 14, 31, 32, 134.

11. Ibid., pp. 29–30.

12. Hollier, *A New History*, p. 700.
13. Quoted in Higonnet, *Paris: Capital of the World*, p. 59.

29. Balzac's Mirror

1. For an account of the early settlement of Algeria, see Alistair Horne, *A Savage War of Peace* (London, 2002), pp. 29–32. See also John Bierman, *Napoleon III and His Carnival Empire* (London, 1989).
2. Mansell, *Paris Between Empires*, p. 357.
3. See Daniela De Agostini, *Il mito dell'angelo: genesi dell'opera d'arte in Proust, Zola, Balzac* (Urbino, 1990).
4. An authoritative account of Balzac's position in French literature is given in David Bellos, *Balzac Criticism in France, 1850–1900* (Oxford, 1976). For an overview of Balzac's political philosophy, see René-Alexandre Courteix, *Balzac et la Révolution française: aspects idéologiques et politiques* (Paris, 1997). This includes useful bibliographical references (p. 429) and indexes. A lucid account of Balzac's politics is also given in Peter Brooks, 'A Monarchist Marxists Could Love', *New York Times Book Review*, 23 May 1999. See also Higonnet, *Paris: Capital of the World*, pp. 207–8.

30. The Age of Contempt

1. See Harvey, *Paris, Capital of Modernity*, pp. 8–9.
2. Mansell, *Paris Between Empires*, pp. 319–20.
3. Ibid.
4. Ibid., pp. 309–10.
5. Ibid., pp. 322–3.
6. Quoted in James Harvey Robinson (ed.), *Readings in European History* (London, 1906), and John Laurence Carr, *Life in France under Louis XIV* (London, 1970).
7. Theodore Zeldin, *France 1848–1945*, 3 vols. (Oxford, 1980), vol. 3, pp. 391–2.
8. Quoted in Mansell, *Paris Between Empires*, p. 393. The figures refer to previous key Revolutionary dates: 1830, 1792 and 1789.
9. Ibid., pp. 401–4.

Part Six: Queen of the World, 1851–1899

Among the main works consulted here are Louis Chevalier, *Labouring Classes and Dangerous Classes in Paris During the First Half of the Nineteenth Century* (New York, 1973); Rupert Christiansen, *Tales of the New Babylon, Paris 1869–1875* (London, 1994); T. J. Clark, *The Absolute Bourgeois* (London, 1973); *Image of the People* (London, 1973), *The Painting of Modern Life* (New York, 1985); Jean Favier, *Paris* (Paris, 1997); P. Parkhurst Ferguson, *Paris as Revolution: Writing the 19th Century City* (Berkeley, CA, 1994); W. Scott Haine, *The World of the Paris Café: Sociability Among the French Working-Class 1789–1914* (Baltimore, MD, 1996); J. Halperin, *Félix Fénéon: Aesthete and Anarchist* (New Haven, CT, 1988); Alistair Horne, *The Fall of Paris: The Siege and the Commune, 1870–1871* (New York, 1965), *Seven Ages of Paris* (London, 2002); Colin Jones, *Paris: Biography of a City* (London, 2004); Joanna Richardson, *The Bohemians: La Vie de Bohème in Paris 1890–1914* (London, 1969); Roger Shattuck, *The Banquet Years: The Arts in France 1885–1918: Alfred Jarry, Erik Satie, Henri Rousseau, Guillaume Apollinaire* (London, 1958); Alexander Varias, *Paris and the Anarchists* (London, 1997); Theodore Zeldin, *France 1848–1945*, 3 vols. (Oxford, 1980).

31. The Cretin's Empire

1. Quoted in Pierre Citron, 'Honoré de Balzac, scènes d'un visionnaire', *Magazine littéraire*, May 1995, pp. 32–5.
2. Walter Benjamin, *The Arcades Project*, trans. Howard Eiland and Kevin McLaughlin, ed. Rold Tiedemann (Cambridge, MA, 1999).
3. John Bierman, *Napoleon III and His Carnival Empire* (London, 1989), pp. 59–65.
4. Quoted in Paul Lafargue, *La Légende de Victor Hugo* (Paris, 1885).
5. Peter Mansell, *Paris Between Empires 1814–1852* (London, 2003), p. 415.
6. Bierman, *Napoleon III*, p. 201.
7. *The Eighteenth Brumaire of Louis Bonaparte*, translated from the German edition of 1869.
8. Quoted in John Russell, *Paris* (London, 1983), p. 32.
9. *Le Ventre de Paris* ('The Stomach of Paris') is the title of a book by Zola, published in 1883.
10. Charles Baudelaire, *Flowers of Evil*, trans. James McGowan (Oxford, 1993), p. 172.

32. Ghosts in Daylight

1. *Paris Guide*, 1867 (Paris, 1999).
2. Quoted in Richardson, *The Bohemians*, p. 43.
3. Jules Janin, *Âne mort* (Paris, 1829), p. 92; Balzac, *C. Birotteau* (Paris, 1837), p. 44.
4. Quoted in Richardson, *The Bohemians*, pp. 142–3.
5. Baudelaire, 'Les sept vieillards', *Flowers of Evil*, p. 177.
6. Baudelaire, 'Le peintre de la vie moderne', *Œuvres complètes* (Paris, 1961), p. 1160.
7. Quoted in Richardson, *The Bohemians*, p. 84.
8. Maxime Rude, *Confidences d'un journaliste* (1876), quoted in ibid., pp. 42–3.
9. Quoted in ibid., p. 87.
10. Baudelaire, *Les petits poèmes en prose* (Paris, 1961), p. 12.
11. Quoted in Richardson, *The Bohemians*, p. 85.
12. Quoted in Horne, *The Seven Ages of Paris*, p. 277.

33. Red Lightning

1. Bierman, *Napoleon III*, p. 184.
2. For a full and authoritative account of the siege and the Commune of Paris, see Horne, *The Fall of Paris*. See also Mme Edmond Adam, *Le Siège de Paris: journal d'une Parisienne* (Paris, 1873); Georges Bourgin, *Histoire de la Commune* (Paris, 1907), *Les Premières journées de la Commune* (Paris, 1928); Gaston da Costa, *La Commune vécue*, 3 vols. (Paris, 1903–5); Karl Marx, *The Civil War in France* (London, 1937); Jacques Rougerie, *Paris Libre 1871* (Paris, 1967).
3. Quoted in Joanna Richardson (ed.), *Paris Under Siege 1870–71* (London, 1982), p. 57.
4. Quoted in ibid., p. 87.
5. Arthur Rimbaud, 'L'Orgie parisienne' and 'Chant de guerre parisien', *Collected Poems* (London, 1986), pp. 131 and 117.
6. Richardson, *Paris Under Siege*, p. 43.
7. Horne, *The Fall of Paris*, pp. 335–6.
8. Ibid., p. 334.
9. Ibid., p. 350.
10. Ibid., pp. 360–61.
11. Quoted in Richardson, *Paris Under Siege*, p. 189.
12. Charles Louandre, *Les Idées subversives de notre temps* (Paris, 1872), p. 93.

34. After the Orgy

1. This song is recorded on the CD *Pour en finir avec le travail: chansons du prolétariat révolutionnaire: anthologie de la chanson française* (Paris, 1998).
2. Quoted in Shattuck, *The Banquet Years*, p. 4.
3. An interesting account of Hugo's funeral is given in ibid., pp. 5–9.
4. See Haine, *The World of the Paris Café*, p. 54.
5. Ibid., p. 18.
6. Octave Mirbeau, *Misère et mortalité* (Paris, 1968), p. 41.
7. Shattuck, *The Banquet Years*, p. 16.
8. Ibid., p. 17.
9. Quoted in Patrice Higonnet, *Paris: Capital of the World* (Cambridge, MA, 2002), p. 286.
10. For the events concerning Boulanger, see Shattuck, *The Banquet Years*, p. 12.
11. A character from Proust's *À la recherche du temps perdu* (1913–27).
12. Shattuck, *The Banquet Years*, pp. 110–11.

Part Seven: Magnetic Fields, 1900–1939

Among the works consulted here are Dudley Andrew and Steven Ungar, *Popular Front Paris and the Poetics of Culture* (Cambridge, MA, 2004); Louis Chevalier, *Montmartre du plaisir et du crime* (Paris, 1987); Jean Favier, *Paris* (Paris, 1997); Nigel Gosling, *Paris 1900–1914: The Miraculous Years* (London, 1978); Andrew Hussey, *The Inner Scar: The Mysticism of Georges Bataille* (Amsterdam, 2000); Maurice Nadeau, *Histoire du Surréalisme* (Paris, 1947); A. Polizotti, *Revolution of the Mind* (New York, 1996); A. Rifkin, *Street Noises* (Manchester, 1995); M. Sheringham (ed.), *Parisian Fields* (London, 1996); Susan Rubin Suleiman, *Subversive Intent* (Cambridge, MA, 1992); Eugen Weber, *The Hollow Years* (London, 1995); Theodore Zeldin, *France 1848–1945*, 3 vols. (Oxford, 1980).

35. New Spirits

1. See Gosling, *Paris 1900–1914*, pp. 13–14.
2. Robert Desnos, 'La Complainte de Fantômas', *Œuvres complètes* (Paris, 1962).
3. Léon-Paul Fargue, *Le Piéton de Paris* (Paris, 1985), p. 44.
4. Guillaume Apollinaire, 'Zone', in *The Penguin Book of French Poetry* (London, 1990), p. 545.

36. New Wars

1. See *La Guerre de 1914–1918 par ceux qui l'ont faite* (Paris, 1968). See also Jean-Michel Bourget, *Les Origines de la victoire: histoire raisonnée de la Guerre Mondiale* (Paris, 1930).
2. Louis-Ferdinand Céline, *Voyage au bout de la nuit* (Paris, 1932), p. 5.
3. Favier, *Paris*, pp. 916–18.
4. Colin Jones, *Paris: Biography of a City* (London, 2004), p. 440.

37. Paris Peasants

1. Tristan Tzara, *Dada Manifesto* (New York, 1978), pp. 78–9.
2. Paul Verlaine, *L'Art poétique* (1871–3).
3. These key Surrealist texts have been beautifully rendered into English by the poet David Gascoyne in André Breton and Philippe Soupault, *The Magnetic Fields* (London, 1985).
4. See, for example, the article 'Black Birds' reprinted in *Encyclopaedia Acephalica* (London, 1996).
5. Pascal Blanchard, Éric Deroo and Gilles Manceron, *Paris Noir* (Paris, 2003), pp. 53–5.
6. Paul Bowles, *Without Stopping* (New York, 1986), p. 123.

38. Darkness Falls

1. See Weber, *The Hollow Years*, p. 88.
2. Ibid., pp. 106–10.
3. Quoted in ibid., p. 102.
4. Ibid., p. 105.
5. See Philippe Alméras, *Les Idées de Céline* (Paris, 1992), p. 128.
6. Weber, *The Hollow Years*, p. 133.
7. Ibid., pp. 159–160. See also Andrew and Ungar, *Popular Front Paris*.
8. Weber, *The Hollow Years*, p. 234.
9. One of the best discussions of the political significance of Bataille's writings can be found in Patrick ffrench, 'Dirty Life', in *The Beast at Heaven's Gate: Georges Bataille and the Art of Transgression* (Amsterdam, 2006).
10. Georges Bataille, *Le Bleu du ciel* (Paris, 1957), p. 172.
11. Bataille, 'Méditation Héraclitéenne', *Œuvres complètes*, vol. 1 (Paris, 1971), p. 557.

Part Eight: The Capital of Treason, 1940–1944

Among the works consulted here are Maurice Bardèche, *Lettre à François Mauriac* (Paris, 1947); Albrecht Betz and Stefan Martens, *Les Intellectuels et l'Occupation, 1940–1944: collaborer, partir, résister* (Paris, 2004); Philippe Boudrel, *L'Épuration sauvage* (Paris, 1988); Julian Jackson, *France, The Dark Years* (Oxford, 2001); Jeremy Josephs, *Swastika Over Paris: The Fate of the French Jews* (London, 1989); Serge Klarsfeld, *Mémorial de la déportation des juifs en France* (Paris, 1978); Maurice Larkin, *Paris Since the Popular Front* (London, 1986); James Macmillan, *Twentieth-Century France* (London, 1992); Peter Novick, *The Resistance Versus Vichy: The Purge of Collaborators in Liberated France* (London, 1986); René Rémond, *Notre Siècle* (Paris, 1988); Henry Rousso, *The Vichy Syndrome* (Cambridge, 1991); Alfred Wahl (ed.), *Mémoire de la Seconde Guerre Mondiale* (Metz, 1984).

39. Night and Fog

1. Eugen Weber, *The Hollow Years* (London, 1995), p. 258.
2. Jean-Pierre Azéma, *De Munich à la Libération 1938–1944* (Paris, 1998).
3. William L. Shirer, *La Chute de la troisième république* (Paris, 1970), p. 454.
4. Josephs, *Swastika Over Paris*, pp. 46–8.
5. Ibid., p. 42.
6. Ibid., p. 40.
7. Ibid., p. 59.
8. Ibid., pp. 72–3.
9. Ibid.
10. Daniel Garcia, 'Y'a des zazous dans mon quartier', *Le Nouvel Observateur*, July 2005.

40. Patriots and Traitors

1. Much of this material is covered effectively in Betz and Martens, *Les Intellectuels et l'Occupation*.
2. Louis Aragon, 'Du poète à son parti', in Germaine Brée and George Bernauer (eds.), *Defeat and Beyond: An Anthology of French Wartime Writing (1940–1945)* (New York, 1970), p. 248.
3. Louis-Ferdinand Céline, *Bagatelles pour un massacre* (Paris, 1938), p. 57, quoted in Philippe Alméras, *Les Idées de Céline* (Paris, 1992), p. 128.
4. Céline, *Bagatelles pour un massacre*, p. 54.

5. Céline, *Guignol's Band* (Paris, 1958), p. 34.

6. Saul Bellow, 'My Paris', *New York Times*, 23 July 1983.

7. See Martin Blumerson, *The Vildé Affair: Beginnings of the French Resistance* (London, 1977), pp. 86–7.

8. Albert Camus, 'Lettres à un ami allemand', in *In Defeat and Beyond*, p. 347.

Part Nine: Society of the Spectacle, 1945–2005

Among the works consulted in this section are David Bellos, *Georges Perec: Life, a User's Manual* (London, 1994), *Jacques Tati: His Life and Work*, (London, 2001); Jean-François Bizot, *Underground: l'histoire* (Paris, 2004); Gavin Bowd, *L'Enterrement interminable* (Paris, 1998); Guy Debord, *La Société du spectacle* (Paris, 1967); Serge Dillaz, *Vivre et chanter en France, 1945–1980* (Paris, 2004); Jonathan Fenby, *France on the Brink* (London, 2002); Patrick ffrench, *The Time of Theory* (Oxford, 1995); Robert Gildea, *France Since 1945* (Oxford, 1998); Andrew Hussey, *The Game of War: The Life and Death of Guy Debord* (London, 2001); Alistair Horne, *A Savage War of Peace* (London, 2002); Sunan Khilnani, *Arguing Revolution* (New Haven, CT, 1993); Tony Judt, *Past Imperfect* (Berkeley, CA, 1992); J. P. Rioux, *The Fourth Republic* (Cambridge, 1991); Keith Reader, *Intellectuals and the Left in France Since 1968* (London, 1987); Patrick Rotman and Bertrand Tavernier, *La Guerre sans nom* (Paris, 1992).

41. Landscapes After the Battle

1. A full account of this period can be found in Antony Beevor and Artemis Cooper, *Paris After the Liberation: 1944–1949* (London, 1994), pp. 88, 158–9, 166–7.

2. Ibid., pp. 179–97.

3. Quoted in ibid., pp. 156–7.

4. Quoted in Germaine Brée and George Bernauer (eds.), *Defeat and Beyond: An Anthology of French Wartime Writing (1940–1945)* (New York, 1970), p. 341, where Brasillach's last days are very effectively described.

5. Beevor and Cooper, *Paris After the Liberation*, p. 158.

6. Ibid., p. 101.

7. An entertaining, authoritative and bracingly opinionated version of this period is given in Herbert Lottmann, *The Left Bank* (London, 1982).

8. Quoted in Dillaz, *Vivre et chanter*, p. 36.

9. Ibid., p. 315.

42. The Seventh 'Wilaya'

1. For accounts of these events, see Horne, *A Savage War*, and David Macey, *Frantz Fanon: A Life* (London, 2000), pp. 241–4.
2. Quoted in Horne, *A Savage War*, p. 27.
3. Pascal Blanchard, *Paris arabe* (Paris, 2004), p. 54.
4. Ibid., p. 55.
5. Charles Baudelaire, 'The Swan', *Flowers of Evil*, trans. James McGowan (Oxford, 1993).
6. Marc Lemonier and Alexandre Dupouy, *Histoire de Paris libertin* (Paris, 2003), p. 32.

43. An Obscure Conspiracy

1. This period in Parisian history is best covered in the compendium of texts collected in Bizot, *Underground*.
2. See, for example, the review by Jean-Baptiste Morain in *Les Inrockuptibles*, September 2004, which describes the film as 'clichéd, ridiculous and superficial'.
3. An authoritative account of the formation of the SI and these opening speeches is given in Ralph Rumney, *Le Consul* (Paris, 1999), pp. 54–7.
4. Debord, *La Société du spectacle*, p. 9.
5. Isidore Isou, *Traité d'économie nucléaire: le soulèvement de la jeunesse* (Paris, 1947).
6. The term 'psychogeography' is used by Libero Andreotti in his article 'Architecture and Play', in Tom McDonough (ed.), *Guy Debord and the Situationist International: Texts and Documents* (Cambridge, MA, 2002), pp. 213–41. In this article, Andreotti analyses the influence of Johan Huizinga's *Homo Ludens* on the nascent Lettriste Internationale.
7. Raoul Vaneigem, *The Revolution of Everyday Life* (San Francisco, 1988), p. 123.
8. Quotations from the 'nurse' and 'young man' in David Caute, *The Year of the Barricades '68* (London, 1988), p. 191.
9. Quoted in Hussey, *The Game of War*, p. 5.
10. Quoted in ibid., pp. 238–9.
11. Ibid., p. 241.

44. The Killing of Paris?

1. Louis Chevalier, *L'Assassinat de Paris* (Paris, 1977), p. 313.
2. *Bazooka* (Paris, 1975).
3. A critical and well-documented survey of this period is provided in John Laughland, *The Death of Politics* (London, 1994).
4. Catherine Millet, *La vie sexuelle de Catherine Millet* (Paris, 2001).
5. Marc Augé, *Un ethnologue dans le métro* (Paris, 1986).
6. Quoted in Patrick ffrench, 'Détournement du flâneur', in *The Hacienda Must Be Built* (Manchester, 1996), p. 31.
7. Peter Ackroyd, 'Glare but not Gloire: Paris', *The Collection* (London, 2001), pp. 104–8.
8. See Jean de Boschère, *Paris Clair-Obscur* (Paris, 1991).

Epilogue: Paris Underground

1. Juan Goytisolo, 'Paris, capital del siglo XXI', in *El bosque de las letras* (Madrid, 1995).

Select Bibliography

On the Growth and Development of Central Paris

Aressy, L., and Parménie, A., *La Cité des épaves* (Paris, 1943)

Bastié, J., *Croissance de la banlieue parisienne* (Paris, 1964)

Bedel, J., *Les Puces ont cent ans* (Paris, 1985)

Brisset, P., *La Zone de Paris et la loi du 10 avril 1930* (Paris, 1932)

Hammonaye, C. de la, *Âme en plein vent* (Paris, 1938)

Jakovsky, Anatole, *Paris, mes puces* (Paris, 1957)

Larguier, Léo, *Marchés et foires de Paris* (Paris, 1953)

Pereire, G., *Note sur l'utilisation des terrains et des fortifications* (Paris, 1901)

Various numbers of architecture and planning reviews: *Architecture, Continuité, Mouvement, Paris Project*

General Historical Works

Babelon, Jean-Pierre, *Paris au XVIe Siècle* (Paris, 1986)

Balon, Hilary, *The Paris of Henri IV: Architecture and Urbanism.* (Cambridge, 1995).

Beaujeu-Garnier, J., *Paris: hasard ou prédestination?* (Paris, 1993)

Beevor, Antony, and Cooper, Artemis, *Paris After the Liberation, 1944–1949* (London, 1994)

Bennet, Arnold, *Paris Nights and Impressions of Places and People* (New York, 1913)

Berlanstein, Leonard, *The Working People of Paris, 1871–1914* (Baltimore, MD, 1985)

Bernier, Olivier, *Fireworks at Dusk: Paris in the Thirties* (New York, 1993)

Bertaut, Jules, *Les Belles Nuits de Paris* (Paris, 1956)

Bierman, John, *Napoleon III and His Carnival Empire* (London, 1987)

Billy, André, *Paris, Vieux et neuf* (Paris, 1909)

Burchell, S. C., *Imperial Masquerades: The Paris of Napoleon III* (New York, 1971)

Cain, Georges, *Promenades dans Paris* (Paris, 1906)

Carco, Francis, *Le Roman de François Villon* (Paris, 1926)

Carnod, André, *Visages de Paris* (Paris, 1912)

Cole, Robert, *A Traveller's History of Paris* (New York, 1998)

Dabit, Eugène, *Ville Lumière* (Paris, 1987)

Daeninckx, Didier, *À louer sans commission* (Paris, 1991)

Delvau, Charles, *Dictionnaire de la langue verte* (Paris, 1866)

— *Dictionnaire érotique moderne par un professeur de la langue verte* (Paris, 1864)

Duchatelet, A., *De la prostitution dans la ville de Paris* (Baillère, 1836)

Dulaure, J.-A., *Histoire physique, civile et morale de Paris*, 12 vols. (Paris, 1837)

Edwards, Stewart, *The Communards of Paris, 1871* (Ithaca, NY, 1973)

— *The Paris Commune, 1871* (Chicago, 1971)

Favier, Jean, *Paris* (Paris, 1997)

Fierro, A., *Histoire et dictionnaire de Paris* (Paris, 1997)

— *History and Dictionary of Paris* (Lanham, MD, 1999)

— *Mémoire de Paris* (Paris, 2003)

— *Mystères de l'histoire de Paris* (Paris, 2000)

Fosca, F., *Histoire des cafés de Paris* (Paris, 1934)

Frégier, H., *Des classes dangereuses de la population dans les grandes villes* (Baillère, 1840)

Horne, Alistair, *The Fall of Paris: The Siege and the Commune, 1870–1871* (New York, 1965)

— *Seven Ages of Paris* (London, 2002)

Jones, Colin, *Paris: Biography of a City* (London, 2004)

Lanoux, Armand, *Introduction to Les Mystères de Paris* (Paris, 1989)

Lapidis, Clément, *Dimanches à Belleville* (Paris, 1884)

Larcher, L., *Dictionnaire historique, étymologique et anecdotique de l'argot parisien* (Paris, 1996)

Leguay, J.-P., *La Rue au Moyen-âge* (Rennes, 1984)

Marrey, B., *Les Grands magasins, des origines à 1930* (Paris, 1979)

Massip, C., *La Vie des musiciens à Paris au temps de Mazarin* (Paris, 1976)

Melly, George, *Paris and the Surrealists* (London, 1992)

Michel, Henri, *Paris allemand, Paris résistant* (Paris, 1982)

Mirot, L., *Les Insurrections urbaines au début du règne de Charles VI* (Paris, 1905)

Moura, J., *Le Café Procope* (Paris, 1929)

Nisard, Charles, *De quelques parisianismes populaires et autres locutions non ou plus ou moins imparfaitement expliquées des XVIIe, XVIIIe et XIXe siècles* (Paris, 185?)

Ozouf, Mona, *La Fête révolutionnaire* (Paris, 1976)

Pernot, M., *La Fronde* (Paris, 1994)

Pinon, P., *Paris: Biographie d'une capitale* (Paris, 1999)

Prendergast, C., *Paris and the Nineteenth Century* (Oxford, 1992)

Rials, S., *De Trochu à Thiers, 1870–1873* (Paris, 1985)

Rougerie, Jacques, *Procès des Communards* (Paris, 1978)

Russell, John, *Paris* (London, 1983)

Sainéan, L., *Le Langage parisien au XIXe siècle* (Paris, 1920)

Shapiro, A. L., *Housing the Poor of Paris* (Paris, 1985)

Shattuck, Roger, *The Banquet Years: The Arts in France 1885–1918: Alfred Jarry, Érik Satie, Henri Rousseau, Guillaume Apollinaire* (London, 1958)

Siegel, Jerrold, *Bohemian Paris: Culture, Politics, and the Boundaries of Bourgeois Life, 1830–1930* (New York, 1986)

Steele, Valerie, *Paris Fashion: A Cultural History* (Oxford, 1988)

Tournier, Michel, *La Goutte d'or* (Paris, 1985)

Tulard, J., *Paris et son administration, 1800–1830* (Paris, 1976)

Vigier, P., *Paris pendant la Monarchie de Juillet* (Paris, 1991)

Walter, G., *La Vie sous l'Occupation* (Paris, 1960)

Essays, Surveys, Theories

Adler, Laure, *La vie quotidienne dans les maisons closes: 1830–1930* (Paris, 1990)

Bandini, Mirella, *L'Estetico, il politico: 1948–1957* (Rome, 1977)

— 'Per loro la società è uno spettacolo', *L'Espresso*, no. 22 (1975)

Brau, Jean-Louis, *Cours camarade, le vieux monde est derrière toi! Histoire du mouvement révolutionnaire en Europe* (Paris, 1968)

Chevalier, Louis, *L'Assassinat de Paris* (Paris, 1977)

— *Labouring Classes and Dangerous Classes in Paris during the First Half of the Nineteenth Century* (New York, 1973)

— *Les Parisiens* (Paris, 1967)

Constant, *New Babylon: Art et Utopie,* (Paris, 2000)

Guilbert, Cécile, *Le Musée National* (Paris, 2000)

Hazan, E., *L'Invention de Paris* (Paris, 2003)

Higonnet, Patrice, *Paris: Capital of the World* (Cambridge, MA, 2002)

Hillairet, Jacques, *Dictionnaire historique des rues de Paris* (Paris, 1957)

Isou, Isidore, *L'Agrégation d'un nom et d'un messie* (Paris, 1947)

Jappe, Anselm, 'La lenta dissipazione del pensiero critico', *Il Manifesto*, 3 December 1994

— *Guy Debord* (Marseilles, 1995)

Jolivet, Merri, 'Nous avons fait ensemble un grand voyage sur place', *Libération*, 6 December 1994

Lewino, Walter, *L'Imagination au pouvoir* (Paris, 1968)

Mension, Jean-Michel, *La Tribu* (Paris, 1998)

Perniola, Mario, 'Arte e revoluzione', *Tempo Presente*, December 1966

Pierini, Franco, 'I partiti non hanno più niente da dirci', *L'Europeo*, December 1966

Rumney, Ralph, *Le Consul* (Paris, 1999)

— *Pourvu que ça dure* (Manosque, 1998)

Stierle, Karlheiz, *La Capitale des signes: Paris et son discours* (Paris, 2001)

Wolman, Gil J., *L'Anticoncept* (Paris, 1994)

Woods, Alan, *The Map Is Not the Territory: The Art of Ralph Rumney* (Manchester, 2000)

Index